Sicily

Vesna Maric

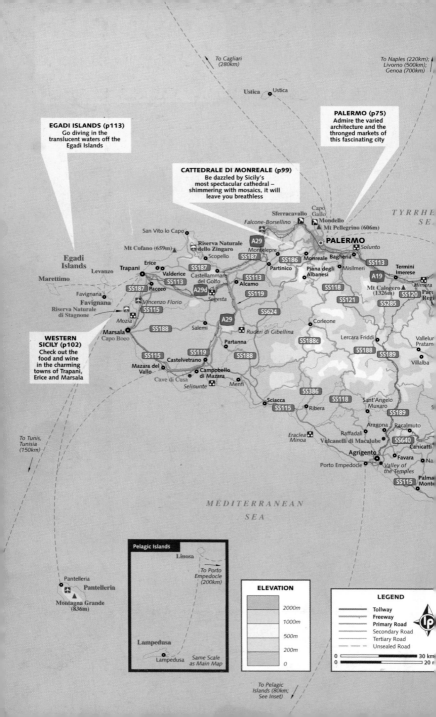

EGADI ISLANDS (p113)
Go diving in the translucent waters off the Egadi Islands

PALERMO (p75)
Admire the varied architecture and the thronged markets of this fascinating city

CATTEDRALE DI MONREALE (p99)
Be dazzled by Sicily's most spectacular cathedral – shimmering with mosaics, it will leave you breathless

WESTERN SICILY (p102)
Check out the food and wine in the charming towns of Trapani, Erice and Marsala

To Cagliari (280km)

To Naples (220km); Livorno (500km); Genoa (700km)

Ustica · Ustica

TYRRHE
SE

Sferracavallo
Capo Gallo
Falcone-Borsellino
Mondello
Mt Pellegrino (606m)
PALERMO

San Vito lo Capo
Riserva Naturale dello Zingaro
Montelepre
Solunto
Bagheria

Egadi Islands
Mt Cofano (659m)
Scopello
Monreale
Misilmeri
Termini Imerese

Marettimo
Erice
Valderice
Castellammare del Golfo
Partinico
Piana degli Albanesi
Mt Calogero (1326m)
Himera
Parc
Regi

Levanzo
Trapani
Paceco
Alcamo
Corleone
Vallelu
Pratam

Favignana
Vincenzo Florio
Segesta
Villalba

Riserva Naturale di Stagnone
Mozia
Salemi
Ruderi di Gibellina
Lercara Friddi

Marsala
Capo Boeo
Partanna
Sant'Angelo Muxaro

Castelvetrano
Campobello di Mazara
Ribera
Aragona · Racalmuto

Mazara del Vallo
Cave di Cusa
Selinunte
Menfi
Sciacca
Raffadali
Canicatti

Eraclea Minoa
Vulcanelli di Macalube
Favara
Na

Agrigento
Porto Empedocle
Valley of the Temples
Palma
Monte

MEDITERRANEAN SEA

Pelagic Islands
Linosa
To Porto Empedocle (200km)

To Tunis, Tunisia (150km)

Pantelleria
Montagna Grande (836m)

Lampedusa
Lampedusa
Same Scale as Main Map

ELEVATION
2000m
1000m
500m
200m
0

LEGEND
Tollway
Freeway
Primary Road
Secondary Road
Tertiary Road
Unsealed Road

0 —— 30 km
0 —— 20 m

To Pelagic Islands (80km; See Inset)

SS29, A29, SS187, SS186, SS113, SS115, SS188, SS119, SS624, SS121, SS118, SS285, A19, SS120, SS188c, SS189, SS386, SS640

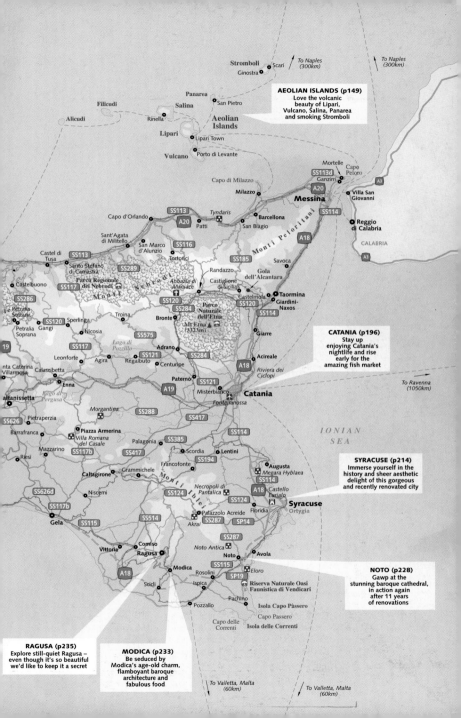

Stromboli
Scari
Ginostra
To Naples (300km)
To Naples (300km)

AEOLIAN ISLANDS (p149)
Love the volcanic beauty of Lipari, Vulcano, Salina, Panarea and smoking Stromboli

Filicudi
Panarea
San Pietro
Salina
Alicudi
Rinella
Aeolian Islands
Lipari
Lipari Town
Vulcano
Porto di Levante

Mortelle
Capo Peloro
SS113d
Ganzirri
A3
Capo di Milazzo
Milazzo
SS113
A20
Tyndaris
Messina
A20
SS114
Villa San Giovanni

Capo d'Orlando
Patti
Barcellona
San Biagio
Reggio di Calabria
CALABRIA

Sant'Agata di Militello
SS116
San Marco d'Alunzio
Tortorici
SS185
Savoca
Monti Peloritani
A18
A3

Castel di Tusa
SS113
Santo Stefano di Camastra
SS289
Randazzo
Gola dell'Alcantara
Abbazia di Maniace
Castiglione di Sicilia
Castelmola
Taormina
Giardini-Naxos

Castelbuono
Parco Regionale dei Nebrodi
SS117
Monti Nebrodi
SS120
SS284
Parco Naturale dell'Etna
SS120
SS114

SS286
Petralia Soprana
SS120
Sperlinga
Troina
Bronte
Mt Etna (3323m)
Giarre

Petralia Soprana
Gangi
Nicosia
SS575
Adrano
Acireale
Riviera dei Ciclopi

19
SS117
Leonforte
Agira
Regalbuto
Centuripe
SS284
A18

nta Caterina Villarmosa
Calascibetta
Enna
SS121
Paternò
SS121
Misterbianco
Fontanarossa
Catania

CATANIA (p196)
Stay up enjoying Catania's nightlife and rise early for the amazing fish market

To Ravenna (1050km)

altanissetta
Lago di Pergusa
A19

SS626
Pietraperzia
Morgantina
SS288
SS417
SS114
IONIAN SEA

Barrafranca
Piazza Armerina
Villa Romana del Casale
Palagonia
SS385
Scordia
Lentini
SS194
Augusta
Megara Hyblaea

Mazzarino
SS117b
Grammichele
Francofonte
SS114
A18
Castello Eurialo

Riesi
Caltagirone
Monti Iblei
Necropoli di Pantalica
SS124
Floridia
Syracuse
Ortygia

SYRACUSE (p214)
Immerse yourself in the history and sheer aesthetic delight of this gorgeous and recently renovated city

SS626d
Niscemi
SS124
SS514
Palazzolo Acreide
SS287
SP14

SS117b
Gela
SS115
Akrai
SS287

Vittoria
Comiso
Ragusa
Noto Antica
Noto
Avola

A18
Modica
Rosolini
SS115
Eloro
SP19

NOTO (p228)
Gawp at the stunning baroque cathedral, in action again after 11 years of renovations

Seicli
Ispica
Riserva Naturale Oasi Faunistica di Vendicari
Pachino

Pozzallo
Isola Capo Pàssero
Capo Passero
Capo delle Correnti
Isola delle Correnti

RAGUSA (p235)
Explore still-quiet Ragusa – even though it's so beautiful we'd like to keep it a secret

MODICA (p233)
Be seduced by Modica's age-old charm, flamboyant baroque architecture and fabulous food

To Valletta, Malta (60km)
To Valletta, Malta (60km)

On the Road

VESNA MARIC Coordinating Author

I'm applying a mud mask to my face at Eraclea Minoa beach (p269), feeling the mud drying and making facial movement impossible. Soon after, I noticed the local children cry and run away in horror. Seeing this picture explained why.

MY SICILY

Sicily is an extraordinary place, and the best place to dive in for me is Palermo (p75). I always dedicate a few days to Salina (p170) and Stromboli (p176) and, if I can, I sneak a visit to Trapani (p105) and Marsala (p120) for some of that fantastic food and wine. Most of all, I love relaxing around Syracuse (p214), Ragusa (p235) and Modica (p233).

ABOUT THE AUTHOR

Vesna has been savouring Sicilian food for many years, and enjoys the region's culture, architecture and atmosphere immensely. Her love of Mediterranean and island life grows with every visit to Sicily. Vesna has travelled up and down Italy, but she's glad there's plenty still to discover.

SICILY

Just when you think you've learned everything there is to know about Italy, along comes Sicily and blows away your certainties. Its land is arid, yet it's a place with fabulously overflowing food markets; it's seated in the comfortable and seemingly risk-free EU, yet it's constantly under the cloud of eruptions, earthquakes and, of course, the Mafia; and its history is richer than a Bond St jeweller, yet its modern disrepair is infamous. Yet with all those discrepancies, the simple truth is that Sicily is a beauty. You'll find your mind and soul snagging on it long after your visit.

Architectural Delights

Centuries under foreign rule have provided Sicily with a treasure trove of architectural riches: its Greek ruins will have classicists in heaven, lovers of baroque can immerse themselves in towns filled with examples of the style, and even the most architecture-weary visitors will be dazzled by the island's mix of Norman, Arabic and Byzantine styles.

5

❶ Cattedrale di Monreale
Breathtaking and spacious, Monreale's cathedral (p99) has one of the most spectacular interiors you'll ever see. Entirely covered in Byzantine mosaics that depict scenes from the Old and New Testaments, this church is unlike any other.

❷ Cappella Palatina, Palermo
You'll have to queue to see this masterpiece of Byzantine-style mosaics, Norman art and Arabic workmanship (p81), but it's worth every moment.

❸ Noto
An entire town dedicated to the baroque style, Noto (p228) was rebuilt by its aristocrats after an earthquake, along with neighbouring (and no less gorgeous) Ragusa and Modica. Its recent renovations have seen the old structures shine anew, so get there and lap it all up (and don't forget to taste some local ice cream too!).

❹ Valley of the Temples
Goethe wrote about these temples (p261) all the way back in 1786, romanticising the remains and putting them onto the world's tourism map. Standing majestically against the blue backdrop of the Mediterranean, the temples still draw thousands of visitors a year.

❺ Catania
Recently restored to its original dazzling state, Catania's lava-rock baroque architecture (p199) is a monochrome delight. From cathedrals to historical theatres, you'll have no end of choice of places to view.

❻ Cappella di Sant'Anna, Castelbuono
Hidden in the enormous castle, this tiny chapel (p140) is like an exquisite baroque soul sheltered inside a robust body. Enter through the heavy curtain and you'll see the wonderful – and slightly dizzying – stuccowork by the legendary Serpotta brothers.

Food for Thought

Whether it's the aubergine-laden *caponata,* the raisin-encrusted and sardine-scattered *pasta con le sarde* or a heap of freshly grilled and garlicky seafood, some of Sicily's greatest pleasures are to be had at the dinner table. The island's major highlight is its fabulous markets, echoing with salesmen's hollers and loaded with fish and meat, and sun-drenched fruit and veggies.

❶ Mercato della Vucciria, Palermo

Depicted in a famous 1974 painting by
Renato Guttuso, this is Palermo's oldest
and most magnetic market (p96). Set in
La Vucciria neighbourhood among ancient
palazzi (palaces or mansions) and drying
washing, the market has everything you've
ever wanted to taste and more. Excellent
for bargain bags of nuts and spices to take
home.

❷ La Pescheria, Catania

As you walk through Catania's fish market
(p200), you're fixed by the gleaming eyes
of swordfish, you hear the fishermen holler
their daily catches and you see squid heaped
up on top of ruby-coloured langoustines.
Any fish- or seafood-lover will feel like
they've died and gone to (a noisy kind of)
heaven.

❸ Modica Chocolate

Unchanged since Aztec times, the chocolate
of Modica (p234) is still prepared in the ancient way, using wooden rolls, lots of love
and raw muscle power. Sweetened with
vanilla, peppered with chilli or tanged-up
with orange peel, it'll turn even the sturdi-
est savoury-lover into a chocoholic.

❹ World's Best Ice Cream, Noto

The baroque town of Noto (p231) is said to
have two of the best *gelaterie* (ice-cream
shops) in the world. Get your lips around
some scoops of pistachio, or go for the
panna cotta (cream and caramel) flavour.

❺ Granita

The ultimate summer freshener, this concoction of crushed ice with flavours like coffee, almond or mulberry will send you into raptures.
It's great anywhere, but we think Colicchia
(p109), in Trapani, is particularly delicious.

③

Islands & Beaches

Sicily has beaches of all kinds: sandy
stretches, pebbly crescents, rocky coves
and hidden inlets. And while the high-
season crowds can be overwhelming,
there's always room for those wanting
to find a bit of peace and quiet by
the sea.

②

❶ San Vito lo Capo

Long, white, sandy and perfectly framed by the rocky mountains, this is one of Sicily's prettiest beaches (p105); unfortunately (and unsurprisingly) it's also one of the most popular. The high season sees thousands of beach beds, umbrellas and hollering salesmen, but things are quieter in July and September.

❷ Scala dei Turchi

Sicily's most stunning 'beach' (it's actually a rock), Scala dei Turchi (p268) will stay with you forever. A chalk-white cliff shaped like a giant staircase, it gorgeously contrasts with the blue sea and sky. Bring lots of sunscreen.

❸ Isola Bella

You won't get more picturesque than this – a tiny, lush island in a small cove reached through crystal-clear shallow waters. The 'Beautiful Island' (p192), once purchased for the bargain price of 5000 lire, now serves as a nature reserve and is a good snorkelling spot. Packed with tourists most of the summer, it's an ideal photo-and-dip opportunity.

❹ Pantelleria

Closer to Tunisia than to Sicily, this island (p117) is where to go if you *really* want to get away from it all. With its wonderful *dammusi* (low-level dwellings made of thick volcanic rock), heavenly wine, azure waters and holidaying A-listers, it's the cream of the Med.

❺ Selinunte

Swimming at this massive, sandy beach (p126) gives you a fabulous view of the ancient Greek temples above. While the main section of the beach can get packed with youngsters in the high summer, there are quieter parts if you head through the small pine forest to the west.

❻ Marettimo

The furthest west of the Egadi Islands, Marettimo (p116) is quiet, small and delightful. It's perfect for walking in lush countryside, sunbathing in coves and eating in wonderful restaurants.

❼ Riserva Naturale dello Zingaro

Totally undeveloped thanks to its protected status, this reserve (p104) has some gorgeous pebbly coves that will guarantee peace and quiet at most times of the year. You'll have to do some work to get here, but once you've arrived, you won't want to leave. If you fancy a livelier scene, go to nearby Scopello's gorgeous (but butt-bothering) beach.

❽ Salina

You won't find such a tiny island with so much character anywhere else in the world. Producing capers and malvasia wine, and consisting of several small villages connected by a single road, Salina (p170) is a beauty.

Erupt 'n' Explode

Sicily is plagued by its volcanoes, but it is also blessed by them. The numerous volcanos provide climbing opportunities, while their fertile soil produces some fabulous wines, fruits and vegetables – and then there's the otherworldly landscapes and underwater biodiversity that send trekkers and divers swooning.

❶ Stromboli

A dangerous time bomb or Sicily's most exciting sight? The dark volcano (p176) is surrounded by the bluest of waters, while the crater puffs on top like an irascible old smoker. The island attracts hardened climbers and international elite alike – why, even Dolce & Gabbana retreat to their Stromboli villa every summer.

❷ Mt Etna

Bellowing and belching almost yearly, Etna (p208) is one of the world's most unpredictable mountains – the volcanic soil, rich with minerals, creates abundant verdancy, but there's always the danger of it being wiped away. Trekking Mt Etna's slopes is one of Sicily's most exhilarating adventures.

❸ Vulcano

Considered 'active' – though it's been sleeping for a long, long time now – this volcano (p167) is an easy climb and interesting experience. Even better is bathing in the sulphuric mud pits, where rheumatic ailments can be relieved, skin diseases soothed and youth (they say) regained. Beware though: it's pretty smelly.

❹ Ustica

This island (p100) is actually the tip of a volcano, meaning it has some of the best diving around; it even hosts an international divers' gathering every year. For more volcanic diving, head to Lipari, Filicudi and Alicudi, which dazzle with colours and rare fish life.

Contents

Regional Map Contents

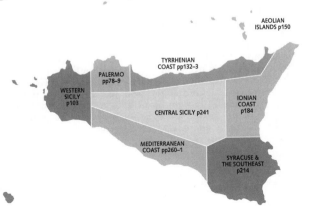

AEOLIAN ISLANDS p150

TYRRHENIAN COAST pp132–3

PALERMO pp78–9

WESTERN SICILY p103

IONIAN COAST p184

CENTRAL SICILY p241

MEDITERRANEAN COAST pp260–1

SYRACUSE & THE SOUTHEAST p214

Destination Sicily

There's a rich history behind Sicily's complex character. Nearly 25 centuries of foreign domination have had a massive impact on the island's cultural output: the Greeks built elegant classical structures, while a unique mix of Byzantine artistry and Norman severity endowed Sicily with some of the most unusual and beautiful buildings in Europe; in later centuries the Spanish topped off this exotic composition with a flourish of baroque. Sicily also has a natural beauty that's astounding: grapevines stretch from the slopes of brooding Mt Etna to the parched landscapes of the west, and the aquamarine waters off the 1000km coastline are splashed with volcanic islands.

The island has often been in the headlines recently, with the explosive violence between rival football fans of Catania and Palermo in February 2007, and the spate of wildfires that scorched the island throughout the summer months of the same year. Etna erupted again in September 2007, and Stromboli barked but had no bite (though we could easily eat our words on this one). Further afield, the immigration crisis continued on the southern island of Lampedusa.

It's also been a busy few years on the anti-Mafia front. The arrest of the big Mafia boss Bernardo Provenzano in April 2006 made ordinary Sicilians and politicians across Italy believe what many previously thought was impossible – that the end of the Mafia might be in sight. Three further anti-Mafia sweeps in December 2007 saw more arrests, including the imprisonment of 37 members of the Catania branch of the organisation. Not only are these events a major step towards the implementation of law and order in Sicily, but many see them as a sign that the Mafia's infrastructure is finally weakening. Experts, however, warn that optimism should be diluted with caution, and that the path to defeating the dreaded organisation is still long and hard.

But these turbulent events will seem like a small cloud on a sunny day as you admire the beautifully restored Noto cathedral and newly scrubbed-up historic centre in Catania.

Aside from history, architecture and natural beauties, one of Sicily's greatest attractions is its food. Every village, town and city has a raucous, sense-exploding food market – all you need to do is walk through Palermo's Mercato della Vucciria or Catania's La Pescheria to work up an appetite. Traditional recipes are wonderfully preserved, and the restaurants that flirt with modern cuisine – such as Catania's Metró or Palermo's Osteria dei Vespri – do so with utter respect for traditional ingredients and methods. The Sicilian attitude towards food is much like its character – a lot of tradition with just a sprinkling of modernity.

Sicily ticks all the right boxes for any visitor: history, architecture, culture, food, beaches, volcanoes – it's all there. But still this island has more. Its special allure is within its people, whose loyalty to tradition keeps their culture aflame.

FAST FACTS

Population: 4.97 million

Area: 25,708 sq km

GDP per head: €15,227

GDP growth: 1.4%

Inflation: 2.6%

Unemployment rate: 20%

Estimated Mafia profits in 2004: €123 billion

Annual pasta consumption per person: 42kg

Getting Started

There are several ways to organise a trip around Sicily besides simply touring the main towns and cities. If you fancy a sea-and-sun holiday, there are plenty of beach resorts and nearby islands. For history and culture it helps to organise travel around a theme – Greek ruins, baroque architecture or volcanoes. An option that is becoming increasingly popular involves renting a house in the countryside. The network of buses is efficient, extensive and cheap. Similarly, hydrofoil and ferry services to the nearby islands are very convenient (and child-friendly) in summer, although their frequency drops off dramatically in winter. In some cases you may be able to cover more ground in Sicily if you rent your own vehicle, although there are also ecofriendly alternatives (see p18 for details).

WHEN TO GO

Sicily is blessed with a sunny climate, with coastal temperatures rarely dipping below 15°C. Beaches and nearby islands warm up relatively early, usually around mid-April, and stay hot well into October.

Inland, in the mountains, temperatures can fall to freezing in winter, but the weather remains gorgeously fresh during the summer months of July and August when coastal temperatures exceed a stifling 30°C. The ideal time for walking in the Madonie and Nebrodi mountains is between April and June, when an explosion of spring flowers covers the mountainsides.

The best times to visit Sicily are between April and June, or September and October, when the weather is usually good, prices are lower and there are fewer tourists. Late July and August are the peak of the high season: the sun broils, prices are inflated and the island's top attractions are awash with a tide of holiday-makers. Most of Italy goes on holiday in this period (known as *Ferragosto*, literally 'the August holiday'), and a significant chunk of the population chooses Sicily as its preferred destination.

You may prefer to organise your trip to coincide with one of the many festivals that fill the Sicilian calendar – Easter is a particular highlight. For more details see p285.

COSTS & MONEY

Sicily isn't as cheap as many travellers assume, but it is one of the few destinations in Italy where the budget-minded can have a comfortable time. A key factor to consider is the huge difference in costs between the high season – usually Easter and from July to September, with the highest prices in August – and the rest of the year. Even the most popular tourist spots, such as Cefalù, the Aeolian Islands and Taormina drop their prices dramatically during the low season. The less visited areas of the island – the west and parts of the interior – generally offer cheaper accommodation and eating options throughout the year.

See p283 for more information on when to visit Sicily.

Admission fees to all the major archaeological sites and museums run by the Regione Siciliana (the Sicilian regional government) are set at the same price, which at the time of research was €6. Most places offer a discount to EU students (€3), while seniors and children go free. You may have to produce some ID (passport or driving licence with a photo) at the more popular sites like the Cappella Palatina in Palermo.

At the bottom end of the price bracket you will pay €15 to €20 per night in youth hostels. The cheapest *pensione* (small hotel) is unlikely to cost much less than €25/50 for a basic single/double. However, you will be able to find comfortable rooms with en suite showers starting from around €55/70 for singles/doubles. Midrange hotels in cities such as Palermo, Syracuse, Agrigento and Taormina can easily cost from €60/80 to €130/180 for singles/doubles.

Eating out is just as variable, depending on the location. In Taormina, Palermo and on the Aeolian Islands you will find the most expensive restaurants; elsewhere food is generally cheaper. You can pay from as little as €20 for a meal of *primo* (first course), *secondo* (second course) and dessert in a little trattoria to more than €40 for the equivalent in an upmarket restaurant, plus wine. Set tourist menus start at around €10, but the food quality on these menus can vary.

A very prudent backpacker might scrape by on €60 per day but only by staying in youth hostels, eating out for only one simple meal per day, keeping transport costs down and minimising visits to museums. Realistically, a traveller wanting to stay in comfortable midrange hotels, eat out for two square meals per day, and not feel restricted to one museum per day should reckon on a minimum daily average of €100 to €120 per person based on two people sharing a room at €80, plus car hire.

Public transport is very reasonably priced, but car hire is expensive (as is petrol) and is probably worth organising before you leave home (see p301). On trains it is cheaper to travel on the *regionale* (slow local train) and *diretto* (slow direct train) rather than the faster Intercity (IC).

HOW MUCH?

Cup of coffee €1

10-minute taxi ride €5-10

Bowl of pasta €8-10

Night in a hostel €25

Night in a 3-star hotel €90-110

See also the Lonely Planet Index, inside front cover.

TRAVELLING RESPONSIBLY

In the grand scale of things, the environmental impact of a single trip might not seem particularly significant, but consider tourism's worldwide context and a different picture emerges: each year there are some 700 million holidays, a figure which is expected to grow to 1 billion by 2010.

Most Mediterranean countries suffer from the overdevelopment of tourism infrastructure to some degree, especially in coastal areas, and Sicily is no exception. The island's main problem is general water shortages, exacerbated by high tourist demands. You can lessen your impact on Sicily's environment and increase the beneficial effects of tourism for the local economy by choosing ecofriendly places to stay, and making use of locally run tours, markets and courses. These are all good ways of engaging with the country and are recommended throughout this guide.

For more on Sicily's environmental issues, see p68.

Fly Less, Stay Longer

While the introduction of cheap flights to Sicily has meant an increase in tourism and a boost to the region's economy, air travel is the fastest growing contributor to climate change. Mile for mile, the amount of carbon dioxide emitted for one person driving a car is about as much as that for one passenger on a plane; the problem with flying, however, is not only the carbon emitted (and other greenhouse gases, such as water vapour), but the fact that at high altitude these gasses have a greater effect on climate change. Offsetting schemes enable you to calculate your emissions so that you can invest in renewable energy schemes and reforestation projects that will reduce the emission of, or remove from the atmosphere an equivalent amount of carbon dioxide.

So what can you do to limit your environmental footprint once you get to Sicily? For a start you might consider a low-emission form of transport once you land. Train travel in Sicily is easy and affordable. Likewise, there is a comprehensive network of coaches running the length and breadth of the island and in many cases this is the preferred mode of transport for Sicilians.

Getting around on a local level is generally fairly easy in Sicily. Most of the towns and cities are easily walkable, meaning zero emissions! Local transport in Palermo is efficient and good value, although blaring horns and peak-time traffic jams are sometimes maddening. The same goes for Catania, Sicily's second biggest city. Syracuse, on the other hand, has had its historic part, namely the island of Ortygia, more or less closed to traffic, making parking possible only for residents – free electric buses circulate around town. This has made Ortygia a great deal more pleasant and has noticeably reduced pollution, so one can only hope that other towns will follow this example.

Madly buzzing scooters remain a firm fixture of Sicilian life and, although scooters don't have a particularly high carbon footprint when compared with most cars, their numbers and the noise they produce do contribute to urban pollution. They are also obviously a lot less environmentally friendly than riding a bicycle. Increasing awareness of ecoissues in Sicily has also prompted a greater number of hotels to offer guests the use of bicycles during their stay.

For more information on ecofriendly travel see p300.

Accommodation

An increasing number of tourism businesses in Sicily are now looking to cash in on the buoyant green euro, so it can be difficult to identify genuinely green options. The eco-labelling scheme Legambiente Turismo has certified nearly 200 hotels, judging each hotel on their use of water and energy resources, reductions in waste production, and the availability of good local cuisine and organic breakfasts. The number of family-run B&Bs is increasing, as are the options for *agriturismo* (accommodation on working farms).

Slow Food

One of the best ways to contribute to local economies is to shop locally. In Italy (including Sicily), this isn't difficult: it is the home of the **Slow Food Movement** (www.slowfood.com), there are many excellent local markets, farm restaurants, and most of the cuisine uses seasonal, organic food. Unlike for the northern areas of Italy, the benefit of visiting (and eating in) Sicily is that the region obstinately retains its culinary traditions. The guidebook *Osterie d'Italia* (published by Slow Food) is an excellent source of information and recommendations on this subject.

'One of the best ways to contribute to local economies is to shop locally'

Responsible Travel Schemes

Agriturismi (www.agriturismi.it) An online guide to farm accommodation.

Fondo per l'Ambiente Italiano (www.fondoambiente.it) The Italian equivalent of the National Trust (in the UK, US and Australia), which restores historic houses and gardens and opens them up to the public.

Legambiente Turismo (www.legambienteturismo.it) Look for their 'Green Swan' eco-label that flags genuinely ecofriendly places to stay.

Parks.it (www.parks.it) The place to look for essential information on all of Sicily's national and regional parks, and other protected areas.

Travel Foundation (www.thetravelfoundation.org.uk) This UK-based sustainable tourism charity provides tips on how to travel more responsibly.

World-Wide Opportunities on Organic Farms (www.wwoof.it) Learn about biodynamic and organic living and farming techniques in return for a few hours' work.

TOP 10

Palermo.
SICILY
Ionian Sea

OUR FAVOURITE FESTIVALS & EVENTS

The Sicilians celebrate their festivals with fervour and great theatrics. Elaborate costumes, profound solemnity, hysterical worship and pagan partying are all par for the course. The following list is our Top 10, but for a comprehensive listing of festivals throughout the island see p285.

1 Festa di Sant'Agata (February); Catania (p201)
2 Sagra del Mandorlo in Fiore (February); Agrigento (p265)
3 I Misteri (March/April); Trapani (p108)
4 Infiorata (May); Noto (p230)
5 La Mattanza (May/June); Favignana (p114)
6 Festival of Greek Classical Drama (May/June); Syracuse (p222)
7 Festino di Santa Rosalia (July); Palermo (p91)
8 Festa di Maria Santissima della Visitazione (July); Enna (p244)
9 Taormina Arte (July/August); Taormina (p193)
10 Festa di Santa Lucia (December); Syracuse (p223)

TOP READS

Grasp a greater sense of people and place by immersing yourself in the following books by some of Sicily's finest writers. See p61 for more information.

1 *Il Malavoglia* (The Malavoglia Family; 1881) by Giovanni Verga
2 *Sei personaggi in ricerca di un autore* (Six Characters in Search of an Author; 1921) by Luigi Pirandello
3 *Conversazione in Sicilia* (Conversations in Sicily; 1941) by Elio Vittorini
4 *Il gattopardo* (The Leopard; 1957) by Giuseppe Tomasi di Lampedusa
5 *Report from Palermo* (1959) by Danilo Dolci
6 *Il giorno della civetta* (The Day of the Owl; 1961) by Leonardo Sciascia
7 *La diceria dell'untore* (The Plague Sower; 1981) by Gesualdo Bufalino
8 *Men of Honour* (1993) by Giovanni Falcone
9 *La luna di carta* (The Paper Moon; 2005) by Andrea Camilleri
10 *A Photographer in Sicily* (1996) by Enzo Sellerio

MUST-SEE MOVIES

Although notably lacking home-grown directors, Sicily has inspired a catalogue of great films heavy on sexual tension, drama and death. See p62 for more details.

1 *La terra trema* (The Earth Trembles; 1948) directed by Luchino Visconti
2 *Stromboli* (1950) directed by Roberto Rossellini
3 *Il gattopardo* (The Leopard; 1963) directed by Luchino Visconti
4 *The Godfather I, II* and *III* (1972, 1974 and 1990) directed by Francis Ford Coppola
5 *Cento giorni a Palermo* (One Hundred Days in Palermo; 1984) directed by Giuseppe Ferrara
6 *Kaos* (Chaos; 1984) directed by Paolo and Vittorio Taviani
7 *Nuovo cinema paradiso* (Cinema Paradiso; 1988) directed by Giuseppe Tornatore
8 *Il postino* (The Postman; 1994) directed by Michael Radford
9 *Respiro* (2002) directed by Emanuele Crialese
10 *Nuovomondo* (The Golden Door; 2006) directed by Emanuele Crialese

TRAVEL LITERATURE

Sicily's complex character, poetic beauty and ancient history have given authors much to write about over the years. The following recommendations will enhance any traveller's understanding of this extraordinary island.

Beautiful Angiola (Laura Gonzenbach; introduction by Jack Zipes) A 19th-century collection of neglected fairy tales gathered from the Sicilian peasantry and translated into English for the first time. This book is full of delightful escapades, sorcery and surprise in the same style as the Brothers Grimm.

The Golden Honeycomb (Vincent Cronin) Considered one of the classic travel accounts of Sicily. The story, essentially a traveller's sojourn on the island in the 1950s, is constructed around the myth of the golden honeycomb, a gift from Daedalus to the goddess Aphrodite at Erice.

In Sicily (Norman Lewis) A slim volume executed in Lewis' typically effortless style. He introduces the reader to a cast of old friends sharing memories and glasses of wine between chasing interviews with councillors and Mafia henchmen. In the end you just don't want him to get back on that plane.

Italian Journey 1786–88 (Johann Wolfgang von Goethe) A weighty tome that presaged the deluge of tourists to Italian shores. It contains the letters and diaries that Goethe wrote during his travels, covering an exhaustive range of interests from art history to politics, painting and personal encounters.

Midnight in Sicily (Peter Robb) A gripping documentary about the Mafia and the 1995 trial of Prime Minister Giulio Andreotti. The skilful narrative weaves political commentary with excellent travel writing and loads of great asides on food, art and culture.

The Normans in Sicily (John Julius Norwich) A magnificent historical account of the Norman conquest of Sicily. Weighty, scholarly and fired with enthusiasm, Norwich's tome skilfully recounts the epic story of the House of Hauteville and one of Europe's greatest adventurers, Robert Guiscard.

On Persephone's Island (Mary Taylor Simeti) An honest and evocative portrait of Sicily's conflicted and complex culture. Simeti's intelligent observations (from a US-expat perspective), scholarly titbits, and in-depth descriptions of people and landscapes bring the island to life.

Sicily: Three Thousand Years of Human History (Sandra Benjamin) An interesting account of immigration to Sicily through the centuries and how the various ethnic groups influenced the island's culture, architecture, cuisine and general character.

For top stories on Sicily, check out *Italy Mag* at www.italymag.co.uk /italy_regions/sicily.

INTERNET RESOURCES

The Lonely Planet website (lonelyplanet.com) has information on Sicily, as well as travel news and links to other travel resources. You may also find these sites useful:

Best of Sicily (www.bestofsicily.com) This detailed site has loads of useful links and tips for travelling throughout Sicily.

CTS Village (www.cts.it; in Italian) This site provides useful information from the Centro Turistico Studentesco e Giovanile (CTS; Centre for Student and Youth Tourists), Italy's leading student-travel organisation.

Regione Sicilia (www.regione.sicilia.it/turismo/web_turismo) The rather poetic website of the regional tourist board has useful transport links and suggested itineraries. You can also inquire about accommodation and guides through the site.

Trenitalia (www.trenitalia.it) The official site of the Italian railways provides fare and timetable information.

Itineraries
CLASSIC ROUTES

WORLD HERITAGE SITES   One to Two Weeks / Catania to Aeolian Islands

Southeast Sicily has a harmonious blend of classical and baroque styles so unique and coherent as to represent the majority of Sicily's World Heritage sites.

In **Catania** (p196), the chiaroscuro baroque of Giovanni Vaccarini combines black lava with white limestone, in complete contrast to the buttery baroque of the Val di Noto towns, including **Caltagirone** (p255), **Palazzolo Acreide** (p227), **Noto** (p228), **Modica** (p233), **Scicli** (p234) and **Ragusa** (p235) – all an extraordinary architectural and artistic achievement of swirling stone sculpture. Although not recognised as a World Heritage site itself, head northeast to civilised **Syracuse** (p214) and visit the **Museo Archeologico Paolo Orsi** (p220), which houses the island's most comprehensive archaeological collection. Then head northwest for **Piazza Armerina** (p249) to enjoy the artistic verve of the mosaics at the **Villa Romana del Casale** (p252), continuing on to Agrigento's famous **Valley of the Temples** (p261).

If you have more time on your hands, take another week to explore Sicily's other notable World Heritage site, the **Aeolian Islands** (p149).

This route will take you through Sicily's World Heritage sites. It is a good week or two of rich sites and short distances that are best enjoyed if you have your own transport.

WILD ABOUT THE WEST   10 Days to Two Weeks / Palermo to Selinunte

Imbued with a profound sense of the past, the west of the island is the most Arabian in attitude, atmosphere and flavour and offers a wonderful 10-day itinerary of sights and activities that are particularly suited to families.

Leave raucous **Palermo** (p75) and head directly west along the A29 to tiny **Scopello** (p104) on the edge of the **Riserva Naturale dello Zingaro** (p104), which has wonderful walking trails and diving. Visit the splendidly sited temple at **Segesta** (p113) on your way to the fishing town of **Trapani** (p105). From Trapani you can do any number of day trips. Be sure to stay overnight in medieval **Erice** (p110), at its best when the day-trippers have deserted the quaint cobbled streets, and visit the chief Phoenician site of **Mozia** (p119).

Alternatively, take to the water and explore the child-friendly **Egadi Islands** (p113) on bicycles and in boats. The more ambitious may take the overnight ferry to **Pantelleria** (p117).

From Trapani the coastal road wends its way to genteel **Marsala** (p120). Don't miss the Carthaginian warship in the **Museo Archeologico Regionale Baglio Anselmi** (p121), then sample some of the town's eponymous wines at the **Cantine Florio** (p123). Push on to scruffy **Mazara del Vallo** (p124) and enjoy the town's treasures in the **Museo del Satiro** (p125). End with the fabulous ruins of **Selinunte** (p126), perched above one of the island's best beaches, then take the fast route back to Palermo along the A29 autostrada (motorway).

This neat circular route is best managed by car, although it is possible to do it by bus and train. With your own car you can stay in some of the excellent *agriturismi* **(farm stays) and enjoy the countryside.**

MAGICAL MOUNTAINS   Two Weeks / Cefalù to Catania

Away from the hot beaches and classical ruins that ring the coastline, the mountainous interior is more representative of traditional Sicilian life than any other area of the island. And its wild, rugged beauty lies well beyond the conventional tourist trail.

Fly into **Palermo** (p75) and head straight for picture-postcard **Cefalù** (p134) with its Arab-Norman **Duomo di Cefalù** (p135) and busy beaches. Take the wonderful day walk to the **Santuario di Gibilmanna** (p139), from where you can view the entire range of the Madonie.

From Cefalù head straight into the heart of **Parco Naturale Regionale delle Madonie** (p139). A landscape of idyllic wooded countryside, the park is full of well-marked walking trails. Then head to the superquaint hilltop town of **Petralia Soprana** (p141), which is a great base for walking.

Head east through **Gangi** (p248) and **Sperlinga** (p248), with its troglodytic caves, to the sun-scorched centre at **Enna** (p241). Delight in its perfectly preserved medieval centre and walk along the heavy fortified walls of the **Castello di Lombardia** (p242). Alternatively, take a short bus ride to the 4th-century **Villa Romana del Casale** (p252) near Piazza Armerina, which has a unique collection of mosaics.

Finish up in **Catania** (p196) and make the long hike up to the main craters of **Mt Etna** (p208) main craters for the most spectacular views on the island.

This 245km route is fairly straight-forward but you will need a car if you don't want to hang around at rural bus stops. Plus, with your own car you can freewheel around the beautiful mountain scenery and make heaps of pit stops to take photographs.

WORSHIPPING IN SICILY

**One Week to 10 Days /
Palermo to Ragusa or Agrigento**

Sicily has some of the world's most spectacular churches, which will inspire awe even in the most irreligious of people.

The most impressive of all is the dazzlingly beautiful **Monreale Cathedral** (p99), situated just above Palermo. Right inside the city itself is its smaller rival, the **Capella Palatina** (p81), another Norman creation that reflects Arab artisanship and Byzantine aesthetics. The gorgeous **Martorana** (p81) is one of Palermo's favourites, with shimmering mosaics and an intimate atmosphere.

Cefalù's duomo (p135) gleams with Norman-era mosaics, and the dramatic cliff-face backdrop frames it beautifully. Syracuse's **Santa Lucia church** (p218) is seated on top of an ancient Greek temple and its baroque façade is gorgeous. **Noto's San Nicoló cathedral** (p229), recently restored to its original glory, has a stunning exterior and glorious stairs leading up to it. Nearby Ragusa's **Cattedrale di San Giorgio** (p236) hosts many a wedding, its baroque style complementing the celebratory mood.

Agrigento's **Chiesa di San Nicola** (p264), with its 13th-century Gothic exterior, is seated inside the Valley of the Temples.

This is an easy route from Palermo to the southeastern side of the island via Cefalù. It's easily done by public transport, though if you decide to head for Agrigento, your own transport may be a better choice.

TAILORED TRIPS

ISLANDS & VOLCANOES

There is no better place to start this itinerary than in **Catania** (p196), a city built of lava. From here frequent buses make the tortuous ascent of Sicily's most famous sight, **Mt Etna** (p208), climbing through its lush national park. From Etna's lofty heights the Cyclops hurled his stones at the fleeing Odysseus, and you can still see their jagged forms along the dramatic **Riviera dei Ciclopi** (p206). Swap Gore-Tex and trekking boots for glad rags in

Taormina (p190), Sicily's foremost international resort, before continuing to **Messina** (p184). If you have small children don't miss the world's largest astronomical clock in the campanile of the attractive **cathedral** (p185).

Another week should allow you to island-hop at your leisure. Start from **Lipari** (p156) to arrange boating and diving activities. Nature lovers should head for **Salina** (p170), while volcano enthusiasts should climb the **Fossa di Vulcano** (p168) and experience the exciting night hike up **Stromboli** (p177). Beach bums will be content to remain idle on the terrace of Hotel Raya on **Panarea** (p175) and those seeking peace and quiet should head for remote **Alicudi** (p181) and **Filicudi** (p180).

To return to Catania via a different route, take the hydrofoil or ferry to Milazzo and make your way back through the **Parco Regionale dei Nebrodi** (p142).

BEACH HOPPING

You'll probably want to start off as near to Palermo as possible, so where better to head than to **Mondello** (p99), a mere 15-minute journey from the capital. Heading further west, you'll reach the **Golfo di Castellamare** (p103) where the **Riserva Naturale dello Zingaro** (p104) hides some pebbly sickle-shaped beaches and **Scopello** (p104) offers a chance to swim surrounded by rusting anchors and dramatic rocks. Nearby **San Vito lo Capo** (p105) is Sicily's most popular beach. Going around the province of Trapani, you'll reach

Selinunte (p126), a stunning archaeological site with a beach to match. Next up is **Eraclea Minoa** (p269), another place made up of the twin attractions of a fabulous beach and an archaeological site. Just southeast further down is the stunning **Scala dei Turchi** (p268).

Going east of Palermo, the first excellent beach is in **Cefalù** (p134). Taormina's **Isola Bella** (p192) is so pretty, it's incredible. Scenic swimming is to be had at **Aci Castello** (p208), where the moody castle broods over the blue waters. Next up is the big sandy stretch of **Fontane Bianche** (p222), just outside Syracuse. Isolation and tranquillity are features of the beaches of the **Riserva Naturale di Vendicari** (p232).

History

From the massively powerful world empires to the wanton hands of feudal rulers and mysterious *mafiosi,* the people of Sicily have long been at the centre of brutal historical events. The island's position in the middle of the Mediterranean, between mainland Italy and North Africa, has meant that it has been involved in nearly every major Mediterranean war. Countless invaders, opportunists and reckless kings and emperors have influenced its language, art, architecture, food, religion and social habits, making Sicily a shimmering mosaic that reflects the entire Mediterranean history and culture.

SETTLING IN

The first evidence of an organised settlement on Sicily belongs to the Stentillenians, who came from the Middle East and settled on the island's eastern shores sometime between 4000 and 3000 BC.

But it was the settlers from the middle of the second millennium BC who radically defined the island's character and whose early presence helps us understand Sicily's complexities. Thucydides (c 460–404 BC) records three major tribes: the Sicanians, who originated either in Spain or North Africa and settled in the north and west (giving these areas their Eastern flavour); the Elymians from Greece, who settled in the south; and the Siculians (or Sikels), who came from the Calabrian peninsula and spread out along the Ionian Coast. Thus cultural divide was created from the start, a divide that was further deepened with the subsequent colonisation of the west of the island by Carthaginians from North Africa (c 850 BC) and the Greeks, who came to Sicily later, in the 8th to 6th centuries BC.

The Italians, the oft-quoted classic by Luigi Barzini, is a wonderful analysis of the history, traditions and attitudes of the Italian people, with an excellent chapter on Sicily.

CITY STATES
Part One: Greeks & Phoenicians (or Civilisation, Splendour, Chaos & War)

The acquisition of the vast Mediterranean territories was a natural next step for the ever-expanding Greek city states. It all started with a group of Chalcidians who landed on Sicily's Ionian Coast in 735 BC and founded a small settlement at Naxos. They were followed a year after by the Corinthians, who built their colony on the southeastern island of Ortygia, calling it Syracoussai (Syracuse). The Chalcidians went further south from their own fort and founded a second town called Katane (Catania) in 729 BC, and the two carried on stitching towns and settlements together until three quarters of the island were in Hellenic hands.

TIMELINE

12,000–10,000 BC	1250–850 BC	735–580 BC
Stone Age settlers live in the caves of Monte Pellegrino and the Egadi Islands, leaving rock art still visible today.	First-known settlers arrive and found small colonies at Stentinello, Megara Hyblaea and on Lipari. They begin the lucrative business of trading obsidian. Carthaginians establish trading ports in the west at Palermo, Solunto and Mozia.	Greek cities are founded at Naxos in 735, Syracuse in 734, Megara Hyblaea in 728, Gela in 689, and Selinunte and Messina in 628. Agrigento is established as a subcolony of Gela in 581.

AN ANCIENT FAMILY

Sicily's past stretches all the way back into the dirt and grime of prehistoric people – rock etchings at Levanzo and Monte Pellegrino attest to human settlements as far back as 12,000 BC. A skeleton discovered in a cave near Messina turned out to have belonged to a woman – later named Thea – who lived 14,000 years ago. Six other skeletons were discovered alongside hers, and are presumably members of her family. Thea's face was reconstructed by a sculptor, aided by anthropologists, at Palermo University in 2007. She was 165cm tall, above average for her time.

Check out the chronology of Ancient Greece and its time in Sicily at www .ancientgreece.com.

Naturally, the growing Greek power in the south and east of the island created uncomfortable tensions with the Phoenicians in the west; in turn, the Phoenicians' alliance with the powerful city-state of Carthage (in modern-day Tunisia) was of serious concern to the Greeks. By 480 BC the Carthaginians were mustering a huge invading force of some 300,000 mercenaries. Commanded by one of their great generals, Hamilcar, the force landed on Sicily and besieged Himera (near Termini Imerese), but the vast army was defeated by the crafty Greek tyrant Gelon, whose troops breached Hamilcar's lines by pretending to be Carthaginian reinforcements. The defeated Hamilcar performed self-immolation.

A much-needed period of peace followed in Sicily. The Greek colonies had lucrative trade deals thanks to the island's rich resources, and the remains of their cities testify to the extent of their wealth and sophistication. But their bad treatment of the native inhabitants (who could never attain citizenship), together with bitter rivalries and parochial politics, constantly undermined the Greeks' civic achievements and inevitably resulted in conflict.

The advent of the Peloponnesian Wars in Greece meant that Athens turned its attention to Syracuse. One hundred years earlier it would have been unthinkable for a Sicilian colony to challenge the hegemony of mainland Greece, but Syracuse was now a direct rival to Athenian power and it decided to challenge the Greek city. Athens, infuriated by the Sicilian 'upstart', decided to attack Syracuse in 415 BC, mounting upon it the 'Great Expedition' – the largest fleet ever assembled. Despite the fleet's size and Athens' confidence, Syracuse fought back and the mainland Greek army suffered a humiliating defeat. The victory over Athens marked the zenith of Syracusan power on the island.

Bone up on Greek tragedy by revisiting the classic plays of Aeschylus, including *Agamemnon*, *Oedipus* and *Prometheus Bound*, all premiered in Syracuse theatre.

Though Syracuse was celebrating its victory, the rest of Sicily was in a constant state of civil war. This provided the perfect opportunity for Carthage to seek its revenge for Himera, and in 409 BC a new army led by Hamilcar's bitter but brilliant nephew Hannibal wreaked havoc in the Sicilian countryside. It completely destroyed Selinunte, Himera, Agrigento and Gela and in 405 BC the Syracusan tyrant Dionysius I (405–367 BC)

227 BC	227 BC – AD 535	530
Sandwiched between the superpowers of Carthage and Rome, Sicily becomes the unfortunate battleground for a war whose outcome is to place it firmly within the Roman Empire.	As the superpower's first colony, Sicily suffers the worst aspects of Roman rule: native inhabitants are refused the right of citizenship and forced into indentured slavery on the *latifondi* – huge landed estates.	A version of ice cream is said to have been championed in Sicily during the Roman rule, with a relay of runners bringing snow from Mt Etna and flavouring it for the wealthy patricians.

launched a counteroffensive that resulted in the complete destruction of Mozia between 398 and 397 BC.

Although relative peace under Timoleon (r 345–336 BC) and later Hieron II (r 265–215 BC) brought stability to the island as its cities were rebuilt and the island repopulated with settlers from Greece and the Italian mainland, the days of Greek domination in Sicily were numbered.

Part Two: The Romans (or Slavery, Rebellion, Trade & Commerce)

Possession of Sicily was essential if Rome were to control the entire Mediterranean basin, and the advent of the First Punic War (264–241 BC) was a turning point for the island. The majority of Sicilians lived in horrifyingly reduced circumstances; native inhabitants were refused the right to citizenship and forced into indentured slavery on the pernicious *latifondi* – huge landed estates that were to cause so many of the island's woes in later years. Rome's less-than-enlightened rule led to a revolt in 135 BC. Led by Eunus of Henna (Enna), the revolt involved tens of thousands of the enslaved men, women and even children. No sooner had the Romans suppressed the first revolt than the Second Servile War broke out (104–101 BC), with the rebellious slaves supported by a large chunk of the island's peasant class.

Although essentially treated as a Roman breadbasket, Sicily regained its status as an important centre of trade during this period. Syracuse experienced a partial rebirth as an important commercial centre, and the period coincided with the construction of some of the finer monuments of the Roman occupation, including the Villa Romana di Casale. And finally, in the 3rd century AD – after some 500 years of Roman rule – Sicilians were granted the right to citizenship.

> If Roman emperors float your boat, click on www .roman-emperors.org to find out all about the lives of these fascinating characters.

A BYZANTINE INTERLUDE

After Rome fell to the Visigoths in AD 410 Sicily was occupied by Vandals from North Africa, but their tenure was relatively brief. In 535 the Byzantine general Belisarius landed an army and was welcomed by a population that, despite over 700 years of Roman occupation, was still largely Greek, both in language and custom. The Byzantines were eager to use Sicily as a launching pad for the retaking of Saracen lands (those lands owned by the combined forces of Arabs, Berbers and Spanish Muslims, collectively known as the Saracens), but their dreams were not to be realised. A new power was emerging in the Mediterranean and its sights were firmly set on Sicily.

ENTER ISLAM

One of Sicily's most formative periods – which lasted over 200 years – started around the year AD 700. The Moors, who already controlled the North African coast, wanted to expand their power by taking charge of the Mediterranean trading routes. Sicily was, naturally, seen as a strategic stepping stone.

535	827–965	1059–72
The Byzantine general Belisarius conquers Sicily. The Byzantines want to use the island as a launching pad for the retaking of Saracen lands; Syracuse temporarily supplants Constantinople as the capital of the empire in 663.	The Saracens land at Mazara del Vallo at the invitation of a Byzantine general rebelling against the emperor. Sicily is united under Arab rule and Palermo is the second-largest city in the world after Constantinople.	Pope Nicholas II and Robert Guiscard sign a concordat at Melfi. Robert vows to expel the Saracens from Sicily. With the help of his younger brother, Roger I, the Normans seize Palermo 'for Christendom' in 1072.

For the most comprehensive coverage of island history invest in Moses Finlay's *A History of Sicily: Ancient Sicily to the Arab Conquest* or Denis Mack Smith's two excellent books, *Medieval Sicily 800–1713* and *Modern Sicily After 1713*.

Although the island had been subjected to repeated raids, it was not until 827 that a full-scale invasion took place when the Saracen army landed at Mazara del Vallo at the invitation of a Byzantine general rebelling against the emperor. In 831 Palermo fell, followed by Syracuse in 878.

The Arab rule was beneficial to the island in general. True, churches were converted to mosques and Arabic was implemented as the common language, but the Arabs also introduced much-needed land reforms and fostered the development of trade, agriculture and mining. New crops were introduced, including citrus trees, date palms and sugar cane, and most importantly, the Saracens developed and perfected a system of water supply and irrigation.

Sicily became an important centre for the expansion of Islam, but a policy of religious tolerance towards non-Muslims was also exercised (though many Sicilians converted to Islam to avoid paying the higher taxes imposed on non-Muslims).

After the invasion, Palermo was chosen as the capital of the emirate and, over the next 200 years, became one of the most splendid cities in the Arab world, a haven of culture and commerce rivalled only by Córdoba in Spain.

THE KINGDOM OF THE SUN

The Arabs called the Normans 'wolves' because of their barbarous ferocity and the terrifying speed with which they were mopping up territory on the mainland. By 1053, after six years of terrifying mercenary activity, Robert Guiscard (c 1015–85), the Norman conquistador, had comprehensively defeated the combined forces of the Calabrian Byzantines, the Lombards and the papal forces at the Battle of Civitate.

The Normans in Sicily is John Julius Norwich's wonderful romp through the Norman invasions, incorporating the earlier title *Kingdom in the Sun*, a detailed account of the Norman takeover of Sicily.

Having established his supremacy, Robert turned his attentions to expanding the territories under his control. To achieve this, he had to deal with the Vatican. But the Normans' relationship with the Vatican underwent a radical turn following the Great Schism of 1054 (which saw a complete break between the Byzantine and Latin churches). In return for being invested with the titles of duke of Puglia and Calabria in 1059, Robert agreed to chase the Saracens out of Sicily and restore Christianity to the island; as backup he summoned his younger brother Roger I (1031–1101) from Normandy that year. Roger landed his troops at Messina in 1061 and captured the port by surprise. In 1064 he tried to take Palermo but was repulsed by a well-organised Saracen army; it wasn't until Robert arrived in 1072 with substantial reinforcements that the city fell into Norman hands.

The great Palermo Mosque was immediately reconsecrated and Roger took on the title of count of Sicily (Conte Ruggero). Although he was an autocratic ruler, his firm hand and formidable army brought about Sicily's most magnificent era. Impressed by the cultured Arab lifestyle, Roger shamelessly borrowed and improved on it, spending vast amounts of money on palaces

1072–1101	1101–30	1145
Sicily's brightest period in history ensues under Roger I, with a cosmopolitan court, reconciliation with the native people and the embracing of several languages. Many significant palaces and churches are built during this time.	Roger II takes over after his father's death and builds one of the most efficient civil services in Europe. His court is responsible for the creation of the first written legal code in Sicilian history.	El Idrisi's famous planisphere (a large, silver global map), the most important medieval geographical work that accurately maps Europe, North Africa and western Asia, is said to have been completed during this year.

and churches and encouraging a cosmopolitan atmosphere in his court. Roger wisely opted for a policy of reconciliation with the indigenous people; Arabic and Greek continued to be spoken along with French, and Arab engineers, bureaucrats and architects continued to be employed by the court. After Roger's death in 1101, Sicily was then governed by his widow, Adelasia (Adelaide), until 1130 when Roger II (1095–1154) was crowned king.

The Enlightened Leader

Roger II was a gifted monarch and a keen intellectual who studied the science of government and built an efficient civil service that was the envy of Europe. He assigned key posts to a number of non-Norman advisers; his finances and army were controlled by Arabs while his increasingly powerful navy was controlled by a Greek, George of Antioch. His court was unrivalled for exotic splendour and learning, while Roger flaunted his multicultural heritage by wearing Arab and Byzantine robes and even keeping a substantial harem. His rule was remarkable not only for his patronage of the arts but also for the creation of the first written legal code in Sicilian history, and his success in enlarging his kingdom to include Malta, most of southern Italy and even parts of North Africa.

But sadly this glorious chapter in the island's history was only to last a mere 64 years, eroded by the incompetence and self-indulgence of Roger's successors.

The Setting Sun

Roger's son and successor, William I (1108–66), inherited the kingdom upon his father's death in 1154. He was nicknamed 'William the Bad' and was a vain and corrupt king who paraded around the court with a bodyguard of black slaves.

The appointment of Walter of the Mill (Gualtiero Offamiglia) as archbishop of Palermo, at the connivance of the pope, was to create a dangerous power struggle between church and throne for the next 20 years – a challenge that was taken up by William II (1152–89) when he ordered the creation of a second archbishopric at Monreale.

William II's premature death at the age of 36 brought about a power grab, and an assembly of barons elected Roger II's illegitimate grandson Tancred (c 1130–94) to the throne. His accession was immediately contested by the German (or Swabian) king Henry VI (1165–97), who laid claim to the throne by virtue of his marriage to Roger II's daughter, Constance. At the same time, jealousy and resentment led Tancred's barons to the foolish decision to expel the local Arab population, thus undermining the efficient bureaucracy of the country. And as if all that wasn't enough, King Richard I ('the Lion Heart') was busy sacking Messina on his way to the Third Crusade in 1190.

For an in-depth look at the fascinating reign of one of Europe's greatest kings, pick up Hubert Houben's *Roger II of Sicily: A Ruler Between East and West*, a comprehensive study of the monarchy's cultured court and the elaborate development of royal government.

For something on the history, heraldry, royalty and nobility of southern Italy and Sicily log on to www.regalis.com.

1154	**1189**	**1194–1250**
William I inherits the kingdom, triggering a power struggle between church and throne. Walter of the Mill is appointed archbishop of Palermo.	William II dies childless and his crown goes to his aunt Constance, wife of Henry VI of Hohenstaufen. Henry VI inherits the German crown of the Holy Roman Empire.	Under Frederick I, Palermo is considered Europe's most important city and Sicily is a key player in Europe. But Frederick imposes heavy taxes and restrictions on free trade, provoking mass rebellion.

Tancred died in 1194, and no sooner had his young son, William III, been installed as king than the Hohenstaufen fleet docked in Messina. On Christmas Day of that year Henry VI declared himself king and young William was imprisoned in the castle at Caltabellotta in southern Sicily, where he eventually died (in 1198).

Wonder of the World

In *Frederick II: A Medieval Emperor* (1988), David Abulafia delves into the life and times of the greatest of the Hohenstaufen rulers of Sicily and finds that he did have chinks in his formidable armour.

As Holy Roman Emperor, Henry paid scant attention to his Sicilian kingdom, and he died prematurely of malaria in 1197. He was succeeded by his young heir Frederick (1194–1250), known as both Frederick I of Sicily and Frederick II of Hohenstaufen.

Frederick was a keen intellectual with a penchant for political manoeuvring, but he was also a totalitarian despot who fortified the eastern seaboard from Messina to Syracuse and sacked rebellious Catania in 1232. He had issued the antifeudal Constitution of Melfi a year earlier, stripping the feudal barons of much of their power in favour of a more centralised authority – his own. He drew up the Liber Augustales, which created a unified legal system based on the legal code promulgated by the Roman emperor Augustus 1200 years earlier. This guaranteed certain rights to the citizenry while reinforcing the unquestionable authority of the monarch. He became an avid patron of the arts and the first official champion of vernacular Italian. In the latter years of his reign Frederick became known as Stupor Mundi, 'Wonder of the World', a none-too-humble recognition of his successful rule. Sicily was now a centralised state and played a key commercial and cultural role in European affairs, and throughout the 13th century Palermo was considered the continent's most important city.

In *The Divine Comedy*, Dante devoted an entire canto to the glory of Frederick's court – to this day Sicilians will insist that the dialect that was the basis for Italian was not Tuscan but Sicilian.

Yet Frederick's rule left substantial scars on the island, most notably in the restriction of free trade, the reappearance of massive landed estates, and a heavy tax burden brought on by the pressures of maintaining the empire. Frederick's death in 1250 left the disaffected barons and their foreign allies, most notably the Pope, in open rebellion against the Hohenstaufens. Frederick's son Manfred (1231–66) tried desperately to hold on to power, but his rule was seriously challenged when in 1255 the pope surreptitiously offered the throne to Prince Edmund of Lancaster.

THE SICILIAN VESPERS

As Edmund had never stepped onto the island, the French pope Urban IV quite rightly decided that he was not the right man for the job and in 1266 offered the crown to the heartless Charles of Anjou, brother of the French King Louis IX (later St Louis). In 1266 the Angevin army defeated and killed Manfred at Benevento on the Italian mainland. Two years later, another battle took the life of Manfred's 15-year-old nephew and heir, Conradin, who was publicly beheaded in Naples.

1226–82	1302	1487
Charles of Anjou is crowned king in 1266. He is ousted in the violent uprising known as the Sicilian Vespers. The war is won by the Spanish, who commence their 500 years in power.	The Kingdom of the Two Sicilies (Sicily and the mainland's southern part) is divided. The Spaniards take Sicily and the French control the mainland. Ruled by absent Aragonese kings and controlled by barons, the island reverts to a feudal regime.	The end of religious tolerance is cemented by the expulsion of Jews from all Spanish territories. The Spanish Inquisition starts terrorising Sicily. The major cities, particularly Palermo and Messina, become centres of protest and unrest.

After such a bloody start, the Angevins were hated and feared. Sicily was weighed down by onerous taxes and religious persecution was the order of the day. Norman fiefdoms were removed and awarded to French aristocrats and Sicilian labourers were further oppressed due to their sympathy with the Hohenstaufens.

Regarded as vicious and venal, the French were hated, and with the alleged rape of a local girl by a gang of French troops on Easter Monday 1282 the population of Palermo exploded in rebellion. The peasants lynched every French soldier they could get their hands on. The revolt spread to the countryside and was supported by the barons, who had formed an alliance with pro-imperial Peter of Aragon, who landed at Trapani with a large army and was proclaimed king. For the next 20 years, the Aragonese and the Angevins were engaged in the War of the Sicilian Vespers – a war that was conclusively won by the Spanish, who would remain in power for nearly all of the next 500 years.

FIVE HUNDRED YEARS OF SOLITUDE

The end of the war between the Angevins and Aragonese came with the Peace of Caltabellotta, a treaty signed in 1302. By the end of the 14th century Sicily had been thoroughly marginalised. The eastern Mediterranean was sealed off by the Ottoman Turks, while the Italian mainland was off limits on account of Sicily's political ties with Spain. As a result the bright light of the Renaissance passed the island by, reinforcing the oppressive effects of poverty and ignorance. Even Spain lost interest in its colony as it turned its attentions away from the Mediterranean to the Atlantic as a preferred channel of trade. After 1458 the Spaniards ruled Sicily through viceroys – the only king to set foot on the island over the next 200 years was Charles V of Germany (a Habsburg), who docked here for a few days in 1535.

By the end of the 15th century Spain had discovered America and was no longer a major participant in the affairs of the Mediterranean. The viceroy's court was a den of corruption, serving only the interests of the nobility. With the expulsion of Jews from all Spanish territories in 1492, the era of religious tolerance ended. The most influential body on the island became the Catholic Church (whose archbishops and bishops were mostly Spaniards), which exercised draconian powers through a network of Holy Office tribunals, otherwise known as the Inquisition.

Reeling under the weight of natural disaster (see the boxed text, p34) and state oppression, ordinary Sicilians demanded reform. But Spanish monarchs were preoccupied by the wars of the Spanish succession and Sicily was subsequently passed around like an unwanted Christmas present: it was traded between Spain, the House of Savoy (1713) and the Austrian Habsburgs, who then traded it for Sardinia in 1720. The Spanish reclaimed the island in 1734, this time under the Bourbon king Charles I of Sicily (1734–59).

In the 1282 massacre of the Angevins, Sicilians identified their French victims by making them say 'ciceri' (chickpeas in dialect), a word the French simply could not pronounce.

If you're Jewish with Sicilian roots, you can now go on a Jewish Heritage Sicily tour – check www.sicilytravel .net/Jewish%20tours .htm.

1669	1806–15	1820–60
The worst eruption in Etna's history levels Catania and the east-coast towns. It is preceded by a three-day earthquake. The eruption lasts four months, leaving disaster in its wake and 27,000 people homeless.	The British occupy Sicily and begin the production of sherry in Marsala. Puppet theatre performances emerge as popular night-time entertainment, particularly in Palermo where more than 25 theatres are chock-a-block with grown men.	The first uprising against the Bourbons occurs in Palermo. It is followed by another in Syracuse in 1837 and Palermo in 1848. The revolutionary committees of Palermo give orders for a revolt in April 1860.

NATURAL DISASTERS, POVERTY & PLAGUE

During the Spanish rule, poverty and ignorance were followed by devastating natural disasters. The Sicilian peasantry suffered greatly, and the decimating effect of the Black Death in 1347–48, along with chronic periods of starvation, hastened the descent into a state of desperate poverty. In addition to plagues and cholera, in 1669 Catania was completely destroyed by the biggest eruption in Etna's history. Barely 25 years later most of the cities on the Ionian Coast were wiped out by a massive earthquake that killed more than 5% of the island's population.

Under the reign of Charles I's successor, Ferdinand IV, the landed gentry vetoed any attempts at liberalisation and turned the screws even tighter. Large exports of grain continued to line the pockets of the aristocracy while normal Sicilians died of starvation. During the 17th and 18th centuries it is estimated that at least one-third of the island's common land was appropriated by the nobility.

Exit Feudalism

Although Napoleon never occupied Sicily, his capture of Naples in 1799 forced Ferdinand to move to Sicily. Spanish domination of Sicily was becoming increasingly untenable and Ferdinand's ridiculous tax demands were met with open revolt by the peasantry and the more far-sighted nobles, who believed that the only way to maintain the status quo was to usher in limited reforms. After strong pressure from Lord William Bentinck, commander of the British forces, Ferdinand reluctantly agreed in 1812 to the drawing up of a constitution modelled on the British one. A two-chamber parliament was formed, feudal privileges were abolished, the king was forbidden to enlist foreign troops without the permission of parliament and a court was set up in Palermo that was to be independent of the one in Naples.

Under the Bourbons the Sicilian nobility owned 280 of the island's 360 villages.

At One with Italy

With the final defeat of Napoleon in 1815, Ferdinand once again united Naples and Sicily as the 'Kingdom of the Two Sicilies' and took the title Ferdinand I. But his time was up. For the next 12 years the island was divided between a minority who sought an independent Sicily, and a majority who believed that the island's survival could only be assured as part of a unified Italy.

On 4 April 1860 the revolutionary committees of Palermo gave orders for a revolt against the tottering Bourbon state. The news reached Giuseppe Garibaldi, who decided that this was the perfect moment to begin his war for the unification of Italy. He landed in Marsala on 11 May 1860 with about 1000 soldiers – the famous *mille* – and defeated a Bourbon army of 15,000 at Calatafimi on 15 May, taking Palermo two weeks later.

Garibaldi and his troops arrived at Marsala in two small paddle steamers. They had sailed 960km with no food or water, and no chart or sextant.

1860	1860–94	1897
Garibaldi lands in Marsala and defeats the Bourbon army, taking Palermo two weeks later. His success at Milazzo completes his victory. The island is free of the Spanish for the first time since 1282.	The emergence of the *mafiosi* fills the vacuum between the people and the state. The need for social reform strengthens the growing trade union, the *fasci*. Feeling threatened, the government imposes martial law on Sicily.	Palermo's famous Teatro Massimo opens, but proceeds to decline soon after. It is re-opened in 1997, after massive renovations and a star performance in *The Godfather*.

Despite the revolutionary fervour, Garibaldi was not a reformer in the social sense, and his soldiers blocked every attempt at a land grab on the part of the ordinary worker. On 21 October a referendum was held that saw Sicily opt for unification with Savoy by a staggering 99%.

FASCISM, CONSERVATISM & WWII

Sicily struggled to adapt to the Piedmontese House of Savoy. Under the new constitution only 1% of the population had the right to vote. The old aristocracy by and large maintained all of their privileges and hopes of social reform soon dwindled. Heavy taxes and military conscription, never before introduced to Sicily, only served to intensify resentment against Savoy.

What the island really needed was a far-reaching policy of agrarian reform, including a redistribution of land. The partial break-up of large estates after the abolition of feudalism still only benefited the *gabellotti* (agricultural middlemen who policed the peasants on behalf of the aristocracy), who leased the land from the owners only to charge prohibitive ground rents to peasants who lived and worked on it. To assist them with their rent collections the bailiffs enlisted the help of local gangs, who then took on the role of intermediary between the tenant and the owner, sorting out disputes and regulating affairs in the absence of an effective judicial system. These individuals were called *mafiosi* and were organised into small territorial gangs drawn up along family lines. They effectively filled the vacuum that existed between the people and the state, comfortably slotting in to the role of local power brokers.

Restlessness for social reform strengthened the growing agrarian trade union known as the *fasci*. Perceiving a very real threat to the status quo, the government imposed martial law on the island in 1894. What was particularly galling to the Sicilians was that the prime minister who made the decision was Francesco Crispi, himself a Sicilian and a one-time leader of the island's independence movement. Crispi sent 15,000 troops to Palermo to suppress any attempt at revolt on the part of the *fasci*. His repressive tactics were followed by an offer of mild reform, but this was discarded by the ruling gentry.

By the turn of the 20th century, Sicily was on its figurative knees. Emigration was draining the island of millions of its inhabitants, and despite localised efforts at land reform the situation was going from bad to worse. In 1908 the Messina earthquake left the city in ruins, 84,000 people dead and tens of thousands of others homeless.

In 1922, Benito Mussolini took power in Rome. With the growing influence of the Mafia dons threatening to jeopardise his dominance in Sicily, Mussolini dispatched Cesare Mori to Palermo with orders to crush lawlessness and insurrection on Sicily. Mori did this by ordering the roundup of individuals suspected of involvement in 'illegal organisations'. For assistance

Gian Carlo Caselli's *A True History of Italy* chronicles the rise of the Mafia and its nefarious influence on the apparatus of state.

1922–43	1928	1943–44
Benito Mussolini brings Fascism and almost succeeds in stamping out the Mafia. He drags Sicily into WWII by colonising Libya. Sicily is the springboard for the recapture of Italy and suffers greatly from Allied bombing.	Lava from Etna's eruption wipes out the coastal village of Mascali, together with huge acres of land and 550 buildings. This is the only place to have been destroyed by Etna's eruptions in the 20th century.	The Mafia collaborates with the Allied forces, assisting the capture of the island. Sicily is taken in only 39 days. The Mafia Don Calogero Vizzini is appointed the island's administrator.

with his efforts, Mori drew on the support of the landed gentry, who were rewarded for their help with the reversal of all agrarian reforms achieved in the previous 50 years. The result was simply to drive the movement dangerously underground.

But by the 1930s, Mussolini had bigger fish to fry – his sights were set on the colonisation of Libya as Italy's Fourth Shore, ultimately dragging Sicily into WWII. Chosen as the springboard for the recapture of mainland Italy, Sicily suffered greatly from heavy Allied bombing. Ironically, the war presented the Mafia with the perfect opportunity to get back at Mussolini and it collaborated with the Allied forces (led by US General Patton), assisting the capture of the island in 1943. The fact that Sicily was taken from the Germans in only 39 days was testament to the Mafia's influence in the countryside. After the war, the prisons were emptied of all those unfairly convicted under Fascism, and the Mafia's authority on the island was firmly re-established with the appointment of Mafia Don Calogero Vizzini as the island's administrator.

POSTWAR WOES & MANI PULITE

Following the war Sicily was in a chaotic state. The widespread support for the separatist movement called for a totally independent Sicily, while the Communist Party, which was also extremely active on the island, organised discontented labourers into protest groups that called for radical reforms and a total redistribution of land. The government responded by granting partial autonomy to Sicily in 1946, and while the new status was met with general approval on a bureaucratic level, it did little to resolve the island's age-old problems. The Mafia, freed from the restraints imposed on it by the Fascist regime, was enlisted by the ruling classes to help suppress the spread of left-wing ideologies in the countryside.

The most powerful force in Sicilian politics in the latter half of the 20th century was the Democrazia Cristiana (DC; Christian Democrats), a centre-right Catholic party that appealed to the island's traditional conservatism. Allied closely with the Church, the DC promised wide-ranging reforms while at the same time demanded vigilance against godless communism. It was greatly aided in its efforts by the Mafia, who ensured that the local DC mayor would always top the poll. In return, the system of *clientelismo*, or political patronage, that became a key feature of Sicily's political activities, guaranteed that Mafia business interests would be taken care of through the granting of favourable contracts.

This constant interference by the Mafia in the island's economy did much to nullify the efforts of Rome to reduce the gap between the prosperous north and the poor south. The well-intentioned Cassa del Mezzogiorno (Southern Italy Development Fund), set up in 1950, was aimed at kick-starting the pitiful economy of the south, and Sicily was one of its main beneficiaries,

For a devastating insight into the continuing poverty of many 20th-century Sicilian towns you can't do better than Danilo Dolci's book *Sicilian Lives*. Equally fascinating is Jerry Magione's *A Passion for Sicilians*, an account of Dolci's life work.

In 1992 the local police force was so busy chasing *mafiosi* on the run that 7000 Italian troops were dispatched from the mainland to deal with street crime.

1946–50	1951–75	1995–99
Partial autonomy is granted to Sicily in 1946, and reforms enforce land redistribution. The Mafia is enlisted to help suppress the spread of left-wing ideologies in the country-side and promote the Christian Democrats.	Sicily's petrochemical industry collapses, the citrus industry implodes and the fishing fleets that provided much of Europe's tinned tuna are diminished. One million Sicilians emigrate to northern Europe in search of a better life.	Giulio Andreotti, the Italian prime minister, is charged with Mafia association, and goes on trial in 1995. He gives nothing away during the four-year pro-ceedings. He is acquitted due to lack of evidence in 1999.

receiving state and EU money for all kinds of projects. However, the disappearance of large amounts of cash eventually led the central government to scrap the fund in 1992, leaving the island to fend for itself.

In the same year, the huge Tangentopoli (Bribesville) scandal (the institutionalisation of kickbacks and bribes, which had been the country's modus operandi since WWII) made headline news. Although largely focused on the industrial north of Italy, the repercussions of the widespread investigation into graft (known as Mani Pulite, or Clean Hands) were inevitably felt in Sicily, a region where politics, business and the Mafia were longtime bedfellows. The scandal eventually brought about the demise of the DC party, throwing the cosy arrangement between political parties and the Mafia – known as Il Terzo Livello (the Third Level) – into disarray, bringing the Italian prime minister, Giulio Andreotti, to trial in Palermo in 1995.

In the meantime, things were changing in regard to how the Sicilians viewed the Mafia, thanks to the investigating magistrates Paolo Borsellino and Giovanni Falcone. They contributed greatly to change the climate of opinion against the Mafia on both sides of the Atlantic, and made it possible for ordinary Sicilians to speak about and against the Mafia more freely. Their tragic murder by huge bombs in the summer of 1992 saw a great loss for Italy and Sicily, but it was these deaths that finally broke the code of silence.

For one of the most up-to-date insights into Italy's machinations pick up Tobias Jones' *The Dark Heart of Italy.*

21ST-CENTURY SICILY

Even though today's Sicily is better off than at any other time in its history and seems more a part of mainland politics and a wider European community, it still has enormous economic, social and political hurdles to jump. With unemployment running officially at 20%, but really more like 30% (double the national average) and the average wage only half of that earned north of Florence, Sicily remains one of the poorest Italian regions.

With limited industrial activity and an age-old reliance on agriculture as a source of income, efforts to modernise the island's economy are painfully slow and outside pressures often undermine limited successes.

The election of Romano Prodi in 2006 put a stop to plans to build a bridge over the straits of Messina at a cost of €4 billion, much to the displeasure of Sicily's centre-right regional government, which launched an online poll in early 2007 to see if people wanted the bridge. While they confidently expected the answer to be positive, in the first few days of voting around 55% said 'no'. Prodi has instead redirected the money back into Sicily's infrastructure, which is in great need of a financial boost.

Hooded Easter marchers were outlawed in Corleone in the 1960s to prevent local mobsters from concealing their identity and shooting each other. The ban was lifted in 2007.

2001–04	2006	2007
Sicilian voters support Silvio Berlusconi's Forza Italia party in the 2001 elections. In 2003 Berlusconi stands accused of laundering Mafia money, only to be acquitted in December 2004.	The Sicilian Godfather, Bernardo Provenzano, is arrested after 40 years on the run. His arrest marks an important milestone in the fight against the Mafia.	Provenzano's successor, Salvatore lo Piccolo, is arrested, together with his son Sandro, on the outskirts of Palermo. Despite general optimism, experts warn of ensuing power-grabbing in the wake of the arrests.

The Culture

It's quite likely that you'll come away from your holiday in Sicily with some extra gesticulations and a heightened appreciation for food; you'll also no doubt return with some memories of hairy driving experiences, with Sicilian drivers overtaking at the most impossible of bends and scooters racing past your legs in narrow streets. But, of course, there's a lot more to Sicily than that.

LIFESTYLE

The local stereotype is that Palermo and Catania stand at opposite ends of the island's character. 'In Palermo, we're more traditional, more conservative', says Massimo, a Palermo shopkeeper. 'The Catanians are more outward looking, and better at commerce.' Some ascribe the Palermitans' conservative character to their Arab predecessors, while the Greeks get all the credit for the Catanians' democratic outlook, their sense of commerce and their alleged cunning. Beyond this divide, Sicilians are thought of as conservative and suspicious (usually by mainland Italians), stoical and spiritual, confident, gregarious and sensitive, and as the possessors of a rich and dark sense of humour.

Colonised for centuries, Sicilians have absorbed myriad traits – so much so, indeed, that writer Gesualdo Bufalino believed Sicilians suffered from an 'excess of identity', at the core of which was the islanders' conviction that Sicilian culture stands at the centre of the world. This can feel terribly exclusive to the visitor, and there is still an awful lot of Sicily that is beyond the prying eyes of the tourist. If you're interested in peeking behind the curtains of Sicily's private life, it's best to have some local friends who might invite you to their home and allow you an insight into a part of local life. Who you know makes all the difference, and any invitation to a Sicilian home should be viewed as a real compliment.

That said, it is difficult to make blanket assertions about Sicilian culture, if only because there are huge differences between the more modern-minded city dwellers and those from the traditionally conservative countryside. It is certain, however, that modern attitudes are changing conservative traditions. In the larger university cities such as Palermo, Catania, Syracuse and Messina, you will find a vibrant youth culture and a liberal lifestyle.

Public Stage & Private Theatre

Family is the bedrock of Sicilian life, and loyalty to family and friends is one of the most important qualities you can possess. As Luigi Barzini (1908–84), author of *The Italians*, noted, 'A happy private life helps tolerate an appalling public life.' This chasm between the private arena and public forum is a noticeable aspect of Sicilian life, and has evolved over years of intrusive foreign domination.

Maintaining a *bella figura* (beautiful image) is very important to the average Sicilian, and striving to appear better off than you really are (known as *spagnolismo*) is a regional pastime. Though not confined to Sicily, *spagnolismo* on the island has its roots in the excesses of the Spanish-ruled 18th century, when the race for status was so competitive that the king considered outlawing extravagance. In this climate, how you and your family appeared to the outside world was (and still is) a matter of honour, respectability and pride. In a social context, keeping up appearances extends to dressing well, behaving modestly, performing religious and social duties and fulfilling all

Travellers who want to get in touch with people rather than places should check out the website of www.authenticsicily.com.

Plug in to all things Sicilian at www .sicilianculture.com, which covers everything from news, politics and the economy to language, culture and the arts.

To organise your very own Sicilian wedding in that private villa or aristocratic palazzo, log on to www.weddings madeinitaly.co.uk.

BLOG OFF

Want to know what it's like to live in Sicily? Here are some locally generated blogs that'll give you a good insight into how things are on the island right now.

- www.ilgiramondo.net/forum/sicilia – an Italian-language forum with tons of travel discussions
- http://liberapalermo.blogspot.com – the Italian-language blog of the anti-Mafia movement; it details the group's daily activities and struggles
- http://siciliamo.blogspot.com – has masses of information on Sicily, ranging from recipes to clubs to current affairs
- http://sicilianodyssey.blogspot.com – a middle-aged US Navy–based teacher's experience of Sicilian life; it's fascinating, really
- www.sicilyguide.com/blog – great for current affairs and an occasional debate
- http://sicilytraveller.blogspot.com – has good stuff on Ragusa and on Sicily in general, with food, drink and travel tips

---

essential family obligations; in the context of the extended family, where gossip is rife, a good image protects one's privacy.

In this heavily patriarchal society, 'manliness' is a man's prime concern. The main role of the 'head of the family' is to take care of his family, oil the wheels of personal influence and facilitate the upward mobility of family members through a system of influence known as *clientelismo,* which basically allows people to secure jobs, contracts and opportunities through association with the Mafia. Women, on the other hand, are traditionally the repository of the family's honour, and even though unmarried couples commonly live together nowadays, there are still young couples who undertake lengthy engagements for the appearance of respectability.

> In order to gain extra subsidies, Sicilian farmers planted their trees in tubs and moved them from field to field as the European Commission counting team advanced.

Traditionally, personal wealth is closely and jealously guarded. Family money can support many individuals, while emigrant remittances have vastly improved the lot of many villagers.

A Woman's Place

'In Sicily, women are more dangerous than shotguns', said Fabrizio Angelo Infanti in *The Godfather.* 'A woman at the window is a woman to be shunned', proclaimed the writer Giovanni Verga in the 19th century. And 'Women are too stupid to be involved in the complex world of finance', decided a judge when faced with a female Mafia suspect in the 1990s. As in many places in the Mediterranean, a woman's position in Sicily has always been a difficult one. Sicilian attitudes towards women have been notoriously conservative, protective and oppressive, and only began to lose currency after the 1980s.

A Sicilian mother and wife commands the utmost respect within the home, and is expected to act as the moral and emotional compass for her family. Although – or perhaps because – male sexuality holds an almost mythical status, women's modesty – which includes being quiet and feminine, staying indoors and remaining a virgin until married – has had to be ferociously guarded. To this day the worst insult that can be directed to a Sicilian man is *cornuto,* meaning that his wife has been unfaithful.

> Despite the landmark decision in 1983 that women were incapable of money laundering, since 1995 over 100 women have been arrested in relation to Mafia crimes.

Divorce was legalised in the 1970s, but remains uncommon (usually requiring at least three years of legal wrangling), despite statistics showing that nearly 70% of Sicilian married couples have had extramarital affairs.

But things are changing for Sicilian women. More and more unmarried women live with their partners, especially in the cities, and enjoy the liberal

For a glimpse of the oppressive social scrutiny Sicilian women were subject to not so long ago, watch Giuseppe Tornatore's film *Malèna,* which chronicles the tragic tale of a village beauty.

lifestyle of many other Western countries. Improvements in educational opportunities and changing attitudes mean that a high proportion of women now have successful careers, although Sicily and Italy have some of the lowest percentages in Europe of women in government.

Boundaries are pushed by Sicily's proactive feminist organisation, Archidonna, which was established in 1986 in order to promote equal opportunities for women. Archidonna champions programmes such as the European Commission's (EC) Mainstreaming programme, which addresses the needs of women entrepreneurs. Women are slowly becoming more active in local politics; for example, Rita Borsellino, the sister of the murdered anti-Mafia judge Paolo Borsellino, has made some serious waves in recent years in the world of politics both by her anti-Mafia efforts, and by the simple virtue of being a woman. In recent years, Archidonna has also started to focus its attention on increasing the presence of women in this arena.

The late legalisation of divorce and the recognition of rape as a crime only in the 1990s reveal just how far women have come in the last couple of decades. Such progress is only emphasised by the publication of novels such as *Volevo i pantaloni* (I Wanted to Wear Trousers; 1989), by Lara Cardella, and the international bestseller *Cento colpi di spazzola prima di andare a dormire* (One Hundred Strokes of the Brush before Bed; 2003), by Melissa Panarello. Cardella's novel, set in 1960s Sicily, deals with the prejudice faced by a young girl who was branded a prostitute because she took the 'revolutionary' step of wearing trousers, while Panarello's book is an account of a teenage girl's sexual experimentation that shocked many Sicilians.

For a humorous insight into the pains of young Sicilians in the 1950s, when divorce was illegal, see *Divorzio all'italiana* (Divorce, Italian Style; 1961), with the excellent Marcello Mastroianni as the unhappy and conniving husband.

SAINTS & SINNERS

Religion is a big deal in Sicily. With the exception of the small Muslim communities of Palermo and the larger Tunisian Muslim community in Mazara del Vallo, the overwhelming majority of Sicilians consider themselves practising Roman Catholics. Even before the 1929 Lateran Treaty between the Vatican and Italy, when Roman Catholicism became the official religion of the country, Sicily was incontrovertibly Catholic, mostly due to 500 years of Spanish domination. In 1985 the treaty was renegotiated, so that Catholicism was no longer the state religion and religious education was no longer compulsory, but this only reflected the reality of mainland Italy north of Rome; in Sicily, the Catholic Church remains strong and extremely popular.

Pilgrimages remain a central part of the religious ritual, with thousands of Sicilians travelling to places such as the Santuario della Madonna at Tyndaris or the Santuario di Gibilmanna in the Madonie mountains.

In the small communities of the interior you will find that the mix of faith and superstition that for centuries dictated Sicilian behaviour is still strong. The younger, more cosmopolitan sections of society living in the cities tend to dismiss their elders' deepest expressions of religious devotion, but most people still maintain an air of respect.

In churches you are expected to dress modestly. This means no shorts (for men or women) or short skirts, and shoulders should be covered; even churches that are also major tourist attractions, such as the cathedrals at Monreale and Palermo, will often enforce strict dress codes. If you visit a church during a service (which preferably you should refrain from doing), try to be as inconspicuous as possible.

IMMIGRATION & EMIGRATION

Immigration and emigration are among the most pressing contemporary issues, and Sicily is no stranger to the subject. Since the end of the 19th century the island has suffered an enormous drain of human resources through emigration. Between 1880 and 1910, over 1.5 million Sicilians left for the US, and in 1900 the island was the world's main area of emigration. In the 20th century, tens of thousands of Sicilians moved northwards to work in the factories of Piedmont, Lombardy and further afield in Switzerland and Germany. Even today emigration continues to be a problem, with over 10,000 people leaving the island for greener pastures each year.

This brain-drain epidemic is the result of the grim unemployment rate, which is officially 20% but is really more like 28%. Furthermore, the entrenched system of patronage and nepotism makes it difficult for young people to get well-paid jobs without having the right connections. Finally, Sicily is the one of the favoured ports of call for the thousands of *extracomunitari* (immigrants from outside the EU) who have flooded into Italy. Mazara del Vallo is home to a substantial Tunisian population (around 9000), most of whom work in the fishing industry, while Palermo has a large number of African, Pakistani and Bangladeshi immigrants. It's also not unknown for large boats to drop many illegal immigrants off at various locations around Sicily (see p271).

Economically beleaguered, Sicily's young people continue to emigrate while their places are filled by foreign nationals prepared to take the low-paid jobs left behind.

THE MAFIA
Origins

The word 'Mafia' took more than 110 years of common usage before it was officially acknowledged as referring to an actual organisation. Although formally recorded by the Palermitan prefecture in 1865, the term was not included in the Italian penal code until 1982.

The origins of the word have been much debated. The author Norman Lewis has suggested that it derives from the Arabic *mu'afah* or 'place of refuge'. Nineteenth-century etymologists proposed *mahjas*, the Arabic word for 'boasting'. Whatever the origin, the term *mafioso* existed long before the organisation known as the Mafia and was used to describe a character that was elegant and proud, with an independent vitality and spirit.

The concept of the *mafioso* goes all the way back to the late 15th century when the restricted commercial opportunities were so stifling that even the overprivileged feudal nobles were forced to make changes in order to survive. They introduced a policy of resettlement that forced thousands of farmers off the land and into new towns; the idea was to streamline crop growth, but it also destroyed the lives of the peasants in the process. Many of the aristocrats moved to big cities such as Palermo and Messina, leaving their estates in the hands of *gabellotti* (bailiffs), who were charged with collecting ground rents. They, in turn, employed the early *mafiosi* – who were small gangs of armed peasants – to help them solve any 'problems' that came up on the way. The *mafiosi* were soon robbing large estates and generally causing mayhem, but the local authorities were inept at dealing with them as they would quickly disappear into the brush.

The bandits struck a mixture of fear and admiration into the peasantry, who were happy to support any efforts to destabilise the feudal system. The peasants became willing accomplices in protecting the outlaws, and although it would be another 400 years before crime became 'organised', the 16th and 17th centuries witnessed a substantial increase in the activities of brigand bands. The bands were referred to as Mafia, while the peasants' loyalty to their own people resulted in the name Cosa Nostra (Our Thing). The early-day Mafia's way of protecting itself from prosecution was to become the modern Mafia's most important weapon: the code of silence.

Five million Sicilians live outside Italy and 18 million Italians of Sicilian origin live in the US, but the current population of the island is only five million.

The demanding responsibilities of farm life and the effects of modernity on an age-old agricultural system are the substance of *On Persephone's Island*, Mary Taylor Simeti's fascinating account of her life in Sicily.

Peter Robb's *Midnight in Sicily* (1998) is an immensely enjoyable treatise on the four pillars of Sicilian society: art, culture, food and the Mafia.

THE 10 COMMANDMENTS OF A MAFIOSO

The Mafia is said to be a God-fearing organisation, a claim which seems ludicrous considering its activities break most biblical rules – its disregard for life, and other people's property and personal freedom, for example. But the recent arrest of Salvatore lo Piccolo, the Cosa Nostra's top boss, unearthed a list of 10 rules for a *mafioso* that has ironically been compared to the Bible's own commandments.

■ No-one can present himself directly to another of our friends. There must be a third person to do it.

■ Never look at the wives of friends.

■ Never be seen with cops.

■ Don't go to pubs and clubs.

■ Always being available for Cosa Nostra is a duty – even if your wife's about to give birth.

■ Appointments must absolutely be respected.

■ Wives must be treated with respect.

■ When asked for any information, the answer must be the truth.

■ Money cannot be appropriated if it belongs to others or to other families.

■ People who can't be part of Cosa Nostra: anyone who has a close relative in the police, anyone with a two-timing relative in the family, anyone who behaves badly and doesn't hold to moral values.

The 'New' Mafia

Up until WWII the Mafia had operated almost exclusively in the countryside, but with the end of the conflict Cosa Nostra began its expansion into the cities. It took over the construction industry, channelling funds into its bank accounts and creating a network of kickbacks that were factored into every project undertaken. In 1953, a one-off meeting between representatives of the US and Sicilian Mafias resulted in the creation of the first Sicilian Commission, which had representatives of the six main Mafia families (or *cosche*, literally meaning 'artichoke') to efficiently run its next expansion into the extremely lucrative world of narcotics. At the head of the commission was Luciano Liggio from Corleone, whose 'family' had played a vital role in developing US-Sicilian relations.

Throughout the 1960s and '70s the Mafia earned billions of dollars from the drug trade. Inevitably, the raised stakes made the different Mafia families greedy for a greater share and from the late 1960s onwards Sicily was awash with vicious feuds that left hundreds dead.

The most sensational assassination was that of the chief prefect of police, General Carlo Alberto Dalla Chiesa, who was ambushed in the heart of Palermo in 1982; his brutal murder led to prosecutors and magistrates being granted wider powers of investigation.

The first real insight into the 'New Mafia' came with the arrest of *mafioso* Tommaso Buscetta, also in 1982. After nearly four years of interrogation, headed by the courageous Palermitan magistrate Giovanni Falcone, Buscetta broke the code of silence. His revelations shocked and fascinated the Italian nation, as he revealed the innermost workings of La Società Onorata (the Honoured Society; the Mafia's chosen name for itself).

In 1986, 500 top *mafiosi* were put on trial in the first *maxiprocesso* (supertrial) in a specially constructed bunker near Palermo's Ucciardone prison. The trial resulted in 347 convictions, of which 19 were life imprisonments and the others jail terms totalling a staggering 2665 years.

Well into the 1970s, *delitto d'onore* (honour killings) were considered acceptable and were punished with only light prison sentences ranging from three to seven years.

Perhaps the most significant development in the fight against the Mafia was the change in the attitude of ordinary people. Angered and disgusted by the tidal wave of savage murders, people began to speak out against organised crime. For more information on the anti-Mafia movement, see below.

Finally in January 1993, the authorities arrested the infamous *capo di tutti capi* (boss of bosses), Totò Riina, the most wanted man in Europe. He was charged with a host of murders, including those of the anti-Mafia magistrates Giovanni Falcone and Paolo Borsellino, and sentenced to life imprisonment.

The Anti-Mafia Movement

The anti-Mafia movement is alive and kicking in Sicily, tracing its roots back to the beginning of today's Mafia. According to historians, the movement first appeared in the late 19th century, and lasted in its first incarnation until the 1950s. The movement strove for agrarian reform, targeting the Mafia, conservative political elites and the *latifondisti* (big landowners), but its efforts were shattered when the lack of economic prospects in the postwar era drove thousands of young Sicilians to emigrate in search of work and a better life.

During the 1960s and 1970s, the anti-Mafia movement was headed by political radicals, mainly members of the left-wing groups disenchanted with the Socialist and Communist parties. Giuseppe 'Peppino' Impastato became famous during this period; the son of a *mafioso,* Impastato mocked individual *mafiosi* on his popular underground radio show. He was assassinated in 1978 and was subsequently the subject of the film *I cento passi* (One Hundred Steps; 2000). Things were at their worst for the anti-Mafia movement in the 1980s, when the Mafia was particularly intolerant of anyone perceived as a potential threat. The assassination in 1982 of General Carlo Alberto Dalla Chiesa, whom the national government had sent to Sicily to direct anti-Mafia activities, is now seen as one of the major elements in sparking a new wave in the anti-Mafia movement, with groups ranging from educators and students to political activists and parish priests becoming involved.

The reformist Christian Democrat Leoluca Orlando, who was elected mayor of Palermo during the 1980s, also helped to increase anti-Mafia sentiment. He led an alliance of left-wing movements and parties to create Palermo Spring, which invalidated the public-sector contracts previously given to Mafia families, restored and reopened public buildings, and aided in the arrests of leading *mafiosi*. During the 1990s, Orlando left the Christian Democrats and set up the anticorruption movement, La Rete (the Network), bringing together a broad collection of anti-Mafia individuals and reform organisations. Some reformers have criticised Orlando, however, for having left office without establishing structures and institutions to continue his work.

Civilian efforts saw housewives hanging sheets daubed with anti-Mafia slogans from their windows, shopkeepers and small entrepreneurs forming associations to oppose extortion, and the formation of groups such as Libera (www.libera.it), cofounded in 1994 by Rita Borsellino, the sister of the murdered judge Paolo Borsellino. Libera managed to get the Italian parliament to permit its member organisations to legally acquire properties that had been seized from the Mafia by the government, establishing agricultural cooperatives and other legitimate enterprises on these lands. Even the Catholic Church, long silent on the Mafia's crimes, finally began to have outspoken anti-Mafia members. The best known was Giuseppe Puglisi, who organised local residents to oppose the Mafia, and who was shot in 1993.

At the time of writing, Sicily's social attitudes were continuing to change: in Gela, the town's remarkable mayor, Enzo Crocetta – an openly

---

For an authoritative and comprehensive insight into the history, structure and traditions of the Sicilian Mafia, look no further than Claire Sterling's *Octopus: The Long Reach of the Sicilian Mafia.*

A Mafia boss, killed in a December 2007 police shoot-out, was found with three *pizzini* (secret messages) in his windpipe and three in his stomach. The police didn't reveal whether the messages were legible or not.

Recent works on the Mafia, such as Norman Lewis' *In Sicily* (2000) and Alexander Stille's *Excellent Cadavers* (1995), have reported the presence of a new organisation composed of *mafiosi* who left Cosa Nostra during the turbulent 1980s.

Head to www.bestofsicily
.com to continue explor-
ing the issues that are
meaningful to Sicilians.

gay, communist and Catholic anti-Mafia activist – was re-elected for a
second term, while Mafia-connected individuals were fired from government jobs in what the Italian daily *La Repubblica* described as 'a small
Sicilian miracle'.

For an interview with Catania's anti-Mafia campaigners, see p164.

The Mafia Today

Since Riina's conviction, other top *mafiosi* have followed him behind
bars, most notably his successor Leoluca Bagarella, arrested in 1995, and
the vicious killer Giovanni Brusca, arrested in 1996. In 1998 top bosses
Vito Vitale and Mariano Troia were arrested and prosecuted, as well as
Mafia accountant Natale d'Emmanuele. In 2003 Salvatore Sciarabba –
right-hand man to Mafia boss Bernardo Provenzano – was arrested in
the heart of Palermo. Provenzano was arrested in 2006, followed by the
arrest of his successor, Salvatore lo Piccolo in 2007. No-one would be so
foolish to suggest that the power of the Mafia is a thing of the past, but
these arrests have meant that the powerful core of the organisation is
being weakened.

Around 150 students
'exorcised' the spirit of
Mafia boss Bernardo
Provenzano from the
town of Corleone by
staging a 'freedom
marathon' down the
dirt track leading to
Provenzano's former
hiding place.

Despite the arrests, Mafia experts warn that the battle is not over.
According to Leoluca Orlando, Palermo's former mayor, the arrests of the
big bosses have only cleared the path for other criminal organisations to
muscle in. He particularly warned of the 'Americans' – the Mafia members
pushed off the island by the Corleone gang during the 1980s Mafia wars –
who might come back to seize control.

Today's Mafia has infiltrated daily life, becoming intertwined with legal
society: its collaborators and their children are now 'respectable' and influential citizens. Whether it's recovering stolen property or getting a permit,
the Mafia still has a hand in it; for example, a legitimate business might
secure a building contract, but the Mafia will then tell it where to buy
cement or where to hire machinery. Palermo's chief prosecutor calls it
'the Invisible Mafia', and points out that a large number of Palermo's
shopkeepers still pay some kind of *pizzo* (protection money). It's hardly
surprising that the Eurispes think-tank in Rome estimated the Mafia's
(including the branches in Calabria, Campania and Puglia) 2004 profits
at €123 billion, 10% of national GDP.

Such is the resistance
in Sicily to wearing a
helmet on a bike or
scooter, in summer 2007
a traffic police officer
fined a motorcycle police
officer for not wearing
a helmet.

A bright note is the significant anti-*pizzo* efforts in Palermo, such as
the 2004 campaign called Addiopizzo, enlisting around 209 businesses that
signed a pledge not to pay the *pizzo* and whose names are listed on the
group's website (www.addiopizzo.org).

The future of Sicily and the Mafia is full of daunting challenges, thanks
to the fact that the Mafia's involvement in the economic, political, and
social life of the island is longstanding and deeply entrenched. But considering the arrests that took place in 2006 and 2007, it is clear that much
has changed, and thankfully for the better.

Food & Wine

'Leave the gun. Take the *cannoli*.' Sicily's food is so good that even the mobsters in *The Godfather* turned to it for comfort. And indeed, in a nation where food is at the centre of existence, the cuisine of Sicily is respected as one of the most exciting and exotic, but also as one of the most traditional. A huge part of anyone's visit to this gorgeous island will be taken up with eating, and with learning the many unwritten (and written) rules of eating the Sicilian way – understanding the strict order of the dining ritual, matching tastes and preparation methods, choosing the right dessert, having the right coffee. But the task should be immensely enjoyable: Sicily's kitchen is packed with fresh ingredients, shiny fish straight out of the Mediterranean, unusual additions such as almonds and pistachios, and delectable combinations such as pasta with sardines, saffron and sultanas.

For more information on food and drink in Sicily, see p286.

Traditional recipes have survived here for centuries, and Sicily's rich pantry was filled over a long period. The abundance of fruit and vegetables has been evident since the times of the ancient Greeks – Homer famously said of the island, 'Here luxuriant trees are always in their prime, pomegranates and pears, and apples glowing red, succulent figs and olives swelling sleek and dark', and wrote about wild fennel and caper bushes growing on the hills. But it wasn't until the Arabs came to the island that the cuisine really took shape. The Saracens brought the ever present aubergine, as well as the citruses, and they are believed to have introduced pasta to the island (rather than Marco Polo bringing noodles from China). They also spiced up the dishes with saffron and sultanas, and contrasted the dishes' delicate flavours with the crunch of almonds and pistachios. In fact, the Arabs were so influential that couscous is present on every menu in western Sicily; *arancini* (deep-fried rice balls) are another staple contributed by the Arabs. And, on top of this, the Saracens brought sugar cane to Sicily, helping it develop all those fantastic sweets; the classic *cassata* comes from the Arabic word *qas'ah*, referring to the terracotta bowl used to shape the cake.

The first cookery book of the Western world, *The Art of Cooking* was written by Mithaecus in Syracuse in the 5th century BC.

What's really impressive about Sicily's cuisine is that most of these amazing tastes came out of poverty and depredation. The extravagant recipes of the *monsù* (chefs; from the French *monsieur le chef*) employed by the island's aristocrats were adapted to fit the budget and means of the less fortunate. Ordinary Sicilians applied the principal of preserving the freshness of the ingredients, and most importantly, never letting one taste overpower another. And that's the crunch of it, so to speak, the key to all of Sicily's dishes: simplicity. Prepare to have your taste buds educated, converted and pampered.

BREAKFAST, LUNCH & DINNER

Sicilians rarely eat a sit-down *colazione* (breakfast); instead they drink a cappuccino and eat a *cornetto* (Italian croissant) while standing at a bar. Cappuccinos or caffè lattes are only drunk for breakfast.

Pranzo (lunch) is traditionally the main meal of the day and most businesses close for several hours every afternoon. Lunch consists of an antipasto, a *primo piatto* (first course) of pasta or risotto, and a *secondo piatto* (second course) of meat or fish. It's rounded off with fresh fruit or *dolci* (dessert), and coffee, often on the way back to work.

Cena (dinner) is eaten late, with many restaurants getting started between 9pm and 10pm. The evening meal used to be simpler, but habits have changed due to the inconvenience of travelling home for lunch every day. Many Sicilians eat out on Fridays and Saturdays, and an increasing number have Sunday lunches in restaurants.

THREE COLOURS

Sicily's favourite ingredients can be grouped according to the *tricolore* – the three colours of the Italian flag. The following are the basics that will be found in the pantry of any Sicilian; through these you can get to the core of the island's cuisine.

The Slow Food Movement (symbolised by a snail) champions traditional cuisine and sustainable agricultural practices. Log on to www.slowfood.com for the best places to eat and drink.

Red

You may think red is the colour of passion, but when it comes to Sicilian cooking, it's also the colour of the most important ingredient of all: the tomato. *Il pomodoro* or *il pomodorino* (cherry tomato) is at the foundation of most sauces, whether it's cooked, blanched or simply scattered fresh over a heap of pasta. Sicilian tomatoes are renowned throughout Italy for their sweet flavour and you'll often see tomatoes hanging in bunches outside the houses (especially on the island of Salina) where the locals claim it's the best way to keep them fresh. Sun-dried tomatoes are another way of preserving tomatoes, and many Sicilians use this version in the winter months, when fresh tomatoes aren't easy to find.

Peppers are another must-have vegetable for Sicilians, and you'll find both the bell-shaped version and the long, pointy type in many starters and antipasti. A favourite dish involving red, green and yellow peppers is *peperonata in agrodolce*, where peppers are stewed with onions, pine nuts, raisins and capers.

The story goes that Sicilians, delighted by the beauty of Bellini's opera *Norma*, started using the superlative *una vera Norma* (a real Norma). When the author Nino Martaglio tasted the pasta dish, he found it so ravishing he called it *pasta alla Norma*.

White

Garlic is, of course, a major ingredient in Sicilian cooking. It is added to around 80% of savoury recipes, and it sometimes forms the main component of a sauce, as in *spaghetti aglio olio* (spaghetti with garlic and oil) – simple and delicious. Sicilians use crushed fresh cloves, most commonly on grilled or baked fish, or fry it thinly sliced to flavour the oil.

'White' is also for cheese. Sicilians like to sprinkle liberal helpings of a strong cheese called *caciocavallo* on their pasta dishes (despite the word

---

HOW TO WIN FRIENDS & INFLUENCE PEOPLE (PART ONE)

Sicily's *pasta a picchi pacchiu* (spaghetti with tomato and chilli sauce) is mind-blowingly good, and it's available on virtually every Sicilian menu. It is unlikely you'll eat a better version of this simplest of pasta dishes anywhere else – and if you cook it at home, all your friends will love you. This is how to make it (enough for two, maybe three people):

250g to 300g spaghetti
6 to 7 large juicy, ripe tomatoes
8 garlic cloves, thinly sliced
12 fresh basil leaves, ripped up
½ cup olive oil
1 tbsp salt
1 tbsp ground black pepper
A sprinkling of chilli flakes

Blanch the tomatoes in boiling water for no more than a minute. Peel and crush them, then place them (and all the lovely juices) in a bowl.

Boil water for spaghetti and cook as per the instructions on the packet. Remember to give the pasta plenty of water to 'breathe', and to always salt the water well.

Pour the olive oil into a pan and, when it has heated, add the garlic and chilli. Keep stirring until the garlic is golden. Add garlic and oil to the tomatoes and stir well, then sprinkle the roughly ripped basil, salt and pepper on top, stirring once again. Drain the pasta and pour into the sauce, mixing well together. Add fresh olive oil to taste.

cavallo, which means 'horse', the cheese is actually made from cow's milk). Parmesan has only recently found its way onto the menu, and Sicilians will shriek with horror if you sprinkle it on the wrong sauce. Ricotta cheese, both dried and fresh, often features on Sicilian menus – along with aubergines and tomatoes, it's one of the main ingredients in *pasta alla Norma.* If you can find it really fresh (as in 24 hours old), it tastes like heaven. *Pecorino* cheese is another favourite. Made of sheep's milk, it has a strong aroma and is often added to sauces.

Mandorle (almonds) usually come blanched. They are widely cultivated throughout Sicily and they add a wonderful crunch to many a dish, such as *pasta Trapanese,* where they are crushed and added to the tomato and basil sauce. Almonds are also used to make one of the most common *granite* (flavoured crushed ice), as well as wonderful cookies. The Sicilians have invented *latte di mandorla,* a delicious cold drink that is basically almond pulp and water; it is drunk mostly in the west, where you can also buy it in supermarkets, and it's freshly made in many bars.

> A wonderful website is www.inmamaskitchen .com, with reams of 'real' recipes, all from a mother's kitchen. Sicilian food is amply represented and membership is free.

Green

Which should go first? Olive oil? Basil? Pistachios?

Good olive oil is one of the prime delicacies of Sicilian cuisine, and several traditional olive varieties have been grown on the island for centuries. The main types are *biancolilla* (southwestern Sicily), *nocellara* and *ogliarola messinese* (northeast), *cerasuola* (between Sciacca and Paceco) and *nocellara del Belice* (Trapani province). Titone oil, produced by a family-run refinery near Marsala, is considered to be one of Sicily's best olive oils. An organic oil made from 50% *nocellara* olives, 25% *biancolilla* olives and 25% *cerasuola* olives, it has an exquisite taste and keeps its freshness for a long time after bottling. Needless to say, you won't cook with this oil, but instead cherish every drop.

> Pistachio nuts are highly flammable in large quantities, and are prone to self heating and spontaneous combustion.

Next onto *basilico* (basil), the 'king of herbs', whose smell you'll detect wafting from most Sicilian kitchens. While the herb is used in northern Italy mainly for making pesto, the Sicilians have taken this a step further, making *pesto alla Trapanese* with its fragrant leaves. In this dish, basil is combined with blanched and peeled tomatoes, grated *pecorino* cheese, a healthy clove or two of garlic and some crushed almonds. The ingredients are bashed together with a pestle and mortar, some good olive oil is added, and the sauce is mixed with short pasta. It's hard to describe how good this sauce is – and the scent of basil is essential (as is good olive oil).

Pistachios are a big deal in Sicily. Brought to Sicily by the Arabs and cultivated on the fertile volcanic-soil plains of the island, the nut is used in both savoury and sweet recipes – some of the best ice cream is made from pistachios. And the good news is that, if eaten regularly, the pistachio can significantly reduce cholesterol (although that unfortunately does not apply to the ice cream). There's an entire festival dedicated to the green nut in the town of Bronte from 29 September to 7 October; it is held every other year (the 15th and 16th festivals are scheduled for 2009 and 2011, respectively) because it takes two years to produce a harvest of pistachios.

> Marrying into a Sicilian family, American-born Mary Taylor Simeti set about learning the history and folklore of the island's food. The result is the fascinating and practical *Sicilian Food,* full of recipes and romantic history.

STAPLES

Bread, pasta, antipasti, fish, meat…with so many delicious staples in Sicilian cuisine, you'll be spoilt for choice.

Bread

Through the island's plagues and power struggles, bread has always been a staple food for the Sicilian peasant. Made from durum wheat, Sicilian bread is coarse and golden, fashioned into a myriad ritualistic and regional shapes from braids to rings to flower shapes. Baked bread is treated with the greatest respect and in the past only the head of the family had the privilege of slicing the loaf.

John Dickie's Delizia! The Epic History of the Italians and their Food *explores Italian (and Sicilian) history through foodie moments and claims that the best food in Italy came from the cities, not the countryside.*

Periods of dire poverty and starvation no doubt gave rise to the common use of breadcrumbs, which served to stretch meagre ingredients and fill up hungry stomachs. Such economy lives on in famous dishes such as *involtini,* in which slices of meat or fish are wrapped around a sometimes-spicy breadcrumb stuffing. Some other popular dishes made with a bread-dough base include *sfincione, impanata* and *scaccie* (see Sicilian Street Food, p51).

Pasta

According to the British *Guardian* newspaper, a poll conducted in 2007 found that almost 50% of Italians preferred a good plate of pasta to sex. Perhaps some will be surprised to hear this, considering the Italians' often flaunted virility, but the fact remains that, aside from Dolce & Gabbana, pasta is Italy's (and Sicily's) most famous export. While fresh pasta is now common on most Sicilian restaurant menus, it is dry pasta that has always been the staple of Sicily and southern Italy – mainly because dry pasta is more economical. But dry pasta may not be the poor man's staple for much longer: the 2007 Italy-wide pasta boycott was triggered by a massive rise in wheat prices, which increased by 20% in only two months.

In 15th- and 16th-century Palermo, pasta cost three times as much as bread and was a dish confined to the aristocracy.

The most famous of all Sicilian pasta dishes is *pasta con le sarde* (pasta with sardines). It is a heavy dish, but the liberal use of wild mountain fennel (unique to Sicily), onions, pine nuts and raisins give the sardines a

---

HOW TO WIN FRIENDS & INFLUENCE PEOPLE (PART TWO)

There's nothing that can add flavour and edge to a dish like a good aubergine. The Sicilians know this well, and the aubergine occupies a mighty place in Mediterranean cuisine. Bitter at first, the aubergine takes on and balances out heavy aromas and flavours while keeping its own in the process. One of the most famous Sicilian aubergine recipes is *pasta alla Norma;* here's how to make it (for four people):

450g to 500g penne
3 aubergines, finely sliced, salted and left to rest for an hour
8 large ripe tomatoes
1 onion
2 cloves of garlic
coarse salt
flour
olive oil
6 to 10 basil leaves
200g crumbled *ricotta salata* (salted ricotta)

Blanch the tomatoes in boiling water for a minute, then peel and slice into a mushy mass. Meanwhile, sauté an onion and two cloves of garlic in 2 tbsp of olive oil until the onion is sweet smelling. Add the tomatoes, a pinch of salt and freshly ground pepper, and cook until the sauce is nice and thick (around 20 minutes).

Rinse and dry the aubergines, then cover them lightly in flour. Heat oil in another pan, throw the aubergines in, then cook them for a few minutes on each side until they are soft and golden.

Cook the pasta and toss it with fresh olive oil in a large bowl. Add the ricotta, mix well, and add the tomato sauce, placing the aubergines on top. Cover with torn basil leaves. Chew and think of Sicily.

wonderfully exotic flavour. Other famous dishes include Catania's *pasta alla Norma*, with its rich combination of tomatoes, aubergines and salted ricotta. In the interior you will find meat (mostly mutton and beef) and cheese sauces. Baroque Modica is where the island's best lasagne (*lasagne cacate*) is made; in this version, two kinds of cheese – ricotta and *pecorino* – are added to minced beef and sausage, and spread between layers of home-made pasta squares.

Antipasti

Sicilians aren't big on antipasti (literally 'before pasta'), but their love of strong flavours and unusual combinations lends itself well to the antipasto platter. It is a great way to explore some of the wonderful Sicilian flavours, ranging from marinated sardines and slivers of raw herring to fruity cheeses and a whole range of marinated, baked and fresh vegetables, the most famous of which is *caponata* (a combination of tomatoes, aubergines, olives and anchovies).

Fish

The extensive development of fishing and – until recent years – the widespread presence of fish such as sardines, tuna and mackerel off the island's shores have ensured that fish is a staple food.

A Palermitan favourite is *sarde a beccafico alla Palermitana* (sardines stuffed with anchovies, pine nuts, currants and parsley). However, the filet mignon of the marine world is the *pesce spada* (swordfish), served either grilled with lemon, olive oil and oregano, or as *involtini* (slices of swordfish rolled around a spicy filling of onions and breadcrumbs).

The best swordfish is caught in Messina, where they serve the classic *agghiotta di pesce spada* (also called *pesce spada alla Messinese*), a mouth-watering dish flavoured with pine nuts, sultanas, garlic, basil and tomatoes. The Egadi Islands are home to two splendid fish dishes, *tonno 'nfurnatu* (oven-baked tuna with tomatoes, capers and green olives) and *alalunga di Favignana al ragù* (fried albacore served in a spicy sauce of tomatoes, red chilli peppers and garlic); it is not uncommon to see the sauce of the latter dish appear as part of your pasta dish. Finally, a popular food throughout the island is calamari or *calamaretti* (baby squid), which is prepared in a variety of ways, including stuffed, fried, or cooked in a tomato sauce.

Meat

Although you can find a limited number of meat dishes along the coast, you won't taste the best until you move further inland. The province of Ragusa is renowned for its imaginative and varied uses of meat, particularly mutton, beef, pork and rabbit. Its most famous dish is *falsomagro*, a stuffed roll of minced beef, sausages, bacon, egg and *pecorino* cheese. Another local speciality is *coniglio all'agrodolce* (sweet-and-sour rabbit), which is marinated in a sauce of red wine flavoured with onions, olive oil, bay leaves and rosemary. In the Madonie mountains, the town of Castelbuono is the home of *capretto in umido* (stewed kid) and *agnello al forno alla Madonita* (Madonie-style roast lamb). The latter is left to soak in a marinade of oil, lemon juice, garlic, onion and rosemary, which gives the meat a particularly delicious flavour. Goat and kid dishes will often appear on the menu as *castrato* – don't be put off! It means the goat was castrated, giving the meat a tender quality. Thankfully, it doesn't refer to what's on your plate.

Travel around Sicily in your kitchen by preparing the specialities from Clarissa Hyman's *Cucina Siciliana*. Recipes are organised by time of the day and there are wonderful insights into the island's pasta, cheese, olive oil and nut producers.

To eat your way around some of the island's most productive farms, head to www.agriturismo-sicilia.it.

FOOD PARTIES

The sharing of food is a central feature of all the most important social occasions, and the Sicilian calendar is dotted with *sagra* (festivals usually dedicated to one culinary item or theme). The classic way to celebrate a feast day is to precede it with a day of eating *magro* (lean), because the feast day is usually a day of overindulgence. The general rule is that a *sagra* will offer food, although you'll normally be expected to pay, while at a *festa* (festival) you may have to bring your own. Here's a list of some of the most famous food festivals:

- Sagra del Mandorlo in Fiore (Festival of the Almond Blossom) – held in Agrigento (p265) on the first Sunday in February
- Festival Internazionale del Cuscus (International Couscous Festival) – held in San Vito Lo Capo (p105) every September
- Sagra del Miele (Honey Festival) – held in Sortino, located between Catania and Syracuse, at the end of September
- Festival of the Pistachio Nut – held in Bronte from 29 September to 7 October every odd year
- Zafferanea Etnea Food Festival (Ottobrata) – held in Zafferanea Etnea in October

However, the biggest Sicilian festivals centre on Carnevale (carnival period between Epiphany and Lent), Pasqua (Easter), Natale (Christmas) and the celebration of saints' days such as Santa Lucia in Syracuse, Sant'Agata in Catania and Santa Rosalia in Palermo.

Sweet Tooth

Sicily's extraordinary pastries are rich in colour and elaborately designed. The queen of Sicilian desserts, the *cassata* is made with ricotta, sugar, vanilla, diced chocolate and candied fruits; in Palermo, they describe a woman as 'lovely as a *cassata*'. In the west you can find *cuccia*, an Arab cake made with grain, honey and ricotta. Most people will have heard of the famous *cannoli*, pastry tubes filled with sweetened ricotta and sometimes candied fruit or chocolate pieces. Also look out for *pasta di mandorle* (almond cookies) and *pasta paradiso* (melting moments).

Other Sicilian sweets to try are *gelso di mellone* (watermelon jelly), *buccellati* (little pies filled with minced fruit), *pupe* (sugar dolls made to celebrate Ognissanti on 1 November), *ucchiuzzi* (biscuits shaped like eyes, made for the Festa di Santa Lucia on 13 December) and *biscotti regina* (sesame-coated biscuits).

Get your kitchen ready for some serious Italian cooking with www.cybercucina.com, where you can order anything from a jasmine-honey spoon to the latest gourmet offerings.

If you are in Palermo around late October, before the festival of Ognissanti (All Souls' Day), you will see plenty of stalls selling the famous *frutti della Martorana*, named after the church that first began producing them. These almond-paste biscuits, shaped to resemble fruits (or whatever takes the creator's fancy), are part of a Sicilian tradition that dates back to the Middle Ages.

Any decent *pasticceria* (pastry shop) will have an enormous spread of freshly made cakes and pastries. It is very common for Sicilians to have their meal in a restaurant and then go to a pastry shop, where they have a coffee and cake while standing at the bar.

Gelati & Granite

Despite Etna's belly of fire its peak is a natural freezer, and snow that falls on Etna lasts well into the searing summer, insulated by a fine blanket of volcanic ash. The Romans and Greeks treasured the snow, with which they used to chill their wine, but it was the Arabs who first started the Sicilian mania for all things icy – *granita* (flavoured crushed ice), *cassata* ice cream, *gelato* (ice cream) and *semifreddo* (literally 'semifrozen'; a cold, creamy dessert).

The origins of ice cream lie in the Arab *sarbat* (sherbet), a concoction of sweet fruit syrups chilled with iced water, which was then developed into *granita* (where crushed ice was mixed with fruit juice, coffee, almond milk and so on) and *cremolata* (fruit syrups chilled with iced milk) and from there to *gelato,* which in Sicily is made with blancmange instead of cream.

The modern manifestation of ice cream – almost-solid pieces of flavoured, iced cream – did not appear until the 18th century. All over Sicily, ice cream is still made at the cafés and bars that sell it, and it is truly delicious, with constant innovations in flavours. Try it like a Sicilian – first thing in the morning in a brioche!

Granite are sometimes topped with fresh whipped cream, and are often eaten with a brioche. Favourite flavours include coffee and almond, though lemon is great in summer. During July, August and September, try a *granita di gelsi* (mulberry), a delicious seasonal offering.

By the 18th century, the preservation of snow was big business. Teams of men were employed to transport snow to grottoes, which were bought or leased, where the snow could be preserved.

WINE

Sicily's vineyards are massive – nearly 290,000 acres – and cover a greater area than that of the vineyards of both Bordeaux and Chile. And while grapes have always been a big feature of the Sicilian economy, Sicilian wine is not well known. Traditionally, the heavy wine was sold as a base to strengthen many French labels, but Sicilian wine is now elbowing its own way onto the table, with white wines fermented at cool, mountain temperatures taking the lead. Whites tend to be light, dry and floral, while reds are heavy and fruity.

For master-chef recipes, try the brilliantly funny *Bruculinu, America: Remembrances of Sicilian-American Brooklyn Told in Stories and Recipes* by Vincent Schiavelli.

The most renowned winery is the Regaleali estate in Caltanissetta province, owned by the Conte Tasca family since 1834. The best of the estate's wines are the Nozze d'Oro (a refined white made to mark the count's 50th wedding anniversary in 1985) and the Rosso del Conte, an intense, full-bodied red.

The wine you'll see on most menus, however, is the Corvo di Salaparuta, a velvety red that is an ideal companion to meaty *falsomagro*. The estate's whites (made with one of the island's best grapes, inzolia) are usually quite fresh and slightly fruity; Corvo Bianco is an excellent and reasonably priced drinking wine.

Rapitalà in Alcamo produces the island's most popular white wine, a soft, neutral white that goes well with most white-fish dishes. The estates around Alcamo also hold a *denominazione di origine controllata* (DOC; see p52).

SICILIAN STREET FOOD

Boy, do these people know how to eat. They're at it all the time, when they're shopping, on the way to work, on the way home from work, when they're discussing business, or any other time of the day. What they're enjoying are the *buffitieri* – little hot snacks, which you'll find at stalls and are meant to be eaten on the spot. You should give it a go.

Kick off the morning with *pane e pannelle,* Palermo's famous chickpea fritters. Or you might want to go for the potato croquettes, the *sfincione* (a spongy, oily pizza topped with onions and *caciocavallo* cheese) or even *scaccie* (discs of bread dough spread with a filling and rolled up into a pancake). In summer, people have a freshly baked brioche filled with *gelato* (ice cream) flavoured with fruits, coffee or nougat.

From 4pm onwards you can pick up some barbecued offal, such as *stigghiola* (goat intestines filled with onions, cheese and parsley) or the Palermo favourite, *frittole* (soup made from meat, marrow and fat). In Catania you can buy all manner of *impanata* (bread-dough snacks) stuffed with meat, vegetables or cheese, as well as *arancini* (deep-fried rice balls).

Another famous street snack is *pani cu'la mensa,* which comes as *schietta o maritata* (literally, 'single or married'). If you choose *schietta,* a bread roll will have ricotta placed in it before being dipped into boiling lard, while the 'married' roll is stuffed with sautéed beef spleen!

Sicilian Home Cooking: Family Recipes from Gangivecchio is a wonderful cookery book by Wanda Tornabene, Giovanna Tornabene and Michele Evans, who run one of Sicily's most highly regarded restaurants.

For something a little more flavoursome you might try one of the whites from Etna, where the cataratto grapes flourish. Their mild fragrance sits well with the spicier snapper dishes. Another good choice from the area is the Rosé Ciclopi, which is known as the best wine to drink with rabbit dishes.

Other excellent reds include those produced by Cerasuolo and Donnafugata. Messina produces the strong Faro red, which goes well with most meat dishes, as well as a good white called Capo Bianco.

From the southwest, the best-known wines are the red Terreforti produced near Catania, and the Anapo white and Eloro and Pachino reds, all produced near Syracuse. From the west, Belice (red and white) and Capo Boeo (white) are good choices. Segesta reds and whites are also popular for their well-balanced body and generous taste.

Most wines are fairly cheap, though (as for any wine) prices vary according to the vintage. In a restaurant a decent wine should cost you around €12 to €20, with a table wine *(vino da tavola)* at around €8.

Sicilian dessert wines are excellent, and are worth buying to take home. Top of the list is Marsala's sweet wine; the best (and most widely known) labels are Florio and Pellegrino. Sweet malvasia (from the Aeolian island of Salina) is a fruity wine whose best producer is Carlo Hauser – just look for his name on the bottle and you know you have a good drop. Italy's most famous moscato is the passito di Pantelleria; it has a deep amber colour, and an extraordinary taste of apricots and vanilla.

For something stronger try a shot of Averna from Caltanissetta or the fiery Fuoco dell'Etna.

There are four main classifications of wine – DOC, DOCG *(denominazione d'origine controllata e garantita)*, IGT *(indicazione geografica typica)* and *vino da tavola* (table wine) – which will be marked on the label. A DOC wine is produced subject to certain specifications, although the label does not certify quality. DOCG is subject to the same requirements as normal DOC, but is also tested by government inspectors for quality. IGT is a recent term introduced to cover wines from quality regions that are of a style or use grapes that fall outside the DOC and DOCG classifications.

The website www .wineofsicily.com should give you a good idea of the range of Sicilian wines and where to get hold of them.

The Slow Food Movement's annually updated *Guide to Italian Wines* is an excellent resource with region-by-region profiles of producers and their wines.

COOKING COURSES

If your interest in Sicilian food extends beyond consuming it, why not try a cooking course? The following are some of our favourites:

Anna Tasca Lanza (http://cuisineinternational.com) The grand dame of Sicilian cookery courses is located on the Regaleali estate, presided over by Anna Tasca. Anna is assisted by her sister and

---

NEW TALENT

Many find the wines from Etna to be the most exciting new offering from Sicily, with the combination of fiery soil and high altitude producing perfumed and vibrant wines.

Here are some worth tasting:

- 2006 Scilio Etna Bianco – complex and minerally
- 2006 Casa Mia Sangiovese – full of flavour and oaky
- 2006 Nerello Mascalese – soft and perfumed
- 2006 Cerrasuolo di Vittoria – a fruity wine made with nero d'Avola grapes
- 2004 Montenero, Abbazia Santa Anastasia – nero d'Avola mixed with 40% merlot and cabernet; it's complex yet cool

---

CAFFÈ ALLA SICILIANA (COFFEE, SICILIAN STYLE)

Sicilians take their coffee seriously; some say even more seriously than in the rest of Italy, which is quite a feat.

First is the pure and simple espresso – a tiny cup of very strong black coffee. *Doppio espresso* is a double shot of the same. If you want the watery version of coffee, similar to filter coffee, ask for a *caffè Americano.*

Enter the milk. A caffè latte is coffee with a reasonable amount of milk. A stronger version is the *caffè macchiato,* basically an espresso with a dash of milk. Alternatively, you can have *latte macchiato,* a glass of hot milk with a dash of coffee. The cappuccino is a stronger, smaller version of the caffè latte, with froth on top.

If you don't want to stick out like a sore thumb, don't order a caffè latte or cappuccino after lunch and dinner – it wouldn't occur to Italians and the waiters are guaranteed to eye you with spite or simply say 'there is no milk'. An espresso or *macchiato* is perfectly acceptable. Of course, if you still want a cappuccino you will get one but you might have to repeat your request a couple of times to convince disbelieving waiters that they have heard correctly.

In summer, the local version of an iced coffee is a *caffè freddo,* served in a long glass and sometimes helped along with ice cubes.

To warm up on those winter nights, a *corretto* might be for you – an espresso 'corrected' with a dash of grappa (grape-based liqueur) or some other spirit.

---

her husband, Venceslao (a specialist in Sicilian history), and highlights include watching shepherds making ricotta and a tour of the acclaimed winery.

Arblaster & Clarke (☎ in Britain 01730-89 33 44; www.arblasterandclarke.com) A Rolls-Royce of a wine tour – you dine in baronial splendour as you tour the island's finest sights and visit its most lauded estates, including Rapitalà, Donnafugata, Regaleali and Barone de Villagrande, with a fully qualified wine expert.

Tasting Places (☎ in Britain 020-746 00 077; www.tastingplaces.com) An excellent tour focusing on the western side of Sicily, it includes accommodation in the 18th-century Villa Ravida at Menfi. Day trips to Mozia, Marsala and Palermo enable you to enjoy the hurly-burly of the marketplace as well as the refined air of the winery.

Anna Tasca Lanza's *The Heart of Sicily* documents a whole year in the life of Regaleali, one of the few feudal estates still in operation, combining beautiful photography and history with authentic recipes.

EAT YOUR WORDS

Get behind the cuisine scene by getting to know the language.

Useful Phrases

I'd like to reserve a table.
  vo·*ray* ree·ser·*va*·re oon *ta*·vo·lo   *Vorrei riservare un tavolo.*

I'd like the menu, please.
  vo·*ray* eel me·*noo* per fa·*vo*·re   *Vorrei il menu, per favore.*

What would you recommend?
  ko·za mee kon·*see*·lya   *Cosa mi consiglia?*

Please bring the bill.
  mee *por*·ta eel *kon*·to per fa·*vo*·re   *Mi porta il conto, per favore?*

Is service included in the bill?
  eel ser·*vee*·tsyo e kom·*pre*·zo nel *kon*·to   *Il servizio è compreso nel conto?*

I'm a vegetarian.
  so·no ve·je·ta·*rya*·no/na   *Sono vegetariano/a.* (m/f)

I'm a vegan.
  so·no ve·je·ta·*lya*·no/na   *Sono vegetaliano/a.* (m/f)

Food Glossary

BASICS

cameriere/a	ka·mer·*ye*·re/ra	waiter (m/f)
cena	*che*·na	dinner

coltello	kol·*te*·lo	knife
conto	*kon*·to	bill/cheque
cucchiaio	koo·*kya*·yo	spoon
enoteca	*e*·no te·ka	wine bar
forchetta	for·*ke*·ta	fork
(non) fumatori	(non) foo·ma·*to*·ree	(non)smoking
pranzo	*pran*·dzo	lunch
prima colazione	*pree*·ma ko·la·*tsyo*·ne	breakfast
ristorante	ree·sto·*ran*·te	restaurant
spuntino	spun·*ti*·no	snack
trattoria	tra·to·*ria*	informal restaurant

STAPLES

aceto	a·*che*·to	vinegar
acqua	*ac*·wa	water
aglio	*a*·lyo	garlic
burro	*bu*·ro	butter
formaggio	for·*ma*·jo	cheese
latte	*la*·te	milk
limone	lee·mo·ne	lemon
miele	*mye*·le	honey
olio	*o*·lyo	oil
olive	o·*lee*·ve	olive
pane	*pa*·ne	bread
panna	*pa*·na	cream
peperoncino	pe·pe·ron·*chee*·n	chilli
riso	*ree*·so	rice
rucola	*roo*·co·la	rocket
sale	*sa*·le	salt
uovo/uova	*wo*·vo/*wo*·va	egg/eggs
zucchero	*dzoo*·ke·ro	sugar

MEAL PREPARATION

arrosto/a	a·*ros*·to/ta	roasted
bollito/a	bo·*lee*·to/ta	boiled
cotto/a	*co*·to/ta	cooked
crudo/a	*croo*·do/da	raw
fritto/a	*free*·to/ta	fried
griglia	*gree*·lya	grilled

MEAT, FISH & SEAFOOD

acciughe	a·*choo*·ge	anchovies
agnello	a·*nye*·lo	lamb
aragosta	a·ra·*go*·sta	lobster
bistecca	bi·*ste*·ca	steak
calamari	ca·la·*ma*·ree	squid
capretto	cap·*re*·to	kid (goat)
coniglio	co·*nee*·lyo	rabbit
cozze	*co*·tse	mussels
fegato	fe·*ga*·to	liver
frutti di mare	*froo*·tee dee *ma*·re	seafood
gamberoni	gam·be·*ro*·nee	prawns
granchio	*gran*·kyo	crab
manzo	*man*·dzo	beef
merluzzo	mer·*loo*·tso	cod

ostriche	os·*tree*·ke	oysters
pesce spada	pe·she *spa*·da	swordfish
pollo	*po*·lo	chicken
polpi	*pol*·pee	octopus
salsiccia	sal·*see*·cha	sausage
sarde	*sar*·de	sardines
seppia	*se*·pya	cuttlefish
sgombro	*sgom*·bro	mackerel
tonno	*to*·no	tuna
trippa	*tree*·pa	tripe
vitello	vee·*te*·lo	veal
vongole	von·*go*·le	clams

FRUIT & VEGETABLES

arancia	a·*ran*·cha	orange
asparagi	as·*pa*·ra·jee	asparagus
carciofi	car·*chyo*·fee	artichokes
carota	ca·*ro*·ta	carrot
cavolo	*ca*·vo·lo	cabbage
ciliegia	chee·*lye*·ja	cherry
fagiolini	fa·jo·*lee*·nee	green beans
finocchio	fee·*no*·kyo	fennel
fragole	fra·*go*·le	strawberries
funghi	*foon*·gee	mushrooms
mela	*me*·la	apple
melanzane	me·lan·*dza*·ne	aubergine
patate	pa·*ta*·te	potatoes
pepe	*pe*·pe	pepper
peperoni	pe·pe·*ro*·nee	capsicum
pere	*pe*·re	pears
pesca	*pes*·ka	peach
piselli	pee·*se*·lee	peas
pomodori	po·mo·*do*·ree	tomatoes
spinaci	spee·*na*·chee	spinach
uva	*oo*·va	grapes

DRINKS

birra	*bee*·ra	beer
caffè	ca·*fe*	coffee
tè	te	tea
vino rosso/bianco	*vee*·no *ro*·so/*byan*·ko	red/white wine

Architecture & the Arts

For nearly 10,000 years Sicily has been accumulating a rich array of architectural and artistic treasures, a distillation of styles, techniques and influences from around the Mediterranean basin. Building for posterity, the Greeks left more Doric temples in Sicily than in Greece itself; the Byzantines introduced a love of ornamentation and symbolism, and the fabulous technique of gold-leaf mosaic; while Arab artisans perfected the skill, adding a love of geometric patterns and fanciful decorative devices. The most original and startling artistic style was developed under the Normans, who married Arab artistry with the austere lines of their French Romanesque background, but it is in the Spanish baroque of the 17th and 18th centuries that the extravagance of Sicilian taste really found its soul mate.

ARCHITECTURE & THE VISUAL ARTS
Hellenistic Sicily

The sheer scale and number of Greek buildings and temples in Sicily are unique in their concentration, and the archaeological museums at Palermo, Agrigento, Gela and Syracuse exhibit a stunning range of artefacts. The founding of Syracuse in 735 BC marked the beginning of the extraordinary collaboration between the Hellenistic world and Sicily's cultural and artistic forces. Undoubtedly, the apogee of their creative talents is the Doric temple, splendid examples of which can be seen at Selinunte, Segesta, Syracuse and at Agrigento's Valley of the Temples.

The best preserved example in the world of a Doric temple is the Temple of Concord in Agrigento, which illustrates perfectly the classic rectangular plan with a divided interior, often with an end space that was occupied by the main altar. Although difficult to imagine now, the temples would have been plastered and brightly painted. Despite a rich architectural legacy, the Greek temples in Sicily had little sculptural relief work. The only notable exception was the unusual metopes (spaces along the frieze) of Selinunte, which can now be viewed in the Museo Archeologico Regionale (p85) in Palermo.

Greek theatres are another highlight, even though most of them were either modified or completely rebuilt during the Roman occupation to allow for gladiatorial games. Taormina's theatre, with its lofty position, is the most spectacular, although the theatre at Segesta is closer to the original Greek design. It is framed by a wonderful, natural setting and shows the peculiar talent of the Greeks for harmonising design and environment.

The range of sculpture in the museums of Palermo and Syracuse and the timescale it covers exhibit perfectly the transformation of Greek sculpture from the static, full-frontal, one-piece archaic sculptures that look very Egyptian in style, to the more fluid and naturalistic depiction of form and movement, which resulted in the exceptional *Landolina venus* (p220) and the exquisite *Il giovinetto di mozia* (The Boy of Mozia).

The artistic achievement of the Sicilian Greeks was not limited to sculpture alone, for they produced a phenomenal amount of pottery, including the beautiful red-and-black *kraters* of Gela, the world's most important and extensive collection.

Rapacious Rome

Sicily benefited little from Rome's imperial building zeal. Seen as the potential breadbasket for the growing Roman army, Sicily's forested land was cleared to make way for fields of wheat and provincial governors grew rich on the

For interesting and up-to-date coverage of Sicilian art history and architecture log on to www.bestofsicily .com/magazine.htm, an excellent online magazine featuring articles on art and architecture by Italian specialists.

profits and plunder of the island. One governor, Verres (73–71 BC), proved so greedy in stripping the temples of their treasures that Cicero pursued him to Rome and prosecuted him before the Senate.

Focused on gaming, hunting, racing and gladiatorial combat, Roman culture *was* popular culture. Both the theatres at Taormina and Syracuse were modified to accommodate these pastimes, and certainly at Taormina it is easy to see a new addition: a rectangular stage with a *scaenae frons* (colonnaded backdrop), a complete diversion from the natural settings preferred by the Greeks.

The most wonderful example of the colonial lifestyle enjoyed by the Romans is the Villa Romana del Casale (p252). This fantastic complex, made up of 50 rooms, galleries and corridors, once belonged to the co-emperor Maximian, who ruled jointly with Diocletian between AD 286 and 305. The villa's ruins are mightily impressive but the real draw is the delightful polychromatic mosaics, which offer an exhaustive portrayal of the pleasures of provincial life.

A Light in the Dark: Eastern Influences

Under the skilful hand of the Byzantine artist, classical naturalism gave way to eastern stylisation. The striving for realism in the mosaics at the Villa Romana di Casale was supplanted by deliberate stylisation and symbolism. Above all the Byzantine world loved gold, giving the Sicilians their first taste of ornamentation, the love of which has remained with them to this day. The same goes for an attachment to religious icons. More importantly, the Byzantine world gave the Sicilian church the basilican plan. This form – with its squat nave and semicircular apse, focusing the worshipper's gaze on the eastern altar – was to reach maturity in the fantastic Norman churches, 300 years later.

The Arabs absorbed the central enigma of Byzantine church architecture, a world of mystery and spirituality, heightened by symbolic colours and contrasts of dark and light. Byzantine symbolism was taken one step further into fanciful geometric designs that offered a coded approach to the mystery of God. Forbidden to reproduce images, the Arabs excelled at abstract decoration: arabesques, pointed arches, marble and mosaic inlay, honeycomb niches and vaults and an excess of latticework are all evident in the Arab palace of La Zisa (p88), which now houses a museum of Arab crafts. In the same way that their decoration creates a maze of interest, the Arabs redrew Sicily's street plans using a 'branching tree' street grid, a deliberately confusing design of blind alleys and offshoots.

The Mosaics of Norman Sicily by Otto Demus offers wonderful coverage and authoritative text on Sicily's unique mosaic heritage.

Love thy Normans: Sicilian Romanesque

The Normans were prodigious builders, but their reference points were the vertical lines of French Romanesque, visible in the sobriety of Palermo's La Magione or the church of San Nicola in Agrigento. Roger I recognised the superior artistry of the Arabs and to his lasting credit employed their substantial skills and aesthetic sense in the monuments of his dazzling kingdom.

The Norman period is characterised by an intoxicating mix of Byzantine, Arab and Norman styles, an organic fusion of the best that each culture had to offer. Known as the Sicilian Romanesque style, it was eagerly patronised by royalty, the clergy and the aristocracy. The early years of Norman rule saw the construction of some of the finest buildings of the era, most notably the cathedrals at Monreale and Cefalù along with the expansion of the Palazzo dei Normanni in Palermo.

The first of the great constructions, the Duomo di Cefalù (cathedral), was commissioned in 1131 by Roger II (1095–1154) in classic Romanesque style (a Latin-cross plan made up of a long, tall nave, a deep choir stall and two flanking chapels). The decoration of the interior, with its extensive mosaics, stands out as being among the finest anywhere in Europe. In the cupola the wide-eyed figure of Christ Pantocrator (All-Powerful) shimmers in a universe of gold.

No less impressive but more Eastern in flavour is the Cappella Palatina (Palatine Chapel) in the enormous Palazzo dei Normanni in Palermo, the stronghold of Norman power in Sicily. The decoration of the chapel owes much to Arab influences with its Eastern-style cupola and wooden *muqarnas* (a decorative device resembling stalactites) ceiling – unique in a Christian church. The exotic concoction of cultural influences is evident in the unusual scenes sourced from Greek, Persian and Indian myths and the lavish zigzagging patterns – of marble with mosaic inlay – that cover every surface.

Less Eastern, but far bigger and grander, is the cathedral at Monreale, created by William II (r 1166–89). With some 6340 sq metres of golden mosaic, the overwhelming scale of the decoration is breathtaking. The work drew artisans from Persia, Asia, Greece and Venice, who executed the entire Bible story from the Fall (at the entrance) to the Last Judgment (at the westernmost end) in golden mosaic. The whole effect is, as Bishop Gregorovius enviously noted, 'so luminous and bright as to appear unbecoming of a Northern god'. Outside, the cathedral is one of the most sumptuous Romanesque cloisters in the world, with elegant arches supported by a dazzling array of more than 200 slender columns decorated in shimmering mosaic. Each column supports an enchanting sculpted capital – each one different – and taken together they represent a unique record of medieval Sicily.

With the demise of the Normans it would be another 400 years before Sicily witnessed as rich a period of architectural creativity.

Gothic & Renaissance Sicily: A Missed Opportunity?

In sculpture and architecture, the dominant school of the 15th and 16th centuries was founded by Domenico Gagini (c 1430–92). A student of the Quattrocento (15th-century) Florentine style, he almost single-handedly dragged Sicilian architecture out of the Middle Ages and created a style that fused local designs with those of the budding Renaissance on the Italian mainland. Traditional styles persisted, particularly in the construction of fortified homes, which copied the Arab-Norman model – medieval appearance, with plenty of rustication and squinches (small arches) – rather than contemporary forms. The 15th century also saw the arrival of the Catalan-Gothic style, a blend of influences that featured horizontal lines and large, flat, bare surfaces and is most obvious in Palermo's cathedral and in the Chiesa di San Giorgio Vecchio in Ragusa.

Although Sicily did not figure too much in the learning and aesthetic principles that swept through Italy and the rest of Europe during the Renaissance – thanks to the fact that it was sealed off from the mainland on account of its Spanish rulers – Sicilian painting and sculpture were very much in the ascendancy; however, their influences were mostly Spanish and Flemish. The first of the great Sicilian artists was Antonello da Messina (1430–79), who trained in the Flemish style but was later influenced by Piero della Francesca (1420–92), one of the earliest luminaries of Renaissance art. Only four of Messina's works of art remain in Sicily, the most notable being *Annunciazione,* in the Museo Regionale d'Arte Medioevale e Moderna in Syracuse.

In the field of sculpture, the work of Francesco Laurana (1430–1502) and Domenico Gagini dominated the 15th and 16th centuries. Both were heavily influenced by the early Renaissance, particularly the 14th-century Florentine school, but their work continued to blend new ideas with late

Palazzi of Sicily (1998) by Angheli Zalapi, with photographs by Melo Minnella, gives a peek into Sicily's magnificent palaces and is particularly interesting for visitors to Palermo.

Gothic precedents. Both produced a prolific amount of work in Sicily's churches. However, it was Antonello Gagini (1478–1536), Domenico's son, who was to become the most popular and prestigious Sicilian sculptor of his day. Working in marble, terracotta and stucco, he covered the whole gamut of ecclesiastical décor from pulpits and altars to large-scale façades and statuary. His work can be seen in churches across the island and in the cathedrals of Palermo, Syracuse, Nicosia and Trapani.

Baroque Brilliance: An Architectural Love Affair

Devastated by the earthquake of 1693, Sicily had a perfect opportunity to experiment with the very latest architectural fashion, the hugely extravagant baroque style. Baroque grabbed the Sicilian imagination and flurries of new urban plans were drawn up to modernise cities. These plans favoured wider streets punctuated by grandiose squares with theatrical vistas of prestigious buildings. The grafting of the Quattro Canti onto the old Arab street plan of Palermo is a perfect example.

The heavy ornamental style allowed for wild experimentation, fanciful balconies, sculpted stonework and spatial symmetry. The aristocracy was mad for it and competed shamelessly, creating ever more opulent palazzi such as the Palazzo Villadorata in Noto. Towns that were almost entirely destroyed were rebuilt in this elegant new style, including Noto, Modica, Ragusa, Catania and large parts of Syracuse.

Spearheading this new style was Rosario Gagliardi (1700–70), the engineer and architect considered to be the father of Sicilian baroque. He was the designer of the splendid Cattedrale di San Giorgio at Ragusa Ibla as well as the Chiesa di San Giorgio in Modica. Giovanni Battista Vaccarini (1702–68) introduced the Roman baroque to Catania and his work shows the distinctive influence of Francesco Borromini; another influential Catania-based (though not Sicily-born) architect was Stefano Ittar (1730–1789), who 'took over' from Vaccarini after his death in 1768. Among many other buildings, Ittar designed the façade of the Collegiata, a church originally designed by Antonio Amato. In Syracuse, Andrea Palma (1664–1730) designed the wonderful façade of the city's cathedral, adding yet another cultural layer to the church and its history.

Interiors of coloured marbles and wildly elaborate stucco decoration were no less fanciful, particularly the extravagant works of Giacomo Serpotta (1656–1732), who worked mainly in western Sicily. The oratories of Santa Zita and San Domenico in Palermo are masterpieces of stuccowork, a writhing mass of allegorical statues, tumbling cherubs and saints.

Other notable architects of this time were Filipo Juvarra (1678–1736), born in Messina, where he designed the festive settings for the coronation of Philip V; Giovanni Biagio Amico (1684–1754), who renovated the 13th-century Church of Carmine in Licata, Agrigento province, in 1748; and Tommaso Maria Napoli, an early-18th-century Dominican monk who imported the fashionable Viennese Baroque to Sicily and designed the beautiful Villa Valguarnera (built between 1713 and 1737) and Villa Palagonia (started in 1709) in Bagheria.

In the 17th century, Sicily benefited artistically from the presence of two non-Sicilian artists. Caravaggio (1571–1610), whose turbulent life led him from mainland Italy to Sicily in the late 1600s, created some important works here. Messina's Museo Regionale has two very fine Caravaggio paintings. The Flemish painter Anthony Van Dyck (1599–1641) was in Sicily in 1624 and you can see his altarpiece of the Virgin with San Domenico in the Oratorio del Rosario di Santa Zita in Palermo.

Curl up and watch Visconti's lush cinematic interpretation of *Il gattopardo* (The Leopard), an insight into Sicily's decadent aristocracy filmed in some of the most opulent baroque villas on the island.

Anthony Blunt's classic *The Sicilian Baroque* (1968) is the key read on the subject, containing a detailed and precise history of the style.

ARTE POVERA & RENATO GUTTUSO

There is an alarming dearth of good 19th- and 20th-century art in Sicily. The one exception to this is the work of the painter Renato Guttuso (1912–87), who became the most sought-after painter in Italy during the heyday of the 1960s. He was renowned for his visceral style, which reminded modern Italy of the poor and passionate life that had been lost. His paintings burst with colour and vigour but are typically tinged with a more ominous atmosphere of anguish and despair. His most famous work is *La vucciria* (1974), a depiction of Palermo's notorious street market of the same name.

Back to the Classics

With the new vogue for all things classical in 18th and 19th century Europe, architects turned away from the flamboyant excesses of baroque to revisit the simpler and more formal styles of classical architecture, and the neoclassical style was born. Palermo's closer links with the mainland put the city at the vanguard of the neoclassical movement championed by architect Venanzio Marvuglia (1729–1814). However, it was Giovanni Battista Basile (1825–91) and his son, Ernesto (1857–1932), who gave Sicily its most famous neoclassical monuments: the Teatro Massimo (built during 1875 to 1897) and the Grand Hotel Villa Igiea (1899), both in Palermo. Patronised by the wealthy and influential Florio family, Basile is perhaps even more famous for his Art Nouveau (or Liberty style) interiors, the dining room of the Villa Igiea being the finest remaining example.

To learn about all the major artistic movements and their chief exponents check out www.art cyclopedia.com.

Shocks to the System: Fascism, Futurism & War

Following the 1908 earthquake Messina had to be rebuilt, and the results are surprisingly good. Wide boulevards, elegant civic buildings and a pleasantly designed waterfront give Messina a 'modern' feeling compared with other Sicilian cities. Since then little of note has been built with the exception of Fascist additions in the Art Deco style (check out the enormous edifice of the Palermo post office, p77). Much damage was sustained by Sicily during the Allies' bombing in WWII and you can still see bombed-out buildings, unreconstructed, in Palermo's old quarter.

Architecture is Dead?

The 21st century hasn't been massively fruitful for Sicilian art and architecture, though many Sicilian towns – Syracuse and Catania in particular – have been beautifully restored. Palermo's old quarter is getting there, though thanks to civic corruption and misappropriated funding, it's lagging behind.

Illegal construction (known as *case abusive*) has long been a Mafia favourite for laundering money and funds. As a result, huge swathes of the island are now covered by incomplete highways and uninspiring housing schemes. The most shocking of these was the illegal granting of construction permits for houses in Agrigento's Valley of the Temples – supposedly a protected park. Even worse, a proposal approved by the Sicilian parliament in October 2004 sanctioned the building of seven new hotels on the Aeolian Islands, a UN World Heritage site, though these plans have been abandoned for the moment thanks to the Unesco's warnings that such works would strike the islands off the prestigious Heritage list.

Another controversial construction project that nearly made it was the bridge over the Straits of Messina. Estimated to cost around €4.6 million but speculated to be a honey pot for the Mafia, the bridge was championed by Berlusconi's administration and dumped by Romano Prodi in 2006. An online voting forum showed that the Sicilian public didn't back the bridge either, and the money was redirected into Sicily's infrastructure, which needs all the help it can get.

LITERATURE

Dogged by centuries of oppression, isolation, lack of education and poverty and divided into an illiterate peasantry and a decadent aristocracy, it is hardly surprising that prior to the 19th century Sicily yielded a complete absence of great literature. The written word remained something of a mystery.

In such a context it is interesting to learn that the first official literature in Italian was written in Palermo in the 13th century at the School of Poetry patronised by Frederick II. But such high-minded works were irrelevant to the illiterate peasantry whose main pleasure was the regular celebration of saint's days and religious occasions and, later, the popular theatre of the *opera dei pupi* (puppet theatre; see p64 for details).

The political upheaval of the 19th and 20th centuries finally broke the silence of the Sicilian pen when the literary colossus Giovanni Verga (1840–1922) emerged onto the scene. Living through some of the most intense historical vicissitudes of modern Italy – the unification of Italy, WWI and the rise of Fascism – his work was to have a major impact on Italian literature. His greatest novel, *I malavoglia* (The Malavoglia Family; 1881), essentially a story about a family's struggle for survival through desperate times in Sicily, is still a permanent fixture on every Sicilian schoolchild's reading list.

Since then Sicilian writers have produced fiction to rival the best contemporary European works. Playwright and novelist Luigi Pirandello (1867–1936) was awarded the Nobel Prize for Literature in 1934 for a substantial body of work that included *Sei personaggi in ricerca di un autore* (Six Characters in Search of an Author) and *Enrico IV* (Henry IV). Poet Salvatore Quasimodo (1901–68) won the award in 1959 for his exquisite lyric verse, which included delightful translations of works by Shakespeare and Pablo Neruda. Elio Vittorini (1908–66) captured the essence of the Sicilian migration north in his masterpiece *Conversazione in sicilia* (1941), the story of a man's return to the roots of his personal, historical and cultural identity.

Sicily's most famous novel was a one-off by an aristocrat whose intent was to chronicle the social upheaval caused by the end of the old regime and the unification of Italy. Giuseppe Tomasi di Lampedusa (1896–1957) published *Il gattopardo* (The Leopard) in 1957 to immediate critical acclaim. Though strictly a period novel, its enduring relevance lies in the minutely accurate observations of what it means to be Sicilian.

Much of Sicily's 20th-century literature is more political than literary. None is more so than the work of Danilo Dolci (1924–97), a social activist commonly known as the 'Sicilian Gandhi'. His *Report from Palermo* (1959) and subsequent *Sicilian Lives* (1981), both detailing the squalid living conditions of many of Sicily's poorest inhabitants, earned him the enduring animosity of the authorities and the Church. (Cardinal Ernesto Ruffini publicly denounced him for 'defaming' all Sicilians.) He, too, was nominated for the Nobel Prize and was awarded the Lenin Peace Prize in 1958.

The other great subject for modern Sicilian writers is, of course, the Mafia. *Men of Honour* (1993) by Giovanni Falcone is a good place to start (Falcone was one of the leading magistrates in the 1990 Mafia supertrials and was murdered in May 1992). But for a real insight into the organisation search out the work of Leonardo Sciascia (1921–89), whose novel *Il giorno della civetta* (The Day of the Owl; 1961) was the first Italian novel to take the Mafia as its subject. Throughout his career, Sciascia probed the topic, practically inventing a genre of his own. His protégé Gesualdo Bufalino (1920–96) won the prestigious Strega Prize in 1988 for his novel *Le menzogne della notte* (Night's Lies), the

When Dante wrote *The Divine Comedy* he chose to use a version of the 'new' Italian developed in 13th-century Palermo rather than the accepted language of high literature, Latin.

A SICILIAN ICONOCLAST

Acclaimed and criticised throughout his life, Leonardo Sciascia is one of the most important Italian writers of the 20th century. He proudly claimed to have been the first Sicilian writer to directly tackle the contentious subject of the Mafia, in *The Day of the Owl*. It was a topic that fascinated and tormented him until the day he died. Although radically opposed to the activities of organised crime, he was sensitive to the paradoxical nature of Cosa Nostra, which he considered to be against Sicily yet an intangible part of its social and cultural fabric.

In his later years, he developed an almost irrational dislike of the activities of Giovanni Falcone's anti-Mafia commission, accusing the magistrate of being vainglorious and nothing more than a headline chaser. A committed left-winger, he dallied with extremist elements during the 1970s and in 1979 published a famous pamphlet called *Il caso aldo moro* (The Aldo Moro Affair) in which he subtly accused the ruling Democrazia Cristiana (DC; Christian Democrats) of collusion in the kidnapping of the Italian prime minister Aldo Moro by the Red Brigades. Although the popular press derided him at the time, much of what he believed was proven to be at least partially true, and Sciascia consolidated his position as a hero of the antiestablishment opposition.

Despite his political activities, Sciascia is still remembered as one of the best writers to have emerged from Sicily. His other great novels include *A ciascuno il suo* (To Each His Own; 1966), and *Il consiglio d'egitto* (The Council of Egypt) and *Todo modo* (One Way or Another), both published in 1974. His simple and direct approach to narrative marked him as one of the great stylists of the 20th century, while his often-black humour made him one of the most widely read authors of his generation.

---

tale of four condemned men who spend the eve of their execution recounting the most memorable moments of their lives. Bufalino went on to become one of Italy's finest writers, mastering a style akin to literary baroque – intense, tortured and surreal. His haunting novel *La Diceria dell'Untore* (The Plague Sower; 1981), which won Italy's Campiello Prize, is the story of a tuberculosis patient at a Palermo sanatorium in the late 1940s. Guiding the reader through a landscape of doom, Bufalino invokes the horrors of wartime and the hopelessness of the patients who come to know each other 'before our lead-sealed freight car arrives at the depot of its destination'.

Lady Chatterley's Lover was written by DH Lawrence in Taormina and was based on events that took place in Sicily.

Novels such as *Volevo i pantaloni* (I Wanted to Wear Trousers; 1988) by Lara Cardella and *Cento colpi di spazzola prima di andare a dormire* (100 Strokes of the Brush before Bed; 2003) by Melissa Panarello created shock waves when they were published. Cardella's novel, set in the 1960s, deals with the prejudice against women in small-town Sicily (she decides to wear trousers and is labelled a prostitute), while Panarello's explicit account of a teenage girl's sexual experimentation became Sicily's best-selling novel after *Il gattopardo*.

Today, one of Italy's most popular novelists is the Sicilian crime writer Andrea Camilleri (born 1925). His immensely popular series, *Il cane di terracotta* (The Terracotta Dog), about police superintendent Salvo Montalbano, including the two latest, *The Patience of the Spider* and *The Paper Moon*, is available in translation. All bookshops stock his work.

CINEMA

The rich emotional, psychological and physical landscape of Sicily has long inspired an impressive list of film-makers, from the talented Luchino Visconti to the illustrious Francis Ford Coppola. Visconti's two classics, *La terra trema* (The Earth Shook; 1947) and *Il gattopardo* (1963), illustrate the breadth of Sicilian tales – the former a story of grinding poverty and misfortune in a benighted fishing family while the latter oozes the kind of grand decadence that one imagines preceded the French Revolution.

In Roberto Rossellini's *Stromboli* (1950), the explosive love affair between a Lithuanian refugee and a local fisherman is aptly viewed against the backdrop of the erupting volcano, while the hypnotic beauty of Michael Radford's *Il postino* (The Postman; 1995), filmed on Salina, seduces one into a false sense of security shattered by the film's tragic denouement.

However, it is Francis Ford Coppola's modern masterpiece, *The Godfather* trilogy (Part I, 1972; Part II, 1974; Part III, 1990), that really succeeds in marrying the psychological landscape of the characters with their physical environment. The varying intensities of light and dark superbly mirror the constant undercurrent of quivering emotion and black betrayal. The *coup de grâce* is the final scene of Part III (played out in Palermo's Teatro Massimo) where Mascagni's opera, *Cavalleria rusticana,* a foreboding story of love and betrayal, is interspersed with scenes of Michael Corleone's final acts of murder that ultimately lead to the death of the person he loves most, his daughter. Other Mafia films are *Cento giorni a palermo* (One Hundred Days in Palermo; 1984), Giuseppe Ferrara's film documenting the murder of police general Carlo della Chiesa, who was killed on the job after only 100 days in Palermo; and Mark Tullio Giordana's *I cento passi* (One Hundred Steps; 2000), the tale of Peppino Impastato, a left-wing activist who repeatedly denounces the activities of local Mafia boss Tano Badalamenti (who lives 100 steps away from Impastato's house) over the airwaves of a small local radio station.

Other Italian-Americans such as the Taviani brothers, who filmed *Kaos* in 1984, sought to reproduce the mad logic of Luigi Pirandello's (p61) universe. The aptly named *Kaos* is a series of tales about loss, lust, love, emigration and death played out through some fantastical story lines – such as the lustful peasant who turns into a wolf at night.

Sicily itself has not produced any directors of note with the exception of Giuseppe Tornatore (born 1956). Tornatore followed up on the incredible success of *Cinema paradiso* (1989) with *La leggenda del pianista sull'oceano* (The Legend of the Pianist over the Ocean; 1998), a quirky tale of a genius piano player born and raised in the bowels of a huge ocean-going liner. His most recent release was *Malèna* (2000), starring Monica Bellucci in a coming-of-age story set in Sicily in the 1940s.

Another fantastic film director who has made Sicily his muse is Emanuele Crialese. He directed two films, *Respiro* (2002) and *Nuovomondo* (The Golden Door; 2006). *Respiro,* filmed on Lampedusa, deals with an eccentric woman who clashes with the villagers, while *Nuovomondo* is a dreamy record of a Sicilian family's emigration to New York at the turn of the 20th century.

Wim Wenders started shooting a new film in Palermo in 2007, so watch this space. It's said not to be about the Mafia, but about a photographer and his woes.

MUSIC

Sicily's popular musical culture has its roots in Arab and Greek laments and ecclesiastical chants, while traditional instruments include the mouth organ, reed pipe, drum and harp. In the past itinerant *cantastorie* (minstrels) travelled from town to town singing their haunting folk songs but this tradition has vanished.

Still, music remains close to the Sicilian soul and both Catania and Palermo have notable opera houses with extensive programmes. The father of bel canto (a style of singing) is, of course, Vincenzo Bellini (1801–35; see boxed text, p200), but before him came the versatile Alessandro Scarlatti (1669–1725). Along with the Venetian Apostolo Zeno and the Roman Pietro Trapassi (or Matastasio), Scarlatti is credited with creating the kind of lyrical opera that

Michelangelo Antonioni's *L'Avventura* (1960) was filmed all over Sicily – you'll recognise the Aeolians, Messina and Noto.

Roberto Rossellini and Ingrid Bergman were the talk of Hollywood with their illicit affair during the filming of *Stromboli* in 1950. Their affair caused such a scandal in the US that Bergman was denounced on the floor of the US senate.

The filming of Giuseppe Tornatore's film *Malèna* was interrupted when equipment disappeared. It emerged that the Mafia was holding it in lieu of payment of the notorious *pizzo* (protection money).

later became known as the 'Neapolitan' style. He wrote more than 100 works, including the oratorios *Il trionfo dell'onore* (The Triumph of Honour; 1718) and *La griselda* (1721).

In contemporary terms, there are virtually no writers of good music in Sicily. Aldo Clementi (born 1925) is a classical composer whose name will be unknown to all but serious students of the avant-garde.

THEATRE

Sicily's Greek heritage is nowhere more palpable than in the Sicilian love of theatre, and ancient sites around the island – Segesta, Agrigento, Syracuse and Tyndaris – maintain a full programme of classical Greek theatre. Syracuse also boasts the only school of classical theatre outside Athens, while Taormina's Teatro Greco is now given over to the island's internationally acclaimed music festival, Taormina Arte. Add to this boisterous street markets and extravagant religious celebrations, and there is no doubt that theatre is at the heart of the island.

In terms of modern theatre, Pirandello (p61) remains Sicily's most famous playwright. His explorations into the world of the absurd and his heavy use of irony set the tone for later playwrights such as Eugène Ionesco (author of the absurdist classic *Rinoceronte,* or Rhinoceros) and Jean-Paul Sartre, while his insightful observations into the arcane ways of his fellow Sicilians did much to inspire his two great successors, Giuseppe di Lampedusa (p61; author of *Il gattopardo*) and Leonardo Sciascia (p61).

PUPPET THEATRE

Sicily's most popular form of traditional entertainment is the puppet theatre, which was first introduced to the island by the Spanish in the 18th century. It provided ordinary people with a chance to attend a 'theatre' of sorts as they were barred from nearly everything else. The puppeteers re-enacted the tales of Charlemagne and his heroic knights, Orlando and Rinaldo, against the baddies (forbidding Saracen warriors) with a supporting cast including the fair Angelica and the treacherous Gano di Magonza. A host of magicians and monsters created constant diversions and distractions that kept storylines running for weeks at a time. All the tales had a modern context, and despite their exotic names the characters represented Sicilians in everyday life. Effectively the soap operas of their day, puppet theatres expounded the deepest sentiments of life – unrequited love, treachery, thirst for justice and the anger and frustration of the oppressed. A puppet could speak volumes where a man could not.

The puppets themselves were the creation of a number of extraordinary artisans. In Palermo there was Gaetano Greco, the first of a long line of puppeteers; in Catania there was Giovanni Grasso and his lifelong rival Gaetano Crimi. The last of the great puppeteers was Emanuele Crimi, who died in 1974.

Carved from beech, olive or lemon wood, the puppets stand some 1.5m high, although their height and construction depends on their provenance. In Palermo, puppets have wire joints enabling them to swing swords and behead dragons more effectively.

Nowadays the puppet theatre is really part of Sicilian folklore, maintained largely for the benefit of tourists and children and for the sake of tradition. However, there are still notable puppet theatres in Palermo, Syracuse and Cefalù (see the relevant regional chapters for details). Good puppeteers are judged on the dramatic effect they can create – lots of stamping feet, thundering and a gripping running commentary – and on their speed and skill in directing the battle scenes.

For up-to-date information on all the latest cultural events, including concerts, live-music venues, theatre and festivals, visit www .sicily-news.com.

For everything you need to know about classical drama log on to the bilingual site of the Syracuse-based National Institute of Ancient Drama, www .indafondazione.org. The organisation's website gives details of performances and ticket purchasing.

Environment

THE LAND

The Arabs thought Sicily was paradise on earth and the great medieval poet Ibn Hamdis described the island as 'clothed by the peacock from its many-coloured mantle of feathers'. Certainly, Sicily exhibits a wonderful diversity of scenery, from awesome smoke-belching volcanoes ringed by pretty garden scenery, to darkly forested mountain slopes and ancient river valleys swathed in springtime flowers. In the tropical heat everything vibrates with a peculiar intensity, heightened by the ceaseless singing of cicadas.

Extending over 25,708 sq km, triangular Sicily is the largest island in the Mediterranean, occupying a central and strategic location halfway between Gibraltar and the Suez Canal, creating a bottleneck between Italy and Cap Bon in Tunisia. Not only culturally, but also physically, the island is a combination of European and North African traits as it straddles two continental shelves: the northeastern half of the island is an extension of the Calabrian Apennines, while the southwestern half is topographically similar to the Atlas mountains of North Africa. Popular theory has it that the island was once part of the Italian mainland and that a quick boot from Italy's 'toe' sent it southwards as sea levels rose. But an alternative theory suggests that, despite it being only 4km from the Calabrian tip, the island was formed immediately following the split between the European and African landmasses between 80 and 90 million years ago; evidence points to the fact that Sicily is inching its way *closer* to the mainland, not further away.

Whatever the truth, this precarious geography has given the island a unique topography, not least in its clutch of volcanic outcrops. Most impressive of these is undoubtedly Mt Etna (3323m), Europe's highest volcano – part of a volcanic chain that extends from Vesuvius on the mainland through the rocky arc of the Aeolian Islands to end in tiny Linosa. Inland, the island is characterised by fertile coastal plains, rising to hilly plateaus and finally balding mountains made up of three distinct

> Get hold of a copy of *Guida Blu* (in Italian) and discover where Sicily's best beaches are located.

> Log on to the website of experienced vulcanologist John Seach, www.volcanolive.com, for the most up-to-date information on Sicily's volcanic activity.

EARTHQUAKES & EXPLOSIONS

Sicily's position over two continental plates makes it a major centre for seismic activity. Although most of the Italian peninsula is at risk, earthquakes largely strike the southern half of the country, including Sicily. The last quake occurred in 1968, when the western Belice Valley was flattened by a powerful tremor. Before that, a cataclysmic quake followed by giant tidal waves levelled Messina and half of Calabria in 1908.

As if tidal waves and earthquakes were not enough, Sicily is literally ringed with volcanoes and there have been over 135 recorded eruptions. The end of 2002 saw spectacular eruptions that dazzled spectators and completely destroyed the refuge on Etna's northern flank; the fiery Etna erupted again in September. 2007, sending an avalanche of lava down the slopes and thankfully not destroying anything this time round. Although the annals of Sicilian history are littered with tales of the volcano's destructive capabilities, the last really devastating eruption occurred in 1669, when Catania was engulfed in lava.

Sicily's two other active volcanoes are in the Aeolian archipelago. Although both Stromboli (924m) and Vulcano (500m) appear to be smaller than Mt Etna, they are actually roughly the same size: both are rooted at a depth of about 2000m below sea level, with only their cones breaking the surface of the sea. Stromboli's large eruption in 2004 was one of the largest for a while, but despite its permanent activity, there hasn't been a large explosion in recent years. Don't say it twice though.

ranges: the Nebrodi (1847m) and Madonie (1979m) ranges, which skirt along virtually the entire length of the Tyrrhenian Coast up to Palermo; and the Peloritani (1370m), which are confined to the northeast corner of the Ionian Coast.

Off the western coast are the three Egadi Islands of Favignana, Levanzo and Marettimo, while 110km south is the island of Pantelleria – closer to Tunisia than it is to Sicily.

Sicily's population is concentrated mainly on the fertile coastal plains, largely due to the island's historical importance as a centre of maritime trade. The coasts are an alternating panorama of rugged cliffs and low sandy shores that make up some of the island's most beautiful scenery.

For many years the Mafia used to dispose of the bodies of its victims down the precipitous gorges of the Rocca Busambra in the Ficuzza forest near Palermo.

WILDLIFE

In ancient times Sicily was bisected by large navigable rivers (the Belice, Simeto and Salso) and cloaked in verdant oak forests. For the Greeks and Romans, hunting large mammals such boars, wolves, deer and wildcats would have been a weekend pastime as seen in the mosaics at the Villa Romana del Casale. But it was the Romans who began the devastating process of deforestation to plant huge wheat fields to feed the Roman army. This ultimately resulted in the silting up of Sicily's rivers, the near-destruction of its limited wildlife and the reduction of its forests to a mere 8% of the total area of the island. Only fish and fowl have managed to escape this devastating scourge and remain in all their abundant variety during the seasonal migrations of the year.

Animals

Sicily's dense population, coupled with deforestation, have had a devastating effect on the island's fauna. Etna's roe deer and the Nebrodi wolves have disappeared, but some smaller forest species cling on for dear life, notably the crested porcupine, fox, pine marten and wildcat, which roam the Nebrodi mountain park. Even the poor dormouse is under threat – not surprising, given that it was once a staple part of the diet. Fortunately, the San Fratello horse, which roams wild in the Nebrodi mountains and is unique to Sicily, is faring somewhat better and is now a protected species.

Italian beekeepers reported that unusual and unstable weather patterns in 2006 caused a 30% drop in honey production.

Sicily has a healthy reptilian population – more hardy than their furry counterparts – of lizards, geckos and snakes. Sicily's only poisonous snake, the viper, can be found slithering around the undergrowth throughout the south of the island – watch out for it at archaeological sites.

Birds

A convenient pit stop on the migration routes south, Sicily makes an excellent spot for bird-watchers. Some 150 species of bird have been recorded on the island, including numerous large birds of prey like the golden eagle, peregrine falcon and red kite, and the rare Bonelli eagle population at Zingaro Reserve. Griffon vultures were also longtime residents in the Nebrodi park but the entire colony was 'accidentally' killed in 1965. They are being reintroduced through Spanish stocks with slow, but successful, results.

In the southeast, the Vendicari park is a well-protected haven for innumerable birds that thrive in the salty marshes, including black-winged stilts, slender-billed gulls and Audoin's gulls. The times to visit are spring (March) and, even better, autumn (September to October), when thousands of waders and ducks, as well as flamingos, storks and egrets, arrive on their yearly migrations.

Plants

Despite the damage to the island's environment through centuries of wide-spread deforestation and mismanagement, Sicily retains a rich diversity of flora. In springtime nothing can quite prepare one for the carpets of wild flowers, clichéd as it sounds. After all, this is where the goddess Persephone was collecting flowers when Hades snatched her away to the underworld.

Very little remains of Sicily's ancient forests, but what does is now protected. This includes the Madonie and Nebrodi parks – both rich in oak, elm, ash, cork, manna, holly and yew trees – and the Bosco della Ficuzza near Palermo, the most extensive wooded area of its kind on the island.

Outside the forests you will quickly become familiar with the weirdly sculptural shape of the prickly pear *(Opuntia),* as well as the ubiquitous oleander, umbrella pine, carob and eucalyptus tree – the very basics of Mediterranean flora. The eucalyptus was introduced to the island by the Florio family in the 19th century in order to combat the numerous malarial marshlands that were taking such a heavy toll.

Along the western coast you will see many vineyards. These were introduced by the Greeks, along with the olive tree, which grows throughout the island. You will also see plenty of citrus groves and – in the west – palm dates, both of which were brought here by the Arabs, who also brought cassava and sugar cane (although these are no longer grown commercially). Along the length of the Mediterranean Coast the terrain is characterised by the presence of *maquis* (a North African brush), interspersed with the occasional vineyard or olive grove. The slopes of Mt Etna are extremely fertile on its lower regions, with large tracts of land given over to the cultivation of olives, grapes, citrus and other fruits. The tree spurge *(Euphorbia dendroides)* is a common wild plant on the lower slopes. From 500m up, you can find nut plantations of pistachio, walnut, almond and chestnut, along with pine, beech, silver birch and oak trees. Dusting the charred lava trails with yellow at the very top (2000m to 3000m) are swathes of broom, always the first sign of life on a lava field. The holy thorn of Etna *(Astragalus aetnensis)* and the Etna violet *(Viola aetnensis)* are unique to the mountain.

NATIONAL PARKS & RESERVES

Despite their poor track record on the environment, Sicilian authorities have gone to great lengths to protect large tracts of land from the bulldozer through the designation of specially protected nature reserves.

The two coastal reserves of Zingaro, northwest of Palermo (see p104), and Vendicari, on the southern coast (see p232) are areas of extraordinary beauty that are well run and easily accessible on foot. Made up of three separate marshes and a splendid crescent-shaped beach, Vendicari National Reserve is full of long sandy and pebble beaches on a wonderful stretch of wild coastline protected from the voracious developers. Crisscrossed by medieval water channels constructed when the saltpans were in use, the reserve protects all manner of water birds.

Also in the southeast is the protected Valle dell'Anapo (Anapo Valley), a deep limestone gorge that is the site of the ancient necropolises of Pantalica.

The Parco Naturale Regionale delle Madonie was established in 1989 to protect a vast area of mountainous woodland east of the capital (see p139). It is the only reserve on the island where people actually live, in small towns dotted throughout the hills. Further east is the Parco Regionale dei Nebrodi (see p142), where San Fratello horses can be found roaming free along with all kinds of farmyard animals including sheep, pigs and cattle.

The only other protected forest is the densely wooded and spooky Bosco della Ficuzza, which covers some 4000 hectares of land a mere 35km from

Walkers should equip themselves with the specialist book *Mediterranean Wild Flowers* by Marjorie Blamey and Christopher Grey-Wilson.

The Orto Botanico (Botanical Gardens) in Palermo contain over 12,000 species of plants, including 600,000 herbs. Many of the plants are unique to Europe.

THIS HEATING PLANET

The Central Institute for Research Applied to the Sea (ICRAM) in April 2007 published the results of research stating that the deep waters of the Mediterranean are heating up as a result of global warming. The research took place in the Sicilian Channel (or the Strait of Sicily) – a stretch of waters where marine changes are felt sooner than in the rest of the Mediterranean. The constant trend in rising temperatures is worrying for the sea's biodiversity, especially since the stretch between southwestern Sicily and Tunisia is home to many species of whale, dolphin and shark. Despite the fact that the Mediterranean accounts for just 0.8% of the Earth's marine waters, it is estimated to contain 9% of global biodiversity.

Scientists believe that Italy and southern Europe are especially vulnerable to climate change, and that average temperatures in this area may rise by a staggering 5°C by the end of the century. It is alarming to learn that as a result of global warming 357 Sicilian species are in danger of extinction.

Palermo. It is full of oak and chestnut trees and was once a royal hunting estate. Above the woodland rises the impressive Rocca Busambra (1613m), a favourite nesting place of the golden eagle.

The island's only national park is the Parco Naturale dell'Etna (see p208), which was set up to protect the volcano from the spread of development threatening its slopes up to the late 1980s. Although there is still a sizable amount of unwelcome construction on the mountain, the area appears to be in good hands.

Visit www.parks.it (in Italian and English) for further information on Sicily's parks.

The saltpans of Trapani and Marsala are partially protected by the Regione Sicilia, while the long beach at Capo Bianco, near Eraclea Minoa, was purchased by the Worldwide Fund for Nature (WWF) in 1991.

In 1986 the island of Ustica became Italy's first marine reserve and it remains a centre for marine research. The tiny isle forms the westernmost cone of the volcanic arc that makes up the Aeolian Islands, and like the six Aeolians, the marine world around Ustica is rich and varied. The Atlantic current through the Straits of Gibraltar keeps the water an incredible azure and attracts divers from around the world.

Sicily's other notable sea reserve is centred around the Egadi Islands (see p113), made up of three islands: Favignana, Levanzo and Marettimo. All the islands are ringed with caves and creeks, making other excellent diving spots.

Watch, or rewatch, Michael Radford's wonderful film *Il postino*. It was filmed largely on the impossibly beautiful Aeolian island of Salina.

The Aeolian Islands are not a designated natural park although they are a listed World Heritage site, protected for their unique volcanic characteristics. However, their World Heritage status was threatened by a shocking proposal to develop seven new hotels. The controversial project was approved by the Sicilian parliament in October 2004 but has since been shelved thanks to massive opposition to the project.

ENVIRONMENTAL ISSUES

Sicily is a dramatically beautiful island, with some of the most splendid scenery to be found anywhere in Europe. Yet humans seem to have done their very best to spoil the natural legacy of the island, both on land and off. One of the big environmental issues in Sicily is the fast depletion of tuna fish off the western coast. Traditionally, tuna traps were set around the coast of Sicily once a year; the scale of tuna caught by this method was relatively small and sustainable, but problems arose with the increase in Japanese commercial fishing in the 1960s, when tuna started being fished year-round and deep waters were exploited using indiscriminate fishing methods that ignored seasons and marine life cycles, thus depleting the oceans' resources.

Throughout most of the 20th century industrialisation and urbanisation resulted in pollution problems that have yet to be dealt with adequately. In Palermo and Catania car emissions poison the atmosphere, creating a yellow smog that is clearly visible on a summer's day. The seas surrounding the island, and therefore many of the beaches, have been fouled to some extent, particularly in the industrialised areas around Gela, Porto Empedocle, Augusta and Trapani, where it is inadvisable to go swimming. Aesthetically, these areas represent shameful scars on the island's otherwise pristine coastlines.

A way in which you can help during your visit is to limit your water usage, as Sicily is often plagued by water shortages in high summer. This is especially the case on the Aeolian Islands and particularly on Stromboli, where huge water tanks are brought to 'feed' the population and growing tourist numbers. Thus, don't leave the water running more than you need to and take showers, not baths.

Sicilians as a whole do not help matters greatly. Although deeply proud of their island, they discard rubbish where and when they please, something that will undoubtedly alarm most litter-conscious visitors.

Since the end of WWII, another major problem on the island has been that of illegal construction, known here as *case abusive* (literally 'abusive houses'). Many of the more modern houses built throughout the island, including most of those in the ugly suburbs that plague Sicily's cities, were constructed illegally. Once the authorities got around to checking whether the builders had permits or not, they were presented with a *fait accompli* and took no further action. Perhaps the most appalling example of this is in the famed Conca d'Oro valley around Palermo, once the Arabs' paradisiacal garden overflowing with citrus trees and olive groves. Today many of the trees have disappeared and the valley is ruined by overdevelopment.

Throughout the rural interior you will see plenty of houses that look half-built, with exposed brick and large metal girders jutting out through the top of the roofs. Plaster façades are intentionally left off to avoid incurring taxes on 'finished' houses, while the ugly girders exist in case the owners' children marry and decide to move in: a 2nd floor is added to the house and the newlyweds simply move upstairs. Although these practices spoil the environment, it must be remembered that they are often born of necessity. Sicilians are by and large not wealthy so they make do with what they have, especially in the poorer rural communities.

The government's record on ecology is poor. The Ministry for the Environment was created only in 1986, and many environmental laws are either badly enforced or ignored altogether. Recycling is almost completely unheard of in Sicily, although in the larger cities you will find the occasional bottle bank – far too few to make any considerable difference, however.

There are many subtle references to the sea's fish depletion in Emanuele Crialese's 2002 film *Respiro*, in which the fishermen fleetingly discuss the damage of deep-sea fishing.

Sicily is to host the world's first power plant that harnesses solar energy and uses it alongside natural gas as a source for generating electricity. Known as the Archimedes project, the plant is planned to be built near Syracuse and will cost €40 million.

Sicily Outdoors

In *Il gattopardo* (The Leopard), Giuseppe Tomasi di Lampedusa compares Sicily's landscape to a stormy sea of constantly changing colours and moods. Few descriptions so aptly encapsulate the diversity of the island, where a day's drive can take you from a Mediterranean coastline lined with fragrant *maquis* (North African brush) to the charred slopes of Etna or the green oases of the Nebrodi and Madonie parks. Increasingly, travellers are seeking out these hidden corners of the island, opting to stay in *agriturismi* (farm stays), spending their days hiking or riding amid beautiful farmland.

The wonder of Sicily is that there is so much that one could do. You can ride or hike through Etna's national park, enjoy the wildly varied landscapes of the Aeolian Islands, each completely different from the others, or scuba dive in the marine reserves of Ustica, the Egadi Islands or fabulous Pantelleria. And if you've had enough of salty hair and sunburnt skin, head inland to the mountain-fresh sanctuaries of the Madonie and Nebrodi parks, where an almost alpine climate makes you feel like you're in a different country. The contrasts are startling and enjoyable.

What's more, the authorities are finally waking up to the preciousness of Sicily's wilderness and more efforts are being made to protect the coast and countryside, if only for commercial reasons. This works well with the strong island tradition of small-scale farming and the parks provide employment for local communities. But this is very much a work in progress and aside from Etna park, infrastructure tends to be haphazard and sometimes poorly organised. Don't let this put you off – the rewards far outweigh the minor inconveniences you may encounter.

HIKING

There are several hiking opportunities in Sicily. The biggest draws for hikers are the Parco Naturale Regionale delle Madonie (p139) and the Parco Regionale dei Nebrodi (p142). The Madonie is the more popular of the two and is therefore better organised (maps can be obtained in the tourist offices of Palermo and Cefalù). Nebrodi, on the other hand, is well off the beaten track, beautifully remote but poorly signposted. The Nebrodi and Madonie nature reserves offer the hiker a completely different experience: gently wooded mountains full of wild flowers and the Heidi-style tinkling of cowbells. The Nebrodi mountains, 'the mountains of the fawn', contain the largest remaining beech forest in Europe and a wonderful lake circuit (see the boxed text, p143).

Another fantastic area for walking is the often overlooked western coast of Sicily, home to Sicily's first nature reserve, the Riserva Naturale dello Zingaro (p104). The most organised reserve for walkers, this is a beautiful swathe of coastline dotted with picturesque coves and well-planned walking trails (maps available at the ticket office). The least discovered, however, is in the southeast of Sicily – the wildly overgrown Valle dell'Anapo (p227), where you can clamber around the Bronze Age cave dwellings of Pantalica.

The best time for hiking is undoubtedly spring, when the flowers are in bloom and the landscape retains a rich, green flush. Early autumn is also good for the Madonie and Nebrodi parks – the temperatures remain high on the coast, but a lovely coolness descends inland. Autumn walking also offers up a wildly different aspect of the landscape: shades of gold contrast with freshly ploughed, chocolate-brown fields, and of course it is the time of grape harvest in the island's vineyards.

Log on to the website of Ente Fauna Siciliana, www.entefaunasiciliana.it (in Italian), for all manner of naturalistic tours and treks.

Landscapes of Sicily by Peter Amann is a handy little pocket-size book full of walks and driving tours around the island.

If planning to walk in the Madonie mountains get hold of the 1:50,000 *Madonie/Carta dei Sentieri e del Paesaggio* from the tourist office in Palermo or Cefalù, or the park headquarters in Petralia Sottana.

WALKING HOLIDAYS & GUIDED WALKS

The most reputable UK-based company offering walking tours in Sicily is **Think Sicily** (www
.thinksicily.co.uk). It runs three very lovely walks covering the west, the Madonie, and the Aeolians
and Nebrodi park combined. Trails are led by multilingual, native Sicilians and combine nature
and culture in equal measure. Another quality walking-tour operator is **Tabona & Walford** (☎ /fax
020 8767 6789; www.tabonaandwalford.com; 19 Crockerton Rd, London, SW17 7HE).

Guided treks can also be organised on the ground with **Magmatrek** (www.magmatrek.it; Stromboli),
Ente Fauna Siciliana (www.entefaunasiciliana.it in Italian; Noto & Syracuse), **Eolie Adventure** (www
.eolieadventure.com; Salina), **Gruppo Guide Alpine Etna Sud** (☎ 095 791 47 55; Via Etnea 49, Catania) and
GeoEtna Explorer (www.geoetnaexplorer.it; Catania). See the relevant chapters for full details.

VOLCANO CLIMBING

The serious climber will relish the chance to ascend a volcano, and Sicily
has these aplenty! The Parco Naturale dell'Etna (p208), established in 1987,
covers some 590 sq km and includes 20 different communities. The park is
fascinating, both for its varied natural environment and its surreal summit.
The other two volcanic experiences are on the Aeolians, where there are trails
up Vulcano – a bald, sulphurous boil of a cone – and Stromboli, whose constant pyrotechnics seen against a velvet night sky take some beating (see p176
for details). If you do plan on walking up either Etna or Stromboli, remember
that they are both active volcanoes and walkers are strongly advised to seek
up-to-date information on their activity and stick to designated safety zones.
Try local tourist and trekking agencies for current information.

Mt Etna (p208) is usually at the top of everyone's list for good reason, and
aside from the hour-long tour of Bocca Nuova included in every summit
ticket, you can spend several days trekking around the 165km circumference
of the mountain. The most extensive trek is the *altomontana* (high trail):
traversing the wooded slopes of the volcano from Rifugio Brunek to Rifugio
Sapienza, at altitudes of between 1300m and 1800m, takes three days (see
the boxed text, p143).

It is also possible to walk right across the mountain from Piano
Provenzano, in the north, to Rifugio Sapienza, in the south (seven to
eight hours, 22.5km); and the Gruppo Guide Alpine Etna Sud takes small
groups up to the Valle del Bove, site of the latest lava trail. A range of
personalised tours can be organised with this outfit or a handful of other
specialist companies (see p210).

Etna has its own microclimate, and generally the best walking is between
March and April, and September and October. Trekking across lava fields
under an unforgiving summer sun can be an uncomfortable experience. At
higher altitudes (above 2000m) a mountain climate sets in, with strong –
sometimes freezing – winds. Snowfall is common between November and
April when the mountain is transformed into a skiing destination (see
p73 for details).

On the Aeolian Islands (p149), the trek up Vulcano is easily done on
your own, while the trek up Stromboli is really enriched by the Magmatrek
guides (see p178). By contrast, Salina is the greenest of the islands and is
a pleasant change after all that fire and brimstone. Pantelleria is another
paradisiacal setting, with treks ending in mud baths and natural saunas.

In the Middle Ages
Christians believed that
Vulcano's crater was the
entrance to hell.

Mt Etna is ringed by a
series of good riding
stables and trails (see
p209 for more details).
Ask at the tourist office
for the booklet *Itinerari
a Cavallo*, which gives
details of all the stables
and the itineraries they
run.

CYCLING

Cycling in Sicily is not for the faint-hearted. Much of the terrain is mountainous and most of the surrounding islands are the vertical cones of submerged volcanoes.

> **CYCLING HOLIDAYS**
>
> A number of organisations specialise in self-guided tours of Sicily. **Hooked on Cycling** (www
> .hookedoncycling.co.uk/Italy/Western_Sicily/western_sicily.html) offers a classic itinerary of Western Sicily,
> as does **Exodus** (www.exodus.co.uk/activities/cyclingitaly.html). **Scottish Cycling Holidays** (www.sol.co
> .uk/s/scotcycl/) also does the western route but offers two others: around Taormina, and Syracuse
> and the southeast.

For those with a recreational interest in cycling, the best area is the relatively flat western coast. Hiring a bicycle on Favignana in the Egadi Islands is a great day out and only costs €5, while the saltpans west of Trapani are flat. Likewise, Syracuse is a cycle-friendly city.

Most cyclists concentrate on routes around Mt Etna (p208), which offer excellent views from every angle. The most popular circuit is a complete loop (121km) around the volcano from Catania (p196), through Linguaglossa, Randazzo and Bronte to Rifugio Sapienza at the summit. Here you take your own time visiting the craters. You can also detour to Rifugio Brunek on the northeastern flank, a route that wends its way through verdant oak, chestnut and pine forests.

A more adventurous itinerary through rural Sicily is to bus your way to Enna (p241) in the centre of the island and then freewheel through Agira, Troina and the Parco Regionale dei Nebrodi. Alternatively, the southeast corner of the island around Syracuse (p214) and the west of the island around Trapani (p105) offer some more gentle routes. The west of the island, in particular, offers the least demanding route alongside some wonderful scenery and sights, taking in Scopello (where you can go walking in the Riserva Naturale dello Zingaro, p104), medieval Erice, the Trapani saltpans, Marsala's vineyards and the gorgeous classical site of Selinunte.

It is possible to ride almost all year round, bar the peak of summer (August) and during the dreary winter rain (December to February). If you are planning a trip over Easter, make sure you make all the necessary bookings beforehand, as Sicily is jam-packed in Easter week.

The most versatile bicycle for most of the roads here is a comfortable all-terrain bike capable of travelling over both paved and country roads. You may well find that you are travelling along isolated roads, so it's wise to be equipped with a kit for essential repairs. Always wear a helmet and have a detailed map of the area.

Hazards on the road are manifold. Off the main routes, roads can be narrow and in summer traffic is quite heavy. Also, Sicilians think nothing of overtaking on hairpin bends so you will need your wits about you. In the cities you will have to adapt to the Sicilians' lack of cycle-awareness. Bikes are not common here and few concessions are made for cyclists. You will also have to negotiate the daredevil scooter riders, an exhausting and ever-present hazard on the roads.

Sicily's two major road races both take place in March. The Rofeo dell'Etna is a 200km circuit around the mountain, and the Rofeo Pantalica, a 170km race near Syracuse.

For an outdoor holiday on an authentic working farm, check out the website www .agriturismo-sicilia.it.

DIVING & SNORKELLING

Sicily is a diver's paradise and its volcanic geography ensures that the surrounding waters teem with a wide variety of fish and a colourful marine landscape. The crystal-clear waters of Ustica (p100) remain the location of choice for hundreds of scuba divers and during the summer months almost the entire island is given over to some sort of waterborne activity. The **Marine**

FINDING YOUR WAY

The Michelin map 1:400,000 (series number 565) is a good all-round road map to the island and excellent for touring purposes. Cyclists should try to get hold of a copy of Touring Club Italia's (TCI) 1:200,000 *Sicily* map. The tourist office in Catania also hands out a free TCI map of Mt Etna and its environs: 1:175,000 *Province of Catania*. For Etna walkers, more detailed maps are available from TCI *Mt Etna* at 1:50,000 and the Istituto Geografico Militare (IGM; 1:25,000), although the latter are nearly 40 years old and show some misleading trails.

In the Zingaro reserve a good, free map (1:25,000) is available from the ticket booth. It clearly marks out all the walking trails and they are easy to follow. On the Aeolian Islands most maps use an old IGM 1:25,000 as their base. This covers all the islands of the archipelago. There is also an excellent clear map available from Litografia Artistica Cartografica (LAC), *Isole Eolie o Lipari* 1:25,000, which covers all the islands. The only detailed map of the Nebrodi park is the TCI 1:50,000 *Parco dei Nebrodi*, produced in cooperation with the park's administration. However, it is not totally reliable on the ground. The 1:50,000 *Madonie/Carta dei Sentieri e del Paesaggio* that covers the Madonie park is much better and available from Cefalù and Palermo Tourist Offices and park headquarters in Petralia Sottana. It costs €1.

Reserve Visitors Centre (☎ 091 844 94 56) is very well organised and there is even a signposted archaeological trail that divers can follow, with underwater plaques explaining your deep-sea finds.

The Egadi Islands (p113) form a marine reserve, with serious diving outlets such as **Atlantide** (www.progettoatlantide.com) operating archaeological and night dives. In addition the islands' fishermen have banded together to offer the tourist service known as *pescaturismo,* whereby you can hire out a fishing boat and explore the islands in between fishing for your supper. Given the remoteness of Marettimo and its relative quietness, the waters around the island are some of the most tranquil and clean in all of Italy.

You don't have to be a serious diver to enjoy Sicily, though: nearly all dive outlets hire out snorkels, and both the Aeolians and Taormina are given over to a more leisurely enjoyment of the marine world. Sure you have your serious outlets like **Diving Centre La Gorgonia** (☎ 090 981 20 60; www.lagorgoniadiving.it) on Lipari, but more popular are boat trips that tour the grotto-lined coastlines, stopping here and there for snorkelling and swimming. One of the best of these is the Grotta del Bue Marino on Filicudi (p180). Hiring a snorkel at **Nike Diving Centre** (☎ 0942 4 75 34; www.divenike.com) at Lido Mazzarò in Taormina (p193) to explore the gorgeous cove of Isola Bella or the Blue Grotto is one the cheapest and nicest experiences on the Ionian Coast.

The most impressive recording of the *mattanza* ritual (the annual tuna fishing season) was caught on film by Roberto Rossellini, in his film *Stromboli.*

SAILING

Although every harbour of the island is chockers with boats, sailing is not such a feature of the Sicilian seascape – far too much hard work and not enough posing potential. Here the motorboat or *gommone* (zodiac; motorised rubber dinghy) are the crafts of choice and they can be hired out on all the islands. **Sailing Team** (☎ 0931 6 08 08; www.sailingteam.biz) in Syracuse is about the best and most serious boat charter on the island and it can tailor-make itineraries around Sicily and even as far as Malta, but they don't come cheap.

Pedalos and jet skis are a feature of all the bigger and more popular beach resorts.

SKIING

Strange as it may seem, Sicily has two winter ski resorts: in the Parco Naturale Regionale delle Madonie (see p140) and on Mt Etna (p210). The tiny resort of Piano Battaglia in the Madonie mountains has very limited infrastructure: a few cosy refuges that rent out equipment, and two ski lifts. One takes skiers up the northern slopes to the Mufara complex (1856m) and its 3.5km of runs, while the other ascends the southwestern slope (Mufaretta; 1657m) with a short run of only 500m. It is a pretty place but there is no real support for inexperienced skiers. Cross-country skiing is also very popular in the forest.

Sicily's main resort is the summit of Mt Etna, which benefits from a good 3m of snowfall in the winter. However, the 2002 eruptions swept away the entire ski lift, which was still being reconstructed at the time of research.

Palermo

Palermo (population 680,000) is a city that's quite apart from the rest of Sicily's urban spaces. Though it's on the traditional end of the scale, it carries with it a sense of unpredictability and adventure: its streets are jam-packed with traffic; its markets are a hive of hollers, smells and countless gastronomic offerings; the winding, palazzo-strewn streets of the old quarter contrast with the wide boulevards and glam shops of the new town. It's a European city with a chaotic nature and a penchant for rule bending.

This is an ancient city that showcases the remains of Sicily's countless invaders: it was once an Arab emirate, the seat of a Norman kingdom and, in the 12th century, Europe's grandest city; later, its fate was more grim than glam. The city is still a real beauty, but its gems often need seeking out. You'll be surprised by the number of gorgeous, swirling palazzi – the fusion of Byzantine, Arab, Norman, Renaissance and baroque architecture is a feast for the eyes.

But it's not just history that makes Palermo so terrific. An increasing number of bars, clubs and great restaurants means it's fun after dark, while Mondello beach is a mere 15-minute bus ride away, making it easy to cool off on summer days. And should the chaotic capital make you crave some peace and quiet, the lonely island of Ustica offers total escape. While you're in the city, don't miss its simple joys, such as watching families stroll and eat ice cream by the seafront, or bargaining with the quick-witted market salesmen. But most importantly, whatever you do, don't miss Palermo.

HIGHLIGHTS

- Feel faint before the beauty of the glittering mosaics at the **Cappella Palatina** (p81) and **Cattedrale di Monreale** (p99)

- Weave through the smells and the yells of Palermo's **street markets** (p96)

- See some breathtaking opera in the impressive **Teatro Massimo** (p88)

- Get up close and personal with Sicily's history and culture in two of the island's finest museums, the **Museo Archeologico Regionale** (p85) and the **Galleria Regionale Siciliana** (p86)

- Admire the underwater beauties in **Ustica** (p101), a world centre for diving

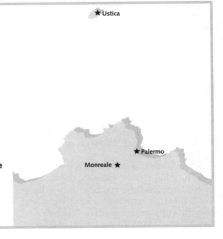

★ Ustica

★ Palermo

Monreale ★

PALERMO

HISTORY

Palermo looks old for a reason – it is. Nearly 3000 years old, at that. It started life as a huddle of Phoenician stores on a peaceful bay surrounded by the fertile Conca d'Oro, a prime piece of real estate that long made it a target for Sicily's colonisers. As the Carthaginians and Greeks began to flex their territorial muscles, the little depot grew in strategic and economic importance. It became Panormus (the Greek word for port).

Conquered by the Arabs in AD 831, the port flourished and became a very fine city. So much so that when the Normans invaded in 1072, Roger I (1031–1101) made it the seat of his kingdom, encouraging the resident Arabs, Byzantines, Greeks and Italians to remain. In Sicily, the Normans found their longed-for 'kingdom of the sun' and under their enlightened rule Palermo became the most cultured city of 12th-century Europe.

The end of Roger's line (with the death of William II in 1189) was to signal the very long and terminal decline of the city to its modern-day nadir. A series of extraordinary and often bloody political struggles saw the island pass from German (Hohenstaufens) to French (Angevins) to Spanish (Aragonese) and English rule. None of these powers – who were nearly always uninterested and removed from Palermo – could regain the splendour of the Norman era. The only physical change to the city occurred under the Spaniards, with the imposition of a rational city plan that disguised the original Moorish layout. If you see the city from an altitude, you'll notice the baroque domes rising like islands above a sea of alleyways.

Industrial entrepreneurs, such as the Florios and the Whitakers, gave the city a brief flash of brilliance in the pre-WWI period by dressing it in the glamorous and decadent structures of art nouveau, resulting in Palermo's final *belle époque*. But two world wars and massive material damage sank the city into despair and disrepair. At the end of 1945, the city was flooded by hundreds of impoverished rural labourers and gripped by Mafia violence.

The middle classes moved out into newly built housing estates, escaping the new wave of violence (and the bad plumbing). By the 1980s the city was virtually a European pariah, notching up weekly murders. It is only since the climax of the Mafia supertrials of the 1990s

that Palermo has begun to emerge from its troubled past. In addition, Palermo's mayors, Leoluca Orlando and Diego Cammarata, have dedicated themselves to restoring the city to its former glory, though cynics say that the Mafia has traded guns and violence for suits and success. In the meantime, you'll see lots of work-in-progress in Palermo's old quarter and on its beautiful palazzi (palaces or mansions). As ever, only time will tell what the future holds in store for Europe's most Byzantine city.

ORIENTATION

Palermo is large but easily walkable – if you can brave crossing the street, that is. Via Maqueda is its central street, extending from the train station in the south before turning into Via Ruggero Settimo. At Piazza Castelnuovo it turns into Viale della Libertà, a lush boulevard lined with late-19th-century apartment blocks that marks the start of the modern half of the city.

Via Maqueda is bisected by Corso Vittorio Emanuele, running east to west from the port of La Cala to the cathedral and Palazzo dei Normanni. The intersection of Via Maqueda and Corso Vittorio Emanuele, known famously as Quattro Canti (Four Corners), divides historic Palermo into four traditional quarters: La Kalsa (east), Vucciria (north), Il Capo (west) and Albergheria (south). These quarters contain the majority of Palermo's sights.

Parallel to Via Maqueda runs Via Roma, a popular shopping street. A one-way system moves traffic north up Via Roma from the train station and south down Via Maqueda.

INFORMATION
Bookshops

Generally, bookshops open from 9am to 2.30pm and 4.30 to 8pm Monday to Saturday, and 10am to 1pm and 3pm to 8pm Sunday. Several stands around Piazza Verdi sell foreign newspapers.

Feltrinelli (Map p82; ☎ 091 58 77 85; www .lafeltrinelli.it; Via Maqueda 395-399) Sicily's best foreign-language book section; it has an excellent choice of classics and contemporary titles, maps and Palermo guides.

Mondadori (Map p82; ☎ 091 32 54 92; www .mondadori.it; Via Roma 287) A small selection of foreign-language books covering romance, mystery and the classics.

Emergency

Central Police (questura; Map pp78-9; ☎ theft & lost documents 091 21 01 11, foreigners office 091 651 43 30;

Piazza della Vittoria) Go here to report thefts and other petty crimes.

City Police (☎ 091 695 41 11) If your car has been towed away, call to find out where to collect it.

Internet Access

Internet cafés come and go rapidly and your best bet is the internet and cheap-phone-call outlets along Via Maqueda (they stay open all day, and some run until midnight). Prices are generally around €6 per hour. As a result of Italy's antiterrorism laws, you'll be asked to provide ID before you can use a computer; a passport photocopy usually suffices.

Aboriginal Café (Map p82; ☎ 091 66 22 22; www .aboriginalcafe.com; Via Spinuzza 51; ☻ 6pm-2am) The most central internet café; it's also an Australian-style bar that gets very busy in the evenings.

Left Luggage

Ferry Terminal (Map pp78-9; Molo Vittorio Veneto; per bag per hr from €1; ☻ 7am-8pm)

Train Station (Map p82; Piazza Giulio Cesare; per bag per 12hr €3.90; ☻ 7am-11pm)

Medical Services

Ambulance (☎ 091 30 66 44)

Farmacia Da Naro (Map p82; ☎ 091 58 58 69; Via Roma 207; ☻ 24hr)

Ospedale Civico (Map pp78-9; ☎ 091 666 11 11; Via Carmelo Lazzaro)

Money

There are plenty of ATMs dotted around the city and on all the major streets.

Cambio Falcone-Borsellino airport (☻ 8am-7pm Mon-Sat); Train Station (Map p82; ☻ 8am-8pm) These places have exchange offices open outside normal banking hours.

Ruggieri & Figli (Map pp78-9; ☎ 091 58 71 44; Via Enrico Amari 40; ☻ 9am-1pm & 4-7pm Mon-Fri, 9am-1pm Sat) Representatives for American Express; will only cash travellers cheques for card-holders.

Post

Main post office (Map p82; Palazzo delle Poste, Via Roma 322; ☻ 8.30am-6.30pm Mon-Fri, 8.30am-12.30pm Sat) This impressive monolithic building, propped up on the largest pillars you'll ever see, is one of the few Fascist-era buildings in Palermo. Smaller branch offices can be found at the train station (Map p82) and on Piazza Verdi. All have the same opening hours.

Tourist Information

Main tourist office (Map pp78-9; ☎ 091 605 81 11; www.palermotourism.com; Piazza Castelnuovo 35;

☻ 8.30am-2pm & 2.30-6pm Mon-Fri, 8.30am-2pm Sat) Sicily's regional tourist office is thin on personal help, but offers some very good brochures on Palermo, the most useful of these being the bimonthly *Agenda Turismo* and the *Lapis Palermo* guide, with listings of cultural events.

Tourist office Falcone-Borsellino airport (☎ 091 59 16 98; ☻ 8am-noon); Train Station (Map p82; ☎ 091 605 81 11; ☻ 8.30am-2pm & 2.30-6pm Mon-Fri, 8.30am-2pm Sat) There are also information booths on Molo Piave (Map pp78-9), Piazza Bellini (Map p82), Piazza Marina (Map p82) and Piazza della Vittoria (Map pp78-9); these are usually open from 9am to 2pm and 3pm to 8pm Monday to Thursday, 8.30am to 8.30pm Friday and Saturday, and 9am to 1pm and 3pm to 7pm Sunday.

Travel Agencies

You can book train, ferry and air tickets at the following agencies:

CTS (Map pp78-9; ☎ 091 611 07 13; www.cts.it in Italian; Via Nicoló Garzilli 28g) A branch of the national youth-travel agency. Also offers tours of the city.

Record Viaggi (Map pp78-9; ☎ 091 611 09 10; Via Mariano Stabile 168)

Sestante CIT (Map pp78-9; ☎ 091 58 63 33; Viale della Libertá 12)

DANGERS & ANNOYANCES

The days when Palermo was known as a dangerous city are over, with its traditional trouble spots – in particular the area from Mercato della Vucciria to the port and La Kalsa – the focus of restoration programmes that have made them more pleasant for residents and tourists alike.

That said, do keep your eye on your belongings, especially in crowded market areas and the main intercity bus station on Via Paolo Balsamo, where pickpockets are known to work their fingers. You should also be aware of the existence of bag-snatchers who – you guessed it – snatch bags from pedestrians, operating from speedy scooters; make sure you carry your daily bag draped across your body rather than having it slung over your shoulder. Stay away from poorly lit streets, particularly late at night or if you are alone.

SIGHTS & ACTIVITIES
Around the Quattro Canti

The busy intersection of Corso Vittorio Emanuele and Via Maqueda marks the **Quattro Canti** (Four Corners; Map p82), the centre of Palermo. This intersection is surrounded by a perfect circle of curvilinear façades that disappear up to the blue vault of the sky in a

PALERMO

0   500 m
0   0.3 miles

INFORMATION
Central Police.................................1 C6
CitySightseeing Palermo..................2 C4
CTS..3 B3
German Consulate...........................4 D3
Information Booth............................5 C6
Information Booth............................6 D3
Main Tourist Office..........................7 C4
Ospedale Civico...............................8 C7
Record Viaggi...................................9 C4
Ruggieri & Figli..............................10 D3
Sestante CIT...................................11 C3

SIGHTS & ACTIVITIES
Cappella Palatina.......................(see 24)
Castello della Zisa.........................12 A5
Catacombe dei Cappuccini............13 A6
Cathedral.......................................14 C6
Chiesa di San Giovanni degli
  Eremiti..15 C6
Chiesa di Sant'Agostino.................16 C5
Complessa di Santa Maria dello
  Spasimo......................................17 E6
Convento dei Cappuccini..........(see 13)
Galleria Regionale Siciliana............18 E5
Hammam..19 C3
Museo Diocesiano..........................20 C3
Museo Internazionale delle
  Marionette...................................21 E5
Orto Botanico.................................22 F6
Palazzo Chiaramonte......................23 E5
Palazzo dei Normanni.....................24 C6
Porta Nuova...................................25 C6
Teatro Massimo..............................26 C5
Teatro Politeama Garibaldi.............27 C4
Tower...28 C6
Villa Giulia.....................................29 F6

SLEEPING
A Casa di Amici B&B.......................30 C5
Albergo Ariston..............................31 C4
Grand Hotel et des Palmes.............32 C4
Hotel Principe di Villafranca...........33 B3
Jolly Hotel.....................................34 F5

EATING
Antico Caffè Spinnato.....................35 C4
Cucina Papoff.................................36 C3
Il Baretto.......................................37 C3
Il Firriato.................................(see 33)
Kursaal Kalhesa..............................38 F5
L'Acanto..39 C4
Massaro...40 C7
Massaro 2......................................41 C7
Trattoria Biondo.............................42 C4

DRINKING
Berlin...43 C3
Exit Drinks.....................................44 C4
Kursaal Kalhesa......................(see 38)
Rocket Bar.....................................45 C4

ENTERTAINMENT
Compagnia Argento........................46 C6
La Cuba..47 A1
Lo Spasimo.............................(see 17)
Teatro Massimo......................(see 26)
Teatro Politeama Garibaldi......(see 27)

SHOPPING
Antico Caffè Spinnato...............(see 35)
I Peccatucci di Mamma
  Andrea.......................................48 D4
Mangia..49 C4
Silvanna Sansone...........................50 C3
Tre Erre Ceramiche.........................51 D3

TRANSPORT
Alitalia...52 C3
Azienda Siciliana Trasporti.............53 C7
Buses for Airport............................54 C4
Buses for Monreale.........................55 B6
Buses for Monte & Monte
  Pellegrino...................................56 C3
Ferry Terminal................................57 E3
Grandi Navi Veloci..........................58 D3
Pietro Barbaro...............................59 D4
Sicily by Car...................................60 D4
Siremar..61 D4
Tirrenia Navigazione......................62 D3

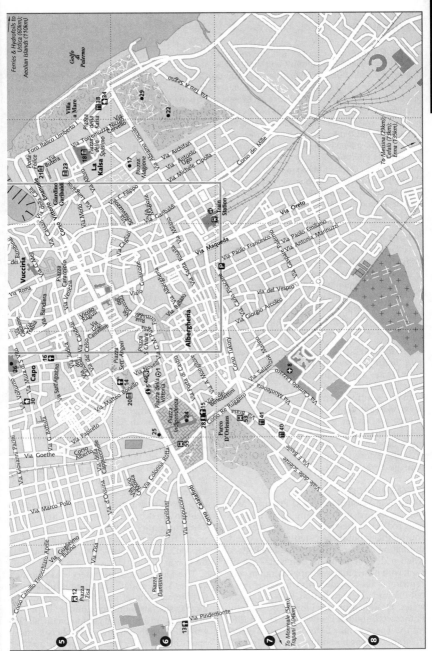

PALERMO IN...

Two Days

Get up early and have a quick breakfast, Sicilian style, and dive straight into the crowds at the **Mercato della Vucciria** (p96), where you can take in Palermo's spirit, and taste local produce as you go along. Emerge at Corso Vittorio Emanuele and start your sightseeing with the chaos and the fun of the market still in your hair. Explore the **Quattro Canti** (p77) and the **Piazza Pretoria** (below), and find tranquillity in the beauty of **La Martorana** (opposite) and **Chiesa Santa Caterina** (below). Walk up Via Maqueda to **Teatro Massimo** (p88) and take a tour around the luxurious building. Finish off your day with a relaxing dinner at **L'Acanto** (p94).

Day two should be another early start. Head for the **Palazzo dei Normanni** (opposite) and the **Cappella Palatina** (opposite), then treat yourself to a coffee and a *cannoli* (pastry shell stuffed with sweet ricotta) at **Massaro** (p94) and gaze at the pink domes of the **Chiesa di San Giovanni degli Eremiti** (p83) on your way back to the centre. Drop into the **cathedral** (p84) on your way to the **Galleria Regionale Siciliana** (p86), where you'll see Sicily's best artwork collection. Spend your afternoon with some classical history at the **Museo Archeologico Regionale** (p85), then sample some imaginative Sicilian cuisine on the terrace of **Kursaal Kalhesa** (p93).

Four Days

Follow the itinerary for the first two days. On the third day take a bus to Monreale, dominated by the huge **Cattedrale di Monreale** (p99); don't miss the beautiful cloister. For views, you can climb up the tower to the roof. When you return to Palermo, book yourself into the **hammam** (p88) and spend a few hours being pampered.

Day four is ideally spent rummaging around one of Palermo's many **markets** (p96) or, if you're a sun fan, heading out to the beach at **Mondello** (p99). Eat at one of the cheap cafés backing the beach or really splash out at the **Charleston** (p99).

---

clever feat of perspective. It is known locally as *Il Teatro del Sole* (Theatre of the Sun) as each façade is lit up in turn throughout the course of the day.

In the southwestern corner is the **Chiesa di San Giuseppe dei Teatini** (Map p82; Corso Vittorio Emanuele; admission free; ☺ 8.30-11am & 6-8pm), topped by a soaring cupola. The monumental interior is baroque at its brashest, and has been lovingly restored after it suffered substantial damage during WWII.

PIAZZA PRETORIA

Across Via Maqueda is Piazza Pretoria (Map p82), a crowd of imposing (and recently restored) churches and buildings that surround the fabulously ostentatious – and, unfortunately, fenced-off – **Fontana Pretoria** (Map p82). The fountain dominates the piazza, with its tiered basins rippling out in concentric circles crowded with nude nymphs, tritons and river gods that leap about the water. Designed by the Florentine sculptor Francesco Camilliani between 1554 and 1555 for the Tuscan villa of Don Pedro di Toledo, the fountain was bought by Palermo in 1573

in a bid to outshine the newly crafted Fontana di Orione installed in Messina. Proudly positioned in front of the **Palazzo Pretorio** (Municipal Hall; Map p82), the fountain's flagrant nudity and leering nymphs proved a bit much for Sicilian churchgoers attending the grandly formal Chiesa di San Giuseppe dei Teatini, and they prudishly dubbed it the *Fontana della Vergogna* (Fountain of Shame).

Closing off the eastern side of the square is the **Chiesa di Santa Caterina** (Map p82; ☎ 338 722 87 75; admission €1; ☺ 9.30am-1pm summer & 25 Nov), Palermo's finest baroque church. Belonging to a Dominican monastery, the church is held in trust by seven very old nuns, who kept the doors of the church shut for 14 years, finally opening them again for visitors on Christmas Eve 2006. The entrance is on Piazza Bellini.

The Dominican monastery was founded around 1310, and it is said that it initially offered refuge mainly to prostitutes. However, the local aristocrats soon took notice of its prominent location and began getting financially involved. With the boost to Catholicism under Spanish rule in the 16th century, the number of nuns and the pious rose, and the ever-expanding monastery effectively swallowed up the existing church. With the old one bursting at the seams, a new one was needed. The Chiesa di Santa Caterina was then built between 1566 and 1596 by an unknown architect. The rich décor was enhanced by a marble coat in the 17th and 18th centuries, and many of the smooth white statues, gilded stucco and whirling frescoes were added in this period, as well as the carved marble presbytery and the amethyst tabernacle behind the main altar, the altar's silver angels and the silver girds on the confessional boxes. Once you view the church you'll understand why the nuns have been so possessive and secretive over this explosion of baroque.

LA MARTORANA & CHIESA DI SAN CATALDO

Palermo's most famous – and beautiful – medieval church is **La Martorana** (Chiesa di Santa Maria dell'Ammiraglio; Map p82; Piazza Bellini 3; admission free; 8am-1pm & 3.30-5.30pm Mon-Sat, 8.30am-1pm Sun), which is often buzzing with wedding ceremonies (always scheduled late morning and usually on Saturdays). This 12th-century structure was the brainchild of King Roger's Syrian emir, George of Antioch, and, like many structures dating from this period, it was originally planned as a mosque. Delicate Fatimid pillars support a domed cupola depicting Christ enthroned amid his archangels, while Arabic script endlessly repeats the name of Allah. The stunning Byzantine mosaics are the legacy of the Greek artisans employed to decorate the church, who brought with them an Orthodox Christian sense of religious décor.

In 1433 the church was given over to a Benedictine order of nuns, founded by Eloisa Martorana (hence its nickname), who tore down the Norman apse, reworked the exterior in a fussy baroque fashion and added their own frescoed chapel, unfortunately at the expense of some of the wonderful mosaic work. Fortunately two of the original mosaics to survive are the portrait of George of Antioch, crouched behind a shield at the feet of the Virgin Mary, and one of Roger II receiving his crown from Christ (the only portrait of him to survive in Sicily).

Mussolini returned the church to the Greek Orthodox community in 1935, and the Greek Mass is still celebrated here.

While La Martorana preserves its interior, the small pink-domed **Chiesa di San Cataldo** (Map p82; Piazza Bellini 3; admission free; 9am-3.30pm Mon-Fri, 9am-12.30pm Sat, 9am-1pm Sun & public holidays) is almost bare inside. It was founded in the 1150s by Maio of Bari (William I's emir of emirs) but Maio's murder in 1160 meant it was not finished – hence the lack of adornment within. However, the main interest lies in the exterior, which illustrates perfectly the synthesis of Arab-Norman styles.

Albergheria

Once inhabited by Norman court officials, Albergheria has been a poor and ramshackle quarter since the end of WWII – indeed, you can still see wartime bomb damage scarring some buildings. The area is now home to a growing immigrant population that has revitalised the streets with its aspirations and homesickness. It is also the location of Palermo's busiest market, Mercato di Ballarò (see p96).

PALAZZO DEI NORMANNI

West along Corso Vittorio Emanuele, past the waving palms in Piazza della Vittoria, rises the fortress palace of **Palazzo dei Normanni** (Palazzo Reale; Map pp78-9; 091 705 43 17; fax 091 705 47 37; Piazza Indipendenza 1; admission incl Cappella Palatina €6; 9am-noon & 2-5pm Mon-Sat, 9am-noon Sun), once the centre of a magnificent medieval court and now the seat of the Sicilian parliament. Guided tours (in Italian only; group visits must be prebooked by fax) take you through the Sicilian parliamentary assembly and to the sumptuous **Sala di Ruggero II**, the king's former bedroom, where some of the only secular mosaics of the day still decorate the walls with Persian peacocks and exotic leopards.

Downstairs, just off the three-tiered loggia, is Palermo's premier tourist attraction, the **Cappella Palatina** (091 705 48 79; 9am-11.45am & 3-5pm Mon-Fri, 9am-11.45am Sat & Sun), designed by Roger II in 1130. The chapel was under restoration at the time of research, with the ceiling and most of the walls covered by scaffolding, but the work is meant to be finished in the summer of 2008, when you should be able to see the mosaics in renewed shiny splendour.

This is one of the busiest tourist sites in Palermo, so be prepared to queue. Once in possession of your ticket you will have to

PALERMO

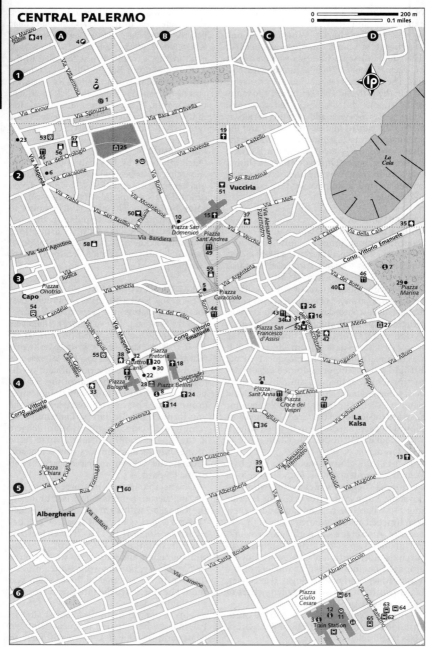

CENTRAL PALERMO

queue once again outside the chapel as minders limit the number of people. The whole process is often badly managed, but don't let yourself be hurried through one of Sicily's finest sights.

The chapel's mosaics are considered one of the world's primary works of art, and with every inch of its bijou interior inlaid with precious marbles and exquisite mosaics the chapel has a jewel-like quality. The mosaics are incredibly sophisticated, capturing expressions, detail and movement with extraordinary grace and delicacy. The bulk of the mosaics recount the tales of the Old Testament, but other scenes recall Palermo's pivotal role in the Crusades, an ironic reference given the fact that the chapel was decorated by Muslim artists. But it's not only the mosaics you should be gazing at – don't miss a good gawp at the wooden *muqarnas* (a decorative device resembling stalactites) ceiling, a masterpiece of honeycomb carving that is unique in a Christian church (and, many speculate, a sign of Roger II's secret identity as a Muslim). The floor too, with its carved marble is breathtaking: marble was as precious as gems during the 12th century, so the value this floor had at the time is almost immeasurable by today's standards.

PORTA NUOVA
Next to the palace is the Porta Nuova (Map pp78–9), built to celebrate the arrival of Carlos V in Palermo in 1535 after a victory over the Tunisians. Designed in the mannerist style, the gate was partially destroyed by lightning in 1667 and rebuilt with the addition of the conical top. More than 400 years later, it still serves as a demarcation line between the old and new city.

CHIESA DI SAN GIOVANNI DEGLI EREMITI
Just south of the Palazzo dei Normanni, the **Chiesa di San Giovanni degli Eremiti** (Map pp78–9; ☎ 091 651 50 19; Via dei Benedettini; admission €6; 9am-1pm & 3-7pm Mon-Sat, 9am-12.30pm Sun & public holidays) is Palermo's best-known example of the Norman-Arab architectural mix. Built under Roger II, it is topped by five red domes and set in a pretty, tree-filled garden with **cloisters** (admission €3) offering temporary respite from the chaos outside. The bare interior of the now deconsecrated church features some badly deteriorated frescoes. The cloisters were undergoing renovation at the time of writing, but were expected to reopen in summer 2008.

There is a **tower** (Map pp78-9; admission free) next door to the church that has lovely views of the pink domes, with the spires of the cathedral thrown in.

Capo

Bordering the Albergheria quarter, Il Capo is another web of interconnected streets and blind alleys. Impoverished like its neighbour, it too has its own street trade, Mercato del Capo (see p96) running the length of Via Sant'Agostino. The centrepiece of the quarter is the imposing monastery of **Chiesa di Sant'Agostino** (Map pp78-9; Via Sant'Agostino; admission free; ☼ 8am-noon & 4-5.30pm), which ran the region in medieval times.

THE CATHEDRAL

Ambitious builders, the Normans converted mosques and palaces, giving rise to the Arab-Norman style that is unique to Sicily. Chief among these is the **cathedral** (Map pp78-9; ☎ 091 33 43 76; www.cattedrale.palermo.it in Italian; Corso Vittorio Emanuele; admission free; ☼ 7am-7pm Mon-Sat, 8am-1.30pm & 4-7pm Sun & public holidays), an extraordinary feast of ziggurat crenellations, majolica cupolas, geometric patterns and blind arches. It's an impressive building that has aesthetically suffered somewhat from the many reworkings during its history (pick from Arab-Norman, Catalan-Gothic, Gothic and neoclassical); with the palms swaying in the foreground, however, the Arab influence is still strong enough to skew your compass.

Construction began in 1184 at the behest of Palermo's archbishop, Walter of the Mill (Gualtiero Offamiglio), an Englishman who was tutor to William II and who held unlimited funds at his disposal and, seemingly, unlimited power in the Kingdom of Sicily. However, he felt his power diminishing with the construction of the magnificent cathedral at Monreale, and thus ordered for Palermo's cathedral to be built. It was erected on the location of a 9th-century mosque (itself built on a former chapel), and a detail from the mosque's original décor is visible at the southern porch, where a column is inscribed with a passage from the Koran. The cathedral's proportions and the grandeur of its exterior became a statement of the power struggle between church and throne occurring at the time, though Walter's death (in 1191) prevented him from seeing the finished building.

Since then the cathedral has been much altered, sometimes with great success (as in

Antonio Gambara's 15th-century three-arched portico that took 200 years to complete and became a masterpiece of Catalan-Gothic architecture), and sometimes with less fortunate results (as in Ferdinando Fuga's clumsy dome, added between 1781 and 1801). Thankfully Fuga's handiwork did not extend to the eastern exterior, which is still adorned with the exotic interlacing designs of Walter's original cathedral. The southwestern façade was laid in the 13th and 14th centuries, and is a beautiful example of local craftsmanship in the Gothic style. The cathedral's entrance is through the three magnificent Catalan-Gothic arches built by Gambara in 1426, which is fronted by gardens and a statue of Santa Rosalia, one of Palermo's patron saints. A recent renovation unearthed a beautiful painted intarsia decoration above the arches, which depicts the tree of life in a complex Islamic-style geometric composition of twelve roundels that show fruit, humans and all kinds of animals. It's thought to date back to 1296.

Although impressive in scale, the interior is a sadly unflamboyant resting place for the royal Norman tombs, which contain the remains of two of Sicily's greatest rulers, Roger II (rear left) and Frederick II of Hohenstaufen (front left). Halfway down the right aisle is a magnificent **treasury** (admission €2; ☼ 8am-6pm Mon-Sat), whose most extraordinary exhibits are the fabulous 13th-century crown of Constance of Aragon (wife of Frederick II), made by local craftsmen in fine gold filigree and encrusted with gems, and a tooth extracted from Santa Rosalia, whose ashes are also kept here in a silver reliquary. For information about the Festino di Santa Rosalia, see p91.

MUSEO DIOCESIANO

Next to the cathedral is the **Museo Diocesiano** (Map pp78-9; ☎ 091 607 72 15; www.diocesipa.it in Italian; Via Matteo Bonello 2; admission €4.50; ☼ 9.30am-1.30pm Tue-Fri & Sun, 10am-6pm Sat), which houses an important and rather extensive collection of artworks from the cathedral and churches destroyed during WWII; these include paintings, and marble, fresco and mosaic fragments. There's a friendly guide who will explain the significance of each piece (they are largely unmarked), though she speaks Italian and French only. The ground floor holds 15th-century frescoes, along with Byzantine paintings and icons, among which the most beautiful is the 1171 *Madonna della*

Perla, rescued from the now-no-more church of San Nicoló Reale. Seek out the room dedicated to the 17th-century Sicilian painter Pietro Novelli (1603–47), who was one of the region's finest and served as a court painter to Spain's ruler, Philip IV. Much influenced by Anthony Van Dyck and Raphael, Novelli often appears in his chiaroscuro paintings. The museum's basement level is a mixture of sculpture, finds from destroyed churches, and paintings of Palermo.

Vucciria

The shabby Vucciria is known throughout Sicily for its rampant Mercato della Vucciria (see p96), a bustling market filled with shrieking vendors, staring silvery fish, swaying carcasses, fresh fruit and vegetables, and smoking meat grills. The market inspired Sicilian painter Renato Guttuso's most important work, *La Vucciria* (1974), described by Leonardo Sciascia as 'a hungry man's dream'.

Once the heart of poverty-stricken Palermo, and a den of crime and filth, Vucciria illustrated the almost medieval chasm that existed between rich and poor in Sicily up until the 1950s. Though it's still pretty shabby, the quarter attracts tons of visitors and is one of Palermo's most fascinating areas to wander around.

MUSEO ARCHEOLOGICO REGIONALE

One of the most important museums of its kind in Europe, the wonderful **Museo Archeologico Regionale** (Map p82; ☎ 091 611 68 05; Via Bara all'Olivella 24; admission €6; ⏰ 8.30am-6pm Mon-Fri, 8.30am-1.30pm Sat, Sun & public holidays) houses an extensive collection of archaeological artefacts. Among its treasures are Phoenician sarcophagi from the 5th century BC, 10,000 Etruscan artefacts, Greek carvings from Selinunte, the Hellenistic *Ariete di bronzo di Siracus* (Bronze Ram of Syracuse), the largest collection of ancient anchors in the world, and finds from archaeological sites throughout the island.

Without a doubt, the museum's most impressive rooms are at the back of the luxuriant cloister. They house the huge, fragmented Gorgon's head (570 BC) from Temple C at Selinunte, and 19 (out of an original 59) of the large lions' heads that formed the spouts of an enormous fountain at Tempio della Vittoria at Himera (see p133), the first Greek colony in Sicily's northern region.

Beyond these is the Sala di Selinunte, featuring the metopes (stone carvings) from the seven Greek temples at Selinunte. The metopes are carved in limestone with marble inserts and were originally vividly colourful – the background was bright blue, while the figures were drenched in crimson. There were originally 12 metopes, but only five remain. Discovered in 1823 by two British archaeologists, they depict scenes full of humour and energy: Heracles fights a wilting Amazon while Actaeon is devoured by his hounds; Perseus, supported by Athena, gleefully beheads the Gorgon (Medusa), who has just given birth to Pegasus; Heracles carries the naughty Cercopes twins on a pole for trying to steal his weapons, while they, hung upside down, laugh at his sunburnt bum.

Upstairs, room after room houses delicate painted vases and a rare collection of Etruscan mirrors. The 1st floor is fantastic for children, with dozens of animal figurines lining the cabinets in the corridors and an entire room dedicated to explaining some of the mythical animal sculptures.

The museum is wheelchair-friendly.

CHIESA DI SAN DOMENICO

About 200m southeast of the museum, off Via Roma, is the **Chiesa di San Domenico** (Map p82; ☎ 091 58 48 72; Piazza San Domenico; admission free; ⏰ 9-11.30am Mon-Fri, 5-7pm Sat & Sun). It was built in 1640 following the design of architect Andrea Cirincione; the façade was added in 1726 after the buildings that once occupied the square were demolished to give the church some space. The church has been the place where Italian VIPs have been buried since the Middle Ages; among the tombs and cenotaphs of notable Sicilians, you'll find the names of parliamentarian Ruggero Settimo, painter Pietro Novelli, and the former Italian prime minister Francesco Crispi.

More exciting than the church is its oratory, **Oratorio del Rosario di San Domenico** (Map p82; Via dei Bambinai 2; admission free; ⏰ 9am-1pm Mon-Fri, 2-5.30pm Sat), which is dominated by Anthony Van Dyck's fantastic blue-and-red altarpiece, *The Virgin of the Rosary with St Dominic and the Patronesses of Palermo.* Van Dyck left Palermo in fear of the plague, and painted the work in Genoa in 1628. There are also paintings by Pietro Novelli, while Giacomo Serpotta's stuccowork (from 1720) is some of the most amazing you'll see; his elaborate work, vivacious and whirling with figures, brought rococo to Sicilian churches. Serpotta's name meant 'lizard' or 'small snake', and he often included one of the reptiles in his work as a sort of signature.

CHIESA DI SANTA ZITA

The nearby 14th-century **Chiesa di Santa Zita** (Map p82; Via Valverde 3; admission free; 🕙 9am-1pm & 3-6pm Mon-Fri, 9am-1pm Sat) church is named after the tired patron saint of domestic servants. The church's funerary chapels are particularly lavish, thanks to the clever idea of the Dominican priests who acquired the church in the 16th century to allow rich families to bury their dead here, thus collecting income for the priests' monastery. There are some fine sculptures by Antonio Gagini here but, again, the real beauty is in the adjoining 17th-century **Oratorio del Rosario di Santa Zita** Map p82; Via Valverde 3; admission free; 🕙 9am-1pm & 3-6pm Mon-Fri, 9am-1pm Sat), where you can see more of Serpotta's breathtaking stuccos. Indeed, this is where his work is at its best. The real masterpiece is the elaborate *Battle of Lepanto* on the entrance wall, depicting the Christian victory over the Turks, a scene that is framed by stucco drapes held by hundreds of naughty cherubs who were modelled on Palermo's street urchins.

La Kalsa

Plagued by poverty, La Kalsa is one of the city's most notorious neighbourhoods and, at least until a few years ago, most visitors were advised to keep away once the sun went down. Certainly Mother Teresa considered it no better than the Third World and even established a mission here. Rightfully shamed, the authorities were galvanised into action and the quarter is now the main beneficiary of the Palermo restoration project.

GALLERIA REGIONALE SICILIANA

The arterial Via Alloro hides Palermo's best museum, the wonderful **Galleria Regionale Siciliana** (Map pp78-9; ☎ 091 623 00 11; Via Alloro 4; admission €6; 🕙 9am-2pm Mon & Fri, 9am-2pm & 3-8pm Tue, Wed & Thu, 9.30am-1.30pm Sat & Sun), full of treasures and paintings from the Middle Ages to the 18th century. The building itself is a gorgeous Catalan-Gothic palace sensitively transformed into an exhibition space in 1957 by Carlo Scarpa, one of Italy's leading designers.

The gallery gives a great insight into Sicilian painting – an art form sadly lacking in more recent years – and numbers among its treasures the *Trionfo della Morta* (Triumph of Death), a magnificent fresco. Mounted on his wasted horse, demonic Death wields a wicked-looking scythe, leaping over his hapless victims (notably the vain and pampered aristocrats of Palermo) while the poor and hungry look on from the side. The huge image, carefully restored, has sensibly been given its own room and can be viewed both at ground level and from a galleried platform.

Other treasures include a remarkable 12th-century Arab doorframe and Antonello da Messina's well-known panel of the *Assunzione* (Assumption). It is interesting to see Messina's work alongside the sculptures of Francesco Laurana, most notably his exquisite bust of *Eleonara di Aragona*, which is exhibited in Room 4. Both artists specialise in an economy of detail that lends their paintings and sculptures a perfect stillness that sets them apart from those of their contemporaries. In Laurana's case this is starkest when compared to the saccharine sweetness of the pearly white Madonnas of Domenico Gagini and his son Antonello. Like the Mona Lisa, Eleonara's grace and beauty are timeless.

GALLERIA D'ARTE MODERNA

Moved from its abode inside the walls of Teatro Politeama, Palermo's **Galleria d'Arte Moderna** (Map p82; ☎ 091 843 16 05; www.galleriadartemodernapalermo.it; Via Sant'Anna 21; adult/child €7/free; 🕙 9.30am-6.30pm Tue-Sun) is located in a wonderfully restored old complex. The building's interior is sleek and very 'modern art', but the art itself is unfortunately not very heartstopping. Divided over three floors, the artwork is dedicated largely to Sicily and Palermo as its subjects, thus ruling out pieces that might be otherwise interesting and brightening to the collection. The gallery's highlights are the paintings of Michele Catti (1855–1914), whose large canvases portray moody scenes of *fin-de-siécle* life in Palermo's streets. The *Ultime foglie* (Last Leaves; 1906) is a beautiful image of a wet Viale della Libertá on a late autumn day. Also interesting is the 1930s painting by Corrado Cagli (1910–76), on the 2nd floor, depicting Mussolini's programme of land irrigation around Rome; in the painting, Cagli combined an ancient wax-painting method and a modernist style. *Il tram,* painted by Mario Sironi (1885–1961) and *Le nozze,* by Massimo Campigli (1895–1971), are fun products of futurism.

MUSEO INTERNAZIONALE DELLE MARIONETTE

With over 3000 puppets, marionettes, glove puppets and shadow figures, the **Museo Internazionale delle Marionette** (Map pp78-9; ☎ 091 32 80 60; www.museomarionettepalermo.it in Italian; Via Butera 1; adult/child €5/2.50; ☒ 9am-1pm & 4-7pm Mon-Fri, 9am-1pm Sat) is almost single-handedly preserving the popular puppet culture that has long been a feature of Sicily's big-city life; see p64 for more information on puppet theatre. Established by the Association for the Conservation of Popular Traditions, the museum's collection derives from Palermo, Catania and Naples, as well as from far-flung places such as China, India, southern Asia, Turkey and Africa. There is also a room where children can play with the puppets and even try to create their own.

The museum stages shows on Fridays at 5.30pm in the autumn and winter months. Every year, puppeteers from all over the world converge on the museum for the Festa di Morgana, which the museum sponsors.

PIAZZA SAN FRANCESCO D'ASSISI

The Piazza San Francesco d'Assisi (Map p82) is Palermo's picture-perfect piazza, overlooked by the charming **Chiesa di San Francesco d'Assisi** (Map p82; Piazza San Francesco d'Assisi; admission free; ☒ 9am-noon Mon, 9am-4pm Tue-Fri, 9am-noon Sat), which features a fine rose window and a flamboyant Gothic portal; it's understandably popular on the wedding circuit. The church's most interesting feature is the rare arch of the **Cappella Mastrantonio** (Chapel of Mastrantonio), carved in 1468 by Francesco Laurana and Pietro da Bonitate, and one of the only true examples of Renaissance art in Palermo. The church also showcases sculptures by the Gagini family, Giambattista Ragusa and Giacomo Serpotta.

Nearby is another of Serpotta's extravagant stucco oratories, the **Oratorio di San Lorenzo** (Map p82; Via dell'Immacolatella; admission free; ☒ 9am-noon Mon-Fri), built in 1569 by the Compagnia di San Francesco. The work includes a series of panels with details from the lives of St Lawrence and St Francis, the best of which is

the *Martirio di San Lorenzo* (Martyrdom of St Lawrence), on the far wall. A large *Natività* (Nativity) by Caravaggio once hung on the wall behind the altar, but it was stolen in 1969 and has never been found.

PIAZZA MARINA

Surrounded on all sides by elegant palazzi, gentrified Piazza Marina (Map p82) is Palermo's quietest piazza, and its small **Giardino Garibaldi** (Map p82; Piazza Marina; admission free; ☒ 24hr) encloses Palermo's oldest tree, a venerable 25m-high, 150-year-old *ficus benjamin.* Dedicated to Garibaldi, the square has witnessed its fair share of bloody executions – something that's unsurprising given that the largest palazzo on the square, the imposing 14th-century **Palazzo Chiaramonte** (Map pp78-9; ☎ 091 33 41 39; Piazza Marina 60) was the headquarters of the Inquisition. Now part of the University of Palermo, it is only open for special exhibitions.

Just off the piazza is one of the only palazzi open to the public, **Palazzo Mirto** (Map p82; ☎ 091 616 75 41; Via Merlo 2; adult/child €3/2; ☒ 9am-6.30pm Mon-Sat, 9am-1pm Sun). Considering Palermitan extravagances, the palazzo is actually pretty modest. Its walls are covered in acres of silk and velvet wallpaper, and vast embroidered wall hangings, while its floors are paved in coloured marbles and mosaics. The real extravagance, however, is the tiny **Salottino Cinese** (Chinese Salon) full of black lacquer, silken wallpaper and a rather conceited ceiling painting of European aristos viewing the room from above.

COMPLESSA DI SANTA MARIA DELLO SPASIMO & CHIESA DELLA MAGIONE

Behind the Galleria Regionale Siciliana is the **Complessa di Santa Maria dello Spasimo** (☎ 091 616 14 86; Via Spasimo; admission free; ☒ 9am-midnight), with its elegant polygonal apse and a tall slender nave that has stood for centuries without a roof. The only example of northern Gothic in Sicily, the church was built by a wealthy doctor, Girolamo Basilicò, on his return from the Holy Land in the early 1500s. The good doctor then commissioned Raffaello Sanzio (1483–1520) to produce a panel painting for the altar, the *Spasimo di Sicilia,* but this is now sadly missing, having been spirited away to Madrid (it now hangs in the Prado) by the viceroy Ferdinado d'Ayala, who bribed the not-so-saintly abbot. The complex is now one of the success stories of the restoration pro-gramme, having reopened in 1995 as a venue for concerts and exhibitions (evenings from June to end of September).

Across Piazza Magione from Lo Spasimo is the **Chiesa della Magione** (Map p82; ☎ 091 617 05 96; Via Magione 44; admission free; ⏱ 9.30am-6.30pm), also known as La Magione. It's a fine example of the more austere Romanesque style that the Normans brought to Sicily.

The 19th-Century City

North of Piazza Giuseppe Verdi, Palermo's streets widen, the buildings lengthen, and the shops, restaurants and cafés become more elegant (and more expensive). Glorious neo-classical and Art Nouveau examples from the last golden age in Sicilian architecture give the city an exuberant and grandiose feel that contrasts with the narrow, introspective feel of the old quarter.

TEATRO MASSIMO

Built between 1875 and 1897 by Giovanni Battista Basile and subsequently his son, Ernesto, to celebrate the unification of Italy, **Teatro Massimo** (☎ 091 605 31 11, toll free 800 65 58 58; www.teatromassimo.it; tours adult/concession €5/3; ⏱ 10am-3.30pm Tue-Sun) has become a symbol of the triumph and tragedy of Palermo itself. Supposedly the third-largest 19th-century opera house in Europe (only the Paris and Vienna Opera Houses are larger), its long history is symptomatic of the conflicting powers that struggle for su-premacy in Palermo society – civic pride and cultural creativity pitted against the sinister bureaucracy and Mafia control (which is said to have been responsible for the ex-traordinary 24 years it took to restore the theatre). Appropriately, the closing scene of *The Godfather III*, with its visually stunning juxtaposition of high culture and low crime, drama and death, was filmed here.

Giovanni Basile was Palermo's most pop-ular architect in the years preceding WWI and, in addition to the theatre, he also de-signed the two kiosks outside it, which now sell newspapers, tobacco and magazines.

Tours run every 30 minutes. See p95 for box-office and performance details.

TEATRO POLITEAMA GARIBALDI

Palermo's second theatre, the **Teatro Politeama Garibaldi** (Map pp78-9; ☎ 091 605 33 15; Piazza Ruggero Settimo), was designed in classical form by Giuseppe Damiani Almeyda between 1867 and 1874. It features a particularly strik-ing façade that looks like a triumphal arch topped by bronze chariots. The theatre is only open for performances.

HAMMAM

You'll hardly need any more heat if you're here in the summer, but you'll surely crave some peace and tranquillity after you've been schlepping around the busy streets of Palermo all day. In case of the latter, head over to the city's only **hammam** (Map pp78-9; ☎ 091 32 07 83; www.hammam.pa.it; Via Torrearsa 17d; admission €30; ⏱ men 10am-10pm Tue, Thu & Sat, women 10am-10pm Mon, Wed & Fri), a modern affair with a lavish marble-faced bath hall and a mean, brick-domed steam room. The changing rooms are spacious and clean, and all the kit you need is supplied: black olive soap, *ghassoul* (a mixture of clay mud, rose petals and lavender), henna for softening the skin, and a vicious scrubbing glove and slippers; there's a one-off charge of €7 to buy your own glove and slippers, which for hygiene reasons can't be borrowed.

After your scrub you can indulge in any number of massages and therapies, which range in price from €15 to €40, or you can simply relax with a mint tea and Arabian sweets in the cooling-off room or café.

Outside the City Centre
CASTELLO DELLA ZISA

A short bus or car journey southwest from Piazza Castelnuovo leads to **Castello della Zisa** (Map pp78-9; ☎ 091 652 02 69; Piazza Zisa; admission €6; ⏱ 9am-6.30pm Mon-Fri, 9am-1pm Sat & Sun), one of the only remaining monuments to the decadence of Moorish Palermo. With *muqarnas* vaults, latticework windows, fountains and even a wind chamber to protect the emir's family from the *scirocco* (the hot African wind), the villa deserves its name, which comes from the Arabic *al aziz*, meaning 'magnificent'. Today it houses a museum of Arabic crafts, the main features of which are some superbly crafted screens and a gorgeous 12th-century bronze basin. Take bus 124 from Piazza Ruggero Settimo.

CATACOMBE DEI CAPPUCCINI

Despite its famous manuscript collection and the tomb of novelist Giuseppe Tomasi di Lampedusa in the adjoining cemetery, the

Convento dei Cappuccini (Map pp78–9; ☎ 091 21 21 17; Via Cappuccini 1; admission to church & catacombs €1.50; ☉ 9am-noon & 3-5pm) is best known for its altogether more macabre catacombs, where the mummified bodies of some 8000 Palermitans who died between the 17th and 19th centuries are on show.

Originally the preserve of monks, the catacombs were eventually opened to a select and moneyed few who made substantial donations of land or money to the monastery. For their pains, these lucky individuals were laid out 'to drain' – ugh – after death, before being washed with vinegar, and powdered with arsenic and milk of lime. They were then dressed in their Sunday best and propped up in their very own niche.

Earthly power, sex, religion and professional status are rigidly distinguished. Men and women occupy separate corridors, and within the women's area there is a first-class section for virgins. The most disconcerting sight is the near-perfectly preserved body of Rosalia Lombardo (just follow the signs for *bambina* or 'baby girl'), who died at the tender age of two in 1920. Gory and perturbing, the catacombs are one of the city's premier tourist attractions.

Public Parks

Palermo has a number of pleasant parks. **Villa Giulia** (Map pp78–9; Via Abramo Lincoln; ☉ 8am-8pm) in La Kalsa is a welcome relief from the claustrophobic streets, although its formal planting scheme is severely challenged by the rampant fecundity of the island.

Laid out by Léon Dufourny and Venanzio Marvuglia, the gorgeous **Orto Botanico** (Map pp78–9; ☎ 091 623 82 41; www.ortobotanico.palermo.it; Via Abramo Lincoln 2b; adult/concession €4/2; ☉ 9am-1.30pm & 2.30-7.30pm) is a tropical paradise, with massive fig trees, tall palms and dazzling hibiscus bushes. There is an avenue of the bizarre-looking bottle, soap and cinnamon trees, as well as coffee trees, papaya plants and sycamores. It's a real haven of silence and fascinating botany, with a large herb garden that focuses on Mediterranean plants. Beware the mosquitos at dusk though.

About 3km to the north of the centre is Palermo's biggest park, the **Parco della Favorita** (off Map pp78–9; admission free; ☉ 24hr). Ferdinand purchased the land in 1799 and commissioned the original layout, and he lived in the extraordinary Chinese pagoda palace,

the **Palazzina Cinese** (☉ closed to the public), with his wife during his exile from Naples. Originally built as Ferdinand's hunting lodge by Venanzio Marvuglia, the *palazzina* is an odd but charming mixture of Chinese and neoclassical styles (if you can imagine such a thing).

The palace also houses the **Museo Etnografico Pitrè** (off Map pp78–9; ☎ 091 740 48 79; Via Duca degli Abruzzi 1; admission €5; ☉ 8.30am-8pm Mon-Thu & Sat), Sicily's best ethnographic museum. It holds over 5000 objects, including traditional costumes, pottery, puppets, votive offerings, torture instruments and a model of the 18th-century Carrozza di Santa Rosalia (a massive cart used to carry the effigy of the saint through the streets during the Festino di Santa Rosalia).

WALKING TOUR

Palermo is a dense city and is best explored on foot. This itinerary covers the eastern half of the city and the labyrinthine alleys of La Kalsa.

Start at Piazza Giuseppe Verdi, dominated by the neoclassical **Teatro Massimo** (**1**; opposite). Facing south, turn left down Via Bara all'Olivella to arrive at the **Museo Archeologico Regionale** (**2**; p85), which houses one of Sicily's finest collections of classical art.

Next head southeast down Via Monteleone towards Via Roma. Walk along Via Roma and then take the steps alongside Chiesa di Sant'Antonio, which should bring you into the heart of **Mercato della Vucciria** (**3**; p96). Exit the market and cross into Via Alessandro Paternostro to arrive at the pretty Piazza San Francesco d'Assisi. Look into the **Oratorio di San Lorenzo** (**4**; p87) for some stupendous stuccowork, then pop into the **Chiesa di San Francesco d'Assisi** (**5**; p87) to see the Cappella Mastrantonio by Francesco Laurana and fine sculptures by the Gagini family.

Heading east down Via Merlo will bring you to **Palazzo Mirto** (**6**; p87), before you emerge at Piazza Marina and the tranquil **Giardino Garibaldi** (**7**; p87). Pick up Via IV Aprile in the southeast corner of the square and walk south. This should bring you to Via Alloro, where a left turn leads to the **Galleria Regionale Siciliana** (**8**; p86).

To finish, head west along Via Alloro, then cross Via Roma to reach Piazza Bellini, with the glittering mosaics of **La Martorana** (**9**; p81) and the peculiar pink domes of **Chiesa**

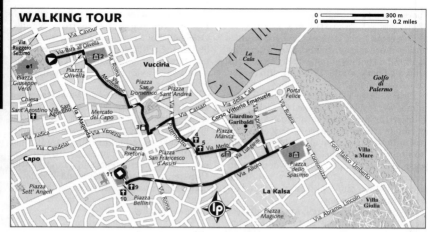

WALKING TOUR

di **San Cataldo** (**10**; p81). Finish up at Piazza Pretoria, where you can see vast **Fontana Pretoria** (**11**; p80).

PALERMO FOR CHILDREN

Palermo is a friendly place for children, though the heavy traffic is not too pleasant for the little ones. There are, however, tons of fun things to do – and there is always good ice cream! Palermo has a couple of good, child-friendly museums: at the Museo Internazionale delle Marionette (p87), Sicily's biggest puppet museum, children can make their own puppets or watch the daily puppet show, while the Museo Archeologico Regionale (p85) is a great introduction to the classical world.

Little ones will be as fascinated as you are by the endless noise and bustle of the Mercato della Vucciria (p96), while a horse-drawn carriage (right) is a great way to take a turn around the historic centre; you can pick them up at Teatro Massimo and Piazza Pretoria.

If the bustle of the city all gets too much for the kids, head for the sandy beaches and waterfront eateries of Mondello (p99). Also located outside the city limits, Ustica (p100) is the perfect place for older children who like to

indulge in all manner of activities, including walking, snorkelling, diving and cycling.

TOURS

You do not need a guide to enjoy Palermo. However, should you want one, the official rate set by the tourist office is a whopping €116 per half-day and €180 per day (up to 50 people). It is better to contact individual guides separately to negotiate a price for smaller groups.

Associazione Guide Turistiche di Palermo e Provincia (☎ 091 30 84 10; www.palermoguide.eu) The first independent guide service set up in Palermo. It has an extensive list of guides on its website.

CitySightseeing Palermo (Map pp78-9; ☎ 091 58 94 29; www.palermo.city-sightseeing.it; Piazza Castelnuovo 6; adult/child €20/10) The pan-European-bus-tour company takes you around central Palermo (Linea A) or out to Giardini Inglese and Castello della Zisa (Linea B). Commentary in eight languages, you can hop on and off the buses, and the tickets are valid for 24 hours. Both tours start at Teatro Politeama.

Horse-drawn carriage (Map p82; tours €50) A fun, though rather *puzzolente* (smelly) way to get around the city. You can find the old carriages, which carry two to four people, at Teatro Massimo and Piazza Pretoria.

FESTIVALS & EVENTS

Palermo hosts tons of religious processions throughout the year. Information about local festivals can be found on the website of the **tourist office** (www.palermotourism.com).

Easter Holy Week This major religious festival is celebrated virtually all over the island. In Palermo there are Greek Orthodox celebrations at La Martorana.

Palermo di Scena Music, theatre, cinema and ballet programmes run throughout the summer.

Festino di Santa Rosalia Held between 10 and 15 July, Palermo's biggest annual festival celebrates Santa Rosalia, the patron saint of the city. The saint's relics are paraded through the city amid four days of fireworks and partying. It's a great time to be in the city.

Festa di Morgana (www.museomarionettepalermo.it in Italian) Puppeteers from all over the world gather at Museo Internazionale delle Marionette (p87) for this festival. Dates vary so check the website.

Opera Season Teatro Massimo (p88) commences its opera season in December; it ends in May.

SLEEPING

Palermo has a wide range of accommodation, though finding really good budget sleeps is a tad more difficult than in the rest of Sicily. Prices in Sicily, and especially in Palermo, fluctuate depending on season and demand. You should book in advance at the better places, particularly between June and October. Prepare to lug suitcases up steep stairs in the older buildings.

All the midrange and top-end hotels are located north of the Quattro Canti, around Piazza Giuseppe Verdi and in the newer part of Palermo. Most of the budget options can be found on Via Roma towards the train station; this is not a good option for lone women travellers.

A useful agency that specialises in B&Bs and apartments in and around Palermo is **Sicily Location** (☎ 347 519 03 15; www.sicilylocation.com).

Budget

A Casa di Amici B&B (Map pp78–9; ☎ 091 58 48 84; www.acasadiamici.com; Via Volturno 6; dm €22.50-25, s with shared bathroom €35-45, d with shared bathroom €55-65; 😧 💻) Palermo's only hostel-type place, this spot has a friendly atmosphere, youthful clientele and a slightly wacky owner named Claudia. It's near Teatro Massimo in a renovated 19th-century palazzo, with four lovely rooms that sleep from two to four people. Each room has a different theme, but all have high ceilings, colourful walls and 'ethnic' décor. There are shared bathrooms and a kitchen.

Hotel Regina (☎ 091 611 42 16; www.hotelregina palermo.it; Corso Vittorio Emanuele 316; s with shared bathroom €28, d with shared bathroom €48-58) You won't find many rooms cheaper than this in Palermo – especially not in such a central location. The

TOP FIVE STYLISH SLEEPS IN PALERMO

- 4 Quarti (p92)
- Allakala (p92)
- BB22 (p92)
- Grand Hotel Villa Igiea (p93)
- Hotel del Centro (p92)

rooms are neat and simple, with nice blue walls, airy gauze curtains, large windows and ceiling fans, but there's no air con and the shared bathrooms are not massively clean come the end of the day; the most inconvenient thing is the midnight curfew.

our pick B&B 316 (☎ 091 611 42 16; www.hotel reginapalermo.it; Corso Vittorio Emanuele 316; s €30-40, d €50-80; 😧) Run by the same family as the Hotel Regina, this is a more upmarket place with a decent breakfast and a lovely roof terrace. The rooms are large, with good bathrooms and views of the roof and church tops of old Palermo; again, the price and location are excellent. Bizarrely, the air conditioning is only available between 5pm and 7am.

Albergo Orientale (☎ 091 616 57 27; www.albergo orientale.191.it; Via Maqueda 26; s €30-50, d €45-70) This fantastic hotel in a crumbling 18th-century palazzo is as atmospheric as you're going to get in the capital. The rooms are clean (the cheapest ones have shared bathrooms), with wrought-iron beds, high ceilings and nice big windows. Check your room before you commit, though, because some can be a bit boxy.

our pick Albergo Ariston (Map pp78–9; ☎ 091 33 24 34; www.aristonpalermo.it; Via Mariano Stabile 139; s €40-49, d €50-69; 😧) Palermo's best budget hotel is set inside an inconspicuous tower block in a great location in the new part of town. The place is impeccably clean and simply decorated, and there's even wi-fi access. The double rooms are spacious. Breakfast is optional (€2.50), and can be brought to your room if you're feeling lazy.

Midrange

Ai Cartari (Map p82; ☎ 091 611 63 72; www.aicartari.com; Via Alessandro Paternostro 62; 2-bedroom apt per person €45-60; 🅿 😧 💻) This B&B comprises two nicely decorated apartments, each with its own front door that's separate from the main building. Both suites sleep up to five people, and secure parking is available for €10 per day. English and French are spoken by the owners.

Ambasciatori Hotel (Map p82; ☎ 091 616 68 81; www .ambasciatorihotelpalermo.com; Via Roma 111; s €55-75, d €85-105; P ⊠) This place was recently renovated to resemble a semiposh hotel, with a gleaming, chandelier-lit reception and breakfast area, but the glitz unfortunately doesn't carry on into the rooms. Sitting on the 5th floor of an old palazzo, the hotel has a marvellous rooftop terrace where you can eat your breakfast in the morning and sip cocktails in the evening.

San Francesco (Map p82; ☎ 091 888 83 91; www .sanfrancescopalermo.it; Via Merlo 30; s/d €60/90; ⊠) Tiny and family run, San Francesco has three lovely rooms, one with a vaulted roof, and the other two with traditional wood-beamed ceilings. Decorated with old radios and bits of antiques, it's a cosy and good-value place to stay in the old town.

Hotel del Centro (Map p82; ☎ 091 617 03 76; www .hoteldelcentro.it; Via Roma 72; s €65-100, d €85-120; P ⊠ ☑) This great little hotel has tasteful, elegant rooms decorated in greens and browns, plus wrought-iron beds, traditional floor tiles and floral prints on the walls. The bathrooms are humungous, and the high ceilings are covered with original 19th-century paintings.

ourpick Allakala (Map p82; ☎ 091 743 47 63; www.allakala.it; Corso Vittorio Emanuele 71; s €75-100, d €95-130; ⊠) A B&B that's a shrine to stylish design, Allakala overlooks the old part of the port and has a fantastic central location. The rooms whisper 'pampering' with their tasteful and soothing whites and blues, the décor is minimal, and the bathrooms are gorgeous. Breakfast is brought to your room on a silver tray.

Hotel Letizia (Map p82; ☎ 091 58 91 10; www.hotel letizia.com; Via dei Bottai 30; s/d €85/115; ⊠) This little hotel off the quaint Piazza Marina has fauxaristo décor that sometimes verges on tacky. There is also a small terrace on which you can enjoy your breakfast (€5). The cheaper B&B Ai Bottai (single/double €65/€85), upstairs, has some screamingly over-the-top rooms with black walls and golden bedspreads; it has the same contact information as Hotel Letizia.

Hotel Tonic (Map p82; ☎ 091 58 17 54; www.hotel tonic.com; Via Mariano Stabile 126; s €85-90, d €110; ⊠) A friendly and efficient hotel, though a little on the impersonal side. The rooms are comfortable, with two reserved for people with disabilities.

ourpick 4 Quarti (Map p82; ☎ 091 58 36 87; www .quattroquarti.it; Corso Vittorio Emanuele 376; s/d €100/120; ⊠) A fabulously decorated B&B in a 17th-century building that belonged to a nobleman's family, 4 Quarti feels like you're the aristocrats' guest, with plush antiques, shiny chandeliers and heavy drapes. The four rooms are supercomfortable, the owners are friendly and the location is excellent.

Jolly Hotel (Map pp78-9; ☎ 091 616 50 90; www .jollyhotels.it; Foro Italico Umberto I; s €117-132, d €136-172; P ⊠ ☑) Large, modern and drab in a 1980s style, the Jolly Hotel's redeeming features are its seafront location opposite the Villa Giulia park, rooms with sea views and its big pool (open from 15 May to 9 September). If you have children, this is a decent option.

ourpick BB22 (Map p82; ☎ 335 790 87 33; www .bb22.it; 22 Largo Cavalieri di Malta; s €100-115, d €130-150, ste s €120-170, d €140-200; ⊠) It calls itself a B&B, but this place is a little palace of luxury, with rooms so elegant and stylish you'll hardly want to go out. It's all virginal whites, silky quilts, quirky designer lamps and plasma TVs. The beds are as firm as Brad Pitt's buttocks, and the suite is pure honeymoon material with its freestanding bath (right in front of the bed), gorgeous wooden floors, antique furniture, a walk-in wardrobe, and a kitchenette with – of course – designer crockery.

Top End

Grand Hotel et des Palmes (Map pp78-9; ☎ 091 602 81 11; www.grandhoteletdespalmes.it; Via Roma 398; s/d €103/191; P ⊠) Like a royal court, this hotel has been the scene of intrigues, doubledealings and liaisons throughout Palermo's history, although it was abandoned by the elite in the 1970s in favour of Villa Igiea. The grand salons still impress with their huge chandeliers and gigantic mirrors, while the rooms are sumptuously decked out.

Centrale Palace Hotel (Map p82; ☎ 091 33 66 66; www.centralepalacehotel.it; Corso Vittorio Emanuele 327; s €130-170, d €160-210; P ⊠) Thoroughly elegant, this renovated 18th-century palazzo right next to the Quattro Canti prides itself on its high level of service. It also has an excellent rooftop restaurant with views over Palermo.

Hotel Principe di Villafranca (Map pp78-9; ☎ 091 611 85 23; www.principedivillafranca.it; Via Turrisi Colonna 4; s €150-206, d €220-332; P ⊠ ☐) Furnished with Sicilian antiques and expensive linens, this hotel is situated just west of Viale della Libertà in one of the most exclusive areas of Palermo.

Its excellent restaurant Il Firriato, cosy library with a huge fireplace, and cutting-edge gym make this the ultimate in discreet luxury.

Grand Hotel Villa Igiea (off Map pp78-9; ☎ 091 54 37 44; www.hotelvillaigieapalermo.com; Salita Belmonte 43; s/d €172/330; ⓟ ⓧ ⓛ ⓡ) What can you say about an Art Nouveau villa that was designed by Ernesto Basile for the Florio family (of tuna and Marsala-wine fame)? You know it's going to be magnificent. It sits 3km north of the city centre, luxuriating in its five stars and its status as the best hotel in Palermo. It has its own beach, swimming pool, tennis court, you name it. Best of all, prices drop by 50% in the low season, so check rates with the hotel before you book.

EATING

There's lots of good food to be had in Palermo, though you'll have to be discerning when choosing a restaurant in the streets around Teatro Massimo. Palermitans generally dine late and although kitchens open around 7.30pm, you'll eat alone if you get to a restaurant before 9.30pm. Eating with the locals makes a huge difference to a restaurant's atmosphere, but make sure you book in advance for dinner after 9pm in most places.

Restaurants

BUDGET

our pick Foccaceria del Massimo (Map p82; ☎ 091 33 56 28; Via Bara all'Olivella 76; meals €8-10; ☒ closed Sun) This is one of Palermo's best places for lunch, and not only for those of you wanting a bit of cheap grub. The *foccacerie* are traditionally workmen's eateries, and the system of choosing and ordering from the counter can be a bit daunting until you get the hang of it. There's a board with the daily specials and an antipasti buffet that you can pick from, so get a plate of antipasti – grilled aubergines, artichokes, green beans and olives – and a *primo* (first course) of the daily pasta (€2 per plate), finishing with a slice of fresh watermelon in the summer months. It's better to get here around 2.30pm, when the lunch crowds have dispersed.

Antica Focacceria di San Francesco (Map p82; ☎ 091 32 02 64; Via Alessandro Paternostro 58; meals €10-15; ☒ closed Mon) A Palermitan institution popular with working men and families, this is one of the city's oldest eating houses; it opened in 1834, and even hosted the first Sicilian parliament. You may find its

---

> **TOP FIVE PLACES TO EAT**
>
> ■ Foccaceria del Massimo (left)
>
> ■ Kursaal Kalhesa (below)
>
> ■ L'Acanto (p94)
>
> ■ Massaro (p94)
>
> ■ Osteria dei Vespri (p94)

---

reputation better than its food, though the age-old Palermitan snack of *panino con la milza* (sandwich of veal innards and ricotta cheese) is worth trying.

Casa del Brodo (Map p82; ☎ 091 32 16 55; Corso Vittorio Emanuele 175; meals €20; ☒ closed Wed) This old-school trattoria (informal restaurant) has had soup as its speciality for more than 100 years, though the fresh fish and seafood are highly recommended by the locals. The *tortellini in brodo* (tortellini pasta in broth) is truly restorative after a hard day's sightseeing.

Les Amis (Map p82; ☎ 091 616 66 42; Piazza San Carlo 9; fixed menu €20; ☒ closed Tue evening) A great spot for a fixed lunch menu of fish, Les Amis has had consistently good recommendations over the years. It's decorated in the classic Italian style, with terracotta walls and peachy lighting.

Sant'Andrea (Map p82; ☎ 091 33 49 99; Piazza Sant'Andrea 4; meals €20-30; ☒ closed Tue & Jan) Right in the heart of Vucciria, this good restaurant serves fresh food from the market. It was the regular haunt of Peter Robb while he researched *Midnight in Sicily*, and the brooding atmosphere of the book mirrors that of the restaurant. The pasta is superb.

MIDRANGE

La Cambusa (Map p82; ☎ 091 58 45 74; Piazza Marina 17; meals €25; ☒ closed Sun) La Cambusa is a local favourite, and its proximity to the old port makes it a serious fish restaurant. You select your fish from the cold counter (around €35 per kilogram) and the staff whisk it off to be cooked. Although the restaurant has a great atmosphere in the evenings, the busier it is, the more inattentive the service becomes.

our pick Kursaal Kalhesa (Map pp78-9; ☎ 091 616 22 82; www.kursaalkalhesa.it in Italian; 21 Foro Italico Umberto I; meals €25-30; ☒ closed Mon lunch & Sun evening) Recline on silk-covered cushions beneath soaring vaulted ceilings or sit outside in the expansive garden while you savour crispy Tunisian *brik* (pastries) and aromatic

PALERMO

fettucine con vongole e gamberi (fettucine with clams and prawns). The mains are meaty, with veal and lamb steaks, and the *granite* (flavoured crushed ice) are perfect for dessert. The cocktail and wine lists are extensive.

ourpick L'Acanto (Map pp78-9; ☎ 091 32 04 44; Via Torrearsa 10; meals €25-35; ☑ closed Mon) The decoration is gorgeous, the food delicious and the staff friendly at this elegant restaurant that sits at the end of a small street in new Palermo. The menu is traditional with a modern twist, sprinkled with some excellent fresh seafood and grilled fish, and there's a decent wine list for boozy dinners. You eat by candlelight under canvas canopies in the leafy back garden.

Trattoria Biondo (Map pp78-9; ☎ 091 57 36 62; Via Carducci 15; meals €25-35; ☑ closed Wed) Be prepared to brave the stares as you ring the bell to gain entry to this trattoria. You are on native turf here and the atmosphere, well oiled with a fine wine list, is darkly intimate.

Cucina Papoff (Map pp78-9; ☎ 091 58 64 60; Via Isidoro la Lumia 32; meals €25-35; ☑ closed Sun & Aug) This is an intimate restaurant with exposed brickwork and an Art Nouveau theme. Despite being founded by a Bulgarian, the restaurant serves imaginative Sicilian dishes such a *u maccu* (broad beans in fennel).

Il Firriato (Map pp78-9; ☎ 091 53 02 82; Via G Turrisi Colonna 4; meals €30-40; ☑ closed Sun) Although Il Firriato is the restaurant for Hotel Principe di Villafranca, it is also open to the public. The restaurant's limited menu is a sign of the care it takes with each dish – the roast lamb is particularly delicious, and the desserts are to die for.

TOP END

ourpick Osteria dei Vespri (Map p82; ☎ 091 617 16 31; Piazza Croce dei Vespri 6; meals €45-55; ☑ closed Sun) If you want to try modern Italian cuisine, this is the perfect place to surrender your taste buds. Add the pleasure of sitting in the shadow of the venerable palazzo where Luchino Visconti filmed parts of *Il gattopardo*, and you have the perfect restaurant. But it's really the cuisine you'll be focusing on – dishes include *anelleti* (pasta ringlets) with octopus poached in nero d'Avola wine and wild fennel, with a hint of saffron; and quail and prunes in Marsala wine on cannellini beans and celery.

Cafés

There are numerous cafés with outdoor tables on Via Principe di Belmonte (which is closed

to traffic between Via Ruggero Settimo and Via Roma).

Massaro (Map pp78-9; ☎ 091 42 05 86; Via E Basile 24-26; sandwiches & cakes €3-5; ☑ 7am-4pm Mon-Sat, closed Sat afternoon) Here's a true Palermo institution – it's a bit out of the way, but it's as traditional and loved by its regulars as it gets. It's excellent for breakfasts or snacks, but it's best for the vast variety of cakes, which range from pistachio balls to pine nut-encrusted rolls to creamy *cannoli* (pastry shells stuffed with sweet ricotta). There's a smaller, more modern Massaro 2 (Map pp78–9; Via Brasa 6–8; open 7am to 4pm Monday to Saturday), where you'll find fewer cakes but delicious ice cream, great coffee, sandwiches and futuristic décor in shiny aluminium. The Via Brasa branch has window stools for people- (and traffic-) watching.

Antico Caffé Spinnato (Map pp78-9; ☎ 091 58 32 31; Via Principe di Belmonte 107-15; breakfast €5, lunch €6-10) Thanks to the café's immense popularity, both with Palermo's professionals and with tourists, the local pigeons are so used to good food lying about they occasionally dive-bomb the tables outside, trying to get to the crisps and olives. Considering this rather unpleasant feature, you're perhaps better off inside the sophisticated tea salon, which serves every imaginable Sicilian drink, plus ice creams and cakes. Great for a late lazy breakfast with the newspaper.

Il Baretto (Map pp78-9; ☎ 091 32 96 40; Via XX Settembre 43; salads & sandwiches €6-8; ☑ closed Sun) This little café with its besuited waiters gives you a good insight into how the other half lives. Rich young Palermitans dressed head to toe in designer labels, ladies with serious hairdos, and eccentric old men with Panamas and shades all congregate here for their light lunch.

DRINKING

In contrast to crazy traffic, the raucous markets and the general buzz of the city during the day, Palermo's night scene can get quite snoozy, especially in the old town. The most lively street is Via Candelai (this is the area to head to if you're under 21), while Piazza Olivella and Piazza San Francesco di Paola are also popular evening areas, with bar crowds spilling out onto the streets.

ourpick Cambio Cavalli (Map p82; ☎ 091 58 14 18; Via Patania 54; ☑ 8pm-1am) Definitely Palermo's coolest and most stylish bar, Cambio Cavalli has candlelit tables under the stars, plus some impressive 16th-century arches. This was one of the city's first bars and the regulars have remained loyal, keeping the atmosphere relaxed and friendly. Cocktails are all €5, and you'll find the usual suspects on the list. It gets busy after 11pm.

Kursaal Kalhesa (Map pp78-9; ☎ 091 616 21 11; Foro Italico Umberto I 21; ☺ 8pm-1am, closed Mon lunch & Sun evening) This gorgeous wine-and-cocktail bar has a bohemian atmosphere and an elegant design under its vaulted exposed-brick ceilings. In winter grab a foreign-language newspaper or a book and toast yourself by the fire; in summer sip on a cocktail under the stars in the lush garden.

Rocket Bar (Map pp78-9; Piazza San Francesco di Paola 42; ☺ 8pm-1am, closed Mon) This is the centre of Palermo's 'alternative' scene, with photographs of Blondie, Elvis, the Ramones, and other kings and queens of rock and punk. The Rocket gets packed after 10.30pm, with the crowds spilling out onto the piazza and staying there until the early hours.

Exit Drinks (Map pp78-9; ☎ 348 400 52 51; www .exitdrinks.com; Piazza San Francesco di Paola 40; ☺ 8pm-1am) Situated right next door to Rocket Bar, but with a distinctly different atmosphere, this is one of the city's favourite gay bars. It's a pretty flamboyant affair, with gilded plush furniture, cocktails and great parties. In the summer months, Exit Drinks moves to Rise Up (off Map pp78-9; Via Ugo la Malfa 95), its outdoor venue, where it hosts regular parties. Check out the website for what is coming up next.

Mi Manda Picone (Map p82; ☎ 091 616 06 60; Via Alessandro Paternostro 59; ☺ 8pm-1am) Set in a fabulous 13th-century building (and with summer seating in the beautiful Piazza San Francesco d'Assisi), this excellent wine bar serves hearty platters of cheese and charcuterie (mains €8 to €12). The walls are lined with an extensive selection of Sicilian wine, and staff are knowledgeable and helpful.

I Grilli Giù (Map p82; ☎ 091 58 47 47; Piazza Cavalieri di Malta 11) This is a popular bar and restaurant where you can sip a cocktail and listen to the latest DJs. It's north of Mercato della Vucciria.

Berlin (Map pp78-9; Via Isidoro la Lumia 21) In the newer part of the city to the north, Berlin is an ultrasleek bar popular with Palermo's gay community.

ENTERTAINMENT
Nightclubs
I Candelai (Map p82; ☎ 091 32 71 51, information 333 700 29 42; Via Candelai 65; ☺ Thu-Sat) Housed in a converted furniture warehouse, this bar-club features live music, impromptu theatre, art exhibitions and a booming sound system.

La Cuba (Map pp78-9; ☎ 091 30 92 01; www.lacuba .com; Viale Francesco Scaduto 12) This place opened in 1997, and has been considered one of Palermo's most fashionable clubs and bars ever since. A difficult place to pigeonhole, La Cuba serves wine and cocktails, as well as food, and hosts parties and live music throughout the year. It has a fantastic outdoor space in the garden of Villa Sperlinga, backed by the villa's dreamy pink domes.

Live Music
Lo Spasimo (Map pp78-9; ☎ 091 616 14 86; Via Spasimo) Fantastic cultural centre in the bombed-out remains of a church (see p87). Hosts interesting art exhibitions and atmospheric live concerts.

Theatre
The daily paper *Il Giornale di Sicilia* has a listing of what's on. Tourist information booths also have programmes and listings.

Teatro Massimo (Map pp78-9; ☎ 091 605 31 11; Piazza Giuseppe Verdi 9) Giovanni and Ernesto Basile's Art Nouveau masterpiece, now restored to its former glory, stages opera, ballet and music concerts. Its programme runs from October to May.

Teatro Politeama Garibaldi (Map pp78-9; ☎ 091 605 32 49; Piazza Ruggero Settimo) This is the main venue for music and ballet.

Teatro della Verdura (off Map pp78-9; ☎ 091 688 41 37; Viale del Fante) Offers a summer-only programme of ballet and music in the lovely gardens of Villa Castelnuovo. Ask at the tourist office for details.

Puppet Theatre
Cuticchio Mimmo (Map p82; ☎ 091 32 34 00; www .figlidartecuticchio.com; Via Bara all'Olivella 52; adult/child €5.50/2.60; ☺ performances 6.30pm Sat & Sun Sep-Jul) This is a good break for young kids, and the elaborate old puppets will endear themselves to adults too. You can visit the workshop (see p96) in the same street.

Other puppet-theatre venues include **Opera dei Pupi Ippogrifo** (Map p82; ☎ 091 32 91 94; Vicolo

---

STREET MARKETS

Palermo's historical ties with the Arab world and its proximity to North Africa are reflected in the noisy street life of the city's ancient centre, and nowhere is this more evident than in its markets.

Each of the four historic quarters of Palermo has its own market. The following three are the most popular. The **Mercato della Vuccria** (La Vucciria; Map p82; Piazza Caracciolo) is the most famous, selling fresh produce and fish. Although it's popular with tourists, many Palermitans shop for their fresh produce and household goods at **Mercato di Ballarò** (Map p82; Via Ballarò), as well as at the flea market **Mercato del Capo** (Map p82), which extend through the tangle of lanes and alleyways of the Albergheria and Capo quarters respectively.

Markets open from 7am to 8pm Monday to Saturday (until 1pm on Wednesday), although they are busier in the morning. Keep an eye on your belongings while walking through the markets.

Ragusi 4) and **Compagnia Argento** (Map pp78-9; ☎ 091 611 36 80; Via Novelli 1). You can also catch performances at the Museo Internazionale delle Marionette (p87).

SHOPPING

Via Bara all'Olivella is good for arts and crafts. Here you will find the puppet workshop of the Cuticchio family, **Il Laboratorio Teatrale** (Map p82; Via Bara all'Olivella 48-50) and the lovely toy shop, **Bottega Ippogrifo** (Map p82; Via Bara all'Olivella 60), with its handcrafted toys.

Tre Erre Ceramiche (Map pp78-9; ☎ 091 32 38 27; Via Enrico Amari 49) has a huge selection of ceramics, and **Silvana Sansone** (Map pp78-9; ☎ 091 32 15 93; Via Torrearsa 9) has some wonderful modern jewellery, although expect high prices.

For homemade jams, sweets and other confectionery, head for **I Peccatucci di Mamma Andrea** (Map pp78-9; ☏ 091 33 48 35; Via Principe di Scordia 67); for wine, there is a huge selection on offer at the wine bar **Mi Manda Picone** (Map p82; ☎ 091 616 06 60; Via Alessandro Paternostro 59; ☏ 8pm-1am) and at **Mangia** (Map pp78-9; ☎ 091 58 76 51; Via Principe di Belmonte 116). For the most skilfully crafted marzipan sweets, look no further than **Antico Caffè Spinnato** (Map pp78-9; ☎ 091 58 32 31; Via Principe di Belmonte 107-15; ☏ noon-3pm & 7.30-11pm).

GETTING THERE & AWAY
Air

Falcone-Borsellino airport (off Map pp78-9; ☎ 091 702 01 11) is at Punta Raisi, 31km west of Palermo. For 24-hour information about domestic flights, call **Alitalia** (Map pp78-9; ☎ airport 091 601 92 50, office 091 601 93 33; www.alitalia.com; Viale della Libertà 39). For international flights call the airport. See p295 for more information about international travel to/from Palermo.

Falcone-Borsellino is the hub airport for regular domestic flights to the far-away islands of Pantelleria and Lampedusa. Alitalia, **Meridiana** (IG; ☎ 199 11 13 33; www.meridiana.it) and **Air One** (AP; ☎ 199 20 70 80; www.flyairone.it) offer a good choice of flights at competitive prices (a one-way fare is usually between €25 and €30).

For more information on tickets and routes, both international and domestic, see p295.

Boat

The ferry terminal (Map pp78–9) is located off Via Francesco Crispi. Ferries depart regularly from Molo Vittorio Veneto for Cagliari (Sardinia), Naples, Livorno and Genoa; see p299 for details.

Tirrenia Navigazione (Map pp78-9; ☎ 091 602 11 11, toll free 199 12 31 99; www.tirrenia.it; Calata Marinai d'Italia; ☏ 8.30am-12.30pm & 3.30-8.45pm Mon-Fri, 3.30-8.45pm Sat, 5-8.45pm Sun) is the main company servicing the Mediterranean, with ferries to Cagliari (€38.50, 13 hours, one weekly) departing at 7pm, and an overnight ferry to Naples (€39, nine hours, one daily). The office is located at the port to the right of the main entrance.

From July to August, **Siremar** (Map pp78-9; ☎ 091 58 24 03; www.siremar.it in Italian; Via Francesco Crispi 118) runs ferries (€10.80, 2½ hours, two daily) and hydrofoils (€15.90, 1½ hours, four daily) to Ustica. It also runs summer-only hydrofoils to the Aeolian Islands (Lipari €32, four hours, one daily).

Ustica Lines (www.usticalines.it in Italian) runs summer-only hydrofoil services to the Aeolian Islands (Lipari €31.30, four hours, one daily) and Cefalù (€12.60, one hour, one daily). Buy tickets from **Pietro Barbaro** (Map pp78-9; ☎ 091 33 33 33; Via Principe di Belmonte 55).

Grandi Navi Veloci (Map pp78-9; ☎ 091 58 74 04; www1.gnv.it; Calata Marinai d'Italia) runs ferries from Palermo to Genoa (high season €99, 20 hours, one daily) and Livorno (€65, 19 hours, three weekly). The office is at the port to the left of the main entrance.

Bus

The main intercity bus station (Map p82) is near Via Paolo Balsamo, east of the train station. Sicily's buses are privatised and different routes are serviced by different companies, all with their own ticket offices.

SAIS Autolinee (Map p82; ☎ 091 617 11 41; Via Paolo Balsamo 20) runs services to Cefalù (€4.50, 1 hour, two daily), Catania (€13.20, 2½ hours, 17 daily Monday to Saturday), Enna (€8.80, 1¾ hours, six daily), Piazza Armerina (€10.80, 1½ hours, eight daily) and Messina (€14.10, 3¼ hours, hourly).

Segesta (Map p82; ☎ 091 616 90 39; www.segesta .it in Italian; Via Paolo Balsamo 26) runs very frequent services to Trapani (€8, two hours, eight daily).

Cuffaro (Map p82; ☎ 091 616 15 10; www.cuffaro .it. in Italian; Via Paolo Balsamo 13) has buses to Agrigento (€8, two hours, seven daily Monday to Saturday, two Sunday).

Azienda Siciliana Trasporti (AST; Map pp78-9; ☎ 091 680 00 11, 222; www.aziendasicilianatrasporti.it in Italian; Via Brasa 4), away from the main terminal, runs buses to Ragusa and Syracuse (€12, four hours, six daily Monday to Saturday, three Sunday). It also operates services to Corleone and Cefalù.

Numerous other companies service points throughout Sicily, and most have offices in the Via Paolo Balsamo area. Their addresses and telephone numbers, as well as destinations, are listed in the *Agenda Turismo*, available at the main tourist office (p77).

See p298 for details of services to destinations throughout the rest of Italy.

Car & Motorcycle

Palermo is accessible on the A20-E90 toll road from Messina, and from Catania (A19-E932) via Enna; the second route is quicker. Trapani and Marsala are also easily accessible from Palermo by motorway (A29), while Agrigento and Palermo are linked by the SS121, a good state road through the interior of the island.

Car hire is not cheap in Sicily, and you will generally get the best deal if you book your rental via the internet before you leave home. A week's car hire will cost anything from €350 to €500 so be sure to shop around first; often it is the larger companies that offer the best deals. All the car-hire companies are represented at the airport and listed in *Agenda Turismo*, which is available at the main tourist office (p77). The local firm **Sicily by Car** (Map pp78-9; ☎ 091 58 10 45; www.sbc.it; Via Mariano Stabile 6a) has good deals and also rents out scooters (€25 per day).

Train

Regular trains leave from the **train station** (Map p82; ☎ ticket office 091 603 30 88; ☼ 7am-9pm) heading for Messina (*diretto* €11, Intercity adult/concession €22/17, *diretto* 3½ hours, every 30 minutes), Catania (*diretto* €12, 3½ hours, six daily) and Agrigento (€7, 2½ hours, 11 daily), as well as nearby towns such as Cefalù (€4, half-hourly, five daily); there are trains to Syracuse (€17.20 to €20.20, six to 10 hours, five daily), but you will need to change at Messina or Catania. There are also Intercity trains to Reggio di Calabria, Naples and Rome; see p299 for the details.

Train-timetable information is available in English at the train station. There are left-luggage and clean toilet facilities (€0.20) inside the station.

GETTING AROUND
To/From the Airport

A half-hourly bus service run by **Prestia e Comandè** (☎ 091 58 04 57) transfers passengers from the airport to the centre of Palermo, dropping people off outside the Teatro Politeama Garibaldi (Map pp78–9) and the train station (Map p82). Tickets for the 45-minute journey cost €5 and are available on the bus. Return journeys to the airport run with similar frequency and pick up at the same points. This is by far the best way to travel to Palermo from the airport.

A train service, the Trinacria Express, also runs from the airport to the train station (€4.50, one hour, every 45 minutes).

There are plenty of taxis outside the airport and the fare for the same trip is about €50.

All the major car-hire companies are represented at the airport including Hertz, Avis and Sicily by Car.

Car & Motorcycle

Palermo has a massive problem with gridlock, and Palermitans have little respect for the rules of the road (though if you have dealt with the roads in Rome or Naples, Palermo will present few difficulties).

Some hotels have small car parks, but they are often full, so book your space in advance. Theft of and from vehicles is a problem, and you are advised to use one of the attended car parks if your hotel has no parking space; you'll be looking at €13 to €16 per day.

See p97 for car-hire information.

Public Transport
BUS

Palermo's orange **city buses** (AMAT; ☎ 091 35 01 11; www.amat.pa.it in Italian) are overcrowded and slow due to the appalling traffic. Ask at the tourist booths for a leaflet detailing the different lines; most stop at the train station. Tickets must be purchased before you get on the bus and are available from tobacconists or the booths at the terminal. They cost €1 and are valid for two hours. Once you get on the bus you need to validate the ticket in the orange machine,

which prints a 'start' time on it. You can be fined if you don't do this, although conductors are lenient with tourists.

There are two small buses – Linea Gialla and Linea Rossa – that operate in the narrow streets of the historic centre and can be useful if you are moving between tourist sights.

METRO

Most visitors will have little cause to use Palermo's metro system, as its 10 stations radiating out from the main train station are a good hike from any destination likely to interest them. There is talk of expanding the system to Falcone-Borsellino airport, which would be useful should it ever happen. A single-trip ticket costs €1.

AROUND PALERMO

Visitors to Palermo will probably welcome a break from this raucous city, which is as exhausting as it is energising. Like the capital, Palermo's environs have a long history,

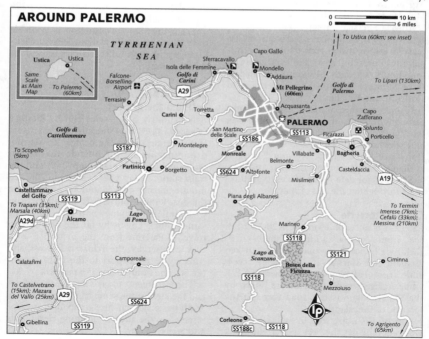

from the prehistoric carvings of the Grotta dell'Addaura and the shrine of Santa Rosalia to the mythology of the Mafia, which envelops towns such as Corleone. And, most famous of all, the Cattedrale di Monreale remains a beacon of medieval brilliance that shouldn't be missed.

MONDELLO

Mondello is Palermo's beach resort, though it's mainly the haunt of Palermitan teenagers who, along with the yelling vendors of jewellery, fruit and plastic toys, crowd the beach during the summer months. If you like quiet beach time, this is not the place for you.

Originally a muddy, malaria-ridden port, Mondello only really became fashionable in the 19th century, when people came to the seaside in their carriages, thus warranting the huge Art Nouveau pier that dominates the seafront. Most of the beaches are private (two loungers and an umbrella per day €9), but there is a wide swath of public beach with all the requisite pedalos (standard/with slide €9/12 per hour) and jet skis (€55 per 20 minutes).

If you want to lounge on the beach yet be able to pop over to Palermo, Mondello provides the best of both worlds. The **Addaura Hotel** (☎ 091 684 22 22; www.addaura.it; Lungomare Cristoforo Colombo 4452; s/d €91/139; P ⌧ ⌧) and the **Splendid Hotel La Torre** (☎ 091 45 02 22, toll free 800 23 61 18; www.latorre.com; Via Piano Gallo 11; s/d €104/136; P ⌧ ⌧) are two good options that both have access to the beach. Or try the B&B **Il Banano** (☎ 091 45 59 26; www.ilbanano.com; Via Stesicoro 3; s €33-40, d €66-80; P).

There are numerous seafood restaurants and snack stalls along the seafront (Viale Regina Elena). One of Sicily's classiest restaurants is the **Charleston** (☎ 091 45 01 71; Viale Regina Elena; meals €35; ⌧ closed Wed), located inside an enormous Art Nouveau palace with a wide terrace jutting out over the sea. It's hosted the great and the good, and the food is suitably fine, with an emphasis on Palermitan favourites. Eating here is a real event – if you don't want to look out of place put on your best outfit. Make a reservation.

With a great location overlooking the harbour, historic **La Locanda** (☎ 091 684 01 27; Via Torre 26; meals €25 ⌧ closed Thu), open since 1865, has a good range of seafood dishes.

To get here take bus 806 from Piazza Sturzo (Map pp78–9; €1.20, 20 minutes).

MONTE PELLEGRINO
elev 606m

Between Palermo and Mondello is Monte Pellegrino (606m) and the **Santuario di Santa Rosalia** (☎ 091 54 03 26; admission free; ⌧ 7am-7pm). One of Palermo's patron saints, St Rosalia, lived on the mountain as a hermit in a cave, which is now the site of a 17th-century shrine. The water, which is channelled from the roof of the cave into a large font, is said to have miraculous powers. It is a fascinating place to visit, but remember that it is a shrine and not a tourist haunt. To get here, take bus 812 from Piazza Sturzo (Map pp78–9).

On the northern side of Monte Pellegrino is the **Grotta dell'Addaura** (☎ 091 696 13 19; ⌧ closed indefinitely due to rock falls), where cave drawings from the Upper Palaeolithic and Neolithic periods have managed to survive into the 21st century. You can see casts of the engravings in the Museo Archeologico Regionale (p85) in Palermo, where you can also obtain up-to-date information on the status of the caves. To get there, head up the road above the beach at Addaura and follow the signposts (the caves are about 400m away).

MONREALE

Inspired by a heavenly vision of the Virgin and driven by earthy ambition, William II set about building the magnificent **Cattedrale di Monreale** (☎ 091 640 44 13; Piazza Duomo, Monreale; admission free; ⌧ 8am-6pm, treasury 9.30am-noon & 3.30-5.30pm) 8km southwest of Palermo. Living in the shadow of his grandfather, Roger II – who was responsible for the cathedral in Cefalù and the Cappella Palatina – and vying with the Palermitan archbishop, Walter of the Mill, William was determined that his cathedral should be the biggest and best. The result was Monreale, considered to be the finest example of Norman architecture in Sicily. The mosaicists were from Sicily and Venice, but the stylised influence of the Byzantines pervades their work. Completed in 1184 after only 10 years' work, the mosaics are an articulate and fitting tribute to the grandeur of Sicilian culture at the time.

The interior is one of the most impressive creations of the Italian Middle Ages. A catalogue of shimmering mosaics depicts essential Old Testament stories from the creation of man

---

DETOUR: CORLEONE

Sixty kilometres south of Palermo, through the tawny landscape of central Sicily, is the town of Corleone, best known through Francis Ford Coppola's classic *Godfather* trilogy, which starred Marlon Brando and Al Pacino. But, tired of living in a town that has suffered centuries of poverty and has a reputation as the home of murderous thugs, residents are trying to reclaim Corleone for themselves.

Take the free town tour and you will hear about not only the local history of organised crime, but also the efforts of those who have fought it and other aspects of the town's history. After all, we were told on the threshold of the impressive 14th-century **Chiesa Madre** that Corleone gave the world two saints. The tour also includes wine tasting at a local cellar and lunch on a farm. The main stop, however, is the anti-Mafia centre, which also houses an archive of documents from major Mafia trials conducted in the 1980s.

The authorities hope that after the tour visitors will take away another impression of Corleone. 'But to be honest,' said the guide, 'they come here because of *The Godfather*'. You can pick up the tour at the **Museo Civico** (☎ 091 846 36 55; Palazzo Provenzano, Via Orfanotrofio; admission free; ◷ 9am-1pm & 3-7pm Mon-Sat, 9am-1pm Sun).

The only hotel in town is the **Hotel Belvedere** (☎ 091 846 49 64; fax 091 846 40 00; Contrada Belverdere; s/d €61/72; P ⊠ ⊠). There are regular Azienda Siciliana Trasporti (AST) buses from Palermo (€3.60, 1½ hours, four daily).

---

to the Assumption in 42 different episodes. The beauty of the mosaics cannot be described – you have to see Noah's ark perching atop the waves or Christ healing a leper infected with large leopard-sized spots for yourself. The story of Adam and Eve is wonderfully portrayed, with a grumpy-looking, post-Eden-eviction Eve sitting on a rock while Adam labours in the background. The large mosaic of Christ, covering the dome, is stunning.

Outside the cathedral is the entrance to the **cloister** (admission €6; ◷ 9am-7pm Mon-Sat, 9am-1.30pm Sun), which illustrates William's love of Arab artistry. This tranquil courtyard is pure Orientalism, with elegant Romanesque arches supported by an array of slender columns alternately decorated with shimmering mosaic patterns. Each capital is different, and taken together they represent a unique sculptural record of medieval Sicily. The capital of the 19th column on the west aisle depicts William II offering the cathedral to the Madonna.

William II succeeded in his ambition of creating the most sumptuous cathedral in Sicily – and it remains so today. He now lies entombed in a white marble sarcophagus in the cathedral.

To reach Monreale take bus 389 from Piazza Indipendenza in Palermo (Map pp78–9; €1, 20 to 30 minutes, hourly). The bus will drop you off outside the cathedral in Piazza Duomo. A taxi from the Quattro Canti in Palermo to Monreale will cost you €20 one way.

SOLUNTO

About 20km east of Palermo are the remains of the Hellenistic-Roman town of **Solunto** (☎ 091 90 45 57; admission €2; ◷ 9am-6pm Mon-Fri), founded in the 4th century BC on the site of an earlier Phoenician settlement. Although the ancient city is only partially excavated, the ruins are beautifully sited on the slopes of Monte Catalfano. Wander along the Roman *decumanus* (main street), and take detours up the steep, paved side streets to explore the ruined houses, some of which still sport their original mosaic floors. Take particular note of the theatre and the Casa di Leda (if you can find it), which has an interesting floor mosaic.

To get there, take the train from Palermo to the Santa Flavia–Solunto-Porticello stop (€1.65, 15 minutes, every 30 minutes) and ask for directions. The ancient city is about a 30-minute uphill walk.

USTICA
pop 1200

If Palermo's bustle becomes so overbearing that all you really want is to have a day or two of peace and quiet, your best bet will be the tiny island of Ustica, which floats alone almost 60km north in the Tyrrhenian sea. Part of the Aeolian volcanic chain, this mini island (8.7 sq km) is actually the tip of a submerged volcano. You'll be mesmerised by its black volcanic-rock landscape, which is sprinkled with blazing pinks and reds of hibiscus flowers and prickly greens of cacti. The limpid waters surrounding the island are kept sparklingly clean by an Atlantic current, so it's a haven for serious divers and a prime spot for anyone wanting to see the multitude of fish and coral.

In 1986 Ustica was made Italy's first marine reserve, and it remains a centre for diving and marine research. In July the island hosts the International Festival of Underwater Activities, drawing divers from around the world. It's best to visit in June and September to appreciate the dramatic coastline and grottoes without the crowds.

Information

The **Marine Reserve Visitors Centre** (Centro Accoglienza; ☎ 091 844 94 56; Piazza Umberto 1; ☷ 8am-1pm & 4-6pm Mon-Fri, 8am-2pm Sat & Sun Oct-Apr, 8am-9pm Mon-Fri Jun-Sep) is in the centre of the village and can advise on activities, boat trips and dive centres. In case of an emergency, call the **police** (☎ 091 844 90 49) or **first aid** (☎ 091 844 92 48).

Activities

Among the most rewarding dive sites are the **Secca Colombara** to the north of the island and the **Scoglio del Medico** to the west. Note that Zone A of the *riserva marina* (marine reserve), taking in a good stretch of the western coast north of Punta dello Spalmatore, is protected; you'll need permission to fish, dive or swim. The reserve's information office can organise diving excursions into the zone.

Most dive-hire outlets operate between April and September. **Profundo Blu Ustica** (☎ 091 844 96 09; www.ustica-diving.it; Via C Colombo), **Katuma Scuola Sub** (☎ 091 844 92 16; www.katuma.it in Italian; Via Petriera 7) and **Tortuga** (☎ 335 833 20 20; www.tortugadiving.eu; Via della Vitoria) are recommended, and all offer a range of itineraries, including a deep-sea archaeological tour that explores wrecks and amphora in their original sites. The cost of dives ranges from around €38 for a single dive to €340 for a full open-water course. All outfits rent wetsuits and equipment. Official guides for snorkelling, diving and boat trips can all be arranged at the visitors centre; the boat trip is particularly worthwhile as it allows you to view the stunning grottoes.

You can hike or cycle along the mountain trails, the most scenic of which passes through pine woods to the summit of **Guardia di Mezzo** (248m), before descending to the best part of the coast at **Spalmatore** where you can swim in natural rock pools.

Sleeping & Eating

There are eight hotels and several *affitta-camere* (rooms for rent) on Ustica.

Hotel Clelia (☎ 091 844 90 39; www.hotelclelia.it in Italian; Via della Vittoria 1; s €35-85, d €60-150; ☷ ☐) This neat three-star hotel has a good restaurant and welcoming management.

Villaggio Punta Spalmatore (☎ 091 844 93 88; Località Spalmatore; r €55-105, 4-person bungalow €65-115; P ☷ ☐) An excellent hotel complex with charming bungalow accommodation amid tumbling gardens. A great choice for families or water-sports enthusiasts.

Grotta Azzurra (☎ 091 844 90 48; www.sicily-hotels.com/siti/framon-hotels/grottazzurra; Contrada San Ferlicchio; s €110-140, d €152-256; ☷ ☐) All the rooms in this clifftop hotel have a romantic terrace overlooking the sea. The hotel's rocky beach has a hydro-massage centre.

A good place to eat and find accommodation and local information is **Trattoria da Umberto** (☎ 091 844 95 42; www.usticatour.it; Piazza Umberto I 26; meals €20). The friendly Tranchina family organise rooms, apartments and villas on the island (doubles from €40) and the son, Gigi, speaks good English.

One of the town centre's best eating options is **Giulia** (☎ 091 844 90 39; Via San Francesco 16; meals €25), which is renowned for its seafood. It's small and busy so book ahead. Also try the fantastic pizza at **Schiticchio** (Via Tre Mulini; pizza €6-8).

Night fun and cocktails can be had at the **220 Bar** (Via Tre Mulini 1; ☷ from 6pm), or you can go partying at the Il Faraglione beach, situated at Cala Santa Marina.

Getting There & Around

Siremar operates a year-round car-ferry service (€14.70, 2½ hours, one daily) from Palermo, and additional hydrofoils run from June to September (€19.90, 1¼ hours, two daily). The office for **Siremar** (☎ 091 874 93 111; Piazza Capitano Longo 9) is in the centre of Ustica.

From June to the end of September you can take the Trapani-Favignana-Ustica-Naples hydrofoil, run by Ustica Lines three days per week. The journey from Naples to Ustica takes four hours and costs €66 one way.

Orange minibuses make a round trip of the island; they leave from the town hall (€1, every 30 minutes). Alternatively, hire a scooter at the **Albergo Ariston** (☎ 091 844 90 42; Via della Vittoria 5) from around €25 to €30 per day.

Western Sicily

NOT ENOUGH TIME

Western Sicily is ancient and rugged, tranquil and sunny, a fascinating insight into the island's history and culture. It's one of the least touristy parts of the region and if you're wanting an off-the-beaten-track experience with good hotels and fantastic food, head straight here. In fact, it could be said without much exaggeration that this is Sicily's prime gourmet area and, with endless fields of Marsala grapes covering the landscape, oenophiles will spend a lot of time in local wine bars.

Though they are irresistible, gastronomic pleasures are not the only highlight of western Sicily – the beautiful coastline is absolutely mesmerising, as are the region's towns. The Riserva Naturale dello Zingaro, Sicily's first nature reserve, is distinguished by coves and rocky beaches washed by the clearest of waters, while offshore Pantelleria and the Egadi Islands hold some 15,000 years of history between them. Trapani, Marsala and Mazara del Vallo are charming, with labyrinthine old quarters sprinkled with gorgeous palazzi and churches.

Historically, the area's roots are firmly in North Africa: the features and physiognomy of the fishermen are almost indistinguishable from the Tunisian immigrants who fill the ports in Trapani and Mazara del Vallo.

For decades, western Sicily was written off as a remote and uninteresting corner of the island, with little to recommend it save a couple of Greek ruins and – for those fascinated by the macabre – its reputation as a hot spot of seismic instability and Mafia activity. Consequently, the area never developed the mass tourist industry of Taormina and Syracuse, but it's been far better off for it.

HIGHLIGHTS

- Feast on fish couscous or tuck into some delicious *pasta alla Trapanese* in **Trapani** (p105)
- Wander through the narrow streets of La Casbah in **Mazara del Vallo** (p124)
- Be mesmerised by the medieval streets of **Erice** (p110) while you fatten up on some fabulous *cannoli* (pastry shells stuffed with sweet ricotta)
- Taste the famed sweet Marsala wine in one of the *enoteche* (wine bars) in **Marsala** (p120)
- Swim, snorkel and island-hop through the **Egadi Islands** (p113)

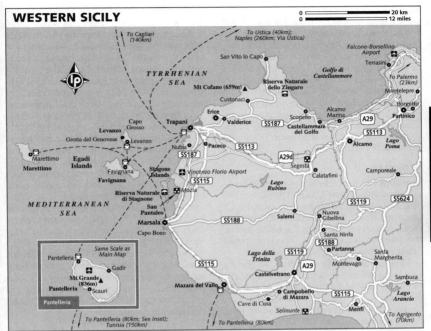

WESTERN SICILY

GOLFO DI CASTELLAMMARE

CASTELLAMMARE DEL GOLFO

pop 14,600

The stunning promontory between Castellammare del Golfo and Monte Cofano (659m) has to be perhaps the most beautiful in all of Sicily, and at its heart lies the fishing village of Castellammare del Golfo. Although it's the least attractive town along the gulf, this place acts as a transport hub. It does have a pleasant harbour that is overlooked by the remains of a 17th-century castle and surrounded by sandy beaches, the best of which is the wide stretch of sand at the lovely **Alcamo Marina**.

Sleeping & Eating

Castellammare del Golfo is a resort town with large hotels catering mainly to Italian families. Two of the best are the **Al Madarig** (☎ 0924 3 35 33; www.almadarig.com; Piazza Petrolo; s €52-82, d €80-124; ✕), on the harbourfront, and

the big, modern **Punta Nord Est** (☎ 0924 3 05 11; www.puntanordest.com; Via Leonardo da Vinci 67; s €50-78, d €78-112; P ✕), with a seafront location.

You'll find good camping facilities at **Nausicaa** (☎ 0924 3 30 30; www.nausica-camping .it; Località Forgia; per person €6-9, camp site €12-20). It is well signposted on roads approaching Castellammare del Golfo.

The **Ristorante del Golfo** (☎ 0924 3 02 57; Via Segesta 153; meals €35-40; ✕ closed Tue) has a Slow Food Movement recommendation, and you can get great seasonal dishes in an elegant setting. Try the excellent fish and seafood, fresh pasta and, in colder months, delicious beans and lentils. You can have your *dolci* (dessert) here, or stroll down to **Gelateria Tropical** (Via Umberto I, 2; sweets from €2-5) for some creamy *semifreddo* (literally 'semifrozen'; a cold, creamy dessert), *cannoli* (pastry shells stuffed with sweet ricotta) and, of course, *gelato* (ice cream).

Getting There & Away

In Castellammare del Golfo buses depart from Via della Repubblica, in the upper part of town. Azienda Siciliana Trasporti (AST) runs a regular service to Trapani (€3.10, eight daily

Monday to Saturday); there's also a Sunday service from June to September. **Russo** (☎ 0924 3 13 64; www.russoautoservizi.it) runs services to Piazza Marina in Palermo (€4.70, nine daily Monday to Saturday, three Sunday), as well as services to Scopello (€1.80, 30 minutes) at 7.10am, 9am, 1.30pm and 4.15pm.

The train station in Castellammare is an inconvenient 3km out of town, although a shuttle bus (€1.40) takes passengers into town. There are frequent trains from Palermo (€4.25, 1½ hours, 13 daily) and Trapani (€3.45, 50 minutes, five daily).

SCOPELLO

The gorgeous Scopello is a two-streets-and-a-square village that couldn't be any more charming if it tried. Built around a *baglio* (manor house) that overlooks the **tonnara** (tuna-processing plant) on the beach below, its white houses and smooth-stone streets feel like they belong in a 1950s Italian movie.

This is pure holiday material, so there's nothing to do except swim by the *tonnara* in one of the most idyllic coves on the island. The place is gorgeous, though somewhat hard on the bum: the abandoned *tonnara* (which only ceased operations in the 1980s, having been in operation since the 1200s) is surrounded by rows of rusting anchors, and the raised stone platform, filled with sun seekers, is lapped by waters of an incredible blue. The cove is protected by rock towers jutting out of the sea. It's a 20-minute (1.5km) walk from the village.

If you prefer a quieter beach, head to the Riserva Naturale dello Zingaro; it's a 2km walk from Scopello, or you can take the bus that heads there at 9am from the village bus stop.

Try to avoid the village in August, when it becomes seriously busy.

If you need a bank, there's a small branch of Banco di Sicilia with an ATM at the *baglio*.

Sleeping & Eating

Considering its size, there is a surprising number of rooms in Scopello; for more accommodation options, check out www.scopellonline.com. Always book in advance. Scopello's eating options are pretty good, and all have gorgeous settings.

Maria (☎ 0924 54 12 16; www.bedandbreakfast maria.com; Piazza Nettuno 3; d €45; 🕸) In a beautiful old house right on the village square, Maria's rooms are airy and comfortable, with

traditional décor. You can use the kitchen, and there's a pleasant common area with a TV.

Hotel-Ristorante Torre Bennistra (☎ /fax 0924 54 11 28; www.hoteltorrebennistra.com; Via Natale di Roma 19; s €60-110, d €70-150; 🕸 🖳) This hotel has newly renovated rooms that are elegant and comfortable, and a restaurant (meals €25 to €35) with wonderful food, sea views and an excellent wine list with offerings from local vineyards.

La Tavernetta (☎ /fax 0924 3 26 60; www.albergo tavernetta.it; Via Armando Diaz 3; r per person €48-80; 🕸) This traditional Scopello house has lovely ochre-coloured rooms with balconies and comfy beds. La Tavernetta also has one of the village's more popular restaurants (meals €25 to €30), serving good fish and seafood indoors or on the little terrace.

Ristorante La Terrazza (☎ 0924 54 11 98; Via Marco Polo 5; meals €25-35) This is the best place to enjoy soaring views down the 106m ridge to the famous cove. The restaurant is elegant, and the service efficient and friendly. Try the excellent mussels in a slightly spicy tomato sauce for a starter, move on to *pasta alle vongole* (pasta with clams), and sink your teeth into a freshly grilled *pesce spada* (swordfish), all with some chilled white wine.

Getting There & Away

There are **Russo** (☎ 0924 3 13 64; www.russoautoservizi .it) buses from Castellammare del Golfo to Scopello (€1.80, 30 minutes) at 7.10am, 9am, 1.30pm and 4.15pm; the 9am bus takes you to Riserva Naturale dello Zingaro (€1.30, 20 minutes) before it reaches Scopello.

Buses to Castellammare del Golfo (€1.80, 30 minutes) depart from the fountain in Scopello at 7.40am, 9.30am, 2pm and 4.45pm.

RISERVA NATURALE DELLO ZINGARO

Saved from development and road projects by local protests, the tranquil **Riserva Naturale dello Zingaro** (☎ 0923 2 61 11; www.riservazingaro.it in Italian; adult/child €3/2; 🕑 7am-9pm Apr-Sep, 8am-4pm Oct-Mar) is the star attraction on the gulf.

Sicily's, and Italy's, first nature reserve, Zingaro was created with the support of local people and ecologists. Now its wild coastline is a haven for the rare Bonelli eagle, along with 40 other bird species and 700 plant varieties, some unique to this stretch of coast. Mediterranean flora dusts the hillsides with wild carob and bright yellow euphorbia, and hidden coves, such as Marinella Bay, provide excellent swimming spots. **Cetaria Diving Centre**

(☎ 0924 54 10 73; www.cetaria.com; Via Marco Polo 3) in Scopello organises dives and underwater tours of the nature reserve from Scopello's *tonnara* in summer.

The main entrance to the park is 2km from Scopello. A walk up the coast between the San Vito lo Capo and Scopello entrances will take about four hours along a clearly marked track (note that the San Vito entrance is 20km from the town of San Vito lo Capo and there is no public transport). There are also several trails inland, which are detailed on the free maps available at the information offices at the park's two entrances. You can also download these from the helpful website, which has lots of good information about the park.

A car is the best way to get to Scopello from Castellammare del Golfo. If you're driving from Trapani, take the SS187. Russo buses run from Scopello (€1.40, 20 minutes, four daily).

SAN VITO LO CAPO
pop 3500

Occupying the tip of the promontory is the seaside town of San Vito lo Capo, full of beachcombers and sun worshippers in summer but virtually dead in winter. The town is renowned for its splendid beach (at the end of Via Savoia) and for its fish couscous, celebrated in the **Festival Internazionale del Cuscus** every September. The most noteworthy sight is the fortresslike 13th-century **Chiesa di San Vito**, about halfway down Via Savoia.

Information
The **tourist office** (☎ 0923 97 24 64; Via Savoia 57) is located in the rather uninteresting Museo del Mare. There's an **internet point** (Via di Bella 17; per hr €6) with around 10 computers, plus telephone and fax services; it's off the main street.

Sleeping & Eating
There are heaps of hotels, B&Bs and restaurants in San Vito but they are heaving July through September.

El Bahira (☎ 0923 97 25 77; www.elbahira.it; Località Makari; per person €5.70-7, camp site €13.50-18.50) This is a good camping ground, 3km south of San Vito lo Capo, with tents shaded by tall eucalyptus trees. There are also apartments for rent (€320 to €990 per week). It's well signposted; ask the bus driver to let you off if you're not coming by car.

our pick **Chiedi La Luna** (☎ 0923 62 14 01; www.chiedi-la-luna.it; Via Santuario 37b; s €45-70, d €60-110; closed Nov-Mar;) The best option in San Vito, this bright little B&B has a cosy atmosphere, terracotta-coloured walls, dark wooden furniture and six rooms with big comfy beds and large windows. Breakfast is served in a pleasant communal area, and the owner speaks English.

Albergo del Corso (☎ 0923 97 28 00; www.albergodelcorso.it; Via Savoia 25; s €55-65, d €75-160; closed Nov, Jan & Feb;) Right on the main drag and perfect for the beach, this no-frills place has 11 rooms that are clean and bright; two come with a terrace. Better value in the lower season.

Capo San Vito (☎ 0923 97 21 22; www.caposanvito.it; s €117-180, d €130-200;) This plush hotel has its own private beach, and classy rooms with an understated Moorish theme. The hotel comes complete with its own wellness centre, so it's a perfect location for splashing out.

Thàam (☎ 0923 97 28 36; www.sanvitoweb.com/thaam in Italian; Via Duca degli Abruzzi 34; meals €35-40; closed Wed Nov) This North African–themed restaurant dishes up its famous fish and chicken couscous beneath tented canopies.

Via Savoia is full of pizzerie and cheap *rosticcerie* (shops selling roast meat and other prepared food). If you fancy some fun, check out **Habana** (☎ 320 85 36 971; Via Piano di Sopra 5), which hosts parties during the summer months – some people even bring their kids!

Getting There & Away
AST Buses serve San Vito lo Capo (€3.25, 1½ hours, eight daily Monday to Saturday, four Sunday) from Trapani. Buses arrive at Via P Matarella, just near the beach and parallel to Via Savoia.

TRAPANI & AROUND

TRAPANI
pop 68,400

The capital of the eponymous province is quiet even in the heights of Sicily's August tourist invasion, which means you can explore its beautiful old quarter at your own pace. Trapani's streets are laden with elegant baroque palazzi (palaces or mansions) and impressive churches, and the

WESTERN SICILY

town's good hotels and restaurants make it an excellent base from which to explore the whole northwest.

Hugging the precious harbour where Peter of Aragon landed in 1282 to begin the Spanish occupation of Sicily, the sickle-shaped spit of land that is Trapani once sat at the heart of a powerful trading network that stretched from Carthage to Venice. Traditionally the town thrived on coral and tuna fishing, salt and wine production, and a healthy injection of Mafia-laundered money; today, arriving in Trapani through extensive and unattractive suburbs, one gets a glimpse of the unbridled, and usually illegal, construction of the last few decades.

Trapani is the main embarkation point for the Egadi archipelago and the remote Moorish island of Pantelleria.

Orientation

Trapani is narrow and relatively compact, bordered on either side by the sea. The main street, Via GB Fardella, runs east–west, splitting the modern city into two neat halves. On either side a chessboard street grid dominates as far as the historic centre, which is a confusing maze of small streets, many of which do not have signposts. All of the sights of interest are concentrated in this area, from where there is also access to the ferry terminal. The main bus station is on Piazza Montalto, in the new town, and the train station is around the corner on Piazza Umberto I.

Information

EMERGENCY
Emergency Doctor (☎ 0923 2 96 29; Piazza Generale Scio 1; ☎ 24hr)
Police (questura; ☎ 0923 59 81 11; Piazza Vittoria Veneto; ☎ 24hr)

INTERNET ACCESS
World Sport Line (Via Regina Elena 26-28; per hr €6; ☎ 10.30am-1pm & 4-8pm Mon-Sat) Three computers and fast connection.

MEDICAL SERVICES
Ospedale Sant'Antonio Abate (☎ 0923 80 91 11, casualty 0923 80 94 50; Via Cosenza; ☎ 24hr)

MONEY
There are dozens of banks in Trapani and nearly all of them have ATMs.

POST
Main post office (Piazza Vittoria Veneto; ☎ 8am-6.30pm Mon-Sat)

TELEPHONE
Public telephone booths are dotted around town, and there are quite a few in front of the ferry terminal. The terminal also has a phone centre on the 1st floor.

TOURIST INFORMATION
Tourist office (☎ 0923 2 90 00; www.apt.trapani .it in Italian; Piazza Garibaldi; ☎ 8am-8pm Mon-Sat, 9am-noon Sun) A well-organised and friendly tourist office with bags of information on the province and a good town map. It provides free audio guides for Trapani's sights.

TRAVEL AGENCIES
Egatours (☎ 0923 2 17 54; Via Ammiraglio Staiti 13) For bus and ferry tickets.
Salvo Viaggi (☎ 0923 54 54 55; Corso Italia 48) For boat and air tickets to Pantelleria.

Sights

Although the narrow network of streets in Trapani's historic centre is Moorish, the city takes most of its character from the fabulous 18th-century baroque of the Spanish period. A catalogue of examples can be found down the pedestrian Via Garibaldi, most notably the **Palazzo Riccio di Morana** and **Palazzo Fardelle Fontana**. The best time to walk down here is in the early evening, when the *passeggiata* (stroll) is in full swing.

Another busy place at *passeggiata* is Corso Vittorio Emanuele, which is punctuated by the huge **Cattedrale di San Lorenzo** (Corso Vittorio Emanuele; admission free; ☎ 8am-4pm), with its baroque façade and iced Christmas cake–style stuccoed interior. Facing off the east end of Vittorio Emanuele is another baroque confection, the **Palazzo Senatorio**.

Off Vittorio Emanuele, south along Via Generale Dom Giglio, is the **Chiesa del Purgatorio** (☎ 0923 56 28 82; Via San Francesco D'Assisi; admission free; ☎ 4-6.30pm), which houses the 18th-century *Misteri* – 20 life-sized wooden figures depicting the story of Christ's Passion. On Good Friday they are carried in procession (see p108).

Further west, on Piazzetta Saturno, is the 14th-century **Chiesa di Sant'Agostino** (Piazzetta Saturno; admission free; ☎ 8am-1pm), its austerity relieved only by its fine Gothic rose window

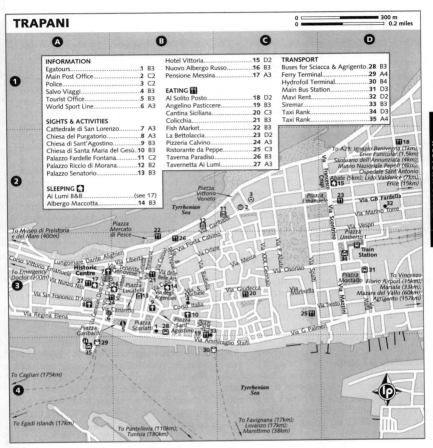

TRAPANI

0 —— 300 m
0 —— 0.2 miles

INFORMATION
Egatours..............................1 B3
Main Post Office...................2 C2
Police.................................3 C2
Salvo Viaggi.........................4 B3
Tourist Office.......................5 B3
World Sport Line...................6 A3

SIGHTS & ACTIVITIES
Cattedrale di San Lorenzo......7 A3
Chiesa del Purgatorio............8 A3
Chiesa di Sant'Agostino.........9 B3
Chiesa di Santa Maria del Gesù..10 B3
Palazzo Fardelle Fontana.......11 C2
Palazzo Riccio di Morana........12 B2
Palazzo Senatorio................13 B3

SLEEPING
Ai Lumi B&B......................(see 17)
Albergo Maccotta................14 B3

Hotel Vittoria......................15 D2
Nuovo Albergo Russo.............16 B3
Pensione Messina.................17 A3

EATING
Al Solito Posto.....................18 D2
Angelino Pasticcere..............19 B3
Cantina Siciliana..................20 C3
Colicchia............................21 B3
Fish Market.........................22 B3
La Bettolaccia......................23 B3
Pizzeria Calvino....................24 A3
Ristorante da Peppe..............25 C3
Taverna Paradiso..................26 B3
Tavernetta Ai Lumi................27 A3

TRANSPORT
Buses for Sciacca & Agrigento.28 B3
Ferry Terminal.....................29 A4
Hydrofoil Terminal................30 B4
Main Bus Station...................31 D3
Mavi Rent...........................32 D2
Siremar.............................33 B3
Taxi Rank...........................34 D3
Taxi Rank...........................35 A4

WESTERN SICILY

---

and portal. Nearby stands something altogether more ornate, the Catalan-Gothic **Chiesa di Santa Maria del Gesù** (Via San Pietro; admission free; ✆ 8am-1pm), which houses the exquisite *Madonna degli Angeli* (Madonna of the Angels), a glazed terracotta statue by Andrea della Robbia.

Trapani's major sight is the 14th-century **Santuario dell'Annunziata** (Via Conte Agostino Pepoli 179; admission free; ✆ 8am-noon & 4-7pm), some way from the centre on Via Agostino Pepoli. Remodelled in baroque style in the 17th century, it retains its original Gothic rose window and doorway. The Cappella della Madonna, behind the high altar, contains the venerated *Madonna di Trapani,* thought to be carved by Nino Pisano.

Next to the Santuario dell'Annunziata, in a former Carmelite monastery, is the **Museo Nazionale Pepoli** (✆ 0923 55 32 69; Via Conte Agostino Pepoli 200; admission free; ✆ 9am-1.30pm Tue-Sat, 9am-12.30pm Sun). It houses the collection of Conte Pepoli, who made it his business to salvage much of Trapani's local arts and crafts, not least the garish coral carvings that were all the rage in Europe before the banks of coral off Trapani and San Vito lo Capo were decimated. The museum also has a respectable collection of sculptures by Antonello and Domenico Gagini, silverwork, archaeological artefacts and religious artwork.

Trapani's other museum is the **Museo di Preistoria e del Mare** (✆ 0923 54 79 22; Via Torre di Ligny; admission €1.50; ✆ 9.30am-1pm & 4.30-7.30pm), located

WESTERN SICILY

I MISTERI

Sicily's most venerated Easter procession is a four-day festival of extraordinary religious fervour. Since the 17th century, the citizens of Trapani – represented by 20 traditional *maestranze,* or guilds – begin the celebration of the Passion of Christ on the Tuesday before Easter Sunday with the first procession of a remarkable, life-sized wooden statue of the Virgin Mary. Over the course of the next three days, nightly processions of the remaining *Misteri* (life-sized wooden statues) make their way through the old quarter and port to a specially erected chapel in Piazza Lucatelli, where the icons are stored overnight. Each procession is accompanied by women following the men (who carry the statues on their shoulders) and a local band, which plays dirges to the slow, steady beat of a drum.

The high point of the celebration is on Friday afternoon, when the 20 guilds emerge from the Chiesa del Purgatorio and descend the steps of the church, carrying each of the statues, to begin the 1km-long procession up to Via GB Fardella; the procession then returns to the church the following morning. The massive crowds that gather to witness the slow march often reach a peak of delirious fervour that is matched only by that which accompanies the Easter *pasos* celebration in Seville, Spain. If you're not around for Easter, you can always see the figures in Chiesa del Purgatorio (p106), where they are stored throughout the year. A guardian is usually on hand to explain the origins of each one.

---

at the tip of the promontory in the Spanish fortress Torre di Ligny. It houses a collection of prehistoric artefacts and medieval objects recovered from shipwrecks off the coast. From the top of the tower there are great views over the town. Highlights are Titian's *San Francesco con Stigmata* (St Francis with Stigmata) and the *Pietà* by Roberto di Oderiso.

Festivals & Events

Trapani is famous throughout Italy for its Easter celebration, the **Procession of the Misteri**. It begins on the Tuesday before Easter and reaches its climax on the night between Holy Thursday and Good Friday. See above for more information.

Sleeping

Trapani has a good choice of small hotels and *pensioni* (guesthouses), with the best options in the historic town centre.

Lido Valderice (☎ 0923 57 30 86; www.campinglido valderice.com; Via del Dentice 15, Località Tonnara di Bonagia; per person/camp site €5/10; ☺ 1 Jun-30 Sep) Located 7km north of Trapani on a shale beach, this is the nearest camping ground to the town and it's pretty good. There are six buses daily that head past here for Erice.

Pensione Messina (☎ 0923 2 11 98; Corso Vittorio Emanuele 71; s with shared bathroom €20, d with shared bathroom €35-40) The basic, grandma-style rooms at Trapani's cheapest sleeping option all share bathrooms; it's very central and a real insight into 1950s Italy. Breakfast is an extra €4 per person. The *pensione* shares a courtyard with Ai Lumi B&B.

our pick Albergo Maccotta (☎ 0923 2 84 18; albergo maccota@comeg.it; Via degli Argentieri 4; s €30-35, d €55-65; ✗) The Maccotta is excellent value, with neat sunflower-coloured rooms decorated with Paul Gauguin prints.

Nuovo Albergo Russo (☎ 0923 2 21 66; fax 0923 2 66 23; Via Tintori 4; s €40-45, d €70-85; ✗) With gilded antiques in the lobby and a classic 1950s vibe, Nuovo Albergo has an eccentric air and a charming owner. Once the best accommodation option in Trapani, it has decayed significantly, and the slow renovations that are taking place are warmly welcomed.

our pick Ai Lumi B&B (☎ 0923 87 24 18; www.ailumi .it; Corso Vittorio Emanuele 71; s €50-70, d €80-100, 4-person apt €130-150; ✗) Situated right on the main drag, this lovely 18th-century palazzo is surrounded by swirling baroque architecture. Some of the stylishly decorated rooms have four-poster beds, and the small apartments are well furnished and spacious. There's wi-fi access, and guests receive a 15% discount at the Tavernetta Ai Lumi (opposite), next door, where the expansive buffet breakfast is served. Francesca speaks impeccable English.

Hotel Vittoria (☎ 0923 87 30 44; www.hotelvittoria trapani.it; Via Francesco Crispi 4; s/d €60/95; ✗) With a total of 65 rooms, Hotel Vittoria is the biggest hotel in the historic centre. All the rooms are comfortable and modern, with big bathrooms, but the hotel does lack the character of some of the smaller sleeping options.

Eating
RESTAURANTS

Sicily's Arab heritage and Trapani's unique position on the sea route to Tunisia has made couscous (or *cuscus*, as they spell it here) something of a speciality, particularly when served with a fish sauce (*cuscus con pesce*) that includes tomatoes, garlic and parsley. Another irresistible staple is *pesto alla Trapanese* (pesto made from fresh tomatoes, basil, garlic and almonds), eaten with *busiate*, a small pasta that is hand-twirled in Trapani. Make sure you try both dishes – you'll find them on the menu of every restaurant in town. You'll need to book in advance on weekend evenings in most places.

Ristorante da Peppe (☎ 0923 2 82 46; Via Spalti 50; meals €20-25; ☺ closed Mon) Lots of stained glass, steaming pasta and fresh seafood. Try the tuna specialities from May to early July.

Tavernetta Ai Lumi (☎ 0923 87 24 18; Corso Vittorio Emanuele 15; meals €25-35; ☺ closed Sun) Converted from the stable block of an 18th-century palazzo, this traditional tavern is rustic to the core. Exposed brickwork and huge arches lend the dining room great character, and the menu is full of unpretentious country fare.

our pick **Cantina Siciliana** (☎ 0923 2 86 73; Via Giudecca 52; meals €25-35) This little trattoria (informal restaurant) is a gastronomic paradise. You'll have to seek it out in the old Jewish ghetto, where scaffolding prevents the alley from collapsing in on itself, but you'll be discovering one of the finest places to eat in the whole of Sicily. It's no wonder it sports the Slow Food Movement badge of approval – just taste the sardine in breadcrumbs for starters, a plate of mind-blowing *pasta alla Trapanese* and the fish platter, followed by a warm *cassatella* (cream horn stuffed with sweet ricotta) or Italy's most famous muscat, the passito di Pantelleria. The restaurant runs the superb *enoteca* (wine bar or shop) next door.

our pick **Al Solito Posto** (☎ 0923 2 45 45; Via Orlandini 30a; meals €30-35; ☺ closed Sun & 15-31 Aug) Tucked at the end of Via Orlandini, this tiny trattoria is another deserved wearer of the Slow Food Movement badge. It's all about fish and seafood here, with an emphasis on the freshest picks of the morning catch. Start with the fish *carpaccio* (thinly sliced fish) and proceed to the delicious *spaghetti con i ricci* (spaghetti with sea urchin meat), which is perfectly followed by a tuna steak covered with sweet caramelised onions. If you can fit in a dessert, try the almond parfait or a creamy *cannoli*.

our pick **La Bettolaccia** (☎ 0923 2 16 95; Via GB Fardella 23; meals €30-40; ☺ closed Sat lunch & Sun) This is a great place to try couscous, prepared here with fish *alla Trapanese* (with garlic, chilli, tomatoes, saffron, cinnamon and nutmeg), a spicy and delightful local speciality. Another excellent *primo piatto* is the *trenette* (short pasta) with prawns and pistachio sauce. Move onto grilled fish or stuffed squid, and finish with ice cream or a *cassata* (sponge cake filled with sweetened ricotta, diced chocolate and candied fruit). No wonder the Slow Food Movement loves the place.

Taverna Paradiso (☎ 0923 87 37 51; Lungomare Dante Alighieri 24; meals €35-40; ☺ closed Jan) Taverna Paradiso serves up good food in a buzzing atmosphere by the seafront. The couscous is plentiful, the fish fresh, there's a good choice of salads, and the service is friendly and multilingual. The clientele stems from the higher levels of Trapani society, so you should dress relatively smartly.

The town's favourite takeaway pizza place is **Pizzeria Calvino** (☎ 0923 2 14 64; Via N Nasi 77; pizzas €3.50-7; ☺ 7pm-midnight Wed-Mon).

CAFÉS

our pick **Colicchia** (cnr Via delle Belle Arti & Via Carosio; granitas €1.55) The *granita* (flavoured crushed ice) here is the best in Trapani. Many flavours are available, including old favourites such as *mandorla* (almond), coffee and *limone* (lemon), but you should also try the seasonal delicacies, such as *gelsi* (mulberry), which is only eaten from July to September.

Angelino Pasticcere (☎ 0923 2 80 64; Via Ammiraglio Staiti 87; cakes €2.50-3.50) This heavenly little café serves excellent *cannoli* and a good array of light savoury meals. Located opposite the hydrofoil dock, it is a great place to pick up a snack before heading off to the islands.

Ignazio Benivegna (☎ 0923 55 55 54; Via Manzoni 99; ice creams & cakes €2.50-3.50) An old-timer among Trapani's *pasticcerie* (pastry shops), this place has been providing tasty *cannoli, cassate* and other delicious cakes since 1939. It's a bit of a walk down towards the Erice funicular.

SELF-CATERING

There's a great open-air **fish market** (Piazza Mercato di Pesce; ☺ morning-early afternoon Mon-Sat) on the northern waterfront. Even if you're not buying seafood, it's a great place to stroll around and take in the sights, smells and sounds.

Getting There & Away

AIR

Trapani's small national airport, **Vincenzo Florio airport** (☎ 0923 84 25 02), is 15km south of town at Birgi. Flights serve Dublin, Rome, Tunis and Pantelleria; see p300 for details.

See right for information on getting to/from the airport.

BOAT

Trapani's **ferry terminal** (☎ 0923 54 54 11) is op-posite Piazza Garibaldi. Inside you will find a money exchange, Tirrenia and Siremar ticket offices, a café, clean toilets and phone facilities.

For hydrofoils you will need to head down Via Ammiraglio Staiti. Hydrofoils run every hour and a half from 7am until around 8pm in the high season.

Siremar (☎ 0923 54 54 55; www.siremar.it in Italian; Via Ammiraglio Staiti 61) runs hydrofoils to Favignana (€5.30, 20 minutes), Levanzo (€5.30, 35 min-utes) and Marettimo (€11.80, one hour). It also runs a daily ferry to Pantelleria (€30, five hours) at midnight June to September; it runs Sunday to Friday through the rest of the year.

Ustica Lines (☎ 0923 2 22 00; www.usticalines.it in Italian; Via Ammiraglio Staiti 23) runs regular hydro-foils to Favignana, Levanzo and Marettimo for similar prices to Siremar, as well as a summer-only service to Ustica (€19, 2½ hours, four weekly), Naples (€83, five hours, four weekly) and Pantelleria (€34, 2½ hours, one daily). Ustica Lines also runs ferries to Tunisia (€72 to €144, nine hours) on Monday, Wednesday and Friday mornings. Get tickets at Egatours (p106), or you can buy directly at the hydrofoil terminal.

Tirrenia (☎ 0923 52 18 96; www.tirrenia.it) runs a ferry service to Cagliari on Sardinia (seat/bed €38/52, 11½ hours, one weekly). Purchase tickets at Salvo Viaggi (p106) or from the ferry terminal.

BUS

All intercity buses arrive and depart from the **main bus station** (Piazza Montalto). Tickets can be bought from kiosks in the station.

Segesta (☎ 0923 2 17 54) runs express buses connecting Trapani with Palermo (€8, two hours, eight daily). **AST** (☎ 0923 2 32 22) serves Erice (€1.80, 45 minutes, 10 daily Monday to Saturday, four Sunday), San Vito lo Capo (€3.50, 1½ hours, eight daily Monday to Friday), Marsala (€3, 30 minutes, eight daily Monday to Friday) and Mazara del Vallo (€4.40, 1½ hours, three daily). Autoservizi Tarantola runs a service to Segesta (€3, 25 minutes, five daily June to September).

Lumia (☎ 0923 2 17 54) has services to Agrigento (€10, four hours, three daily Monday to Saturday, one Sunday) and Sciacca (€7.50, two hours, two daily). You can pick up these buses outside Egatours (p106), where you purchase the tickets.

Services decrease dramatically on Sundays, public holidays and in the low season (October to May). Timetables are always posted at the bus station, or you can get copies at the tourist office.

TRAIN

Trapani is linked to Palermo (€7, 2½ hours, 10 to 12 daily), Castelvetrano (€4.50, one hour 10 minutes, 20 daily), Marsala (€3, 30 min-utes, 20 daily) and Mazara del Vallo (€4, 50 minutes, 20 daily).

Getting Around

AST buses (€3.50, 20 minutes) leave for the Vincenzo Florio airport from the main bus station on Piazza Montalto to coincide with flights. **Segesta** (☎ 0923 2 17 54) has buses to Palermo's Falcone-Borsellino airport (€5.50, one hour and 10 minutes, two daily Monday to Saturday).

You can hire bicycles from Albergo Maccotta (p108) for €5 per day.

Bus 11 does a free circular trip through Trapani from the town centre to the Museo Nazionale Pepoli, leaving from the bus sta-tion and stopping at the train station on the return leg.

Mavi Rent (☎ 0923 2 86 55; www.mavirent.com in Italian; Via Marino Torre 21/23; per day 50cc scooter/500cc motorcycle €25/40, per week Fiat Punto car €330) has a wide range of scooters and a car-rental service with competitive rates. It also has an office at Vincenzo Florio airport.

There are taxi ranks on Piazza Umberto and at the ferry terminal.

ERICE

pop 28,900 / elev 751m

Erice watches over the port of Trapani from the legendary mountain of Eryx, situated

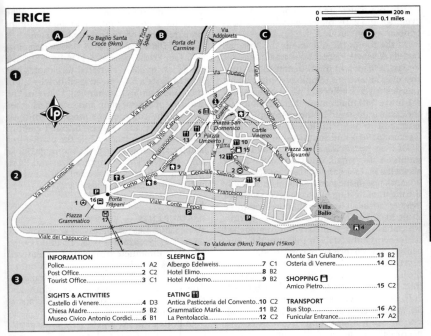

ERICE

INFORMATION		
Police	1	A2
Post Office	2	C2
Tourist Office	3	C1

SIGHTS & ACTIVITIES		
Castello di Venere	4	D3
Chiesa Madre	5	B2
Museo Civico Antonio Cordici	6	B1

SLEEPING		
Albergo Edelweiss	7	C1
Hotel Elimo	8	B2
Hotel Moderno	9	B2

EATING		
Antica Pasticceria del Convento	10	C2
Grammatico Maria	11	B2
La Pentolaccia	12	C2

Monte San Giuliano	13	B2
Osteria di Venere	14	C2

SHOPPING		
Amico Pietro	15	C2

TRANSPORT		
Bus Stop	16	A2
Funicular Entrance	17	A2

WESTERN SICILY

a giddy 750m above sea level. It's a mesmerising medieval town with stern-looking forts and churches, and its mountain charm is enhanced by the unpredictable weather that can take you from a sunny afternoon to a foggy evening. The town has sweeping views of the valley beneath it and the sea, and offers some pretty good restaurants and cake shops. Add to that the wonderful journey up on the funicular from Trapani, and a visit to Erice becomes a real mini-adventure. Shame about the enormous communication towers spoiling the surroundings, though.

The town has a notorious history as a centre for the cult of Venus (Astarte to the Phoenicians and Aphrodite to the Greeks). The mysterious Elymians claimed descent from Venus' famous Trojan son, Aeneas, who mentions the sanctuary as a holy landmark in the *Aeneid*. Inside the holy temple acolytes practised the peculiar ritual of sacred prostitution, with the prostitutes accommodated in the temple itself. Despite countless invasions the sacred site long remained inviolate – no guesses why!

Orientation

The town is shaped like a triangle and all vehicles arrive in Piazza Grammatico, from where you enter the town through the Porta Trapani. This puts you on Corso Vittorio Emanuele, the town's main road, which heads up to Piazza Umberto I, the central piazza. The other main road, which branches off Vittorio Emanuele, is Via Generale Salerno. This eventually brings you out at the castle.

Information

The friendly **tourist office** (☎ 0923 86 93 88; Via Tommaso Guarrasi 1; ✆ 8am-2pm Mon-Sat) is in the centre of town, as is the **post office** (Via Guarnotti; ✆ 8.15am-1.30pm Mon-Fri). The **police** (questura; Piazza Grammatico; ✆ 24hr) are at the main entrance to the old town.

Sights

Virgil once compared Eryx to Mt Athos for its altitude and spiritual pre-eminence. Not that Erice remains a sanctuary today – temples and convents have given way to carpet shops and souvenir stalls. Still, Erice is all about wall-hugging alleys, votive niches and secret

WESTERN SICILY

courtyards, which are best appreciated in the evenings and early mornings, when the day-trippers are not around.

At the top of the hill stands the Norman **Castello di Venere** (Castle of Venus; donations expected; 8am-7pm), built in the 12th and 13th centuries over an ancient temple of Venus, which was destroyed by Roger I when he captured the town. Not much more than a ruin today, the castle is upstaged by the panoramic vistas northeast to San Vito lo Capo and Monte Cofano (659m), and southwest to Trapani.

Of the several churches and other monuments in this small, quiet town, the **Chiesa Madre** (Via Vito Carvini; admission free; 9.30am-1pm & 3-5.15pm), just inside Porta Trapani, is probably the most interesting by virtue of its **campanile** (bell tower; admission €1) with mullioned windows. Built in 1314, the church had its interior, which has a lovely vaulted ceiling, remodelled in the neo-Gothic style in 1865, but the 15th-century side chapels were conserved.

At the top of Corso Vittorio Emanuele is the heart of the city, and the place where you'll find the **Museo Civico Antonio Cordici** (0923 86 91 72; Piazza Umberto I; admission free; 8.30am-1.30pm Tue, Wed & Fri, 8.30am-1.30pm & 2.30-5pm Mon & Thu). The museum houses finds from the town's necropolis, including a 4th-century head of Venus. The other piece worth seeing is an elegant *Annunciation* by Antonello Gagini.

Sleeping

Erice has some excellent hotels, and a quiet night in this medieval stronghold is an attraction in itself.

Albergo Edelweiss (0923 86 94 20; a.edelweiss @libero.it; Cortile Vincenzo 5; s/d €61/82) A good budget option with large rooms, spacious beds and small windows that look onto the plain below.

Baglio Santa Croce (0923 89 11 11; www.bagliosanta croce.it; Contrada Ragosia da Santa Croce, Valderice; s €54-65, d €108-130; P) This converted 17th-century *baglio* is located 9km east of Erice in Valderice. Set amid citrus groves and lush gardens, the hotel is full of authentic details, with exposed stone walls, original terracotta-tiled floors and olive-wood antiques. The swimming pool is a great addition in summer.

Hotel Moderno (0923 86 93 00; www.pippocatalano .it; Corso Vittorio Emanuele 63; s €75-95, d €100-130;) This is a cosy small hotel with a friendly owner who speaks impeccable English and rooms that feature bright rugs and mismatched

pieces that somehow work together. The hotel has a good *enoteca,* and the restaurant prepares some of the best food in town.

Hotel Elimo (0923 86 93 77; www.charmerelax .com; Corso Vittorio Emanuele 75; s €80-110, d €130-150; P) A stylishly cluttered reception gives way to Erice's best-positioned hotel – all of the rooms enjoy enchanting views of the windswept coastal plain and shimmering sea below. The communal rooms are intimate and full of shady alcoves, beamed ceilings and marble fireplaces, while the plant-filled and terracotta-tiled terrace is sunny and looks onto the sea. The rooms are neat and light, with smooth, cream-coloured walls and expansive, comfortable beds.

Eating
RESTAURANTS

Monte San Giuliano (0923 86 95 95; Viccolo San Rocco 7; meals €25-35; closed Mon) Tucked behind Corso Vittorio Emanuele, this eatery is entered through a crumbling arch that leads onto a cool patio graced with drooping hydrangeas. The terrace has a canopy of green vines, and the pasta, fish and seafood are as delicious as the surroundings.

La Pentolaccia (0923 86 90 99; www.ristorante lapentolaccia.it; Via Guarnotti 17; meals €30-35; closed Tue) This is a smart, atmospheric restaurant inside a former 16th-century monastery. It can get swamped by tour groups but the food is good, with *pasta con le sarde* (pasta with sardines) and other favourites featuring on the menu.

Also recommended, away from the busy main street, is **Osteria di Venere** (0923 86 93 62; Via Roma 6; meals €20-25), a traditional tavern of the checked-tablecloth variety.

CAFÉS

Antica Pasticceria del Convento (0923 86 90 05; Via Guarnotti 1; sweets €1.50-3) Heavenly pastries and sweets mean it's hard to go past this little *pasticceria.* And since it's in an old convent, this is one time when gluttony doesn't really count as a sin.

our pick Grammatico Maria (0923 86 93 90; Via Vittorio Emanuele 14; cannoli €2.50) This café is run by Maria Grammatico, Sicily's most famous pastry chef. She was even the subject of Mary Taylor Simeti's book *Bitter Almonds,* a series of recipes and recollections from her childhood, which was when she learnt her considerable skills from the nuns of Erice. Try the exquisite *cannoli* in the leafy back garden – they are some of the best you'll taste.

Shopping

Erice is justifiably famous for its *frazzate* (bright rugs made from colourful cotton rags), which are sold all along the main street. Erice also has a number of fairly good antique shops, one of the best being **Amico Pietro** (☎ 0923 86 92 44; Via Guarnotti 54/58), which sells quality ceramics, some lovely lacework and *presepi* (Nativity figurines).

Getting There & Away

The best way to get to Erice is on the **funicular** (☎ 0923 56 93 06, 0923 86 97 20; www.funiviaerice.it; Piazza Umberto I; one way/return €2/3.75; ☒ 8am-1am 2nd half Jul & Aug, 7.30am-8.30pm Mon-Fri, 9.45am-midnight Sat & Sun Sep-1st half Jul). To get to the funicular from Trapani, catch bus 23 from Via GB Fardella down to the end of Via Alessandro Manzoni, which is the point where Trapani ends and Erice begins. You can walk to the funicular station, but it takes around 30 minutes from/ to the centre of Trapani.

There is a regular AST bus service to/from Trapani (€1.80, 45 minutes, 10 daily Monday to Saturday, four Sunday). All buses arrive and depart from Porta Trapani.

Metered parking is available along Viale Conte Pepoli (€1 per hour).

SEGESTA

elev 304m

The ancient Elymians must have been great aesthetes if their choice of sites is any indication. Set on the edge of a deep canyon in the midst of wild, desolate mountains, this huge 5th-century-BC temple is one of the world's most magical ancient sites. On windy days its 36 giant columns are said to act like an organ, producing mysterious notes.

The city was in constant conflict with Greek Selinunte, whose destruction (in 409 BC) the Elymians pursued with bloodthirsty determination – perhaps understandably, if the Elymians were indeed descended from the Trojans. Such mutual antipathy was to have fatal consequences, and more than 100 years later the Greek tyrant Agathocles slaughtered over 10,000 Elymians and repopulated the city with Greeks.

There are two outstanding surviving sites: the theatre high up on the mountain, with commanding views out to Castellammare

del Golfo, and the never-completed **Doric temple** (☎ 0924 95 23 56; adult/concession €6/3; ☒ 9am-4pm Nov-Mar, 9am-7pm Apr-Aug). The latter dates from around 430 BC and is remarkably well preserved.

From mid-June to mid-September, performances of Greek plays are staged in the theatre. For information, contact the **tourist office** (☎ 0923 2 90 00; www.apt.trapani.it in Italian; Piazza Saturno; ☒ 8am-8pm Mon-Sat, 9am-noon Sun) in Trapani.

Segesta is accessible by **AST** (☎ 0924 3 10 20) bus from the main bus station in Trapani (€3, 25 minutes, five daily in summer, reduced service October to May). Otherwise, you can catch an infrequent train from Trapani (€3, 25 minutes, 10 daily) or Palermo (€5.50, one hour 40 minutes, three daily) to Segesta Tempio; the site is a 20-minute walk away. There are signs to direct you.

A shuttle bus runs every 30 minutes from the entrance 1.5km uphill to the theatre and costs an additional €1.20. If you've got the energy, walk up instead – the views are spectacular.

OFFSHORE ISLANDS

THE EGADI ISLANDS

pop 4280

For centuries the Egadi Islanders have lived from the sea, as the prehistoric cave paintings on Levanzo illustrate. Later, when the islands were a key Carthaginian stronghold, one of the most critical battles of the Punic Wars was fought in 241 BC at Cala Rossa (Red Cove), which earned its name from the amount of Carthaginian blood spilt.

The Arabs used the Egadi Islands (Isole Egadi) as a stepping stone en route to their invasions, and the lucrative tuna industry caused subsequent conquerors to fortify the islands heavily. In the 17th century the islands were sold to Genovese bankers, who then in turn sold them to the business tycoon Ignazio Florio in 1874. The Egadi Islands only became part of the Italian state in 1937.

Nowadays, the Egadi Islands are magnificent for swimming, diving, eating and general relaxing. Unfortunately, the waters around the islands have been terribly overfished, and the tuna fishery (once the only

WESTERN SICILY

LA MATTANZA

An ancient tradition, the Egadi Islands' *mattanza* (ritual tuna slaughter) survives despite the ever-decreasing number of tuna swimming into the local waters each year.

For centuries schools of tuna have used the waters around western Sicily as a mating ground. Locals can recall the golden days of the island's fishing industry, when it was not uncommon to catch giant breeding tuna of between 200kg and 300kg. Fish that size are rare these days and the annual catch is increasingly smaller due to the worldwide commercial overfishing of tuna.

Traditionally, tuna traps were set around the coast of Sicily once a year. The number of tuna caught by this method was relatively small and sustainable – the fact that the *mattanza* took place for around 900 years without overfishing is testament to this. Problems arose with the increase in commercial fishing in the 1960s: tuna was caught year-round, and deep waters were exploited using long-line fishing and indiscriminate means such as drift and gill nets. Anything that passed by was caught, and thus the oceans' fish resources were depleted.

According to some scientists, additional problems such as high legal fishing quotas and illegal fishing are causing 'irreversible' damage to bluefin tuna stock. Fishermen have largely lost their livelihoods, so some have reinvented La Mattanza as a tourist attraction.

From around 20 May to 10 June, tourists flock to the Egadi Islands to witness the event. For a fee you can join the fishermen in their boats and watch them catching the tuna at close hand, but keep in mind that nets have been known to come up empty in the last few years.

If you do decide to go, remember that this is no ordinary fishing expedition. The fishermen organise their boats and nets in a complex formation designed to channel the tuna into a series of enclosures, which culminate in the *camera della morte* (chamber of death). Once enough tuna are imprisoned, the fishermen close in and the *mattanza* begins. It is a bloody affair – up to eight or more fishermen at a time will sink huge hooks into a tuna and drag it aboard. Anyone who has seen Rossellini's classic film *Stromboli* will no doubt recall the *mattanza* scene, one of the most famous accounts of this ancient tradition.

---

cannery in Europe) is now a distant memory, causing a dent in the local economy.

GETTING THERE & AWAY

Siremar and Ustica Lines run hydrofoils to the islands from Trapani; see p110. In summer, there is also a daily service to Favignana and Levanzo from Marsala; see p124 for details.

Services between the islands are cheap and quick. From Favignana you can connect easily to Levanzo (€2.50, 10 minutes) and Marettimo (€6.90, 30 minutes).

Favignana

The largest of the islands is the butterfly-shaped Favignana, which is dominated by Monte Santa Caterina (287m) to the west. You can easily explore it on a bicycle, as the eastern half of the island is almost completely flat. Around the coast tufa quarries are carved out of the crystal-clear waters, most notably around **Cala Rossa** and **Cavallo**.

INFORMATION

Banco del Popolo (Piazza Europa) Has an ATM.
Internet Elyos (☎ 0923 92 25 87; Piazza Madrice 37; per hr €6) A good place with an ADSL connection and several computers.

Police (questura; Palazzo Florio) In the old home of the Florios, just up from the dock.
Post office (Via Marconi; ☒ 8am-1.30pm Mon-Fri, 8am-noon Sat)
Tourist office (☎ 0923 92 16 47; www.egadiweb .it/proloco in Italian; Piazza Madrice 8; ☒ 9am-12.30pm & 4.30-7pm Mon-Sat, 9.30am-12.30pm Sun Jun-Sep) Helpful office in Favignana town.

SIGHTS & ACTIVITIES

The first thing you'll see as you step off the boat is the abandoned **Stabilimento Florio tonnara**. It was shut down in 1977 due to the general crisis in the local tuna-fishing industry and, although there are plans to restore it as a cultural centre, the plans seem to be permanently stalled for lack of funding.

Around the harbour you can sign up for some diving and boating. Unsurprisingly, the crystal-clear waters are a favourite with divers, and **Atlantide** (☎ 0923 92 21 81, 347 050 44 92; www.progettoatlantide.com; Piazza Marina) runs international diving courses, as well as archaeological and night-time dives. For boats try next door at **Catalano** (☎ 339 691 66 18; Piazza Marina), where a dinghy/boat costs €80/110 per day.

If fishing is your thing, ask at the tourist office about **pescaturismo** (per person per day around €30), where local fishermen can take a group for a three-day jolly around the islands.

The best beaches are on the southern side of the island at **Miramare** and **Lido Burrone**.

SLEEPING

There are plenty of accommodation options on Favignana, but during La Mattanza and in August you'll have trouble finding a bed if you don't book in advance. Many locals rent out rooms.

Camping Egad (☎ 0923 92 15 55; www.egadi.com /egad in Italian; Località Arena; camp site per person €5-7, 2-bed bungalow €34-80, 4-bed bungalow €64-130) This well-equipped camping ground is situated in the centre of the island. The two-bed bungalow is not available in August.

Miramare (☎ 0923 92 13 10; www.villaggiomiramare .it; Località Costicella; per person camp site €9-16.50, bungalow €37-62) This four-star camping ground has well-equipped bungalows and tent area. Its large playground and proximity to the beach makes it excellent for families.

Albergo Aegusa (☎ 0923 92 24 30; www.aegusahotel .it; Via Garibaldi 11, Favignana town; s €45-90, d €70-150; ⊠) An attractive converted palazzo with comfortable, well-furnished rooms right in the centre of Favignana. There is also a good restaurant in an outdoor courtyard.

our pick **Albergo Egadi** (☎ /fax 0923 92 12 32; www .albergoegadi.it in Italian; Via Colombo 17, Favignana town; s €50-100, d €100-200) It's a real treat staying at Albergo Egadi, with its lush beds, antique furniture and gushing showers. Decorated in French countryside style, the upstairs rooms have massive terraces and are painted in electric blues and salmon pinks. In addition, the sisters who run this small hotel are friendly and welcoming. The hotel also has the island's best restaurant (closed Wednesday and February), which specialises in a five-course tasting menu (€50 per head) that serves a different speciality each night. Advance bookings for the restaurant are essential in summer.

L'Approdo di Ulisse Club (☎ 0923 92 50 00; www .aurumhotels.it; Cala Grande; s €85-210, d €170-348, all incl full board; ⊠ ⊠) On the western side of the island, this place offers a series of white-washed bungalows set around the hotel's own private beach. The facilities here are excellent, and include a huge pool, tennis courts and professional diving courses. The price includes room, meals, drinks and sporting activities.

EATING & DRINKING

Not surprisingly, tuna is the thing to eat on the islands, served in a multitude of ways. The best restaurant is at Albergo Egadi (left), but the following places are also good.

La Tavernetta (☎ 0923 92 16 39; Piazza Madrice 54; meals €20-25) A popular restaurant with a terrace on the buzzing main square. Fish and seafood are the specialities here, as well as fresh pasta.

El Pescador (☎ 0923 92 10 35; Piazza Europa 38; meals €25-30; ⊠ closed Wed & Feb) A local favourite that rustles up great pasta dishes, nearly all with a fish theme. Try the *spaghetti con ricci*.

Zazzamita (Zona Cavallo; ⊠ 7pm-late) For a laid-back evening, grab a chair in the candlelit garden and enjoy the live music.

SHOPPING

There are plenty of shops that specialise in tuna-related products if you want to stock up on your way home from Favignana. One great little deli you should make a stop at is **Casa del Tonno** (☎ 0923 92 22 27; 12 Via Roma); it's not only filled to the rafters with smoked and canned bluefin tuna, it also sells a host of other fishy delicacies such as *bottarga* (roe) and sardines.

GETTING AROUND

A bicycle or a scooter is a very good way to get around Favignana, giving you access to all the little coves and beaches dotting the island. There are plenty of places offering bikes for hire, including **Il Noleggione** (☎ 0923 92 54 09; Piazza Matrice 29) and **Da Rita** (11 Piazza Europa). The standard hire charge for bicycles/scooters is €5/25 per day.

Tarantola run buses around the island (€1, eight daily) from Piazza Marina in Favignana town. There is a coastal route and an inland route, both of which leave from near the main port.

Levanzo

There are two main reasons to visit Levanzo: to examine the prehistoric cave paintings at the Grotta del Genovese, and to spend some time swimming off its pebbly beaches in the crystal-clear waters.

SIGHTS & ACTIVITIES

The Upper Palaeolithic wall paintings and Neolithic incised drawings at the **Grotta del Genovese** (Genovese Cave) were discovered by accident in 1949. Between 6000 and 10,000 years old, the images mostly feature animals; the later ones also include men and tuna. To get there, you can try to follow the path across the island, but be warned that it is rough going on your own. You can check with the custodian, **Signor Natale Castiglione** (☎ 0923 92 40 32, 0339 741 88 00; ncasti@tin.it; tour €6-15; ☺ 10am-1pm & 3-6pm), who is available for guided tours. You will find him in his souvenir shop on the elevated street directly behind the port. Alternatively, you can take the sea route by hiring one of the several sea taxis that advertise in the town's two bars: it should cost you €15 per person at most. The sea taxis can also be hired for trips around the island.

There are three great spots to go swimming, all a healthy walk from the town. To get to **Faraglione**, take a left through the town and walk about 1km west along the road until you see a couple of rocks sticking out of the water a few metres offshore. If you fancy something a little quieter, keep going until you get to **Capo Grosso**, on the northern side of the island, where there is also a lighthouse. Alternatively, take a right out of town and walk along the dirt road. The road forks 300m past the first bend; take the rocky path down towards the sea and keep going until you get to **Cala Minnola**, a small landing bay with crystal-clear water where, outside the month of August, you can swim in peace and tranquillity.

SLEEPING & EATING

There are two hotels in Levanzo.

Albergo Paradiso (☎ 0923 92 40 80; Via Lungomare; s €35-50, d €70-90; ✖) The most attractive place to stay, with a pretty geranium-clad terrace where you can eat well (meals €30 to €35). Rooms are simply furnished.

Pensione dei Fenici (☎ /fax 0923 92 40 83; Via Calvario 11; s €60-70, d €120-140, all incl half board; ℗ ✖) Right behind the Paradiso is the Fenici, a massive concrete block of a hotel with a cavernous dining hall. Rooms have a Spartan feel, but there are great views from the terrace.

There are a couple of small cafés where you can get coffee, snacks and gelato. There's also a small *alimentari* (grocery store) on Via Lungomare.

Marettimo

The most westward of the Egadi Islands, Marettimo is a collection of green mountain peaks and white-washed houses dipping into a little harbour packed with bobbing fishermen's boats. Marettimo is also the wildest and least developed of the islands. However, with the overfishing of tuna affecting fishermen's incomes, the villagers are starting to see the economic potential in tourism. This doesn't mean that you'll find it packed at any time of the year – on the contrary, this tiny island is pretty much wilderness personified – but more accommodation options have cropped up in the last few years.

Do note that the island virtually shuts down in the winter months.

ACTIVITIES

Marettimo is a perfect place for relaxation and swimming – there are good beaches at **Cala Sarda**, **Cala Nera** and stunning **Cala Bianco**. For fishing trips, contact the local fishermen's association, **San Giuseppe Association** (☎ 0923 92 32 90; www.isoleegadi.it/S.Giuseppe). You can also go walking in unspoilt nature; there's only one road on the island and not that many cars – the main mode of transport is electric carts.

SLEEPING

Marettimo's accommodation is mainly composed of apartments, though private rooms are an option. All the options listed following are in Marettimo town. Book in advance in the summer months, especially August.

Marettimo Residence (☎ 0923 92 32 02; www .marettimoresidence.it; Via Telegrafo 3; s €52-124, d €64-150; ✖ ✖) This small apartment complex shaded by bougainvillea and palm trees caters mostly to families. Each apartment comes with a full kitchen and a small porch, and there's a breakfast bar (€6 per person) that also serves coffee, water and juice all day. There's a small swimming pool and a barbecue area, and, if you're staying for longer than a week, the staff will do your laundry too. It's open year-round.

Le Conchiglie (☎ 333 12 13 66 3; www.leconchiglie .org in Italian; 2-person apt €80-100, 4-person apt €100-120; ☺ closed Nov-Apr; ✖) This newly built small block overlooking the port has apartments with well-equipped kitchens; some have small terraces. Options range from small studios to family apartments that sleep between four and six people.

WESTERN SICILY

You can contact **Rosa dei Venti** (☎ 0923 92 32 49; www.isoladimarettimo.it in Italian) if you wish to arrange private rooms or tours of the island. Expect to pay between €55 and €65 for a double in private accommodation, depending on the season.

EATING
Marettimo's restaurants are few but of a high quality.

ourpick Il Veliero (☎ 0923 92 32 74; Via Umberto 22; meals €30-35) A cosy, intimate restaurant that makes food like (you wish) your mother made it, only better, because the chef goes to the market daily, picking out the freshest catches. Thanks to his labours, you get to start with an octopus salad or marinated sardines, move onto fish couscous or a nice plate of spaghetti with *frutti di mare* (seafood), tuck into some grilled squid for a main, and have fruit or ice cream as your finale. Il Veliero sports its Slow Food Movement badge with pride and deserves every bit of it.

ourpick Il Timone (☎ 0923 92 31 42; Via Garibaldi 18; meals €35-40; ☺ closed Nov-Apr) Another Slow Food Movement champion, this family-run trattoria has the parents, son and daughter all working hard to prepare fabulously tasty food. The antipasti are delicious, mostly focusing on seafood – try the clam-and-mussel soup – and the fresh pasta is Il Timone's pride and joy. Try it in *busiate con i ricci* (short pasta with sea urchin meat), or with a sauce of swordfish and almonds. The mains are all about fresh fish and seafood.

Another recommended restaurant is **Il Pirata** (☎ 0923 92 30 27; Via Scalo Vecchio; meals €25-30), which also focuses on fresh fish and seafood dishes.

PANTELLERIA
pop 7300
Called Bint el-Rhir (Daughter of the Winds) by the Arabs, Pantelleria is characterised by jagged lava stone, low-slung caper bushes, dwarf vines and steaming fumaroles – as well as A-list celebrities and Italian fashionistas. What, you may wonder, is the attraction? Is it the remote location? The exoticism of an island known as the 'Black Pearl of the Mediterranean'? Or the simple fact that the island is breathtakingly beautiful? Drive around on a sunny day and the stunning visual juxtaposition of black lava stone against velvet green vineyards and psychedelic splashes of bougainvillea, all framed by the deepest blue sea, will probably explain it – you won't want to leave, either.

The Arabs settled here in the 8th century, leaving an indelible mark on the island with their odd, domed *dammusi* (low-level dwellings made of thick volcanic rock) to the rather un-Islamic cultivation of the zibibbo grape, used in the production of the local wine moscato di passito di Pantelleria. Many of their habits remain, with the result that Pantelleria is the only truly agricultural community remaining in the Med.

Orientation
Apart from Malta, this is the largest of the islands surrounding Sicily, so you'll need to use some kind of motorised transport to get around. The town of Pantelleria occupies the northwestern tip; the airport is 6km southeast of town. Most of the island's places of interest are along the southwestern and northeastern coasts.

Information
Banks can be found along Via Borgo Italia in Pantelleria town.
Agenzia Rizzo (☎ 0923 91 11 04; www.agenziarizzo .com; Via Borgo Italia 12) Come here for Siremar and Tirrenia tickets, or for accommodation in *dammusi*.
Ambulance (☎ 0923 91 11 10)
First Aid (☎ 0923 69 92 84; ☺ flight times) At the airport.
Internet Point (Via Dante 7; per 30min €6; ☺ 9.30am-1.30pm & 5-8.45pm) Youth centre with gaming machines and internet access.
La Cossira (☎ 0923 91 10 78; www.lacossira.it in Italian; Via Borgo Italia 19) Travel agency dealing with all flights off the island and *dammuso* lettings.
Police (questura; ☎ 0923 91 11 09)
Tourist office (☎ 0923 91 18 38; www.pantelleria.it in Italian; Piazza Cavour; ☺ 9.30am-12.30pm & 5.30-6.30pm Mon-Sat, 9-11am Sun) In a corner of the municipal hall. Good information on the island, and the website has a good range of *dammusi* to rent.
Valenza Libreria (Via Borgo Italia 69) Sells the book *L'ABC* (€7.80), which outlines walking itineraries and has a town plan tucked in the back. Also sells the most comprehensive map of the island (€7).

Sights & Activities
Pantelleria is less a place to see than to experience. Aside from the 16th-century **Castello Barabacane** (admission free; ☺ 6-8pm Jun-Sep), at the end of the harbour, there is little of interest in Pantelleria town – it was flattened during

WWII and rebuilt with modern, cube-shaped houses. The other main towns are Gadir (the prettiest of the towns), Rekale (in the remote south of the island) and Scauri (the island's second port). You can take in all the villages during a day's drive.

More curious are the island's natural phenomena, including the 24 **cuddie** (ancient craters of red volcanic rock) surrounding the main volcano, Monte Grande (836m), which dominates the centre of the island. At the summit is the **Stufa del Bagno di Arturo**, a steaming natural sauna, and the milky white **Specchio di Venere** (Mirror of Venus), where the bodies beautiful (most famously a pregnant Madonna) come to wallow in the volcanic mud; the Stufa del Bagno di Arturo can get extremely hot, so beware. Another of these milky turquoise lakes, much bigger in size and more accessible, is the **Bagno dell'Aqua** (Lago di Venere), which can be viewed from the ancient village of Bugeber. In August horse races are held around the lake.

If you can't face steaming caves, boiling mud baths and baking volcanic mountains, plunge into the cool green of the **Valle di Monastero**, south of Monte Grande, or the **Valle di Ghirlanda**, southeast of Monte Gibele. Both are carpeted by vines that are harvested in September. This is the perfect place for hiking or riding.

Also worth checking out are the *sesi*, massive Neolithic funeral cairns with low passages leading to the centre. The most impressive of them is the **Sese del Re**, about 15 minutes' walk south of the Cuddie Rosse on the northwestern coast. The island was once dotted with these mounds but over the years most were dismantled and the stones used in the construction of modern *dammusi*. These dwellings have been modelled on the *sesi*, with thick, whitewashed volcanic-rock walls and shallow cupolas keeping the inside nice and cool.

The island is equally famous for its secluded coves and sea grottoes, which are perfect for snorkelling and diving. The northeastern end of the island provides the best spots, with a popular **acquacalda** (hot spring) at Gadir. Boat excursions, such as those offered by **Minardi Adriano** (☎ 0923 91 15 02; Via Borgo Italia 5; day trips per person €20), are available at the dock and are the perfect way to visit some of the more inaccessible grottoes around the island. Divers should get in touch with **Green Divers** (☎ 0923 91 82 09; www.greendivers.it in Italian; Mursia), which

can arrange exciting archaeological dives and night-time dips.

Sleeping
HOTELS
Summer bookings should be made at least a month in advance.

Bue Marino (☎ 0923 91 10 54; Contrada Bue Marino; s €36-50, d €72-100) Roughly a 1km walk out of town, this small, intimate hotel has an impressive clifftop location. The restaurant is also good, and it sells a lot of the island's produce, including capers, oil and wine.

Albergo Papuscia (☎ 0923 91 54 63; www.papuscia .it in Italian; Corso da Sopra Portella 48, Localitá Tracino; s €42-70, d €84/140; ✖) Situated on the eastern side of the island, this lovely little *albergo* (hotel) in a typical *dammuso* is surrounded by a flower-filled garden. It's run by a mother and daughter, and the hotel's restaurant (meals €25 to €30) serves up Mamma's own cooking.

Hotel Mursia (☎ 0923 91 12 17; www.mursiahotel .it; Località Mursia; s €50-105, d €100-210; P ✖ ✪) Pantelleria's only large modern hotel has a waterfront location and all the expected facilities including two massive pools, tennis court, a diving centre and its own private beach. It also runs the Hotel Cossyra (singles €35 to €80, doubles €70 to €160), which is set back from the seafront and offers cheaper rooms; it also has a pool, parking and air-con.

RENTAL ACCOMMODATION
If you're in a group you should consider renting a *dammuso*.

our pick Zubeb Resort (☎ 0923 91 36 53; www .zubebi.it; Contrada Zubebi; 2–4-person apt €800-1600; P ✖ ▯ ✪) This is a beautifully styled complex made up of traditional *dammusi* overlooking the harbour. Inside, the décor is austerely minimalist, with smooth concrete walls and tactile Indian furnishings. There is also an uberstylish (though slightly impractical) crescent-shaped pool, a massage parlour inside an old Arab garden and on-site scooters. Each *dammuso* has its own cubbyhole kitchenette on its terrace.

Most bars and restaurants have notices advertising rentals. Expect to pay about €800 to €1500 per week for four people in August. **Agenzia Rizzo** (☎ 0923 91 11 04; www.agenziarizzo.com; Via Borgo Italia 12, Pantelleria town) organises renovated *dammusi* all over the island; a two-/four-bedroom apartment costs €800/1600.

Eating

Habibi Club (☎ 333 739 90 63; Località Mursia; couscous €14; ☾ evening Jul & Aug) Bookings are essential at this converted *dammuso* next to the Mursia Hotel. It only serves the famed fish couscous and it's all freshly prepared for you.

Il Cappero (☎ 0923 91 26 01; Via Roma 31, Pantelleria town; meals €25-30; ☾ closed Mon Oct-Apr) Wonderfully unpretentious, with excellent pasta and fish dishes. Try the local speciality, *ravioli con menta e ricotta* (ravioli with mint and ricotta cheese). Bookings recommended for Saturday.

Trattoria Favarotta (☎ 0923 91 43 47; Contrada Favarotta; meals €25-30; ☾ closed Wed & winter) Trattoria Favarotta has an excellent reputation for tasty, local fare including *spaghetti con pesto pantesco* (spaghetti with a tomato, garlic, pepper and basil sauce), and roast hare.

I Mulini (☎ 0923 91 53 98; Contrada Tracino; meals €30-35; ☾ closed Jan & Feb) Located in a converted mill, this is one of Pantelleria's best restaurants. The most famous dish on the menu is the *baci*, a dessert composed of crispy layers of pastry stuffed with ricotta.

Entertainment

Oxidiana (☎ 0923 91 23 19; Contrada Kuddie Rosse; ☾ 4pm-4am Jun-Sep) Pantelleria's only disco is full to the gunwales in summer. The building is built from black lava, which gives it an eerie atmosphere at night. It also runs a popular pizzeria.

Shopping

Pantelleria has a healthy supply of slips and sandals shops to cater for all those fashion victims. What you *should* stock up on is the island's own range of cosmetic products, Linea Cosmetica Lago di Venere, made from the mineral-rich mud of the Bagno dell'Aqua. They are available from **Il Mirto e la Rosa** (☎ 0923 91 19 21; Via Catania 3), just off Via Borgo Italia.

For all that sweet, sweet wine and jars full of pickles and preserves, excellent **La Nicchia** (☎ 0923 91 29 68; Via Messina 22) can cater to your every craving.

Getting There & Away

Pantelleria is 30 minutes by plane with Air Sicilia from Palermo (€28.50, one hour 20 minutes, one daily); **Air One** (☎ 848 84 88 80) and Alitalia fly from Rome (from €172). The local bus connects Pantelleria town with the **airport** (☎ 0923 84 12 22).

All boats arrive at the port in Pantelleria town. Ustica Lines has hydrofoils departing from Trapani (€34, 2½ hours, one daily) from June to September. Siremar also runs a ferry from Trapani (€30, five hours, one daily) and a fast boat from Mazara del Vallo (€34, 2½ hours, one daily) between June and September. There are reduced services from October to May, but they are dependent on the weather conditions.

For agents selling plane and ferry tickets, see p117.

Getting Around

Local buses (€0.85, Monday to Saturday) depart from Piazza Cavour in Pantelleria town at regular intervals and service all the towns on the island.

You can rent scooters and cars from **Autonoleggio Policardo** (☎ 0923 91 28 44; Vicolo Messina 35; per day scooters €10-25, Fiat Panda cars €15-40), just down the alley to the left of the Port Hotel as you approach from the harbour.

SALINE DI TRAPANI

Driving along the SS115 coast road between Trapani and Marsala you will find yourself in a bleached landscape of *saline* (shallow pools) and softly shimmering heaps of salt. Flat and featureless, the only interruption on the coastal saltpans are small *mulini* (windmills), which were used to grind the salt. The salt from these marshes is considered the best in Italy and has been big business since the 12th century; now, however, salt production has fallen off massively and only a cottage industry remains, providing for Italy's more discerning dinner tables.

SIGHTS & ACTIVITIES

The most attractive spot along the coast, where the saltpans glitter undisturbed by modern construction, is the **Riserva Naturale di Stagnone**, a noted wetlands area taking in the Stagnone Islands (Isole delle Stagnone) and the long arm of Isola Lunga, which protects the shallow waters of the lagoon.

In the foreground floats the site of ancient **Mozia** (also known as Motya or Mothia), on the tiny island of San Pantaleo. The island is connected to the mainland by a Phoenician road, which can be seen at a depth of 1m below the water. San Pantaleo was bought by

WESTERN SICILY

the amateur archaeologist Joseph Whitaker, who was intrigued by the unusual fragments of pottery that had been unearthed. He built a villa here, and spent decades excavating the island and assembling the unique collection of Phoenician artefacts that now appear in the museum. What his weekend archaeology revealed was one of the most important Phoenician settlements in the Mediterranean, coveted for its strategic position. It is also the best-preserved Phoenician site in the world as the Romans utterly destroyed Carthage, sowing the ground with salt so that no living thing should remain. You can take a pleasant stroll around the island, following the path to various excavations, including the ancient port and dry dock, where you can see the submerged road. Afterwards, visit the **Whitaker Museum** (☎ 0923 71 25 98; admission €6; ⏲ 9am-1pm Oct-Feb, 9am-1pm & 3-6.30pm Mar-Sep). Its main treasure is *Il Giovanetto di Mozia*.

On the mainland near the pier is the small **Museo Saline Ettore e Inferza** (☎ 0923 96 69 36; admission €3; ⏲ 9.30am-1.30pm & 3-7pm), a salt museum housed in an old windmill that shows a video of the whole salt-making process; it even runs its windmill from 4pm to 6pm Wednesday to Saturday. In summer, ask at the reception about renting canoes (€5 per hour) so that you can weave your way in and out of the saltpans.

SLEEPING & EATING

La Finestra sul Sale (☎ 0923 73 30 03; fax 0923 73 31 42; Contrada Ettore Infersa 55; s/d €100/130; 🅿) Run by the Museo Saline Ettore e Inferza, this spot has three lovely rooms located above a café, overlooking the saltpans, their windmills and San Pantaleo. The rooms are nicely decked out with terracotta floors and neat blue-and-yellow furnishings.

There is also a busy café opposite the pier, with outdoor tables overlooking San Pantaleo and the lagoon. It is a lovely place for an evening drink as the sun turns the saltpans rosy pink.

GETTING THERE & AWAY

San Pantaleo is accessible by a private boat (€3 return), which operates 9am to around 6pm; in winter, it only operates in the morning. To get to the embarkation point from Marsala, take local bus 4 from Piazza del Popolo (€4.25, 25 minutes, one daily Monday to Saturday).

THE SOUTHWEST

MARSALA
pop 78,000
Many know about its sweet dessert wines, but few people realise what a charmer the town of Marsala is. Elegant and full of stately baroque buildings, with a busy main square guarded by an imposing cathedral, tranquil Marsala is all about the simple pleasures – food, wine and, judging by the crowds in the square, lots of family fun.

Marsala was founded by the Phoenicians who escaped from Mozia. They settled here on Capo Lilibeo, calling their city Lilybaeon and fortifying it with 7m-thick walls that ensured it was the last Punic settlement to fall to the Romans. In AD 830 it was conquered by the Arabs, who gave it its current name Marsa Allah (Port of God).

It was here in 1860 that Garibaldi landed in his rickety old boats with his famous 1000-strong army, a claim to fame that finds its way into every tourist brochure in the city.

Orientation
The city of Marsala hugs a small promontory looking out onto the vast Mediterranean Sea. The old city is clustered around the tip, separated from the sea by Via Lungomare Boeo. The main entrance to the old city is through the Porta Nuova (New Gate) at one end of Viale Vittorio Veneto, which runs southeast from Via Lungomare Boeo. Alternatively, from Piazza Piemonte e Lombardo walk north along Viale dei Mille and enter the old city through the older Porta Garibaldi. Piazza della Repubblica is halfway up Via Garibaldi. You'll find the train station situated southeast of the old city.

Information
You'll find banks with ATMs all over the town of Marsala.
Ambulance (☎ 0923 95 14 10)
Biblioteca Comunale (Town Library; 100 Via XI Maggio; per hr €6; ⏲ 9am-1pm Mon-Fri, 9am-noon Sat) Has internet access.
Information booth (Via Lungomare Boeo; ⏲ 9am-2pm & 4-8pm Tue-Sun) Next to the Museo Archeologico Regionale Baglio Anselmi.
Ospedale San Bagio (☎ 0923 71 60 31; Piazza San Francesco; ⏲ 24hr)
Police (questura; ☎ 0923 92 43 71; Corso Antonio Gramsci; ⏲ 24hr)

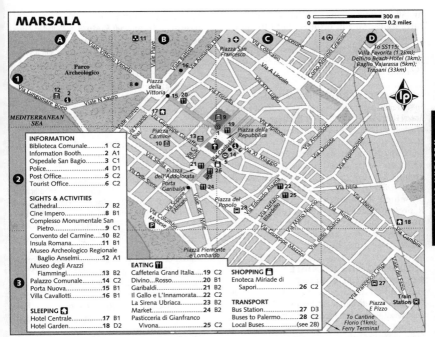

MARSALA

0 — 300 m
0 — 0.2 miles

MEDITERRANEAN SEA

Parco Archeologico

To SS115;
Villa Favorita (1.2km);
Delfino Beach Hotel (3km);
Baglio Vajarassa (5km);
Trapani (33km)

Piazza San Francesco

Piazza della Vittoria

Piazza Carmine

Piazza della Repubblica

Piazza dell'Addolorata

Porta Garibaldi

Piazza del Popolo

Piazza Piemonte e Lombardo

Piazza E Pizzo

To Cantine Florio (1km);
Ferry Terminal

Train Station

INFORMATION	
Biblioteca Comunale	1 C2
Information Booth	2 A1
Ospedale San Bagio	3 C1
Police	4 D1
Post Office	5 C2
Tourist Office	6 C2

SIGHTS & ACTIVITIES	
Cathedral	7 B2
Cine Impero	8 B1
Complesso Monumentale San Pietro	9 C1
Convento del Carmine	10 B2
Insula Romana	11 B1
Museo Archeologico Regionale Baglio Anselmi	12 A1
Museo degli Arazzi Fiammingi	13 B2
Palazzo Comunale	14 C2
Porta Nuova	15 B1
Villa Cavallotti	16 B1

SLEEPING	
Hotel Centrale	17 B1
Hotel Garden	18 D2

EATING	
Caffeteria Grand Italia	19 C2
Divino...Rosso	20 B1
Garibaldi	21 B2
Il Gallo e L'Innamorata	22 C2
La Sirena Ubriaca	23 B2
Market	24 B2
Pasticceria di Gianfranco Vivona	25 C2

SHOPPING	
Enoteca Miriade di Sapori	26 C2

TRANSPORT	
Bus Station	27 D3
Buses to Palermo	28 C2
Local Buses	(see 28)

Post office (Via Garibaldi; 8am-6.30pm Mon-Sat)
Just southeast of Piazza della Repubblica.

Tourist office (0923 71 40 97; Via XI Maggio 100;
8am-2pm & 3-8pm Mon-Sat, 9am-noon Sun) A
friendly tourist office with a good map and brochures.

Sights

MUSEO ARCHEOLOGICO REGIONALE BAGLIO ANSELMI

Marsala's finest treasure, and definitely
worth the trip alone, is the partially reconstructed Carthaginian warship in its **Museo
Archeologico Regionale Baglio Anselmi** (0923 95
25 35; Via Lungomare Boeo; admission €3; 9am-1.30pm
Mon, Tue & Thu, 9am-1.30pm & 4-6.30pm Wed & Fri-Sun).
The warship was sunk off the Egadi Islands
during the First Punic War nearly 3000 years
ago, and these delicate remnants are the only
remaining physical evidence of Phoenician
seafaring genius. The wreck was discovered
in 1971 in the Stagnone lagoon; it's actually
only a small part of the original ship, carefully
reconstructed to give an impression of what it
would have looked like. Manned by 68 oars-
men, the 35m-long warship is thought to have
been part of the Carthaginian fleet attacked by

the Romans in 241 BC at the Battle of Egadi.
If you visit here after viewing the excavations
on Mozia the ship resonates with history, providing a glimpse into a civilisation that was
extinguished by the Romans.

The exhibition also includes objects
found on board: ropes, ceramic fragments,
corks from amphorae, a brush and a sail-
or's wooden button. In an adjacent room are
two beautiful mosaics from the 3rd and 5th
centuries AD, as well as other bits and bobs
recovered from the nearby dig of the **Insula
Romana** (closed indefinitely), a 3rd-century
Roman villa.

PIAZZA DELLA REPUBBLICA

Walking or driving from Capo Lilibeo, you
will enter the historic centre through **Porta
Nuova**, a grand Renaissance arch that sets the
tone of the town. At the town's heart is the
elegant Piazza della Repubblica, dominated
by the imposing **cathedral**. Although started
in 1628, the church's façade wasn't completed until 1956 (courtesy of a cash donation by a returning emigrant). The cavernous
interior, divided into three aisles highlighted

by tall columns, contains a number of sculptures by the Gagini brothers but little else.

On the eastern side of the square is the arcaded **Palazzo Comunale** (Town Hall), formerly known as the Palazzo Senatorio (Senatorial Palace).

MUSEO DEGLI ARAZZI FIAMMINGI

Just behind the cathedral is the **Museo degli Arazzi Fiamminghi** (☎ 0923 71 29 03; Via Guiseppe Garraffa 57; admission €2.50; 🕑 9am-1pm & 4-6pm Tue-Sun), with its eight magnificent Flemish tapestries. They were made in Brussels between 1530 and 1550, and were gifted to the Marsala-born archbishop of Messina, Antonio Lombardo (1523–95), by Felipe II. Lombardo in turn presented them to the cathedral in 1589. Representing the Roman capture of Jerusalem from the Saracens, the tapestries have been carefully restored and are now on display across three dimly lit floors.

COMPLESSO MONUMENTALE SAN PIETRO & CONVENTO DEL CARMINE

Housed in a beautiful restored building, the **Complesso Monumentale San Pietro** (☎ 0923 71 87 41; Via Ludovico Anselmi Correale; admission free; 🕑 9am-1pm & 4-8pm) attracts locals and visitors alike. A former Benedictine monastery (dating from the 16th century), it has permanent exhibitions on Garibaldi, an archaeological section with an interesting fragment of a sculpture of Eros catching a ride on the back of a duck, and items from Lilibaeo's necropolis. Another area is dedicated to folk traditions.

Another attractive gallery is the restored **Convento del Carmine** (☎ 0923 71 16 31; Piazza Carmine; admission free; 🕑 10am-1pm & 5-7pm). Parts of the building date from 1155, when the Carmelites first came to Marsala with Roger I's widow Adelaide. After years of neglect and a spell as a police barracks, the convent has been returned to its former glory, and is now an art gallery and a centre for civil weddings.

OTHER SIGHTS

On the western edge of Piazza della Vittoria is the **Cine Impero** (Empire Cinema), a marvellous example of Italian futurist architecture popular during the Fascist era.

If you're travelling with small children, they might enjoy the **Villa Cavallotti**, a large park just outside Porta Nuova that has a playground and acres of space for a relaxing walk.

Festivals & Events

Processione del Giovedì Santo (Holy Thursday Procession) Held on the Thursday before Easter, this is Marsala's most important annual event and a centuries-old tradition. Actors depict the events leading up to Christ's crucifixion, and many children dress in colourful costumes as saints.

Marsala Jazz Festival Held in the historic centre in July, this festival is sponsored by Marsala wine companies and increasingly attracts major artists.

Sleeping

Marsala has few hotels situated within the city centre; most tend to be on the roads exiting the city.

Hotel Garden (☎ /fax 0923 98 23 20; Via Gambini 36; s/d with shared bathroom €35/45, d with private bathroom & air-con €55; P) A grey block of flats disguises this good old-fashioned *pensione*, run by a sweet old couple. It has neat, clean rooms with mismatched furnishing. Friendly, quiet and cheap.

Hotel Centrale (☎ 0923 95 17 77; www.hotelcentrale marsala.it; Via Salinisti 19; r per person €35; P ❄) A simple hotel in an excellent location near Porta Nuova. It's run by a friendly manager and the unexciting rooms, which all have a safe and fridge, are centred on an internal courtyard.

Delfino Beach Hotel (☎ 0923 75 10 76; www.delfinobeach.com; Via Lungomare Mediterraneo 672; s €45-75, d €65-130; P ❄ 🏊) At the turn-off to Petrosino, a mere 3km south of Marsala, is the sumptuous Delfino, situated on a wonderful sandy beach. Dotted around the gardens, the rooms are cheerfully decorated in blue and yellow and equipped with all modern amenities.

Baglio Vajarassa (☎ /fax 0923 96 86 28; www.bagliovajarassa.com; Contrada Spagnola 176; r per person incl half board €60) If you have your own car, the Vajarassa winery is a great choice. It's in a traditional manor house 6km north of Marsala, near Mozia, and has lots of good food, wine and traditional furnishings. There are only four rooms in the manor, so booking in advance is a good idea.

Villa Favorita (☎ 0923 98 91 00; www.villafavorita.com; Via Favorita 27; s €65-85, d €95-120; P ❄ 🏊) This slightly faded 19th-century villa is very popular with families. The accommodation is in small bungalows amid the huge landscaped gardens, and there is a good-sized pool; the hotel also has a good restaurant (opposite). You will find it on the SS115 as you enter Marsala from Trapani.

WINE, SWEET WINE

Fresh out of sherry country in southern Spain, John Woodhouse's 'sweet nose' knew a business opportunity when he smelt it. The soap merchant set up shop in Marsala to market the local wines to the seemingly insatiable sweet palate of 18th-century England, but the only problem was how to get the wine to England without it going bad? He added a dash of pure alcohol and, voila, Marsala's fortified wines were born.

The real success of the wines came when the British Navy used it as an alternative to port in order to supply the sailors' ration of one glass of wine per day. Nelson placed a huge order after the Battle of the Nile (1798), and by the 19th century other entrepreneurs wanted to get in on the action. Benjamin Ingham and his nephew, Joseph Whitaker, set up the first rival winery, exporting to the USA and Australia in 1806. The third big producer was canny Vincenzo Florio, who already owned the Egadi Islands and their lucrative tuna plants. All of the wineries were eventually bought by Cinzano in 1920, which merged them under the Florio label.

Eating

RESTAURANTS

Garibaldi (☎ 0923 95 30 06; Piazza dell'Addolorata 35; meals €20-30; closed Sat lunch & Sun evening) One of Marsala's Slow Food Movement electees, the Garibaldi is a traditional trattoria that serves a wide antipasti buffet; try the sun-dried tomatoes or the delicious *caponata* (a combination of tomatoes, aubergines, olives and anchovies). The *primi* (first courses) range from fish couscous to fresh pasta with seafood, while the mains are mainly about grilled fish. Don't miss a glass of sweet Marsala for the end.

Il Gallo e L'Innamorata (☎ 329 29 18 50 3; Via Stefano Bilardello 18; meals €35-40; closed Jul-Sep) Perfect for simple but fabulously delectable dishes, this fun little restaurant (another bearer of the Slow Food Movement badge) serves up fun starters such as *arancinette* (small deep-fried rice balls) stuffed with meat or fish, homemade ravioli, and fresh pasta with sardines or *ricci* (sea urchin meat). Tuna and swordfish dominate the mains; try the *involtini de pesce spada* (swordfish roulade stuffed with breadcrumbs). For dessert, try the *testa di Turco* (Turk's head; blancmange with puff pastry in the middle) or, if that's too sweet, go for a – you guessed it – glass of Marsala.

Villa Favorita (☎ 0923 98 91 00; Via Favorita 27; meals €35-40; 8-11pm) The most classy eating option in Marsala is the restaurant on the beautiful terrace of this Liberty-style villa. Eat beneath a canopy of tree branches and sample a whole range of dishes drenched in Marsala wine.

An excellent option in the historic centre, **Divino…Rosso** (☎ 0923 71 17 70; Via XI Maggio; pizzas €6.50-10; 7-11pm) is a restaurant-cum-wine bar serving superb pizza. Try the *prosciutto crudo con rucola* (Parma ham with rocket) or something with fresh tomatoes. Dine out on the pavement, overlooked by the imposing Palazzo Fici.

La Sirena Ubriaca (☎ 328 10 53 52 2; www.sicilywine.com; Via Garibaldi 39; aperitivi €8) is a great place for predinner aperitifs and snacks, with a fantastic selection of wine, olive oil, dips and other local delicacies. You can sit at the bar or at the outside tables, and taste the wine/oil/pesto, which you can later purchase.

CAFÉS

Pasticceria di Gianfranco Vivona (Via Stefano Bilardello 21; sweets from €1.50) One of the better places for sweets and traditional cakes. The almond biscuits are perfect for taking home.

Caffeteria Grand Italia (☎ 0923 95 68 28; Piazza della Repubblica 3; sandwiches €3.50; closed Sun) This is one of the most popular cafés in Marsala, though its customers are mainly in the 80-plus age bracket. It has a good-value *tavola calda* (hot table) and some mean ice creams.

SELF-CATERING

Marsala's open-air fresh produce **market** (morning) is held on a square off Piazza dell'Addolorata, situated next to the municipal offices.

Shopping

Marsala likes its wine (even the non-Marsala sort), and it's the best place to sample and purchase wines from the region. *Enoteche* can be particularly helpful in this regard.

Cantine Florio (☎ 0923 78 11 11; fax 0923 98 23 80; Lungomare Florio; 3-5pm Mon-Thu, 10am-noon Fri) On the road to Mazara del Vallo, this is the place to buy the cream of Marsala's wines.

Florio opens its doors to visitors to explain the process of making Marsala, giving them a taste of the products; fax to make a reservation for one of the tours. Take bus 16 from Piazza del Popolo.

Enoteca Miriade di Sapori (Via Garibaldi 30) This little *enoteca* offers good wines for tasting in convivial surrounds.

Getting There & Away

There are buses from Trapani (€3, 30 minutes, eight daily Monday to Friday), Agrigento (€10, four hours, three daily Monday to Saturday, one Sunday) and Palermo (€8, 2½ hours), but the best way to travel along this part of the coast is by train. Palermo buses arrive at Piazza del Popolo, off Via Mazzini, in the centre of town. All other buses stop at the bus station in Piazza E Pizzo, in front of the train station.

Regular trains serve Marsala from Trapani (€3, 30 minutes, 20 daily), Mazara del Vallo (€2.30, 20 minutes, 10 daily) and Palermo (€8, three hours, six daily).

Between June and September, **Sandokan** (☎ 0923 71 20 60, 0923 95 34 34) runs a service from Molo Dogana to the Egadi Islands (Favignana €5.30). Ustica Lines also runs daily hydrofoils to the islands (Favignana and Levanzo €5.30, to Marettimo €11.80).

MAZARA DEL VALLO
pop 50,700

Mazara's old quarter is like a North African kasbah (in fact, it's known as La Casbah), full of narrow little streets that go around each other, and sprinkled with magnificent baroque and Norman-period buildings. It's small enough that you won't ever really get lost, and the dilapidated old buildings give it a rugged charm (though some renovations would be welcomed). This little town is a fantastic spot to see Sicily's North African face, and to get away from the tourist trail almost completely.

Mazara was one of the key cities of Saracen Sicily and the North African influence is still strongly felt here – the town is said to have one of the highest percentages of immigrants in Italy, with hundreds of people from Tunisia and Maghreb arriving annually, mainly to work on Mazara's fishing fleet. Most of the immigrants live within the labyrinth of the old town streets, giving the town a really multicultural feel.

MAZARA DEL VALLO

INFORMATION	
Tourist Office..1	A3

SIGHTS & ACTIVITIES	
Castle...2	B4
Cattedrale del San Salvatore........................3	A4
Chiesa di San Nicolò Regale........................4	A3
Chiesa di Sant'Ignazio.................................5	A4
Museo Civico..6	A4
Museo del Satiro..7	A4
Museo Diocesano...8	A4

SLEEPING	
Foresteria Monastica San Michele Arcangelo...........9	B3
Hopps Hotel...10	B4

EATING	
Alla Kasbah..11	A3
Baby Luna..12	A4
Il Gambero...13	A4
Lo Scoiattolo...14	A4

TRANSPORT	
Agenzia Punica..15	B3
AST Bus Stop...16	A4
Ferry Terminal..17	A4
Lumia Bus Stop..18	B3
Siremar..19	A4

Orientation

Mazara's main street, Corso Umberto I, runs north–south from Piazza Matteotti down to Piazza Mokarta on the waterfront. La Casbah is in the old city, northwest of Piazza Mokarta. The train station is east of Corso Umberto I.

Information

Banks and ATMs can be found on Piazza Mokarta.

BeliceNet (☎ 0923 90 98 40; per 30min €3; Via Castelvetrano 4; ⏲ 9.30am-1pm & 4.30-9pm Mon-Sat) Has a good number of fast computers.

Tourist office (☎ 0923 94 17 27; www.comune .mazara-del-vallo.tp.it in Italian; Piazza Santa Veneranda; ⏲ 8am-2pm Mon-Sat, & 3-6pm Wed) In the historic centre.

Sights
MUSEO DEL SATIRO & MUSEO CIVICO
For a city that has such a rich history, Mazara's sights are few and sometimes badly maintained. The exception to this is the **Museo del Satiro** (☎ 0923 93 39 17; Piazza Plebiscito; admission €6; ⏲ 9am-2pm & 3-7pm), held in the deconsecrated shell of the Chiesa di Sant'Egidio.

Even if you drive into Mazara, curse the lack of signs and want to get the hell out of there, you must go to this museum and watch the fascinating video about its prize piece, the bronze statue *Il Satiro Danzante* (the Dancing Satyr). It is really exciting – don't peek at the statue before you see the video! In Italian, with English subtitles, it tells the story of how a bunch of fishermen, only 40km off the shores off Tunisia, pulled up the bronze leg of a statue. Time elapsed and they continued to fish there wondering if they would ever find the rest of the statue. Extraordinarily, they did in 1998. Overcome by romanticism, Captain Giuseppe Asaro tells the camera: 'Lying on the deck with its face turned to the sky, it looked like someone who'd clung on, waiting to be rescued'. What followed was 4½ years of painstaking restoration, during which time Mazara strenuously tussled with the powers in Rome to ensure the return of the city's satyr, which only came home in 2003.

And what a beauty. It is believed to be a rare original casting, and is the only statue of its kind depicting a bacchanalian satyr, dancing wildly like a whirling dervish, arms outstretched, head flung back, the centrifugal force evident in his flowing hair. It is supported by a clever internal structure that allows it to stand upright, towering over bemused tourists who try to sneak forbidden photos.

The **Museo Civico** (Civic Museum; ☎ 0923 94 17 77; Piazza Plebiscito 2; admission free; ⏲ 9am-1pm daily & 3-6pm Tue & Thu, 4-7pm Sat & Sun) is on the same piazza, and houses a small collection of sculpture, local paintings and Roman artefacts. Next to it is the baroque **Chiesa di Sant'Ignazio**.

PIAZZA DELLA REPUBBLICA
Nothing else in Mazara even comes close to the Museo del Satiro but it is pleasant enough to wander around the town, and the central piazza, Piazza della Repubblica, is an attractive set piece. Stick your head in the 11th-century **Cattedrale del San Salvatore** (Piazza della Repubblica; admission free), which was completely rebuilt in the 17th century in the baroque style. Over the portal is a relief from the 16th century of Count Roger trampling a Saracen. Inside, there is a heavily ornamented altar featuring the Transfiguration, surrounded by a bevy of statues by Domenico and Antonello Gagini, and stuccowork by Antonio Ferraro. In the chapel to the right of the altar is a rare 13th-century painted cross.

Other buildings on the square include the elegant, two-storey Seminario dei Chierici (dating from 1710); it houses the **Museo Diocesano** (Diocesan Museum; ☎ 0923 90 94 31; Via dell'Orologio; admission free; ⏲ 9am-1.30pm Mon-Sat), whose library contains a number of 18th-century texts.

NORMAN MONUMENTS & LA CASBAH
On Piazza Mokarta, the ragged remains of Count Roger's Norman **castle** have definitely seen better days, although their forlorn ruination is wonderfully atmospheric at night (when they are floodlit). The same goes for the twee little **Chiesa di San Nicolò Regale** (Porta Palermo; admission free), which overlooks the bustling fish market. A perfect cube, it has remained virtually unchanged since its construction in 1124.

Northwest of the church is **La Casbah**, a maze of tiny streets and alleyways that was once the heart of the Saracen city. The most important street was **Via Bagno**, the old city's main thoroughfare, which still has its *hammam* (public baths). Today, the area is run-down but interesting, if only because it retains a strong Arab connection through the Tunisians who now live here.

Sleeping
Mazara is a business town with few hotels.

Foresteria Monastica San Michele Arcangelo (☎ /fax 0923 90 65 65; www.foresteriasanmichele.com in Italian; Piazza San Michele Arcangelo 6; dm €15-30, d €30-50) Essentially a youth hostel, this central place is set in a converted monastery with a lovely exterior. Its rooms are simple, but have a kindly atmosphere. Enter at the side.

Hopps Hotel (☎ 0923 94 61 33; www.hoppshotel .it; Via G Hopps 29; s €52-68, d €75-95; P ⏲ ⏲) Set around a nice pool, this is a big, white, modern hotel with a good seafront location. Rooms are comfortable, with olive bedspreads and apricot walls, and the service is very friendly and efficient.

DETOUR: CAVE DI CUSA

From Castelvetrano take the SS115 south through wine-making country to Campobello di Mazara. Turn off at Principe-Torre Cusa to head for the Greek quarries, known as the Cave di Cusa (or Rocche di Cusa), where most of Selinunte's buttery yellow stone was hewn. The site is charming – overgrown and wild, it's the domain of foraging goats nibbling the wildflowers.

Round about are huge column drums forever awaiting transport to Selinunte. About 400m in from the gate are two carved columns ready for extraction. Around each is a gap of 50cm to allow the stonemason access to the column. When removed, the columns would have been transported to Selinunte across wooden logs by oxen or slaves. Archaeology aside, the site is perfect for a picnic.

Eating

Eating well in Mazara isn't much of a problem. Head to the public gardens on Via Lungomare Mazzini for a host of restaurants and bars, all with terraces overlooking the water:

Lo Scoiattolo (☎ 0923 94 63 13; Via Lungomare Mazzini; meals €20-25; ☽ closed Thu) This spot has reasonable prices and pretty good food. The antipasto buffet is a vegetarian dream, and the pasta and fish are good, too. Pizza is served in the evenings.

Il Pescatore (☎ 0923 94 75 80; Via Castelvetrano 191; meals €25-30; ☽ closed Mon) Gourmets gather at Il Pescatore, Mazara's best restaurant, to sample the delectable fish. The restaurant is an elegant affair and the service is impeccable.

Alla Kasbah (☎ 0923 90 61 26; Via Itria 10; meals €25-30; ☽ closed Mon) For something different, head to the historic centre. The fish couscous here is especially good here, as are the vegetarian dishes.

Also recommended are **Baby Luna** (☎ 0923 94 86 22; Via Lungomare Mazzini; meals €20-25; ☽ closed Mon) and **Il Gambero** (☎ 0923 93 29 32; Via Lungomare Mazzini; pizzas €6; ☽ closed Thu), both on the seafront.

Getting There & Away

AST has buses to Trapani (€4.40, 1½ hours, three daily), Marsala (€2.15, 25 minutes, two daily) and Castelvetrano (€1.65, 20 minutes, two daily). The AST bus stop is beside the train station; you can buy a ticket on the bus. Lumia also has buses serving Marsala, Trapani and Castelvetrano, leaving from Piazza Matteotti; buy your tickets at **Agenzia Punica** (Corso Vittorio Veneto) around the corner.

There are train connections every hour or so with Trapani (€4, 50 minutes), Marsala (€2.30, 20 minutes) and Castelvetrano (€2.15, 20 minutes). Coming from Palermo, you must change at Alcamo Diramazione (€3.85, one hour, 10 daily).

Siremar runs a fast boat to Pantelleria (€34, 2½ hours, one daily) between June and September.

CASTELVETRANO
pop 30,500 / elev 187m

On the road to Selinunte, Castelvetrano is of limited interest save for the small **Museo Civico** (☎ 0924 90 49 32; Via Giuseppe Garibaldi; admission €3; ☽ 9am-1pm & 3.30-7.30pm), home of the *Efebo di Selinunte*, a bronze statue of a young man from the 5th century BC. Up the street, on Piazza Garibaldi, is the 19th-century **Teatro Selinus** (admission free; ☽ 9am-1pm & 3.30-7.30pm), built by Giovanni Battista Basile as a smaller-scale model of the Teatro Massimo (p88), his Palermo masterpiece. It is built on the site of a hotel where Goethe stayed in 1787.

Those familiar with the story of the bandit Salvatore Giuliano might want to check out the completely unremarkable **courtyard** (Via Mannone 94-100) where his body was found in 1950. Norman Lewis gives a fascinating account of the macabre incident – when Giuliano's mother knelt on the ground to lick her son's blood from the paving stones – in his book *In Sicily*.

There are regular bus services to Castelvetrano from various places in the region and around it, including Agrigento (€4.40, two to 2½ hours, three daily Monday to Saturday), Selinunte (€0.77, 20 minutes, five daily Monday to Saturday) and Marsala (€2.40, one hour, three daily).

SELINUNTE

The ruins of Selinunte are some of the most impressive of the ancient Greek world, and the site is one of the most captivating in Sicily.

In its heyday, the huge city had over 100,000 inhabitants, and for two centuries it was one of the richest and most powerful cities in the world. The spectacular remains of its many temples are proof of its influence.

No visit to Selinunte is complete without a walk along the stunning stretch of beach below, from where there are marvellous views of the clifftop temples. The path down is to the left of the Acropolis parking area.

History

Selinunte was the most westerly of the Greek colonies, established by a group of settlers from nearby Megara Hyblaea in 628 BC. It had a wonderful location atop a promontory between two major rivers (now silted up), the Modione and Cottone, the latter forming a secure natural harbour. The plains around were overgrown with celery (*selinon* in Greek), so the Greeks named their new colony Selinunte.

Originally allied with Carthage, it switched allegiance after the Carthaginian defeat by Gelon of Syracuse at Himera in 480 BC. Under Syracusan protection it grew in power and prestige. The city's growth resulted in a litany of territorial disputes with its northern neighbour, Segesta, which ended abruptly in 409 BC when the latter called for Carthaginian help. Selinunte's former ally happily obliged and arrived to take revenge.

Troops commanded by Hannibal utterly destroyed the city after a nine-day siege, leaving only those who had taken shelter in the temples as survivors; these were spared not out of a sense of humanity but because of the fear that they might set fire to the temples and prevent their looting. In a famous retort to the Agrigentan ambassadors who sought to negotiate for the survivors' lives, Hannibal replied that as they hadn't been able to defend their freedom, they deserved to be slaves. One year later, Hermocrates of Syracuse took over the city and initiated its recovery. In 250 BC, with the Romans about to conquer the city, its citizens were relocated to Lilybaeum (Marsala), the Carthaginian capital in Sicily, but not before they destroyed as much as they could. What they left standing, mainly temples, was finished off by an earthquake in the Middle Ages.

The city was forgotten until the middle of the 16th century, when a Dominican monk identified its location. Excavations began

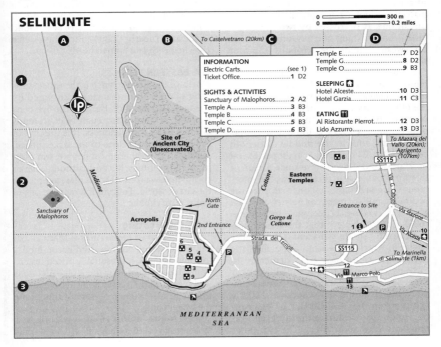

WESTERN SICILY

SELINUNTE

0 ——————— 300 m
0 ——————— 0.2 miles

To Castelvetrano (20km)

INFORMATION
Electric Carts.........................(see 1)
Ticket Office.............................1 D2

SIGHTS & ACTIVITIES
Sanctuary of Malophoros........2 A2
Temple A..................................3 B3
Temple B..................................4 B3
Temple C..................................5 B3
Temple D..................................6 B3

Temple E..................................7 D2
Temple G..................................8 D2
Temple O..................................9 B3

SLEEPING
Hotel Alceste.........................10 D3
Hotel Garzia..........................11 C3

EATING
Al Ristorante Pierrot.............12 D3
Lido Azzurro.........................13 D3

Site of
Ancient City
(Unexcavated)

To Mazara del
Vallo (20km);
Agrigento
(107km)

SS115

Modione

Cottone

Eastern
Temples

Entrance to Site

Via C. Caboto

Via Stazione

Sanctuary of
Malophoros

North
Gate

Acropolis

2nd Entrance

Gorgo di
Cottone

Strada dei Templi

SS115

To Marinella
di Selinunte (1km)

Via Alceste

Via Marco Polo

MEDITERRANEAN
SEA

in 1823, courtesy of two English archaeologists, William Harris and Samuel Angell, who uncovered the first metopes.

Orientation & Information

The archaeological site is divided into the acropolis, the ancient city, the eastern temples and the Sanctuary of Malophoros. It is spread out over a vast area dominated by the hill of Manuzza, the site of the ancient city proper. You can access the site via two entrances: one leads to the eastern temples, while the other requires a 15-minute hike across the depression known as the Gorgo di Cottone.

You can get information about the site at the **ticket office** (☎ 0924 4 62 51; adult/concession €6/3; ☺ 9am-1hr before sunset Mon-Sat, 9am-noon & 3-6pm Sun), near the eastern temples. Just behind the ticket office you can pick up an **electric cart** (per person €5). The carts take you around the whole site, dropping you off at each point and arranging a pick-up time to suit each person.

Sights

THE ACROPOLIS

The acropolis, the heart of Selinunte's political and social life, occupies a slanted plateau overlooking the now-silted-up Gorgo di Cottone. It is crossed by two thoroughfares – one running north–south, the other east–west, dividing the acropolis into four separate sections.

Huddled in the southeastern part are five temples (A, B, C, D and O). The northernmost is **Temple D**, built towards the end of the 6th century BC and dedicated to either Neptune or Venus. Virtually the symbol of Selinunte, **Temple C** is the oldest temple on the site, built in the middle of the 6th century BC. The stunning metopes found by Harris and Angell were once a part of this formidable structure, as was the enormous Gorgon's mask that once adorned the pediment; both of these can be viewed in the Museo Archeologico Regionale in Palermo (p85). Experts believe that the temple was dedicated to Apollo. Adjacent is the smaller **Temple B**, which dates from the Hellenistic period and could have been dedicated to the Agrigentan physiologist and philosopher Empedocles, whose water-drainage scheme saved the city from the scourge of malaria (a bitter irony for William Harris, who contracted the disease during the initial excavations and died soon after). The two other

temples, **Temple A** and **Temple O**, closest to the sea, are the most recent, built between 490 and 480 BC. They are virtually identical in both style and size, and it's been suggested that they might have been dedicated to the twins Castor and Pollux.

THE ANCIENT CITY

Occupying the hill of Manuzza, to the north of the acropolis, the ancient city, where most of Selinunte's inhabitants lived, is the least excavated of all the sites. Exploration of the area has only begun in recent years, and evidence suggests that survivors of the destruction of 409 BC may have used the city as a necropolis.

THE SANCTUARY OF MALOPHOROS

If you walk west from the acropolis across the now-dry river Modione (formerly the Selinon) and up a dirt path, you'll reach the ravaged ruins of the temple dedicated to Demeter, the goddess of fertility. Amid the debris, two altars can be made out; the larger of the two was used for sacrifices. Although they're not much to look at, these are some of the most important finds of the site as they provide an insight into the social history of Selinunte. Thousands of votive offerings to Demeter have been found in the area (nearly 12,000), including stelae crowned with real human heads.

THE EASTERN TEMPLES

North of the site entrance is the most stunning of all Selinunte's ruins, crowned by the majestic **Temple E**. Built in the 5th century BC and reconstructed in 1958, it stands out due to its completeness. It is the first of the three temples close to the ticket office. **Temple G**, the northernmost temple, was built in the 6th century BC and, although never completed, was one of the largest temples in the Greek world. Today it is a massive pile of impressive rubble.

Sleeping & Eating

The nearest town to the ruins is Marinella di Selinunte, where you can find accommodation and a couple of reasonably priced restaurants. The restaurant at the Hotel Alceste is well regarded and serves an extensive menu; there are also plenty of restaurants along the beachfront.

Hotel Alceste (☎ 0924 4 61 84; www.hotelalceste.it; Via Alceste 21; s €45-60, d €70-90; P ✿) This small family-run hotel has an excellent restaurant and tidy rooms decked out with pine furnishings. It is within walking distance of the archaeological park, and the rooms on the upper floors have sea views.

Hotel Garzia (☎ 0924 4 60 24; www.hotelgarzia.com; Via Antonio Pigafetta 6; s €50-100, d €90-120; ❄) This modern hotel is very close to the ruins and is situated right on the seafront within easy reach of the restaurants. Excellent value.

Al Ristorante Pierrot (☎ 09244 62 05; Via Marco Polo 108; meals €25-30) This place does a fantastic buffet and good fish, and it's so popular that you can hear the contented hubbub down the road.

Lido Azzurro (☎ 0924 4 62 11; Via Marco Polo 51; meals €30-35; ❄ closed Mon) Teetering right above the water, Lido Azzurro is also recommended.

Getting There & Away

AST and Salemi buses link Marinella di Selinunte to Castelvetrano (€0.77, 20 minutes, five daily), which can be reached by Lumia buses from Agrigento, Mazara del Vallo and Trapani. If travelling by car, take the Castelvetrano exit off the A29 and follow the brown signposts for about 6km. If you're driving from Agrigento, take the SS115 and follow the signposts.

Tyrrhenian Coast

This is holiday central. The coastal stretch between Palermo and Milazzo, which takes in the small town of Termini Imerese and gorgeous Cefalù, is a constant succession of resorts, beaches and towns that live and breathe for the Italian tourist industry. During August, when the whole of Italy goes on holiday (and prices jump sky-high), the beaches and hotels here are tightly packed with vociferous families and youngsters. One of the most attractive spots for a day or two is the beautiful town of Cefalù, despite the summer crowds – though it advertises itself as a traditional fishing village, its popularity as a holiday destination is second only to Taormina.

But it's not all sun, sea and stentorian voices: move away from the coast and you'll discover an intriguing and less tourist-inundated interior that encompasses two massive natural parks dotted with tiny mountain villages with a quiet and old-fashioned air. Stretching across the Madonie and Nebrodi mountains, and taking their names from the ranges, the parks are a haven if you love walking and bird-watching. Add to this the slightly cooler temperatures and rustic accommodation options that offer locally produced food, and you might just forget about the beach altogether.

If the pull of the surf is too strong, however, head east of Cefalù for the coast's best beaches, which are clean, unpolluted and relatively uncrowded (except in August), especially around Capo d'Orlando and Capo Tindari, the location of the gorgeously sited ruins of Tyndaris. At the end of this stretch of coast is Milazzo, with its apocalyptic power station and its port for the Aeolian Islands; while it's often overlooked by tourists, it has some lovely unspoilt coastline on its narrow peninsula.

HIGHLIGHTS

- Discover enchanting **Cefalù** (p134): swim at its long sandy beach, admire its beautiful medieval town and sigh over the magnificent mosaics in the Duomo
- Go walking in the **Parco Naturale Regionale delle Madonie** (p139)
- Lose yourself in the huge **Parco Regionale dei Nebrodi** (p142)
- Explore the isthmus, fine castle and very good waterfront restaurants at **Milazzo** (p146)
- Take the pilgrimage trail to **Tyndaris** (p145) and enjoy the best views on this coast

PALERMO TO CEFALÙ

A part of greater Palermo, this stretch of coastline shares the city's deep history and is the site of ancient Phoenician settlements – Solunto, Termini Imerese and Caccamo – and the ruins of Greek Himera. East of Palermo, beyond ancient Solunto (see p100), is the beautiful Capo Zafferano, the first stretch of the Tyrrhenian Coast. It's a bit of a mess both visually and conceptually, ending up as an unhappy mix that's part resort, part industrial zone. Yet the grotty edge is softened with the dramatic backdrop of Monte Calogero (1326m) and the brilliant waters that lap the very foot of this intense urbanisation.

TERMINI IMERESE
pop 26,800

The town dates from prehistoric times, though its name is derived from the two neighbouring Greek settlements of Thermae and Himera. The latter was destroyed by the Carthaginians in 409 BC and its inhabitants moved to Thermae, which was then renamed Thermae Himerensis. The town flourished for another 150 years, ruled for a time by local boy Agathocles, who went on to bigger and better things as the first tyrant of Syracuse. It was then taken by the Romans in 252 BC and became a famous Roman spa. Until the 19th century, Termini Imerese was enclosed within a set of protective walls but it has since spilled out into the outlying countryside. The largely industrial growth has somewhat spoilt the town's appearance and, unless you want to immerse yourself in the therapeutic waters for a few days, you may not want to spend much time here once you've seen the sights.

Orientation & Information

Like so many of Sicily's older settlements, Termini Imerese has an upper and lower town. The upper half is where you'll find all of the sights of interest, while the lower half is home to the town's hotels and day-to-day activity. The train station is southeast of the town centre along the coast; all buses arrive and depart just in front of the train station.

The **tourist office** (☎ 091 812 82 53; Piazza del Duomo; ☺ 9am-1pm & 3.30-6pm Mon-Fri) is in the town hall on the main square.

Sights

At the heart of the upper town is **Piazza del Duomo**, the original Roman forum, dominated by the 17th-century **cathedral** (admission free; ☺ 9am-7pm). The façade was designed to display four 16th-century-saint statues, and although the statues that now adorn it are copies, you'll be able to find the originals inside in the third chapel, on the north side. This chapel also contains sculptures from the Gagini school. In the fourth (southern) chapel there is a wonderful relief by Ignazio Marabitti, *Madonna del ponte* (Madonna of the Bridge).

Opposite the cathedral is the **Museo Civico** (☎ 091 812 82 79; Via del Museo; admission free; ☺ 9am-1pm & 3.30-5.30pm Tue-Sun), established in 1873. It has different sections devoted to archaeology, art and natural history.

Backed up against the museum is the **Chiesa di Santa Maria della Misericordia** (Church of Our Lady of Mercy). The entrance is off Via Mazzini, which heads west from Piazza del Duomo. Inside is a marvellous triptych of the *Madonna con Santi Giovanni e Michele* (Madonna with Saints John and Michael; 1453), attributed to Gaspare da Pesaro.

Northwest of the cathedral, down Via Ianelli, is the **Chiesa di Santa Caterina**, home to a very good fresco of the *La Vita della Santa Caterina d'Alessandria* (Life of St Catherine of Alexandria) by Giacomo Graffeo. The church keeps very irregular hours; check at the tourist office or at the church itself. From here there are some lovely views of the citrus groves and the sea beyond; there are also good views off Via Belvedere, north of the cathedral.

Just beyond the Chiesa di Santa Caterina are the public gardens of **Villa Palmieri**, laid out in 1845. Inside are the remains of a public building known as the Curia, which was built sometime during the 2nd century AD, and the faint traces of the town's Roman amphitheatre.

To see something of Termini's famous mineral baths, check into the Grande Hotel delle Terme (p132).

Festivals & Events

Termini Imerese celebrates **Carnevale**, Sicily's oldest festival, in February. Decorated floats and enormous papier-mâché figures parade the streets.

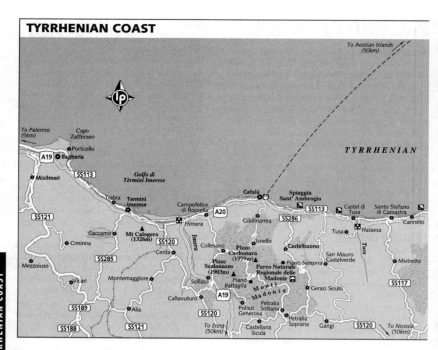

TYRRHENIAN COAST

Sleeping & Eating

Hotel Il Gabbiano (☎ 091 811 32 62; www.hotel gabbiano.it; Via Libertà 221; s €62-75, d €88-110; **P** ⌧) Only 90m south of the train station, the Gabbiano has recently had a timely face-lift, resulting in a modern little hotel. The rooms are well decorated, each with its own balcony, simple but tasteful furniture, writing desks, and facilities such as wi-fi access and satellite TVs.

Grand Hotel delle Terme (☎ 091 811 35 57; www .hotelbenessere.it; Piazza Terme; s €83-130, d €130-220; **P** ⌧ ⌧) This lovely Art Nouveau building nestled in a pine wood houses the remaining marble baths of the Roman spa, as well as a gym and a pool. Enjoy the plush rooms and take to the waters with recuperating Italians.

The selection of restaurants in Termini Imerese is surprisingly poor for a resort town. However, two fair options are the fish restaurant **La Petite Marseilles** (Via Porta Erulea; meals €25), above the Grand Hotel delle Terme, and **Da Giovanni** (Via Nogara 4; meals €25), a friendly trattoria (informal restaurant) in the lower city.

Getting There & Away

SAIS Autolinee (☎ 091 617 11 41) runs buses Monday to Saturday between Termini Imerese and Palermo (€2, 30 minutes, six daily) and Cefalù (€3, 30 minutes, four daily).

The best way to get here is by train. The town is a stop on the Palermo–Messina and Palermo–Agrigento lines; there are departures every 20 minutes from Palermo station (€2.65, 30 minutes).

CACCAMO
pop 8500 / elev 521m

Lorded over by its imposing **castle** (admission free; ☉ 9am-noon & 3-5.30pm), the hilltop town of Caccamo is a popular day trip from Termini Imerese or Cefalù. A Carthaginian stronghold that served as a constant thorn in Himera's side, the town wasn't officially founded until 1093, when the Normans began building the castle on a rocky spur overlooking a cliff. The castle was enlarged by the Chiaramontes in the 14th century and is now one of Italy's largest. The best parts are the walls and original fortifications, which included some ingenious traps for any intruder who might have breached the

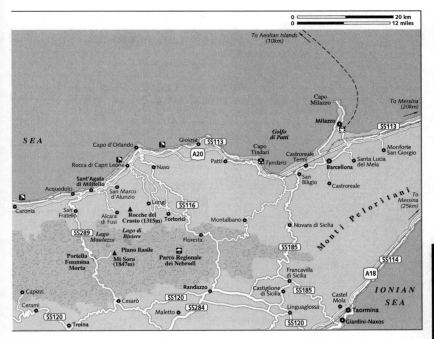

outer perimeter. Unsurprisingly, there are fabulous views of the surrounding countryside.

Since the 1950s, the town has lost almost half of its inhabitants to emigration, but you'd never know it wandering through the traffic-filled streets. The attractive 11th-century cathedral was remodelled twice, in 1477 and 1614. Inside, the sacristy has some lovely carvings of the *Madonna con bambino e angeli* (Madonna with Child and Angels) and *Santi Pietro e Paolo* (Saints Peter and Paul), both by Francesco Laurana.

On the left-hand side of the cathedral is the **Chiesa dell'Anime del Purgatorio** (Church of the Souls of Purgatory), featuring some fine stuccowork in the eastern end and an 18th-century organ. A local tour guide is almost always on hand to explain the history of the church and guide you downstairs to the musty catacombs.

A great place for lunch is **La Castellana** (☎ 091 814 86 67; Piazza del Monumento 4; meals €25), located in the grain stores of the castle. It has a great atmosphere and an inexpensive menu, dishing up local favourites such as pasta with fennel. It also does pizzas in the evening.

To get to Caccamo, take the bus from in front of the train station in Termini Imerese (€2.80, 30 minutes, 14 daily Monday to Saturday).

HIMERA

Founded in 648 BC by Greeks from Zankle (now Messina), **Himera** (admission free; 🕒 9am-6pm) was named after the river Imera, which flows nearby. It was the first Greek settlement on this part of the island and was a strategic outpost on the border of the Carthaginian-controlled west. In 480 BC the town was the scene of a decisive battle, with the combined armies of Theron of Agrigento and Gelon of Syracuse defeating a sizable Carthaginian army led by Hamilcar, who threw himself on the funeral pyre of the Carthaginian dead in a heroic act of self-immolation. The Carthaginians had intended to take Himera and then wrest control of the island from Greek hands, but the Greek victory put an end to all that. As for Himera, in 409 BC it paid the price for Carthage's defeat, when Hamilcar's nephew Hannibal destroyed the town in revenge for his uncle's death.

Compared with other Greek sites around the island, the remains here are disappointing. The only recognisable ruin is the **Tempio della Vittoria** (Temple of Victory), a Doric structure supposedly built to commemorate the defeat of the Carthaginians. Whatever its origin, Hannibal did a good job of destroying it. To the south of the temple is the town's necropolis, currently under excavation.

Some artefacts recovered from the site are kept in the small **antiquarium** (☎ 091 814 01 28; admission €2; ☽ 9am-6pm Mon-Sat, 9am-1pm Sun), about 100m west of the site's entrance (it's up a small lane off the other side of the main road). Although the more impressive pieces are in Palermo's Museo Archeologico Regionale (p85), you can see well-sculpted lion-head spouts that were used to drain water off the temple's roof.

Buses (€1.60, 15 minutes, four daily Monday to Saturday) run from in front of the train station in Termini Imerese, 8km to the west of Himera.

CEFALÙ

pop 13,800

If you've seen Giuseppe Tornatore's *Cinema Paradiso*, one of the classics of Italian cinema, you'll remember the charming town it was filmed in – yep, it was Cefalù. The town is so pretty and picturesque it'll knock your socks off, though you won't be alone in admiring its beautiful squares, streets and churches, for every year Cefalù becomes more like its competitor resort town, Taormina, with hundreds of tour buses emptying onto the streets for a day of photo snapping and ooh-aahing.

It's no wonder that crowds descend upon the town, especially considering that, as well as its unspoilt medieval streets and historic sights, Cefalù has a fantastic sandy beach running almost the entire length of the town. Add to that the fact that it is just over an hour by train or bus from Palermo, and you get what is now the top spot on the Tyrrhenian Coast. But despite the crowds, the town's fantastic location, backed up against the towering mass of a crag known simply as La Rocca (the Rock), gorgeous architecture and atmospheric streets make it a lovely spot for a few days of swimming, sunbathing and strolling.

ORIENTATION

The focus of all activity in historic Cefalù is Corso Ruggero and the alleys that branch off it. The working port, which is also the dock for hydrofoils, is on the eastern side of La Rocca.

From the train station take any of the opposite roads (north) down to Via Roma, then turn right to reach Via Matteotti, which heads directly into the old town centre. If you are heading for the beach, turn left from the station and walk along Via Gramsci, then take a right down Via N Martoglio and Via Vazzano, which will bring you to the western end of the *lungomare* (seafront promenade).

INFORMATION

Bookshops

Antica Cartolibreria del Corso (☎ 0921 42 30 96; Corso Ruggero 98) A large newsagent on the main drag that sells foreign-language newspapers, books about Cefalù and maps.

Emergency

Ambulance (☎ 0921 42 45 44)
Police (questura; ☎ 0921 92 60 11; Via Roma 15)

Internet Access

Internet access is sorely lacking in Cefalù. You'll have to wait a while before you get access to a computer.

Bacco on Line (☎ 0921 42 17 53; Corso Ruggero 38; per 30min €3) Only one computer; it's also a very nice deli and wine shop.
Vodafone (☎ 0921 92 39 70; 122 Corso Ruggero 122; per 30min €3) One computer, long waits but, eventually, fast connection.

Medical Services

Farmacia Battaglia (☎ 0921 42 17 89; Via Roma 13; ☽ 8am-1pm & 4-8pm Mon-Sat)
First Aid (☎ 0921 42 36 23; Via Mazzini 8)
Hospital (☎ 0921 92 01 11; Contrada da Pietra Pietrapollastra) On the main road out of town in the direction of Palermo.

Money

There are plenty of ATMs in town along Corso Ruggero and one in Piazza del Duomo. It's not a good idea to exchange money at any of the *cambio* (exchange) booths around town as they generally charge higher commissions than banks. The post office changes money, and the rates are pretty good.

Banca di Sicilia (Piazza Garibaldi 2)
Banca S Angelo (Via Roma) Has an exchange office.

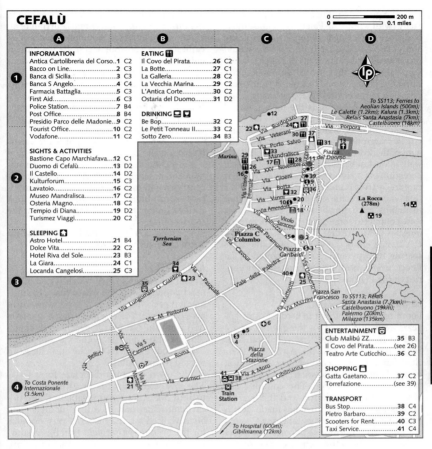

CEFALÙ

TYRRHENIAN COAST

Post

Post office (Via Vazzana 2; 8.30am-6.30pm Mon-Fri, 8.30am-12.30pm Sat)

Tourist Information

Presidio Parco delle Madonie (0921 92 33 27; www.parcodellemadonie.it in Italian; Corso Ruggero 116; 8.30am-1.30pm & 4.30-7.30pm Mon-Sat) The official office for the Madonie park. It has leaflets on walking and driving tours, and you can buy the 1:50,000 *Madonie/Carta dei Sentieri e del Paesaggio* map (€1).

Tourist office (0921 42 10 50; www.cefalu-tour.pa .it; Corso Ruggero 77; 8am-7.30pm Mon-Sat, 9am-1.30pm Sun) English-speaking staff, lots of leaflets and good maps.

SIGHTS

Most of Cefalù's sights are within the picturesque old town, and though you'll have to walk a little to get to La Rocca, it is worth it for the fabulous views.

Duomo di Cefalù

Along with the Cappella Palatina and the Cattedrale di Monreale, this is the final jewel in the Arab-Norman crown. Legend has it that the **duomo** (0921 92 20 21; Piazza del Duomo; donations appreciated; 8am-noon & 3.30-7pm) was built by Roger II in the 12th century to fulfil a vow to God after his fleet was saved during a violent storm off Cefalù; however, it is more likely the result of Roger's tempestuous relationship with the Palermitan archbishopric. Eager to curb the growing influence of the papacy in Sicily (with whom the Palermo archbishopric had close ties), Roger thought that building a mighty church so far from Palermo would prove an effective smack in the chops. Hardly surprising then that, from the outside, the cathedral looks more like a massive fortress.

Inside, in the central apse, a towering figure of Christ All Powerful is the focal point of the elaborate Byzantine mosaics. In his hand he holds an open Bible bearing a Latin and Greek inscription from John 8:12: 'I am the light of the world; he who follows me shall not walk in darkness.' It is easily the best mosaic depiction of Christ in Sicily, and the artist has captured a truly human expression on Christ's face – no mean achievement considering that these mosaics, dating between 1150 and 1160, were completed some 20 to 30 years before the mosaics of Monreale.

You can enjoy the view of the cathedral's soaring twin pyramid towers, framed by La Rocca, over a morning coffee or evening aperitif in the Piazza del Duomo.

La Rocca

Looming over the town **La Rocca** (278m) appears a suitable home for the giants that are said to have been the first inhabitants of Sicily. It was here that the Arabs had their citadel until 1063, when the Norman conquest brought the people down from the mountain to the port below. The combination of this dramatic backdrop and the narrow Moorish streets of the town has made Cefalù a popular film set, most notably for *Cinema Paradiso*. An enormous staircase, the **Salita Saraceno**, winds up through three tiers of city walls in a 30-minute climb to the summit. From here you have wonderful views of the town below, whilst nearby the 4th-century **Tempio di Diana** (☼ 24hr) provides a romantic getaway for young lovers. Apart from a few loose rocks there is nothing left of the **Il Castello**, a Norman castle that once crowned the rock's peak, or the Arab citadel.

The steps are to the right of the Banco di Sicilia on Piazza Garibaldi. From here the way is clearly signposted.

Other Sights

Off the Piazza del Duomo is the private **Museo Mandralisca** (☎ 0921 42 15 47; www.museomandralisca.it; Via Mandralisca 13; admission €6; ☼ 9am-8pm). Its collection of Greek ceramics and Arab pottery is rather faded, with the notable exception of the *Ritratto di un uomo ignoto* (Portrait of an Unknown Man; 1465), Antonello da Messina's earliest known portrait. His smirk is almost as enigmatic and thought provoking as the Mona Lisa's – but without the attendant hype.

Turn left outside the museum and walk down Via Mandralisca towards the sea. On Via Vittorio Emanuele is the **lavatoio**, a 16th-century wash house built over a spring that was well known in antiquity.

The town's other main sight is the **Osteria Magno**, on the corner of Corso Ruggero and Via Amendola. This imposing 14th-century mansion has been heavily renovated over the centuries and today is only open for temporary art exhibitions. If you want to get a look inside at other times, ask for the keys at the tourist office.

For great sea views, head to **Bastione Capo Marchiafava**, off Via Bordenaro.

ACTIVITIES

Cefalù's crescent-shaped beach is one of the most popular along the whole coast. In summer it is packed so be sure to get down early to get a good spot. You can rent a beach umbrella (€3) from the bar on the beach; deck chairs (€5) are also available. Some sections of the beach require a ticket, but the area closest to the old town is public.

The town is a splendid place for a walk. The lovely little port is lined with narrow fishing boats, and you might find the occasional fisherman mending his nets. The boardwalk along the beach is very popular for the evening *passeggiata* (stroll); in summer the cafés and restaurants that line it are almost always full.

COURSES

Cefalù is well known for its language courses. **Kulturforum** (☎ 0921 92 39 98; www.kulturforum.it; Corso Ruggero 55) runs Italian courses of one to four weeks, plus French and German courses; a one- to two-week Italian course costs €160 to €280. Private lessons can also be arranged.

TOURS

From Cefalù port, **Turismez Viaggi** (☎ 0921 42 12 64; Corso Ruggero 83; adult/child half day €20/10, full day €50/25; ☼ half day 9.30am-1.30pm & 2.30-6.30pm, full day 7.30am-7.30pm) runs personalised tours and excursions along the coast; the full-day tour includes lunch on the boat.

SLEEPING

Between June and August cheap accommodation is like gold dust and there is no such thing as value for money. It is essential to book ahead at this time.

The good news is that out of season (between October and April) the hotels that remain open drop their rates substantially, some even by half. Unless otherwise indicated, the accommodation listed following is open year-round.

Costa Ponente Internazionale (☎ 0921 42 00 85; Località Contrada Ogliastrillo; camp sites per tent/person €5/8; P ⬛) Situated 4km west of the town, this camping ground is one of the best-maintained sites in Sicily. It has a tennis court and a swimming pool, and is in a shady spot. To reach it, take the bus from the train station heading for La Spisa, or follow the SS113 if you are in a car. Note: the train tracks run directly behind the camping ground.

Locanda Cangelosi (☎ 0921 42 15 91; www.locanda cangelosi.it; Via Umberto I 26; s with shared bathroom €25, d with shared bathroom €35-40) This private house is the cheapest place in town – and with only four rooms, you will have to book in advance. If the owners run out of rooms in the house, they have a couple of apartments nearby. Rooms are clean and simple, and there is a shared TV room.

Dolce Vita (☎ 0921 92 31 51; www.dolcevitabb.it; Via Bordonaro 8; s €25-50, d €45-110; ⬛ 🖵) A lovely little B&B that has to be booked in advance during the summer months, the Dolce Vita has only five rooms, all of which are airy and light, with nice, comfy beds. You can have your breakfast on the roof terrace and enjoy the sweeping sea views. There's the added bonus of internet access too.

La Giara (☎ 0921 42 15 62; fax 0921 42 25 18; www .hotel-lagiara.it; Via Veterani 40; s €47-90, d €55-130; ⬛) This small place, set on top of an old house off Corso Ruggero, has a perfect location – it's within spitting distance of Piazza del Duomo. It is fairly comfortable, and the reception is efficient and friendly. Better value out of season.

Astro Hotel (☎ 0921 42 16 39; www.astrohotel .it; Via Roma 105; s €60-100, d €80-200; P ⬛) This three-star hotel is convenient for the train station and only 100m from the *lungomare*, but its rooms could do with a facelift sometime soon. The hotel has its own private beach, which can help justify the high-season prices.

Kalura (☎ 0921 42 13 54; www.hotel-kalura.com; Via Vincenzo Cavallaro 13, Località Caldura; s €70-140, d €80-270; P ⬛ ⬛) This small resort-style hotel has been managed by the same family for over 30 years. Situated on a rocky outcrop, it has its own private beach and most rooms have good views. It is a good choice for families, with tons of activities – mountain bikes, canoes and pedalos, scuba diving and riding – and a large pool.

Hotel Riva del Sole (☎ 0921 42 12 30; www.rivadelsole .com; Via Lungomare G Giardino 25; s €90-150, d €145-170; P ⬛) Situated right on the beachfront next to a string of restaurants, this ugly modern hotel has fair rooms and great views. There is also a garden and a swinging disco.

Le Calette (☎ 0921 42 41 44; www.lecalette.it; Via Vincenzo Cavallaro 12, Località Caldura; r per person incl half board €95-150; P ⬛ ⬛) On the eastern side of the headland, about 2km out of town, Le Calette is set in its own grounds above a pebbly beach, and is a very good-looking place. It offers a number of different excursions and has promotional offers for families.

A beautiful option only 7km from Cefalù is the Relais Santa Anastasia (see p140 for details).

EATING

Although the town is packed with restaurants, the food can be surprisingly mundane. Still, there are a few spots that stay ahead of the crowd. The restaurants overlooking the sea (on Via Vittorio Emanuele) have sea-view terraces on the rocks for outdoor dining. Most restaurants fill up between 8.30pm and 10pm, so book your table in advance (a few hours' notice is sufficient).

Il Covo del Pirata (Via Vittorio Emanuele 59; sandwiches & snacks €4-6) A cheap spot for a quick lunch. Il Covo serves sandwiches, a limited number of pasta dishes and filling salads. Ask for a seat on the tiny terrace overlooking the port. At night it turns into a club (p138).

L'Antica Corte (☎ 0921 42 32 28; Corso Ruggero 193; tourist menu €11.90; 🕑 closed Thu) Housed in a lovely old *cortile* (courtyard), this is one of the better restaurants in town but it can get very busy.

EATING ON THE CHEAP

A cheap alternative to restaurant eating is to grab some supplies and eat at Bastione Capo Marchiafava (opposite).

Go for a plate of traditional Sicilian pasta or a simple pizza.

La Vecchia Marina (☎ 0921 42 03 88; Via Vittorio Emanuele; tourist menu €18; ☒ closed Tue & Nov) Overlooking the cute little fishermen's beach, this is the best fish restaurant in town. It serves an array of freshly caught beauties, which you can enjoy with a delightful view.

La Botte (☎ 0921 42 43 15; Via Veterani 6; pasta €20; ☒ closed Mon) Although it doesn't have a sexy beachfront location, this eatery just off Corso Ruggero continues to send out good food. It has excellent antipasti and pasta dishes, and its house special, *casarecce alla botte* (short pasta with a meat sauce), is good if you fancy a change from fish.

Ostaria del Duomo (☎ 0921 42 18 38; Via Seminario 5; mains €25; ☒ closed Mon) Right on Piazza del Duomo, with outdoor tables facing the cathedral, Ostaria del Duomo seems as if it would be the most overpriced restaurant of them all. But this tavern serves up beautifully prepared food at very reasonable prices, and there's live piano music for that extraromantic touch. Simple, tasty, fresh ingredients and an excellent wine list.

our pick La Galleria (☎ 0921 42 02 11; Via XXV Novembre 22-24; meals €25-30) A new restaurant, café, gallery and bookshop, La Galleria is a lovely space with a big, elegant garden and excellent cuisine. Try its antipasto of marinated fish, and for starters go for the risotto with asparagus or the fresh tagliatelle with prawns, cherry tomatoes and crushed pistachio. The mains, which usually consist of grilled fresh fish, are palate-bendingly good. We recommend a glass of sweet Marsala for an ending with style.

DRINKING

Cefalù has a number of pretty good bars that are popular in summer.

Le Petit Tonneau II (☎ 0921 42 14 47; Via Mandralisca 66; ☒ closed Tue Oct-Mar) Just down from the Museo Mandralisca is this French-owned bistro (the name means 'Little Tuna') that's fun for a late-night drink.

Be Bop (☎ 0921 92 39 72; Via Botta 4; ☒ 11am-4am, closed Mon Oct-Mar) An English-style pub with live rock and pop music on summer weekends.

Sotto Zero (Via Lungomare G Giardino) A very cool bar at the beginning of the *lungomare*. Its Buddha Bar–inspired décor is dreamy: seating on low cushions, stairs covered in soft carpets and candles, and the sound of the sea lapping

below. A great place for aperitivi, cocktails and chatting till late. During the day, the stairs lead to the beach beneath.

ENTERTAINMENT
Nightclubs

Club Malibú ZZ (☎ 3470405132; www.zetazetaitalia.it; Via Lungomare G Giardino; entry €10, free for women before 1am; ☒ 10pm-3am Aug, 10pm-3am Wed-Sun Sep-Jul) Cefalù's hottest club and the place where Palermitans often flock in the summer, Malibú is full of youngsters keen on big nights out. With lots of decent DJs and plenty of cocktail swigging, the party really gets heaving in August. The best place to go if you're after a good night's dancing.

Il Covo del Pirata (Via Vittorio Emanuele 59) This is the town's version of an 'alternative' club, with soul, hip-hop and beats played by DJs nightly throughout the summer (music from 10.30pm).

Puppet Theatre

Teatro Arte Cuticchio (☎ /fax 0921 42 22 30; www.teatroarte-cuticchio.com; Corso Ruggero 92; tickets €5.50; ☒ performances 6.30pm Wed, Sat & Sun) Cefalù's *opera dei pupi* (puppet theatre) is run by the Cuticchios of Palermo (see p95). There is also a small puppet museum (admission €2.60; open 9am to 1pm and 4pm to 10pm).

SHOPPING

Like Taormina, Cefalù is something of a shopping snare. The medieval streets are lined with jewellery boutiques and some very good delis where you can stock up on wine and oil – but beware, as much of it is overpriced.

One very good place is **Torrefazione** (☎ 0921 92 23 48; Corso Ruggero 120), which stocks olive oil, freshly ground coffee, preserves, wine, liqueurs and a good range of locally made biscuits and nougat. Very different is **Gatta Gaetano** (☎ 0921 42 31 56; Corso Ruggero 152), a tiny cubbyhole of a shop full of strong-smelling Madonie cheese and some extraordinary gourmet pastas.

GETTING THERE & AWAY

Buses run from outside the train station Monday to Saturday. **SAIS Autolinee** (☎ 091 617 11 41) buses service Palermo (€4.50, one hour, two daily) and Termini Imerese (€3, 30 minutes, three daily).

The best way of getting to and from Cefalù is by train, which links Cefalù with

Palermo (€4, one hour, half-hourly) and virtually every other town on the coast.

You can also get a hydrofoil from Cefalù to the Aeolian Islands between 1 June and 16 September. **Ustica Lines** (www.usticalines.it) has hydrofoils that depart Cefalù for Alicudi at 8.10am (€14.50, one hour, one daily), then serves all the other islands. During the same period, Ustica Lines runs hydrofoils to/from Palermo (€12.60, one hour, one daily). You can buy tickets at **Pietro Barbaro** (☎ 0921 42 15 95; Corso Ruggero 82).

GETTING AROUND

Cefalù is small enough to walk around. If you find yourself heading further afield, a **taxi service** (☎ 0921 42 25 54) operates out of Piazza della Stazione, next to the train station. Rates depend on where you want to go, but a 5km trip, for instance, should cost no more than €5. Be sure to fix the rate before you leave.

If you are driving, parking can be a problem. You should be able to find somewhere on the roads that run parallel to the long beach southwest of the town centre.

Scooters for Rent (☎ 0921 42 04 96; www.scootersforrent.it; Via Matteotti 13b; per day/week 50cc Vespas €25/175, mountain bikes €10/45) rents out bikes as well as scooters.

PARCO NATURALE REGIONALE DELLE MADONIE

This 40,000-hectare nature reserve, between Palermo and Cefalù, incorporates the Madonie mountain range and some of the highest mountains in Sicily after Mt Etna (the highest peak in the Madonie is Pizzo Carbonara at 1979m). Established in 1989 by the Regione Sicilia, the park also takes in numerous small towns and villages, and plenty of farms and vineyards. It is an area where people live, rather than simply a nature reserve, so you can combine walking with visits to some of its more interesting towns, such as Castelbuono and lovely Petralia Soprana. Also worth exploring is the small town of Gibilmanna, where there are some good walking trails.

In summer, the Madonie is a popular destination for Palermitans armed with picnic baskets, who tend to make a day of wandering or driving through the expanse of the park. In winter it is the only place in Sicily, other than Etna, where you can go skiing.

Orientation & Information

From Termini Imerese head east for 22km along the coastal SS113 to Campofelice di Roccella and then turn off for Collesano, 13km inland. From Cefalù it is even easier: just follow the directions for the Santuario di Gibilmanna (Sanctuary of Gibilmanna), 14km to the south.

The body responsible for the park is **Ente Parco delle Madonie** (☎ 0921 68 40 11; www.parcodellemadonie.it in Italian; Corso Paolo Agliata 16, Petralia Sottana; ☺ 8.30am-1.30pm & 4.30-7.30pm Mon-Sat), which has its headquarters (the Presidio) in Petralia Sottana and a branch office, **Presidio Parco delle Madonie** (☎ 0921 92 33 27; Corso Ruggero 116; ☺ 8.30am-1.30pm & 4.30-7.30pm Mon-Sat) in Cefalù. The offices have details about the park and several one-day walks, as well as information about transport and accommodation. They also stock the 1:50,000 *Madonie/Carta dei Sentieri e del Paesaggio* map, which highlights the region's walking trails.

Getting There & Away

Getting around the Madonie by bus can be a time-consuming business, but **SAIS** (☎ 091 616 60 28) does run services from Palermo to Cefalù and from Cefalù to most of the mountain towns, including Castelbuono, Geraci Siculo, Gangi, Isnello and Gibilmanna. The most frequent services run to the larger town of Castelbuono (€1.80, 45 minutes, seven daily Monday to Saturday, two Sunday) and the popular Gibilmanna (€1.20, 20 minutes, three Monday to Saturday, morning only).

If you are planning on travelling in the Madonie consider renting a car for a couple of days from Cefalù or Palermo – this will give you the freedom to enjoy the scenery and walking more freely.

GIBILMANNA

The main reason most people visit Gibilmanna is to appreciate the wonderful view from the belvedere in front of the 17th-century **church**. You can see the superb spread of the Madonie and the peak of Pizzo Carbonara. While you're in town, you will probably meet a few visitors who have come on a pilgrimage to pray at the elaborately decorated baroque **Santuario di Gibilmanna**, a shrine to the Virgin Mary. During the shrine's coronation on 17 August 1760 (a day which also marked the official consecration of the church), the Virgin is supposed to have shown signs of life, namely restoring sight to two blind worshippers and speech to a mute. The miracle was later confirmed by the Vatican and consequently, the church is one of Sicily's most important shrines.

CASTELBUONO
pop 9600 / elev 423m
Castelbuono is the capital of the Madonie and has a lovely setting amid ancient manna ash and chestnut forests. It is known as the town of the Ventimiglias, a powerful noble family who ruled the town between the 14th and 16th centuries.

Castelbuono is serviced by a helpful **tourist office** (☎ 0921 67 11 24; www.comune.castelbuono.pa.it in Italian; Via Umberto).

In 1316, Francesco I Ventimiglia built the absolutely enormous **castle** (☎ 0921 67 12 11; Piazza Castello; admission €2; ☒ 9am-1pm & 4-8pm Tue-Sun) that gave the town its name (from *castrum boni*), and which soars above the golden patchwork of houses. The castle is divided into areas that cover archaeology, and the castle's and Castelbuono's history (with religious artefacts and jewellery), and several rooms are dedicated to modern and contemporary art exhibitions; sadly, none of the paintings is marked or explained.

The castle is supposed to be haunted by Queen Constance Chiaramonte, who it is said runs along the corridors, regular as clockwork, every first Tuesday of the month. Right in the heart of the castle is the extraordinary **Cappella di Sant'Anna** (Chapel of St Anne), containing some of the greatest stuccowork of Giacomo and Giuseppe Serpotta.

The other excellent sight in Castelbuono is the **Museo di Mina Palumbo** (☎ 0921 67 65 96; Via Roma 52; adult/concession €6/3; ☒ 9am-1pm & 3-7pm), named after the naturalist Francesco Minà Palumbo. His collection gives an exhaustive insight into the Madonie mountains, and their botany, natural history, minerals and archaeology.

Relais Santa Anastasia (☎ 0921 67 22 33; www.santa-anastasia-relais.it; Contrada Santa Anastasia, Castelbuono; d/ste €200/350; ☒ ☒) is a simply gorgeous 12th-century abbey – superlatives are not enough to describe it. Set among working vineyards, and

with an ancient cobbled courtyard straight out of a storybook, the abbey boasts beautiful rooms, exquisite attention to detail, and fabulous food and wine from the vineyards. It is 9km from Castelbuono in the direction of Cefalù.

our pick Nangalarruni (☎ 0921 67 14 28; Via Alberghi delle Confraternite 5; meals €35; ☒ closed Wed) is famous throughout Sicily for its exquisite mountain dishes of mushrooms and roast meats, including wild boar. Try its mushroom-and-warm-polenta cake for starters, then move onto a light plate of pasta with pistachios, cherry tomatoes, basil, mint and garlic. Your main should definitely be the wild boar and potatoes with porcini mushroom sauce. The wine list is excellent – you're in for a real treat.

Also recommended is **Romitaggio** (☎ 0921 67 13 23; Contrada da San Guglielmo, Castelbuono; meals €25-30; ☒ closed Wed), located in an ancient Benedictine monastery 4km from Castelbuono on the San Guglielmo road.

Two of the best delis in Castelbuono are **Fiasconaro** (www.fiasconaro.com; Piazza Margherita 10; cakes & snacks from €1.50), home of *mannetto* (manna cake), a local speciality, and **Antica Gelateria del Corso** (Corso Umberto 46; cakes & snacks from €1.50), maker of *testa di Turco* (Turk's head; blancmange with puff pastry in the middle), chocolate-covered almonds and tasty ice cream. All products are handmade and delicious.

PIANO BATTAGLIA
More Swiss than Sicilian, the little ski resort at Piano Battaglia (near Pizzo Carbonara) is dotted with chalets that play host to an ever growing number of Sicilian downhill skiers in winter.

The Mufara (northern slopes) skiing complex goes up to heights of 1856m and serves 3.5km of runs, while the Mufaretta (southwest slopes) reaches 1657m, with a run about 500m long. There are two ski lifts up to the ski runs. You can also do cross-country and alpine skiing.

With the advent of spring and summer Piano Battaglia becomes an equally good walking area, with plenty of signposted paths. One such walk starts at the Rifugio Ostella della Gioventù Piero Merlino (opposite) in Piano Battaglia and heads north-northwest taking in Pizzo Scalonazzo (1903m) and Pizzo Carbonara to end in an area of oak woodland at Piano Sempria (1300m). All the hostels listed here can help you with itineraries and guides.

Luigi Orestano (☎ /fax 0921 66 21 59; www.rifugi orestano.com/orestano; Località Piano Zucchi; r per person incl breakfast/full board €28/45), approximately halfway between Piano Battaglia and Cefalù, is run by the friendly Mogavero family and is open year round. Its guides can help you with trails and itineraries, and the website is a good source of information on the mountains.

Closed for refurbishment at the time of research, **Rifugio Giuliano Marini** (☎ 0921 64 99 94; www.palermoweb.com/caipalermo/cai_rifugio.html in Italian; Località Piano Battaglia; r per person incl half/full board €23.50/28.50) is right at Pizzo Carbonara, with chalet-style rooms and good facilities. It also rents out ski equipment (skis and boots per day €26).

Rifugio Ostello della Gioventù Piero Merlino (☎ 0921 64 99 95; www.rifugiopieromerlino.it; Località Piano Battaglia-Mandria Marcate; r per person €30, incl full board €50) is an alpine chalet with wood-panelled rooms and classic mountain décor. It's not quite a youth hostel in the proper sense, because it caters to all visitors. It also has eating and drinking areas, and lots of info on cycling and walking.

PETRALIA SOPRANA
pop 3650 / elev 1147m
Beautifully positioned at the top of a hill above a tree line of pines, Petralia Soprana (from the Italian word *sopra*, meaning 'on' or 'above') is one of the best-preserved little towns in north-central Sicily, with rough stone houses and curling wrought-iron balconies brimming with geraniums. It is also the highest village in the Madonie. At the heart of the main square is Piazza del Popolo, a WWI memorial built by Antonio Ugo in 1929. The most beautiful church in town is the 18th-century **Chiesa di Santa Maria di Loreto**, at the end of Via Loreto, off the main square. Inside is an altarpiece by Gagini and a *Madonna* by Giacomo Mancini. To the right of the church through an arch is the town's belvedere. The **cathedral**, off Piazza dei Quattro Cannoli, was consecrated in 1497 and has an elegant 18th-century portico.

PETRALIA SOTTANA
pop 3310 / elev 1000m
Below Petralia Soprana, the town of Petralia Sottana (from the Italian *sotto*, meaning

'under') is the gateway to the Madonie and the headquarters of the **Ente Parco delle Madonie** (☎ 0921 68 40 11; www.parcodellemadonie .it in Italian; Corso Paolo Agliata 16; ☺ 8.30am-1.30pm & 4.30-7.30pm Mon-Sat), which supplies maps and walking itineraries in the park. It is another quiet country town with a clutch of churches, including the **Chiesa Matrice**, which towers above the town.

Rustic and welcoming, **Albergo Il Castello** (☎ 0921 64 12 50; www.il-castello.net in Italian; Via Generale di Maria 27; s/d €40/65; ▣) is a sweet stone-built hotel with shuttered windows and simple but comfortable rooms.

The tiny, traditional **Trattoria-Pizzeria 'da Salvatore'** (☎ 0921 68 01 69; Piazza San Michele 3; pasta & pizza €6-8; ☺ closed Tue) has an open wood-fire pizza oven and bags of semolina propped up around the place. There is no menu at lunchtime, but the generous antipasto of grilled vegetables, pungent cheeses and olives is delicious. Pizzas are an evening-only affair, and a very popular one at that.

POLIZZI GENEROSA
pop 4080 / elev 917m
At the start of the Imera valley, Polizzi Generosa is a charming town that was given the nomenclature *generosa* (generous) by Frederick II in the 1230s. The town is a trekking base for the Madonie, and is riddled with churches that are often shrouded in mist. One sight worth visiting is the **Chiesa Madre**, with a Flemish depiction of the *Madonna and Child with Angels* from the early 16th century, and a *Madonna of the Rosary* by Guiseppe Salerno.

It's a good idea to pick up some pastries from **L'Orlando** (Via Rampolla 1; pastries from €1) and satisfy your sweet tooth while you stroll.

CEFALÙ TO MILAZZO

The 83km stretch of coastline between Cefalù and Capo d'Orlando to the east is dotted with little coves, clean beaches and a couple of resorts that are quite popular, including the ceramics centre of Santo Stefano di Camastra and Sant'Agata di Militello. Beyond Capo d'Orlando the coast becomes more developed and industrialised the closer you get to Milazzo, the main point of departure for the Aeolian Islands. Inland lies the rugged, wooded 85,000-hectare Parco Regionale dei

Nebrodi, the largest and most inaccessible of Sicily's surviving forest communities.

CASTEL DI TUSA
pop 3400 / elev 600m

About 25km east of Cefalù, just inside the province of Messina, is this little resort village. Just above the town (at 600m) are the ruins of the **castle** that gave the resort its name. A small road (9km) leads inland to the parent village of **Tusa**. Between the coastal resort and the village you'll see a signpost for **Halaesa**, a Greek city founded in the 5th century BC. Beautifully positioned on a hill, it commands fine views of the surrounding countryside and – on a clear day – the Aeolian Islands. The most conspicuous remains are those of its agora (marketplace) and its massive, rusticated walls. Just down the hill are the barely recognisable remains of a small theatre. The site was first excavated in the 1950s and again in 1972, but nothing has been done since then.

Atelier sul Mare (☎ 0921 33 42 95; www.ateliersul mare.it; Via C Battisti 4; s €50-65, d €70-100, art room €70-105) was designed by local artists who some years ago caused village controversy with their Fiumara d'Arte (Art in the River) project, which saw large, provocative sculptures embedded in the river – and you too can be part of the living art by staying in this hotel. Each 'art room' is an artistic installation, and you can stay in a different room each night if the hotel isn't full. Thankfully the artists don't play with your food like they do with your mind – the restaurant is very good.

The town is served by frequent trains from Palermo (€6.45, 1¼ hours), Cefalù (€2.15, 20 minutes) and Messina (€7.10, 2½ to three hours).

SANTO STEFANO DI CAMASTRA
pop 4600

About 8km east of Castel di Tusa, Santo Stefano di Camastra is a popular bus-tour stop on account of its bustling ceramics industry, which grew up as a result of numerous clay quarries in the hills above the town. Until 1693 the town was further up the hill and was called Santo Stefano di Mistretta; it was destroyed by a landslide in 1692 and a new town was built closer to the coast.

If you're interested in the process of manufacturing ceramics, you can pop your head into the **Museo Civico delle Ceramiche** (Civic Museum of Ceramics; Palazzo Trabia, Via Palazzo; admission free; ☒ 9am-1pm & 4-8pm) stationed towards the sea.

SANT'AGATA DI MILITELLO
pop 12,900

This relatively new town (founded in the 18th century), 30km east of Santo Stefano di Camastra, is a popular resort and a gateway for the Parco Regionale dei Nebrodi. In summer it's usually crammed with Italian holiday-makers eager to make the most of the nice long stretch of beach. The only sight really worth mentioning is the **Chiesa del Carmelo**, in the centre of town, which has a handsome 18th-century gable. If you're heading into Nebrodi, you may want to visit the **Museo Etno-Antropologico dei Nebrodi** (☎ 0941 72 23 08; Via Cosenz 70; admission free; ☒ 9am-noon Mon-Fri), which has some information on the area, including maps.

There are only two hotels in town, **Hotel Parimar** (☎ 0941 70 18 88; Via Medici 1; s/d €35/55) and **Roma Palace Hotel** (☎ 0941 70 35 16; hotelroma@tiscalinet .it; Via Medici 443; s/d €36/67), both of which offer reasonable, if unexceptional, accommodation.

You can get here by frequent trains from Milazzo (€6.85, 1¼ hours). There is also an ISEA bus from Catania (€10.55, 2½ hours, one daily Monday to Saturday).

PARCO REGIONALE DEI NEBRODI

The Nebrodi park was established in 1993 and constitutes the single largest forested area in Sicily. In fact, this is Sicilian author Gesualdo Bufalino's real 'island within an island', so long cut off from the outside world that Nebrodi villagers still retain something of their French-Lombard dialect.

The forest ranges in altitude from 1200m to 1500m, and is an undulating landscape of beech, oak, elm, ash, cork, maple and yew trees that hide the remnants of Sicily's wildlife: porcupines, San Fratello horses and wildcats, as well as a healthy population of birds of prey such as golden eagles, lanner and peregrine falcons and griffon vultures (recently reintroduced into the park). The high pastures have always been home to hardworking agricultural communities that harvest delicious mushrooms, churn out creamy ricotta, and graze cows, sheep, horses, goats and pigs.

The highest peak in the park is Monte Soro (1847m), and the Lago di Biviere is a lovely natural lake supporting herons and stilts. The

TYRRHENIAN COAST

few villages in the park each have something to offer and represent an authentic insight into traditional Sicilian life.

Information

Finding information on this park is very difficult. Few, if any, general tourist offices keep any information on the area, while the park's visitors centres are relatively inaccessible to anyone relying on public transport. The most useful centre for information is the **park office** (☎ 095 69 60 08; Strada Nazionale) in Cesarò, which stocks publications on the park and maps, including the Touring Club Italiano *Parco dei Nebrodi* map. There is a second **information office** (☎ 0941 79 39 04; Via Ugo Foscolo 1) in Alcara di Fusi. For more information, see www.parks.it /parco.nebrodi or www.parcodeinebrodi.it (in Italian).

Sights & Activities

If you take the enchanting SS289 from Sant'Agata di Militello you will arrive at San Fratello after about 18km. This typical Nebrodi town was originally founded by Roger I's third wife, Adelaide di Monferrato, for her Lombard cousins (thus the strange local dialect). The church was founded in the 12th century, **Santuario del SS Fratelli**, still survives. The town is renowned for its esoteric **Festa dei Giudei** (Feast of the Jews), which takes place on Maundy Thursday and Good Friday. Continuing on the SS289 you will pass Monte Soro (1847m) on your left-hand side and eventually arrive at Cesarò and the park office.

Another route through the park heads east from Sant'Agata di Militello on the road to Capo d'Orlando, then takes the first turn-off inland, towards **San Marco d'Alunzio**. San Marco was founded by the Greeks in the 5th century BC and was later occupied by the Romans, who named it Aluntium. At the town's entrance is the spectacularly situated **Tempio di Ercole** (Temple of Hercules), which has terrific views over

---

THE LAKE CIRCUIT WALK *Emily Coles*

Take the SS289 to Portella Femmina Morta (the ISEA bus from Catania and Sant'Agata di Militello stops at Villa Miraglia, just 300m to the south). Just before the pass (on the northern side) take the forest track that heads east. The track winds through wood and meadow, with tantalising glimpses of Mt Etna in the distance, climbing gently to meet the main road at Portella Calacudera (1562m), a little more than 1km later.

Here the route divides: the left fork goes to Lago Maulazzo and the right is signposted 'Monte Soro'. Take the right-hand fork and continue along a sealed road that climbs up through a hunting reserve. Higher up are views to Troina and Enna.

About 1km before the summit, just as the road begins a tight curve to the south, turn off to the left and head along a leafy track. After 50m the track passes through a wooden gate, then a second, as it descends north then east through a thicket of beech trees. Stay on the main track and cross two streams, then head through a third gate. The trail starts to head north again as the wood opens out into a small meadow, then swings back east to cross another stream with a paved crossing. Shortly afterwards the trail forks. Take the left, descending track, which opens out onto another magnificent view of Mt Etna. Five minutes later you will reach the meadow of Piano Basile, where on a fine day you can see the outline of Rocche del Crasto to the north.

Continue to the end of the meadow, where there is a T-intersection with a north–south cart track. Follow this track left (north), descending steeply through more woodland for 2km to the shores of Lago di Biviere. As it nears the lake the trail opens out onto a grassy slope and swings left to meet a track running parallel to the shore's edge. Go left to pass a small tile-roofed building, then turn almost immediately right onto a track that leads to the lake's edge. This is a perfect spot to kick off your shoes and have a sandwich. You can walk around the lake on a track that heads southeast (20 minutes).

To return to the walk's starting point, head for the western end of the lake, cross the fence next to the lake track and walk across the small field to a cart track that follows the northern edge of Lago di Biviere. Turn left (west) here for Lago Maulazzo (5km, one hour); when you reach Lago Maulazzo a sign will direct you around the western edge of the lake back to Portella Femmina Morta.

the sea. A Norman church, now roofless, was subsequently built on the temple's red marble base. Virtually all of San Marco d'Alunzio's older buildings and its 22 churches were made using this locally quarried marble. The best of the churches is the **Chiesa di Santa Maria delle Grazie**, where you can find a beautiful Gagini statue of the *Madonna con bambino e San Giovanni* (Madonna with Child and St John). At the top of the hill are the scant remains of the **castle** built by Robert Guiscard in 1061; it was the first castle built by the Normans in Sicily.

A short distance south of San Marco by the Chiesa di San Teodoro is the **Museum of Byzantine & Norman Cultures** (☎ 0941 79 77 19; Badia Nica, Via Ferraloro; admission free; ☺ 9am-1pm & 3.30-7pm), which contains a number of lovely frescoes from the town's churches.

Southeast of San Marco is the trekking base, **Longi**, and southwest is **Alcara di Fusi**, a small village where there is an **information office** (☎ 0941 79 39 04; Via Ugo Foscolo 1). Alcara is situated beneath the impressive **Rocche del Crasto** (1315m), a nesting site of the golden eagle.

The third route through the park follows the SS116, which heads south from Capo d'Orlando. This is a fabulous (and tiring) driving road that takes you up to **Floresta** (1275m), the highest village in the park. From there you make a spectacular descent to Randazzo, with unforgettable views of Mt Etna.

Sleeping & Eating

Villa Nicetta (☎ 0941 72 61 42; www.villanicetta .it; Contrada Nicetta, Acquedolci; r per person incl half/full board €50/60) Located just before Sant'Agata di Militello, inland from Acquedolci, is this lovely rural retreat, which is actually a fortified farmhouse with its very own church. You can get involved with farm activities or take one of the trekking, mountain bike or horseback excursions.

Villa Miraglia (☎ 095 773 21 33; www.villamiraglia .it; SS289, Cesarò; r per person incl half/full board €50/62) This lovely stone *albergo* (hotel), once a hunting lodge, is situated just beneath Portella Femmina Morta. It is a refuge in the true sense of the word: warm, welcoming and stuffed full of knick-knacks (ceramics, cart panels and the like). It also serves up hearty, simple food (meals €25

to €30). You will need to book ahead on weekends and in summer.

Casali di Margello (☎ 0941 48 62 25; www.casalidi margello.it; Km9, SP155; s €40-55, d €80-110; P ⤫) This huge farm that's actually more like a hamlet has restored cottages that sleep two to four people. You can help with the farm work, pick mushrooms, make ricotta or take any number of excursions in the park; it's a wonderful environment to get lost in. It's on the road to San Salvatore di Fitalia; check out the website for good directions.

Getting There & Away

As a rule, you'll need your own transport to get around the park. The SS116 connects Capo d'Orlando with Randazzo, while the SS117 connects Santo Stefano di Camastra with Nicosia. Cutting through the heart of the park is the SS289, which links Sant'Agata di Militello with Cesarò in the interior.

The only public transport is the once-daily **ISEA** (☎ 095 53 68 94) bus between Catania and Sant'Agata di Militello. It makes a stop in the middle of the park near the Portella Femmina Morta, from where you can embark on the lake circuit walk (see p143 for more details). The bus departs Sant'Agata di Militello at 5am and Catania at 2pm.

CAPO D'ORLANDO
pop 12,700

The busiest resort town on the coast after Cefalù, Capo d'Orlando was founded – at least according to legend – when one of Charlemagne's generals, a chap called Orlando, stood on the headland and declared it a fine place to build a castle. The ruins of the castle are still visible. In 1299 Frederick II of Aragon was defeated here by the rebellious baron Roger of Lauria, backed up by the joint forces of Catalonia and Anjou. Recent rebels include the town's shopkeepers and traders, who made a name for themselves in the 1990s with their stand against the Mafia's demands for *pizzo* (protection money) – sadly, an all-too-rare bit of resistance.

Visitors come here for the beaches, both sandy and rocky, that are on either side of town. The best swimming is to the east. It's also the best option for accommodation if you don't wish to make the trip to Cefalù or Milazzo.

There is a **tourist office** (☎ 0941 91 27 84; www .aastcapodorlando.it in Italian; Via Piave; ☼ 9am-1pm & 3-7pm Mon-Fri, 9am-1pm Sat).

Sleeping & Eating

There is no shortage of hotels or restaurants in Capo d'Orlando.

Il Mulino (☎ 0941 90 24 31; www.hotelilmulino.it; Via A Doria 46; s €55-70, d €85-110; ☒ ☒) A popular hotel in the centre of town, with modern and comfortable rooms. There's a nice public beach with deck chairs just opposite.

La Tartaruga (☎ 0941 95 50 12/13/14; www.hotel tartaruga.it; Lido San Gregorio; s €70-80, d €120-135; ☼ closed Nov-Feb; ☒ ☒) This is a largish resort hotel with good, comfortable rooms and a nice swimming pool. It is situated to the east of town, overlooking a wide, sandy beach. The hotel's restaurant is highly regarded (meals €25 to €30).

Apart from the restaurant at La Tartaruga, a couple of other places are worth a visit.

A Uletta (☎ 0941 91 17 00; Piazza Duca degli Abruzzi 21; meals €20-25; ☼ closed Mon) has an ample buffet and a range of fish and meat dishes – you'll dine well here, even if you're on a tight budget.

Da Enzo (☎ 0941 90 17 00; Via Lo Sardo; pizza €6-8) is a good pizzeria with a fine selection of pasta dishes.

Getting There & Away

The best way to get here is by train from Palermo (€9.70, two hours, hourly) or Milazzo (€3.45, one hour, hourly).

PATTI

pop 13,000 / elev 157m

After a landslide in the 1st century AD the refugees of Tyndaris established a new town at Patti. Here you'll find the 18th-century **Cattedrale di San Bartolomeo**, built on the site of Roger II's Norman church, which he founded to house the remains of his mother Adelasia (Adelaide), who died here in 1118. Her remains were later transferred to a fine Renaissance sarcophagus, which you can see in the right transept.

However, most people come to Patti to visit the remains of the **Roman villa** (☎ 0941 36 15 93; admission €2; ☼ 9am-1hr before sunset), which is located on the eastern outskirts of town beneath the motorway viaduct. Built in the 4th century AD, it was destroyed by an earthquake 100 years later. It was only uncovered in 1973 when the Palermo–Messina motorway was being built. Sadly, the site is badly positioned, although an ugly plastic roof has been erected to protect the polychrome mosaics from the scorching sun and the fumes emanating from the motorway overhead. The mosaics are very faded and explanations of the site are pretty much nonexistent. A small room near the

TYRRHENIAN COAST

DETOUR: TYNDARIS

To visit the beautiful ruins at Capo Tindari, turn off the autostrada at the sign for Oliveri, from where brown signs will direct you to the **Santuario della Madonna** (Sanctuary of the Madonna) via scenic hairpin bends. If you're coming from the west, it is 6km from Patti on the SS113.

You can see the enormous church from miles around: it sits right on the cape, its dome glistening in the sun. A sanctuary has been here since the 16th century, when a boat carrying the sacred relic of the Madonna Nera (Black Madonna), thought to have come from Asia Minor, docked here. Legend has it that the boat would go no further until the icon was unloaded. The inscription underneath the icon reads *Nigra sum, sed hermosa*, which means 'I am black, but I am beautiful'.

From the sanctuary, a path leads to the entrance of a more ancient holy place, **Tyndaris** (☎ 0941 36 90 23; admission €2; ☼ 9am-1hr before sunset), one of the most beautiful and peaceful archaeological sites on the island. The ruins (a basilica, Roman house and theatre) are actually very small, but are set on the cliff edge amid prickly pears, olives and cypress trees in perfect seclusion. In summer you can clearly see the Aeolian Islands and the lovely Oliveri lagoon in the bay below.

At the far end of the town's main street is the **theatre**, originally a Greek structure but substantially modified by the Romans. From July to September it hosts a festival of Greek drama, ballet and music. For information ask at the **ticket office** (☎ 0941 36 91 84; Via Teatro Greco 15) at the entrance to the site or visit www.pattietindari.it.

There are buses to Tyndaris from Patti (€1.55, four daily, morning only).

ticket office houses some artefacts (labelled in Italian) found during renovations.

There is a **tourist office** (☎ 0941 24 11 36; Piazza Marconi 11; 9am-1pm Mon-Sat) in the town centre.

To get to Piazza Marconi from the train station, take a bus (€0.85) or walk uphill for about 20 minutes (signposted).

MILAZZO
pop 32,100

Hardly Sicily's prettiest town, Milazzo is hemmed in on its eastern perimeter by industrial development that can make even the most determined visitor run for the nearest hydrofoil. Indeed, the prime reason for setting foot in this town is to get to the Aeolian Islands. But, away from the refineries and busy dock, Milazzo has a very pretty Spanish quarter, while the isthmus that juts out to the north is an area of great natural beauty dotted with rocky coves.

Orientation

Everything of interest is within walking distance of the ferry and hydrofoil port. The train station is on Piazza Marconi, about 3km south of the port along the seafront. Orange AST buses run between the station and the quayside; see p148 for details.

Information

Banco di Sicilia (Via dei Mille) Opposite the hydrofoil dock; has an ATM.

First Aid (☎ 090 928 11 58)

Mail Boxes (☎ 090 922 47 17; Via dei Mille 7; per 30min €3) Internet access; one miserable computer.

Pharmacy (Via Luigi Rizzo; 24hr)

Police (questura; ☎ 090 928 17 20)

Tabacchi Edicola (Via dei Mille) Excellent newsagent selling good foreign-language books on the Aeolians; it also has a useful map.

Tourist Office (☎ 090 922 28 65; Piazza C Duilio 10; 8am-2pm & 4-7pm Mon-Fri, 8am-2pm Sat) Behind Via Crispi; limited information.

Sights & Activities

The strategic position of Milazzo is obvious from the enormous **castle**, built by Frederick II in 1239 and added to by Charles V Aragon. It constitutes the nucleus of the old town and was originally the site of a Greek acropolis, then that of an Arab-Norman citadel. At one time the whole of Milazzo fitted within its huge walls, which command great views of the bay and the Aeolians. The castle contains the city's **Duomo Vecchio** (old cathedral) and the ruins of the **Palazzo dei Giurati** (the old town hall). It is a lovely site to clamber around, full of flowers and crumbling structures. To reach the castle climb the **Salita Castello**, which rises up through the atmospheric Spanish quarter.

If you have a car and a bit more time, take a drive along the **Strada Panoramica** around **Capo Milazzo**; the rugged coastline is beautifully unspoilt. Alternatively you can arrange a boat trip (ask at the tourist office) around the rocky cape to **Baia del Tonno** on the western side of the isthmus. Right at the end of the isthmus is the lighthouse, from where you can make a short walk down to the **Santuario Rupestre di San Antonio da Padova** (signposted from the car park), situated beside the crystal-clear waters.

There's good swimming to be had at Capo Milazzo, but the most easily accessible spot is the long stretch of pebbled **beach** that can be reached at the end of Via Colombo; follow the signs to Baia del Tonno from the end of Via Colombo, then pass the ugly stadium.

Sleeping

Riva Smeralda (☎ 090 928 29 80; www.rivasmeralda.it; Strada Panoramica; tents €2.50-4.50, camp sites per person €5-10, 2-bedroom bungalows €30; Apr-Oct) A well-equipped camping ground with a seafront location and its own beach, Riva Smeralda is situated a mere 3km north of Milazzo. Take the bus from Piazza della Repubblica and ask the bus driver to drop you off.

Hotel Garibaldi (☎ 090 924 01 89; www.hotel garibaldi.net; Via Lungomare Garibaldi 160; s €65-85, d €90-130; P X) Situated on the edge of the historic town, the Garibaldi has tons of character, very swish rooms and its own private beach. There is a residence next door with self-catering apartments. It's probably more convenient if you have a car.

Hotel Riviera Lido (☎ 090 928 34 56; www.hotelriviera lido.it; Strada Panoramica; s €70-80, d €100-130; P X) This modern hotel has a lovely position with its own private beach, plus balconied seaview rooms. Staff can help arrange water sports and boat trips. It's located on Strada Panoramica heading north out of Milazzo.

Petit Hotel (☎ 090 928 67 84; www.petithotel.it; Via dei Mille; s €70-90, d €100-145; P X) The hotel of choice in Milazzo is right opposite the

MILAZZO

INFORMATION
Banco di Sicilia.....................**1** D1
Mail Boxes...........................**2** D1
Pharmacy............................**3** B4
Tabacchi Edicola................(see 9)
Tourist Office.......................**4** B3

SIGHTS & ACTIVITIES
Castle.................................**5** B1
Duomo Vecchio...................**6** B1
Palazzo dei Giurati...............**7** B1

SLEEPING
Hotel Garibaldi.....................**8** C1
Petit Hotel...........................**9** D2

EATING
Al Pescatore........................**10** C1
Il Covo del Pirata..................**11** B2

DRINKING
Washington Bar....................**12** C1

TRANSPORT
AST Buses............................**13** B3
Bus Stop..............................**14** B3
Eolie Garage........................**15** D1
Ferry to the Aeolian Islands..**16** B4
NGI Ticket Office..................**17** D2
Siremar Ticket Office............**18** D1
Ustica Lines Ticket Office.....**19** D2

hydrofoil dock. The hotel is obsessively ecofriendly, using renewable energy sources, latex mattresses and serving a delicious homemade breakfast. It has very friendly staff, and you can leave your luggage and car here (€10 per day) while you visit the islands.

Eating & Drinking
For something to eat, head for Lungomare Garibaldi, which runs along the seafront.

Il Covo del Pirata (☎ 090 928 44 37; Via San Francesco 1; mains €20-25; closed Wed) This is one of Milazzo's best restaurants. The ground-floor section is a very popular pizzeria at night, and the service is as smooth as silk. Reservations are advised.

Al Pescatore (☎ 090 928 65 95; Lungomare Garibaldi 176; mains €25; closed Tue) The seafood here is definitely recommended, as is the efficient service (staff members are used to dealing with hordes about to catch boats to the Aeolian Islands). The *involtini di pesce spada* (swordfish roulade stuffed with breadcrumbs; €8.25) is delicious.

Salamone e Mare (☎ 090 928 12 33; Strada Panoramica; mains €30-35; closed Mon) A wonderful restaurant north along the isthmus. Its terrace juts out over the water, giving it attractive views, which are accompanied by a delicious array of seafood, including a lobster speciality.

Washington Bar (☎ 090 922 38 13; Via Marina Garibaldi 94) This very pleasant bar is a great spot to unwind with a drink while you watch the *passeggiata* go by. The excellent nibbles that accompany drinks only add to the charm. You can also get great gelato here.

Getting There & Around

Milazzo is easy to reach by bus or train from Palermo and Messina. **Giuntabus** (☎ 090 67 37 82) runs an hourly service to/from Messina (€3.70, 50 minutes, hourly Monday to Saturday from 6.30am to 8pm, one Sunday). All intercity buses run from Piazza della Repubblica.

Trains are more frequent, with two departures and arrivals hourly from/to Palermo (€9.20, 2½ to three hours), and around 10 daily to Messina (€2.65, 45 minutes).

The main ferry and hydrofoil operators, Siremar, Ustica Lines and NGI, all have ticket offices along Via dei Mille opposite the port. See p151 for details of ferry travel to and from the island.

AST buses run between the station and the quayside. They depart every 30 minutes or so between 5.30am and 8.40pm. Tickets (€0.85, valid for two hours) can be bought inside the train station or at the shop opposite the quayside bus stop with the AST sign.

If you want to leave your car here while you island-hop, you can park long term at the **Eolie Garage** (Via Giorgio Rizzo; per day €10), next to Hotel Capitol.

TYRRHENIAN COAST

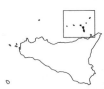

Aeolian Islands

Cobalt-blue sea, wild, windswept mountains swathed in flowers and steaming volcanoes – these go some way to explaining why the Aeolians (Isole Eolie) are the European holy grail for island lovers. Part of a huge volcanic ridge, the seven Aeolian Islands represent the very pinnacle of a 3000m-high outcrop that was formed one million years ago. Created by successive explosions – first Panarea, Filicudi and Alicudi, then Lipari and Salina, and finally the still-boiling Vulcano and Stromboli – the islands exhibit an extraordinary variety of landscape. Hillsides of silver-grey pumice and lush green vineyards give way to jagged veins of black obsidian. A wilderness of flowers and plants enriched by the volcanic soil, as well as an abundance of sea life, make these islands a paradise for naturalists and scuba divers alike. Recognising their unique volcanic characteristics, Unesco declared the islands a World Heritage site in 2000.

The Aeolians' natural beauty and unpredictable nature have tempted and repelled people throughout the centuries. Myths name the island as the home of the god of the winds, Aeolus, and they were also thought to be home to the monster Polyphemus and the god of fire, Vulcan. Modern hedonists, including the international jet set and film stars, arrive in droves in the summer to swim, hike, dive and party in this playground. The best time to come is in May and early June or late September and October; prices soar in July and August, when the population doubles.

AEOLIAN ISLANDS

HIGHLIGHTS

- Go for a night-time climb on fiery **Stromboli** (p176) – an unforgettable experience for the eyes, legs and lungs
- Visit Lipari's dazzling **Museo Archeologico Eoliano** (p153), with its wealth of artefacts
- Climb to the top of Vulcano's mineral-encrusted **Fossa di Vulcano** (p168) and go for an atmospheric mud bath after dusk to heal those bones
- Take a trip around all of the fascinating villages on **Salina** (p170) and taste the sweet Malvasia wine
- Enjoy the wild natural beauty of Filicudi's huge **Grotta del Bue Marino** (p180)

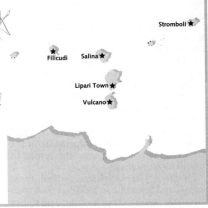

Stromboli ★

Filicudi ★   Salina ★

Lipari Town ★

Vulcano ★

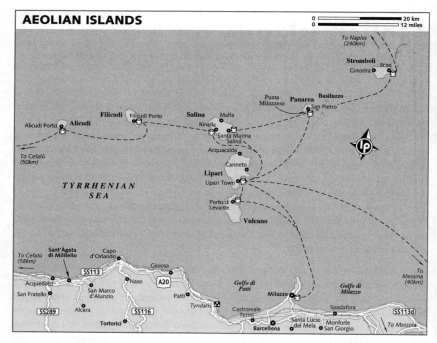

AEOLIAN ISLANDS

HISTORY

There are two types of history when it comes to the Aeolian Islands: the mythical (which is very exciting) and the real (almost equally eventful). The mythical story is responsible for many of the islands' names. The Greek keeper of the winds, Aeolus, who famously gave Odysseus a bag of winds (not a wind bag, mind) to take along on his trip, gave the archipelago its name. Aeolus' father-in-law, the mythical King Liparus, gave his name to Lipari, the 'capital' island. Jupiter's son, Vulcan, the god of fire and metalworking, had his workshop on Vulcano island, giving it not only its name, but also its fiery character.

The more plausible version of the past testifies that the first settlers came to the islands to make tools out of obsidian, a hard volcanic glass that provided the mainstay of the islands' economy for more than 5000 years. Obsidian drew Sicily's first-known inhabitants to the Aeolians, the Stentillenians, who settled in the 4th millennium BC.

The first Greek settlers arrived from Segesta and Selinunte in 580 BC, creating an effectively run system of farming, commerce and ship-looting, which brought much wealth to the islands. The Greeks also used the islands as ports on the east–west trade route between the Aegean and Tyrrhenian seas, and built their acropolis on the promontory where you can still visit the Neolithic and classical ruins.

The Aeolian Islands were a base for the Carthaginians and Greeks in the First Punic War, until they finally fell to Rome between 252 and 251 BC. The Romans impoverished the islands by charging high taxes on exporting obsidian. Population decline continued as the inhabitants fled the increasingly active volcanoes, especially on Lipari. Between Roman rule and the Arab lootings in AD 863, the islands frequently changed hands. The Arab attacks destroyed the islands' homes, enslaved the population and famously scattered the remains of St Bartholomew, the guardian of the Aeolians.

The islands lay unpopulated for over a hundred years, until a group of monks was sent to settle there in 1083. They announced that St Bartholomew's remains had miraculously reappeared, and that this was a sign that the islands should be repopulated under his protection. But it proved difficult to lure people back to the volatile islands, and rightly so – North African pirates attacked the islands frequently. The notorious pirate Barbarossa (tyrant of all of the Mediterranean) burnt Lipari Town to the ground and took off with its entire population in 1544 (some say he imprisoned as many as 10,000 people). The future of the Aeolians was not looking bright. However, the Viceroy Pedro of Toledo quickly rebuilt the island, setting up plentiful civilian privileges, which helped lure settlers from mainland Italy.

The 19th century saw a further population decline, with many islanders fleeing the poor living conditions and emigrating to Australia. During the same period Lipari's citadel became a prison and continued in this role until Fascist times, when Mussolini's political opponents were incarcerated here. With hardly any population and sparse agriculture, the Aeolians were a sad sight until the 1950s, when their wild beauty grabbed the attention of the tourist industry, propelling them to their present-day guise as one of the most attractive parts of Italy.

GETTING THERE & AWAY

Ferries and hydrofoils leave for the islands on a regular basis in summer from Milazzo and Messina. In Milazzo all the ticket offices are along Via dei Mille, at the port, and in Messina the office is halfway up Via Vittorio Emanuele II. You have to purchase your tickets at the port ticket offices before boarding; telephone bookings are not accepted unless they are done weeks in advance. Hydrofoils are twice as frequent and faster than ferries, although more expensive. Peak season is from June to September and, although ferries and hydrofoils operate year-round, the winter services are much reduced and sometimes cancelled – to the outer islands at any rate – due to heavy seas. All the following prices were one-way high-season fares at the time of writing.

Air

For some brilliant Aeolian-style luxury, book yourself (and four friends) a helicopter transfer with **Air Panarea** (☎ 090 983 44 28; www .airpanarea.com; Via Iditella, Panarea). From Palermo to Lipari it works out about €560 per person.

Air Panarea also operates a scheduled transfer to the Reggio Calabria airport (€176, Monday and Friday) departing from Panarea at 9am and returning at 2pm.

An excursion around the islands, with a tour over Stromboli costing €480 per person (for a group of five), is just about one of the most exciting things you can do.

Boat

Both Ustica Lines and Siremar (for contact details for Lipari see p166, Vulcano p170, Salina p174, Panarea p175, Stromboli p180, Filicudi p181 and Alicudi p182) run hydrofoils to Lipari from Milazzo (€11.30), and then on to the other islands. From 1 June to 30 September hydrofoils depart almost hourly (from around 7am to 8pm) to Lipari, and also stop at Vulcano (€10.50, 45 minutes) and either Santa Marina or Rinella (€12.80, 1½ to two hours) on Salina. Services to the other islands are less frequent unless you change in Lipari: combined there are nine departures daily for Panarea (€13.30, two hours) and Stromboli (€16.20, 2½ hours). There are four daily departures for Alicudi (€21.30, three hours) and Filicudi (€17.50, two hours 20 minutes).

Ustica Lines hydrofoils also connect the islands with Messina (€16.50, 1½ hours from Lipari, five daily) and Reggio di Calabria (€17.50, two hours from Lipari, five daily), as well as Naples (€75, 5½ hours, one daily, summer only) and Palermo (€32, four hours, one daily, summer only).

Siremar runs car ferries from Milazzo to the islands (€7.30, small cars €24.40, two hours, five daily), but they are slower and less regular. **NGI Traghetti** (Map p147; ☎ 090 928 40 91; Via dei Mille 26, Milazzo) also runs a thrice-daily car-ferry service for the same rates.

GETTING AROUND
Boat

Regular hydrofoil and ferry services operate between the islands but they can be disrupted by heavy seas. In Lipari Town nearly all hydrofoil and ferry services arrive at and depart from Marina Lunga (also known as Porto Sottomonastero). Siremar and Ustica Lines have ticket offices in the same cabin opposite the port. Full timetable information is available at all offices. On the other islands, ticket offices are at or close to the docks.

AEOLIAN ISLANDS

Single fares and approximate sailing times from Lipari are as follows:

Destination	Cost	Duration
Alicudi	€14.10	2hr (hydrofoil)
	€8.95	3¾hr (ferry)
Filicudi	€11.30	1½hr (hydrofoil)
	€6.40	2¾hr (ferry)
Panarea	€6.90	50min (hydrofoil)
	€3.85	2hr (ferry)
Salina	€5.30	35min (Santa Marina, hydrofoil)
	€6.10	45min (Rinella, hydrofoil)
	€3	45min (Santa Marina, ferry)
	€3.40	1½hr (Rinella, ferry)
Stromboli	€13.30	1hr (hydrofoil)
	€7.70	3¾hr (ferry)
Vulcano	€2.50	10min (hydrofoil)
	€1.30	25min (ferry)

Car & Motorcycle

If you are only visiting the islands for a couple of days it'll work out too expensive to take your own car. It's best to garage it in Milazzo for €10 per day (see p148 for details). If you're thinking of taking in the sights for longer than two or three days, taking your own vehicle will work out cheaper than hiring one. You can take cars onto Lipari, Vulcano and Salina, all of which also have scooter- and car-rental outlets (scooter hire per day €12, car hire per day €45). On Panarea, Stromboli and Filicudi you can use the electric-cart taxis to transport luggage. On Alicudi, their methods of transport are lovely and old-fashioned: mules and donkeys.

THE ISLANDS

LIPARI

pop 10,500 / elev 602m

The 'capital' of the islands, Lipari is the most populated and most popular of the Aeolians, not least because it's at the centre of the archipelago. With a good variety of hotels and restaurants it's the best-equipped base for hopping to the rest of the islands. Lipari Town is a delightful maze of pastel-coloured houses but the high level of tourism means that the main street is a little too crowded with beachwear and surf-gear shops. The town's real charm can be found in its back streets and the area around the cathedral.

The town's soaring castle was built as a defence against the attacks of pirates like Barbarossa who were eager to get their hands

on the revenue from the lucrative obsidian and pumice mining. You can see the still-active pumice mines north of Lipari Town, between the popular pebbly beaches of Canneto and Porticello.

The rest of the island hides some good beaches, though you'll have to make an effort to get to some of the more isolated coves.

Orientation

Tourists arrive at one of two ports in Lipari Town: Marina Lunga or Marina Corta. The ports are situated either side of the cliff-top citadel (known as the *castello*). Here you'll find the cathedral and the archaeological museum. The town centre extends between the ports. The main street, Via Vittorio Emanuele, runs roughly north-south to the west of the castle. This area is where you'll find banks, bars, offices and restaurants.

Information

BOOKSHOPS

La Stampa (Via Vittorio Emanuele 170) Selection of foreign-language newspapers – usually English, German and French – and some novels.

EMERGENCY
Ambulance (☎ 090 988 52 67)
Emergency Doctor (☎ 090 981 24 27; Via Sant'Anna)
At the hospital (Ospedale Civile di Lipari Centralino).
Police (☎ 090 981 13 33; Via Guglielmo Marconi)

INTERNET ACCESS
Prices start at €3 per half-hour or €6 an hour.
Internet Point (☎ 090 981 34 94; Via Vittorio
Emanuele 53; 🕒 10.30am-1.30pm & 6.30-11.30pm Mon-
Sat, 6.30-11.30pm Sun)
Net C@fe (☎ 090 981 35 27; Via Garibaldi 61; 🕒 10am-
late) Serves snacks and regularly screens football matches.

INTERNET RESOURCES
www.isole-eolie.com (in Italian) Full of information
about island hotels and offers a secure online booking
service.

LEFT LUGGAGE
Siremar Ticket Office (Marina Lunga; per bag per hr €3;
🕒 8am-8pm)

MEDICAL SERVICES
The *farmacie di turno*, a timetable showing
which pharmacy is on night duty, is displayed
in the window of each pharmacy.
Farmacia Internazionale (☎ 090 981 15 83; Via
Vittorio Emanuele 128; 🕒 9am-1pm & 5-9pm Mon-Fri)
Ospedale Civile di Lipari Centralino (☎ 090 988 51
11; Via Sant'Anna) Also operates a first-aid service.

MONEY
Via Vittorio Emanuele is lined with ATMs.
Outside banking hours you can change cash
at the post office and travel agencies.

POST
Post Office (Via Vittorio Emanuele 207; 🕒 8.30am-
6.30pm Mon-Fri, 8.30am-1.20pm Sat)

TOURIST INFORMATION
Main Tourist Office (☎ 090 988 00 95; www.aasteolie
.info; Via Vittorio Emanuele 202; 🕒 8.30am-1.30pm &
4.30-8pm Mon-Fri year round, 8.30am-1.30pm Sat & Sun
Jul & Aug) This office provides information for all the
islands and can assist you with finding accommodation.
Pick up a free copy of *Ospitalità in Blu*, which contains
details of accommodation and services on all the islands.
Off-peak, the office is randomly closed in the afternoon.

Sights
CITADEL (UPPER TOWN)
Following Barbarossa's murderous rampage
through the town in 1544, the Spaniards
rebuilt and fortified Lipari. Although the citadel never had to defend the town from further
marauders, its fortifications look impregnable
and are still relatively intact.

Along the streets of the castle, plaques
explain the different strata that excavations
have revealed. The neat layers, preserved by
the slow accumulation of windblown earth,
provide a fantastic timeline that archaeologists
use to date finds elsewhere in the Med.

You enter the castle via a set of steps (Via del
Concordato) that leads up to the 17th-century
Cattedrale di San Bartolomeo. It was built to replace
the original Norman cathedral, which was destroyed by Barbarossa who, despite his Arab
name (Khair-ed-din Barbarossa), was actually
an Italian mercenary. The only original element to survive is the 12th-century Benedictine
cloister. The interior is hung with chandeliers
and features: in the northern transept is a silver
statue of St Bartholomew (1728) with his flayed
skin tucked under his arm.

Around the cathedral are a couple of other
ruined baroque churches, but the real area of
interest is the **archaeological dig** in the southern half of the citadel where finds from the
Neolithic period to the Roman era have been
unearthed. You won't make much sense of
what's here without visiting the museum.

Museo Archeologico Eoliano
If you're at all interested in Mediterranean
history, the **Museo Archeologico Eoliano** (☎ 090
988 01 74; adult/concession €6/3; 🕒 9am-1.30pm & 3-6pm)
is an absolute must, as it contains a collection of finds that is among the most complete
in Europe. The **Archaeological Section** (Sezione
Archeologica) is divided into two buildings.
Just south of the cathedral, the former Palazzo
Vescovile (Bishop's Palace) is devoted to artefacts found on Lipari, beginning with the
Neolithic and Bronze Ages upstairs and continuing in chronological order to the Roman
era downstairs. Amid the plethora of artefacts is some finely sculpted obsidian, telling
evidence of the relative sophistication of the
island's prehistoric civilisation. Prehistoric
finds from the other islands are housed in the
small pavilion directly in front of the palace.

On the other side of the cathedral is the
Classical Section (Sezione Classica). It houses
finds from Lipari's 11th-century-BC necropolis. These are beautifully displayed and
include a sizable collection of burial urns
as well as models of a Bronze Age burial

AEOLIAN ISLANDS

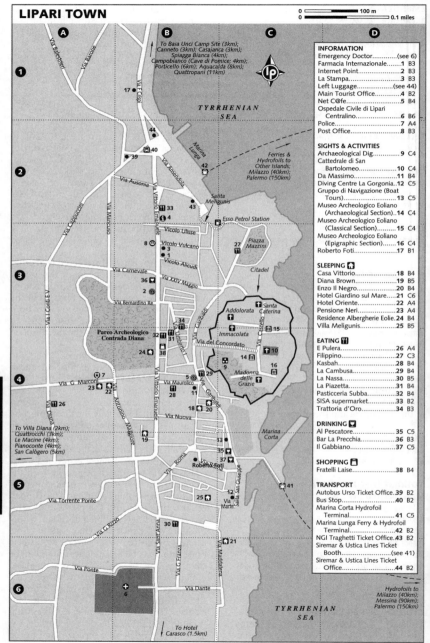

LIPARI TOWN

| 0 | 100 m |
| 0 | 0.1 miles |

To Baia Unci Camp Site (3km);
Canneto (3km); Casajanca (3km);
Spiaggia Bianca (4km);
Campobianco (Cave di Pomice; 4km);
Porticello (6km); Aquacalda (8km);
Quattropani (11km)

TYRRHENIAN
SEA

Marina
Lunga

Ferries &
Hydrofoils to
Other Islands;
Milazzo (40km);
Palermo (150km)

Salita
Meligunis

Via Ausonia

Esso Petrol Station

Vicolo Ulisse

Piazza
Mazzini

Vicolo Vulcano

Vicolo Alicudi

Citadel

Via Carnevale

Via XXIV Maggio

Via Bernardino Re

Addolorata   Santa
                 Caterina

Immacolata

Parco Archeologico
Contrada Diana

Via del Concordato

Madonna
delle
Grazie

Via G. Marconi

Via Maurolico

Via Nuova

Marina
Corta

To Villa Diana (2km);
Quattrocchi (3km);
Le Macine (4km);
Pianoconte (4km);
San Calògero (5km)

Roberto Foti

Via Torrente Ponte

Via G. Rizzo

Via Ponte

Via Dante

+
6

Hydrofoils to
Milazzo (40km);
Messina (90km);
Palermo (150km)

TYRRHENIAN
SEA

To Hotel
Carasco (1.5km)

INFORMATION
Emergency Doctor............(see 6)
Farmacia Internazionale.......1 B3
Internet Point....................2 B3
La Stampa.........................3 B3
Left Luggage................(see 44)
Main Tourist Office............4 B2
Net C@fe.........................5 B4
Ospedale Civile di Lipari
    Centralino.....................6 B6
Police..............................7 A4
Post Office........................8 B3

SIGHTS & ACTIVITIES
Archaeological Dig............9 C4
Cattedrale di San
    Bartolomeo..................10 C4
Da Massimo.....................11 B4
Diving Centre La Gorgonia..12 C5
Gruppo di Navigazione (Boat
    Tours).........................13 C5
Museo Archeologico Eoliano
    (Archaeological Section)..14 C4
Museo Archeologico Eoliano
    (Classical Section).........15 C4
Museo Archeologico Eoliano
    (Epigraphic Section)......16 C4
Roberto Foti....................17 B1

SLEEPING
Casa Vittorio....................18 B4
Diana Brown.....................19 B5
Enzo Il Negro....................20 B4
Hotel Giardino sul Mare......21 C6
Hotel Oriente....................22 A4
Pensione Neri...................23 A4
Residence Albergherie Eolie.24 B4
Villa Meligunis..................25 B5

EATING
E Pulera...........................26 A4
Filippino..........................27 C3
Kasbah............................28 B4
La Cambusa......................29 B4
La Nassa..........................30 B5
La Piazzetta......................31 B4
Pasticceria Subba..............32 B4
SISA supermarket..............33 B3
Trattoria d'Oro..................34 B3

DRINKING
Al Pescatore.....................35 C5
Bar La Precchia..................36 B3
Il Gabbiano......................37 C5

SHOPPING
Fratelli Laise.....................38 B4

TRANSPORT
Autobus Urso Ticket Office.39 B2
Bus Stop...........................40 B2
Marina Corta Hydrofoil
    Terminal......................41 C5
Marina Lunga Ferry & Hydrofoil
    Terminal......................42 B2
NGI Traghetti Ticket Office.43 B2
Siremar & Ustica Lines Ticket
    Booth....................(see 41)
Siremar & Ustica Lines Ticket
    Office.........................44 B2

AEOLIAN ISLANDS

ground and Lipari's necropolis. Upstairs is an impressive array of decorated vases and the museum's most treasured items: the most complete collection of Greek theatrical masks in the world. There are also a number of statuettes of dancers and actors – the one of *Andromeda con Bambino* (Andromeda with Child) is particularly beautiful – and some elegant jewellery. The next room contains polychromatic vases decorated by an artist simply known as 'Il Pittore Liparoto' (the Lipari Painter; 300–270 BC).

The museum's last part is the **Epigraphic Section** (Sezione Epigrafica), which is housed in a smaller building located south of the Archaeological Section. Here you will find a little garden of engraved stones and a room of Greek and Roman tombs.

AROUND LIPARI TOWN

The only worthwhile sight outside the citadel is the **Parco Archeologico Contrada Diana**, west of Via Vittorio Emanuele, which has revealed part of the original Greek walls (5th and 4th centuries BC) and Roman houses. At the southwestern end of the park is the necropolis, where the tombstones are still visible in the overgrown grass. The park, alas, is rarely open but all of the important finds are in the museum.

AROUND LIPARI ISLAND

Although Lipari Town is so self-contained that you could easily spend your entire holiday there, the rest of the island is worth checking out, especially if you want to find the best swimming spots. The island is small enough that a grand tour of its perimeter should take about an hour by car.

The Observatory

Just south of the town is Lipari's observatory, a small place with a big job – monitoring all the volcanic and seismic activity in the Mediterranean. Follow signs south to the Hotel Carasco and Porto delle Gente, which will lead you out to a promontory formed by Monte Giardina and Monte Guardia. From here a track leads through the vineyards to the **Observatory** (☎ 090 981 10 81; by appointment) with fantastic views across the water to Vulcano. The route is clearly marked on the *Isole Eolie o Lipari* 1:25,000 map produced by Litografia Artistica Cartografica (available in the Tabacchi Edicola in Milazzo, see p146).

North of Lipari Town

Only 3km north of Lipari Town, at the end of a short tunnel, **Canneto** is a relatively quiet village. The long pebbled beach is also the most accessible beach from Lipari for swimming and you can hire deck chairs, umbrellas, kayaks and canoes (€5 per hour).

About 1km further north of Canneto is **Spiaggia Bianca** (White Beach), the most popular beach on the island. Its name derives from the layers of pumice dust that once covered it. These have been slowly washed away by the rough winter seas, leaving it a darker shade of grey. Another good beach is the one at **Porticello** (north again). Beware, the pebbles are murder on your feet so come equipped with sandals or beach shoes.

Between Spiaggia Bianca and Porticello lie the pumice quarries of **Campobianco**. The slopes of the vast mines run along the side of the road, and pumice is still shipped from the dock below **Monte Pilato** (476m). This unlikely place is one of the better spots to splash into the sea, via one of the pumice chutes that allow you to slide from the hillside above directly into the azure water. Such a scene features in the Taviani brothers' classic film *Kaos*. You can only get to the chutes by boat and most tours will stop here to allow you some time to slide.

Monte Pilato is actually the source of all of the pumice, which exploded from the crater in the last eruption in AD 700. Also around the cone are fields of solidified obsidian known as the **Rocche Rosse** (Red Rocks). You can reach the crater via a path from the northern end of Campobianco (about 1.2km).

Northwest to Quattropani

West of Lipari Town (and accessible by bus from the Marina Lunga), through some lush vegetation, the road climbs for about 3km to the belvedere known as **Quattrocchi** (Four Eyes, although you'll only need two to appreciate the stunning views of Vulcano to the south). Less than 1km north is the small village of **Pianoconte**; a side road before the village proper veers off to the Roman baths of **San Calogero**, famous in antiquity for the thermal spring that flowed at a constant temperature of 60°C. The last stop on the bus route is at **Quattropani**, from where you can walk the 5km north to **Acquacalda** and catch a bus returning to Lipari.

TOP FIVE DIVING SPOTS AROUND LIPARI

- **Punta Castagna** (difficult, depth 10m to 40m) A spectacular dive with a 10m white pumice platform interrupted by multicoloured channels
- **Secca del Bagno** (difficult, depth 40m to 45m) A breathtaking collection of colourful walls that are swathed with schools of technicolour fish
- **Pietra Menalda** (medium, depth 18m to 40m) See the home of octopuses, eel, groupers and other sea critters on the southern side of the island
- **Pietra del Bagno** (all levels, 20m to 40m) Circumnavigate the Bagno rock, while witnessing colourful rock surfaces and sea life
- **La Parete dei Gabbiani** (medium, 20m to 45m) An almost black 'n' white dive: the black lava rock is streaked with white pumice stone, hiding cracks that are home to lobsters

---

Just before you reach Lipari Town from the eastern side is the island's best beach, **Spiaggia di Vinci**, a peaceful pebbled cove with wonderful clean waters for swimming in. You'll need to make an effort to get here, so it's not a place for a quick dip. From the main road, watch out for the sign down to the beach. You'll have to leave your car/scooter after some 150m and walk down for about 10 to 15 minutes through an idyllic landscape of long grass, flowers and cacti. There's not a peep of traffic or any kind of noise down here; perfect if you want a quiet day on the beach. Alternatively, get a boat to drop you off (and pick you up). There's a little hut that serves food and drinks, or just bring your own picnic.

Activities

Snorkelling and scuba diving are incredibly popular, given the crystal-clear waters. For information on courses or to rent equipment, contact **Diving Center La Gorgonia** (☎ 090 981 26 16; www.lagorgoniadiving.it; Salita San Giuseppe, Marina Corta; single dive/basic beginner's course €32/60; mask & fin per day €10). If taking your first scuba course you will need a medical certificate from your doctor to say you are in good health.

Tours

Gruppo di Navigazione (☎ 090 982 22 37; www.navigazioniregina.com; Via Garibaldi; Stromboli by night €35, Alicudi & Filicudi €40; ☼ tours Mar-Oct) conducts boat tours of and to all the islands, including one to Stromboli to see the Sciara del Fuoco (Trail of Fire).

You can take excursions from **Da Massimo** (☎ 090 981 17 14, 3332986624; www.damassimo.it; Via Maurolico 2; Stromboli by night €35, Alicudi & Filicudi €45, Panarea €30; ☼ tours Mar-Oct). It also hires boats and dinghies. Another outlet is **Roberto Foti** (☎ 090

981 13 70; www.robertofoti.it in Italian; Via Francesco Crispi 31; motorised rubber dinghy 3-/6-seater per day €70/120).

Sleeping

Lipari provides plenty of options for a comfortable stay. However, prices increase on average by 30% in July and August and you may have to commit to a multiday stay and/or half board. The low (October to March) and high (July and August) season prices for a double room are given here as they vary so wildly.

In peak season, if all else fails, the staff at the tourist office will billet new arrivals in private homes on the island. The touts (who swarm around the port when you arrive) usually also have decent rooms in private houses. To rent an apartment contact the tourist office for a list of establishments.

BUDGET

The *affittacamere* (rooms for rent) operators renting furnished rooms are a good deal (you usually have use of a kitchen).

Baia Unci (☎ 090 981 19 09; www.baiaunci.com; Marina Garibaldi 2, Località Canneto; per person €7-12, per tent €7-13.50; ☼ 15 Mar-15 Oct) The island's only camp site is at Canneto, about 3km north of Lipari Town and accessible by bus from the Esso service station at Marina Lunga. It has sites underneath shady eucalyptus trees (although the road runs nearby) and there is a self-service restaurant. Reserve for August.

Casa Vittorio (☎ 090 981 15 23; www.casavittorio.it in Italian; Vico Sparviero 15; r per person €18-40) These basic furnished rooms are in a tiny alley off Via Garibaldi near Marina Corta. You'll find the owner at Via Garibaldi 78, on the way from

(Continued on page 165)

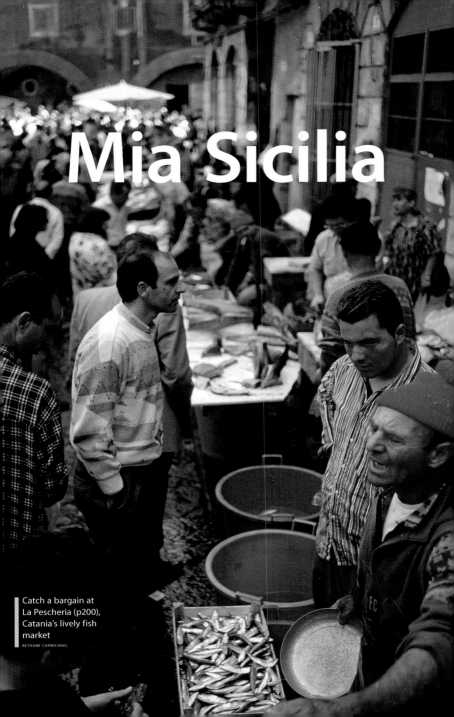

Mia Sicilia

Catch a bargain at
La Pescheria (p200),
Catania's lively fish
market

BETHUNE CARMICHAEL

Young, Gifted & Sicilian

NAME	Graziano Puglisi
AGE	27
OCCUPATION	Student
RESIDENCE	Catania

It's easy to go out on a weeknight and come back at 5am when you're a student – you have nothing to do in the morning. That's why student nights are always during the week – Wednesday is typical.

I love going to Zo, which is a cultural centre with lots of music and theatre. Another good club is Mercati Generali. It hosts lots of interesting concerts and international DJs. We don't listen to a lot of Italian music, because there aren't so many modern bands. There are some bands that are more experimental, like Africa Unite – it mixes Jamaican music with electronica.

It's very difficult to get work when you finish university. Lots of young people come out of university with big ideas and ambitions, but find all the doors closed. If people don't know you, it's hard to get a job. It's not a totally bad thing, it's just the way the people are here. They think that if they know you, they can trust you. Many move to the north of Italy because there are more opportunities. I think there's a risk of not coming back once you've gone somewhere like Milan. Things work better there.

AS RELATED TO VESNA MARIC

'Lots of young people come out of university with big ideas and ambitions, but find all the doors closed'

Fireworks light up the night sky at a beach concert near the town of Noto (p228)
RICHARD BARONESSA

Moving with the times: mobile phones and motorcycles on the streets of Catania
HELENE ROGERS/ALAMY

PARTY TIME

Zo (p205) A fab club, restaurant and bar in an old palazzo (palace or mansion) just off Via Vittorio Emanuele in Catania. Go there for live music, food and fun till late.

Mercati Generali (p205) Proper clubbing, just outside Catania, with international DJs and open-air dancing during the summer months.

I Candelai (p95) An old warehouse with impromptu live music and theatre, plus lots of scheduled shows.

The grand Palazzo dell'Università (p201) is home to Catania's university
BOB TURNER/ALAMY

Bars are at their busiest on weeknights in the university town of Syracuse (p214)
RAI MONITTO

A Recipe for Success

NAME	Franco Ruta
OCCUPATION	Sixth-generation owner of Antica Dolceria Bonajuto
RESIDENCE	Modica

'We think that [today's] chocolate has 'lost the memory' of the original chocolate through the modern preparation methods'

This [style of chocolate] is the first chocolate that people knew in Europe. It was brought to Sicily by the Spanish from the New World, and it's the chocolate that the Aztecs used to eat and drink. We think that [today's] chocolate has 'lost the memory' of the original chocolate through modern preparation methods. We work to preserve that memory.

We didn't invent anything, we just continued the use of the original instruments, ingredients and methods. Some would say our method is primitive and vulgar. But we're the only ones producing pure chocolate.

People always ask what our secret is. And we say that our secret is not to have any secrets. As a family, we've simply always stuck to the philosophy of never working industrially, and of remaining artisan producers – that's why we just have a dozen people working in the workshop, and everyone knows everyone else. It's a small business, but we have many customers because people trust us and our quality.

We have worked on reintroducing the original production methods back to our cocoa producers in Ecuador and Peru because we want to get to know them better, pay them better and help them understand our product. This will help them to keep growing good cocoa. Quality cocoa makes good chocolate and that's what our livelihood depends on.

AS RELATED TO VESNA MARIC

A taste of history: 16th-century Spanish rulers introduced the Aztec way of making chocolate to Modica

CUBOIMAGES SRL/ALAMY

SWEET SICILY

Antica Dolceria Bonajuto (p234) Try Franco's fabulous and ancient chocolate recipes, and taste the cardamom, chilli or orange-spiced chocolate for a real kick.

Grammatico Maria (p112) Erice's (and Sicily's) most famous sweet shop has some of the best *cannoli* (pastry tubes stuffed with sweet ricotta) and almond cookies around.

Corrado Costanzo and Caffè Sicilia (p231) These are deemed to be Sicily's best *gelaterie* (ice-cream shops), so head over to Noto to taste the pistachio or chocolate flavours, or to indulge in a *granita* (flavoured crushed ice).

Family-run Antica Dolceria Bonajuto has been satisfying Sicily's sweet tooth for six generations

RAFAEL ESTEFANIA

Island of Artisans

NAME	Antonio Delfino and Concetta Busacca
OCCUPATION	Ceramicists and teachers at the Luigi Sturzo School of Ceramics
RESIDENCE	Caltagirone

'we had healthy competition, and original and quality design. We didn't have so many shops, but there were more artists'

The art of ceramics has always been quite sophisticated. In the old times people used olive pips to fire the ceramics. Each time they fired a collection of pots, they'd build a new brick wall for the kiln, and when it was finished they had to destroy it to get the pots out. The kiln was heated up to 900°C and the temperature was controlled by looking through a spyhole and checking the colour of the bricks and the tiles.

Our school is one of the main ones in the country for ceramicists, but lots of students are often quite disillusioned when they realise that everyone wants traditional designs. We had a couple of students from Brazil a few years ago. They did wonderful things with bright colours and tropical designs, but that would never sell here. Unfortunately, there isn't much room for artistic creation in Caltagirone.

Before tourism impacted on Caltagirone's ceramics, we had healthy competition, and original and quality design. We didn't have so many shops, but there were more artists. But then it all turned towards making souvenirs and lots of shops opened up, abandoning quality and wanting to sell as much as possible.

AS RELATED TO VESNA MARIC

Artists throughout Sicily are still creating memorable mementos (p290)

PETER HORREE/ALAMY

Ancient art: ceramics have been produced in Caltagirone for more than 1000 years

RAFAEL ESTEFANIA

CHINA TOWN – CERAMICS IN CALTAGIRONE

Scalinata di Santa Maria del Monte (p255) A 142-step stairway to heaven, all with hand-painted ceramics depicting Sicilian history.

Museo Regionale della Ceramica (p255) Discover the history of ceramics from prehistoric times to the present day.

Le Maioliche (p256) If you want to see creative and innovative ceramics, head to Le Maioliche.

The colourful steps of Scalinata di Santa Maria del Monte (p255), Caltagirone

PAT BEHNKE/ALAMY

Mafia? Just Say No

NAME	Puccio La Rosa and David Migneco-Brandt
AGE	31 and 24
OCCUPATION	Anti-Mafia campaigners
RESIDENCE	Catania

'Don't think like the Mafia, and don't tolerate the Mafia. If you see something suspicious, report it to the police'

People used to be very afraid of the Mafia, but this is not so much the case any more. We raise awareness by telling people: 'Don't think like the Mafia, and don't tolerate the Mafia. If you see something suspicious, report it to the police.' It's about changing the way people think, what they find acceptable. We have practically won the fight against *omertá* [code of silence] – if someone goes into a shop today and asks for *pizzo* [protection money], the owner will report it to the police. Fifteen years ago, this would never happen. You'd pay up and keep quiet.

We can't beat the Mafia with demonstrations and slogans only, however. It's important to see political and economical reforms. Sicily has a huge unemployment problem, and we need to deal with this so that the Mafia doesn't find it easy to recruit young people. If people can work and earn money legally, they won't go for criminality.

We promote the concept of working together and of adopting the rule of law. The Mafia as people know it from 15 or 20 years ago doesn't exist any longer. But we need to pay attention.

AS RELATED TO VESNA MARIC

Anti-Mafia sweeps have put many former *mafiosi* heavies behind bars (p44)

AFP/GETTY IMAGES

(Continued from page 156)

Marina Corta to the town centre. Some rooms sleep up to five people and there is a communal kitchen and two terraces with views.

our pick **Diana Brown** (☎ 090 981 25 84; www.diana brown.it; Vico Himera 3; s €30-80, d €40-100; 🔀) Diana Brown's spotless, bright and comfortable rooms (some with small kitchens) are the best budget choice on the island. The B&B is tucked behind Via Vittorio Emanuele in a small alleyway. South Africa–born Diana is a fount of local information. She also does laundry (for longer stays) and operates a book exchange.

MIDRANGE

Enzo Il Negro (☎ 090 981 31 63; www.enzoilnegro .altervista.org; Via Garibaldi 29; s €40-60, d €60-130; 🔀) Enzo Il Negro has clean, comfortable rooms with traditional tiled floors, good bathrooms and little fridges. All rooms have a balcony, but it's the roof terrace that's the spectacular feature – overlook the little marina while you have breakfast.

Hotel Oriente (☎ 090 981 14 93; www.hoteloriente lipari.com; Via G Marconi 35; s €40-80, d €60-130; 🔀) An eccentric joint, full of funny, bizarre and often scary bric-a-brac that crowds the reception. The rooms are minimal in terms of décor, but each has a little porch in the lush garden that's bursting with jasmine and hibiscus bushes. There are large rooms for families too.

our pick **Casajanca** (☎ 090 988 02 22; www.casajanca .it; Marina Garibaldi 115, Località Canneto; d €60-200; 🔀) You'll struggle to find a more charming hotel on the whole of Lipari. Once the home of Aeolian poet Ruccio Carbone, it has only 10 rooms, all of which are decorated in an impeccably stylish mix of antiques and French countryside style. The dappled courtyard is a relaxing place to enjoy breakfast and it hides a natural thermal water pool that's perfect for winter stays. Run by Silvia and Massimo, Casajanca is located just behind the waterfront at Canneto.

Pensione Neri (☎ 090 981 14 13; www.pensioneneri.it; Via G Marconi 43; d €70-130; 🔀) Although a touch expensive, this patrician pink villa is conveniently located right in the historic centre. It also has views over the archaeological park from its balconies. The interior is decorated in typical Aeolian style and feels like someone's home.

Villa Diana (☎ 090 981 14 03; www.villadiana.com; Via Tufo 1; s €40-75, d €75-130; Ⓟ) An old Aeolian house, bought by the Swiss artist Edwin Hunziker in the 1950s, was renovated into this lovely hotel. It stands above Lipari Town in a garden of citrus and olive trees and there are lovely views from its terrace. The artist's family still owns and runs it in the same bohemian spirit.

Residence Alberghiere Eolie (☎ 090 981 70 47; www.residenceeolie.it; Corso Vittorio Emanuele 101; s €65-90, d €90-150; 🔀) Brilliantly located off the main street with an attractive terracotta courtyard, the rooms here are spacious (though lacking in character a little) and with views of the archaeological park. There are apartments too (per person €40 to €70) and a solarium on the rooftop terrace. The service is friendly and helpful.

Hotel Carasco (☎ 090 981 16 05; www.carasco.it; Porto Delle Genti; s €60-136, d €80-220; 🕑 Apr-Oct; 🔀 🏊) The Carasco's a real mixed bag. It has an undeniably wonderful location, right on a cliff edge, a large pool and its own private jetty. But it is inconveniently located for the town and restaurants and could do with a facelift.

TOP END

Villa Meligunis (☎ 090 981 24 26; www.villameligunis.it; Via Marte 7; s €110-240, d €150-300; 🔀) A converted 18th-century villa, the Meligunis is Lipari's top hotel, offering luxurious accommodation, great facilities and a scenic rooftop terrace. Diving and water sports can also be arranged at reception.

Hotel Giardino sul Mare (☎ 090 981 10 04; www .giardinosulmare.it; Via Maddalena 65; d €196-300; 🕑 Mar-Nov; 🔀 🏊) An attractive small hotel with chichi décor – cane furniture and the like. The poolside terrace, situated on a cliff edge, is fabulous. The hotel is family-run and has a friendly atmosphere.

Eating

The waters of the archipelago abound with fish, including tuna, mullet, cuttlefish and sole, all of which end up on restaurant tables at the end of the day. Try *pasta all'eoliana*, a simple blend of the island's excellent capers with olive oil and basil. Swordfish is a particular favourite and you can also find 'black' risotto (rice stained with the dye of ink fish).

The local wine is malvasia, which has a DOC *(denominazione di origine controllata)* accreditation and a sweet taste of honey (see p51).

Many restaurants close at the end of October for the winter season.

RESTAURANTS

La Piazzetta (☎ 090 981 25 22; off Via Vittorio Emanuele behind Pasticceria Subba; pizza €4-7; ☒ closed for lunch Sep-Jun) A popular pizzeria restaurant that has served the likes of Audrey Hepburn. Great location and lively atmosphere.

La Cambusa (☎ 349 476 60 61; Via Garibaldi 72; meals €20-25) A tiny one-room restaurant with good, unpretentious cooking that strives for a homemade feeling. Although it specialises in fish it also does mean pasta and lasagne.

La Nassa (☎ 090 981 13 19; Via G Franza; meals €25-30; ☒ closed Mon Nov-Mar) Genuine Aeolian cuisine is served in this family-run trattoria away from the main drag. Favourites include fish such as *cernia, sarago* and *dentice*, or try the Aeolian sausages, which are a house speciality.

Trattoria d'Oro (☎ 090 981 13 04; Via Umberto I 28-32; meals €25-30; ☒ closed Sun Nov-Mar) This is a good small restaurant with fresh seafood dishes. Popular with the locals.

Le Macine (☎ 090 982 23 87; Pianoconte; meals €35-40) This Slow Food–awarded restaurant is located outside Lipari just as you enter Pianoconte. Creative Aeolian cooking includes fish in *ghiotta* sauce: a blend of olive oil, capers, tomatoes, garlic and basil. Lobster-filled ravioli or the fresh grilled swordfish are great too. The presentation is nicely low-key, but the portions could be bigger.

our pick **Kasbah** (☎ 090 981 10 75; Via Maurolico 25; pizzas €8, meals €35-40; ☒ 7pm-3am Mar-Oct) The Kasbah is a sleek place with a North African décor and a fantastic back garden where candlelit dinners take place under canopies. The food is excellent – this place does some of the best pizzas in Sicily (try the *tre formaggi* – mild cheeses with basil and fresh tomatoes) and delicacies such as *linguine con bottarga* (linguine with dried pressed fish roe), almonds and fennel.

Filippino (☎ 090 981 10 02; Piazza Municipio; meals €45-50; ☒ closed Mon Oct-Mar) Occupying a big chunk of Piazza Municipio, this is Lipari's most classy restaurant. The menu is based on old-fashioned Sicilian cooking and is full of surprising tastes. Dress appropriately and book ahead.

E Pulera (☎ 090 981 11 58; Via Diana, Filippino; meals €45-50; ☒ evenings only Jun-Sep) You can dine in the middle of a garden at Filippino's popular summer restaurant.

CAFÉS

Pasticceria Subba (☎ 090 981 13 52; Via Vittorio Emanuele 92) Open since 1930, this is a historic café where you can enjoy a delicious selection of mouthwatering Sicilian pastries and cakes.

SELF-CATERING

People with access to a kitchen can shop for supplies at the grocery shops and **SISA supermarket** (Via Vittorio Emanuele).

Drinking

Most of the town's nightlife is concentrated in and around the Marina Corta, where there are a handful of bars with outdoor seating. Try **Il Gabbiano** (☎ 090 981 14 71; Marina Corta) and **Al Pescatore** (☎ 090 981 15 37; Marina Corta) – both are popular places for people-watching.

If you fancy a late-night drink or want to be in the right place for crowd gazing during *passeggiata* (evening stroll), **Bar La Precchia** (☎ 090 981 13 03; Via Vittorio Emanuele 191) is a local favourite. It has an enormous menu of drinks, from *café frappe* and fruit milkshakes to cocktails and wine. In summer it's open until 3am and often has live music.

Shopping

Lipari is full of shops, particularly jewellery shops selling (sadly) truckloads of precious coral alongside all manner of obsidian and turquoise trinkets. There are also a number of great gourmet delicatessens: a couple as you walk up Via Garibaldi from Marina Corta, and the tempting **Fratelli Laise** (☎ 090 981 27 31; Via Vittorio Emanuele 118), which sells fresh fruit and veg and a whole range of wines, sweets, *anis* (aniseed) biscuits, pâtés, capers and oil.

Getting There & Away

The main port is Marina Lunga where you will find the main **Siremar** (☎ 090 981 13 12) and **Ustica Lines** (☎ 090 981 24 48) ticket offices. There is also another ticket booth at the Marina Corta hydrofoil terminal. NGI Traghetti is located at Marina Lunga.

For details of ferry and hydrofoil departures for Milazzo and the other islands, see p151 and p151.

Getting Around

BUS

Autobus Urso Guglielmo (☎ 090 981 12 62, 090 981 10 26; Via Cappuccini 9) runs an efficient and frequent service around the island, departing from just near the Esso service station at Marina Lunga. You can pick up timetables from the office. There are frequent departures for Canneto (€1.30, 30 minutes, nine daily), Acquacalda, Porticello and Quattrocchi. During July and August the service increases. If you plan on using the bus a lot buy a booklet of tickets (six/10 for €6/9.80) to use when you like.

The company also offers tours of the island (€3.70, one hour, departures 9.30am, 11.30am and 5pm from 1 July to 30 September), which are a good way of seeing the sights if your time is limited.

CAR & MOTORCYCLE

Roberto Foti (☎ 090 981 23 52; www.robertofoti.it; Via F Crispi 31; scooters per day €15-30, Fiat Panda/Uno per 24hr €45/55) rents out scooters and cars. Otherwise, there are half a dozen rental outfits by the port.

VULCANO

pop 720 / elev 500m

Only 1km south of Lipari, across the Bocche di Vulcano, sits the steaming crater of Fossa di Vulcano (or Gran Cratere, 'Large Crater') on Vulcano island. Worshipped by the Italian jet set for its therapeutic mud baths and hot springs, this little island is a great place to spend a day or two, enjoying the sulphur baths, taking a boat around the wild coast, and climbing up to the sleeping crater to see the steaming yellow sulphuric rocks. It's not a place to come and enjoy traditional sights – Vulcano is all about taking the time to relax and enjoy the tranquil beaches at Gelso and Cannitello.

Orientation

Boats dock at the Porto di Levante. To the right, as you face the island, is the small Vulcanello peninsula. To reach the mud baths turn right and walk right along the *lungomare* (seafront promenade); the pools are at the end, hidden behind a small hillock. All facilities are concentrated between the Porto di Levante and the Porto di Ponente, where you will find the Spiaggia Sabbia Nera (Black Sand Beach), a nice long stretch of black sand.

Of Vulcano's three volcanoes, the oldest lies on the island's southern tip and was already extinct in ancient times, although the fumarole constantly emits a wisp of sulphurous gases.

Information

EMERGENCY

Emergency Doctor (☎ 090 985 22 20; Via Lentia)
Police (☎ 090 985 21 10)

MEDICAL SERVICES

Bonarrigo Pharmacy (☎ 090 985 22 44; Via Favoloro 1)

MONEY

Banco di Sicilia (☎ 090 985 23 35; port area; 8.30am-1.30pm & 2.45-3.45pm Mon-Fri Jun-Sep only) Has an ATM.
Thermessa Agency (☎ 090 985 22 30; Via Provinciale) Changes money and sells tickets for Ustica Lines hydrofoils.

POST

Post Office (☎ 090 985 30 02; Contrada Piano)

TOURIST INFORMATION

Tourist Office (☎ 090 985 20 28; Via Provinciale 41; 8am-2pm Jun-Oct) A domelike building on the main street, 50m back from the dock. It provides information on rented rooms.

A SMELLY PIT OR NATURE'S HEALING SPA?

The *fanghi* is a large natural pool of thick, warm, sulphurous mud water that has long been considered an excellent treatment for all kinds of rheumatic pains and skin diseases. It's also incredibly smelly in certain places, sending people running and thinking of rotten eggs. Those with sulphite allergies are at risk here, so if you know you suffer, stay away.

If you're on good terms with life's essential element and don't mind smelling funny for a few days, rolling around in the mud can be a tantalising experience. Dip into the warm, pale green water, and mind you don't step on any of the hot air vents that spring from the ground on the way into the pool – they can scald your feet, so take flip-flops.

Once you have had time to relax in the muddy water, get some soft clay from the bottom of the pool and apply it to your skin (body and face). Don't let any of the mud get in your eyes as the sulphur is acidic and can be damaging to the retina (keep your hair mud-free too). Wait for the clay mask to dry, wash it off in the pool, and run to the natural spa around the corner, where there are hot, bubbling springs in a small natural sea-water pool. You're advised to spend another five to 10 minutes lolling about. Finally, take a shower (get a token in advance, for €1) and make sure not to use your favourite fluffy towel – if you're staying in a hotel, the staff can usually provide you with 'special' *fanghi* towels. The same goes for your swimsuit – wear something that you don't mind destroying because once the smell gets in it's near impossible to get rid of.

Remember to remove watches and jewellery with stones, as the mud will ruin them. Experts have advised that prolonged immersion can be bad for you on account of the pool's slight radioactivity. You should not stay in for more than 10 or 15 minutes and pregnant women should avoid it altogether.

Have fun!

Sights & Activities

PORTO DI LEVANTE & AROUND

Once you've disembarked, head over to the **Laghetto di Fanghi** (admission €2, groups of 10 €1; 7am-11pm) mud baths. They're right (north) of the dock at the bottom of a *faraglione* (a long stone finger jutting up into the sky).

Just next to the baths is the cone of Vulcanello, where you can see the **Valle dei Mostri** (Valley of the Monsters), a group of wind-eroded dark rocks that have formed grotesque shapes.

FOSSA DI VULCANO

The island's other main attraction is climbing Fossa di Vulcano (391m). The walk up to the crater is self-evident. Follow the intermittent signs for 'Al Cratere' (or ask for directions), which take you south out of the port area along Via Provinciale. About 500m further, a track slopes off to the left (not well signposted; look out for a gravel track) which leads up to the crater. Before you start the ascent you'll have to buy a ticket (€3) and take note of the official plaque (in four languages), which announces the dangers of the crater. If you proceed (which everyone does) you won't have any problem with officialdom but you do need to be aware that this is a 'sleeping' volcano.

It's about one hour's scramble to the lowest point of the crater's edge (290m). The going is a bit tough in the first part of the climb, where the ground is covered with black sandy soil, so it feels as if you're walking uphill on a sandy beach. The sand turns clay-like further up, with the final part of the path becoming quite rocky. There's a bit of dust blowing around, so it's a good idea to have a tissue handy. The way is also very exposed, so make sure you wear strong, closed shoes, apply sunscreen and bring plenty of water, though there is a small café halfway up the path, which sells water, juice, ice cream and coffee. When you've reached the top, you can lean over a ledge and look into the main crater. The bottom of the volcano is clearly visible less than 50m below. A steep trail descends (it takes three minutes to reach the bottom) and many go down for a walk along the hard crater floor.

For stunning 360-degree views of all the islands lined up to the north, walk clockwise around the crest of the crater. Along the path you will pass fumaroles that constantly vent gases. Don't walk too close to them as the temperature of the escaping gas can be searing.

Though it's not really necessary since the climb is not very tough, you can hire a guide. Contact the **Gruppo Nazionale Vulcanologia** (☎ 090

AEOLIAN ISLANDS

985 25 28) or **Gruppo Trekking Vulcano** (☎ 339 418 58 75). The latter organises daily hikes up the volcano as well as other treks, including an ascent of Stromboli (€50) and snorkelling outings. It has a stand by the restaurant Da Maurizio (see p170).

PORTO DI PONENTE & AROUND
On the far side of the peninsula from Porto di Levante at **Porto di Ponente** is the **Spiaggia Sabbia Nera** (Black Sand Beach), a smooth, sandy beach, with stunning *faraglioni* jutting into the sky. Paddleboats are usually available for hire on the beach (€8 for one hour).

PIANO & CAPO GRILLO
Piano is the plain where most of Vulcano's population lives, and from there you can get to Capo Grillo, where there are breathtaking views of the coast and out to sea. **Scaffadi** has seven buses from Porto di Levante to Piano and Capo Grillo between 8am and 6pm Monday to Saturday (two on Sunday and public holidays).

GELSO
On the island's southern coast is Gelso, a gorgeous little port with a couple of black-sand beaches that are never crowded. There's a little eatery here (see p170) and if you fall in love with the isolation, peace and quiet, you can rent an apartment (see p170). Most people come here for the day only, in order to enjoy the splendid beaches. There are two excellent tranquil beaches near Gelso, approached by signposted steep dirt tracks (pedestrians only) that branch off before the town. The first crescent sweep of black sand and inviting waters is **Spiaggia dell'Asina** (Donkey Beach); the second, which is surrounded by lush, almost tropical greenery, is **Spiaggia Cannitello**. Both have a rudimentary bar/café, where you can also hire sun lounges (€8) and umbrellas (€5). Keep in mind that both these beaches are loved for their tranquillity and take a bit of time getting to and from the main port.

To get to Gelso and the beaches by public transport is pretty limiting, so hiring a scooter is a much better idea. The **Vulcania Tour bus** (€1.95; ⏰ departs Porto di Levante 10.15am, 11.35am & 4.30pm, 15 Jun-15 Sep) transports passengers up and down the steep curves (20 minutes). If you are going to either of the beaches, ask the driver to let you off at the dirt track. Buses from Gelso leave at 11am, 12.10pm and 5pm, picking up

passengers from the pier. Boat tours of the island also call in here and are happy to take passengers on a tour, but disembark at Gelso for €10. A taxi from Porto Levante costs a whopping €30.

Tours
Gente di Mare (☎ 3334577446; Via Comunale Levante; boat trip per person €15)
Gioielli del Mare (☎ 090 985 21 70; Porto di Levante; 2hr tour per person €15) The proprietor of this outfit organises bus tours around the island in his red transit Ford. Make a booking and wait for a group of 10 people to form.
Pino & Giuseppe (☎ 090 985 24 19; Via Comunale Levante; boat trip per person €15) In front of the tobacconist.

Sleeping
Vulcano's hotels are mostly on the large side, and it's worth staying here mainly if you want to take advantage of the mud baths or the quiet beaches at Gelso. The best hotels are situated around the Spiaggia Sabbia Nera.

Camping Togo Togo (☎ 090 985 21 28; www .campingtogotogo.it; Porto Ponente; per person/site €10/15; ⏰ Apr-Sep) This decent camp site at the end of the Spiaggia Sabbia Nera is shaded with eucalyptus trees and has a tranquil atmosphere. There's a cinema, solarium, bar and pizzeria for supplies and entertainment.

Hotel Torre (☎ 090 985 23 42; Via Favaloro 1; d €40-80; ❄) This good-value hotel has large rooms that all come with a kitchen and a terrace. Its proximity to the beach at Laghetto di Fanghi may prove too potent for some.

Hotel Arcipelago (☎ 090 985 20 02; Vulcanello; s €58-102, d €116-204; ⏰ Mar-Oct; ❄ ⛱) This is one of the smaller big hotels, 2km from the village on Vulcanello. Bright, breezy rooms have views over the gardens and sea. Those on the seaward side have good views of all seven islands.

Eolian Hotel (☎ 090 985 21 51; www.eolianhotel .com; Via Porto di Ponente; s €62-88, d €124-176; ⏰ Mar-Oct; ❄ ⛱) The Eolian offers small bungalows dotted throughout a landscaped garden. The rooms are fine but not fantastic; the real draw is the excellent facilities, including tennis, water sports, boat trips and even a private sulphurous pool.

Hotel Les Sables Noirs (☎ 090 985 24 54; www .framon-hotels.com; Porto di Ponente; s €110-140, d €152-256; ⏰ Apr-Oct; ❄ ⛱) The best hotel on the island, with a beach-front location overlooking the Spiaggia Sabbia Nera. The large pool is surrounded by gardens and palms and the rooms have flower-bedecked balconies. The restaurant's panoramic terrace is fantastic at sunset.

Nando e Carla Marraro (☎ 339 711 77 95; Gelso; 2-bed apt per week Jun & Jul, Sep €600, Aug €1400; ☺ Jun-Sep) Gelso's only accommodation is a modern apartment that can sleep from four to six people, overlooking the little port from its gorgeous terrace. Owned by a lovely couple, it's a heavenly location and fantastic value for a group in the low-season months. Booking in advance is essential.

Eating & Drinking

Vulcano's eating scene is pretty poor, though there are a couple of good picks.

our pick Ritrovo Remigio (Porto di Levante; cannolo €1.80) This place sells the best *cannoli* ever. Fresh, with the perfect contrast of soft ricotta and crispy biscuit, it'll send you *cannoli* crazy. Don't leave Vulcano without getting at least one. It's right by the port, as you get off the ferry.

Cantine Stevenson (☎ 090 985 32 47; Via Porto di Levante; pizza €6-8) Like some ill-advised transplant of Scottish décor onto a Sicilian island, Cantine Stevenson is, visually, sorely out of place. But take a tipple in James Stevenson's wine cellars and you'll be thanking the Scotsman who bought most of Vulcano in the 19th century with a view to exploiting its natural resources. He also planted the first vineyards.

our pick Trattoria Maniaci Pina (☎ 090 985 22 42; Gelso; meals €20-22; ☺ closed Nov-Easter) Gelso's only trattoria is as traditional as they get, with blue chequered tablecloths and wooden tables. The food is delicious and simple, with a couple of daily changing *primi* and *secondi*. It has the best atmosphere of any restaurant on the island.

Da Maurizio (☎ 090 985 24 26; Via Porto di Levante; tourist menu €15.50, meals €30-35; ☺ closed Nov-Easter) This pleasant restaurant in an attractive garden has a good reputation on the island. Try the excellent cuttlefish pasta.

Da Vincenzino (☎ 090 985 20 16; Via Porto di Levante 125; meals €30-35; ☺ closed Nov-Apr) Just near Da Maurizio, this place is close to the port and OK for lunch or dinner. The service is friendly and the portions generous.

Caffè Piazzetta (☎ 090 985 32 67; Piazzetta Faraglione; ice cream from €1.50) This large outdoor café is convenient for a drink or gelato. In the summer, music booms out from the sound system

and in July and August there is live music in the evenings.

Getting There & Away

Vulcano is an intermediate stop between Milazzo and Lipari and a good number of vessels go both ways throughout the day. See p151 for details.

Getting Around

You can hire boats on the island. One company that offers this service is **Centro Nautico Baia di Levante** (☎ 090 982 21 97, 3393372795; zodiac 4-/8-person per day €60/80). You will find it in a shed on the beach to the left of the hydrofoil dock.

Scooters, bikes and small motorised cars can be rented from **Da Paolo** (☎ 090 985 21 12) or **Sprint** (☎ 090 985 22 08) at the intersection of Via Provinciale and Via Porto di Levante. Scooters cost around €25 per day although this varies with season and demand. Cars cost around €50 per day.

See p169 for details of travel on Scaffadi buses. Call ☎ 3396005750 (24 hours) if you need a taxi.

SALINA
pop 2300 / elev 962m

It's striking how, despite their proximity, each of the Aeolian Islands is so different from the others. This little island is unique: its twin craters (Monte dei Porri and Monte Fossa delle Felci) are lushly wooded, with wild flowers, thick yellow gorse bushes and serried ranks of vines carpeting the island in vibrant colours and cool greens. Its high coastal cliffs plunge into dramatic beaches and its stylish and quiet towns are a world away from the tourist bustle of Lipari. And it's not only that Salina is different from the rest of the islands, it's incredibly diverse on its own (and for its size). Santa Marina Salina, the island's main port and town, is worlds away from Lingua, its closest neighbour. If you take the winding road around the island to Malfa or Rinella you'll find another two villages that have their own atmosphere and style.

Although it owes its modern name to the *saline* (saltworks) of Lingua, Salina is defined and shaped by the two volcanoes that gave it its ancient Greek name of Dydime, meaning 'double'. Despite being extinct since antiquity, previous eruptions combined with plenty of water (Salina is the only island that has natural springs) have rendered the island the most

fertile in the archipelago. The famous Aeolian *capperi* (capers) grow plentiful here, as do the grapes used to make malvasia wine.

Orientation

Boats dock at Santa Marina Salina, where you will find most accommodation, or at Rinella, a fishing hamlet on the southwest coast. The other main villages on the island are Malfa, on the northern coast, and Leni, slightly inland from Rinella.

The road south from Santa Marina Salina port leads to Lingua (see right), and the buses for the rest of the island depart from the bus stop at the corner of the main square.

Information

In summer tourist booths operate at Rinella, Malfa and Santa Marina Salina; the rest of the year, contact the Lipari bureau. You will find public phones at the island's ports.

Banco Antoveneta – Malfa (Via Provinciale 2; ☾ 8.40am-1.20pm Mon-Sat).

Banco Antoveneta – Santa Marina Salina (Via Lungomare Notar Giuffre; ☾ 8.40am-1.20pm Mon-Sat) To the right along the *lungomare;* has an ATM.

Emergency Doctor (☎ 090 984 40 05)

Farmacia Cucinotta (☎ 090 980 90 53; Via Libertà, Santa Marina Salina)

Police (☎ 090 984 30 19)

Post Office (☎ 090 984 30 28; Via Risorgimento, Santa Marina Salina) Can also change money.

Salina Computers (Via Risorgimento, Santa Maria Salina; per hr €6; ☾ 10am-2.30pm & 6-8.30pm Mon-Sat, 6-8.30pm Sun) Half a dozen computers and a fast connection.

Sights

SANTA MARINA SALINA

Santa Marina Salina is Salina's main port and town. The town is bisected by the main street, Via Risorgimento, which is lined by gorgeous Aeolian houses – varicoloured cubes with round windows – design shops, some cafés and a few *alimentari* (grocery shops). It runs parallel to the *lungomare,* off Piazza Santa Marina and the port. If you turn right from the docking area and head along the *lungomare,* you can swim off the large-pebble beach (though the pebbles are somewhat stabbing). Santa Marina is a great base from which to explore the rest of island.

MADONNA DEL TERZITO & MONTE FOSSA DELLE FELCI

If you're feeling energetic, climb the **Fossa delle Felci** (962m) volcano and visit the nature reserve. The **Santuario della Madonna del Terzito** (Sanctuary of the Madonna of Terzito) is at Valdichiesa, in the valley separating the two volcanoes. It is a place of pilgrimage, particularly around the Feast of the Assumption on 15 August. From the church you can follow the track (signposted) all the way to the peak (about two hours).

Along the way you'll see plenty of colourful flora, including wild violets, asparagus and a plant known locally as *cipudazza* (Latin *Urginea marittima*), which was sold to the Calabrians to make soap but used locally as mouse poison! Once you've reached the top (the last 100m are particularly tough), you have unparalleled views of the entire archipelago. You can get to the sanctuary by taking a bus from Santa Marina Salina to Rinella or Leni, and asking the driver to let you off at the sanctuary.

LINGUA

Only a 3km walk along the main road or a bus ride from Santa Marina Salina, Lingua is a romantic seaside village with some hotels – one notably luxurious – a few trattorie and a small beach. Its *lungomare* street, Via Manzoni, runs from the end of Via Umberto, which takes you into the village. Lingua's houses are Aeolian cubes, painted with whitewash and light sky-blues, with bunches of fresh tomatoes and drying herbs hanging outside. There's a salt lagoon near the lighthouse and the beach, and it is this that gave Salina its name. It's a beautiful sight at dusk.

AEOLIAN ISLANDS

A TASTE OF HONEY

Salina's fortune is its freshwater springs. It is the only Aeolian island with natural water sources, the result of which is the startling greenery. The islanders have put this to good use, producing their own style of wine, malvasia. It is thought that the Greeks brought the grapes to the islands in 588 BC, and the name is certainly derived from Monenvasìa, a Greek city.

The wine is still produced according to traditional techniques using the malvasia grape and the now-rare red Corinthian grape. The harvest generally occurs in the second week of September when the grapes are picked and laid out to dry on woven cane mats. The drying process is crucial; the grapes must dry out enough to concentrate the sweet flavour but not too much, which would caramelise them.

The result is a dark golden or light amber wine which tastes, some say, of honey. It is usually drunk in very small glasses and goes well with cheese, sweet biscuits and almond pastries.

To experience a working vineyard you can stay at the luxurious **Capo Faro** (☎ 090 984 43 30; www.capofaro.it; Via Faro 3, Malfa; d €190-290; 🏊), a small resort of Aeolian-style cottages on the 13-acre Tasca d'Almerita vineyard. Aside from its beautiful location and elegant rooms, you can sample the home-brew and explore the vineyards.

You can also head from Lingua by path up to Monte Fossa delle Felci (follow the signs for Brigantino). Corn and barley are the main crops around Brigantino, but as soon as you start climbing (take the path to the right), you'll see plenty of olive trees that eventually give way to vineyards. A century ago the hilltops were covered in vines, but local industry has suffered greatly at the hands of competition from the Sicilian mainland, leaving only a few cultivators of the famed malvasia wine.

MALFA

If you're after a relaxing time in stylish, elegant and/or luxurious hotels, where you can read, get pampered and have a swim, Malfa is the place for you. Totally different from Santa Marina, Lingua and Rinella, Malfa is built on a cliff that overlooks the crashing waves, and its atmosphere is quiet and reserved. The main road snakes down into town and the wonderful hotels are scattered along its narrow streets. Malfa is the largest town on the island and has a small shingle beach, backed by destroyed fisherfolk's houses. It never gets really crowded.

The **Museo dell'Emigrazione Eoliana** (Emigration Museum; ☎ 090 984 43 72; admission free; 🕑 9am-1pm Mon-Fri Jun-Sep) in Palazzo Marchetti gives visitors an idea of the scale and effect of emigration from the Aeolian Islands.

If you come to Malfa by bus, you'll be dropped off at the top of the town, by the church, but the bus coming back will pick you up just below Hotel Punta Scario (see opposite).

POLLARA & RINELLA

Don't miss a trip to the beach at Pollara, the setting for much of the film *Il Postino*. The climb down is quite tricky but the beach itself with its backdrop of volcanic cliffs is absolutely unbeatable (visit in the afternoon as the beach is in shadow in the morning). If you're coming here by bus, get off at the stop before Pollara village, where the steps take you down to the beach. Otherwise it's quite a hike from Pollara village.

The road to Rinella spirals all the way down to the tiny port. From there, a small black-sand grin of a beach extends to the side, and above the beach the miniature village clambers up the same hills you just descended. The village is a picture of beauty, with salmon pinks, pearly whites and sea-blue houses huddled together. Rinella is a popular underwater spearfishing spot (for information ask at the tourist booths). If the sandy beach gets too cramped, you can always go to the rocky spot near the Campeggio Tre Pini camp site or walk past the camp site for 20 minutes along the paved sea-view path to the other big (large-pebble) beach. You can use the bus to get here, or take one of the hydrofoils from Santa Marina Salina.

Activities

Eolie Adventure (☎ 090 984 41 34, 3334699530; www .eolieadventure.com; information stand at Santa Marina harbour during summer; hike per person 1-day €20, 3-day to Filicudi incl tent & sleeping bag €75) organises excellent nature hikes on Salina as well as the other islands. If you feel adventurous you can take the wonderful hike to Filicudi, which involves crossing a lava trail.

Sleeping & Eating
SANTA MARINA SALINA

Salina remains relatively undisturbed by mass tourism, generally offering only upmarket accommodation in a few small hotels. The majority of restaurants are located in these hotels although it is possible to eat in them if you are not a guest by making a reservation.

Hotel Bellavista (☎ 090 984 30 09; Via Risorgimento 8; s €70-110, d €90-190; ☉ Apr-Sep; ✖) This hotel has panoramic views of the sea and three-star facilities.

Hotel Mercanti di Mare (☎ 090 984 35 36; www .hotelmercantidimare.it; Piazza Santa Marina 9; d €100-180; ✖) A new outfit that follows the stylish line of Salina's hotels, this is a gorgeous white cubic building, decorated in the typical Aeolian style of curving walls and minimalist décor. The rooms have good wrought-iron beds and some have views of the sea. The lovely terrace is perfect for relaxing in the evening.

Pensione Mamma Santina (☎ 090 984 30 54; www .mammasantina.it; Via Sanità 40; d €110-210; ✖ 🍴) A family atmosphere, colourful rooms with tiled floors and great views make Mamma Santina one of the favourites. Head for Via Risorgimento (the narrow main street) and walk north for a few hundred metres. Its highly regarded restaurant has been featured in *Cucina Italiana*.

Though the choice of restaurants is limited, the food is great.

our pick Cucinotta Rita (☎ 090 984 35 23; Via Risorgimento 6; meals €25) Salina's best restaurant is this small place at the end of Via Risorgimento. Sit at one of the elegantly set tables alfresco, while the attentive waiters serve fantastic food such as stuffed squid, grilled swordfish sprinkled with parsley, and hearty chocolate cake desserts. You can also pop in here for breakfast – the croissants are freshly baked.

Portobello (☎ 090 984 31 25; Via Bianchi 1; Santa Marina; meals €25-30; ☉ Tue-Sun) Sit on the terrace overlooking the sea and tuck into the *spaghetti al fuoco* (fiery spaghetti) in this excellent restaurant.

LINGUA

A Cannata (☎ 090 984 31 61; www.acannata.it; Via Umberto 1; r per person €50) Situated on a wild, green bluff, A Cannata has 10 simple rooms and some apartments in a nearby house. Its restaurant

has a Slow Food recommendation and focuses on fish and seafood, with a simple, down-to-earth approach (meals €25 to €30). You'd be advised to book in advance in summer.

our pick La Salina Borgo di Mare (☎ 090 984 24 41; www.lasalinahotel.com; Via Manzoni; s €120-200, d €150-200; ✖) A stunning new hotel built in the converted old saltworks complex, Borgo di Mare is divided into five low, cubic Aeolian buildings, all of which are connected by little paths in the fragrant gardens full of jasmine and hibiscus. The hotel is quiet and relaxing and the houses – whose traditional Aeolian style has been carefully preserved – are painted in light pastel colours. The rooms are luxurious and stylish, each with its own little terrace. It's right next to the large pebble beach – sunset swims are essential if you stay here.

Da Alfredo in Cucina (☎ 090 984 33 07; Via Pantano; meals €25-30) A new outfit run by the son of Alfredo, Lingua's masterly *granita* maker (of 'Da Alfredo' on Via Manzoni, around the corner). This is a simple and elegant restaurant with a large terrace where each table is lit by an individual overhanging light. It overlooks the salt lagoon and is tucked away from the bustle of the other restaurants and cafés. A wonderful addition to the village.

MALFA

our pick Hotel Santa Isabel (☎ 090 984 40 18; www .santaisabel.it; Via Scalo 12; d €90-235; ☉ Apr-Oct; ✖) A white complex consisting of ten furnished apartments with one and two bedrooms, mezzanine sleeping areas and kitchenettes. The interiors are a blinding white with vibrant bedspreads and large black-and-white film stills covering a wall in each. The clifftop position is best appreciated from the bar, where many nonguests come for *aperitivi* in the early evening.

Hotel Punta Scario (☎ 090 984 41 39; www.punta scario.it; Via Scalo 8; d €100-150; ✖) Another gorgeous Malfa hotel, the Punta Scario is simple, good-looking and with great views of the sea and Stromboli from its massive rooftop terrace.

our pick Hotel Signum (☎ 090 984 42 22; www .hotelsignum.it; Via Scalo 15; d €110-240; ✖ 🍴) Surrounded by vineyards overlooking the sea, the Signum is the best hotel on Salina. The building is a series of interlinking Aeolian houses and the interior is decorated with antiques. The rooms cluster around the stunning swimming pool with its invisible edge and views straight out to smoking Stromboli.

AEOLIAN ISLANDS

RINELLA

Campeggio Tre Pini (☎ 090 980 91 55; www.trepini .com in Italian; Frazione Rinella-Leni; per tent/person €7.70/8; ☺ May-Sep) The island's only camp site has good amenities and the terraced sites overlook the sea. You can get here by ferry or hydrofoil (walk up and left from the port for about 100m), or by regular buses from Santa Marina. Reservations recommended in July and August.

Hotel L'Ariana (☎ 090 980 90 75; www.hotelariana .it; Via Rotabile 11; d €80-210) A patrician villa overlooking the sea at Rinella is the setting for this lovely little hotel. Its huge terrace is the place to be for malvasia-sipping sundowners as the sun sets on this side of the island. L'Ariana has a bar and restaurant and good deals on half/full board in summer.

Getting There & Away

Hydrofoils and ferries service Santa Marina Salina and Rinella. There are at least eight hydrofoil connections per day between Santa Marina Salina and the other islands and four daily from Rinella from 1 June to 30 September, including to/from Panarea (€6, 25 minutes, five daily) and Stromboli (€11.80, one hour, five daily). Service is reduced at other times.

Siremar (Santa Marina Salina ☎ 090 984 30 04; Rinella ☎ 090 980 91 70) has ticket booths at the harbours as does **Ustica Lines** (Santa Marina Salina ☎ 090 984 30 78; Rinella ☎ 090 980 92 33). For information on arrivals and departures from Milazzo, see p148.

Getting Around

Regular **Citis** (☎ 090 984 41 50) buses run from Santa Marina Salina to Lingua (€1.30), Malfa (€1.30), Rinella (€1.85), Pollara (€1.30), Valdichiesa and Leni (€1.85). Timetables are posted at the ports and around the island. If you're going to Rinella or Pollara from Santa Marina Salina, you'll have to change at Malfa, where the buses convene and take passengers on their particular routes.

Motorcycles and scooters can be hired from **Antonio Bongiorno** (☎ 090 984 34 09; Via Risorgimento 240, Santa Marina Salina; per day around €25). If you feel like hiring a scooter in Rinella (given the steepness of the road from here to the rest of the island, it's a good idea), check out **Eolian Service** (☎ 090 980 92 03; per day from €18) at the port.

Ask at the tourist office for hydrofoils between Santa Marina Salina and Rinella. Boats are available for hire from June to August at **Nautica Levante** (☎ 090 984 30 83; Via Risorgimento, Santa Marina).

PANAREA

pop 320 / elev 421m

Tiny Panarea is 3km long and 2km wide and feels more like a Greek island with its adobe-style whitewashed houses. Exclusive and expensive, it is popular with the international jet set who come here for one reason only – Hotel Raya. In summer luxury yachts fill the tiny harbour while flocks of day-trippers dock at San Pietro.

Orientation & Information

The island's population lives almost exclusively on the eastern side of the island, in one of the three former hamlets of Ditella, San Pietro and Drauto, although you'll hardly notice the difference between them as they have all merged into one strip of tangled lanes and pretty seafront houses. Addresses here are approximate as the intimacy of the place makes them unnecessary – everyone knows everyone else by name, and even the *forestieri* (outsiders) are known by their place of origin. ('Oh, you mean that fellow from Turin who owns the fancy villa up past Piero's?')

All boats dock at San Pietro, where you'll also find most of the accommodation (very expensive in high season), plus an ATM and public phones.

There is a pharmacy, **Sparacino** (☎ 090 98 31 48; Via Iditella), and in a medical emergency call ☎ 090 98 30 40. You can only call the **police** (☎ 090 98 31 81) between June and September. A good online resource is www.amapanarea .it (in Italian).

Sights & Activities

AROUND THE ISLAND

Head south to Punta Milazzese, about a 30-minute walk past a couple of beaches, to see the **Bronze Age village**, made up of 23 huts, which was discovered in 1948. It is reckoned that the headland here was inhabited as far back as the 14th century BC, while pottery found at the site shows distinctly Minoan influences, lending credence to the theory that there were ties between the islanders and the Cretans. The artefacts found here are on display in the Museo Archeologico Eoliano on Lipari (p153).

From the Punta Milazzese a set of steps leads down to the **Cala Junco**, a beautiful little cove where the swimming is excellent and the water a deep aquamarine. The island's other beach is to the north of Ditella, at the end of a track – just follow the signposts for **Spiaggia Fumarola**. The 'Stone Beach' here is isolated and a perfect place for a quiet swim, except in July and August, of course, when the ringing of mobile phones is incessant.

OFFSHORE
Panarea's own little archipelago consists of five tiny islets off the eastern shore, which can only be reached by boat (see opposite). The largest island, **Basiluzzo**, is also the furthest away and is given over to the cultivation of capers. At the back of the island, visible from land, is the impressive wreck of a Roman ship.

Nearest to Panarea is **Dattilo**, which has a pretty little beach called **Le Guglie**. Of the three islands south of Dattilo, you should make for **Lisca Bianca**, the one furthest away, where you can indulge in your own little spot of wreck-hunting if you're equipped with scuba gear. Contact **Amphibia** (☎ 090 98 33 11; Via Iditella, San Pietro, Panarea) to hire gear. Crossing the narrow channel from the islet of **Bottaro** (actually nothing more than a protruding rock) to Lisca Bianca, you will notice there is a small white beach on Lisca Bianca's southern side. Proceed left past the beach and continue around the sharp point of the island. Here, at a depth of perhaps 40m or 50m, you will find the wreck of an old English ship that sank in the 19th century. The last islet, **Lisca Nera**, lies south of Dattilo.

Sleeping & Eating
Finding accommodation on Panarea can be an expensive nightmare in July and August. Out of high season everything quietens considerably and the prices drop dramatically.

Hotel La Piazza (☎ 090 98 31 54; www.hotelpiazza.it; Via San Pietro; s €115-265, d €155-325; 🅿 🅰) Draped in bougainvillea and situated on the eastern side of the island, La Piazza offers exclusive and tranquil accommodation. Cool and elegant rooms, all with spectacular views of Caletta Bay, are full of rattan furnishings. There's also a gorgeous swimming pool terrace and an excellent restaurant.

Pensione Rodà (☎ 090 98 32 12; Via San Pietro; d €180-290) The first boarding house on the island opened just after WWII. The Rodà is located in the centre of the island amid a pleasant garden setting and has a welcoming atmosphere.

Lisca Bianca (☎ 090 98 30 04; www.liscabianca.it; Via Lani 1; d with/without sea view €310/280; 🅰 Apr-Oct) One of the loveliest places to stay on Panarea, Lisca Bianca's prices drop by over 50% in the low season. With whitewashed walls, sea views, a terrace and a great Arabia-themed bar, you may find it hard to leave.

Hotel Raya (☎ 090 98 30 13; www.hotelraya.it; Via San Pietro; d €320-480; 🅰 🅿) This is *the* hotel on Panarea. A complex of whitewashed villas climbing up the seashore, the Raya is pure understated luxury. Each room has its own sunbathing terrace with views of Stromboli. In the evening diners eat by the intimate light of oil lamps and tables are in such demand that you need to reserve them (meals €35 to €40). Its disco (open July to August) is known all over the islands.

Trattoria da Pina (☎ 090 98 30 32; Via San Pietro; meals €30; 🅰 12.30-3.30pm & 8.30-11pm Tue-Sat) Just up from the harbour, tables spill out onto a large covered terrace at this family-run restaurant. It attracts a good crowd in season and is definitely worth a try.

Da Francesco (☎ 090 98 30 23; Via San Pietro; meals €30-35) A good-value terrace restaurant overlooking the dock. Try the speciality *spaghetti con le cozze* (spaghetti with mussels). In summer they also rent out some inexpensive rooms (doubles €120).

Getting There & Away
In summer hydrofoils and ferries link the island with Stromboli (€7.50, 30 minutes, five daily) to the northeast, and Salina (and on to Lipari and Milazzo) and Filicudi (€18.10, 1½ hours, one daily) to the west. Both **Siremar** (☎ 090 98 30 07) and **Ustica Lines** (☎ 090 98 30 09) have offices along the harbour on Via San Pietro.

Getting Around
Cars are not allowed on Panarea, but you don't need them as the island is small enough to get around on foot. The preferred mode of transport is golf carts (the island's taxis). You can pick one up at the port, or call **Paolo & Angela** (☎ 3333138610; one-way fare per person €4, rental per day Sep-Jul/Aug about €26/36; 🅰 24hr).

To explore the islands, coves and beaches you'll need to hire a boat. **Tesoriero Roberto** (☎ 090 98 30 33; Via San Pietro) does all kinds of boat rentals, from rubber dinghies to wooden longboats with outboard motors. Expect to pay around €52 for half a day.

STROMBOLI
pop 400 / elev 924m

Seeing Stromboli from a distance strangely conforms to one's childhood ideas of a volcano: a cone-shaped thing with smoke coming out of the top. This is the furthest and most isolated of the Aeolian Islands, but also the most captivating, largely because it is the only place in Europe to have a permanently active volcano. Its relative isolation is a large part of its appeal to Italy's (and Europe's) social elite who come to holiday on Stromboli (Dolce & Gabbana have a holiday home here). The island is a unique picture among the Aeolians – the black soil, black beaches (some very good, with excellent sand) and the black, towering volcano are in contrast to the gleaming white houses, all of which are breathtakingly beautiful and shrouded in Mediterranean gardens.

Stromboli's sense of isolation isn't just a matter of romantic illusions, it is in fact an island whose infrastructure is as fragile as ever. The town doesn't have 'proper' electricity – it's powered by massive generators – hence no streetlights at night, except in a couple of main streets and the church square (bring a torch). The same goes for the island's water situation – potable water is brought in from the mainland, so water saving is essential. And should the weather roughen up and the sea go a bit wild, no boats, ferries or hydrofoils head over to Stromboli. There are no roads across the island, so the tiny village of Ginostra (of around 30 houses) is only accessible by sea. It's that kind of place. Pure magic.

And we haven't mentioned that lively volcano yet. Its most recent eruption, in February 2007, was quite harmless as eruptions go, but it reminds the locals and visitors alike that living under this fiery giant is not a laughing matter. Yet, despite the fact that the volcano can potentially endanger lives, it's been providing a livelihood for the local mountaineers, climbing guides and trekking agents who take dozens of visitors up to the crater every night of the week.

Orientation

Boats arrive at Porto Scari/San Vincenzo, downhill from the Stromboli 'town' (formed by the villages of San Bartolo, San Vincenzo and Scari). Accommodation is a short walk

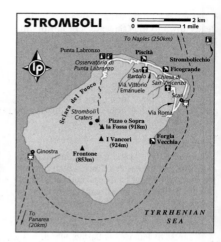

up the Scalo Scari to Via Roma or, if you plan to head straight for the crater, follow the road along the waterfront (see opposite for details).

Information

BOOKSHOPS

La Libreria sull'Isola (☎ 090 986 57 55; Via Vittorio Emanuele; ☿ 10.30am-1pm & 5.30-7pm Mon-Fri, 5.30-7pm Sat) A lovely little bookshop with some literary, foreign-language offerings and open-air film screenings (tickets €5) in its little garden.

EMERGENCY

Emergency Doctor (☎ 090 98 60 97; Via Vittorio Emanuele)

Police (☎ 090 98 60 21; Via Roma) On the left as you walk up Via Roma.

INTERNET ACCESS

La Libreria sull'Isola (☎ 090 986 57 55; Via Vittorio Emanuele; ☿ 10.30am-1pm & 5.30-7pm Mon-Fri, 5.30-7pm Sat; per hr €6) Two computers with a fast connection and printing and CD-burning facilities.

Totem Trekking (Piazza San Vincenzo 4; per hr €6; ☿ 10am-1pm & 4-8pm) Climbing shop that will let you use its painfully slow computer.

MEDICAL SERVICES

Farmacia Simone (☎ 090 98 60 79; Via Roma)

MONEY

You'll find an ATM on Via Roma, on the approach to Piazza San Vincenzo from the port.

Le Isole e Terme d'Italia (☎ 090 98 62 74; Via Roma)
This travel agency near the port has exchange facilities.

POST
Post Office (☎ 090 98 60 27; Via Roma; ✆ 8.20am-
1.20pm Mon-Sat)

TOURIST INFORMATION
Vulcanalogical Information Centre (Porto Scari;
✆ 10.30am-1pm & 5-7.30pm) This very interesting
information centre dedicated to the volcano is 150m to
the right of the port. A video (in Italian) is usually shown
in the afternoon. It is well worth a visit.

Sights & Activities
There is little to see here other than a couple
of churches. Just outside the town (follow
Via Roma, which then becomes Via Vittorio
Emanuele), a couple of doors down on the
right from **Chiesa di San Vincenzo** but before
the Barbablù hotel, is a **pink-red house** where
Ingrid Bergman and Roberto Rossellini lived
during the filming of *Stromboli* in 1949.
Film buffs will be familiar with the scandal
provoked by their liaison – Rossellini was
a married man – which was the talk of the
film world for a long time thereafter.

Stromboli's **beaches** are the best on all the
islands – the massive stretch of black sand
beneath the main hotels is ideal, while there
are little sandy coves to be discovered further along the northern coast.

THE VOLCANO
The Stromboli crater was formed only
40,000 years ago and, like a champagne
bottle, is full of gases, which is why it almost constantly launches showers of incan-
descent lava into the air. Technical volcano
language, taking this kind of activity as a
model, has come to include the term *attività
Stromboliana* (Strombolian activity).

The most recent eruptions took place on
27 February 2007, opening two new craters
on the summit. No real damage was endured
in the last eruption, and the lava descended
the western flank of the volcano. The lava
flow is confined to the Sciara del Fuoco
(Trail of Fire), leaving Stromboli town to
the east and Ginostra to the south quite
safe. Before that, the eruptions in April 2003
showered the town of Ginostra with rocks,
and the December 2002 eruption produced a
mini tsunami, causing damage to Stromboli

town, injuring six people and closing the
island to visitors for a few months.

Some 5000 people lived on the island until
the massive eruption of 1930, when most
took fright and left. Permanent residents now
number about 400.

Recent crater activity has made it illegal to
attempt to climb the volcano without a guide,
and local authorities have limited the number
of people allowed to go up in a day. You must
book in advance (a day before is usually fine,
but allowing a couple is advisable in August),
and the limit is 20 people per guide.

It is once again possible to go all the way
up to the crater, after the post 2002/03 eruption period limited climbs to 400m. You'll
meet your guide between 4.30 and 5.30pm,
depending on the time of the year, and start
your trek up, reaching the peak just in time
for sunset. The sight of the sun dipping into
the sea, with the flaming gut of the volcano in
front of you, is magnificent. You're allowed to
spend about 40 minutes on the top (usually
resting, eating and drinking), before starting
the descent. It is estimated to take about two
hours to get down to Piazza San Vincenzo,
normally arriving around 10.30pm. The climb
is not massively demanding, though you'll
have to have a reasonable level of fitness to
keep up and find it enjoyable (and get there
for the sunset!).

To undertake the climb you will need
proper walking shoes and clothing for cold
wet weather, a change of T-shirt, a torch and
a good supply of water and some food. Worry
not if you haven't got any of those and still
want to climb. **Totem Trekking** (☎ 090 986 57 52;
Piazza San Vincenzo 4; climb kit €14.50) hires out all the
necessary equipment (which is well main-
tained), and thanks to the limited climbing
numbers, there's plenty to go around. You'll
need to go up with your spectacles on and not
contact lenses, especially for the way down
when lots of dust gets blown around.

If you don't fancy going all the way, you can
go up to 400m, from where you get fabulous
views of the **Sciara del Fuoco** and the explosions
at the crater. You're allowed to go to the Sciara
on your own, but do bring a torch if you're
walking at night. The explosions usually occur
every 20 minutes or so and are preceded by
a loud belly-roar as gases force the magma
into the air. It is incredibly exciting. On a still
night the livid red Sciara and exploding cone
are dramatically visible.

DID YOU KNOW?

■ Stromboli is the youngest volcano in the Aeolian archipelago.

■ There are usually two major explosions per year.

■ The island has been inhabited since Neolithic times but the volcano has never destroyed Stromboli town.

■ Stromboli was used to control important trade routes in the Tyrrhenian Sea, as it overlooks the other Aeolian Islands, the Italian mainland and the Straits of Messina. Because of this and its exploding crater, it was known as the 'Lighthouse of the Mediterranean'.

■ The pinnacle of rock known as Strombolicchio, which can be seen just off the coast near Ficogrande, is the remnants of the original volcano that collapsed into the sea. Strombolicchio is what is left of the central cylinder (the neck) of the volcano, in which the lava solidified.

■ The word 'sciara' comes from the Arabic *sharia* (meaning 'street'), thus the Sciara del Fuoco is a 'Street of Fire'.

■ The Sciara del Fuoco depression descends 700m below sea level, although the debris from the volcano descends to a depth of 2200m.

■ The 2003 state of emergency was caused by an underwater landslide on the Sciara del Fuoco that caused a 7m-high tidal wave to land on Stromboli town, damaging many houses (none of the older houses, built at a height of 10m, were affected).

■ The landslide caused the crater to collapse and blocked the normal activity of the volcano. The subsequent build-up of gases and magma finally exploded in July 2003 like a small bomb.

■ The 2003 eruptions increased the crater size from 35m to 125m.

■ The 2007 eruption opened two new craters on the summit.

The still less ambitious can follow the road leading right along the waterfront to the **Osservatorio di Punta Labronzo** (the observatory, follow the signs), which has good views of the volcano. The ascent to the summit starts here.

For up-to-date information on volcanic activity, check www.volcanolive.com.

Guides

Magmatrek (☎ 090 986 57 68; www.magmatrek.it; Via Vittorio Emanuele; excursion per person €28) can put together any number of tailor-made treks for individual groups. Experienced guides, speaking English, German and French, will take groups of up to 20 people to the crater. You need to book the day before you want to do the climb.

Down the steps from Piazzale San Vincenzo is **AGAI** (Associazione Guide Alpine Italiane; ☎ 090 98 62 63; Via Pola 1; ☺ Apr-Oct), the volcano's own information office. Guides take groups of up to 20 people to the crater. Contact the office to make a booking a day before you want to climb.

BOAT TOURS & DIVING

Although **La Sirenetta Diving Center** (☎ 090 98 60 25; La Sirenetta Hotel, Via Marina 33) offers diving courses, alternatively you can make your way to the beach of rocks and black volcanic sand at Ficogrande to swim and sunbathe.

If you want a more gentle view of the volcano from the safety of a boat, contact **Società Navigazione Pippo** (☎ 090 98 61 35; Via Roma 47) or **Antonio Cacetta** (☎ 090 98 60 23; Vico Salina 10, near Porto Scari). Both companies take visitors for a 2½-hour gander at the Sciara del Fuoco from the sea (€15 per person). Both leave at 10pm from the port. You can also enjoy a number of other tours; a circuit around the island (€20, five hours) takes in some swimming at Strombolicchio.

Sleeping

Most accommodation on Stromboli is pricey, but there are also some good budget and midrange alternatives.

Casa La Pergola (☎ 090 98 61 27; www.casalapergola .it; Via Roma; d & tr per person from €25) A great budget place operated by an older couple who also run a greengrocer, La Pergola is in a fantastic central location. The newer rooms are simple, while the older ones feature scary Catholic figurines and ancient wardrobes. There's also a good shared terrace. No breakfast.

Casa del Sole (☎ 090 98 60 17; Via Soldato Cincotta; dm/d per person €25/30) Off the road to the volcano, before you reach Ficogrande, Casa del Sole offers five cottages that are used as dorms, sleeping four to six people. There's also a few new en-suite doubles and triples. Surrounded by bougainvillea and broom, this is a wonderfully peaceful place, though it's a bit of a (dark) walk at night from the centre.

La Lampara (☎ 090 98 64 09; Via Vittorio Emmanuele 27; d & tr per person from €35) A new B&B with reasonable rooms, a lovely roof terrace for breakfast, and a surly, 'do not disturb between 1.30pm and 4.30pm' landlady.

Pedra Residence (☎ 090 98 64 13; www.pedra residence.it; Via Nunziante; d €80-120, apt €180-300; ⊠) A new complex with great self-catering rooms (breakfast included in the price) that have big bathrooms, well-equipped kitchenettes, heavy wooden furniture and a slightly 'eastern' design. An expansive communal terrace fronts the rooms.

Hotel Sirenetta (☎ 090 98 60 25; www.sirenetta.it; Via Marina 33; s €90-140, d €100-150; ⊠ Apr-Oct; ⊠ ⊠) This hotel is perfectly sited on the beach at Ficogrande in front of Strombolicchio. Although the décor is rather dated – think floor-to-ceiling posters of sunsets – the rooms are comfortable and the hotel is well known as a diving centre.

our pick **La Locanda del Barbablù** (☎ 090 98 61 18; www.barbablu.it; Via Vittorio Emanuele 17-19; d €120-210; ⊠ Mar-Oct) This dusky-pink Aeolian house is an inn in the true sense of the word. It is not only one of the best restaurants on the island, but also has some fabulously eccentric rooms with silk coverlets, painted ceilings, water glasses on silver trays and antique tiles. Eat on the terrace looking out at the volcano.

Eating

Ritrovo Ingrid (☎ 090 98 63 85; Piazza San Vincenzo; pastries & cakes from €1, pizza €8; ⊠ 8am-midnight, 8am-3am Jul & Aug) Situated at the high point of Piazza San Vincenzo (also the location of the Chiesa di San Vincenzo, p177) with scenic views all around from its terrace, Ritrovo Ingrid is the heart of Stromboli. Trekkers come here for sundowners and pizza as well as the day's gossip, and it's the best place for breakfast.

La Lampara (☎ 090 98 64 09; Via Vittorio Emanuele 27; pizza €8-10; ⊠ 6pm-late) A noisy, vine-draped terrace with great pizzas and some decent seafood baked in aluminium foil for extra succulence. This place is much loved by families for its relaxed atmosphere. You will find it beyond Barbablù.

L'Osservatorio (Observatory; ☎ 090 98 63 60; meals around €25) About 20 minutes' walk up the lower slope of the volcano, this is where you get the unique opportunity to watch the volcano's activity as you eat. The food is traditional pasta, fish and seafood, and there is some good pizza too.

Punta Lena (☎ 090 98 62 04; Via Marina 8; meals €25-30) Punta Lena, on the *lungomare* walking away from the northern port towards the volcano, has a terrace overlooking the sea and Strombolicchio. Great fish and lots of lovely grilled vegetables.

our pick **Ai Gechi** (☎ 090 98 62 13; Vico Salina 12, Porto Scari; meals €30-35; ⊠ 6.30-11pm, Tue-Sun) An excellent place that's a deserved favourite with the locals, Ai Gechi is a tastefully outfitted Aeolian house whose terrace serves as the dining area. Ship lamps light the tables, and the friendly barefoot waitstaff give you the lowdown on the day's menu. The food is traditional with a slightly modern twist. As you walk up from the port you will see a sign pointing down a small lane to your left. The restaurant is right at the end of the lane.

La Tartana (☎ 090 98 60 25; Via Marina; à la carte meals €35) It's hard to tell how to recommend La Tartana: as a bar, semi-disco or restaurant. It's all of those, plus it has great sea views from its terrace. During the day it has a good buffet lunch of fish and vegetables (€30 per kilo) that shouldn't cost you over €15. The evening affair is a different ball game, with an upmarket menu and crowd. *Aperitivi*, cocktails and a bit of dancing happen after dusk on the bar terrace.

La Locanda del Barbablù (☎ 090 98 61 18; www.barbablu.it; Via Vittorio Emanuele 17; tasting menu per person €45; ⊠ 7-11.30pm) By far the island's fanciest restaurant, serving only a tasting menu (no à la carte) that changes according to the chef's desires. You will have to book if you want to dine here.

The terrace restaurant at Hotel Sirenetta (see left) is another good choice with beautiful views.

There are a couple of bars at the port, where you can get light snacks, and there is a supermarket on Via Roma. For night fun, La Tartana is your best bet.

Getting There & Around

It takes four hours by ferry to reach the island from Lipari or 1½ to two hours by hydrofoil. Ticket offices for **Ustica Lines** (☎ 090 98 60 03) and **Siremar** (☎ 090 98 60 16) are at the port. In winter or in bad weather the service is often disrupted or cancelled altogether.

Sirocco (☎ 3355219446) runs an electric cart service that is useful to transport luggage when you arrive (if you don't have a back-pack). However, it randomly charges you between €5 and €10 per trip. It is possible to hire scooters from **Motonautica Mandarano** (☎ 090 98 62 12; Via Marina; per day €20). From the port follow the road to your left; you will find it after about 300m.

FILICUDI

pop 300 / elev 774m

Filicudi is arguably the wildest and the prettiest of the Aeolian Islands, with crystal-clear waters and deep grottoes. Disembarking at Filicudi's port gives no real indication of what a beautiful island it is. The area is a huddle of concrete houses and one large resort hotel. Most of the island's limited facilities are here, including a general store.

Information

Emergency Doctor (☎ 090 988 99 13)
Pharmacy (☎ 090 988 90 77)
Police (☎ 090 988 99 42; Contrada Pecorini)
Post Office (☎ 090 988 90 53; Contrada Pecorini; ☽ 9am-1pm Mon-Fri)

Sights & Activities

Once you've moved on from the port, the disappointment will definitely fade. The main road goes south towards Capo Graziano and the **prehistoric village** (☽ 24hr), discovered in 1952, a smattering of Bronze Age huts that predate Panarea's Punta Milazzese by a few hundred years. From the village you can descend to Filicudi's only real **beach**, a stony affair that offers the easiest swimming on the island – if you want to take a dip elsewhere, you'll have to clamber down some jagged rocks or rent a boat.

At the port, via a set of steep steps, you'll find the path to the centre of the island. After about 10 minutes (just past La Canna and Villa La Rosa), the road forks. You can go

north (right) to **Valdichiesa**, a little village with a pretty church on a hillside terrace. Above the village is the peak of the **Fossa dei Felci** (774m), which you can climb – just keep walking in the general direction of the peak.

Alternatively, you can take the road that leads south (left) at the fork and make your way down via the donkey path to the little hamlet of **Pecorini**, which is nothing more than a cluster of one-storey houses huddled around a church. There are a couple of restaurants here (see below) and you can swim in the water.

The best way of visiting the island is by boat. There's usually someone around the port who rents boats out for around €20 per person during the high season for a two-hour trip. If you can't find anyone to help you at the port, call **Giuseppe Taranto** (☎ 090 988 90 11, 3683461315).

On the uninhabited western side of the island is the natural arch of the **Punta del Perciato** (Perciato Point) and the nearby **Grotta del Bue Marino** (Cave of the Monk Seal). This cavity is 37m long by 30m wide, and named after the seals that once lived here. You won't see any now, though, as the last one was harpooned in the 1960s, but you will see one of the most luminous light shows caused by the sunlight's reflection in the clear turquoise waters. To the northwest is the **Scoglio della Canna** (Cane Reef), a long, thin stack of rock 71m high that is perhaps the Aeolians' most impressive *faraglioni*.

Sleeping & Eating

All the following hotels and *pensioni* have good restaurants attached. Mains generally cost between €9 and €15.

Hotel Phenicusa (☎ 090 988 99 46; www.hotel phenicusa.com; Via Porto; r per person hill/sea views from €34/42; ☽ May-Sep) This boxy modern hotel dominates the port and provides pleasant enough accommodation and friendly staff.

Hotel La Canna (☎ 090 988 99 56; www.lacannahotel .it; Via Rosa 43; d €64-140; ✴ ⬛) After an exhausting uphill walk (you can be picked up from the port) the Hotel La Canna appears like a private paradise. Minimalist white rooms, magnificent panoramic views and some wonderful homemade cooking make this a highly recommended hotel. Reservations are advised.

Villa La Rosa (☎ 090 988 99 65; www.villalarosa.it in Italian; Via Rosa; d €100-160) Just beyond Hotel La Canna at the junction of Via Rosa is Villa La Rosa, a private residence that rents out

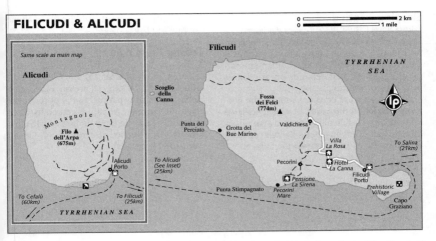

FILICUDI & ALICUDI

lovely rooms, all with bathroom and terrace. Adelaide Rando's food is also very good. If you're desperate for some – nay, any – type of nightlife, then the disco here is the only place to boogie.

Another good *pensione*-cum-trattoria is **Pensione La Sirena** (☎ 090 988 99 97; www.pensionela sirena.it; Via Pecorini Mare; d €130-180) towards the sea just outside Pecorini.

Getting There & Away

Filicudi can be tricky to reach for short visits. The intermittent ferry and hydrofoil service is virtually nonexistent in winter, and in summer can be cancelled due to rough seas. **Siremar** (☎ 090 988 99 60) and **Ustica Lines** (☎ 090 988 99 84) both have ticket offices on Via Porto, which runs along the port. At the height of summer Filicudi is served by three hydrofoils and one ferry daily. See p151 for details.

ALICUDI

pop 100 / elev 675m

When the French novelist Alexandre Dumas visited Alicudi during the 19th century, he wrote to his wife: 'It is hard to find a sadder, more dismal and desolate place than this unfortunate island…a corner of the earth forgotten by creation and which has remained unchanged since the days of chaos.' The barren nature of the northeast of Alicudi clearly was not to Mr Dumas' liking or taste, and in some respects he wasn't far wrong. However, if you're looking to get away from it all and revel in some sun, sea and solitude,

Alicudi is the best place for it. The flood of summer tourists that visit the Aeolian Islands is reduced to a mere trickle on Alicudi.

The island is as isolated a place as you'll find in the entire Mediterranean basin, with minimal facilities (one hotel and one restaurant) and no marked roads. For a time it served as the Italian equivalent of Devil's Island, with Mafia prisoners being sent here to serve lengthy prison sentences. Today it is home to a handful of farmers and fishers who only saw the arrival of electricity and TV in the 1990s. There are a couple of grocery shops, and a **post office** (☎ 090 988 99 11) by the port keeps erratic hours. The doctor can be contacted on ☎ 090 988 99 13.

Sights & Activities

The central peak of the **Filo dell'Arpa** (String of the Harp; 675m) is climbable; it's a hardy, two-hour trek up a pretty rocky path. At the top you can view the crater of the extinct Montagnole volcano and the **Timpone delle Femmine**, huge fissures where women are said to have taken refuge during pirate raids. Be sure to wear sturdy shoes and bring plenty of water as there is absolutely no shade along the way. There is not much else to do save potter around and find a peaceful place to sunbathe – the best spots are to the south of the port, where you will have to clamber over boulders to reach the sea. As you would expect, the waters are crystal clear and there's nothing to disturb you save the occasional hum of a fishing boat.

Sleeping & Eating

Ericusa Hotel (☎ 090 988 99 02; www.alicudihotel.it; Via Regina Elena; d €130-170; ☒ Jun-Sep) This pleasant hotel has 12 rooms and a good restaurant where you'll eat well, although the menu is a bit of a mystery as it depends on provisions brought from the mainland.

For longer stays consider renting the gorgeous **Casa Ibiscus** (www.alicudi.net in Italian; weekly rate €1000-1400), a typical Aeolian house in a paradisaical setting. It sleeps up to four. Rentals run from Saturday and bookings are via the website.

The only restaurant on Alicudi is **Airone** (☎ 090 988 99 22; meals €25-30).

Getting There & Away

Alicudi is the most difficult Aeolian Island to reach. Both **Siremar** (☎ 090 988 97 95) and **Ustica Lines** (☎ 090 988 99 12) are on Via Regina Elena, which runs parallel to the port. At the height of summer, Alicudi is served by three hydrofoils and one ferry daily (see p151). A summer-only service also runs from Cefalù (see p138 for details).

AEOLIAN ISLANDS

Ionian Coast

Magnificent, overdeveloped and unruly, the Ionian Coast is Sicily's most popular tourist destination, its commercial engine room and home to 20% of the island's population. Thriving cities like Messina and Catania do the Greeks proud – they are still centres of trade and business and house two of the largest universities on the island. Moneyed entrepreneurs have built their villas and hotels up and down the coastline, eager to bag a spot on Sicily's equivalent of the Amalfi Coast, a fortunate few owning the luxury homes of Taormina's Monte Tauro.

Above it all towers the muscular peak of Etna (3323m). With puffs of smoke billowing from its snow-covered cone, it's an ever-present reminder of the superficiality of success that rings its base. Like Californians, Etna's residents enjoy the good life to the full, waiting for the 'big one' that might sweep it all away. Nowhere is this more palpable than in the city of Catania, the capital of the Ionian Coast, destroyed by Etna in 1669 and rebuilt again in lava.

For tourists the Ionian Coast is an exciting destination, home to Europe's largest active volcano and its 590 sq km of well-managed national park. Within its boundaries it shelters some 20 farming communities, a far cry from the profiteering coastline. It is the largest unspoilt wilderness left in Sicily, home of the Titans and, as Aeschylus saw it, the column that holds up the sky.

HIGHLIGHTS

- Check out the chiaroscuro, baroque, cacophonous fish market and boisterous nightlife in **Catania**'s (p199)
- Climb up to magnificent and volatile **Mt Etna** (p208) but don't lean into the crater!
- Admire the Scoglie dei Ciclopi as you swim, snorkel and sunbathe on the **Riviera dei Ciclopi** (p206)
- Pose on Piazza IX Aprile in the mini medieval town in **Taormina** (p190), or savour the views from the Teatro Greco
- Take a ferry across the **Straits of Messina** (p184) and enjoy the views as you leave or enter Sicily.

IONIAN COAST

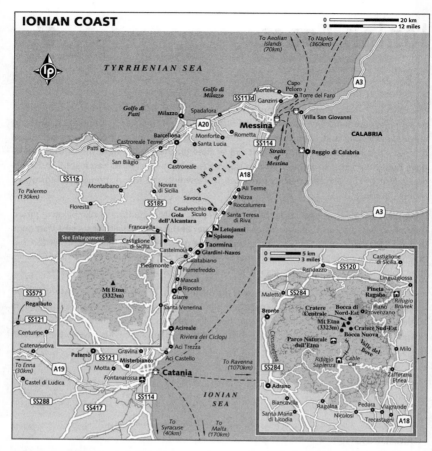

MESSINA & AROUND

MESSINA

pop 250,000

Known to the ancient Greeks as Zankle (Sickle) for its beautiful curved harbour, Messina is situated at the northernmost point of the Ionian Coast and is staggeringly close to the Italian mainland. Wide boulevards, a practical grid system and elegant turn-of-the-century buildings make Messina an easy and pleasant city to get around, though you'll mainly find yourself here to catch a ferry to the Aeolian Islands or if you've entered Sicily from Reggio Calabria.

The Greeks mythologised the clashing currents of Messina's straits as the twin monsters of Charybdis (the whirlpool) and Scylla (the six-headed monster), but the tremendous earthquake of 1908 altered the course of the treacherous waters and now the straits are a veritable highway of seafaring traffic. Strategically located at the heart of the trading routes that linked the Tyrrhenian Sea with the Mediterranean, Messina has always been prosperous and in the 18th century was famous for its four-storey mansions that overlooked the harbour. But all that was destroyed with the 1908 earthquake, one of the worst natural disasters to hit Sicily – it sank the shore by half a metre and killed 84,000 people. A new, earthquake-proof city had barely been rebuilt when it was flattened by Allied bombing in 1943. In 2005 Messina nearly got an ill-conceived suspension bridge over the straits (see boxed text, p187) but the plan was thankfully cancelled by the new government.

Orientation

The main transport hub is at Piazza della Repubblica, at the southern end of the long waterfront. You will find the train station here and the Trenitalia (FS) ferries also arrive near here. The main intercity bus station is outside the train station, to the left on the piazza. To get to the city centre from Piazza della Repubblica, walk either straight across the piazza and directly ahead along Via I Settembre to the Piazza del Duomo, or turn left into Via Giuseppe La Farina and take the first right into Via Tommaso Cannizzaro to reach Piazza Cairoli.

Those coming by hydrofoil from Reggio di Calabria arrive about 1km north of the city on Via Vittorio Emanuele II, while drivers on the private car ferry (Caronte) from Villa San Giovanni land 3km further along, just north of the trade-fair area (Fiera).

Information

EMERGENCY

Police (☎ 090 3 66 11, foreigners 090 36 65 19; Via Placida 2)

INTERNET ACCESS

Paritel Telecommunicazioni (Via Centonze 74; per hr €6; ☺ 9am-8pm) Telephones and internet connection.

MEDICAL SERVICES

Ospedale Piemonte (☎ 090 222 42 38; Viale Europa) Has a casualty service.
Pharmacy (☎ 090 34 54 22; cnr Via Cesare Battisti & Via Camiciotti; ☺ 24hr)

MONEY

There are numerous banks in the city centre – most with ATMs – and a currency exchange booth at the timetable-information office at the train station.

POST

Post Office (Piazza Antonello, Corso Cavour; ☺ 8.30am-6.30pm Mon-Sat)

TOURIST INFORMATION

Main Tourist Office (☎ 090 67 42 36; www.provincia .messina.it in Italian; Via Calabria 301; ☺ 9am-1.30pm & 3-5pm Mon-Thu, 9am-1.30pm Fri) Friendly, English-speaking staff with good information about Messina and onward travel.

TRAVEL AGENCIES

Messina is full of travel agencies.
CTS (☎ 090 292 67 61; Via Ugo Bassi 93) Student travel group with special deals for students and those under 26.
Lisciotto Viaggi (☎ 090 71 90 01; Piazza Cairoli 13) Can assist with theatre tickets.

Sights

PIAZZA DEL DUOMO

Messina's Norman **cathedral** (Piazza del Duomo; admission free; ☺ 8am-6pm) is one of the most attractive churches in Sicily and if it hadn't been for its unfortunate history it would probably be on a par with the cathedrals of Cefalù (p135) and Monreale (p99).

Built in the 12th century, it suffered its first disaster in 1254 at the funeral of Conrad IV (son of Frederick II), when a mass of candles set the church on fire. Devastating earthquakes in 1783 and 1908 and a WWII incendiary bomb in 1943 put paid to the rest. The fire caused by the bombing destroyed all the frescoes and mosaics, incinerated the choir stalls and ruined the royal tombs. But the Messinese picked up the pieces and rebuilt it faithfully in the style of the original basilica with three mosaic apses. Some of the few original elements that were salvaged are the lovely stripy marble inlay and tracery of the façade and the Catalan-Gothic portal.

Inside the church is an impressive carved altar and an inlaid organ. Other treasures, such as the magnificent **Golden Mantle** (1668) designed by Innocenzo Mangani as a 'cloak' for the picture of *La Madonna della Lettera* (The Madonna of the Letter) that now sits on the altar, are kept in the cathedral's **treasury** (admission €3; ☺ 9am-1pm Mon-Sat). The letter the Madonna is supposed to have written was a blessing on the city of Messina, which suffered a terrible famine after converting to Christianity in AD 42.

Outside, the 60m campanile houses the world's largest **astronomical clock**, built in Strasbourg in 1733. The clock strikes at noon, setting in motion a slow-moving procession of bronze automata that have various historical and allegorical meanings (pick up the brochure from the tourist office for an explanation of each one) – watch out for the comical roaring lion and crowing cockerel. You can climb the **campanile** (admission €3.50; ☺ 8am-6pm) to see the enormous figures up close.

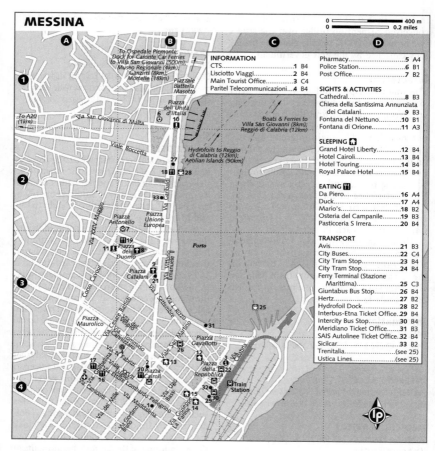

MESSINA

0	400 m
0	0.2 miles

INFORMATION
CTS	1	B4
Lisciotto Viaggi	2	B4
Main Tourist Office	3	C4
Paritel Telecomunicazioni	4	B4
Pharmacy	5	A4
Police Station	6	B1
Post Office	7	B2

SIGHTS & ACTIVITIES
Cathedral	8	B3
Chiesa della Santissima Annunziata dei Catalani	9	B3
Fontana del Nettuno	10	B1
Fontana di Orione	11	A3

SLEEPING
Grand Hotel Liberty	12	B4
Hotel Cairoli	13	B4
Hotel Touring	14	B4
Royal Palace Hotel	15	B4

EATING
Da Piero	16	A4
Duck	17	A4
Mario's	18	B2
Osteria del Campanile	19	B3
Pasticceria S Irrera	20	B4

TRANSPORT
Avis	21	B3
City Buses	22	C4
City Tram Stop	23	B4
City Tram Stop	24	B4
Ferry Terminal (Stazione Marittima)	25	C3
Giuntabus Bus Stop	26	B4
Hertz	27	B2
Hydrofoil Dock	28	B2
Interbus-Etna Ticket Office	29	B4
Intercity Bus Stop	30	B4
Meridiano Ticket Office	31	B3
SAIS Autolinee Ticket Office	32	B4
Sicilcar	33	B2
Trenitalia	(see 25)
Ustica Lines	(see 25)

Facing the tower, the pale marble **Fontana di Orione** (1553) depicts a lounging Orion, the mythical founder of Messina. The fountain was constructed by Giovanni Angelo Montorsoli (pupil to Michelangelo) to commemorate the construction of Messina's aqueduct – the city's houses were the first in Sicily to receive running water. The figures that adorn it represent the Rivers Tiber, Nile, Ebro and Camaro.

OTHER SIGHTS

Tiny by comparison, the 12th-century **Chiesa della Santissima Annunziata dei Catalani** (Piazza Catalani; ☿ special services only) is a jewel of Arab-Norman construction. The statue in front of it is a monument to Don John of Austria,

who beat the Turks at the Battle of Lepanto in 1571.

Further north, where Via Garibaldi spills into Piazza dell'Unità d'Italia, is Messina's other great fountain, the 16th-century **Fontana del Nettuno** (Neptune's Fountain), also by Montorsoli. The figures are actually copies: the originals are housed in the museum. Opposite the fountain is Piazzale Batteria Masotto where you can enjoy views over the harbour and admire the huge golden statue of the **Madonnino del Porto**.

Picking up the city tram at Piazza Cairoli or the train station, you can take a pleasant gander up the sickle-shaped harbour. It is also the easiest way to reach the **Museo Regionale** (☎ 090 36 12 92; Viale della Libertà 465; adult/concession

IONIAN COAST

DIRE STRAITS

When you see the tiny Messina Straits, you'll no doubt hear about the controversial plans of building a bridge across the waters, plans that were discussed during the 1960s and almost realised under Berlusconi, but finally dropped when Romano Prodi came to power in 2006.

The project was in the offing for some 30 years and made the EU's list of priority projects in 2004 but it was never a happy affair. The number of arguments against it was vast, starting with concerns by environmental organisations that feared that the enormous construction work would damage the delicate freshwater lagoons of Ganzirri and Mortelle and destroy the marine ecosystem. The residents weren't happy either, as nearly 800 homes would have been destroyed to make way for the mighty pylons (each as high as New York's Empire State Building) and more than 1200 people looked set to lose their jobs on the ferries. The bridge was estimated not to be able to withstand earthquakes, and its building was rumoured to be a vehicle for the enrichment of organised-crime networks from Sicily and Calabria.

The bridge was to be the world's longest suspension bridge, spanning a record-breaking 3300m (Japan's Akashi Kaikyo Bridge currently holds the title at 1991m) and rising 64m above sea level. An estimated 6000 vehicles per hour would have whizzed along its six lanes, while 200 high-speed trains would have traversed the two rail tracks each day.

But thankfully, Romano Prodi's ministers bagged the plans – much to the dismay of the centre-right Forza Italia party – after a total of 272 MPs voted in favour of abandoning the bridge proposal (232 voted for the building to continue). It is now planned that some of the estimated €4.4 billion which was to be spent on the bridge is going to be used to reinforce Sicily's infrastructure and better the ferry service across the straits.

€6/3; ☾ 9am-1.30pm Mon, Wed & Fri, 9am-1.30pm & 3-5.30pm Tue, Thu & Sat, 9am-12.30pm Sun). The gallery's most famous work is the *San Gregorio* (St Gregory) polyptych by local boy Antonello da Messina (1430–79). Although in pretty shabby condition, the five panels of the piece are wonderfully figurative. Other highlights include *Madonna con bambino e santi* (Virgin with Child and Saints) by the same artist and two splendid works by Caravaggio (1571–1610): *L'Adorazione dei pastori* (Adoration of the Shepherds) and *Risurrezione di Lazzaro* (Resurrection of Lazarus). The works in the gallery are arranged chronologically and there are sculptures and stone fragments in the surrounding gardens and central courtyard.

Sleeping

Despite being a major transport hub, Messina is not a tourist city and hotels and restaurants cater mainly for businesspeople and residents.

Hotel Touring (☎ 090 293 88 51; www.hoteltouring-me.it; Via N Scotto 17; s €20-50, d €40-70; ❄) A cute little hotel near the station, newly renovated, with a slightly eccentric reception and decent rooms. The cheaper rooms share bathrooms, but most are spacious, simple and tasteful, with bits of antique furniture and (some with) traditional tiles. A good budget option.

Hotel Cairoli (☎ 090 67 37 55; www.hotelcairoli.it; Viale San Martino 63; s/d €45/80; ❄) Just off Piazza Cairoli, this is a convenient and comfortable budget hotel in Messina, though the décor is pretty nondescript. The owner is friendly, the beds hard and some rooms have sweet pieces of antique-style furniture.

Royal Palace Hotel (☎ 090 65 03; www.framon-hotels.com; Via Tommaso Cannizzaro 224; s/d from €89/125; P ❄) Messina's most popular hotel is a real homage to the 1970s idea of hotel aesthetics: 106 rooms that line long and narrow corridors, low sofas and round lamp shades in the reception, along with lots of browns and oranges. The rooms are comfortable and James Bond would have loved all the buttons on the bed head and the electric shutters.

Grand Hotel Liberty (☎ 090 640 94 36; www.framon-hotels.com; Via I Settembre 15; s/d from €115/200; P ❄) This is the most comfortable hotel in Messina. The Grand is a renovated corner palazzo with an old-world sense of luxury in the rooms and lots of marble, chandeliers and plush sofas and armchairs in the reception. The staff are helpful and speak English.

Eating

There are few good restaurants accessible on foot in the town, and on top of this many of them close in August. Messina is most famous for its quality swordfish. It is typically served *agghiotta,* a ravishing dish with pine nuts, sultanas, garlic, basil and tomatoes.

Pasticceria S Irrera (☎ 090 67 38 23; www.irrera .it in Italian; Piazza Cairoli 12; sweets from €1) An excellent *gelateria/pasticceria* (ice-cream/cake shop), which is famous for the Messinese snack *pignolata* (doughnut sticks covered with chocolate).

Duck (☎ 090 71 27 72; Via Ettore Lombardo Pellegrino 107A; sandwiches €4, steaks €12-14; ☽ Mon-Sat) This noisy bar/restaurant is about the most authentic pub in Sicily, with a well-priced menu and a long wooden bar crammed full of young professionals. Steaks are the big thing here; it is a mistake to order anything else.

Osteria del Campanile (☎ 090 71 14 18; Via Loggia dei Mercanti 7; meals €20-25; ☽ closed Sun Sep-Jun) This cosy hostelry with its warm wooden interior is a good choice if you are up near the cathedral. In summer, tables flood the outside area. Again, swordfish is the highlight of the menu.

Mario's (☎ 090 4 24 77; Via Vittorio Emanuele II; meals €25; ☽ Tue-Sun Oct-Aug) Opposite the hydrofoil dock, this specialist fish restaurant is highly regarded and popular with the locals. The antipasti are laid out on a buffet – a delicious mixture of fish and vegetables. This is also a great place to while away the time before the hydrofoil leaves.

Da Piero (☎ 090 71 83 65; Via Ghibellina 121; meals €35-45; ☽ 8-11pm Mon-Sat) A classy restaurant frequented by well-heeled Messinese who come here for a big night out. It is an excellent place to try the swordfish *agghiotta*. You'll need to make a reservation and dress stylishly – time to get that designer garb out.

Getting There & Away
BOAT
Messina is the main point of arrival for ferries and hydrofoils from the Italian mainland, only a 20-minute trip across the straits.

Trenitalia (☎ 090 66 16 74; www.trenitalia.it; Ferry Dock; passenger one-way/return €3/5, small car eg Fiat Punto €18) runs at least 20 fast boats a day to Reggio di Calabria (10 on Sunday). It also operates services to Villa San Giovanni on the Italian mainland. The boats bear either the old FS (Ferrovia dello Stato) or a new Bluvia insignia.

Meridiano Lines (☎ 090 641 32 34; Via L Rizzo) also runs hourly boats to Reggio di Calabria (24 hours Monday to Friday) for similar prices.

Caronte (☎ 090 371 83 24; Viale della Libertà; passengers/ cars €1.50/9) has car ferries between Messina and Villa San Giovanni (40 minutes, 12 daily). The Caronte ferries are 1.5km north of the ferry dock; just follow the signs along Via Vittorio Emanuele II.

Ustica Lines (☎ 090 36 40 44; www.usticalines.it in Italian; Via Vittorio Emanuele II) runs daily hydrofoils to Reggio di Calabria (€2.80, 15 minutes, five daily). In summer Ustica Lines hydrofoils also connect Messina with Lipari in the Aeolian Islands (€16.50, 1½ hours, five daily).

BUS
Interbus (☎ 090 66 17 54; Piazza della Repubblica 6) runs a regular service to Taormina (€3, 1½ hours, hourly Monday to Saturday) and has a weekly connection to Rome (€33, 9½ hours, Saturday).

SAIS Autoline (☎ 090 77 19 14; www.saisautolinee.it in Italian; Piazza della Repubblica 6) serves Palermo (€14.10, two hours, eight daily Monday to Saturday, two Sunday), Catania (€7.10, 1½ hours, half-hourly Monday to Saturday, two Sunday) and Catania's airport. The Catania bus travels via Taormina, Giardini-Naxos, Giarre and Acireale. SAIS Autolinee also offers a number of national services from Messina, including three weekly buses to Pisa (€60, 15 hours) and Bologna (€60, 14 hours via Florence and Siena). You can buy these online.

Giuntabus (☎ 090 67 37 82; Via Terranova 8) runs a service to Milazzo (€3.70, 50 minutes, half-hourly Monday to Saturday between 6.30am and 8pm, one Sunday). From there you can catch the ferries and hydrofoils to the Aeolian Islands.

CAR & MOTORCYCLE
If you arrive in Messina by Trenitalia ferry with a vehicle it is simple to make your way out of town. For Palermo, Milazzo and the Aeolian Islands turn right from the docks, get onto Via Garibaldi and follow it along the waterfront. After about 1km, turn left into Viale Boccetta and follow the green autostrada (motorway) signs. To reach Taormina and Syracuse, turn left from the docks into Via Giuseppe La Farina and follow the autostrada signs for Catania.

If you arrive by private ferry, turn right along Viale della Libertà for Palermo and Milazzo and left for Taormina and Catania –

follow the green autostrada signs. Messina's streets are well signposted so you should find your way around easily.

If you arrive without a vehicle and decide to hire one, the usual car-rental companies are represented:

Avis (☎ 090 67 91 50; Via Garibaldi 109)

Hertz (☎ 090 36 37 40; Via Vittorio Emanuele II 75)

Sicilcar (☎ 090 4 69 42; Via Garibaldi 187)

TRAIN

Hourly *diretto* (direct) passenger trains connect Messina with Catania (2nd/1st class €8/10, 1½ to two hours), Taormina (2nd/1st class €6/7.50, 40 minutes, hourly), Syracuse (2nd/1st class €13/19 intercity or €9/12 *diretto*, 2½ to three hours) and Palermo (€17/22 intercity or €11 *diretto*, 3½ hours). You can also get the train to Milazzo (€2.65, 45 minutes, 10 daily), but buses are generally faster. The train stations for Milazzo and Taormina are inconveniently located some distance from their respective town centres.

From Messina you can also take the train across the straits for Rome and Milan.

Getting Around

The easiest way to get around Messina is on the city tram that runs up and down the length of the town from Piazza Cairoli, via the train station (Piazza della Repubblica) up to the Museo Regionale. Like the bus, you buy a ticket for two hours (€0.90, from a ticket conductor at the stop).

City buses run from outside the train station to Ganzirri (79 and 81) and Mortelle (79 and 80). A two-hour ticket costs €0.90.

GANZIRRI

pop 170

Only 8km north of Messina, Ganzirri is a pleasant town that on summer evenings plays host to crowds of youths from the city, who come to gossip and flirt in the town's bars and restaurants.

It's a very pretty setting: the town rings a salty inland lake famous for its mussels, which is why it is a favourite dinner alternative to Messina. One of the most popular restaurants is the family-run **La Napoletana-Salvatore** (☎ 090 39 10 32; Via Lago Grande 29; meals €30-35). It has fabulous views and serves up a huge antipasti buffet and excellent pasta with clams.

Buses 79 and 81 serve Ganzirri from Messina's Piazza della Repubblica.

MORTELLE

pop 240

A further 10km from Ganzirri (around the tip of the island) is the area's most popular summer resort, *the* place the Messinese go to sunbathe and hang out. On summer evenings, you can hardly walk around for the number of scooters and motorcycles, while during the day you'll generally have to get down to the beach early if you want to get a good spot. It only takes about 40 minutes to get here by bus from Messina (No 79 or 80 from Piazza della Repubblica).

MESSINA TO TAORMINA

Squeezed by the long range of the Peloritani mountains to the west and the straits that separate Sicily from the mainland to the east, the thin ribbon of coastline that runs from Messina to Taormina is traversed by a spectacular cliff-hugging road. Although the coastal strip appears as one long development, tucked away in the Peloritani are a couple of quiet villages. Most interesting is tiny **Savoca**, located 4km inland from the grey pebble beaches of Santa Teresa di Riva.

If the village seems familiar it is because it appeared in *The Godfather,* as the picturesque setting for Michael Corleone's marriage to Apollonia. At the entrance to the town is the **Bar Vitelli**, also used in the film. This is the place to go for virtually everything in town: the keys to the churches and stories of when the Americans came to make 'that film'. The town also has a Capuchin monastery with its own miniature **catacombs** (admission by donation; ⏰ 9am-1pm & 3-7pm) complete with a few mummified local bigwigs.

Three kilometres above Savoca is another hilltop village, **Casalvecchio Siculo**. If you drive through the village and turn left (after 700m), you descend through citrus groves to **Chiesa di San Pietro e Paolo di Agrò**, a monastery built of brick and lava. It was built for Greek Orthodox monks in 1172 and has a beautiful interior with stalactite vaulting and lavish polychromatic marbles. The setting is also gorgeous, on the banks of the Agrò river.

THE HIGH ROAD

Sicily has one autostrada running between Catania Nord and Messina and continuing to Sant'Agata di Militello. Here you must get off the autostrada and onto the SS113 as there is a huge gap in the motorway between Sant'Agata and Cefalù – another example of Sicily's ambitious and corrupt road projects that were never completed.

In order to access the autostrada you have to pass through a ticket barrier (press the button and take a ticket; there's no operator). You pay at the barrier where you exit.

You don't have to take the autostrada; you can make the same journeys along the traffic-logged SS113 (north to Milazzo) and the SS114 (south to Taormina).

- Messina–Taormina costs €1.70
- Messina–Catania costs €3
- Messina–Milazzo costs €1.70
- Messina–Sant'Agata di Militello costs €5.50

TAORMINA & AROUND

TAORMINA
pop 10,800 / elev 204m

Taormina's glitz and tourism inundation might make some visitors flinch, especially if coming from the quieter parts of Sicily. Spectacularly located on a terrace of Monte Tauro and with dominating views west to Mt Etna, the city is beautiful. However, its character is marred by the fact that it exists mainly to please the tourist troupes who pound the city's pavements, shop in its upmarket boutiques and eat in its high-priced restaurants most of the year. Taormina's gorgeous churches are the most popular wedding venues in Sicily, and its stunning architecture is snapped by thousands of digital cameras per day.

Over the centuries Taormina has seduced an exhaustive line of writers and artists, aristocrats and royalty, and these days it is host to a summer film festival that packs the town with the international jet set. The city is far removed from the banal economic realities of other Sicilian cities, as it is cushioned by some serious wealth. The capital of Byzantine Sicily in the 9th century, Taormina is an almost perfectly preserved medieval town.

In July and August the town is packed with tourists; it is difficult to find accommodation and even dining can be a problem. Though it only gets really quiet in November – when most of Taormina's hotel and restaurant proprietors apparently go to Thailand for a month – a good time to come is at either end of the high season (April to May or September to October), when everything quietens down a bit.

Orientation

The train station (Taormina-Giardini) is at the bottom of Monte Tauro. You'll need to hop on an Interbus (€0.85) to the bus station (for local and intercity services) on Via Luigi Pirandello. You'll arrive at Via Luigi Pirandello anyway if you come by bus. A short walk uphill from there brings you to the old city entrance and Corso Umberto I, which traverses the town.

Information
BOOKSHOPS

Mazza Giuseppe (Corso Umberto 9) A big newsagent selling all the foreign newspapers and a selection of foreign-language books.

EMERGENCY

Police (☎ 094 261 11 11; Piazza Badia 4)
Tourist First Aid (☎ 094 262 54 19; Piazza San Francesco di Paola; ☒ 24hr 16 Jun-15 Sep) Free medical service.

INTERNET ACCESS

Las Vegas (Salita Alexander Humboldt 7; per hr €6; ☒ 8am-1pm & 7pm-2am Tue-Sun) A slick internet bar with a bunch of fast computers and cocktails.

MEDICAL SERVICES

British Pharmacy (☎ 094 262 58 66, night call-out 3381587988; Piazza IX Aprile 1; ☒ 8.30am-1pm & 4.30-8.30pm) Offers a night call-out service.
Ospedale San Vincenzo (☎ 094 25 37 45; Piazza San Vincenzo) Call the same number for an ambulance. It is outside Porta Catania.

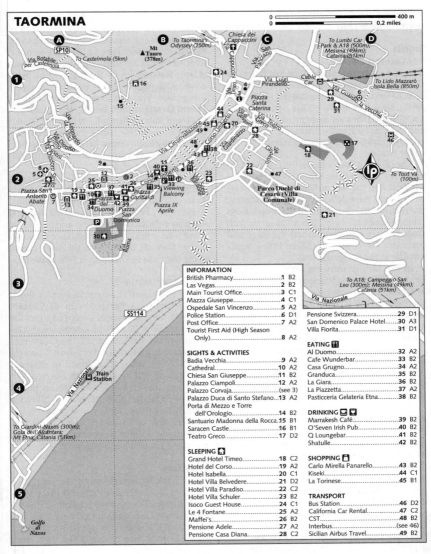

TAORMINA

INFORMATION

British Pharmacy	1 B2
Las Vegas	2 B2
Main Tourist Office	3 C1
Mazza Giuseppe	4 C1
Ospedale San Vincenzo	5 A2
Police Station	6 D1
Post Office	7 A2
Tourist First Aid (High Season Only)	8 A2

SIGHTS & ACTIVITIES

Badia Vecchia	9 A2
Cathedral	10 A2
Chiesa San Giuseppe	11 B2
Palazzo Ciampoli	12 A2
Palazzo Corvaja	(see 3)
Palazzo Duca di Santo Stefano	13 A2
Porta di Mezzo e Torre dell'Orologio	14 B2
Santuario Madonna della Rocca	15 B1
Saracen Castle	16 B1
Teatro Greco	17 D2

SLEEPING

Grand Hotel Timeo	18 C2
Hotel del Corso	19 A2
Hotel Isabella	20 C1
Hotel Villa Belvedere	21 D2
Hotel Villa Paradiso	22 C2
Hotel Villa Schuler	23 B2
Isoco Guest House	24 C1
Le 4 Fontane	25 A2
Maffei's	26 B2
Pensione Adele	27 C1
Pensione Casa Diana	28 C2
Pensione Svizzera	29 D1
San Domenico Palace Hotel	30 A3
Villa Fiorita	31 D1

EATING

Al Duomo	32 A2
Cafe Wunderbar	33 B2
Casa Grugno	34 A2
Granduca	35 B2
La Giara	36 B2
La Piazzetta	37 A2
Pasticceria Gelateria Etna	38 B2

DRINKING

Marrakesh Café	39 B2
O'Seven Irish Pub	40 B2
Q Loungebar	41 B2
Shatulle	42 B2

SHOPPING

Carlo Mirella Panarello	43 B2
Kiseki	44 C1
La Torinese	45 B1

TRANSPORT

Bus Station	46 D2
California Car Rental	47 C2
CST	48 B2
Interbus	(see 46)
Sicilian Airbus Travel	49 B2

MONEY

You will find plenty of banks in Taormina situated along Corso Umberto I; all of them have ATMs (bancomat). There are also some currency-exchange places located along the same street. Compare the commissions, as these can vary between outlets.

POST

Post Office (Piazza Sant'Antonio Abate, far end of Corso Umberto I; 8.30am-6.30pm Mon-Sat)

TOURIST INFORMATION

Main Tourist Office (☎ 094 22 32 43; www .gate2taormina.com; Palazzo Corvaja, Corso Umberto I; 8.30am-2pm & 4-7pm Mon-Sat) Busy tourist office

IONIAN COAST

with multilingual staff. Loads of brochures on activities and services but you may have to queue to speak to someone.

Sights

TEATRO GRECO

Taormina's most famous sight just has to be the heavenly **Teatro Greco** (Greek Theatre; ☎ 094 223 22 20; Via Teatro Greco; adult/concession €6/3; ⌚ 9am-7pm Apr-Oct, 9am-4.30pm Nov-Mar). This perfect horse-shoe-shaped theatre, suspended between sea and sky, was built in the 3rd century BC and is the most dramatically situated Greek theatre in the world.

The Greeks had originally intended to make the most of the breathtaking views of Mt Etna and the Bay of Schisò, but the brutish Romans remodelled it in AD 1, obscuring the natural backdrop with a tall *scaenae frons* (colonnaded backdrop). None too taken with tragedy, they also demolished the stage and orchestra pit, converting them into a semi-circular arena for gladiators.

In the 12th century the family of Spain's Costanza d'Aragona fancied the site as its villa and built a house over part of the theatre (to the right as you face the stage). Fortunately, time has swept many of these alterations away, and the crumbling backdrop once again reveals the stunning panorama.

In summer the theatre is used as the venue of the international arts festival, Taormina Arte (see opposite for details). In peak season the site is *very* busy and best explored early in the morning to avoid the crowds.

AROUND CORSO UMBERTO I

One of the chief delights of Taormina is simply wandering through its narrow medieval main drag, browsing the antique and craft shops, delis and designer boutiques. When these have exhausted their charms most folk retire to the gorgeous **Piazza IX Aprile** from where you can enjoy stunning panoramic views of Etna and pop your head into the cutest rococo church, **Chiesa San Giuseppe** (Piazza IX Aprile; ⌚ 9am-7pm).

At the western end of Piazza IX Aprile is a 12th-century clock tower, **Porto di Mezzo e Torre dell'Orologio**, which leads you through into the Borgo Medievale, the oldest quarter of the town. Head down here to **Piazza del Duomo** where teenagers congregate around the ornate baroque fountain (1635), which sports a two-legged centaur with the bust of an angel, the symbol of Taormina. On the eastern side of the piazza is the **cathedral** (Piazza del Duomo;

admission free; ⌚ 8am-noon & 4-7pm), constructed in the 13th century. It has survived much of the Renaissance remodelling undertaken by the Spanish aristocracy in the 15th century, which is better illustrated in the **Palazzo Duca di Santo Stefano** with its Norman-Gothic windows. Although it is not possible to access this palace, you can look at others such as **Palazzo Corvaja** (which houses the tourist office) and **Palazzo Ciampoli** (☎ 094 22 30 33; Salita Ciampoli 9), now the Hotel Palazzo Vecchio. The nearby **Badia Vecchia** (Old Abbey; Via Leonardo da Vinci) is a 14th-century Gothic building with Norman-Arab elements.

Above the town, and accessible by a tortuously steep staircase, is the peak of Monte Tauro (378m). It is adorned with the wind-swept ruins of a **Saracen castle** and the **Santuario Madonna della Rocca**. The castle and sanctuary are of little interest but the views are fantastic. By car they are 500m from the town centre along the road to Castelmola (see opposite).

VILLA COMUNALE

To get away from the crowds, wander down to the luxuriant Parco Duchi di Cesarò, which is more commonly referred to as the **Villa Comunale** (Via Bagnoli Croci; admission free; ⌚ 9am-midnight summer, 9am-10pm winter). They were created for Lady Florence Trevelyan Cacciola (1852–1907), who left England in disgrace after having had an affair with Edward VII. Now they are some of the most lovely public gardens in Sicily, full of magnolias, hibiscus, bougainvillea, cacti and cypress trees. Perfect for picnicking on a summer's day, the gardens afford some glorious views over the bay below and there is a children's play area.

Activities

To reach **Lido Mazzarò**, directly under Taormina, you need to take the *funivia* (cable car) on Via Luigi Pirandello (one way/return €1.80/3; ⌚ 8am to 1am). This beach is well serviced with bars and restaurants, and private operators charge a fee for a space with umbrella and deck chair (€5 per person or between €10 and €12 for two deck chairs and an umbrella). To the right of the beach past the Sant'Andrea hotel and round the cape is the miniscule **Isola Bella** set in a stunning cove. You can walk here in a few minutes but it is more fun to rent a small boat from Mazzarò to paddle round Capo Sant'Andrea. Isola Bella was bought by Florence Trevelyan for a mere 5000 lire.

IONIAN COAST

It is her house that you can see on the island. Now it is run as a nature reserve by the World Wildlife Fund and the craggy base is a wonderful snorkelling spot.

Given its size, this cove is best enjoyed out of season. Still, you can bag some personal space by renting a deck chair and umbrella (€5 per person). Mendolia Lido has changing facilities but the spot over by the Nike Diving Centre is quieter.

Nike Diving Centre (☎ 094 24 75 34, 3391961559; www.divenike.com; Lido Mazzarò; single dive €30, snorkelling equipment per day €10) can be found at the northern end of the beach. It offers a whole range of courses from Introductory (€40) to Advanced Open Water Diver (€260).

For a real sandy beach you will have to go to **Spisone**, just beneath the autostrada exit (left from the cable-car station and about a 10-minute walk). When you reach the Le Capinera restaurant, take the staircase on the right, go through a tunnel and out onto the large sandy beach.

Other activities involve short excursions around Taormina, one of the most popular being to the **Gola dell'Alcantara** (see the boxed text, p197). Panorama fanatics should head 5km up the hill to **Castelmola**, literally the high point of the area, with a ruined castle and sweeping views of, well, everything. Interbus makes an (almost) hourly run from Taormina (€1.30).

Tours

It is possible to take any number of excursions from Taormina. They are well organised, time saving and hassle free but it may be cheaper to rent a car for the day.

CST (☎ 094 262 60 88; Corso Umberto I 101) Runs coach excursions to destinations including Mt Etna (€27), Piazza Armerina (includes the Villa Romana di Casale and Caltagirone, €50), Palermo (includes Monreale, €45) and Panarea and Stromboli in the Aeolian Islands (€75). Prices exclude admission to museums and archaeological sites.

Sicilian Airbus Travel (SAT; ☎ 094 22 46 53; www.sat-group.it; 73 Corso Umberto I) Provides almost identical tours to CST for very similar prices.

Festivals & Events

Raduno del Costume e del Carretto Siciliano A parade featuring traditional Sicilian carts and folkloric groups. Usually held in autumn. Ask at the tourist office for details.

Taormina Arte (☎ 0942 2 11 42; www.taormina-arte.com) Films, theatrical events and music concerts in July and August from an impressive list of international names. Contact them for details, programmes and bookings.

Sleeping

Taormina has plenty of (expensive) accommodation; in summer it is essential to book in advance.

BUDGET

The cheapest option in Taormina is to go for a room in a private house. The tourist office has a full list.

Campeggio San Leo (☎ 094 22 46 58; Via Nazionale, Località San Leo; per person/tent €4.15/14.45) Near the beach, this camp site has minimal facilities. Take the bus from Taormina to the train station and ask the driver to drop you off at the entrance. Children go free.

Taormina's Odyssey (☎ 094 22 45 33; www.taorminaodyssey.com; 2 Traversa A, Via G Martino; dm/d €18/50) Taormina's only hostel and one that has earned a flurry of complimentary letters from LP readers who rate highly its friendly atmosphere, lack of curfew and open kitchen. A seven-minute walk from the town centre.

Pensione Casa Diana (☎ 094 22 38 98; Via di Giovanni 6; s/d €25/50;) The ancient and lovely Signora Diana has only four simple rooms, and at these prices they are snapped up quickly. It is within spitting distance of the Greek theatre.

Le 4 Fontane (☎ 094 262 55 20; www.le4fontane.it; Corso Umberto 231; s €40-50, d €60-80;) Another excellent budget B&B, on the top floor of an old palazzo, Le 4 Fontane is run by a friendly couple and has three spacious, well-equipped rooms, two of which have views of Piazza del Duomo.

our pick **Pensione Adele** (☎ 094 22 33 52; www.pensioneadele.it; Via Apollo Arcageta 16; s €34-50, d €65-90;) One of the best budget options in town, Adele's is a huge pastel-pink palazzo converted into a *pensione*. It's clean, the rooms are spacious and simple, and the location is pretty much perfect. It also has a very cheap shuttle to the beach, which includes chairs and umbrella for a mere €5 per person.

MIDRANGE

All midrange hotels offer a beach shuttle and have some parking, but you need to phone in advance and book a space. Prices vary between €10 and €14 per day.

our pick **Isoco Guest House** (☎ 094 22 36 79; www.isoco.it; Via Salita Branco 2; s €60-95, d €80-115;) If you think of accommodation as more than just a place to lay your head, then you'll love Isoco. Run by the friendly Michele (also responsible for most of the furniture and decoration), this is Taormina's best little hotel. Isoco sits on a small cliff, just minutes from the centre, with five rooms featuring a different artist. The Keith Haring room has the artist's famous beaming figurines supporting a table and being chairs, and the Herb Ritts room is like a photo-shoot set, with old cameras serving as lamp shades. Michele prepares a good breakfast and the garden has a small Jacuzzi for guests' use. Book well in advance.

Pensione Svizzera (☎ 094 22 37 90; www.pensione svizzera.com; Via Luigi Pirandello 26; s €60-95, d €85-125; P ⊠ ⊒) A very popular B&B teetering on the edge of a cliff with views over Mazzarò bay. Many of the rooms have balconies. The hotel can also organise tennis and diving.

Hotel Isabella (☎ 094 22 31 55; www.gaishotels .com; Corso Umberto I 58; s €72-100, d €112-152; P ⊠) Situated on the *corso*, the Hotel Isabella has a pretty exterior. Inside it's not quite as impressive and rooms are impersonally modern, although comfortable enough. It has its own private beach, Lido Caparena, and meals are served on the rooftop terrace.

Hotel Villa Paradiso (☎ 094 22 39 21; www.hotelvilla paradisotaormina.com; Via Roma 2; s €95-120, d €150-200; P ⊠) Tucked around the back of Taormina, the Paradiso, with its charming, individually decorated rooms, is often overlooked. It has a relaxed atmosphere and each room has a balcony complete with two sun lounges.

Hotel del Corso (☎ 094 262 86 98; www.hoteldel corsotaormina.com; Corso Umberto I 238; s/d €98/125; P ⊠) A modest family-run hotel with a welcoming character. It is one of the few hotels located in the Borgo Medievale, overlooking the stately Palazzo Duca di Santo Stefano and the Golfo di Naxos.

Villa Fiorita (☎ 094 22 41 22; www.villafioritahotel .com; Via Luigi Pirandello 39; s/d €110.50/125; P ⊠ ⊒) A slightly dated hotel on the road into town. Still, it is reasonably priced and comfortable and has the added bonus of a swimming pool. The rooftop terrace is particularly lovely with all its flowers and gorgeous views of Mazzarò bay.

Hotel Villa Schuler (☎ 094 22 34 81; www.villaschuler .com; Piazzetta Bastione, Via Roma 1; d garden view €124-136, d sea view €148-178; P ⊠) Surrounded by shady terraced gardens and with views of Mt Etna, the rose-pink Villa Schuler is family-owned and preserves a homely atmosphere. A lovely

breakfast is served on the panoramic terrace. A great choice.

OUR PICK Hotel Villa Belvedere (☎ 094 22 37 91; www.villabelvedere.it; Via Bagnoli Croce 79; s €100-200, d €118-220; ⊙ 11 Mar-19 Nov; P ⊠ ⊒) Built in 1902, the jaw-droppingly pretty Villa Belvedere was one of the original grand hotels, well-positioned with fabulous views and luxuriant gardens, which are a particular highlight. There is also a swimming pool with a 100-year-old palm tree rising from a small island in the middle.

TOP END

San Domenico Palace Hotel (☎ 094 261 31 11; www .thi.it; Piazza San Domenico 5; d €240-500; P ⊠ ⊒ ⊒) Originally a Dominican monastery, the San Domenico is Taormina's second luxury hotel and a historical monument in itself. Over the years it has hosted an illustrious list of names, from Marshal Kesselring who used it as his WWII headquarters, to Francois Mitterrand. The views may be unsurpassed but so are the prices.

Grand Hotel Timeo (☎ 0942 2 38 01; www.framon -hotels.com; Via Teatro Greco 59; d/ste from €250/360; P ⊠ ⊒ ⊒) The line of sleek Mercedes Benzes with personal drivers should be enough to tell you that this is Taormina's premiere hotel. Surrounded by spectacular panoramic views, the rooms feature baroque-style furnishings, which are dark and sumptuous, and the terrace is truly glamorous.

Eating

Eating out in Taormina isn't necessarily the best value or best quality you'll find, but there's a lot of posing to be done, if that's your thing. Be discerning about where you eat, because there are many overpriced restaurants.

RESTAURANTS

La Piazzetta (☎ 094 262 63 17; Via Paladini 5; meals €30; ⊙ closed Mon winter) Tucked in the corner of the very picturesque Piazzetta Paladini. Recommended.

Granduca (☎ 094 22 49 83; Corso Umberto 172; pizza €10, meals €30-35; ⊙ Thu-Tue) Eating delicious oven-baked pizza on the spectacular terrace of Granduca is an experience not easily forgotten. It also has a wide-ranging international menu. It's very popular so a reservation is highly recommended if you want to be sure of getting a table.

Al Duomo (☎ 094 262 56 56; Vico Ebrei 11; meals €35-40; ⊙ Mon-Sat) The discreet Al Duomo has an intimate terrace that overlooks the cathedral and has hosted a number of celebrities. The stewed lamb and fried calamari are simply delicious. Reservations are required.

Casa Grugno (☎ 094 22 12 08; Via Santa Maria dei Greci; meals €35-40) With an Austrian chef in the kitchen, don't expect typical Sicilian fare. The food at Casa Grugno is international and this remains Taormina's most fashionable eatery. The Catalan farmhouse where the restaurant is ensconced gives it great atmosphere.

Maffei's (☎ 094 22 40 55; Via San Domenico de Guzman 1; meals €40-45; ☒ Tue-Sun) A small restaurant with a pretty courtyard garden and some of the best fish dishes in Taormina. Here you can enjoy a cornucopia of fish, cooked to your liking, however, it is always a good bet to go for the house special.

La Giara (☎ 094 22 33 60; Vico la Floresta 1; meals €40-45; ☒ 8.15-11pm, Tue-Sun Sep-Jul) This stylish Art Deco restaurant and piano bar serves grilled fish and delicious pasta with inventive sauces such as lemon and shrimp. It has a well-heeled clientele (Ava Gardner used to dine here) and the sniffy maître d' will turn you away if you're not dressed appropriately. Reservations are required.

CAFÉS

Cafe Wunderbar (Piazza IX Aprile 7; coffees €3.50, alcoholic drinks €5.50-7) A poseur paradise on Piazza IX Aprile, serving the most delicious *latte di mandorla* (almond milk). Perfect for a warm summer's evening.

Pasticceria Gelateria Etna (112 Corso Umberto) A quaint little coffee shop–cum-*pasticceria* selling traditional sweets, cakes and liqueurs.

Drinking

Marrakesh Café (☎ 094 262 56 92; Piazza Garibaldi 2; cocktails €5.50; ☒ 6pm-3am) An Arabian-themed cocktail bar with candlelit, mosaic-topped tables. Its outdoor tables draw a cosmopolitan crowd in summer.

Shatulle (☎ 094 262 61 75; Piazza Paladini 5; cocktails from €5.50) A gay and lesbian bar that has one of the best terraces around. A great atmosphere and it's open all year round.

Q Loungebar (☎ 094 22 12 96; Piazzetta Paladini 6; cocktails €5.50-7; ☒ Tue-Sun) Another stylish bar in this busy piazza. White and brown leather stools and banquettes give it a sleek modern look. Drinks are served with olives, nuts and crisps. Don't bother with the food.

O'Seven Irish Pub (Largo Giuseppe La Farina; snacks €2.60-5.20; ☒ 24 hr) Tucked behind the Torre dell'Orologio is this pleasant pub with outdoor seating – perfect for watching the *passeggiata* (evening stroll).

Shopping

Taormina is a shoppers' paradise full of high-quality ceramic goods, lace and linen tableware, antique furniture and jewellery. Corso Umberto I is where the better shops are; Via Teatro Greco tends to be much more touristy although it does have a couple of gourmet grocery shops. Shops in Taormina tend to stay open late (until around 10pm) and can often arrange packing and shipping to your home address (for a fee).

La Torinese (☎ 094 22 33 21; Corso Umberto I 59) A good deli that stocks lots of wine, conserves, capers, liqueurs and honey.

Kiseki (☎ 094 262 88 61; www.kisekijewels.com; Corso Umberto I 55) One exceptional jeweller that utilises natural materials like shells, coral, semiprecious stones and lava.

Carlo Mirella Panarello (Via A Marziani) If ceramics are your thing, this workshop produces original designs that have a lovely naive quality. Ring the bell to be admitted.

Getting There & Away

BUS

The bus is the easiest way to reach Taormina. **Interbus** (☎ 094 262 53 01; Via Luigi Pirandello) services leave for Messina (€3, 1½ hours, five Monday to Saturday) and Catania (€4.50, 1½ hours, four Monday to Friday). The Catania bus also services the train station and Giardini-Naxos (€1.60). There are also services to the Alcantara Gorge (€4.70 return, four daily) and up to Castelmola (€1.30, 15 minutes, four daily).

CAR & MOTORCYCLE

Taormina is on the A18 motorway and SS114 between Messina and Catania. Parking is a complete nightmare and Corso Umberto I is closed to traffic. The **Lumbi car park** (☎ 094 22 43 45; ☒ 24hr) is north of the town centre. It provides a shuttle service to the centre from Porta Messina.

California Car Rental (☎ 094 22 37 69; Via Bagnoli Croce 86; Fiat Punto with air con per day/week €78/339, Vespa 125 per day/week €30/189) rents out cars and motorcycles at reasonable prices, with added

IONIAN COAST

extras such as unlimited kilometres, free child seats and hotel drop-off.

TRAIN

There are regular trains along the Ionian Coast, but the awkward location of Taormina's station is a strong disincentive. If you arrive this way, catch an Interbus bus up to the town. The buses run roughly every 30 to 90 minutes (much less frequently on Sunday). Bear in mind that in summer, the bus pulls up close to full, so you may have to wait for the next one. Trains run from Taormina to Messina (2nd/1st class €6/7.25, 40 minutes, hourly). From Taormina to Catania is just as regular (2nd/1st class €3/4.25, 45 minutes).

GIARDINI-NAXOS
pop 9270

This small town 5km south of Taormina is a popular alternative for accommodation and though it has one of the longest pebbly beaches on the Ionian Coast the town itself is nothing to write home about. Giardini-Naxos' economic engine is tourism and the summer months see the long beach packed with Italian families and package tours. If you're after a quieter place, head down the coast towards Catania and the Riviera dei Ciclopi.

Giardini-Naxos is the location of the first Greek settlement in Sicily. According to legend, the Greeks stayed well clear of the Sicilian coastline, believing it to be inhabited by monsters. This belief was encouraged by Phoenicians eager to keep the Greeks away from the western Mediterranean, but when the Athenian, Theocles, was shipwrecked along the eastern shore he found that the stories were untrue. He returned soon after with a group of Chalcidian settlers and the town of Naxos was founded in 735 BC.

The Naxos ruins are not nearly as impressive as those in other Sicilian excavations. Apart from a 300m stretch of wall, a small temple and a couple of other structures, the best part of a visit is simply to amble through the lemon groves. A small **museum** (☎ 094 25 10 01; Via Schisò; admission €2; ☽ 9am-7pm) has bits and bobs uncovered during the excavation.

The **tourist office** (☎ 094 25 10 10; Via Tysandros 76; ☽ 8.30am-2pm & 4.30-7.30pm Mon-Sat) can help you with accommodation lists and handy maps of the area.

Regular Interbus buses leave from the Taormina bus station on Via Luigi Pirandello (see p195) for Giardini-Naxos. To get to the town from its train station, turn left as you exit the station and follow the signs for about 10 minutes.

Sleeping & Eating

Giardini-Naxos is chock-full of accommodation. If you want to be close to the sea, try the following.

Hotel Nike Giardini-Naxos (☎ 094 25 12 07; www .hotelnike.it; Via Calcide Eubea 27; s €35-54, d €70-109; P ☒) A larger, Mediterranean-style hotel, situated about 3km from the train station in a small rocky bay near the Naxos site. It has marvellous views of Taormina and Etna, and its terraced gardens descend to its own pier and private beach.

Hotel La Riva (☎ 094 25 13 20; www.hotellariva .com; Via Tysandros 52; s €55-77, d €70-110; P ☒) A lovely little family-run hotel with 40 rooms, all individually decorated with traditional Sicilian furnishings. It has great character for Giardini-Naxos and your hosts are charming, making you feel like a guest rather than a paying customer.

Giardini-Naxos is also full of cheap restaurants, most of which are along the waterfront. One good example is **La Cambusa** (☎ 094 25 14 37; Via Schisò 3; pizza €2.60-8). With sea views, ocean breezes and a good list of pizzas, this is one of the town's better choices.

CATANIA & AROUND

CATANIA
pop 310,000

Catania is Sicily's most vibrant (and second-largest) city, the modern, forward-looking sister to traditional Palermo. Much renovated over the last five years, Catania's lava stone buildings are dramatic against the blue skies, its piazze and boulevards are wide and inviting and, come night time, the streets are full of students having fun at the zillion bars and clubs. The city's famous fish market is one of Sicily's most impressive – you'll find yourself outstared by massive swordfish first thing in the morning, and invited to witness sea creatures you never knew existed. All this happens under the watchful puff of Etna which, having erupted once again in September 2007, keeps the city's inhabitants on their toes.

DETOUR: GOLA DELL'ALCANTARA

A relatively short drive up the winding SS185 from Naxos will get you to this series of vertiginous lava gorges known as Gola dell'Alcantara (derived from the Arabic *al qantara,* meaning bridge). The weirdly shaped twisting rock formations were created when a red-hot lava flow hit the water, splintering the basalt into lava prisms. The lava went on to create Capo Schisò at Giardini-Naxos.

The gorge is now protected. The water is freezing, even in summer, and in winter (November to March) it is forbidden to enter the gorge due to the risk of flash flooding. The **Gola Alcantara office** (☎ 0942 98 50 10; admission €4.50) hires out the necessary waders (€5). The lift down into the gorge is beside the car park. It is also possible to reach the gorge by the stairs on the main road, 200m uphill from the lift entrance.

You could stop off here on your way to Mt Etna. Otherwise, Interbus has buses from Taormina to Gola dell'Alcantara (€4.70 return, one hour, four daily Monday to Saturday).

There are great places to eat in the city and some gorgeous B&Bs to go home to. Combine these with the nightlife, friendly people, amazing architecture and some impressive sights, plus the proximity of beaches, and you get Sicily's best city by a mile.

History

Katane was founded by the Chalcidians in 729 BC. For 300 years it tussled with Syracuse for control of the region, before it was sacked by the Romans in 263 BC, and occupied by the Byzantines (AD 535), the Saracens (878) and the Normans (1091). By the mid-17th century Catania was a prosperous urban centre that enjoyed a sophisticated trading network with the rest of the island.

Mt Etna's eruption in 1669 covered most of Catania in boiling lava, killing 12,000 people, destroying the city and reconfiguring the landscape. The fertile countryside was devastated and the starving local population was finished off by the 1693 earthquake, which killed 20,000 people.

The following year Giuseppe Lanza, the duke of Camastra, organised a committee to rebuild the city with a view towards minimising the potential damage of another Etna eruption. Under the supervision of the brilliant architects Giovanni Vaccarini and Stefano Ittar, a new street grid was created that allowed for spacious squares and streets of differing widths, all of which would provide escape routes and greater shelter when Etna stirred once more. In keeping with the dominant architectural style of the period, the new city was thoroughly baroque in appearance. Years of neglect had left many of Catania's elegant palaces and churches in decay but recent renovations, which started around 2002, have brought back the beauty of the city's flamboyant baroque style.

Orientation

Catania's main train station and intercity bus terminal are situated a 15-minute walk east of the city centre, near the port on Piazza Giovanni XXIII. Southwest of the square is Via Vittorio Emanuele II, which runs east–west through the heart of the city, while Via Etnea runs north–south from Piazza del Duomo. Most sights are concentrated around and west of Piazza del Duomo, while the commercial centre of Catania is further north, around Via Pacini and Via Umberto I.

Information

EMERGENCY

Police (☎ 095 736 71 11; Piazza San Nicolella)

INTERNET ACCESS

Prices are €6 per hour.

La Internetteria (Via Penninello 44; ☾ noon-midnight Mon-Sat, 6.30-11.30pm Sun) A nice café serving snacks and drinks. Speedy computers.

LEFT LUGGAGE

Train Station (per bag per 12hr €3.90; ☾ 24 hr)

MEDICAL SERVICES

Farmacia Del Centro (☎ 095 31 36 85; Via Etnea 107; ☾ Sep-Jul) Late-night pharmacy.

Ospedale Garibaldi (☎ 095 759 43 66; Piazza Santa Maria di Gesú)

Ospedale Vittorio Emanuele (☎ 095 743 54 52; Via Plebiscito 628) Has a 24-hour emergency doctor.

IONIAN COAST

CATANIA

IONIAN COAST

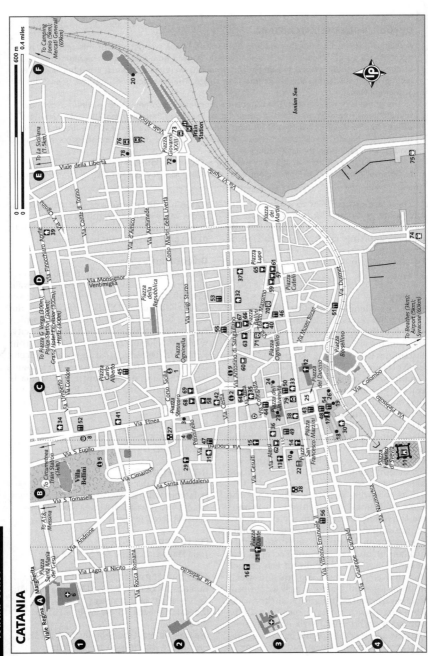

INFORMATION
Banca Nazionale del Lavoro &
  ATM....................................**1** C2
CIT..**2** C3
Farmacia del Centro..................**3** C2
La Internetteria.........................**4** C2
Main Information Office............**5** B1
Ospedale Garibaldi....................**6** A1
Ospedale Vittorio Emanuele......**7** A3
Post Office.................................**8** C1
Sestante Vacanze.....................(see 2)
Tourist Office............................**9** C3

SIGHTS & ACTIVITIES
Arco di San Benedetto..............**10** B3
Castello Ursino.........................**11** B4
Cathedral..................................**12** C3
Chiesa di San Benedetto..........**13** B3
Chiesa di San Francesco...........**14** B3
Chiesa di San Giuliano.............**15** B3
Chiesa di San Nicolò all'Arena..**16** A3
Fontana dell'Amenano..............**17** C3
Fontana dell'Elefante..............(see 25)
Food Market..............................**18** C4
La Pescheria..............................**19** C3
Le Ciminiere..............................**20** F2
Monastero di San Nicolò
  all'Arena.............................**21** A3
Museo Belliniano......................**22** B3
Museo Civico.........................(see 11)
Odeon.....................................(see 28)
Palazzo dell'Università.............**23** C3
Palazzo Sangiuliano.................**24** C3
Piazza del Duomo.....................**25** C3
Porta Uzeda..............................**26** C4

Roman Amphitheatre................**27** C2
Roman Theatre.........................**28** B3
Sant' Agata al Carcere..............**29** B2
Teatro Massimo Bellini...........(see 71)

SLEEPING 🛏
Agorà Hostel............................**30** C4
B&B Crociferi...........................**31** B2
B&B Opera................................**32** D3
Hotel del Duomo.......................**33** C3
Hotel Etnea 316........................**34** C1
Hotel La Collegiata...................**35** C3
Hotel Moderno..........................**36** C3
Hotel Novecento.......................**37** D3
Hotel Savona............................**38** C3
Katane Palace Hotel..................**39** D1
Pensione Bellini........................**40** D3
Pensione Rubens.......................**41** C1
UNA Hotel Palace......................**42** C2

EATING 🍴
Ambasciata del Mare................**43** C3
Café Charmant..........................**44** C3
La Fiera....................................**45** C1
Marrakesh.................................**46** D3
Metrò.......................................**47** B2
Osteria Antica Marina...............**48** C3
Osteria i Tre Bicchieri...............**49** C3
Pasticceria Caprice...................**50** C3
Sicilia in Bocca.........................**51** D4
Spinella....................................**52** C1
Trattoria Casalinga...................**53** D2
Trattoria La Paglia....................**54** C3
Via Coppola..............................**55** D2
ZenZero....................................**56** B3

DRINKING 🍷 🍺
Agorà Bar...............................(see 30)
Heaven.....................................**57** D3
Joyce..**58** C2
L'Incognito...............................**59** D3
Lino's Coffee Shop....................**60** C3
L'Insonnia................................**61** D3
Nievski Pub...............................**62** B3
Over Time Pub..........................**63** C3
Perbacco! Wine Bar..................**64** C3
Rendez Vous Wine Bar..............**65** D3
Stag's Head..............................**66** D3
Tertulia....................................**67** D3
Waxy O'Connors........................**68** C2
Wine Bar...................................**69** C2

ENTERTAINMENT 🎭
Ixtlan......................................**70** D3
Teatro Massimo
  Bellini................................**71** C3
Zo..(see 20)

TRANSPORT
AST...**72** E2
City Buses................................**73** E2
Ferry Terminal (TTT Lines Ferries to
  Naples)..............................**74** D4
Ferry Terminal (Virtu Ferries to
  Malta)................................**75** E4
Interbus-Etna Transporti...........**76** E1
Intercity Bus Station.................**77** E2
SAIS Autolinee Ticket
  Office.................................**78** E1
Taxi Rank...............................(see 73)
Taxi Rank..................................**79** C3

MONEY

Banks are along Corso Sicilia and several have currency exchanges. There is also an exchange office at the train station. Plenty of ATMs can be found along Via Etnea.
Banca Nazionale del Lavoro (Corso Sicilia; 🕑 8.30am-1.30pm & 2.30-4pm Mon-Fri) Has an ATM.

POST

Post Office (Via Etnea 215; 🕑 8am-6.30pm Mon-Fri, 8.30am-12.30pm Sat)

TOURIST INFORMATION

Tourist Office (www.apt.catania.it in Italian; 🕑 8am-8pm Mon-Fri, 8am-2pm Sat) airport (☎ 095 730 62 66); city centre (☎ 095 730 62 33; Via Etnea 63); train station (☎ 095 730 62 55); Via Cimarosa (☎ 095 730 62 22, 095 730 62 11; Via Cimarosa 10-12) Has brochures and maps on the city and Etna. Some English is spoken. You can get the *Lapis* leaflet here, which lists all sorts of entertainment events, live music, jazz, theatre, art exhibitions, restaurants and bars.

TRAVEL AGENCIES

You can book train, ferry and air tickets at the following agencies:

CIT (☎ 095 31 35 77; Via Antonino di Sangiuliano 205)
Sestante Vacanze (☎ 095 31 35 17; Via Antonino di Sangiuliano 208)

Sights

PIAZZA DEL DUOMO

The central square of Catania, **Piazza del Duomo**, is a World Heritage site. Surrounded by magnificent, sinuous buildings, the piazza is a sumptuous example of Catania's own style of baroque with its contrasting lava and limestone. In the centre of the piazza is the city's most memorable monument, the smiling **Fontana dell'Elefante** (Fountain of the Elephant; 1736). This comical statue is composed of a naive elephant, dating from the Roman period, surmounted by an improbable Egyptian obelisk. The elephant, with its upturned trunk, is known locally as Liotru and is the symbol of the city. It belonged to the magician Eliodorus (8th century AD), who reputedly made his living turning people into animals, and thus is believed to retain some magical powers that help calm the restless activity of Mt Etna.

Facing the statue is Catania's other defence against the volcano, St Agata's **cathedral** (☎ 095

IONIAN COAST

THE MASTER OF SONG

In his short life (he died when he was 34) Vincenzo Bellini composed 10 operas, including the trio that made his fame: *La sonnambula* (The Sleepwalker), *I puritani* (The Puritans) and *Norma*. Unlike his bel canto contemporaries, Bellini refused to rely on the tried-and-tested seductive melodies that made such hits out of operas like Rossini's *Il barbiere di siviglia* (The Barber of Seville) and Donizetti's *Lucia di lammermoor*. Unperturbed by the ease with which his fellow composers reeled off operas (Rossini wrote an average of one opera every two weeks!), Bellini tried to write works that didn't rely on pretty melodies at the expense of a well-crafted story. Although successful during his short career, Bellini's style fell out of favour after his death and his operas struggled for recognition until the 1950s and the revival of the bel canto style. Wagner, however, recognised Bellini's genius and wrote that his music was 'strongly felt and intimately wound up with the words', a powerful emotional combination brought to dramatic life by Maria Callas in her 1953 performance in the title role of *Norma*.

32 00 44; Piazza del Duomo; admission free; 8am-12pm & 4-7pm), with its impressive marble façade sporting two orders of columns taken from the Roman amphitheatre (see opposite). Inside the huge vaulted interior lie the remains of the city's patron saint, the young virgin Agata, who resisted the advances of the nefarious Quintian (AD 250) and was horribly mutilated (her breasts were hacked off and her body was rolled in hot coals). The saint's jewel-drenched effigy is ecstatically venerated on 5 February in one of Sicily's largest *festas* (festivals; see opposite).

Today the best show in town is **La Pescheria** (Piazza del Duomo; 5-11am), the bustling fish market and the adjoining **food market** (Piazza del Duomo; all day). The shouts of the fishmongers, the hundreds of gleaming fish, the massive swordfish and dozens of squid displayed on the wooden tables are unforgettable (and delicious too!). This street show is not to be missed at any cost and if you're staying in self-catering accommodation it is heaven for a fantastic lunch. The **Fontana dell'Amenano** at the entrance of the food market is Tito Angelini's commemoration of the River Amenano, which once ran overground and on whose banks the Greeks founded the city of Katane.

EAST OF PIAZZA DEL DUOMO

A few blocks northeast, you'll stumble onto the lovely Piazza Bellini, dominated by **Teatro Massimo Bellini** (Via Perrotta 12). It is named after Vincenzo Bellini, Catania's most famous export and the father of a vibrant modern musical scene (see boxed text, above), and is one of the largest theatres in Europe, with a sumptuous, gilt-encrusted interior.

Further east on Viale Africa is the renovated sulphur refinery building, **Le Ciminiere**

(095 734 99 11). The renovation involved transforming the refineries into a cultural centre while preserving their original character – a bit like the Tate Modern in London. It houses a collection of modern art and a permanent exhibition of WWII memorabilia, art and photography. Enquire at the tourist office about temporary exhibitions and cultural events, or pick up the *Lapis* leaflet.

CASTELLO URSINO

If you walk south from Piazza del Duomo, through the impressive **Porta Uzeda** (built in 1696) and down to Piazza Federico di Svevia, you'll come across the imposing fortifications of the 13th-century Castello Ursino, built by Frederick II. The grim-looking fortress, surrounded by a moat, was once on a cliff top overlooking the sea; following the earthquake of 1693 the whole area to the south was reclaimed by the lava and the castle became landlocked. Inside is the **Museo Civico** (095 34 58 30; Piazza Federico di Svevia; admission free; 9am-1pm & 4-8pm Mon-Sat), the repository of the valuable archaeological collection put together by Catania's most important aristocratic family, the Biscaris. It also houses treasures from the monastery of San Nicolò and some Roman artefacts.

WEST OF PIAZZA DEL DUOMO

The city's most interesting street is probably Via Crociferì. At the southern end, on Piazza San Francesco, is the **Museo Belliniano** (095 715 05 35; admission free; 9am-1.30pm Mon-Sat, 9am-12.30pm Sun & public holidays), the former home of Vincenzo Bellini, now a small museum with a good collection of the composer's memorabilia, including original scores, photographs and his death mask.

Opposite the museum is the 18th-century **Chiesa di San Francesco** and just up the street is the **Arco di San Benedetto**, an arch built by the Benedictines in 1704. According to legend, the arch was built in one night to defy a city ordinance against its construction on the grounds that it was a seismic liability. On the left past the arch is the imposing **Chiesa di San Benedetto**, built between 1704 and 1713. Inside is some splendid stucco and marble work.

Past the church, off Via Crociferì, are the ruinous remains of the **Roman theatre** and a small rehearsal theatre, the **Odeon** (Via Vittorio Emanuele II 266; theatre & odeon €2; ☾ 9am-1.30pm & 3-7pm).

Back on Via Crociferì, you'll find the **Chiesa di San Giuliano** (1738–51), designed by Vaccarini, about halfway up the street on the right-hand side. The convex central façade makes for an interesting effect. Further on you'll notice the excavations that have resulted in the whole street being closed off to traffic: here, at the crossroads with Via Antonino di Sangiuliano, a section of the old Roman road and a sizable floor mosaic have been uncovered. You can peer over the boarding to take a look.

CHIESA DI SAN NICOLÒ ALL'ARENA
Directly opposite Chiesa di San Giuliano is the tiny Via Gesuiti, which leads west to Piazza Dante and Sicily's largest church, the Chiesa di San Nicolò all'Arena. Commissioned in 1687, work on the building was interrupted by the earthquake of 1693 and then by problems with its size – it is 105m long, 48m wide and its cupola is 62m high. The church was never completed. It has a terribly ugly façade, a stark contrast to the rich embellishments that adorn the city's other baroque structures. The cavernous interior is equally devoid of frills, the long walls interrupted by a series of altars that are almost completely bare. The presbytery features a splendid organ crafted by Donato del Piano.

Directly behind the church and part of the same complex is the massive Benedictine **Monastero di San Nicolò all'Arena**, built in 1703 and now part of the city's university. It is the second-largest monastery in Europe and has some lovely internal cloisters and one of the most valuable libraries on the island,

complete with its original bookcases and 18th-century majolica-tiled floors.

VIA ETNEA
Via Etnea is an impressive wide boulevard and Catania's main north–south artery. It runs from Piazza del Duomo right up through the city and into the foothills of Mt Etna. Via Etnea is a bright street with lots of shops and cafés, and at its heart is Piazza dell'Università. Facing each other on the square are two buildings designed by Vaccarini – the **Palazzo dell'Università** to the west and the **Palazzo Sangiuliano** to the east. The former is the city's university.

A further 300m north is the large and modern Piazza Stesicoro, whose western side is dominated by the sunken remains of the **Roman amphitheatre**. It doesn't look like much today, but in its heyday (around the 2nd century BC) it could seat up to 16,000 spectators and was second in size only to the Colosseum in Rome. What you see from the street is only a part of the once-massive structure, which extended as far south as Via Penninello. You can explore part of the vaults and get an idea of the true size of the theatre from a diagram.

A little walk away from Piazza Stesicoro you will find the church of **Sant'Agata al Carcere** (admission free; ☾ 8am-12pm & 4-7pm Tue-Sat), built above the dungeons where the saint was imprisoned and tortured. You can ask the custodian for permission to take a peak at the gloomy prison cell below the church.

For relief from the madding crowd, continue north along Via Etnea and cut in left behind the post office for the lovely gardens of the **Villa Bellini**, with loads of trees and places to sit, and a floral clock.

Festivals & Events
Festa di Sant'Agata Hysterical celebrations where one million Catanians and tourists follow the Fercolo (a silver reliquary bust of the saint covered in marvellous jewels) as it is carried along the main street of the city. There are also spectacular fireworks during the celebrations. Held 3 to 5 February.

Catania Musica Estate Classical music festival in July.

Etna Jazz Ask at the tourist office for information on this jazz festival, also held in July.

Settimana Barocca A week of baroque concerts, pageants and other performances in July.

Sleeping
Catania is probably the best place in Sicily for reasonably priced, stylish hotels. This makes

it an excellent base for exploring the Ionian Coast and Etna. Quality top-end hotels, however, are a bit thin on the ground.

BUDGET

Camping Jonio (☎ 095 49 11 39; www.camping.it/italy /sicilia/jonio; Via Villini a Mare 2; per adult €6-10, per tent €6-12, bungalow per person €20-50) This place is about 5km northeast of Catania, close to a beautiful rocky beach. To get there, catch bus 334 from Via Etnea. It also has bungalows. The services are decent here and if you fancy the beach and don't mind not being inside Catania, it's a good budget option.

Agorà Hostel (☎ 095 723 30 10; www.agorahostel .com; Piazza Currò 6; dm €18-20, d €40-50; 🖵) A classic youth hostel with rooms of six to 10 beds and some doubles. There is no lockout, an internet point is provided (€3 per hour) and you can do laundry (€4 per wash). Its location near La Pescheria makes it a good base for self-caterers, and its bar is one of the coolest in Catania (see p204). The hostel (and its website) is a mine of information about itineraries on Etna and around Catania.

Pensione Bellini (☎ 095 715 09 69; www.bellinihotel .com; Via Landolini 41; s €35-45, d €49-60; 🔀) This friendly little *pensione* just off Piazza Bellini is an excellent budget option and provides good, comfortable accommodation. The young couple running it is friendly and helpful. Breakfast is included if requested.

our pick **B&B Opera** (☎ 3492689998; www.bbopera .it; Via Antonino di Sangiuliano 129; s €40-50, d €60-70; 🔀) B&B Opera is what happens when you get gorgeous décor, good prices, fab location and great management in one place. Sitting on the top of an old palazzo, this converted space has five large rooms with domed ceilings, modern and stylish furnishings and gleaming bathrooms. There's a kitchen that you can use freely as well as a small terrace. The friendly manager, Lydia, is a dream. If only every town had as good a place as this...Book in advance.

Pensione Rubens (☎ 095 31 70 73; www.rubenshotel .it; Via Etnea 196; s/d €45/75; 🔀) Seven huge, spacious rooms are kept in tiptop condition by the affable Signor Caviezel. The wide windows are double-glazed and the rooms are quiet and restful, with floral furniture and tall ceilings. There's a large pink reception, a coffee room where black-glass chandeliers swing from the ceiling, and aristocratic furniture glams up the space. A great choice.

Hotel Moderno (☎ 095 32 65 50; www.albergomoderno .it; Via Alessi 9; s/d €59/79; 🔀) The Moderno is more modern in name than in appearance, with drab 1970s rooms that can be a bit sad. It's only good if there's nowhere else; its saving grace is its location, near Via Crocierì, and the fact that the manager is friendly.

our pick **B&B Crociferi** (☎ 3478975729; www.bbcroci feri.it; Via Crociferì 81; s €50-65, d €65-85; 🔀) Another stunning B&B, consisting only of three rooms (so book in advance), all of which have domed and frescoed ceilings and small balconies looking at the street below. The owner Teresa is a lover of all things Indian, and the décor – which could easily feature in a style magazine – reflects this. There's a gorgeous, plant-filled kitchen with traditional Sicilian ceramics where you have your breakfast.

MIDRANGE

Hotel La Collegiata (☎ 095 31 52 56; www.lacollegiata .com; Via Paolo Vasta 10; s €45-50, d €75-85; 🔀) With lovely rooms in terracottas and burgundies, some overlooking Piazza dell'Università and others a peaceful courtyard, La Collegiata is great value for its excellent location and pleasant atmosphere. You need a coupon (€3) from reception to get breakfast from one of the bars on Via Etnea.

Hotel Etnea 316 (☎ 095 250 30 76; www.hoteletnea316 .it; Via Etnea 316; s €55-65, d €75-90; 🔀 🖵) The charming Hotel Etnea is opposite the Bellini gardens and has really good rooms with comfy wrought-iron beds, big windows, traditional tiles or wooden floors, and ochre walls. It's a peaceful place with a sunny lounge and breakfast room. The service is good and discreet.

Hotel del Duomo (☎ 095 250 31 77; www.hoteldel duomo.it; Via Etnea 28; s/d €75/100; 🔀) The very central Hotel del Duomo occupies the whole wing of an ancient palazzo. Front rooms have great views over Piazza del Duomo, which is particularly lovely at night. The décor is classic and the service friendly.

Hotel Novecento (☎ 095 310 48 88; www.hotelnovecento catania.it; Via Monsignor Ventimiglia 37; s/d €85/100; 🔀) An elegant hotel at very reasonable prices. Inside, the Art Nouveau interior gives it a classy feel and bedrooms are decorated with turn-of-the-century furnishings. There is no restaurant but breakfast is served in the hotel café.

Hotel Savona (☎ 095 32 69 82; www.hotelsavona.it; Via Vittorio Emanuele 210; s/d €100/140; 🔀) Another good hotel located just off Piazza del

---

EATING & DRINKING IN THE STREET

One of Catania's best features is that, come evening, the market area (p200) turns out a number of food stalls that cook and serve the meat and fish they didn't sell during the day. Head here after 7pm and you'll see several of the daytime stalls turned into plastic-chair outdoor diners. Pick your piece of meat/fish and enjoy a plate of antipasti and some house wine. You'll pay around €15 for a plate of antipasti and a main, followed by some watermelon or whatever is in season. It's simple, delicious food, the proprietors are friendly, and the atmosphere always jolly. Perfect.

Another speciality of Catania is the tubular kiosks that dot the streets (Via Etnea has many) and serve the traditional nonalcoholic drink: a lemon, orange or mandarin cordial, or a very special fizzy lemon concoction. Stop by in the evening (they usually open after 6pm) and be refreshed the Catanian way.

Duomo. Back rooms overlook a quiet inner courtyard while other rooms have views over scattered rooftops backing the hotel. There's no lift and the stairs are very steep, so watch out if you have heavy bags.

Katane Palace Hotel (☎ 095 747 07 02; www .katanepalace.it; Via Finocchiaro Aprile 10; s €127-160, d €147-160; P 🞬 🖳) A restored palazzo with discreet, elegant, top-class service. The rooms are warmly furnished and the restaurant, Il Cuciniere, is excellent, with a menu drawn from local ingredients and wines.

TOP END

Grand Hotel Excelsior (☎ 095 53 70 71; www.thi.it; Piazza G Verga; s/d €195/345; 🞬 🖳) Catania's only five-star hotel is the Excelsior, in an ugly Fascist-era building on Piazza G Verga. It is much less attractive on the outside than it is on the inside and has a floor for nonsmokers and an internal garden.

UNA Hotel Palace (☎ 095 250 51 11; www.unahotels .it; Via Etnea 218; r from €358; 🞬) A new, white, gleaming six-floor, four-star hotel from the UNA chain, with sleek, blindingly white rooms, black and gold furniture and a rooftop garden bar that serves cocktails and aperitivi at sunset. It's posh all right, but you can get a great bargain if you book online.

Eating

Like true sybarites the Catanians love to eat, and dining out in Catania is a real pleasure. Pretension is set aside for quality food and a noisy, companionable atmosphere.

Don't miss the savoury *arancini* (fried rice balls), *cartocciate* (bread stuffed with ham, mozzarella, olives and tomato) and *pasta alla Norma* (pasta with tomatoes, aubergine and salted ricotta), which originated here.

RESTAURANTS

Marrakesh (Via Landolina 52; dishes €6-9; 🕑 8pm-1.30am Thu-Tue) A North African eatery and bar near Piazza Bellini. Serves couscous, *makluba* (a spicy chicken stew with aubergines, tomatoes, onions and almonds with rice) and *tagine*. In summer tables are set up outside and there is nearly always live music or belly dancing.

Via Coppola (☎ 095 31 29 09; Via Coppola 39; pizza €6.50-8) The best thing about this place is its atmospheric setting in a quiet street, where the tables are covered by a canopy and surrounded by flickering candles. It's popular with Catanians for its good pizza and is great for a low-key dinner.

Osteria i Tre Bicchieri (☎ 095 715 35 40; Via S Giuseppe al Duomo 31; cheese plates €10, fondue €20; 🕑 8pm-midnight Tue-Sun) The dark wood-panelled interior creates the perfect atmosphere for this classy wine bar, which stocks over 1000 different labels. Huge glasses of wine are served with tasty crudités, and the fondue is great fun on evenings of live jazz.

Trattoria La Paglia (☎ 095 34 68 38; Via Pardo 23; meals €20-25; 🕑 Mon-Sat) This is a great-value, simple trattoria with a nice view of the La Pescheria market, from which it gets its fish and seafood. It serves straightforward fresh pasta and fish dishes and is good for lunch or dinner.

our pick Metró (☎ 095 32 20 98; www.ristorante metro.it; Via Crociferì 76; meals €25-30; 🕑 Mon-Fri, lunch Sat) A gastronomic delight sitting right near the top of Via Crociferì, with outdoor tables. The food here is to die for: traditional Sicilian with a modern touch. No wonder Metró gets a shining review in Slow Food. Try the *pasta alle vongole* to start and go for the succulent *tonno a cipollata* (tuna steak topped with caramelised onions) as a main. Finish with seasonal fruit or the pistachio-and-chocolate *semifreddo*. The wine list is great too.

IONIAN COAST

Trattoria Casalinga (☎ 095 31 13 19; Via Biondi 19; meals €25-30; ✆ Mon-Sat) A homely, family-run, Slow Food–awarded restaurant presided over by patron Nino, this is a good place for a simple Sicilian dinner of pasta with seafood, tuna steak or a seafood platter with a hearty green salad. Finish with some fruit.

Sicilia in Bocca (☎ 095 250 02 08; Via Dusmet 31/35; meals €25-30; ✆ Tue-Sun) Fabulous medieval atmosphere in the old sea wall. A favourite of the bohemian crowd, which flocks here for its famous traditional fish recipes.

ourpick Osteria Antica Marina (☎ 095 34 81 97; Via Pardo 29; meals €30; ✆ Wed-Mon) A rustic-style trattoria near the fish market, this is the place for fresh fish of the day. Slow Food praises the local favourite, a raw anchovy salad, and rightly so. The décor is solid wooden tables and rough stone walls. Reservations are essential.

ZenZero (☎ 095 32 01 11; Via Vittorio Emanuele II 201; meals €30; ✆ 8-11pm Tue-Sun) Set on the roof terrace of an old palazzo that overlooks a peaceful square off the main road, ZenZero is the young people's eating place of choice in Catania. It's a welcome change from the world of pasta, serving international dishes like tempura or Argentine steak. It's also a good place for an aperitivo, and the flower-laden terrace is divine.

Ambasciata del Mare (☎ 095 34 10 03; Piazza Duomo 6; meals €30-35; ✆ Tue-Sun) A tiny restaurant on the side of Piazza Duomo (right by the fountain), this is a great spot for the fish market offerings, so tuck into the sardines, or the swordfish cooked in sea water (amazing). If you can fit in a *cannoli* (pastry shell stuffed with sweet ricotta), go for it: they are delicious. Another Slow Food champion.

La Siciliana (☎ 095 37 64 00; Viale Marco Polo 52; meals €35-40; ✆ closed Sun evening) Considered one of Catania's best restaurants, La Siciliana serves traditional fare cooked to perfection. Try the breaded cutlets, roast lamb or the huge selection of seafood. Reservations are required and you will need a taxi or car to get here.

CAFÉS

Pasticceria Caprice (Via Etnea 30) An old-style *pasticceria*, this café is highly recommended. Located on Via Etnea, it is the perfect place to come during *passeggiata*. Try a selection of minitarts filled with fresh fruit.

Spinella (☎ 095 32 72 47; Via Etnea 300) This is probably Catania's most famous *pasticceria*;

one taste of its produce – especially the ricotta-filled *cannoli* – will tell you why.

Café Charmant (Via Etnea 19-23; ✆ 24hr) An elegant, modern café good for morning snacks and breakfast with street-side tables for people-watching.

SELF-CATERING

Every morning except Sunday, Piazza Carlo Alberto is flooded by the chaos of a produce market, known locally as **La Fiera** (✆ 7am-noon Mon-Sat), not dissimilar to a Middle Eastern kasbah. The other major market is **La Pescheria** (off Piazza del Duomo; ✆ 5-11am Mon-Sat). It is a huge fish market set out over several courtyards and alleys where fishers shout out their catch of the day. You can buy fresh mussels and sea urchins to eat on the spot.

Drinking

Not surprisingly for a busy university town, Catania has a reputation for its great nightlife. There are dozens of cafés and bars serving cheap and tasty snacks and offering a good mix of music and drinks. Via Vasta, off Via Etnea, and Piazza Bellini is where a lot of the action takes place and Wednesday nights are big student nights out. Opening hours are generally from around 9pm to 2am.

Tertulia (Via Mario Rapisardi 1-3; ✆ 4.30pm-1.30am daily Sep-Jul) This nocturnal bookshop and café is a mix between a stylish teahouse and bar. There is occasional live music, literary evenings and book presentations. There is also internet access.

Agorà Bar (☎ 095 723 30 10; www.agorahostel.com; Piazza Currò 6) The bar and restaurant of the Agorà Hostel are a great venue for a drink. This neon-lit cave 18m below ground where a stream bubbles to the surface was used by the Romans as a spa. Now a cosmopolitan crowd lingers over drinks in the lava cavern.

Perbacco! Wine Bar (☎ 347 093 79 88; Via Vasta) Quite a large bar with sofas and cushions laid out under burgundy canopies, Perbacco! is a real hit with the Catanians, who hang out here until the wee hours, enjoying the variety of wines.

Lino's Coffee Shop (☎ 095 31 51 60; Via Antonino di Sangiuliano 225; ✆ 9am-midnight) An excellent coffee shop attached to the Mondadori bookshop, Lino's has a massive variety of coffees. The *granite* (flavoured crushed ice) are also popular and this is a perfect place for reading your book in a quiet, cool atmosphere.

Wine Bar (☎ 3387602772; Via Montesano 19) With simple décor and a loyal crowd of glass-whirlers, this lovely and simply named bar serves a massive variety of Sicilian and international wines, as well as some snacks to go with the booze.

Rendez Vous Wine Bar (40 Via Teatro Massimo) An elegant place with a modern look and canary-coloured lamp shades, the Rendez Vous is right at the end of the Via Teatro Massimo bar strip. It has tables and chairs on the little balcony outside, but the crowd spreads out onto the street below too.

L'Insonnia (Via Teatro Massimo 1) Opposite the elegant Rendez Vous, L'Insonnia is home to those lovers of night fun, Catania's boho crowd, who sit on the benches outside the bar and chat, drink and smoke till dawn breaks.

Heaven (Via Teatro Massimo 39) A cool lounge bar with massive leather sofas in the street and electric-blue lighting inside. Disco music is favoured by the young crowd, though not much dancing goes on.

L'Incognito (Via Teatro Massimo 22) Woven chairs and palm trees make L'Incognito's outdoor area feel like a tropical corner despite the fact that it's right on Piazza Bellini. It's a popular place for a drink and chat and starts getting busy only after 10pm.

Over Time Pub (☎ 3491678469; Via Rapisardi 16-18) A unique place in the city, Over Time brings out real poker tables on Monday nights and the local crowd puts poker faces on and comes out to play. Check it out, it's quite fun just to watch.

Stag's Head (Via Rapisardi 7-9) Opposite Over Time, the Stag's Head has huge speakers out the front and the tables are permanently full, mostly with students drinking beer and mouthing the words to whatever song is playing.

Nievski Pub (☎ 095 31 37 92; www.nievski.it in Italian; Scalinata Alessi 15; mains €5-6.50; ☺ 1-4pm & 8pm-2am Tue-Sat) On the heaving Scalinata Alessi, this is a good place to mingle with Catania's alternative crowd. Cuban revolutionary posters adorn the walls and the menu uses organic, fair-trade produce for its Greek and Cuban dishes.

Joyce (☎ 3498107896; Via Montesano 46; ☺ 9pm-2am Tue-Sun 16 Aug-19 Jul) Joyce is an Irish pub where you can enjoy pints of Guinness in a pleasant courtyard. It's quite a popular place and quieter than the wacky Waxy's across the street.

Waxy O'Connors (Piazza Spirito Santo 1) A really popular place, where many come to listen to (sometimes pretty dodgy) live music and watch the dancers shake their booties. It doesn't appeal to everyone, but many love it. Across from Joyce.

Entertainment

To see what's going on (jazz, opera, theatre, puppet shows etc) pick up a copy of *Lapis* (free and available throughout the city).

LIVE MUSIC & CLUBBING

Ixtlan (Via Teatro Massimo 33; ☺ 6pm-2am) A legendary pub, putting on impromptu jazz performances and jamming sessions. Good bar- and buffet-style snacks from 6pm to 9.30pm.

our pick **Zo** (☎ 095 53 38 71; www.zoculture.it; Piazzale Asia 6; ☺ 1pm-2am Sep-Jul) Part of a cultural complex hosting events and exhibitions, the bar/café/restaurant serves good food in an impressive venue – the converted sulphur works, Le Ciminiere. The weekends host live music and dancing.

Mercati Generali (☎ 095 57 14 58; www.mercatigenerali.org; Km69, SS 417; ☺ 11pm-late) The student population's favourite club, this place is out of town (so you'll need your own transport or a taxi) and it hosts the best parties around. DJ Talvin Singh has played here, as well as many good international and local DJs. You'll find Ninja Tunes–released artists on the list, as well as some of Berlin's promising names.

THEATRE

Teatro Massimo Bellini (☎ 095 730 61 11; www.teatromassimobellini.it; Via Perrotta 12) Ernesto Basile's Art Nouveau masterpiece, restored to its brilliant former glory, stages opera, ballet and music concerts. Its programme runs from October to May and you can book tickets online.

Getting There & Away

AIR

Catania's airport, **Fontanarossa** (☎ 095 30 45 05; www.aeroporto.catania.it) is 5km southwest of the city centre and has domestic services and European flights (mostly via Rome or Milan). Air Malta, Lufthansa and Alitalia all have regular flights to Fontanarossa, while British Airways and Air Berlin offer direct flights from London and Berlin respectively. In the summer you may be able to pick up some cheaper charters with British Midland, JMC or Hapag-Lloyd Flug (see p296 for more details). To get to the airport, take the special Alibus (bus 457, €0.85) from outside the

IONIAN COAST

train station, although many of the services from Catania to, say, Taormina or Syracuse, will also stop at the airport. There is also an hourly shuttle to Taormina (€5, one hour, 7am to 8pm). All the big car-hire companies are represented at the airport.

BOAT

The ferry terminal is south of the train station along Via VI Aprile.

Virtu Ferries (☎ 095 53 57 11; www.virtuferries.com) runs express ferries from Catania to Malta. Ferries depart Catania's Molo Centrale at the port at various times (one departure a week March to May and four a week between 24 July and 3 September). The ferry trip takes around three hours and tickets cost from €83 one way, €104 return and from €130 if you take a car.

Società Adriatica (☎ 095 713 91 41) connects Catania with Ravenna (Emilia-Romagna; €90, 36 hours). You can buy tickets at the Sestante Vacanze travel agency (for details see p199).

TTT Lines (☎ 095 746 21 87; www.tttlines.it in Italian) has a daily ferry from Naples to Catania leaving at midnight Monday to Saturday and 7.30pm on Sunday (€28/76 passenger/car, €125 double cabin, 10½ hours,).

BUS

Intercity buses terminate in the area around Piazza Giovanni XXIII, in front of the train station, and depart from Via d'Amico, which is one block up. Although intimidating at first glance, Catania's bus station is superefficient and easy to navigate, far surpassing the rather plodding train service.

AST (☎ 095 746 10 96; Via L Sturzo 230) runs similar services to SAIS and Interbus, as well as to many smaller provincial towns around Catania, including Nicolosi (€3.55, 50 minutes, half-hourly).

Interbus-Etna Trasporti (☎ 095 53 27 16; Via d'Amico 181) runs buses to Syracuse (€4.50, 1¼ hours, half-hourly Monday to Saturday, eight Sunday), Piazza Armerina (€20, 1½ hours, nine Monday to Saturday) and Taormina (€4.30, 1½ hours, four Monday to Friday).

SAIS Autolinee (☎ 095 53 62 01; Via d'Amico 181-187) serves Palermo (€13.20, 2½ hours, 17 daily), Agrigento (€13, three hours, 14 daily Monday to Friday, seven Saturday and Sunday) and Messina (€7.10, 1½ hours, half-hourly Monday to Saturday, two Sunday). It also

has a service to Rome (€45, 14 hours) which leaves at 8pm.

CAR & MOTORCYCLE

Catania is easily reached from Messina on the A18-E45 autostrada (see boxed text, p190) and from Palermo on the A19. From the autostrada, signs for the centre of Catania will bring you to Via Etnea. Bear in mind that driving in Catania is only for the brave (or heavily insured). If you must drive, the best time to arrive and leave is between 2pm and 4pm or on Sunday, when everyone is safely at home and not in their cars.

TRAIN

Frequent trains connect Catania with Messina (2nd/1st class €8/10, 1½ to two hours, hourly) and Syracuse (€5, 1½ hours, 18 daily).There are less frequent train services to Palermo (€12, 3½ hours, six daily *diretto*) and Agrigento (€11.50, an agonisingly slow 3½ to 4½ hours, five per day). The private Circumetnea train line circles Mt Etna, stopping at the towns and villages on the volcano's slopes. See p208 for more information.

Getting Around

Many of the more useful **AMT city buses** (☎ 095 736 01 11) terminate in front of the train station. These include: Alibus (station to airport every 20 minutes); buses 1 to 4 (station to Via Etnea); buses 4 to 7 (station to Piazza del Duomo). A two-hour ticket costs €0.85. In summer a special service (D) runs from Piazza G Verga to the sandy beaches. Bus 334 from Via Etnea takes you to the Riviera dei Ciclopi and the beautiful Norman castle at Aci Castello (admission is free).

For a taxi call **CST** (☎ 095 33 09 66). There are taxi ranks at the train station and on Piazza del Duomo.

RIVIERA DEI CICLOPI

One pleasant surprise for visitors to Catania is the quality swimming and little-visited towns a little north of the city.

To travel along the coast, take one of the regular Interbus services from Catania to Messina (€1.30; about 30 minutes). In Acireale, the buses stop along outside the public garden at the end of Corso Umberto. In Aci Trezza and Aci Castello the buses stop along the main road.

IONIAN COAST

Acireale

About 17km north of Catania, and occupying a magnificent position on the Ionian Coast, Acireale is a true discovery for lovers of Sicilian baroque, and could be said to be one of the few 'off-the-beaten-track' towns on the island. It's surprisingly tourist-free, considering its position between Taormina and Catania, and it has fantastic baroque architecture, thermal baths, good food and a lively morning market. Acireale, like much of this coast, was destroyed in the 1693 earthquake, and its baroque beauty owes its dues to the city's aristocrats and merchants who financed the rebuilding effort.

ORIENTATION & INFORMATION

The **tourist office** (☎ 095 89 52 49; Via Romeo 1; ☾ 8am-2pm & 3-9pm) is just off Piazza Duomo, and the staff are friendly and speak good English. Piazza Duomo is the heart of the city, with Corso Umberto, Acireale's main drag, running north, while Via Ruggero Settimo trickles south and out of town. Via Cavour takes you to Piazza San Domenico and the market area.

SIGHTS & ACTIVITIES

To see Acireale's stunning architecture, start at the very centre of town, the **Piazza Duomo**, where the tall spires of the restored **cathedral** watch over the city. The cathedral is richly frescoed by the work of Pietro Paolo Vasta and it's hugely popular for hosting wedding parties. The **Basilica dei Santi Pietro e Paolo** sits on the eastern corner of the square, and on its right is the impressively long **Palazzo Municipale** (Town Hall), stretching down Via Romeo. One of the city's arteries, Via Ruggero Settimo, takes you south to the gorgeous **Basilica di San Sebastiano**, one of the most beautiful examples of Acireale's baroque architecture. It has a breathtaking altar, and its dome is adorned by Pietro Paolo Vasta's frescoes. Don't miss the **Chiesa di San Domenico** and the *pescheria* (fish market) area that surrounds it – Acireale's market is the perfect place to explore all the goods without the crowds (like those in Palermo or Catania). If you're into puppets, Acireale has some great shows at the **Teatro dell'Opera dei Pupi** on Via Alessi (between Piazza Duomo and Piazza San Domenico). The theatre is also a puppet museum, hosting performances every Sunday at 6pm. For performances on other days check the tourist office.

DETOUR: SANTA MARIA LA SCALA

For a real track (even) less beaten, head down to the tiny fishing village of Santa Maria La Scala, 2km downhill from Acireale. If you follow Via Romeo down from Piazza Duomo, across the small road and down onto the small towpath, you'll soon find yourself in tranquil surroundings with gorgeous coastal views. The village consists of a tiny harbour crowded with technicolour fishing boats, a church, some houses and a black lava-rock beach next to the harbour. Check out one of the trattorie for daily fish offers.

For a bit of sulphur bathing, a tradition and a must-do in Acireale, head to **Terme di Santa Vénera** (☎ 095 768 61 11; www.terme-acireale.com; Via delle Terme 1; treatments from €21; ☾ 7am-1pm Mon-Sat).

FESTIVALS & EVENTS

Acireale hosts one of Sicily's best **carnivals** (during Lent), when the streets are filled with flowers and floats and the whole town is out in the street. There's also a jazz festival, **Made in Sicily**, in September (dates change so check www.comune.acireale.ct.it, in Italian, for details), hosting Italian and international jazz talent.

SLEEPING

Acireale has a dozen decent B&Bs, should you decide to stay the night.

San Sebastiano Holidays (☎ 3333258894; www.sansebastianoholidays.com; Piazza Odigitria 3; s €30-45, d €55-80; 🐱) A very simple place with clean rooms and white furniture, close to the central Piazza Marconi and the fish market.

our pick **Al Duomo** (☎ 3479078323; www.alduomo.org; Via Cali 5; s €50-60, d €70-80; 🐱) The best pick of Acireale's places to stay is this four-room apartment in a restored palazzo just off Piazza Duomo. It's colourful and stylish, with a luxurious feel. There's a communal living room and window seating, and the (included) breakfast is eaten in the bar across the street.

EATING

Fish is the best thing to go for here, thanks to the restaurants stocking up daily on fresh catches from the market.

L'Oste Scuro (☎ 095 763 40 01; Piazza Lionardo Vigo 5-6; meals €25) Fish, pasta and good desserts are accompanied by views of the Basilica di San Sebastiano. Try the generous antipasti for two (for a bargain €10), consisting of lemony anchovies, amazing *caponata*, sweet aubergines and other small-dish delights, followed by grilled squid or one of the fresh daily catches prepared in sea water.

La Taverna (Piazza Marconi; meals €25-30) A good lunchtime option right on the fish market square. You can savour the daily catches here – the locals recommend its simple but delectable dishes.

La Casa del Grecale (☎ 095 60 51 05; www.lacasadel grecale.it in Italian; Via Santa Caterina 51; set menu €30) An excellent reason for visiting Acireale is a superspecial lunch at this gorgeous 18th-century villa perched on the hillside behind the town in its own lemon grove. If driving, turn off the SS114 at the signpost for Acireale into the village of Santa Caterina. After 20m you will find the villa on your left-hand side, adjacent to Hotel Aloha d'Oro.

Aci Trezza

A few kilometres south of Acireale is Aci Trezza, a fishing village and a good place to satisfy your seafood appetite. It's famous for the surreal, jagged basalt rocks, **Scogli dei Ciclopi**, that protrude from the sea and bejewel the coast. They were supposedly thrown by the blinded Cyclops (who lives in Etna) at the fleeing Odysseus. The rocks are best observed from the tiny Piazza Bambini del Mondo, just along the main *lungomare*, where you can plonk yourself down on a bench and watch fearless local kids diving off the rocks.

Aci Trezza is also popular with young crowds in the summer, who come here to sunbathe on the wooden platforms. There's nothing to do here apart from swim, sunbathe and read.

If you decide to stay the night, a decent option is **Grand Hotel i Faraglioni** (☎ 095 093 04 64; www.grandhotelfaraglioni.com/it/; Lungomare Ciclopi; s €95-110, d €105-130;), in a futuristic building with comfortable rooms. It's equally popular for La Terrazza, where locals and visitors head for pizza, aperitivi and the fabulous views.

Another good place to eat is **Ristorante Il Pontile** (☎ 095 711 68 16; www.ilpontilecapodacqua.it; Lungomare Ciclopi 133; couscous €24-28, meals €25-30), with a terrace over the water, overlooking Cyclops' rocks. It specialises in fish and couscous.

There are tons of trendy lounge bars along the beach. Check out **Café de Mar** (Lungomare Ciclopi; 8pm-late) right next to Grand Hotel i Faraglioni, where white sofas and armchairs are scattered across a palm-tree shaded garden. **La Scivola** (Lungomare Ciclopi; 9pm-late) has DJs and hosts parties in the summer.

Aci Castello

Aci Castello is a small town only 1km from Aci Trezza, and is a popular destination for swimming, sunning and snorkelling. It's also only 9km from Catania's city centre (take AMT bus 334 from Piazza Borsellino), so you can head out here for your day's swimming if you're staying in Catania. It's a lava **beach** (sharp on the bum!) and in summer wooden platforms are erected for sunbathing ease.

Apart from swimming, the real attraction in Aci Castello is the **castle** (adult/concession €2.50/1; 9am-1.30pm & 3.30-7pm Tue-Sun May-Sep, 9am-1pm & 3-5pm Tue-Sun Oct-Apr) that gives the town its name. Another popular wedding venue, the dark, brooding castle resembles an abandoned ship overlooking the sea. It was built in the 13th century and was the base for the rebel Roger di Lauria in 1297, who was replaced by Frederick II of Aragon after some serious battling over the castle. It's in surprisingly good shape considering the assaults it has endured in battles and from volcanic fury. It's a moody and atmospheric building, with sweeping, windy views of the horizon.

MT ETNA & AROUND

MT ETNA
elev 3323m

Sicily's most prominent landmark is Europe's largest live volcano and one of the world's most volatile. At 3323m it towers over the Ionian Coast, dwarfing everything beneath it; its smoking peak is visible from almost everywhere on this side of the island, and is a heart-stirring (and sometimes heart-stopping!) sight. As a symbol of power, creation and destruction it's hard to beat, and the effect of this extraordinary volcano should not be underestimated.

Since 1987 the volcano and its slopes have been part of a national park, the Parco Naturale dell'Etna, a territory that encompasses a fascinatingly varied natural environment from its severe, almost surreal summit, with its breathtaking panoramas, to deserts of lava and alpine forests.

History

Triggered by a combination of volcanic and regional tectonic activity more than half a million years ago, a number of eruptive centres appeared off the east coast of Sicily. The most recent phase of volcanism, about 35,000 years ago, created the present-day stratovolcano known as Etna.

In ancient times Etna's summit was frequently lit up by spectacular pyrotechnic displays. Not surprisingly, the eruptions featured in some very early writing. The classical world saw the volcano in mythological terms as the home of the god Plutone and of the Titans who predated Zeus and rebelled against him. In the 18th century BC, Homer mentioned Etna in his story of Ulysses (Odysseus) and the Cyclops, and in *Prometheus,* Aeschylus describes Etna as a 'column holding up the sky', with the giant Tifone (Typhoon) at its base.

Recorded history is littered with eruptions, including major ones in 475 BC, AD 1169, 1329 and 1381, all of which saw molten rock flow right down to the sea. The most devastating eruption occurred in 1669 and lasted 122 days. A massive river of lava poured down Etna's southern slope, destroying 16 towns and engulfing a good part of Catania.

The first documented visitor to Etna was in 1493: Pietro Bembo, who wrote *De Aetna* telling of his adventures. This encouraged an influx of English, German, French, Dutch and Danish travellers. In 1773 English physicist, Patrick Brydone, published his *Tour Through Sicily & Malta,* and his lyrical descriptions of the ascent to the crater inspired many aristocrats to visit.

In more modern times Etna has claimed its fair share of victims, despite the fact that it is monitored by 120 seismic activity stations and is under constant satellite surveillance. In 1971 an eruption destroyed the observatory at the summit, and another in 1983 finished off the old cable car and tourist centre. Nine people died in an explosion at the southeastern crater in 1979, and two died and 10 were injured in an explosion at the same crater in 1987. In 1992 a stream of lava pouring from a fissure in the southeastern slope threatened

to engulf the town of Zafferana Etnea. The town was saved when the Italian Air Force dropped a pile of breeze blocks in the lava's path. In 2001–02 and 2003 Mt Etna's most spectacular explosions in 40 years caused immense damage to the infrastructure on the southern side of the mountain (see p210). Luckily the reconstruction of the villages was not damaged in the September 2007 eruption, which lasted for two days and caused nothing more than a fantastic night scene of lava fountains, which were several hundred metres high (available for viewing on YouTube or www.volcanoetna.com).

Orientation & Information

The two main approaches to Etna are from Piano Provenzano on the northern flank and Rifugio (Refuge) Sapienza on the southern flank. The 2001–03 eruptions of the volcano destroyed the refuge at Piano Provenzano and the village is being slowly reconstructed. You can pick up information at a number of sources, the most convenient being the main tourist office in Catania (see p199).

The official office of the **Parco Naturale dell' Etna** (☎ 095 82 11 11; www.parcoetna.ct.it in Italian; Via del Convento 45, Nicolosi; ☒ 9am-2pm & 4-7.30pm) is in Nicolosi on the south side. Further up at Rifugio Brunek is another **information point** (☎ 095 64 73 52; Rifugio Brunek; ☒ 9am-3pm); and at Rifugio Sapienza you will find the **Etna Sud Tourist Office** (☎ 095 91 63 56; ☒ 9am-4pm).

On the northern side of the mountain the local **tourist office** (☎ 095 64 73 52; www .prolocolinguaglossa.it in Italian; Piazza Annunziata 5; ☒ 9am-3pm) in Linguaglossa is the best source of information.

For up-to-date information on eruptions and weather forecasts, and for a detailed account of the mountain's geology and history, take a look at www.etnaonline.it (in Italian).

Sights & Activities

The volcano is made up of four summit craters and is surrounded by 200 major and secondary cones dotting its flanks. Measuring roughly 7km by 5km, the Valle del Bove, a depression on the eastern side of Etna, is a caldera formed after a cone collapsed several thousand years ago.

It is absolutely forbidden to approach the summit craters and after all the activity it would very foolish to do so. At the summit it is always windy and temperatures can fall below

IONIAN COAST

WHAT TO TAKE

■ Solid comfortable walking boots are essential for walking on the craters. The loose gravel-like lava is very slippery to walk on and in many places the ground underfoot is hot. The Parco Naturale dell'Etna even prints a disclaimer on its tickets abdicating responsibility for people who do not wear hiking boots – you'd be surprised at how many people actually wear their sandals up there!

■ For trips up Stromboli and Etna you will need all the high-altitude gear: warm clothes, a wind jacket, warm headgear, gloves and a compass.

■ Bring a mat, sleeping bag, fire-lighting equipment and a torch if you plan on camping. Note that this is only permitted at official camp sites.

■ Pack sun-block, sunglasses and a hat. It's really easy to burn up there, and that's the sun we're talking about, not the lava.

■ Bring bottled water – the local supplies are limited and often not reliable.

■ A mobile phone is an excellent safety precaution, although it may not work in certain locations.

---

freezing, so come prepared. Do wear suitable footwear. Jackets and boots can be hired at the cableway station at Rifugio Sapienza.

RIFUGIO SAPIENZA

With a daily bus link from Catania via Nicolosi, the southern side of the volcano presents an easy option for an ascent towards the craters. The AST bus drops you off at the Rifugio Sapienza (1923m) from where **Funivia dell'Etna** (☎ 095 91 42 09; www.funiviaetna.com; cable car €23, cable car, bus & guide €42.50; ☼ 9am-4.30pm) runs a cable car up the mountain to 2500m. (The ticket office accepts credit cards and cash.)

Once out of the cable car you can attempt the long walk (3½ to four hours return) up the winding track to the authorised crater area (2920m). If you plan on doing this, make sure you leave yourself enough time to get up *and* down before the last cable car. Otherwise you can hop on one of the Mercedes–Benz trucks (bus with obligatory guide €19.50).

On a clear day the landscape above the cable-car station is simply stunning, the perfect black cone of the Cratere Sud-Est offset by a bright blue sky. The guided tour takes you on a 45-minute walk around the Bocca Nuova, a new crater formed in the latest eruptions. Along its rim the ground is still hot, the magma in its crater simmering at 400°C. On the eastern edge the Valle del Bove falls away in a precipitous 1000m drop, smoke billowing up from its depths and enveloping you on the ridge above. You feel like you have reached the very edge of the world.

PIANO PROVENZANO

Before the eruptions in 2001–03, Piano Provenzano (1800m) was Etna's main ski resort. The eruptions changed all that – the refuge, five ski lifts, ski runs and hotels were all swept away in a huge lava flow. On your way up you can see how the lava flattened the trees that line its edges at peculiar angles.

Now things are slowly getting back on track and all the infrastructure is once again being rebuilt. There are small wooden kiosks selling water, food and souvenirs and a portacabin sells tickets (€37) for regular truck excursions to the summit craters. Again, you can make the three-hour walk if you start early enough.

This side of the mountain is considerably quieter than Rifugio Sapienza and the landscape is quite different, with thick, dappled pine forest (the Pineta Ragabo) full of holidaying Italians with their barbecues. You need your own car to get here as there is no public transport from Linguaglossa, 16km away.

Tours

Acquaterra (☎ 095 50 30 20; www.acquaterra.com; Via A Longo 74, Catania) Excellent guided tours around the northern side of the volcano, from where you see a different volcanic landscape.

Centro Ippico Amico del Cavallo (☎ 095 46 18 82; www.amicodelcavallo.com; Via A Gramsci 27, Misterbianco) This well-run stable is 8km west of Catania. Horse trails include a seven-hour trek through Etna farmland, a two-day trek along the Simeto river and a five-day trek around the summit. For other stables pick up the booklet *Itinerari a Cavallo* from the tourist office in Catania (p199).

Etna Experience (☎ 095 723 29 24; www.etna experience.com) A well-regarded agency with tours to Bove Valley and hikes up to the craters.

Ferrovia Circumetnea (FCE; ☎ 095 54 12 50; www .circumetnea.it; Via Caronda 352a, Catania; ☺ 8am-5pm) FCE has some good tours to Mt Etna and the surrounding area. You can also take the train around the base of the volcano.

Gruppo Guide Alpine Etna Nord (☎ 095 64 78 33; www.guidetnanord.com; Piazza Santa Caterina 24, Linguaglossa) Runs a similar service as the Etna Sud (below), only to the north side.

Gruppo Guide Alpine Etna Sud (☎ 095 791 47 55; www.etnaguide.com; Via Etnea 49, Nicolosi) The official guide service on the mountain runs day or multiday itineraries for around €180 per day with a guide. It also has a hut at Rifugio Sapienza from where it runs a daily trek into the Valle del Bove (€55, four hours, departs 9am).

Sleeping & Eating

Accommodation on Etna is limited. Catania is the best alternative base. If you do plan to stay around the mountain be sure to book in advance as rooms are at a premium, especially in summer.

SOUTH

Camping Etna (☎ 095 91 43 09, fax 095 791 51 86; Via Goethe; per person/tent €4.40/9.20; ☺ Apr-Oct) A camp site set in woodland within easy walking distance of Nicolosi (signposted).

Ostello della Gioventù Etna (☎ 095 791 46 86; etnahostel@hotmail.com; Via della Quercia 7; dm €26) If you don't fancy camping but need a cheap bed, this very good Nicolosi hostel is the answer to your prayers. It's close to both Catania and the volcano.

Gemmellaro (☎ 095 91 13 73, fax 095 91 10 71; Via Etnea 160; s €27-50, d €40-79; ❄) Located in Nicolosi, the three-star Gemmellaro is an acceptable hotel choice offering comfortable rooms.

Rifugio Sapienza (☎ 095 91 63 56; www.rifugiosa pienza.com; Piazzale Funivia; s/d €49/98) Completely refurbished after the 2001–03 eruptions, the Sapienza refuge offers very comfortable accommodation right next to the cable car. It also has a restaurant.

Airone (☎ 095 708 18 19; www.hotel-airone.it; Via Cassone, Zafferana Etnea; s €70-80, d €100-120) A sweet little hotel in the bustling market town of Zafferana Etnea, full of rustic charm. The hotel also has a good restaurant and nice location.

WHO'S AFRAID OF ETNA'S HOT BREATH? *Vesna Maric*

To an outsider, living under Etna seems like a disconcerting business. As a child you learn about the historical lava wipe-outs and that the big old volcano erupts almost annually. To your average neurotic, this must mean anxiety aplenty. I asked Pascal Bresson, one of the people from the Acquaterra agency who takes people up and down Etna on a daily basis, how people cope with living under such a potentially dangerous volcano.

'Local people aren't really scared of the activities of the volcano. Etna is part of their landscape. They know that places were destroyed by Etna, and it's just part of their history. No one gets caught up by fears over the smoke on top of Etna and what might happen next.' And what about the tourists, do they get frightened of going up? 'You see, Etna is an effusive volcano, which means that there are no explosions, ie no general possibility of flying rocks landing uncomfortably close to wandering tourists. That means that it's safe to go up to the top and look at it.' I give him an unsettled look. 'Basically, no, most people have no fears about it. In fact, there are so many people who travel from all parts of Italy when Etna erupts, coming over to see the 'lava show'. It can be very beautiful.'

It's all very well to say that, I point out, but what about the Piano Provenzana and the damage done there? 'Well, it's true that despite all the monitoring there was no forecast for the Piano Provenzana activity,' says Pascal. 'But having said that the scientists knew there was a fracture – an east to west fracture that could be subject to activity at any point – it's just that they weren't expecting lava to come and cover Piano Provenzana. I guess it's just not a very precise science.' I thank him and go off on my clamber up the old volcano, anxiously watching the puff on top of the cone in case it gets any larger. But as the walk progresses, my fears melt away as if covered by, erm, lava, and I conclude that Pascal is right. It's a beautiful place indeed.

NORTH

Rifugio Brunek (☎ 095 64 30 15; Bosco Ragabo; B&B/half board €26/39) A rustic refuge situated in the tranquil Ragabo pine forest on the eastern slopes of Etna. Designed as a chalet, it has pleasant rooms and a dedicated and helpful host. The restaurant serves fresh local produce.

Hotel Scrivano (☎ 095 92 11 26; www.hotelscrivano .com; Piazza Loreto, Randazzo; s/d €45/85; P 🔀) A very pleasant hotel in quiet Randazzo, run by the Scrivano family. Its rooms are modern and comfortable and the restaurant is well regarded locally.

Getting There & Away

Having your own transport will make life much easier around Mt Etna, but there are some public transport options.

BUS

AST (☎ 095 53 17 56) runs buses from Catania to Rifugio Sapienza (€3.80, one hour). It leaves from the car park in front of the main train station in Catania at 8.15am, travelling via Nicolosi. It returns from Rifugio Sapienza at 4.30pm. You can buy your tickets on the bus. You can also drive this route (take Via Etnea north out of Catania and follow the signs for Nicolosi and Etna).

SAIS and FCE buses connect Linguaglossa with Fiumefreddo, on the coast (from where other SAIS and Interbus buses run north to Taormina and Messina and south to Catania). There was no public transport up to Piano Provenzano at the time of research. If driving, follow the signs for Piano Provenzano out of Linguaglossa; it is 16km.

TRAIN

Another option is to circle Mt Etna on the private train, **Ferrovia Circumetnea** (FCE; ☎ 095 54 12 50; www.circumetnea.it; Via Caronda 352a, Catania). You can catch the metro from Catania's main train station to the FCE station at Via Caronda (metro stop: Borgo) or catch bus 429 or 432 going up Via Etnea and ask to be let off at the 'Borgo' metro stop.

The train follows a 114km trail around the base of the volcano, from where you get great views of the mountain and the lush vegetation

at its base. It also passes through many of Etna's unique towns like Adrano, Bronte and Randazzo (see below). It takes two hours to reach Randazzo (€4). To continue from here you will need to get another train for Giarre on the coast (another hour).

AROUND MT ETNA

The villages around Etna's base make for a wonderful tour right off the beaten track. They all have a unique character influenced by their proximity to the volcano. The countryside is also extremely pretty, especially in springtime when the orchards and citrus groves are in full flower. Heading west out of Catania along the SS121 you will come to baroque **Paternò**, surrounded by orange groves and dominated by a huge 14th-century **Norman castle**, where Frederick II took his last breath. North of Paternò is **Biancavilla**, founded by Albanian refugees in 1480, and 3km further north is scruffy **Adrano**, home of the Sicel god of fire, Adranus. Adrano is a formal market town, like Randazzo, with all activity centred around Piazza Umberto. This town's **Norman castle** rises from a huge fortified base and is powerfully impressive. It was once a Bourbon prison but now houses a minor museum.

From Adrano, the SS284 heads directly north through acres of nut groves (chestnuts, walnuts, pistachios and almonds) to **Bronte**. Here the landscape becomes more rugged, interspersed with chunks of lava flow dating to 1823. Bronte itself is trapped between two lava flows, and you can detour from here to the Abbazia di Maniace (see p247 for details).

By far the most interesting town around the volcano is grey **Randazzo**, a small medieval town that has consistently escaped destruction despite its proximity to the summit. Its crenellated churches were the focus of three embattled communities: the Italians in **Cattedrale di Santa Maria**, the Greeks in **Chiesa di San Nicolò** and the Lombards in **Chiesa di San Martino**. Until the 16th century each of the churches took turns to act as the cathedral for a three-year term, until the Italians won out. The heart of Randazzo is Piazza Municipio.

From Randazzo the SS120 will take you back to the coast through Linguaglossa.

Syracuse & the Southeast

One of the most magical corners of Sicily, Syracuse and the southeastern part of the island brim with Sicilian baroque, historical remains, amazing food and some beautiful beaches and landscapes. At the same time this part of the world somehow manages to remain unflooded by tourism – how perfect is that?

Starting with glorious Syracuse which, like some noble and elegant dame, just gets better with age, you'll likely find it hard to pull yourself away from this gorgeous city. But make sure you do, for a little further from Syracuse you'll reach the 'baroque triangle': Noto, a renovated shrine to Sicilian baroque and a paradise for lovers of the style; the friendly and charming Modica, where you'll eat and drink well, admire the dramatic baroque and sigh over the landscape of cluttered pastel-coloured palazzos; and finally, the knockout that is the largely undiscovered Ragusa, abundant with baroque and teeming with dozens of delightful B&Bs and great restaurants.

If that's not enough, the coastline running underneath Modica and Ragusa all the way east to Riserva Naturale Oasi Faunistica di Vendicari is full of long sandy and pebble beaches – most of which are relaxed and not too crowded in high season – so swimming opportunities in this area are top class too. There's no two ways about it: the southeast is a stunner.

HIGHLIGHTS

- Stroll down the magical streets of Syracuse's **Ortygia** (p217), where ancient Greece and 18th-century baroque jostle for space
- Delight in the beauty of baroque architecture and delicious food as you explore the relatively undiscovered **Ragusa** (p235)
- Indulge in the rich dark chocolate and the equally extravagant architecture in **Modica** (p233)
- Bask in the golden reflection of **Noto** (p228), a voluptuous baroque town, restored to its utmost glory
- Find some of Sicily's wildest and quietest beaches at the **Riserva Naturale Oasi Faunistica di Vendicari** (p232)

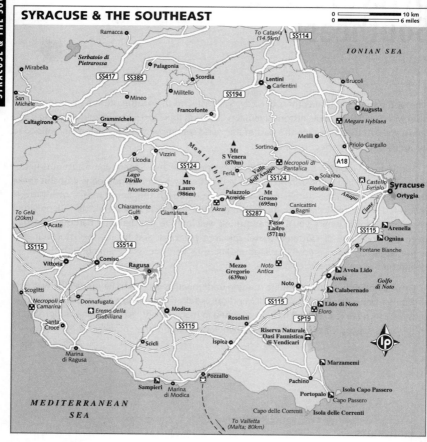

SYRACUSE & THE SOUTHEAST

SYRACUSE

pop 122,900

It's quite possible that there isn't a more
picture-perfect city than Syracuse (Siracusa)
in the whole of Sicily. This oddly shaped
city, sticking out on Sicily's southeastern
tip, is divided into 'mainland' Syracuse and
Ortygia island – the old part of town, which
is connected to the mainland by a bridge.

Syracuse's history is hard to forget when
you're walking through the narrow streets
of Ortygia or getting sunstroke at the Greek
and Roman amphitheatre and archaeological
digs in the mainland part of town. It was,
after all, a rival to Athens in power and
prestige during the Greek period and its

illustrious past is visible in every nook, street
and palazzo.

But Syracuse's modern guise is just as delicious: the city is a perfect mix of history,
beauty, seaside fun and gastronomic delights,
and a recent spring-clean of the historic centre has made it shine with a renewed beauty.
Syracuse isn't a city you'll come to for the
nightlife – it's in fact favoured by families
and those looking for quiet pleasures – but if
you want beauty and history sprinkled with
summer delights and Mediterranean delicacies, you're in for a treat.

HISTORY

Syracuse is rightly proud of its illustrious
history, which dates back 3000 years to the

time when the island of Ortygia was settled by Siculian tribes. However, the foundations of the modern city weren't laid until the arrival of the Corinthians (734 BC) who expanded onto the mainland with a second town called Acradina four years later. The growing city of Syracoussai derived its name from a torrential stream, called the Syrakò, which flowed nearby.

Well protected and increasingly prosperous, Syracuse soon cut its ties with Corinth and began trading on its own, a new rival to the Mediterranean powers of Athens and Carthage. In 485 BC the 'tyrant of Gela', Gelon (540–478 BC), seized the city and ordered that the populations of all other Sicilian colonies transfer to Syracuse, triggering a sharp increase in the city's population. But the real turning point for the city's fortunes came with the defeat of the Carthaginians at the Battle of Himera (480 BC), which allowed the city to dominate trade in the Mediterranean basin. Understandably the successes of this upstart colony didn't go down well in Athens, embroiled as it was in the Peloponnesian War.

In 415 BC Athens assembled the largest fleet ever put together, to deliver Syracuse into its hands, but overconfidence, poor planning and weak supply lines were no match for Syracusan strategy and the fleet was almost completely destroyed. Syracuse's revenge was unmerciful: those prisoners who escaped execution were incarcerated for seven years in the city's notorious quarries.

Cruel and vicious though they often were, Syracusan tyrants commissioned an impressive programme of public works and patronised the finest intellectuals of the age. Luminaries flocked to Syracuse, cultivating the sophisticated urban culture that was to see the birth of comic Greek theatre. Pindar and Aeschylus were invited by Hieron I (r 478–66 BC); Dionysius II (r 367–343 BC) was greatly taken with the 'philosopher-king' theories expounded by his tutor Plato; and Hieron II (275–216 BC) patronised Archimedes.

Following Dionysius' death, the city entered a series of unsteady alliances aimed at preserving the status quo in the face of the new Roman threat. But not even the ingenious defences devised by Archimedes were enough to stave off the ransacking of the city by the Romans in 211 BC.

Under Roman rule Syracuse remained the capital of Sicily and was the seat of the praetors, but the city was in decline. It was briefly the capital of the Byzantine empire in AD 663 when Constans set up court here, but was sacked by the Saracens in 878 and reduced to little more than a fortified provincial town. The population fell drastically, and famine, plague and earthquakes marked the next 800 years. The Val di Noto earthquake in 1693, however, was the catalyst for energetic urban renewal as planners took advantage of the damaged city to undertake a massive programme of reconstruction in the baroque style.

Following the unification of Sicily and Italy in 1865 Syracuse was made a provincial capital and the city began to expand once more, a trend that continued with the ugly urban development of the postwar years.

ORIENTATION
Tidy and compact, Syracuse is a very manageable city to visit. The main sights are in two areas: on the island of Ortygia, and 2km across town in the Neapolis Archaeological Park. The train station is located to the west of the busy shopping street, Corso Gelone, and this is where you'll be dropped off if you arrive by bus. Walking to Ortygia will take you about 15 to 20 minutes – head down Corso Gelone and continue down Corso Umberto until you reach the bridge. Via Roma is the main street running through the centre of Ortygia. Free electric buses are now operating on Ortygia, starting from Piazza della Posta, and no nonresidents are allowed to park on the island. There is talk of making Ortygia totally pedestrian, though this is still being discussed. Stay on Ortygia for the atmosphere, great restaurants and good-quality hotels.

INFORMATION
Emergency
Police (☎ 0931 49 51 11; Via San Sebastiano)

Internet Access
Prices are around €6 per hour.
Eureka Web (☎ 0931 6 07 67; Via Castello Maniace 23, Ortygia; 9.30am-1.30pm & 4.30-9pm Mon-Sat) Other multimedia services available.
Internet Train (☎ 0931 46 87 97; Via Roma 122, Ortygia; 7.30pm-midnight Tue-Sat) Fifteen fast, flat-screen computers, colour printing, digital downloads and scanning. Also rents out mobile phones.

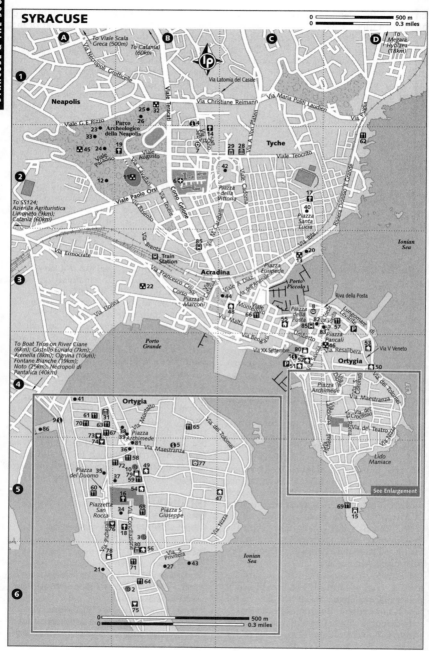

SYRACUSE

0 — 500 m
0 — 0.3 miles

Neapolis

To Viale Scala Greca (500m)

Via Necropoli Grotticelle

To Catania (60km)

Via Latomia del Casale

Via Christiane Reimann

Via Maria Politi Laudien

Via Puglia

Tyche

Via von Platen

Via Teocrito

Via G. E. Rizzo

Parco Archeologico della Neapolis

Viale Paradiso

Via Cavallari

Viale Augusto

Corso Gelone

Via Paolo Orsi

Via Bainsizza

Via Tevere

Viale Cadorna

Via M. Citabem

Piazza della Vittoria

Via Isola

To SS124; Azienda Agrituristica Limoneto (9km); Catania (60km)

Piazza Santa Lucia

Rivera Dionisio II Grande

Ionian Sea

Via Brenta

Via Ermocrate

Via Francesco Crispi

Train Station

Acradina

Corso Umberto

Piazza Euripede

Piazzale Marconi

Viale A. Diaz

Via dell'Arsenale

Porto Piccolo

Riva della Posta

Via Elorina

Viale Montedoro

Via Malta

Piazza della Posta

Lungomare di Levante

Via Piave

Via Bengasi

Corso Umberto

Piazza Pancali

P

To Boat Trips on River Ciane (6km); Castello Euriala (7km); Arenella (8km); Ognina (10km); Fontane Bianche (19km); Noto (25km); Necropoli di Pantalica (40km)

Via XX Settembre

Via Resalibera

Via V Veneto

Ortygia

Porto Grande

Piazza Archimede

Via Maestranza

Via dei Tolomei

Lido Maniace

See Enlargement

Ortygia

Via Montalto

Piazza Archimede

Via dei Tolomei

Piazza del Duomo

Via Maestranza

Piazzetta San Rocco

Via della Conciliazione

Piazza S Giuseppe

Via S Nizza

Via Pichera

Via S Privitera

Ionian Sea

0 — 500 m
0 — 0.3 miles

Web & Work (Via Roma 16-18, Ortygia; 🕑 10am-2pm & 4-10pm Mon-Fri, 11am-2pm & 4.30-9.30pm Sat, 6-10pm Sun) Other multimedia services available.

Medical Services
Ospedale Generale Provinciale (☎ 0931 6 85 55; Via Testaferrata 1)

Money
Numerous banks (all with ATMs) line Corso Umberto and there are banks on Corso Gelone. Ortygia is a little less prolific with its ATMs, but there are a couple around Via XX Settembre and on Via Roma.

Post
Post Office (Piazza della Posta 15; 🕑 8am-6.30pm Mon-Fri, 8am-1pm Sat) Also offers currency exchange.

Tourist Information
Main Tourist Office (☎ 0931 48 12 00; www.apt -siracusa.it; Via San Sebastiano 43; 🕑 8.30am-1.30pm & 3.30-6.30pm Mon-Sat) English-speaking staff and a useful city map – ask about the cumulative tickets for the sites.

There is also an information booth at the Chiesa San Nicolò dei Cordari in the Parco Archeologico.
Ortygia Tourist Office (☎ 0931 46 42 55; Via Maestranza 33; 🕑 8am-2pm Mon-Sat & 2.30-5.30pm Mon-Fri) English-speaking staff and lots of good information.

Travel Agencies
Boccadifuoco (☎ 0931 46 38 66; Viale Mazzini 8) For information and tickets to Malta from Pozzallo.
Syrako Tourist Services (☎ 0931 2 41 33; www .syrako.it in Italian; Largo Porta Marina; 🕑 9am-1pm & 3-8pm Mon-Sat, tours Jul-Sep) Can help carless people to see more of the province. See p222 for tour details.

SIGHTS
Ortygia
The island of Ortygia is the spiritual and physical heart of the city. It is a living museum of a succession of epochs – Greek, Norman, Aragonese and baroque – purposefully combined in a harmonious symmetry. You can access the island across the Ponte Nuovo, past the inner harbour of quietly bobbing boats and rust red Venetian palazzi (palaces). In

recent years Ortygia has undergone some serious renovations, making it shine with a bright new lustre; it has also gone car-free (except for local parking), which means that the town now breathes with clean lungs (and so will you).

PIAZZA DEL DUOMO

Despite its baroque veneer, Syracuse's Greek essence is much in evidence, and particularly so in disguised architectural relics such as the Piazza del Duomo, the one-time acropolis of the Greek city, surrounded as it now is by baroque mansions constructed after the 1693 earthquake.

The piazza's centrepiece is the lofty façade of the **cathedral** (Piazza del Duomo; admission free; ☙ 8am-noon & 4-7pm), a Spanish shell of dramatic columns and Marabitti statuary designed by Andrea Palma, which thinly disguises the original Greek temple of Athena. The original 5th-century-BC Doric columns are visible both inside and out, and their weathered contours still support the cathedral roof. Even more extraordinary is an altar (ara) built by the Siculi three centuries earlier, the only surviving evidence of the island's first settlers.

The original Greek temple was renowned throughout the Mediterranean, in no small part thanks to Cicero, who visited Ortygia in the 1st century BC. The doors were adorned in gold and ivory, while the interior was lined with magnificent paintings of Agathocles fighting the Carthaginians. The roof was crowned by a golden statue of Athena that served as a beacon to sailors at sea; nowadays a statue of the Virgin Mary stands in the same spot.

North of the cathedral is the **Palazzo Municipale** or Palazzo Senatoriale, built in 1629 by the Spanish architect Juan Vermexio, nicknamed 'Il Lucertolone' or 'the lizard'. On the left corner of the cornice is the architect's signature: a small lizard carved into a stone. In recent years, excavations beneath the building have uncovered the unfinished remains of an Ionic temple, better known as the 'couch of Artemis', to whom Ortygia was dedicated. The mansion now serves as the city hall. To see the temple's remains, just ask at the gate. Attached to the cathedral's southern side is the elegant, 17th-century **Palazzo Arcivescovile** (Archbishop's Palace; ☎ 0931 6 79 68), which is home to the Biblioteca Alagoniana and some rare 13th-century manuscripts.

In the northwestern corner of the square is the **Palazzo Beneventano del Bosco**, which has a pretty 18th-century façade, while at its southern end is the **Chiesa di Santa Lucia alla Badia**, dedicated to St Lucy, the city's patron saint, who was martyred at Syracuse during the reign of the Roman emperor Diocletian.

FONTANA ARETUSA

Just south of Piazza del Duomo, along Via Picherali, is the Fontana Aretusa, where fresh water bubbles up as it did in ancient times when it was the city's main water supply. Legend has it that the goddess Artemis transformed her beautiful handmaiden Aretusa into the spring to protect her from the unwelcome attention of the river god Alpheus. In her watery guise Aretusa fled from Arcadia under the sea, hotly pursued by Alpheus, their waters mingling as she came to the surface in Ortygia. Now populated by ducks, grey mullets and papyrus plants, the fountain is *the* place to hang out on summer evenings.

MUSEO REGIONALE D'ARTE MEDIOEVALE E MODERNA

Housed in Ortygia's finest Catalan-Gothic mansion, the 13th-century Palazzo Bellomo, the **Museo Regionale d'Arte Medioevale e Moderna** (☎ 093 16 96 17; Via Capodieci 14; adult/concession €6/3; ☙ 9am-1.30pm Mon-Fri, 9am-12.30pm Sun) has a sizable collection of sculpture and painting dating from the Middle Ages up to the 20th century. Highlights include Byzantine icons and Spanish paintings and lots of bloodthirsty religious painting, of which *La Strage degli Innocenti* (The Murder of the Innocents) stands out for its ferocious energy.

Other exceptional pieces here are Antonello da Messina's *Annunciazione* (Annunciation; 1474) and Caravaggio's *La Sepoltura di Santa Lucia* (The Burial of St Lucy; 1609), which is presented in its own room. It is a huge work, half of which is a dark and brooding background, the composition a simple triangle of two gravediggers framing the lifeless body of St Lucy, the light catching her upturned chin. The brutish efforts of the gravediggers contrast starkly with the stillness of the spectators; the eye is naturally drawn to the central mourner whose red cloak provides the only splash of colour in an otherwise golden brown expanse. It is the highlight of the collection.

PIAZZA ARCHIMEDE & AROUND

Walking through the tangled maze of alleys that characterises Ortygia is an atmospheric experience. Right at the heart of the island is the handsome Piazza Archimede, with its 19th-century **fountain** (by Giulio Moschetti) of Artemis (the goddess of hunting) surrounded by handmaidens and sirens. The square is Syracuse's 'drawing room' and is surrounded by Catalan-Gothic palazzi, including **Palazzo Lanza** and the **Palazzo Platamone**, now home to the Banca d'Italia.

East of the piazza is Via Maestranza, the heart of the old guild quarter, behind which lies the labyrinth of the crumbling *Giudecca*, the old Jewish ghetto. During the renovations of Alla Giudecca hotel, an ancient Jewish **miqwe** (ritual bath; ☎ 0931 2 22 55; Alla Giudecca, Via GB Alagona 52; admission €5; ⏰ 10am-7pm) was discovered some 20m below ground level. The baths were once connected to the synagogue, but were blocked up by members of the Jewish community when they were expelled from the island in 1492. It is a fascinating sight – the three deep pools intended for total immersion constantly bubble with freshwater, which now has to be pumped out of the chamber to prevent flooding. There is a separate, private pool that was for the sole use of the rabbi.

Also in the Jewish quarter is Syracuse's own brand of **Piccolo Teatro dei Pupi** (☎ 0931 46 55 40; www.pupari.it in Italian; Via della Giudecca 17), managed by the charming Mauceri brothers (see p225).

OTHER SIGHTS

At the entrance to Ortygia lies the **Tempio di Apollo** (Temple of Apollo; Piazza Pancali), one of the first Greek structures built here. Little remains of the 6th-century BC Doric structure, apart from the bases of a few columns.

At the southern tip of the island is the 13th-century **Castello Maniace**, built by Frederick II as part of a massive programme of construction that turned Ortygia into an island fortress. Still used as a barracks, the castle is generally off-limits to the public, except during the Ortygia and Greek Classical Drama Festivals (see p222) when it is the atmospheric venue for musical and theatrical performances.

The Mainland

Although it's not nearly as picturesque as Ortygia, you should still devote time to exploring the sights on the mainland. The Acradina quarter, directly across the bridge from Ortygia, is the modern city, built on the site of the ancient settlement of the same name. To the northeast in the Tyche quarter are the city's extensive catacombs and the renowned Museo Archeologico Paolo Orsi. To see the real thing, go west to Neapolis and the archaeological park.

ACRADINA

Bombed twice during WWII (by the Allies in 1943 and then by the Luftwaffe in 1944), most of the Acradina quarter bears the unmistakable stamp of the postwar aesthetic: functional and not too pleasing on the eye. Near Piazzale Marconi the old **Syracusan Forum** (Foro Siracusano), once the site of the agora (marketplaces), is now bisected by a number of busy streets and overshadowed by some hideous architecture.

A few hundred metres west of the forum along Via Elorina, however, is a sight well worth visiting (though few ever seem to): the ruins of the **Ginnasio Romano** (Roman Gymnasium; admission free; ⏰ 9am-1pm Mon-Sat), built in the 1st century. Despite the name, this was actually a small theatre at the heart of a building that also contained a large atrium and another theatre directly behind the stage.

Along the water to the east of the forum (take Via dell'Arsenale) are the fenced-off remains of the ancient **arsenal**, once a set of rectangular pits into which ships would be pulled for re-provisioning. Adjacent are the ruins of the **Edificio Termale** (Thermal Building), a Byzantine bathhouse where it is claimed the Emperor Constans was assassinated with a soap dish in 668.

North of the arsenal is one of the city's biggest squares, **Piazza Santa Lucia**, whose northern end is dominated by the **Chiesa di Santa Lucia al Sepolcro**. The 17th-century church is built on the spot where the city's patron saint, Lucia, an aristocratic girl who devoted herself to saintliness after being blessed by St Agatha, was martyred in 304. Underneath the church is an impressive network of **catacombs** (not open to the public) that are the largest in Italy after those in Rome.

CATACOMBS OF TYCHE

According to Roman law, Christians were not allowed to bury their dead within the city limits (which during the Roman occupation did not extend beyond Ortygia). Forced to go elsewhere, Christians conducted their burials in the outlying district of Tyche and its underground aqueducts, unused since Greek times. New tunnels were carved out and the result was a labyrinthine network of burial chambers, most of which are inaccessible except the ones underneath the **Basilica di San Giovanni** (Via San Sebastiano; admission church/catacombs free/€4; 9am-12.30pm & 2.30-5pm Wed-Mon), directly opposite the main tourist office. The church itself is pretty, with its skeletal rose window open to the sun. In the 17th century it served as the city's cathedral and is dedicated to the city's first bishop, St Marcian, who was tied to one of its pillars and flogged to death in 254.

The **catacombs** here are, for the most part, dank and a little spooky. Thousands of little niches line the walls and tunnels lead off from the main chamber *(decumanus maximus)* into *rotonde*, round chambers used by the faithful for praying. All of the treasures that accompanied the dead on their spiritual journey fell victim to tomb robbers over the centuries bar one: a sarcophagus unearthed in 1872 and now on exhibition in the Museo Archeologico Paolo Orsi.

MUSEO ARCHEOLOGICO PAOLO ORSI

At the top of Viale Cadorna (which runs north from Piazza Euripede) is Sicily's most extensive archaeological museum, the **Museo Archeologico Paolo Orsi** (0931 46 40 22; Viale Cadorna; adult/concession €6/3; 9am-2pm Tue-Sat). Located in the grounds of the Villa Landolina, the museum (named after the archaeologist Paolo Orsi, who arrived in Syracuse in 1886 and devoted the next 45 years to uncovering its ancient treasures) contains a thoroughly well-organised and extensive collection. The museum is wheelchair accessible. At the centre of the building is a large atrium that serves as a reference point with information on the three sections of the museum.

The collection runs the gamut from prehistoric artefacts (such as the earthenware pots from Pantalica in Sector A), to early Greek settlements such as Megara Hyblaea, the most thoroughly excavated site on the island, to Syracuse itself and its satellite settlements at Eloro, Akrai, Kasmenai and Kamarina (showcased in Sector C). The star of the show is undoubtedly the sculpture, the development of which can seen between the archaic work from Megara Hyblaea (Sector B), most notably the statue of a mother suckling twins, and the immodest modesty of *Venere Uscendo dell'Acqua* (Venus Emerging from the Water),

also known as the *Landolina Venus* (named after Saverio Landolina, who found it in 1806). Other treats are the lovely terracotta votive offerings to Demeter that were excavated next to the Madonnina delle Lacrime (once a sanctuary to Demeter), and more famously the grimacing terracotta face of the Gorgon with Pegasus. There is also an interesting selection of material found in the major Doric colonies of Gela and Agrigento.

Visiting the museum will easily take a whole morning, while the afternoon can be pleasantly spent in the Parco Archeologico della Neapolis (opposite).

MUSEO DEL PAPIRO

The small **Museo del Papiro** (0931 6 16 16; Viale Teocrito 66; admission free; 9am-1.30pm Tue-Sun) has exhibits including papyrus documents and products. The plant grows in abundance around the River Ciane, near Syracuse, and was used to make paper in the 18th century. The museum also features some interesting papyrus canoes and a copy of the Rosetta Stone.

SANTUARIO DELLA MADONNA DELLE LACRIME

Supposedly modelled on the shape of a tear drop, Syracuse's newest landmark building (it opened in 1994 and reaches a height of 102m) is a rather ugly architectural conceit. The cavernous **Santuario della Madonna delle Lacrime** (Sanctuary of Our Lady of the Tears; Viale Teocrito; admission free; 8am-noon & 4-7pm) was commissioned to house a statue of the Virgin that allegedly wept for five days in 1953 and bestowed over 300 miraculous cures within a matter of months.

The **Museo delle Lacrimazione** (Museum of the Lacrymation; admission €1.55; 9am-12.30pm & 4-6pm), underneath the sanctuary, explains the events of the miracle and objects associated with it.

During the construction of the church, work revealed an extensive network of houses and streets from the Greek and Roman periods, as well as the remains of another sanctuary to the goddesses Demeter and Kore (5th–4th century BC). Near the sanctuary some 5000 terracotta votive statues were found, the best of which are now in the museum. You can view the excavations, in Piazza della Vittoria, from outside the fence.

PARCO ARCHEOLOGICO DELLA NEAPOLIS

About 500m west of the museum is the extensive **Parco Archeologico della Neapolis** (☎ 0931 6 62 06; admission €6; ☒ 9am-2hr before sunset), Syracuse's most visited site – not surprising given its mighty, rough-hewn quarries, spectacular theatre and impressive, tumbledown ruins. Once past the entrance lined by souvenir stalls and drink stands, you can lose yourself in the shady groves of the quarries and the ample space around the ruins. The tourist information desk is disguised in the entrance to **Chiesa San Nicolò dei Cordari**, itself hidden behind a restaurant/café. You can pick up information and buy the cumulative ticket here (€6 archaeological park and museum, €8 archaeological park, museum and the Museo Regionale). The park is wheelchair accessible.

To get there, take buses 1, 4-6, 8, 11, 12 or 15 from Piazza della Posta to Corso Gelone/ Viale Teracati. The walk from Ortygia will take about 30 minutes. If you have a car, you can park along Viale Augusto for €1 (no time limit).

Latomia del Paradiso (Garden of Paradise)

Enter the Latomia del Paradiso, a limestone quarry full of huge hollows and caves, planted with orange and olive trees, via the northern site. In Greek times the quarry was vaulted by a 'roof' of earth that collapsed in the 1693 earthquake, leaving it open to the sunlight. It was only after this that the gardens were planted. The Greeks ran the quarries along the lines of a concentration camp, putting prisoners to work cutting blocks of limestone out of the subterranean caves. The Athenians captured after the great sea battle of 413 BC were imprisoned here and held for seven years before being branded with the mark of the Siracusan horse and sold into slavery.

A renowned curiosity at the heart of the garden is the ear-shaped artificial grotto known as the **Orecchio di Dionisio** (Ear of Dionysius). According to Caravaggio, Dionysius must have had it built so he could listen in on the conversations of the prisoners, but it is most likely that the grotto – 23m high and 65m deep – was dug out as a rock quarry and later used as a sounding board for theatrical performances.

Next to it is the now-closed **Grotta dei Cordari** (Rope-makers' Cave), a grotto, supported by pillars, once used in the manufacture of rope;

in antiquity, humidity was an essential ingredient in rope manufacture and the cave had plenty of it. Linked to the Latomia del Paradiso by a tunnel is the **Latomia Intagliatella**, while a rocky path continues on to the **Latomia di Santa Venera**, another citrus-scented quarry. At the highest, most easterly point you will reach the **Necropoli dei Grotticelli**, a honeycomb of Hellenistic and Byzantine tombs, one of which is wrongly ascribed to Archimedes. These catacombs, like the catacombs of Tyche (see p219), were once part of the underground aqueducts designed by the Greeks.

Teatro Greco

For the classicist, the highlight of the Neapolis is the lustrous white Teatro Greco, hewn out of the rocky hillside. A masterpiece of classical architecture, the ancient theatre could seat 16,000 people and saw the work of Sophocles, Euripides and the last tragedies of Aeschylus, including *The Persians*, *Prometheus Bound* and *Prometheus Unbound*, which were first performed here in his presence. When the Romans took Syracuse in the 3rd century they made alterations to the theatre, mostly so that they could stage gladiatorial combats and *naumachiae* (mock naval battles) in the flooded arena. Some of the seats bear inscriptions to Syracuse's notables, namely Hieron II's family, and the gods. For the best views climb up to the tomb-riddled Via dei Sepolcri.

Every summer the theatre is brought to life again with a host of classical dramas, details of which you can obtain from the tourist office or the **Museum of Ancient Greek Theatre** (☎ 0931 48 33 78; Palazzo Greco, Corso Matteotti 29, Ortygia; ☒ 9am-6pm Wed-Mon). The museum showcases some of the wealth of material housed in the archives of the Instituto Nazionale Dramma Antico, including models, designs, playbills and costumes.

Anfiteatro Romano (Roman Amphitheatre)

In the southern zone of the Neapolis (same ticket), across the other side of the Viale Paradiso, is the 2nd-century-AD Roman amphitheatre, the third-largest in Italy after the Colosseum in Rome and the amphitheatre in Verona. It was used for gladiator fights and horse races. Roman punters used to park their chariots in the area between the amphitheatre and Viale Paolo Orsi. The Spaniards, little interested in archaeology, destroyed the site in

---

THE GREATEST SHOW ON EARTH?

Performances in Syracuse's theatre were pretty intense affairs, particularly during the six-day Feast of Dionysus, god of wine and merriment. Daily performances of a *tetracycle* (three tragedies and a satirical work thrown in for good measure) and no less than five comedies kept audiences glued to their seats from dawn till dusk. As the festival was essentially a hedonistic religious ceremony, the high point of the day's performance (usually during the third tragedy) saw the audience whipped into a frenzy of delirium described by Aristotle as 'catharsis', after which they were made to laugh for a few more hours and then sent home. After nearly 20 centuries without a festival, 1914 saw the start of a new series of productions.

Nowadays, the **Teatro Greco di Siracusa Festival** is held in May and June every year, with two Greek tragedies usually performed on alternate nights. Tickets start from €18 and go all the way up to €56 for seats on weekend evenings. You can splash out or get a standing ticket, but make sure you go and catch a show if you're in town during the festival. Find out what's on from the tourist office or the Museum of Ancient Greek Theatre (p221).

---

the 16th century, using it as a quarry to build the city walls at Ortygia. West of the amphitheatre is the 3rd-century-BC **Ara di Ierone II** (Altar of Hieron II). The monolithic sacrificial altar was a kind of giant abattoir where 450 oxen could be killed at one time.

ACTIVITIES

Syracuse is all about urban pleasures and there are few outdoor activities. However, what there is lives up to the high standards of everything else in this town. You can go swimming at one of the island's platform 'beaches' – a good **swimming spot** is a five-minute walk down Via S Privitera. It's local, free and there's decent swimming to be done.

If you want something more glam (though also a bit squashed) rent a pew on Syracuse's tiny **Lido Maniace** (www.lidomaniace.it in Italian; 2 people €10) – a rocky platform of sun beds and shades where you can dip into the water. Bigger, sandy beaches can be found at **Arenella** (bus 23), the best beach on the coast, with a blue-flag classification (which denotes it as an environmentally pristine beach; visit www .blueflag.org). A bit further south are the rock pools and inlets of **Ognina**, and further still the popular **Fontane Bianche** (bus 21 or 22 from Piazza della Posta).

TOURS

Like Palermo, Syracuse has a host of professional tour guides. They generally escort groups so prices are steep, ranging from €110 for half a day to €155 for a whole day (groups of up to 18 people). The tourist office has a list of guides and their numbers – you can negotiate directly for smaller groups.

Ente Fauna Siciliana (☎ 0931 71 73 35, 328 885 70 92; www.entefaunasiciliana.it in Italian; Viale Montedoro 79; per person mountain-bike trip to Cava Cardinale €10, trekking on Etna €6) Landlubbers should definitely undertake one of the excursions, including archaeological and botanical itineraries, run by this conservation group. The website should be your first port of call, as tours change and it supplies phone numbers for tour operators so you can make your bookings. Note: most tours are in Italian.

Sailing Team (☎ 0931 6 08 08, 335 785 03 44; www .sailingteam.biz; Via Savoia 14; 4-6 people €25) Departing at 10am and returning at 6pm, you can organise a sexier boat trip than the Selene to explore the coastline and snorkel to your heart's content. Sailing Team also charters boats and operates an exciting excursion to the Aeolians and Malta, a holiday in itself that runs into thousands of euros (check the website for prices).

Selene (1hr cruise per person €10; ⏱ 12.30pm & 1.30pm Apr-Oct) This takes passengers around Ortygia on a ride that offers splendid views of the city. Don't forget to bring along a picnic lunch. The cruise departs from the dock near the Grand Hotel.

Syrako Tourist Services (☎ 0931 2 41 33; www .syrako.it; Largo Porta Marina; per person Castello Eurialo & archaeological park €15, Pantalica & Noto or Buscemi & Palazzolo Acreide incl lunch €45; ⏱ 9am-1pm & 3-8pm Mon-Sat, tours Jul-Sep) Syrako can help you arrange guides and runs good tours, from classical to baroque itineraries, around the Neapolis and Ortygia.

FESTIVALS & EVENTS

Festival of Greek Classical Drama (☎ 0931 44 93 58; www.indafondazione.org; tickets €15-35) Today, Syracuse boasts the only school of Classical Greek drama outside Athens and the productions attract some of Italy's finest performers. Performances are held in May and June and are in Italian. Tickets are available online, from the tourist office or at the booth at the entrance to the Museum of

Ancient Greek Theatre (☎ 0931 48 33 78; Palazzo Greco, Corso Matteotti 29, Ortygia; open 9am to 6pm Wednesday to Monday).

Ortygia Festival (☎ 0931 48 36 48; www.ortigia festival.it in Italian; Castello Maniace) Set in the dramatic castle, this September festival showcases avant-garde and experimental theatre, musical events and exhibitions.

Festa di Santa Lucia This annual procession on 13 December commemorates the city's patron saint. During the festival the enormous silver statue of the saint wends its way from the cathedral to Piazza Santa Lucia accompanied by fireworks.

SLEEPING

Syracuse prides itself on discerning tourism and this is certainly reflected in its excellent hotels. Most of the best options are on Ortygia, which is the location of choice due to its seductive atmosphere and great selection of restaurants. All the no-frills, cheaper options cluster around the train station.

Budget

ourpick Viaggiatori, Viandanti e Sognatori (☎ 0931 2 47 81, 333 897 83 51; www.bedandbreakfastsicily.it; Via Roma 156, Ortygia; s €35-50, d €55-75; 🌂) An old palazzo at the end of Via Roma cradles Syracuse's loveliest B&B. Recently refurbished, this is a tasteful and stylish outfit with rooms decorated with shells, books and old postcards. The beds are super comfy, the bathrooms are gleaming and the two front-facing rooms have a joint balcony that looks onto Via Roma. The sunny roof terrace is perfect for breakfast and the friendly dog Nina will put a smile on anyone's face.

B&B Casa Mia (☎ 0931 46 33 49; www.bbcasamia .it; Corso Umberto 112; s €30-48, d €60-80; P 🖳) This home-away-from-home is a great choice on the mainland. Casa Mia is situated in an old mansion on Corso Umberto. Its rooms are furnished with family antiques and named after various family grandmas, and the family is adding 10 extra rooms to the existing 13. A good traditional breakfast is served on the internal patio.

Milano (☎ 0931 6 69 81; Corso Umberto 10; s/d €37/60; 🌂) A cheap option near the station and not too far from Ortygia. The rooms are plain but decent, with TV.

B&B L'Acanto (☎ /fax 0931 46 11 29; www.bebsicilia .it; Via Roma 15, Ortygia; s/d €50/75; 🌂 🖳) The family-run L'Acanto is a very popular, value-for-money *albergo* (hotel). It has delightful, traditionally decorated rooms with artistic prints on the walls and embroideries above the beds. It's set around a pretty internal courtyard.

Midrange

Alla Giudecca (☎ 0931 2 22 55; www.allagiudecca.it; Via Alagona 52, Ortygia; s €60-75, d €96-120; 🌂) A gorgeous set of houses in the old Jewish quarter contains these 23 wonderful apartments. Inside is a warren of vaulted rooms full of wonderful antiques and enormous tapestries, while cosy sofas cluster around huge fireplaces. During renovations an ancient Jewish *miqwe* was discovered (see p219).

ourpick Hotel Gutkowski (☎ 0931 46 58 61; www .guthotel.it; Lungomare Vittorini 26, Ortygia; s/d €80/110; 🌂 🖳) You could say this is Sicily's most stylish hotel and you'd not be exaggerating. Designed with utmost simplicity and minimalism, the rooms are in soft olives and teals, many overlooking the vast stretch of sea outside (others are courtyard-bound), and the look is a mix of the marine and rustic. The hotel offers excellent excursions (€40 per person) to natural beauty spots, as well as Italian lessons. Booking in advance is advised.

Azienda Agrituristica Limoneto (☎ 0931 71 73 52; www.emmeti.it/Limoneto; Via del Platano 3; d €80-120; P 🌂) This big country farm set amid attractive citrus and olive groves, is noted for its organic produce and excellent restaurant. It's a lovely alternative to the city and a great base for exploring the countryside; the employees will help you with trekking itineraries. You will find it 9km from Syracuse along the SS124.

Hotel Gran Bretagne (☎ 0931 6 87 65; Via Savoia 21, Ortygia; s €85-90, d €110-115; 🌂) This handsome, small hotel has friendly management and is situated in a great location at the beginning of Ortygia. The rooms are spacious and airy in blues and whites, some with fresco-covered ceilings. There's a nice and big communal area with massive oval sofas around a glassed-in underground medieval wall.

Domus Mariae (☎ 0931 2 48 54; www.sistemia .it/domusmariae; Via V Veneto 76, Ortygia; s €110-115, d €150-155; P 🌂) This former school for nuns has been transformed into an elegant, comfortable hotel. It has huge rooms with sea views and balconies, and the toffee-coloured bathrooms are sizable too. The street-view doubles are cheaper (€135 to €140). The nuns, who run the place, really know how to turn out an impeccable room.

Top End

Hotel Roma (☎ 0931 46 56 26; www.hotelroma.sr.it; Via Minerva 10, Ortygia; s €99-130, d €149-200; P ✗) Right in the centre of Ortygia just behind the cathedral is the beautifully restored Hotel Roma. Intimate, efficient and convenient, this is an excellent luxury option with helpful staff.

Grand Hotel (☎ 0931 46 46 00; www.grandhotelsr.it; Viale Mazzini 12, Ortygia; s/d €155/250; P ✗) Big and brash, the Grand Hotel is Ortygia's top-class hotel with all the requisite amenities and none of the character of some of the smaller hotels. It caters to a well-heeled, largely American clientele and has a spectacular rooftop restaurant that is great in the evenings. A shuttle bus transfers guests to the hotel's private beach.

EATING

Ortygia is the place for restaurants, and you'll find little reason to go and eat on the mainland part of town.

Restaurants

Solaria Vini & Liquori (☎ 0931 46 30 07; www.enotecasolaria.com; Via Roma 86, Ortygia; snacks from €5) The perfect place if you want to buy wine and taste it before you commit, or if you just want to have a bit of a snack and a good glass of wine. It's a small, rustic winery on the main street, with snacks of cheese, olives, prosciutto, anchovies, sardines and other Mediterranean delicacies, and the choice of wine is excellent and wide-ranging.

Sicilia in Tavola (Via Cavour 28, Ortygia; pasta €6-8; ☽ closed Sun) A tiny rustic restaurant that specialises in fresh pasta dishes (try the speciality of the house, seafood ravioli). It fills up quickly in the evenings so reservations are advised.

Il Gattopardo (Via Cavour 67a, Ortygia; meals €15-20, pizza €3.50-7) Tucked away in Via Cavour this hugely popular, unpretentious restaurant specialises in simple and delicious dishes and in the evening everyone comes here for a pizza. Great fun and full of weird African and South American souvenirs – someone did too much shopping on their travels.

our pick La Gazza Ladra (☎ 340 060 24 28; Via Cavour 8; meals €20; ☽ closed Mon & Jul & Aug) A favourite of students and young professionals, this place is as informal as they get, while still making such excellent food that it features in the Slow Food guide. Try the *pasta alla siracusana* (with anchovies, breadcrumbs and almonds), a local speciality, and tuck into the fresh fish of the day.

Trattoria Archimede (☎ 0931 6 97 01; Via Gemellaro 8, Ortygia; meals €25; ☽ closed Sun evening & 3 weeks in Jul) The most authentic restaurant in Ortygia, with B&W photographs of the island as it once was. Three formal dining rooms serve an array of seafood dishes and pasta. The menu changes often so you never get bored.

Trattoria Pescomare (☎ 0931 2 10 75; Via Landolina 6, Ortygia; meals €25) Near the cathedral, the Pescomare serves up a pleasing selection of local fish dishes and a wide range of pizza. Grab a spot in the vine-covered courtyard and feast on the *spaghetti alle cozze* (spaghetti with mussels).

Le Baronie (☎ 0931 6 88 84; www.ristorantelebaronie .com; Via Gargallo 26, Ortygia; meals €25; ☽ closed Mon) Offering a boisterous atmosphere in an old Catalan-Gothic mansion, Le Baronie prides itself on traditional cuisine with a twist, such as swordfish with a pepper-and-brandy sauce. There is also a pleasant garden dotted with sarcophagi.

La Medusa (☎ 0931 6 14 03; Via S Teresa 21-23; meals €25) A traditional restaurant run by a mother-and-daughter duo who take pride in the size and presentation of the dishes – the huge risotto is served in a big white shell (yes, shell) and the salads are brought out in dishes the shape of a boat. The sizable *primi* (first courses) are enough for two, so be aware of the danger of over-ordering. The fish and seafood are delicious and reasonably priced, and the wine is decanted into apothecarylike bottles. Good, no-nonsense service and great food.

Jonico-a Rutta 'e Ciauli (☎ 0931 6 55 40; Riviera Dioisio il Grande 194; meals €25-30, pizza €3.50-8; ☽ closed Tue) Very inconvenient but worth the trek or taxi ride, Jonico is right on the sea with a wonderful terrace and a hearty Syracusan menu including steak with tomato, eggplant and white-wine salsa. The roof garden serves pizza in the evening.

our pick Taberna Sveva (☎ 0931 2 46 63; Piazza Federico di Svevia 1-2; meals €30) A fantastic place to eat, with a big terrace in a peaceful square and excellent food. Try the *gnocchi al pistachio* or the *cassarecie* (short, curled pasta) with fresh tomatoes for *primi*, and follow it with a tuna steak covered in sesame seeds. The tiramisu is excellent, as is the local wine. The service is relaxed and friendly, and you'll get to enjoy your food whilst listening to tarantellas (traditional music written to accompany a dance named tarantella) belting out of the stereo – a very Sicilian experience.

Trattoria la Foglia (☎ 0931 6 62 33; www.lafoglia .it; Via Capodieci 21, Ortygia; meals €30) An eccentric owner/chef and her vegetarian husband have made this place into something of a cult Syracusan restaurant, but the tiny portions and relatively high prices make the eclectic interior take a back seat. The menu features whatever seafood and vegetables are fresh that day and the bread is home-baked. They also have a one- to two-bedroom flat to rent on Ortygia, its décor in the same eclectic style as the restaurant.

The **Antico Mercato** (old market; www.anticomercato .it in Italian; ☿ daily) is in the streets near the post office. The market is busy until about 1pm; there is also a market restaurant.

Cafés

Gran Caffè del Duomo (Piazza del Duomo 18, Ortygia; tourist menu €12) You'd normally avoid a place like this, thinking it screams 'location + expense', but a reasonable tourist menu and prime position in this beautiful square makes it a viable option.

our pick **Biblios Cafe** (Via del Consiglio Reginale 11, Ortygia; ☿ 10am-1.30pm & 5-9pm, closed Wed, Sun & Sep) This café is nestled in a bookshop that supports a range of cultural activities (readings, language courses and dance lessons). It has a cosy, relaxed atmosphere and internet access, and turns into a nice little bar in the evenings.

Caffè Minerva (Via Roma 58, Ortygia) A popular, people-watching café serving a good range of Sicilian cakes and pastries, the best cup of tea on the island and a nice, frothy cappuccino.

If you want a good café on the mainland, the **Pasticceria Tipica Catanese** (Corso Umberto 46) is a great option.

DRINKING

Syracuse is a big university town and as a result weekdays are buzzing (most of the students go home on weekends, so things are a little quieter then). The most popular drinking spot on Ortygia is Piazzetta San Rocca with its cluster of bars with outside tables.

San Rocca (Piazzetta San Rocca, Ortygia; cocktails €5) This is the smoothest of a bunch of bars that take up this whole piazza. Great spot for early-evening drinks before heading on to a restaurant – if you can fit anything else in after that many crisps and olives.

Café Giufá (☎ 0931 46 53 95; Via Cavour 25, Ortygia; ☿ closed Mon winter) A fun bar that spreads onto the tiny square at the back, the Giufá has some good DJs who like reggae, jungle and dub beats, and the crowd – including the bar staff – are jolly and friendly. Beer's the name of the game here.

Il Sale (Via dell'Amalfitania 56/2, Ortygia) Here you'll find a little disco-oriented place with crowds sitting outside on the small terrace under an olive tree. Drink beer or cocktails (€5) and enjoy the night sky above.

Peter Pan (☎ 0931 46 89 37; Via Castello Maniace 46/48, Ortygia; glass of wine €4-7; ☿ 10am-2.30pm & 7.30pm-2am) Brunch, beer, books, cocktails and live music make this tiny wine bar an excellent place to while away some time. It also serves a limited menu of cheese and charcuterie to soak up those huge glasses of wine.

ENTERTAINMENT

Apart from the healthy programme of Classical Greek and contemporary theatre, and live music that is staged in various venues throughout the city (see p222), Syracuse has its own very popular puppet theatre.

Piccolo Teatro dei Pupi (☎ 0931 46 55 40; www.pupari .it in Italian; Via della Giudecca 17; tickets €5; ☿ 9.30pm Tue, Thu & Sat, 5pm Sun) Managed by the Mauceri brothers, Syracuse's puppet theatre is thriving. Beware with very small children as the shows can be a bit violent: lots of noise and beheading of dragons. The workshop, where you can purchase puppets, is at No 19 and the company also has a small museum (which was moving location at the time of research, so check the website for updates).

SHOPPING

Shopping in Syracuse is as pleasant as everything else; the alleys of Ortygia are full of sweet little boutiques selling quality products that will not look out of place once you get them home.

Izzo Oro (☎ 0931 2 23 01; Via Roma 30/32, Ortygia) You will find handmade jewellery here; Carlo and Massimo work with Sciacca coral and gold. Some of the pieces are very ostentatious but some are lovely, modelled on Greek coins and theatre masks.

Two contemporary ceramic shops are **Circo Fortuna** (☎ 0931 6 26 81; Via Capodieci 42, Ortygia) and **Lecomarí** (Via Salvatore Chindemi 21, Ortygia).

GETTING THERE & AWAY

Boat

There are a number of services from Malta to Pozzallo (see p235). For information in Syracuse, check with the Boccadifuoco travel agency (see p217).

Bus

Unless you're coming from Catania or Messina, more often than not you'll find buses faster and more convenient than trains. **Interbus** (☎ 0931 6 67 10; Via Trieste 28) buses leave from the main bus station, located on Corso Gelone. They connect with Catania (€4.50, 1¼ hours, half-hourly Monday to Saturday, eight Sunday) and its airport, and Palermo (€14, four hours, four daily Monday to Saturday, three Sunday).

AST (☎ 0931 46 27 11; bus station at Corso Gelone) runs a local network to Piazza Armerina (€8, four hours, one daily), Noto (€3, one hour, 12 daily Monday to Saturday) and Ragusa (€6, two hours, nine daily Monday to Saturday). Buses leave from the bus stop on Corso Gelone. AST also run buses to Palermo (€12, four hours, six daily Monday to Saturday, three Sunday).

Car & Motorcycle

By car, if arriving from the north, you will enter Syracuse on Viale Scala Greca. To reach the centre of the city, turn left at Viale Teracati and follow it around to the south; it eventually becomes Corso Gelone. The road between Catania and Syracuse is the SS114 and between Syracuse and Noto it's the SS115. A motorway is supposed to connect the SS114 and SS115, but it starts and ends virtually in the middle of nowhere some kilometres out of Syracuse.

There is a very large underground car park on Via V Veneto (free) on Ortygia and another at the marina (€1). Please note that as at the time of writing you can enter Ortygia to drop off and pick up your luggage, but you must leave your car at the designated parking area, since the island allows resident parking only.

Train

More than a dozen trains depart daily for Messina (1st/2nd class €17/12, 2½ to three hours) and Catania (€5 to €7.50, 1¼ hours). Some go on to Rome, Turin, Milan and other long-distance destinations. For Palermo (€17.20, six to 10 hours) you will have to change at either Catania or Messina.

There are several slow trains from Syracuse to Noto (€2.65, 30 minutes) and Ragusa (€5.85, 2¼ hours).

GETTING AROUND

If you arrive by bus, you'll be dropped at the bus station at Corso Gelone. Electric (free) buses go around Ortygia from Piazza della Posta. To get to the archaeological park, get bus 1 from the main bus stop. Bus 11 goes to Castello Eurialo (below). City buses cost €0.85 for two hours, irrespective of the number of buses you take.

You can hire a bicycle or scooter at **Allakatalla** (☎ 0931 6 74 52; Via Roma 10; bicycle/scooter per day €10/30) travel agency. It does get very busy so try and book in advance.

AROUND SYRACUSE

Castello Euralio

Seven kilometres west of the city in the outlying quarter of Epipolae is the **Castello Euralio** (☎ 0931 71 17 73; admission free; ☉ 9am-1hr before sunset), the stronghold of Syracuse's Greek defensive works. Built during the reign of Hieron II, Castello Euralio (Euryalus Castle) was adapted and fortified by Archimedes and was considered impregnable. Unfortunately for Syracuse, the castle was taken by the Romans without a fight. The views back to Syracuse make it worth the trip. To get here take bus 11 from the main bus station on Corso Gelone or the archaelogical park.

Megara Hyblaea

The area north of Syracuse is a largely unattractive sprawl of refineries and heavy industry, but right in the middle of it are the ruins of the ancient settlement of Megara Hyblaea, founded in 728 BC by Greeks from Megara. Its history is largely unfortunate: razed to the ground and all its inhabitants evicted in 483 BC by the tyrant Gelon, it was rebuilt on the same spot by Timoleon in 340 BC but only survived until 213 BC when it was destroyed for the second time by the Roman general Marcellus. A small population continued to live there until the 6th century, but it has been abandoned ever since. You'll need your own car to get there – it's 25 minutes (20km) north of Syracuse on the SS114.

DETOUR: THE RIVER CIANE & THE OLYMPEION

A popular diversion between May and September is a boat trip up the Fiume Ciane, a mythical river dedicated to the nymph Ciane, who tried to thwart the abduction of Persephone by Hades – the spring, 2km upriver, is said to have been formed by her tears. The river habitat, a tangle of lush papyrus, is unique and endangered – the only place outside North Africa where papyrus grows wild. The plant was originally a gift to Hieron II by the Egyptian Pharoah, Ptolemy. Along the way, you can check out the ruins of the Olympeion, a temple from the 6th century BC.

The embarkation point for the boats is 5km outside Syracuse on the SS115. Turn left just after you cross the bridge over the River Ciane. With **boat rentals** (☎ 0931 6 90 76, 368 729 60 40; per boat up to 8 people from €40), the bigger the group the better. In summer it is constantly busy so this shouldn't be a problem for individuals. To get there, take bus 21, 22 or 23 from the main bus station on Corso Gelone.

THE SOUTHEAST

The mountainous interior of the southeast, dominated by Monti Iblei, lacks the popular appeal of the coastline and has, therefore, preserved its rural atmosphere. The landscape here is gently rugged, characterised by weathered limestone cliffs and cut through by deep gorges and valleys, one of which contains the mysterious Pantalica necropolis, the largest pre-Greek necropolis on the island. Although the region is difficult to explore without your own transport, it is worth the effort. Amid the dry-stone walls is a catalogue of Unesco World Heritage sites: Sicilian baroque towns, each with its own eccentricities, from noble Noto to chocolate-eating Modica and groovy Palazzolo Acreide.

VALLE DELL'ANAPO

For some beautifully wild and unspoilt countryside take the SS124 (via Floridia) northwest from Syracuse and turn off onto the byroad for Ferla. After about 36km this will bring you into the **Valle dell'Anapo** (Anapo Valley; signposted), a deep limestone gorge protected by the **Forestry Commission** (☎ 0931 46 24 52; near Cassaro; ☉ 7am-1hr before sunset). Should you want to explore the area you must leave your car at the car park near the Forestry hut and take one of the walking maps provided (paths marked A are unchallenging; paths marked B are harder). In spring, the valley is awash with flowers between the rock faces, and picnic tables dot your route.

Necropoli di Pantalica

A further 10km from the Valle dell'Anapo, on a huge plateau above the valley, is the site of Sicily's most important Iron and Bronze Age necropolis, the **Necropoli di Pantalica** (admission free; ☉ 9am-sunset), with more than 5000 tombs of various shapes and sizes honeycombed along the limestone cliffs. The site is terribly ancient, dating between the 13th and 8th century BC, and its origins are largely mysterious although it is thought to be the Siculi capital of Hybla, who gave the Greeks Megara Hyblaea in 664 BC. Very little survives of the town itself other than the **Anaktron** or prince's palace.

GETTING THERE & AWAY

The site is a difficult place to reach unless you have your own transport. If you don't, your best bet is to ask at the tourist office in Syracuse or at a travel agent to see if any tours of the area are available. These deals can come and go – see p222 for details of tour operators.

PALAZZOLO ACREIDE

pop 9000 / elev 670m

Almost completely off the beaten track, Palazzolo Acreide is a charmingly down-to-earth town full of surprising baroque architecture. The original medieval town was abandoned after the 1693 earthquake and a new Palazzolo was built in the shadow of Akrai (see p228).

The handsome town is centred on Piazza del Popolo, itself dominated by the massive bulk of the 18th-century **Chiesa di San Sebastiano** and the **Palazzo Municipale**, which is home to the **tourist office** (☎ 0931 88 20 00; www.palazzolo-acreide.it; ☉ 9.30am-1pm & 3.30-6.30pm Mon-Sat). To get to Piazza del Popolo from Piazza Pretura (where buses depart and arrive), walk up Via San Sebastiano. North of the square, at the end of a tight lane, is Piazza Moro and two other exquisite baroque churches: on the northern side of the square is the **Chiesa Madre** and on the southern side the **Chiesa di San Paolo**. At the top of Via Annunziata (the main road leading right out of Piazza Moro) is the fourth of the town's baroque treasures, the **Chiesa dell'Annunziata**, with a richly adorned portal of twirling columns.

Off Piazza del Popolo is the **Casa-Museo di Antonino Uccello** (☎ 0931 88 14 99; www.antoninouccello.it; Via Machiavelli 19; admission free; 🕒 9am-1pm), formerly the home of the poet and scholar (1922–79) and since 1984 a museum. Uccello devoted himself to preserving what he feared was disappearing from Sicilian life, so this is the place to go if you want to see what 18th-century farmers would have worn or how they ground olives to make oil. The museum houses a traditional stable, bedroom and living quarters. Only 10 people are allowed in at a time, and a custodian will escort you. Ring the doorbell to gain admission.

Akrai

The **archaeological park** (☎ 0931 88 14 99; admission €2; 🕒 9am-7pm) is a 20-minute walk southwest of the modern town along Corso Vittorio Emanuele. It covers the site of ancient Akrai, Syracuse's first inland colony established to defend the overland trading route to other Greek settlements such as Akragas.

The most impressive ruin is the **Greek theatre**, built at the end of the 3rd century BC and later altered by the Romans, who needed it for sittings of the local senate. This perfect semicircle once had an audience capacity of 600. Behind the theatre are two *latomie* (quarries). The quarries were later converted into Christian burial chambers – a fascinating sight, especially when you think about how many bodies were in there. The larger of the two catacombs, the **Intagliata**, has catacombs and altars cut into its sides, while the narrower one, the **Intagliatella**, has a wonderful relief of a large banquet cut into the rock face; it is thought to date from the 1st century BC. Other remains are the hardly recognisable **Tempio di Afrodite** (Temple of Aphrodite), south of the Intagliata, and the **Tempio di Persefone** (Temple of Persephone), off to the west of the theatre.

South of the archaeological zone are the stone sculptures known as the **Santoni** (Holy Men). The 12 statues are set in rock and devoted to the goddess Cybele, herself depicted on a seat. The largest figurative complex devoted to this particular goddess was created sometime during the 3rd century BC. It's a five-minute walk down to the statues, but you'll need to wait for a group to go with the guide, who'll want to drive down – see if you can cadge a lift. The area around the statues is closed to the general public.

Sleeping & Eating

Senatore (☎ 0931 88 34 43; fax 0931 88 34 44; Largo Senatore Italia; s/d €39/60; **P** ❄) One of Palazzolo's few hotels, the Senatore is fairly modern and has comfortable, if uninspiring, rooms with TV.

Hotel Santoro (☎ 0931 88 38 55; fax 0931 88 36 92; www.hotelsantoro.com in Italian; Via San Sebastiano 21; s €35-45, d €55-65; ❄) Not exactly luxurious, but a hop, skip and a jump from Piazza del Popolo. The rooms have a TV, a fridge and heating.

Alfredo (☎ 0931 88 32 66; Via Duca d'Ao-sta 27; tourist menu €15) A good choice just off Piazza del Popolo where the focus is on Sicilian meat dishes. The *salsiccia e costata di maiale* (sausages and roast pork chop) will fill you up.

Il Portico (☎ 0931 88 15 32; Via Orologio 6; meals €25, set menu €35; 🕒 closed Tue & Nov) This formal little restaurant has swagged rose curtains, high-backed chairs and florid painted ceilings. The menu focuses on Iblean mountain dishes with lots of roasted and grilled meats and mushrooms.

Getting There & Away

Unless you have your own transport, the only way to get here is by AST bus from Syracuse's main bus station (€3.25, one hour, 14 daily Monday to Saturday). You can buy tickets onboard.

NOTO

pop 23,100 / elev 160m

Flattened by the 1693 earthquake, Noto was rebuilt by its noble families in the grand baroque style and is now the finest and most coherent baroque town in Sicily – its exuberant style tamed by the rational grid work and an innate sense of symmetry. It's been almost completely renovated since 2002, and the gleaming baroque architecture is dazzling. You'll see Noto in its 1960s guise in Michelangelo Antonioni's film *L'Avventura* (1960), where the postcoital Monica Vitti wanders through the main square, glared at by Noto's entire male population.

Orientation

Intercity buses drop you at the Giardini Pubblici (public gardens), a nice shady park that meets Porta Reale at the beginning of Corso Vittorio Emanuele, the town's main street.

Information

EMERGENCY

Ambulance (☎ 0931 89 02 35)
Police (☎ 0931 83 52 02; Via Maiore) On the eastern extension of Via Aurispa.

INTERNET ACCESS

Salvo Cataneo Photography Lab (☎ 0931 83 52 51; Via Cavour 100; per hr €6; 🕑 9am-1pm & 4-7pm Mon-Sat) Two laptops with a fast connection at a photographer's studio.

MEDICAL SERVICES

Hospital (☎ 0931 57 12 25; Via dei Mille) On the way out of town towards Noto Antica.

MONEY

There are banks with ATMs on Corso Vittorio Emanuele, near Porta Reale.

POST

Post Office (Via Zanardelli 2; 🕑 8.30am-5pm Mon-Fri, 8.30am-1.30pm Sat)

TOURIST INFORMATION

Tourist Office (☎ 0931 57 37 79; www.comune.noto .sr.it; Piazza XVI Maggio; 🕑 8am-2pm & 3.30-6.15pm Mon-Sat) An excellent and busy office with multilingual staff, a free map and loads of information on the province.

TRAVEL AGENCIES

Allakatalla (☎ 0931 83 50 05; Corso Vittorio Emanuele 47; bicycle/scooter per day €10/30) Wears various hats including that of tour guide.

Sights

Most of the important monuments line Corso Vittorio Emanuele. A structural report commissioned in 1986 revealed the precarious state of Noto's buildings – the result of decades of neglect and plenty of minor earth tremors – many of which were on the brink of collapse. In fact, in 1996 the dome of the cathedral did collapse, although thankfully no one was inside at the time. Apparently local authorities knew that it was cracked but did nothing to repair it. The incident did, however, galvanise the authorities into action, resulting in many of Noto's most important buildings being carefully restructured. The town is now looking as good as new.

Pride of place is naturally given to the recently renovated **San Nicoló Cathedral**, which stands centre stage in Noto's most graceful square, the Piazza Municipio. Following its dome's collapse and subsequent restructuring, the cathedral was scrubbed of centuries of dust and dirt and is now once again gleaming in its peachy glow. The June 2007 reopening was a major event in town, with the inhabitants keen to see the cathedral looking brand-new. A fabulous place from which to see the cathedral

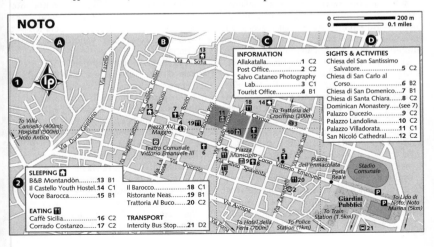

NOTO'S NATIVITY

Although a town called Noto or Netum has existed here for many centuries, the 'modern' town dates back to the devastating earthquake of 1693. One week after the event, architect Giuseppe Lanza, duke of Camastra, was given the biggest commission of his life: build a town from scratch. He set about his task with a stubborn single-mindedness and a blatant disregard for the wishes of the now homeless townspeople, who were horrified when they heard that the new town was to be 15km away.

In rebuilding Noto, Lanza's true genius lay in his choice of collaborators. With the help of the Flemish military engineer Carlos de Grunemberg, master craftsman Rosario Gagliardi and the architects Vincenzo Sinatra and Paolo Laisi, the new Noto put into practice a revolutionary idea based on the creation of two quarters, one for political and religious administration, the other a residential area. Both quarters were built with a careful emphasis on symmetry and visual harmony; indeed, the warm gold and rose hues of the local stone soften the heavily embellished palazzi and churches, giving the town a permanent sunset-light hue.

Despite the townspeople's initial reservations, the final results must have made them fall in love with their new town: what they saw was an almost perfect urban plan of crisscrossing parallel streets, tricks and treats of perspective and grand set-piece piazze, and indeed, the finest baroque town around.

is **Chiesa di Santa Chiara** (Corso Vittorio Emanuele; admission to roof adult/concession €1.50/1; 10am-7pm) on the opposite side of the street. You get excellent views of the cathedral and the whole of Noto from the top of the church.

The cathedral is surrounded on all sides by elegant town houses such as **Palazzo Ducezio** (Town Hall; 0931 83 52 01; admission free; 8.30am-2pm & 3-7pm Mon-Fri) and **Palazzo Landolina**, once home to Noto's oldest noble family. The only palazzo to be restored to its former glory is the **Palazzo Villadorata** (Palazzo Nicolaci; 0931 83 50 05; Via Corrado Nicolaci; adult/concession €3/1.50; 10am-1pm & 3-7pm Tue-Sun), whose wrought-iron balconies are supported by a swirling pantomime of grotesque figures – mythical monsters, griffins, cherubs and sirens. Inside, richly brocaded walls and frescoed ceilings give an idea of the sumptuous lifestyle of Sicilian nobles.

Two other piazze break up the long *corso*: to the east, Piazza dell'Immacolata and, more notably, to the west, Piazza XVI Maggio, overlooked by the beautiful **Chiesa di San Domenico** and the **Dominican monastery**, both designed by Rosario Gagliardi. On the way to Piazza XVI Maggio, climb the campanile of **Chiesa di San Carlo al Corso** (bell tower; admission €1.55; 9am-12.30pm & 4-7pm) for some excellent views over Noto.

In the opposite, easterly direction, towards the grand Porta Reale is the **Chiesa del Santissimo Salvatore** with its adjoining nunnery, which was reserved for the daughters of local nobility. The interior is the most impressive in

Noto, but it is unfortunately closed to the public. The fountain suspended on a wall next to it remained after Noto's streets were lowered in 1840 to facilitate the movement of carriages.

Festivals & Events

Infiorata Noto's colourful flower festival, held on the third Sunday in May, is when artists line the length of Via Corrada Nicolaci with works of art made entirely of flower petals.
La Notte di Giufà Music and storytelling from dusk until dawn with musical acts from around the world. Held at the end of July.

Sleeping

There is very limited hotel accommodation in Noto, but there's a plethora of good B&Bs. Ask at the tourist office for a detailed list, otherwise check out www.notobarocca.com (in Italian).

Il Castello Youth Hostel (/fax 0931 57 15 34; ostellodinoto@tin.it; Via Fratelli Bandiera 2; dm €15) Right in the centre of things in a beautiful old building, this place is the pride of Noto and great value for money. There are 68 beds and an open-all-day policy.

our pick B&B Montandòn (0931 83 57 93; www .b-bmontandon.it; Via A Sofia 50; s €25-40, d €50-75;) A beautiful B&B in a crumbling old palazzo – real old Noto. You enter via imposing vaulted hallways and the bedrooms are lovely and light with elegant furnishings. Upper rooms have panoramic views over the town.

Voce Barocca (0931 57 33 29; www.vocebarocca.com in Italian; Via Bruno 15; s €25-40, d €50-80;) A small, two-room B&B in an old palazzo right off the main street, Voce Barocca has a traditional, mismatching décor, a nice little roof terrace and good breakfasts that keep the punters happy. Book in advance.

Villa Canisello (☎ 0931 83 57 93; www.villacanisello.it; Via Pavese 1; d €70-90; P ✗) This quiet farmhouse is at the western end of Corso Vittorio Emanuele, past Piazza N Bixio, about 15 minutes' walk from the centre. It has a nice garden, but quite stuffy rooms that don't justify the price. The breakfast is decent and the food home-grown.

Hotel della Ferla (☎ 0931 57 60 07; www.hotelferla.it; Via A Gramsci; s €48-78, d €84-120; P ✗) This small hotel with 15 rooms is modern, efficient and within easy walking distance of the historic centre. It also has invaluable parking facilities and very helpful management to help with itineraries and recommendations around town.

Eating

The people of Noto are serious about their food: take time to enjoy a meal and follow it up with a visit to one of the town's excellent pastry shops, where the *gelati* and *dolci* (sweets) are divine.

Trattoria Al Buco (☎ 0931 83 81 42; Via Zanardelli 1; mains €20; ✗ closed Mon) This bustling and popular place is a good cheap option in Noto, and the locals like it as well. There are several vegetarian options and the fish is fresh and delicious.

our pick Trattoria del Crocifisso (☎ 0931 57 11 51; Via Umberto 46-48; meals €25) The best restaurant in Noto (and for miles around), this Slow Food–selected trattoria serves such good food that you'll immediately forgive the slightly stroppy service. Try the linguine with *vongole* (clams) and tuna steak in an orange, cinnamon and sesame sauce or tuna in a pistachio and sesame sauce – both are equally exquisite. A dessert must is the pistachio *semifreddo* (ice-cream cake), creamy and encrusted by gem-green pistachio pieces.

Il Barocco (☎ 0931 83 59 99; Via Cavour 8; meals €25) Another brilliant place to eat in Noto, tucked into a converted stable block of the Palazzo Astuto-Barresi. The eccentric character of the owner and chef is everywhere – from the graffitied walls (signatures from appreciative clientele) to the spaghetti with limpets.

Ristorante Neas (☎ 0931 57 35 38; Via Rocco Pirri 30; meals €25-30; ✗ closed Mon) You'll find a high standard of both food and service at this place, which opens up its terrace in summer. Try the *linguine allo scoglio* (with mixed seafood), or the legendary fish soup.

Getting There & Away

Noto is easily accessible by AST and Interbus buses from Catania (€5.75, 2¼ hours, 12 daily Monday to Saturday, seven Sunday) and Syracuse (€2.75, one hour, 12 daily Monday to Saturday). From June to August only, buses run frequently between Noto and Noto Marina (in the winter there is a school bus service). Trains from Syracuse are frequent (€2.65, 30 minutes, 11 daily), but the station is located 1.5km south of the bus-station area, so it's not as good an option for coming or going.

I SCREAM, YOU SCREAM, WE ALL SCREAM FOR ICE CREAM

People have said that Noto has the two best *gelaterie* (ice-cream shops) in the world. And, having tried them both, we can't argue with this statement. It's now up to you to decide if you agree. The famous **Corrado Costanzo** (☎ 0931 83 52 43; Via Silvio Spaventa 9) has the best ice cream, and you should indulge in at least a lick of the pistachio, a bite of the chocolate, or a chomp of the *amaro* (a dark liqueur) flavour. Around the corner, **Caffè Sicilia** (☎ 0931 83 50 13; Corso Vittorio Emanuele 125), which has been operating since 1892, excels in the art of the *granita* (a drink made of crushed ice with fruit juice). Depending on the season, try the *fragolini* (tiny wild strawberries) or *gelsi* (mulberry) flavours, or go for the classic *caffè* (coffee) or *mandorla* (almond). If you're not worried about calories, throw in a brioche and a bit of fresh cream on top, and you'll have a real Sicilian experience.

Both places make superb real *cassata* (made with ricotta cheese, chocolate and candied fruit), *dolci di mandorle* (almond cakes and sweets) and *torrone* (nougat), which are perfect for sharing (or not) with your friends back home.

AROUND NOTO

Noto Marina

If you fancy a swim, there's the pleasant **Lido di Noto** at Noto Marina, 15 minutes (5km) from Noto by car or bus – there are four buses per day to Noto Marina from July to September (one way/return €1.50/3), but ask at the tourist office for bus service out of the summer season.

An attractive hotel in Noto Marina is the **Villa Mediterranea** (☎ 0931 81 23 30; www.villa mediterranea.it; Viale Lido; s €75-125, d €90-150; P ✕ ⊠), located right on the seafront.

Eloro

On the coast 9km southeast of Noto are the ruins of the ancient Syracusan colony of Helorus, or **Eloro** (admission free; ☿ 8am-2pm). The town, founded in the 7th century BC, is still in the early stages of being excavated, but so far a portion of the city walls, a small temple dedicated to Demeter (Ceres in Roman mythology) and a theatre have been uncovered. When the site is closed you can still get a look at the place through the fence. You'll need your own transport to get there, or you may fancy walking from Noto Marina. The walk is about 4km long and there are lovely views of the coastline along the way.

On either side of the hill where the sparse ruins lie are long, sandy beaches comparatively free of the usual crowds. Unfortunately, a storm-water drain spills into the sea at the beach to the south.

Riserva Naturale Oasi Faunistica di Vendicari

Less than 1km south of Eloro is the northern boundary of the **Riserva Naturale Oasi Faunistica di Vendicari** (☎ 0931 57 14 57; admission free; ☿ 9am-6pm Apr-Oct, 9am-5pm Nov-Mar), a wonderful stretch of wild coastline protected from voracious developers. The reserve is made up of three separate marshes and a splendid crescent-shaped, sandy beach. You'll have to walk about half an hour to get to the beach, but once you get there, you'll feel like you're in heaven.

Crisscrossed by medieval water channels constructed when the saltpans were in use, the reserve is replete with old fortifications, an abandoned tuna plant and a rugged Swabian tower. More importantly, the reserve protects all manner of water birds, including the black-winged stilt, slender-billed gull and Audoin's gull; bird-watchers are well catered for by special observatories. Marked tracks meander through the marshes.

It is possible to reach the park by taking the SAIS bus connecting Noto and Pachino, or on the Interbus bus from Largo Pantheon, the street behind the public gardens in Noto.

Avola

With a reputation for producing excellent almonds (nicknamed *pizzuta*), Avola is a pleasant day trip from Syracuse or Noto. Town-planning buffs will appreciate the hexagonal shape of the town's design, created when the town had to be rebuilt after the earthquake. The open and harmonious nature of its architecture and public places is pleasing – look for **Chiesa Madre San Nicolo** in Piazza Umberto I.

To get there, take an AST bus from Syracuse (€2.10, 12 daily Monday to Saturday, four Sunday) or Noto (12 daily Monday to Saturday, four Sunday). In Noto, buses arrive at and depart from Piazza Vittorio Veneto, about five minutes' walk from Piazza Umberto, down Corso Vittorio Emanuele.

Trains connect Avola with Syracuse and Noto, although the train station is not quite as handy as the bus station.

The Cape Area

Sicily's southeastern cape doesn't offer much in the way of excitement, but the various African, Maltese and Arabic accents that pervade the area make it a sensual place to visit. **Pachino** is a wine-growing area surrounded by sandy beaches, while **Marzamemi**, 5km away, is a rather lovely fishing town with an old tuna fishery and tuna-based gift/craft shops. **Portopalo di Capo Passero** is popular in summer and has a nightly fish market from sunset at the port. The small island off the coast is Isola Capo Passero, with a castle and nature reserve. **Isola delle Correnti**, at the bottom of the cape area, really *is* the end of the line, and has a charming bay, thankfully free of pollution.

Interbus has buses to Pachino from Syracuse and Noto (11 daily Monday to Saturday).

If you're coming by car, take the SS115 to Noto, then follow the signs south to Pachino. Marzamemi is northeast of Pachino, while Portopalo di Capo Passero is southeast.

MODICA

pop 52,900 / elev 296m

Modica is blooming into a wonderful base for any discerning traveller: it's a beautiful town with sun-bleached, pastel-coloured houses that tumble down from Modica Alta (High Modica) to Modica Bassa (Low Modica). There are fantastic places to eat, the baroque architecture is breathtaking, the chocolate produced here is known throughout Italy, and to top it all off, there are some great beaches nearby. It's a town that really allows you to see and live life as it's lived by the locals, and many an unsuspecting visitor has fallen in love with Modica's wily charms.

Once a powerhouse in the region and the personal fiefdom of the Chiaramonte family, Modica lost its pre-eminent place to Ragusa. Despite this, Modica's inhabitants feel proud of their town's illustrious history, and will no doubt mention – in a fit of local patriotism – that Modica is better than Ragusa.

Orientation

Modica is divided into two parts: Modica Alta tumbles into a deep valley where once a raging river flowed right through the town, and becomes Modica Bassa. Following a devastating flood in 1902, the river was transformed into Corso Umberto I and Via Giarrantana, the main axes of the town. The huge hill will test your legs, especially if you intend to walk around the entire town in a day (not advisable).

The train station is located just over 500m west of Corso Umberto I, past Via Vittorio Veneto. It's better to get the bus, as you'll be dropped off near the intersection of Corso Umberto I and Via Garibaldi. The bus trip is also better in terms of scenery.

Information

Police (☎ 113; Piazza Matteoti)
Post Office (Corso Umberto I) Just near Chiesa di San Domenico.
Tourist Office (☎ 0932 76 26 26; Via Grimaldi 32; ☼ 8.30am-1.30pm & 3-7pm Mon-Sat, 8.30am-1.30pm Sun) Can supply the odd map or list, but no English is spoken.

Sights

The highlight of a trip to Modica is the **Chiesa di San Giorgio** (Modica Alta; admission free; ☼ 9am-noon & 4-7pm), easily one of the most extraordinary baroque churches in the province. Gagliardi's

(of Noto and Ragusa fame) masterpiece, it is a vision of pure rococo splendour perched at the top of a majestic 250-step staircase. Erected in the early 18th century, the church has a daringly tall façade, while the interior is full of polychromatic marbles. Viewed from below, the swirling confection looks as if it might float away. Its counterpart in Modica Bassa is the **Cattedrale di San Pietro** (Corso Umberto I; admission free), another impressive church atop a rippling staircase lined with life-sized statues of the apostles.

Walking down Corso Umberto I, with its many fine mansions and churches, is a very pleasant experience. Heading south you will pass the **Chiesa Santa Maria del Carmine** (Piazza Matteoti), the **Chiesa di San Giovanni Evangelista** (off Piazza San Giovanni), ending at **Chiesa Santa Maria delle Grazie**, whose convent (Palazzo dei Mercedari) has since been converted into the **Museo Civico** (Via Mercè; admission free; ☼ 9am-1pm Mon-Sat), with a well-ordered display of finds from Modica and Cava d'Ispica. Upstairs is the separate and private **Hyblean Museum of Arts & Crafts & Popular Traditions** (☎ 0932 75 77 47), which is only open on request. It is worth phoning up to arrange entrance as it houses a wonderful ethnographical collection set out in workshop context. Especially good is the laboratory for making chocolate, which will set you up nicely for a chocolate feast at Antica Dolceria Bonajuto (p234).

Another noteworthy church is **Chiesa di Santa Maria di Betlem** (Via Marchesa Tedeschi), where a marker points out the highest point of the 1902 flood.

Courses

Arts and crafts courses in mosaics (per person one week €750) and painting (per person one week €650) were set up by a worthy local initiative aiming to integrate tourism with local development. The courses are run through the **Albergo i Tetti di Siciliando** (☎ 0932 94 28 43; www.siciliando.it; Via Cannata 24, Modica Bassa), which also provides accommodation (see below).

Sleeping

our pick **Albergo i Tetti di Siciliando** (☎ 0932 94 28 43; www.siciliando.it; Via Cannata 24, Modica Bassa; s €24-34, d €42-60; ☒) Hidden away in a small street off Corso Umberto, this *albergo* must be the most welcoming, intimate place in town (and possibly in Sicily), thanks to its owners, Valeria and Rosa. They'll not only tell you everything there is to know about Modica (in excellent English), but you'll get a good breakfast, your own key, and you can attend one of the courses they organise here. The rooms are simple and sizable, many with dreamy views of Modica's tightly packed houses that seemingly teeter on top of each other. You can rent mountain bikes for €10 per day (or €50 per week).

Carrube e Cavalieri (☎ 0932 94 18 37; www.carrubee cavalieri.it; Corso San Giorgio 111, Modica Alta; s €30-35, d €60-65; ❄) A new B&B right next door to the Chiesa di San Giorgio, with predictably awesome views, this place has seven rooms that are all spacious, simply decorated and have gleaming new bathrooms. Ask for a room with a balcony-view of the church and you'll risk spending far too much time gazing at the gorgeous baroque curves. The owner is friendly and speaks English.

Dei Ruta (☎ 0932 75 56 00; www.deiruta.it; Via Moncada 9, Modica Alta; r per person €30-35; ❄) Another San Giorgio church–gazing B&B, with huge rooms in an old palazzo. The atmosphere is of a family house, with a communal kitchen and friendly landlady. The traditional tiles on the floors give the rooms character, and it's all flawlessly clean.

Hotel Relais (☎ 0932 75 44 51; www.hotelrelaismodica .it; Via Tommaso Campanella, Modica Bassa; s/d €60/95; ❄) Housed in a converted palazzo (just off Corso Umberto I, near Teatro Garibaldi), this attractive hotel in the historic centre has individually decorated rooms with all the mod cons and large French windows. There is an elegant rooftop garden – perfect for an aperitif.

ourpick **Hotel Mohac** (☎ 0932 75 41 30; www.hotel demohac.it; Via Tommaso Campailla 15; s €55-65, d €90-105; ❄) A swanky new joint, Hotel Mohac dedicates its 10 rooms to different poets and writers (such as Pablo Neruda and Salvatore Quasimodo), decorating each with good-looking antiques, chaise longues, writing tables, and big comfortable beds. There's a nice, greenery-shrouded balcony that doubles as a breakfast area, and the downstairs bar/café is relaxing and cool. A good, stylish place to stay.

Eating & Drinking

Modica has some very good restaurants, many of which are modestly priced.

Antica Dolceria Bonajuto (☎ 0932 94 12 25; www .bonajuto.it; Corso Umberto I 159) Mass production of chocolate has meant that the chocolate industry has moved on since the early days, but not in Modica. Here the method remains the same and to taste the crunchy, black stuff – flavoured with cinnamon, vanilla and orange peel – head straight for the famous Antica Dolceria Bonajuto. Also try the famous 'mpanatigghi (South American empanadas filled with meat and chocolate). See p160 for an interview with the owner.

ourpick **I Baccanti** (☎ 0932 94 11 33; Via Grimaldi 72; meals €15-20) This little-sister restaurant to Taverna Nicastro offers the chance to try all the delicious food served in the big restaurant, but at deflated prices. The fresh pasta is excellent, and you can get meaty dishes like rabbit here, as well as fish and seafood. Try some wine too, and if you can't choose for yourself, ask the friendly sommelier.

Taverna Nicastro (☎ 0932 94 58 84; Via S Antonino 28; meals €25) The traditional *taverna* where Modica's families go for lunch and dinner is selected in the revered Slow Food guide for its excellent wine list and fine food. The menu is quite meaty, with sausages, rabbit and pork, though you'll find green beans and tomato stews there too. Desserts are good, though a glass of sweet wine is even better.

Fattoria delle Torri (☎ 0932 75 12 86; Vico Napolitano 14, Modica Alta; mains €30-35; ❄ closed Sun evening & Mon) Worth going to only if you're wanting to splash out, this very upmarket restaurant offers food that is exquisite, but small of portion and high on eye-pleasing presentation. The seafood is gorgeous, wonderful when combined with a crisp, dry white wine such as Cerasuolo di Vittoria, and heart-warming broad-bean-and-ricotta ravioli.

Hemingway (☎ 340 093 52 28; Via Grimaldi 36; ❄ 7pm-late) This is Modica's coolest bar, with books and cushioned outdoor seating, where everyone gathers after 11pm to drink beer and chat away to friends, and where you're likely to find a DJ party several times a month.

Getting There & Away

There are plenty of buses and trains to Modica from Syracuse (10 daily buses Monday to Saturday) and Ragusa (all under €5.20).

AROUND MODICA

Modica is surrounded by pretty countryside full of rambling lanes leading you to interesting sights and pleasant country towns. **Scidi** is just such a town, full of more wonderful baroque architecture – in particular Palazzo

Beneventano and Palazzo Fava – and framed by rocky cliffs. It is well off the beaten track and there is seldom another tourist in sight.

Head down to **Modica Marina** (€1.20, six buses daily) and **Sampieri** (€1.50, three buses daily) for long sandy beaches, as well as rocky coves. Both are popular with the town's youth, with bars and loungers (bed and umbrella for two €10) on the sand, though there are vast unpopulated areas if you walk along the beaches, where you can be undisturbed by the crowds.

A similar town, southeast of Modica, is **Ispica**, located at the head of the 13km-long gorge known as **Cava d'Ispica** (☎ 0932 95 11 33; admission €2; ☼ 9am-1.30pm & 3-6.30pm). Long used as a Neolithic burial site, the caves were later transformed into cave dwellings in the Middle Ages. The gorge is tranquil and verdant and you can follow an overgrown path along the whole length of the valley.

South of Ispica is **Pozzallo**, a pleasant resort town, where you can catch the ferry to Malta.

Getting There & Around

Scicli, Pozzallo and Ispica are all accessible by bus and train from both Modica and Ragusa. If you're driving from Syracuse, take the SS115 and follow the signs to the towns.

Virtu Ferries has services between Pozzallo and Malta (single/return high season €93/125, 1½ hours, two daily except Tuesday and Saturday). Departures are usually at 9am and 9.30pm. The **Virtu office** (☎ 0932 95 40 62; www.virtuferries.com; Via Studi 80) is in front of Via Lungomare Raganzino. In Pozzallo, there's a free courtesy bus that will take you from the ferry dock to the town centre (to the train station it's €2.75).

RAGUSA
pop 69,700 / elev 502m

Classic, quiet and dignified, Ragusa is a delightful provincial town almost completely overlooked by tourists, though judging by the renovations and the town's resulting appeal, not for much longer. Dozens of B&Bs, fantastic restaurants, ice-cream parlours and bars have sprouted, and staying a few days here is an absolute dream. You can walk from the steep heights of Ragusa Superiore (Upper Ragusa), down the curving streets and countless stairs that lead to Ragusa Ibla (Ragusa's old town) and count the baroque spires as you descend.

Like every other town in the region, Ragusa Ibla (the old town) collapsed after the 1693 earthquake and a new town, Ragusa Superiore, was built on a high plateau above the original settlement. But the old aristocracy was loathe to leave the tottering palazzi and rebuilt Ragusa Ibla on exactly the same spot. The two towns were only merged in 1927, thus creating the two towns in one that prevails today. A perilous bus ride or some very steep and winding steps connect the two towns.

Orientation

The train station is on Piazza del Popolo and the intercity bus station is on the adjacent Piazza Gramsci. From the train station, turn left and head along Viale Tenente Lena, across the bridge (Ponte Nuovo) and straight ahead along Via Roma to reach Corso Italia, the upper town's main street. Turn right on Corso Italia and follow it to the stairs to Ibla, or follow the winding road to the lower town.

Information

EMERGENCY
Ambulance (☎ 113)
Police (☎ 0932 62 49 22; Via Raspardi) Next to the town hall.

MEDICAL SERVICES
Hospital (☎ 0932 62 14 10; Piazza del Popolo) Opposite the train station.

MONEY
ATM (Piazza del Duomo)
Banco di Sicilia (Via Roma) Has an ATM; located opposite Mediterraneo Palace.

POST
Main Post Office (Via Ecce Homo, Ragusa Superiore; ☼ 8.30am-5pm Mon-Fri, 8.30am-1.30pm Sat)
Post Office (Piazza Pola, Ragusa Ibla; ☼ 8.30am-5pm Mon-Fri, 8.30am-1.30pm Sat)

TOURIST INFORMATION
Tourist Office (☎ 0932 22 15 11; www.ragusaturismo .it in Italian; Via Capitano Bocchieri 33; ☼ 9am-1.30pm & 3.30-6pm Tue-Sun) Helpful tourist office in Palazzo La Rocca. Also has an excellent map of the town and an interesting booklet, In Barocco, about baroque buildings throughout the province.
Tourist Office (Largo Camarina 5; ☼ 9am-1.30pm & 3.30-6pm Tue-Sun) Staff here can help with booking rooms in the old town.

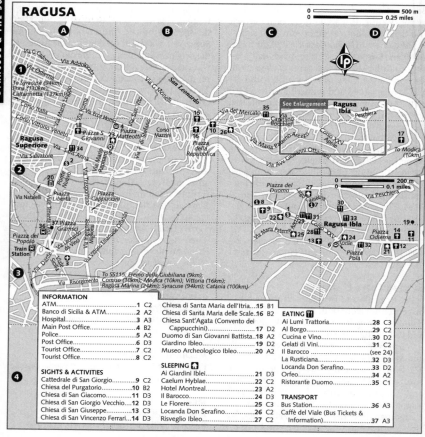

Sights

RAGUSA IBLA

Your first sight of Ragusa Ibla will be the
breathtaking views from the hairpin bends
of Corso Mazzini. It is a lovely picture, the
austere grey of the buildings nestled amid the
green countryside, lifted by splashes of colour
here and there from painted palazzi and the
majolica-tiled dome of the **Chiesa di Santa Maria
dell'Itria**. If you have the time, the old town is
best accessed via the *salita commendatore,* a
winding pass made up of stairs and narrow
archways taking you past the remains of the
15th-century **Chiesa di Santa Maria delle Scale**,
from where there's a good viewing point.
Keep going down and you come to Piazza
della Repubblica and the **Chiesa del Purgatorio**,

whose main altar features a depiction of
Anime in Purgatorio (Souls in Purgatory) by
Francesco Manno.

Aside from the churches and palazzi that
literally line your route wherever you go, the
best thing to do about town is to wander
through its narrow streets and sun-drenched
squares, which look even better on a soft
summer night. If you continue east along
Via del Mercato (which has great views of
the valley below) you'll get your first side
view of palm-planted Piazza del Duomo,
whose western end is dominated by the
Cattedrale di San Giorgio (1744). It is one of
Gagliardi's most elegant churches and its
convex façade is the focal point of the piazza.
The wedding-cake structure is divided into

three tiers, each level supported by gradually narrowing Corinthian columns and punctuated by jutting cornices. The interior is not quite as sumptuous, although there are two paintings by Dario Guerci and a statue of St George on horseback. A close second is the smaller **Chiesa di San Giuseppe**, east of Piazza del Duomo. The elliptical interior is topped by a cupola decorated with a fresco of the *Gloria di San Benedetto* (Glory of St Benedict; 1793) by Sebastiano Lo Monaco.

At the eastern end of the old town is the **Giardino Ibleo** (8am-8pm), a pleasant public garden laid out in the 19th century, perfect for a picnic lunch. In its grounds are the remains of three medieval churches: **Chiesa di San Vincenzo Ferrari**; **Chiesa di San Giacomo** (9am-1pm & 3.30-7pm), the 1563 church with a badly damaged but interesting painted ceiling; and **Chiesa Sant'Agata** (Convento dei Cappuccini; 9am-1pm & 3.30-7pm), with an fine altarpiece and three great examples of painter Pietro Novelli's work *(Assumption of the Virgin, Sant'Agatha* and *Santa Caterina d'Alessandria)*. There's also the Catalan-Gothic portal of what was once the large **Chiesa di San Giorgio Vecchio**, but is now mostly ruined. In the lunette there is an interesting bas-relief of St George killing the dragon.

RAGUSA SUPERIORE

The centrepiece of Ragusa Superiore, and a symbol of its urban renewal, is the enormous **Duomo di San Giovanni Battista**, built between 1718 and 1778. An elegant, terraced square fronts the ornate façade made asymmetrical by Mario Spada's pretty campanile.

South of the cathedral, off Via Roma, is the **Museo Archeologico Ibleo** (0932 62 29 63; Via Natalelli; admission €3; 9am-1.30pm), an important archaeological museum housing finds from prehistoric times and from the Greek site at Camarina on the coast. Also of interest are the ceramics from the caravan centre of Scornavacche, including a reconstructed kiln. Don't miss the mosaic-floor remains from Santa Croce Camerina, near the end of the loop around the museum. Unfortunately, if you don't read Italian, gleaning information about the finds will be a problem.

Sleeping

Most of Ragusa's large hotels are in the upper town; however, there are tons of new,

small hotels and B&Bs in Ragusa Ibla and this is certainly the best place to stay.

Ai Giardini Iblei (338 286 18 58; www.aigiardini.it in Italian; Via Normanni 4, Ragusa Ibla; s €30-50, d €60-70;) As the name suggests, this delightful little B&B is right by the Giardino Ibleo, and next door to the portal of Chiesa di San Giorgio Vecchio. Run by an Italian-Brazilian family, the welcome is warm and the four rooms are simple but comfortable, with blush-coloured walls and large bathrooms (the triple has a bath). Breakfast is served in the small kitchen. Book in advance.

ourpick Risveglio Ibleo (0932 24 78 11; www.risveglioibleo.com; Largo Camerina 3, Ragusa Ibla; r per person €34-42;) An excellent B&B in an old palazzo, this place sports a large apartment on the 1st floor that's decorated like a 1960s novelist's pad. It sleeps two to four people, and it's perfect for a couple who want to spend some time pretending they live in Ragusa. There's also a double room on the ground floor, with high ceilings, antique furniture, wooden floors and a wrought-iron bed. The owner is friendly and speaks good English. It's true value for money here, so book in advance.

Le Fiorere (0932 62 15 30; www.bblefiorere.it; Via Maria Paternò Arezzo 104, Ragusa Ibla; s €40-45, d €65-75; P) Just around the corner from Piazza del Duomo, Le Fiorere has three sweet rooms, each with fridge and stove. The owner even brings you fresh pastries and bread for breakfast, and you can park for free in the internal courtyard. Only one room has air conditioning, so specify if that's your preference.

ourpick Caelum Hyblae (0932 22 04 02; www.bbcaelumhyblae.it; Salita Specula 11, Ragusa Ibla; s €45-50, d €90-100) A stylish, family-run B&B, with seven immaculately turned out rooms with white walls, pristine beds, and an airy, marine atmosphere. The reception is all books, writing tables and a piano, and the place breathes quiet sophistication. The rooms have views of the cathedral, as does the roof terrace. Note that there is no air conditioning, but the family guarantees that the building's thick walls are enough to keep things cool.

Hotel Montreal (0932 62 11 33; www.hotelmontreal.sicily-hotels.net; Corso Italia 70, Ragusa Superiore; s/d €70/9; P) In the upper town, this place is easy to find and comfortable – stay here if you don't want to go hunting around the old town. Rooms are modern and the service is efficient and friendly.

ROYAL RAGUSA

Eremo della Giubiliana (☎ 0932 66 91 19; www.eremodellagiubiliana.it; Contrada Giubiliana, SP per Marina di Ragusa 7.5km; d/ste €240/820; P 🏊) The Eremo is a wonderful homage to history and authenticity. Its white tower dominates the highland above Ragusa Marina in a ruggedly wild estate of carob trees and dry stone walls. The estate used to be part of the old fief of Renna and the structure was a fortified hermitage. The Knights of St John used the hermitage in the 16th century after which it was bought by the Nifosì family, whose last heir, Vincenza Iolanda Nifosì, is responsible for its sensitive restoration. Nowadays it is a luxurious retreat offering a catalogue of wonderful excursions on foot, by 4WD or even in the estate's private plane (to Lampedusa, Tunisia, Mt Etna and Palermo).

To reach it, take the road from Ragusa to Ragusa Marina and after 9km turn off right and follow the signs.

Il Barocco (☎ 0932 65 23 97; www.ilbarocco.it; Via S Maria La Nuova, Ragusa Ibla; s/d €80/125; 🏊) Owned by the Cabibbo family, which also runs the massively popular restaurant of the same name (see opposite), this was once a carpenter's workshop. It's a tastefully done-up hotel, with unfussy and comfortable rooms.

Locanda Don Serafino (☎ 0932 22 00 65; www.locandadonserafino.it; Via XI Febbraio 15, Ragusa Ibla; d from €148; 🏊) A plush three-star hotel that prides itself on its upmarket service, with comfortable rooms, vaulted ceilings, and a stylish décor all-round. A good splash-out opportunity, especially considering that the hotel has its own beach at Marina Ragusa, 20km from here. The eponymous restaurant (see opposite) is very popular.

Eating

Like Modica, Ragusa has a good selection of restaurants, all of them located in the old town.

ourpick Gelati Di Vini (☎ 0932 22 89 89; www.gelatidivini.it in Italian; Piazza del Duomo 20, Ragusa Ibla; ice cream from €1.50) The name of this place indicates that (some of) the ice cream is wine-flavoured, and it plays with the idea that they are 'divine' of flavour. And dare we say it, it's some of the best ice cream we've tasted in Sicily. There are such adventurous and marvellous-tasting flavours here that you might just find yourself unable to leave Ragusa without trying another one. The carob is powdery and subtle, the peach is like eating the fruit itself, the cinnamon is sweet and exotic, and the cardamom aromatic and seductive. Try the moscato d'Asti wine flavour (sweet wine) for a real Ragusa ice-cream experience. Divine indeed.

Al Borgo (☎ 0932 65 12 03; Piazza del Duomo 3, Ragusa Ibla; bruschetta €5) Right in front of the lovely cathedral, Al Borgo is the ideal place to catch the afternoon sun while you snack on one of the sizable bruschettas, topped with tomatoes, ham, olives or anchovies. You'll be sure to witness a wedding from here, and it's the perfect people-watching place.

La Rusticana (☎ 0932 22 79 81; Corso XXV Aprile 68, Ragusa Ibla; meals €20-25) A great budget option that serves meat and fish dishes to a boisterous crowd of loyal locals who come here for the generous portions and the relaxed vine-covered terrace. Try the *spaghetti con le cozze* (spaghetti with mussels).

Ai Lumi Trattoria (☎ 0932 62 12 24; Corso XXV Aprile 16, Ragusa Ibla; meals €25) Right on the main street, where the *passeggiata* (stroll) unfolds before your dining table, Ai Lumi is a great opportunity to eat well in elegant surroundings, without having to pay a lot for the experience. The fish soup is a favourite here, and the fish and meat menus offer local delicacies. Enjoy some wine too and watch Ragusa stroll.

ourpick Cucina e Vino (☎ 0932 68 64 47; Via Orfanotrofio 91, Ragusa Ibla; meals €25-30) One of Ragusa's foremost restaurants, this Slow Food electee is a friendly place with pleasant terrace seating that overlooks the street. The menu is unusual, with things like rigatoni in a lamb sauce or ricotta ravioli in pork juices. The mains are in a similar vein, with stews of pork belly and tomato, or lamb and artichokes. Great for a rich dinner, enjoyed with some potent red wine.

Orfeo (☎ 0932 62 10 35; Via Sant'Anna 117, Ragusa Superiore; meals €25-30) Another Ragusa Slow Food–championed restaurant, this time in the upper part of town. Orfeo goes for the simple Sicilian cuisine that sports seafood and fish, but also likes to offer lamb, veal and pork, and it serves some fabulous sausages with Nero

D'Avola wine sauce. The climb up or down to the restaurant will certainly aid digestion.

Il Barocco (☎ 0932 65 23 97; Via Orfanotrofio 29, Ragusa Ibla; meals €25-30) Il Barocco is so popular that reservations are essential and eating in the vaulted dining room or on the kerbside is a boisterous, enjoyable affair. You simply must try the delicious and excellent-value grilled-meat platter (€22 for two people).

Locanda Don Serafino (☎ 0932 24 87 78; Via Orfanotrofio 39, Ragusa Ibla; meals €30-35; ☺ closed Tue) An excellent restaurant in the atmospheric barrel-vaulted caverns of an old stable block. Head right to the back to the furthest and most intimate room and dine on rabbit stuffed with pistachios or tender pork and mushrooms.

Ristorante Duomo (☎ 0932 65 12 65; Via Capitano Bocchieri 31, Ragusa Ibla; meals €70, tasting menu €100; ☺ closed Mon) This five-star restaurant is one of Sicily's poshest, with a friendly, though extremely formal, service and atmosphere. The Duomo combines ingredients in an imaginative and unconventional fashion while sticking close to traditional favourites such as tomatoes, pistachios, fennel and almonds. Five small dining rooms keep things intimate.

Getting There & Around

Ragusa is accessible by train from Syracuse (€5.70, 2¼ hours, eight daily), Noto (€4.25, 1¾ hours, eight daily) and Gela (€3.80, 1¼ hours, six daily).

Interbus-Etna Trasporti (information and tickets at Caffè del Viale, Viale Tenente Lena 42), runs daily buses to Catania (€6.60, 1¾ hours, 10 daily Monday to Friday, five Saturday and Sunday). **AST** (☎ 0932 68 18 18) runs the local network to Modica (€1.95, 20 minutes, 16 daily Monday to Saturday), Noto (€3.15, two hours, 11 daily Monday to Saturday) and

Syracuse (€5.50, 2½ hours, 10 daily Monday to Saturday). There is usually only one bus to each destination on Sunday. An AST timetable is posted on Piazza Gramsci where AST and SAIS buses stop.

City buses run from Piazza del Popolo in the upper town to Piazza Pola and the Giardino Ibleo in the lower town of Ragusa Ibla.

AROUND RAGUSA

Ten kilometres west of Ragusa, on the SS115, is the town of **Comiso**, with plenty of baroque buildings and churches to look at, including a rare survivor of the earthquake of 1693, the Chiesa di San Francesco (13th century). Six kilometres west of Comiso is **Vittoria**, founded in 1603 by Vittoria Colonna, hence the name. The town has baroque buildings and is a wine-making centre for the region.

North of Comiso (take the SS514) is **Chiaramonte Gulfi**, with churches, decent views of the countryside and delicious ham. It was founded by Manfredi Chiaramonte, the Count of Modica, and is famous both for its high-quality olive oil (accredited by the *Denominazione d'Origine Protetta*; DOP), cured hams and pasta, and its eight **museums** (www.comunechiaramontegulfi.it; ☺ 5-8pm Sat, 10am-1pm & 3-7pm Sun).

Approximately 20km southwest of Ragusa is **Castello di Donnafugata** (admission free; ☺ 9am-1pm Tue-Sun), a 19th-century building with some remnants of its 17th-century predecessor. It looks even older than that though, as it was designed in the Venetian-Gothic style – don't confuse it with the Donnafugata of *Il Gattopardo* (The Leopard) though!

A car is definitely the best way to see these towns; although train and bus services exist from Syracuse, frequency can be a problem.

Central Sicily

CENTRAL SICILY

The centre of Sicily is a place of subtle moods and dramatic scenery, a place where severe mountain ridges cloaked in a patchwork of farms are interspersed with a series of atmospheric mountain towns. It is an ancient landscape redolent of the huge feudal estates from an era not long past, when hunger drove men to work in the harsh sulphur mines that surround Caltanissetta.

Today it is a place of great beauty and harsh economic realities, where farming and mining continue to power the local economy and create close-knit communities. These physically and culturally isolated towns retain the remnants of traditional Sicilian life, creating a fascinating province on an already fascinating island: Enna is the natural crossroads of the island; Lago di Pergusa is the source of the powerful myth of Persephone and Demeter; Piazza Armerina holds a famous Roman villa; and Caltagirone is a typical provincial town.

For more than a decade now, tour operators have been touting the area as the next big destination. Walking enthusiasts love this area too, as do people keen to get a break from the scorching summer temperatures, but tourist droves won't be crowding this area any time soon. It's still a region for independent travellers, especially those with their own vehicle – the public transport isn't as good as in the rest of Sicily.

HIGHLIGHTS

- Spot a bikini-clad trio, leaping leopards and a tiny rhino in the breathtaking polychrome mosaics of the **Villa Romana del Casale** (p252)

- Lose your breath climbing Caltagirone's **Scalinata di Santa Maria del Monte** (p255), and see Sicilian history portrayed on the steps' ceramic tiles

- Get some fresh mountain air in Enna as you walk the ramparts of the **Castello di Lombardia** (p242)

- Catch the extraordinary rituals of Enna's **Holy Week** (p244), when religious confraternities parade the streets

- Learn to cook like a *monsù* under the tutelage of Anna Tasca Lanza at her home on the vast **Regaleali estate** (p258)

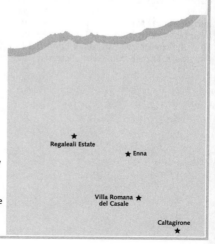

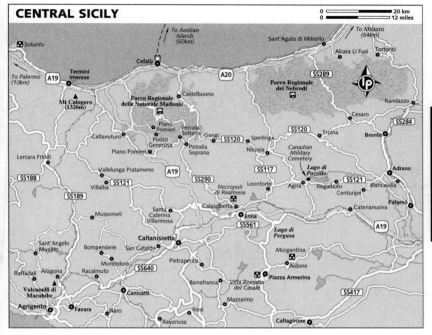

CENTRAL SICILY

ENNA & AROUND

ENNA
pop 28,800 / elev 948m

Shrouded in myth, the township of Enna dominates the centre of the island with its monumental demeanour, grandiose palazzi (palaces or mansions) and churches and a crisp mountain air. Its unmatched views of the surrounding valley suggest that this has traditionally been the top dog in the province. The atmosphere here is different to that of other Sicilian towns, with the workaday feel of a town unperturbed by tourism.

Enna has long been the seat of a sacred cult of Demeter (also called Ceres; the goddess of fertility and agriculture) and in springtime the countryside surrounding the town is filled with the flowers that attracted Demeter's daughter Persephone (also known as Proserpina) to the shores of Lago di Pergusa. Throughout the Greek, Roman and Arab periods Enna supplied places far and wide with necessities such as grain and wheat, cotton and cane. It's a tradition that

continues today, as Enna supplies a large proportion of the durum wheat used by the Italian pasta-manufacturing industry.

Orientation

The town of Enna is divided into two main areas: the historic centre on the summit of the hill (Enna Alta), and the modern town at its base (Enna Bassa). From the south you enter the lower part of Enna along the SS561, which becomes the main road, Via Pergusa. This road takes you all the way up to the historic centre. From the north (on the Palermo–Catania autostrada), you enter the historic town via the hairpin bends of the SP2. Turn left at the T-junction for Via Roma, which is the main street of historic Enna.

The intercity bus station is on Viale Diaz. To get to the town centre from the bus station, turn right from the station and follow Viale Diaz to Corso Sicilia. You then need to turn right again and follow it to Via Sant'Agata, which leads to Via Roma.

The train station is about 3km out of the town centre.

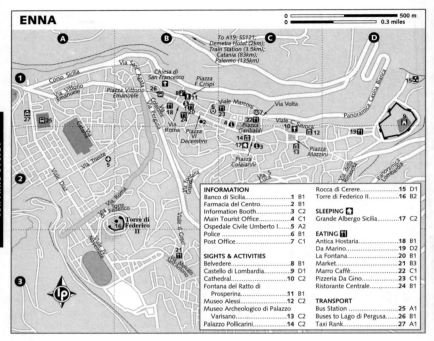

ENNA

To A19; SS121;
Demetra Hotel (2km);
Train Station (3.5km);
Catania (83km);
Palermo (135km)

INFORMATION		Rocca di Cerere.....................15 D1
Banco di Sicilia.........................1 B1		Torre di Federico II................16 B2
Farmacia del Centro...............2 B1		
Information Booth (..................3 C2		**SLEEPING**
Main Tourist Office.................4 C1		Grande Albergo Sicilia..........17 C2
Ospedale Civile Umberto I......5 A2		
Police......................................6 B1		**EATING**
Post Office..............................7 C1		Antica Hostaria......................18 B1
		Da Marino...............................19 D2
SIGHTS & ACTIVITIES		La Fontana..............................20 B1
Belvedere................................8 B1		Market....................................21 B3
Castello di Lombardia.............9 D1		Marro Caffè............................22 C1
Cathedral..............................10 C2		Pizzeria Da Gino.....................23 C1
Fontana del Ratto di		Ristorante Centrale................24 B1
Prosperina...........................11 B1		
Museo Alessi.........................12 C2		**TRANSPORT**
Museo Archeologico di Palazzo		Bus Station 25 A1
Varisano.............................13 C2		Buses to Lago di Pergusa......26 B1
Palazzo Pollicarini................14 C2		Taxi Rank...............................27 A1

Information

EMERGENCY
Ambulance (☎ 0935 4 52 45)
Emergency Doctor (☎ 0935 50 08 96)
Police (questura; ☎ 0935 52 21 11; Via San Giovanni 2)

MEDICAL SERVICES
Farmacia del Centro (☎ 0935 50 06 50; Via Roma 315)
Ospedale Civile Umberto I (☎ 0935 4 51 11, first aid
0935 50 08 96; Via Trieste)

MONEY
There are plenty of banks along Via Roma.
Banco di Sicilia (Via Roma 367)

POST
Post office (Via Volta 1; 🕑 8am-6.30pm Mon-Fri,
8am-12.30pm Sat)

TOURIST INFORMATION
Information booth (Piazza Colaianni; 🕑 9am-1pm
Mon-Sat) Next door to the Grande Albergo Sicilia.
Main tourist office (☎ 0935 52 82 88; www.apt
-enna.com; Via Roma 413; 🕑 9am-1pm & 3.30-6.30pm
Mon-Sat) Helpful staff with good maps and information.

Sights

CASTELLO DI LOMBARDIA
Cloaked by mist, the streets of Enna feel
like they might just float away if it weren't
for the solid mass of the rampart walls and
the steadying bulwark of **Castello di Lombardia**
(Piazza Mazzini; admission free; 🕑 9am-8pm). The original castle was built by the Saracens and
later reinforced by the Normans; Frederick
II of Hohenstaufen ordered that a powerful
curtain wall be built with towers on every
side. The wall is still intact but only six of
the original 20 towers remain. Within the
walls is a complex structure of courtyards;
the closest one to the entrance, **Cortile di San
Martino** (Courtyard of St Martin), is used in
summer as an outdoor theatre (see p244).
From the same courtyard you can climb up
Torre Pisano, from where there are fabulous
views – at least when the fog, an enduring
element of Enna's weather, has lifted. Across
the valley is the town of Calascibetta and to
the distant northeast you can just about
make out the towering peak of Mt Etna.
Secret passageways once led to the octago-
nal **Torre di Federico II** (Tower of Frederick II; Via Torre

di Federico; admission free; 8am-6pm), which now stands in the town's public garden; once part of the town's old defence system, it stands nearly 24m high.

ROCCA DI CERERE

To the north of the castle a small road leads quickly down to the superbly sited foundations of the Temple of Demeter (Ceres to the Romans), the goddess of fertility and agriculture. In classical times it was the centre of a massive fertility cult, and in 480 BC the tyrant Gelon built a temple here lest his plans for the capture of Syracuse be foiled by a couple of bad harvests. The temple is also supposed to have featured a statue of King Triptolemus, the only mortal to witness the rape of Demeter's daughter Persephone by Hades, god of the underworld (see boxed text, below). In return for spilling the beans, Demeter taught Triptolemus the secrets of agriculture, from which Enna has benefited ever since. The temple's remains are not enclosed, and it's a great spot for a picnic or to take in the sunset.

ALONG VIA ROMA
Cathedral
Back in town, Via Roma extends westwards from the castle (and also down to the south-west of town), and is lined with most of the town's more important sights.

The best of these is the **cathedral** (admission free; 9am-noon & 4-7pm), which has a composite style that's the result of the waves of invaders who sought to possess the mountain eyrie. In 1446 a fire destroyed the church, which was slowly rebuilt in early baroque style over the next 200 years. The curious façade (complete with 17th-century bell tower) covers its Gothic predecessor, while the rich interior is almost entirely baroque in design. The dark grey basalt columns are worth looking at for their highly ornamented bases, which are carved with a series of grotesques such as snakes with human heads. Other points of interest are the Graeco-Roman remains (the base of the pulpit and stoup) from the Temple of Demeter; the medieval walls and Gothic transepts and some Renaissance artwork like the presbytery paintings (dating from 1613) by Filippo Paladino; and the altarpieces by Guglielmo Borremans. Ironically, the iron gate to the sacristy was taken from the *seraglio* (harem) in the Castello di Lombardia.

Museo Alessi & Museo Archeologico di Palazzo Varisano
Near the cathedral is the **Museo Alessi** (0935 50 13 65; Via Roma 465; closed to the public until further notice),

---

A DEVIL'S BARGAIN

The ancient cult of Demeter (called Ceres by the Romans; the goddess of fertility and agriculture) is all about the need to explain the workings of the natural world, and is influenced by the fundamental human concern with food. The central story of the cult, the tale of Hades' capture of Demeter's daughter Persephone (as known as Proserpina), is one of the most famous Greek myths.

According to a Homeric hymn of the 7th century BC, Hades (also called Pluto; the god of the underworld) asked Zeus for Persephone's hand in marriage. He was not refused and, emboldened, he raped and kidnapped her while she was gathering flowers around the Lago di Pergusa. When Demeter couldn't find Persephone she wandered the world distraught, forbidding the earth to bear fruit. Triptolemus, who had witnessed the rape, told her what had happened and in return Demeter granted him the secret of agriculture. She then went straight to Zeus to demand the release of her daughter, threatening the entire human race with never-ending famine. Stuck between a rock and a hard place, Zeus ordered Hades to release Persephone and sent Hermes to escort her back to earth. Hades agreed on the condition that she had not tasted anything in the underworld.

Persephone had not eaten during her time in the underworld, but Hades gave her a pomegranate for her journey back and she nibbled six of its seeds on the way. Hades immediately demanded her return and, in a spirit of compromise, Zeus decreed that Persephone would have to spend six months of the year in the underworld and six months with her mother. Demeter still mourns during Persephone's time in the underworld, bringing winter to the world; her joy at her daughter's return is heralded by the blossoms of springtime.

which houses the valuable contents of the cathedral's treasury. It was unfortunately closed in April 2007 due to a lack of funds, and locals and visitors are eagerly awaiting its reopening, which is due as soon as funds are found.

The museum's collection was originally the property of Canon Giuseppe Alessi (1774–1837), who left the collection to his brother with the intention that he then donate it to the Church. Eager to make a tidy profit, Alessi's brother actually sold it to the Church in 1860. Some of the pieces are stunning, such as the golden crown of the Madonna, encrusted with jewels and enamels, by Leonardo and Giuseppe Montalbano; it dates from 1653.

On the far side of Piazza Mazzini from the cathedral is the **Museo Archeologico di Palazzo Varisano** (☎ 0935 2 47 20; admission €2; ☉ 8am-7pm), which has a good, if small, collection of artefacts (labelled in Italian) excavated from throughout the region. Of particular interest is the Attic-style red-and-black *krater* (drinking vases) found in the town itself.

About 100m further down Via Roma, on the southwestern side of Piazza Colaianni next to the Grande Albergo Sicilia, is the Catalan-Gothic **Palazzo Pollicarini**, one of Enna's most handsome buildings. Although it has been converted into private apartments, you can still nip in to take a peek at the medieval staircase in the central courtyard.

Belvedere

All roads in Enna must eventually lead one to Piazza F Crispi and the wonderful belvedere (viewing point) that overlooks the opposite hilltop town of Calascibetta. In the evenings the piazza is absolutely heaving with Enna's smooching teenage population, but hustle your way through the crowd to enjoy the sunset over the rust-red buildings of Calascibetta. In the centre of the piazza is the **Fontana del Rato di Prosperina** (the Fountain of the Rape of Proserpina), commemorating Enna's most enduring legend. It is actually a copy of Giovanni Lorenzo Bernini's original, which is in the Galleria Borghese in Rome.

Festivals & Events

Holy Week Held in April, this is a living reminder of Enna's esoteric past, smacking of pagan rites and occultism. Thousands of people wearing hoods and capes representing the town's different religious confraternities participate in a solemn procession to the cathedral.

Grand Prix (☎ 0935 2 56 60) Between April and October, Formula 3 racing takes place at the Autodromo di Pergusa, 9km south of Enna. Take bus 5.

Festa di Maria Santissima della Visitazione On 2 July an effigy of Enna's patron saint was traditionally dragged through the town on a cart called La Nave d'Oro (Golden Ship) by farmers wearing just a white band over their hips! Today the band has been replaced by a long sheet. The feast is accompanied by fireworks.

Castello di Lombardia Hosts nightly plays and performances of a medieval nature during summer. Ask the tourist office (p242) for details.

Sleeping

Enna has only one hotel in the historic centre. There is a second hotel on the way out of town on the SP2.

Demetra Hotel (☎ 0935 50 23 00; Contrada Misericordia SS121; s €51-78, d €83-110; ⓟ ⌘) Demetra offers a modern standard of accommodation: laminate floors; neat, sterile rooms; and all the mod cons. It is some way out of the historic centre so it's only really viable if you have a car.

Grande Albergo Sicilia (☎ 0935 50 08 50; fax 0935 50 04 88; www.hotelsiciliaenna.it; Piazza Colaianni 7; s €55-72, d €70-120; ⓟ ⌘) Enna's only hotel has a crude concrete façade that disguises an Art Nouveau interior with lots of coloured glass and gold-framed pictures. Refurbished in 2005, the rooms are nicely decorated, with warm colours and good, firm beds, though the bathrooms are still waiting for the next wave of renovations. The same is the case with the balconies, which are crumbling.

Eating

Unlike the coast, the staple here is meat, and local specialities usually involve some cut of mutton or beef and a tasty array of mushrooms and grilled vegetables. Local dishes include *castrato* (charcoal-grilled castrated ram) and *polpettone* (stuffed lamb or meatballs). Soups and sausages are also a feature.

RESTAURANTS

La Fontana (☎ 0935 2 54 65; Via Volturo 6; meals €20; ☉ closed Fri) Right opposite the fountain on the little piazza, this little restaurant is run by an eccentric older couple who've decorated the place in a mixture of kitsch and Art Nouveau. Mostly frequented by tourists, it's friendly and the food is straightforward Sicilian fare. It has outdoor seating on the piazza in summer.

Ristorante Centrale (☎ 0935 50 09 63; www .ristorantecentrale.net; Piazza VI Dicembre 9; meals €20-25;

closed Sat) Very central (hence the name), this friendly, family-run place has a feast-like buffet of antipasti, and cooks up typical mountain dishes of meat, sausages, mushrooms and vegetables. The menu of Sicilian specialities changes daily. The décor is a cacophony of pictures and plates.

our pick **Antica Hostaria** (☎ 0935 2 25 21; Via Castagna 9; meals €30; closed Tue) Enna's best restaurant has made it into the Slow Food Movement bible thanks to its pork *ragù* (sauce), an ancient mountain staple. The chef only makes it in the winter months, however, so you can opt for simpler things if you're here in the summer. The *orecchiette* (ear-shaped pasta) with broccoli and black olive paste is very good, as is the pasta carbonara with asparagus. Also try the *castellane* (conical macaroni) with mussels and mushrooms.

Historic **Pizzeria Da Gino** (☎ 0935 2 40 67; Viale Marconi 6; pizza €6-8; closed Wed) has outdoor seating, and is absolutely buzzing with teenagers. Good atmosphere and great views.

Another good pizzeria is **Da Marino** (☎ 0935 2 52 22; Viale C Savoca 62; pizza €6-8; closed Wed); it's near the castle.

CAFÉS
Marro Caffè (☎ 0935 50 23 36; Piazza Vittorio Emmanuele 21) This is a good café for both the summer and winter months. It's popular with a 25-and-up crowd, who come here for coffee, snacks, drinks and aperitivi. The interior is sleek and there's a covered outdoor seating area for the cooler months.

SELF-CATERING
There is a **market** (Via Mercato Sant'Antonio; Mon-Sat) every morning where you can find basics such as fresh fruit, bread and cheese.

Getting There & Around
There is a **bus station** (☎ 0935 50 09 05; Viale Diaz) in the historic town, from where **SAIS Autolinee** (☎ 0935 50 09 02) runs services to Catania (€10.30, 1½ to two hours, 10 daily Monday to Saturday, three Sunday) and its airport, and to Palermo (€8.80, 1¾ hours, six daily Monday to Saturday, one Sunday). It is possible to reach Agrigento via Caltanissetta (€3.30, one hour, three daily Monday to Friday), and regular buses also run to Piazza Armerina (€2.75, 45 minutes, eight daily Monday to Saturday, two Sunday).

The train station is inconveniently located at the bottom of a steep hill 3.5km northeast of the town centre. Trains service Caltanissetta (€2.65, 40 minutes, seven daily), Catania (€4.65, seven daily) and Palermo (€7.50, four daily), and you can purchase tickets from the machine on the platform. That said, you're best off not bothering with the train at all.

Local buses (single trip/day pass €1.35/2.10) make the run from the train station to town hourly (except Sunday, when you might have to wait a couple of hours between buses).

You can call for a taxi on ☎ 0935 50 09 05. There is also a **taxi rank** (Viale Diaz) near the bus station.

LAGO DI PERGUSA
Lago di Pergusa, 9km south of Enna, is Sicily's only natural lake, and the source of all that mythology (see boxed text, p243). It seems incredible that developers have been allowed to destroy the lake, which was first ringed by a motor-racing track in the 1950s and then further diminished by the excessive development of its shores. Now it seems Persephone's lake is disappearing fast, with the vegetation and bird life on its shores all but vanished. Brackish water laps against the sandy beaches, which in summer are crammed with tourists escaping from Enna. It must be one of the most sacrilegious and shameful fates visited on any classical site.

The area around the lake has a few hotels that are a popular alternative to those in Enna.

Park Hotel La Giarra (☎ 0935 54 16 87; www .parkhotellagiarra.it; Via Nazionale 125; s €60-80, d €90-109; P ⊠ ⊠) is a nice, small hotel in a quiet location on the lake. Rooms are comfortable, with all the mod cons, and the restaurant is also good.

To get there, take bus 5 from Piazza Vittorio Emanuele in Enna (€1.35, every hour from 7am to 9.30pm).

NORTH OF ENNA
The winding SS121 makes its way out of Enna in a northeasterly direction through some of the most splendid inland scenery on the island before it eventually reaches Catania. There are a couple of towns, such

as Calascibetta and Nicosia, that are worth a stop, if only to get a sense of what Sicilian life is like away from the tourist trail. All the towns mentioned are reachable by bus from Enna; check at the tourist office or the bus terminal for departure details and prices. Without a doubt, the best way to explore this area is with your own transport, as some services are nonexistent after the morning peak hours.

CALASCIBETTA
pop 4800 / elev 691m

A mere 2km north of Enna across a valley and the A19 motorway lies the hilltop town of Calascibetta, built by the Arabs who laid siege to Enna in 951. More than 100 years later, in 1087, Roger I also camped on the hill when he besieged the Arabs. Seemingly ambivalent about the influence of modernity, Calascibetta is a densely packed maze of little streets above an enormous drop (on its eastern side) to the valley below. The 14th-century **cathedral** (admission free; ☺ 9am-1pm & 3-7pm), dedicated to St Peter, is worth popping your head into.

Only 1km or so northwest of town is the well-signposted **Necropoli di Realmese** (admission free; ☺ 24hr), where some 300 rock tombs dating from 850 to 730 BC have been found.

The town is within easy access from Enna by SAIS Autolinee bus (€1.35, 11 daily Monday to Saturday, two Sunday) from the main bus terminal.

LEONFORTE
pop 14,100 / elev 603m

A further 18km northeast along the SS121 is this attractive baroque town, founded in 1610 and once renowned for its horse breeding. Leonforte's most imposing building is the **Palazzo Baronale**, which has an ornate façade. The town's **cathedral** houses some good wooden sculptures, but the real sight of interest is the **Granfonte**. Built in 1651 by Nicolò Branciforte, this lavish fountain is made up of 24 separate jets against a sculpted façade. The fountain is about 300m down a small road from the cathedral; follow the signpost.

Interbus has frequent departures between Enna and Leonforte (€2.70, 35 minutes, 12 daily Monday to Friday, two Saturday). Buy tickets on the bus or at Bar Venticinque in Leonforte.

AGIRA
pop 8300 / elev 650m

From a distance, Agira rises up in an almost perfect cone, with the ruins of its medieval Norman castle at the top. The town was colonised by Timoleon in 339 BC and was later captured by the Romans, who added substantially to the existing Greek settlement. The Augustan historian Diodorus Siculus was born here and declared that the amphitheatre was matched in beauty only by that of Syracuse. Apart from a few unremarkable traces, there is little that remains of the town's distinguished past (it had an important mint for 500 years), although its churches house some precious artefacts: **Chiesa di Santa Maria Maggiore** holds a 15th-century triptych, while the treasury of **Chiesa di San Salvatore** has a jewel-encrusted medieval mitre.

From Enna, SAIS buses head to Agira (€2.85, 1¾ hours, 10 daily Monday to Friday, two Saturday). There are also SAIS buses between Agira and Troina (three daily).

REGALBUTO

The road to Regalbuto (about 14km northeast of Agira) is more interesting than the town at the end of it. A couple of kilometres out of Agira (signposted to your left), atop a little hill, is a well-tended **Canadian Military Cemetery**, where the bodies of 480 soldiers killed in July 1943 lie. Further on, still to your left, is a large artificial lake known as the **Lago di Pozzillo**. This is a great spot for a picnic amid the almond trees and prickly pears. Under no circumstances try to pick one of these pears without gloves: although they look harmless enough, they are covered in tiny, painful needles that are very difficult to remove from your skin.

CENTURIPE
pop 5800 / elev 730m

About 13km past Regalbuto on the road to Adrano and Mt Etna is a turn-off south for this little town, known as the *Balcone di Sicilia* (Balcony of Sicily) on account of its commanding position on a ridge in front of Mt Etna. The approach from the turn-off (you will need your own transport) brings you through 7km of lovely citrus groves and then uphill into the town, which has been fought over many times due to its strategic importance. The last battle occurred in 1943; when the Allies captured the town, the

Germans realised that their foothold in Sicily had slipped and they retreated to the Italian mainland. The town centre was partially destroyed by Allied bombs and much of it is now a collection of uninspiring modern buildings. The sole exception is the 17th-century pink-and-white **cathedral**.

NICOSIA

pop 14,800 / elev 724m

Of all the hill towns, Nicosia is the quietest and most fascinating. Set on four hills, this market town has played its part as a Greek city, Byzantine bishopric, Arab fort and Lombard stronghold. During the Norman era it was the most important of a series of fortified towns that stretched from Palermo to Messina, but the new autostrada (motorway) has sunk Nicosia into profound solitude. Between 1950 and 1970 nearly half the village emigrated and now only old men linger in the piazze, talking in their own blend of Gallo-Italico (a Lombard dialect unique to Nicosia, Aidone, Piazza Armerina and Sperlinga).

Sights

Although the town is full of fine buildings and churches, Nicosia's architectural legacy is in an alarming state of decay. Many of the buildings were damaged in the 1968 earthquake, and the elegant portico of the **Cattedrale di San Nicolò** still sports headless statues, as yet unrepaired. The cathedral dominates the central piazza, Piazza Garibaldi, and incorporates a Catalan-Gothic campanile built on an original Moorish tower. Inside is a baptismal font by

Domenico Gagini and a wooden crucifix by Fra Umile di Petralia, which is carried through the town on Good Friday.

From Piazza Garibaldi, pick up Nicosia's most impressive street, Via Salamone, lined with crumbling Franco-Lombard palaces and convents. At the top of the steep hill is the 19th-century **Chiesa di Santa Maria Maggiore**. It's another reconstruction, as the original 13th-century church was destroyed by a landslide in 1757. In 1968 the bell tower was demolished by an earthquake and its bells rehung on a low iron bracket – the chime you hear is electric. Inside is a lovely marble polyptych by Gagini. From the terrace the ruins of a Norman **castle** are visible on a rocky crag above the town.

Sleeping & Eating

Accommodation is in short supply here, and is usually to be found in the form of converted farmhouses. Though the farmhouses are generally charming, you almost always need your own transport to reach them.

Baglio San Pietro (☎ /fax 0935 64 05 29; www.bagliosanpietro.com in Italian; Contrada San Pietro, Nicosia; s/d €40/80; P) Only 750m from the entrance to Nicosia (on the SS117 to Agira) this large country *baglio* occupies a lovely rural setting and has 10 comfortable rooms. It's a working farm, and offers mountain biking and horse riding – it's perfect if you fancy a quiet, relaxing time with the option of a bit of muscle work.

La Cirata (☎ 0935 64 05 61; SS117, Contrada Cirata; meals €25; ⊙ closed Mon) The cavernous La Cirata,

---

DETOUR: NICOSIA TO ABBAZIA DI MANIACE

From Nicosia the SS120 skirts the border of the Parco Regionale dei Nebrodi, travelling across some of the most beautiful scenery on the whole island. For 32km the tortuous road climbs the mountains until the lofty village of **Troina** comes into sight. Situated on a 1120m ridge, this is Sicily's highest town. This austere and scruffy medley of houses was Roger's first Norman diocese, won in 1082 when Roger and his new bride Adelaide took refuge in the Chiesa Madre.

Continuing in an easterly direction on the SS120 you enter the volcanic landscape of Etna's northeastern slopes, with views over the 1823 lava flow. The hills are covered with nut orchards; in fact, nearly 80% of Italy's pistachios come from here. After 37km, just past Cesaro, you will arrive at the **Abbazia di Maniace** (☎ 095 69 00 18; Maniace; admission free; ⊙ 9am-1pm & 3-7pm), a fortified abbey set in a wooded hollow. It was also established by Roger (the chapel still has its Norman ceiling) and named after the Byzantine general Maniakes, who helped him defeat the Saracens. However, the estate is better known for its connection to Nelson, who was awarded the title of duke of Bronte in 1799, a title only relinquished by his descendants in 1981. The castle keeps lots of Nelson memorabilia and looks more like an English manor house than a Sicilian palazzo (palace or mansion).

5km south of town, is the best place to eat around Nicosia. In summer the place is a popular stop for bus tours and local wedding parties, all of whom come here for the solid rustic cuisine, including a lip-smacking lamb roast.

There are a couple of bars on Piazza Garibaldi that can rustle up a sandwich or even a hot dish at lunch.

Getting There & Away

Nicosia is served by Interbus buses from Enna (€5.80, 40 minutes, three daily Monday to Friday), Catania (€5.80, two hours, 10 daily Monday to Friday, three Sunday) and other towns throughout the region. Buses arrive and depart from Piazza Marconi. You can buy your tickets from Bar del Passeggero by the bus stop.

SPERLINGA

A 15-minute drive west along the SS120 (about 13km) from Nicosia will bring you to Sperlinga, an interesting small town nestled beneath its impressive castle rock. The castle was the only place in Sicily to give refuge to the French during the Sicilian Vespers (1282), hence the saying 'Whatever pleases Sicily, only Sperlinga denies'. The town is also famous for its prehistoric cave system, which makes the sandstone mountain look like a piece of Swiss cheese. Both the caves and the **castle** (☎ 0935 64 31 77; admission €2; 🕑 9.30am-1.30pm & 4-6.30pm) are accessible.

GANGI

This beautiful hilltop town is definitely worth a visit if you like soaking up a quiet atmosphere. The town produced two well-known 17th-century painters, Gaspare Vazano and Giuseppe Salerno, the latter nicknamed *Lo Zeppo di Gangi* (the Cripple of Gangi). You can see Salerno's impressive *Last Judgement* (1629) in the town's lovely **Chiesa Madre**. On the second Sunday of August, the whole town is decorated with ears of wheat for the **Sagra delle Spighe**, an ancient festival that goes all the way back to the Greek cult of Demeter.

From Gangi it is only 12km to Petralia Sottana, the gateway to the Parco Naturale Regionale delle Madonie.

There is some excellent rural accommodation around Gangi, and many of the *agriturismi* (farm stays) in the area have good restaurants.

Tenuta Gangivecchio (☎ 0921 64 48 04; fax 0921 68 91 91; www.tenutagangivecchio.com; Contrada Gangi Vecchio; r incl half board per person €60; P 🍴) is a former 14th-century Benedictine convent now run by the Tornabene sisters, who also run a highly regarded cookery course. It is a perfect base from which to explore the Madonie park. Children aged under 10 aren't accommodated at Easter and New Year.

Casale Villa Rainò (☎ 0921 64 46 80; www.villaraino.it in Italian; Contrada Rainò; s/d €45/70; P 🍴) is a wonderful brick-built manor house in a

A REGION BLIGHTED

By the end of the 19th century Sicily was officially the chief area of emigration in the world, with nearly 1.5 million Sicilians trying their luck elsewhere. Although it was an islandwide problem, the effect of the depopulation was greatest in the western interior. Novelist Leonardo Sciascia captured the huge emigration with his stories *The Long Crossing* and *The Test*. You can find them, with other great stories about Sicily, in his collection *The Wine Dark Sea*.

It is hardly surprising that Sciascia was able to capture the Sicilian longing for a better life so vividly. He grew up in Racalmuto, and his own grandfather worked in the sulphur mines that once dominated the countryside of Caltanissetta. By 1900 Italy had a world monopoly on the trade, but life was not so rosy for the 16,000 miners working in 300 mines. At the age of nine, Sciascia's grandfather went to work down the mine – children were used as they were the only ones small enough to crawl through the suffocating galleries at a depth of 60m. Naked, maltreated, clawing the sulphur out of the pits with their bare hands – it must have been a hellish existence, and many only saw the light of day once a week. The grandfather of Sicily's greatest novelist taught himself to read and write in the evenings, enabling his son (Sciascia's father) to become a mine clerk.

By the end of the 19th century American sulphur was beginning to dominate the markets and the consequent collapse of the Sicilian industry started the huge exodus of rural poor.

gorgeous rural setting. The interior is cosy and intimate, with rugs and roaring fires, and all the rooms are individually styled with antiques and family knick-knacks. The restaurant is famous and it attracts diners from all around.

To get to Gangi by car, take the SS120 from Nicosia (19km) or from the Tyrrhenian Coast. Sais Autolinee has a bus connecting Gangi with Enna (via Sperlinga and Calascibetta; €7.90, two hours, one daily Monday to Saturday).

SOUTH OF ENNA

South of Enna the landscape alters from severe mountain scenery to gentler cultivated fields dotted with busy market towns. Piazza Armerina and Caltagirone are typically provincial, and both have an attractive historic centre and a bustling atmosphere that's independent of tourism. The remains of the Greek city of Morgantina, east of Aidone, are considerable and worth more than the trickle of visitors they receive. The real highlight, however, is just outside Piazza Armerina at Casale, the site of one of the most extraordinary finds from antiquity: a sumptuous Roman villa with the largest and best-preserved collection of mosaic works of art in the world.

PIAZZA ARMERINA
pop 20,900 / elev 697m

Set amid some of the most fertile territory on the island, this town (simply called Piazza until the 18th century) takes its name from the Colle Armerino, one of the three hills on which it is built. It is actually two towns in one: the original Piazza was founded by the Saracens in the 10th century on the slope of the Colle Armerino, while a 15th-century expansion to the southeast was redefined by an urban grid established in the 17th century.

You can easily spend a day or two wandering around its labyrinthine streets and seeing the extraordinary Roman villa. With the addition of a couple of nice hotels and restaurants, Piazza Armerina becomes an unexpected treat.

Orientation & Information

The small **tourist office** (☎ 0935 68 02 01; Via Cavour 15; ◷ 8.30am-12.30pm & 3-7pm Mon-Fri) is in the town centre just off the central Piazza Garibaldi. Members of staff speak only Italian. There

is a helpful **information point** (☎ 0935 68 70 27; www.guardalasicilia.it in Italian; Via Umberto 1; ◷ 9am-7pm) with English-speaking staff, who can give you free town guides and maps of the Roman Villa (maps are often unavailable at the site itself). If you continue up Via Cavour you will reach the cathedral, which sits dramatically right at the top of the hill.

The main road into town is Via Garibaldi, and a one-way system takes you out along Via Roma. The main shopping street is Via G Mazzini, where you will find internet access at **S@binet** (☎ 0935 68 73 85; Via G Mazzini 35; per hr €6; ◷ 4-8pm Mon, 9.30am-1pm & 4-8pm Tue-Sat).

The **post office** (Piazza Falcone e Borsellino; ◷ 8am-6.30pm Mon-Fri, 8am-12.30pm Sat) is on Piazza Falcone e Borsellino.

Sights

Piazza Armerina is an elegant town although many of its palazzi are quite rugged-looking. Its fate is to be upstaged by the Roman villa 5km to the south, but take your time and spend a day or two at the town's lovely historic centre.

You can spot the dramatically sited dome of the huge **cathedral** from a few kilometres away. It rises majestically from the hilltop and the terraced houses skirt its base in descending tiers. Make your way up here to enjoy the belvedere. The façade dates from 1719 and the dome was added in 1768. The airy blue-and-white interior contains an altar, behind which is a copy of a Byzantine painting, *Madonna delle Vittorie* (Virgin of the Victories), the original of which was supposedly presented to Count Roger I by Pope Nicholas II. Opposite the cathedral is the baronial **Palazzo Trigona**, and a **statue of Baron Marco Trigona** – who financed the cathedral's construction – stands in the square.

Off Piazza Duomo is **Via Monte**, the arterial road of the 13th-century city, with its warren of tiny alleys fanning out like the ribs of a fish bone. This is the town's most picturesque quarter. Alternatively, take Via Floresta, beside Palazzo Trigona, to arrive at the ruins of the 14th-century **Castello Aragonese**.

From the castle, Via Vittorio Emanuele leads you down to the heart of the town, where Piazza Garibaldi is overlooked by the elegant **Palazzo di Città** (Town Hall; ◷ closed to the public) and the **Chiesa di San Rocco** (known as the Fundrò); the latter has an impressive doorway carved out of tufa.

PIAZZA ARMERINA

INFORMATION	
Information Point	1 B2
Post Office	2 C2
S@binet	3 B2
Tourist Office	4 B2

SIGHTS & ACTIVITIES	
Castello Aragonese	5 B3
Cathedral	6 B2
Chiesa di San Rocco	7 B2
Palazzo di Città	8 B2
Palazzo Trigona	9 B2
Statue of Baron Marco Trigona	10 B2

SLEEPING	
Hotel Suite D'Autore	11 A2
Ostello del Borgo	12 C2

EATING	
Da Totò	13 B2
Del Teatro	14 C2
Garibaldi 62	15 C2
La Tavernetta	16 B2

DRINKING	
Club La Belle Aurore	17 B3

Festivals & Events

Held on 13 and 14 August, **Palio dei Normanni** is a medieval pageant celebrating Count Roger's capture of the town from the Moors in 1087. There are parades and other festivities, as well as a joust. See the tourist office (p249) for details.

Sleeping

Piazza Armerina has limited accommodation on offer.

Ostello del Borgo (☎ /fax 0935 68 70 19; www .ostellodelborgo.it; Largo San Giovanni 6; dm/s/d €17/45/60; 🖳) This restored convent is a great budget option if you don't mind the crucifixes above your head and the bare, austere interior. The staff are friendly and speak

English, and there's internet access (€3 per hour) and bicycle rental. It is right in the historic centre.

Azienda Agriturista Savoca (☎ 0935 68 30 78; www.agrisavoca.com; Contrade da Polleri; r per person €30-40; P 🖳) This is a good rural retreat, located about 3km from Piazza Armerina on the road to Mirabella.

Azienda Agrituristica Gigliotto (☎ 0933 97 08 98; www.gigliotto.com; Contrada Gigliotto, SS117; s €70-80, d €80-100; P 🖳) An ancient *masseria* (manor farm) dating back to the 14th century, Gigliotto is set in rolling countryside 9km south of Piazza Armerina. It is a fantastic rural retreat where you can learn how to make ricotta, help pick grapes, go horse riding or swim in the farm's lake. Everything is organic.

A ROOM WITH A VIEW *Vesna Maric*

It's not often that you can go into a hotel and walk out with a bed, chair, mirror or lamp without being chased by security. And it's even less common that you'll be encouraged by the owner to do so. OK, I've fibbed a little: Ettore Messina, the owner of Piazza Armerina's extraordinary hotel-cum-gallery Suite D'Autore, won't be happy if you simply walk out with his furniture – you do have to pay for it – but it is true that you can buy every single thing you see in the hotel. 'Where did this idea come from?' I asked Ettore.

'I befriended a couple of teachers at the University of Art and Design in Palermo, and we had this idea to start a competition for the design students to come up with innovative bits of furniture for the hotel. We'd wanted to sell the pieces and make the competition work both for the students and for us. Soon after, we had 100 people working on the art for the hotel. There were Italian and international artists and students, and people who'd approach me wanting to exhibit and sell their work here.'

And indeed, as you walk into the hotel, you're already coveting the bicycle-seat bar stool or the nutty lampshade that looks like a flock of birds flying off into the sun. But where does he keep getting this great art from? 'I find the art and the artists as I travel. I was on holiday in Belarus, and I found these amazing artists there. I invited them all to the hotel and 40 of them came to Piazza Armerina on a bus from Belarus to produce and exhibit their work here. It was amazing. There are artists approaching me almost every day. It's something new for our town, and the locals seem to like it.'

He shows me around the seven rooms, flicking all the switches on and off, letting me sit on the champagne cork stool, demonstrating the sliding walnut cupboard that glides across the wall and cleverly hides blankets. Each room has *Nessun Dorma* (No-One Shall Sleep) etched across the mirror. Is this some sort of homage to Puccini or Pavarotti? 'No, no,' Ettore laughs. 'It's a message to our guests that this isn't the place to sleep, but to enjoy the space. We don't mean it literally, of course. The guests should sleep very well indeed.'

our pick Suite D'Autore (☎ 0935 68 70 27; www .suitedautore.com; Via Monte 1; d €100-140; 🎝) Suite D'Autore is a playful, beautiful and original hotel that doubles as a gallery, meaning that everything you use, lie or sit on is produced by artists and can be bought. Opened in July 2007, it's a fantastic place to stay, especially if you like to spend time in your room. Each of the seven rooms is themed after a period in design, so Fluidità features the famous Bocca (Mouth) sofa and a snazzy round bed, while Stravaganza has pop art and futuristic elements, and so on. The welcoming owner (see A Room with a View, above) is bound to pass on his passion for the project.

Eating & Drinking

Da Totò (☎ 0935 68 01 53; Via G Mazzini 27; meals €20; 🎝 closed Mon) A popular and down-to-earth trattoria (informal restaurant) with traditional and uncomplicated pasta dishes, risottos and meat mains. It's a good place for a simple lunch or dinner with a bit of local wine.

Del Teatro (☎ 0935 8 56 62; Via Teatro 1; meals €20-25; 🎝 closed Mon) Tucked down the side of the local theatre is this good trattoria, which serves excellent pizzas and good pasta dishes; try the *pappardelle alla Norma* (pasta with tomatoes, aubergines and salted ricotta). Tables are set outside in summer.

La Tavernetta (Via Cavour 14; meals €20-25; 🎝 closed Sun) On the way up to the cathedral, this unpretentious, popular local trattoria is much loved for its simple, good-quality food. Try a plate of delicious pasta with tomatoes, followed by a piece of meat (usually lamb or veal). A carafe of local red is a great addition.

La Ruota (☎ 0935 68 05 42; Contrada Paratore Casale; meals €30; 🎝 12.30-3pm) About 1km from the Roman villa is this exceptional restaurant, renowned throughout central Sicily for its hearty rural fare. The house speciality is the *coniglio all stemperata* (rabbit stewed with tomatoes, olives and capers).

Garibaldi 62 (☎ 0935 68 85 37; Via Garibaldi 62; meals €30-35; 🎝 closed Sun evening & Mon) This is a new restaurant that's currently the hottest spot on Piazza Armerina's restaurant map. The interior is elegant, with a relaxed up-market atmosphere, and the terrace, dotted with palms and shielded by white canopies, is lovely. The kitchen has a modern take on traditional seasonal cuisine and the wine list is patriotic, with Sicilian wines ruling the roost.

Club La Belle Aurore (☎ 0935 68 63 33; Piazza Castello 5) If you're looking for a good bar head up to the castle, where you will find this funky place. Behind its somewhat dilapidated exterior is a stylish bar with an internal patio.

Getting There & Away

SAIS buses connect Piazza Armerina with Enna (€2.75, 45 minutes, eight daily Monday to Saturday, two Sunday); bear in mind that some of these buses arrive in Enna Bassa, not the historic centre. There is also an AST bus to Syracuse (€7.75, two hours, one daily) and frequent services to Catania (€19.30, 1½ hours, nine daily Monday to Saturday).

AROUND PIAZZA ARMERINA
Villa Romana del Casale

The extraordinary Unesco World Heritage–listed **Villa Romana del Casale** (☎ 0935 68 00 36; www .villaromanadelcasale.it; adult/concession €6/3; ⏰ 8am-7pm, ticket office shuts at 6pm) is easily the most important Roman site in Sicily. It was thought to be the property of Maximian (Maximianus Herculeus), coemperor during the reign of Diocletian (AD 286–305) – hence its other name, the Villa Imperiale. Although other surviving villas testify to the magnificent lifestyles enjoyed by wealthy Romans – for example, Hadrian's villa at Tivoli and Diocletian's getaway retreat in Split, Croatia –the Casale country residence stands out for its sheer size coupled with the breathtaking extent (3535 sq metres) of its polychrome floor mosaics.

Given the early date of the mosaics, what impresses scholars most is their naturalism, range and fluidity – they cover every aspect of provincial Roman life. Erotic, playful and full of vitality, the scenes are very human; they lack the frosty symbolism of Byzantine mosaic work and, consequently, the detail is striking. A leopard pounces on the back of a deer and blood flows from a deep gash, silly putti (cherubs or cupids) smirk and children play, while ladies lounge in seductive poses. You could spend hours here spotting all the different and amusing scenes.

HISTORY

The villa is made up of four connected groups of buildings, which date from the early 4th century and were built on the site of a more modest 2nd-century home (possibly a hunting lodge). Scholars believe that the buildings were maintained until about the year 1000, after which they were abandoned to local squatters and destroyed by the Norman king William the Bad in 1160.

In the 12th century the entire area was covered by a landslide that left the villa under 10m of mud for some 700 years. From 1761 onwards, intermittent attempts were made at excavation, but it wasn't until the 1950s that serious work began revealing the main structure and the mosaics.

The work continues today and large parts of the estate – including the extensive slave quarters and outbuildings – remain covered. The fact that the mosaics have been underground for so long has largely proven to be a blessing in disguise; in 1991 they were badly damaged by a flood, which suggests that had they not been covered they would hardly have survived nearly 2000 years of inclement weather and petty vandalism.

However, the perspex roof that now covers the mosaics creates a sweltering greenhouse effect in summer, with temperatures reaching nearly 40°C and humidity at 80%. Unesco is so concerned that it has now deemed the mosaics 'at risk'.

INFORMATION

The villa is located in a wooded valley 5km southwest of Piazza Armerina. There is an official car park at the top of the road that descends to the villa; it costs €1 and a guardian is on duty. It is about a five-minute walk down to the ticket office, which enters the site directly. Near the entrance there is a café with toilets.

Unfortunately, the villa is besieged by hordes of tourists in the summer – some 2000 per day are deposited by bus tours. This can make the experience very frustrating as the raised walkways are narrow. Get here early if you want to avoid the tour groups (they start arriving at 9.30am); another good time is the lunch hour between 1pm and 2pm. There is no wheelchair access to the site.

There is an explanatory plan of the site, which is sometimes available at the ticket office. Otherwise you can get hold of a copy at

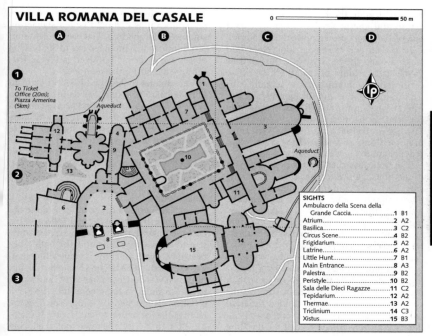

VILLA ROMANA DEL CASALE

0 ─────────── 50 m

SIGHTS		
Ambulacro della Scena della		
Grande Caccia	.1	B1
Atrium	.2	A2
Basilica	.3	C2
Circus Scene	.4	B2
Frigidarium	.5	A2
Latrine	.6	A2
Little Hunt	.7	B1
Main Entrance	.8	A3
Palestra	.9	B2
Peristyle	.10	B2
Sala delle Dieci Ragazze	.11	C2
Tepidarium	.12	A2
Thermae	.13	A2
Triclinium	.14	C3
Xistus	.15	B3

the tourist office in Piazza Armerina (p249) or at one of the many souvenir stalls that line the road down.

The site's raised walkways carry visitors through the house's many rooms in a particular sequence. The description below follows the order of that sequence.

SIGHTS

The **main entrance** leads through the remnants of a triumphal arch into an elegant **atrium** (forecourt). To the west are the substantial **thermae** (baths), all-important in a Roman house. They incorporate a **tepidarium** (warm room), where you can now see the exposed brickwork and vents that allowed hot steam into the room, and a **frigidarium** (cold room), where the radiating apses contained cold plunge pools. The small **latrine** is a good indication of the house's elegance – it is adorned with a brick drain, a marble washbasin and rich mosaics.

As you walk through the villa proper, the western side of the massive **peristyle** is lined with amusing animal heads. This was the central courtyard, where guests would have been received before being taken through to the **basilica** (throne room), which you can view through a window. As you walk along the west side of the peristyle you can look down into the **palaestra** (gymnasium), which has a splendid mosaic depicting a **circus scene** from the Circus Maximus in Rome (the room is also known as the Salone del Circo or Circus Room). Of the rooms on the northern side of the peristyle, the most interesting is the second-last one called the **Little Hunt**, depicting a hunting scene in exquisite detail. But this is merely an appetiser for what follows.

A small staircase brings you to the eastern side of the peristyle and the **Ambulacro della Scena della Grande Caccia** (Ambulacrum of the Great Hunting Scene), a long corridor (64m) depicting the hunt and capture of the Romans' favourite gaming animals – tigers, leopards, elephants, antelopes, ostriches and a rhino – animals they eventually hunted to extinction in North Africa. The first figure is resplendent in a Byzantine cape and is flanked by two soldiers, most likely Maximian himself and two members of his personal legion, the Herculiani. The detail, action and energy of the mosaic makes it one of the finest pieces of work ever found.

At the far end of the corridor, steps lead south around the peristyle and the **Sala delle Dieci Ragazze** (Room of the 10 Girls), home of the famous bikini girls – actually athletes pumping iron and lifting tiny bell jars. Interestingly, in the far left-hand corner you can see that the mosaic covers a second mosaic floor; Maximian wanted the very latest in home décor and ordered the entire place redone, an extraordinary extravagance.

The walkways then lead through the rest of the house. On the other side of the long corridor is a series of apartments, whose floor illustrations reproduce scenes from Homer, as well as mythical subjects such as Arion playing the lyre on a dolphin's back, and Cupid and Faunus wrestling. Of particular interest is the **triclinium** (banquet hall), with a splendid depiction of the labours of Hercules, where the tortured monsters are ensnared by a smirking Odysseus. It is far larger in scale than the previous rooms and reminiscent of the epic work of Michelangelo. To view the **xistus** (elliptical courtyard), which you can see from the triclinium, you have to exit the building and walk around the apse. As it is uncovered, the mosaic work here is not well preserved.

GETTING THERE & AWAY
Autolinee Urbane runs buses from Piazza Armerina to the villa in the summer only (€0.70, 30 minutes, six daily 1 May to 30 September). Buses depart from Piazza on the hour (9am to 11am and 3pm to 5pm), and return on the half-hour (9.30am to 11.30am and 3.30pm to 5.30pm).

Outside summer you will have to walk the signposted 5km; it's downhill, not too strenuous and takes about an hour. The walk back is only steep in the last part. Taxis (parked all over town) will take you there, wait for an hour and drive you back to Piazza Armerina for about €20 – not bad value if you're in a group.

If you have your own car, head south along the SS117.

Aidone
If you're in Aidone, it's worth popping into the **Museo Archeologico** (☎ 0935 8 73 07; Convento dei Cappuccini; admission €3; ☾ 8am-1hr before sunset). This collection houses finds from the excavations

at Morgantina but it's not nearly as large or significant as it should be – a staggering amount of the good stuff has been stolen from Morgantina and smuggled out of Sicily. One object worth seeing, however, is a large 3rd-century-BC bust of Persephone.

You can get to Aidone by SAIS bus from Enna (€3.25, 50 minutes, two daily Monday to Friday). AST buses run from Piazza Armerina to Aidone (€0.70, 15 minutes, 10 daily Monday to Friday, two Saturday and Sunday). There is no central taxi service in Aidone, just individual taxi drivers. You could, however, ask the **local tourist office** (☎ 0935 8 65 57; Via Mazzini 1) to help you.

Morgantina
About 4km beyond the town of Aidone are the noteworthy **remains** (☎ 0935 8 79 55; admission €3; ☾ 8am-6.30pm) of this sizable Greek colony, spread across two hills and the valley between. Morgeti, an early Sicilian settlement, was founded in 850 BC on Cittadella hill, but this town was destroyed in 459 BC and a new town was built on the second hill, the Serra Orlando. It reached its apogee during the reign of the Syracusan tyrant Hieron II (269–215 BC). In 211 BC the town took the losing Carthaginian side during the Second Punic War and was delivered by the Romans into the unmerciful hands of a Spanish mercenary called Moericus, who promptly stripped it of its wealth. By the reign of Emperor Augustus, it had lost all importance and was eventually abandoned. In 1955 archaeologists identified the site and began its excavation, which continues to this day.

The centre of the town is the **agora** (marketplace), spread over two levels. A trapezoidal stairway linking the two was also used as seating during public meetings. The upper level had a **market**; you can still see the walls that divided one shop from the next. The lower level was the site of the **theatre**, which has been preserved in excellent condition.

To the northeast are the **residential quarters** of the city, holding what must have been houses for the town's wealthier class, as testified by the ornate wall decorations and handsome mosaics in the inner rooms. Another residential quarter has been found behind the theatre and its considerable ruins are well worth checking out.

Morgantina is an easy detour if you have your own transport but a difficult proposition if you don't. There is no way of getting there by public transport; you can get an SAIS bus from Enna to Aidone (€3.25, 50 minutes, two daily Monday to Friday) and either take a taxi or walk 3km along the SS288.

CALTAGIRONE
pop 37,500 / elev 608m

The elegant baroque town of Caltagirone is renowned throughout Sicily for its ceramics, which have been produced here for more than 1000 years thanks to the high-quality clay found in the area. Although the town's earliest settlers worked with terracotta, the arrival of the Arabs in the 10th century saw the beginnings of a lucrative ceramics industry. Not only did the Arabs give the town its name (from the Arabic *kalat* and *gerun,* meaning 'castle' and 'cave'), but they introduced the wide array of glazed polychromatic colours, particularly yellow and blue, that have distinguished local ceramics ever since.

The town was destroyed in the earthquake of 1693 and rebuilt in the baroque style that now characterises the whole of the southeast. In Caltagirone this is given its own unique twist with the liberal use of majolica tiles; the Ponte San Francesco is even adorned with ceramic flowers.

The ceramics industry might have died out in the early 20th century if it weren't for the efforts of Luigi Sturzo (who later moved into politics and campaigned actively for land reforms); he founded the prestigious School of Ceramics, and today tourism ensures that ceramics are once again big business in the town.

Orientation

Caltagirone is divided into an upper and lower town. All buses stop on Piazza Municipio in the upper town, where most of the town's sights are located. AST buses depart from in front of the Metropol Cinema on Viale Principe Umberto in the lower town, but stop at Piazza Municipio on the way. The train station is located in the lower town, at the western end of Viale Principe Umberto, along with Caltagirone's accommodation options. If you are travelling by bus and just planning a quick visit, you can go right up to Piazza Municipio, but if you plan on staying here overnight you should get off in the lower town.

Information

The **Tourist Office** (☎ 0933 3 41 91; www.comune .caltagirone.ct.it; Via Duomo 7; ☼ 9am-1pm & 4-7pm Mon-Fri, 9am-1pm Sat) is conveniently located just off Piazza Duomo. It has an excellent website and helpful staff who hand out a free map of the town.

Sights

Caltagirone's upper town is a bustling centre of activity with some gorgeous baroque buildings and churches. The most evocative sight is a set of steps, **Scalinata di Santa Maria del Monte**, which rises up from Piazza Municipio to the **Chiesa di Santa Maria del Monte**, at the top of the town. Each of the 142 steps is decorated with hand-painted ceramics, and no two are the same. On either side of the steps are rows of ceramic workshops where you can watch local artisans ply their handiwork. Some shops also make the traditional terracotta *presepi* (crib figurines), which are formally exhibited between 6 December and Christmas. The steps are also the focus of the Feast of St James (Festa di San Giacomo), the town's patron saint (see below).

In the south of the upper town is the **Museo Regionale della Ceramica** (Regional Ceramics Museum; ☎ 0933 5 84 18; Via Roma; admission €6; ☼ 9am-6.30pm), where you can trace the history of ceramics from prehistoric times to the present day.

Festivals & Events

During the **Festa di San Giacamo**, held on 24 and 25 July, the Scalinata di Santa Maria del Monte is lit up by more than 4000 oil lamps while a religious procession makes its way through town from Chiesa di Santa Maria del Monte.

Sleeping

There are some sweet B&Bs in Caltagirone's old town. Prices are the same year-round.

Gualtiero (☎ 0933 3 42 22; Piazza San Francesco d'Assisi 20; d €55) A small, six-room place with a slightly dingy feel and low beds. Its main bonus is the fabulously picturesque views of the Chiesa dell'Immacolata from its balconies.

Il Piccolo Attico (☎ 0933 2 15 88; Via Infermeria 82; 2-4 person apt €60) An excellent option for two or four people, this little attic apartment is homy, cosy and superclean, with fantastic views over Caltagirone. The elderly couple who run the place are friendly enough, and Mamma makes the breakfast in the morning.

TESTA DI MORO

You'll see the *testa di Moro* (Moor's head) in almost any Sicilian institution, shop, hotel or restaurant, usually with a plant sticking out of it. The man's head – usually with African features, a moustache, and wearing a turban – is often coupled up with a woman's head, and the woman sports grapes, oranges and other Mediterranean fruit on her head. The roots of this design are a little less lustrous, however. It symbolises the beheadings of the ruling Arabs by the invading Inquisitionist Spaniards, who saw it as their 'holy duty' to rid Europe of anything non-Christian. The heads were hung around Sicilian towns as warnings to the Arabs and represented signs of victory for the Christians. They somehow came to be replicated in clay, supporting Sicily's flowerpots along the way.

La Pilozza Infiorata (☎ 0933 2 21 62; www.lapilozzainfiorata.com; Via SS Salvatore 97; s/d €70/90; 🕮) This airy, bright B&B has welcoming rooms decorated in white and sky blue, and is scattered with bits of tasteful antique furniture, so that you feel like you're walking into a French countryside maison. Breakfast is served on the sweet terrace in the warmer months. A great, central location.

Grand Hotel Villa San Mauro (☎ 0933 2 65 00; www.framon-hotels.com; Via Porto Salvo 14; d/ste from €98/174; 🅿 🕮 🛋) One of the luxury Framon chain, the Villa San Mauro is extremely comfortable and has a wonderful panoramic terrace with views over the town. You'll find it at the southern end of town, near Chiesa di Santa Maria di Gesù.

Eating

Caltagirone's restaurants may not be two a penny, but what's there is good.

La Piazzetta (☎ 0933 2 41 78; Via Vespri 20; meals €20; 🕮 closed mid-Aug–mid-Sep) This small restaurant specialises in strictly regional cuisine, with fantastic dishes such as fresh pasta with pistachio pesto for *primo* (first course), and a fillet with asparagus for mains. A real treat.

Non Solo Vino (☎ 0933 3 10 68; Via Vittorio Emanuele 1; mains €20; 🕮 closed Mon) Though it looks pretty uninviting from the outside, this place is a good working-man's diner where you can get wine *and* a decent mixed grill. It's the perfect cure for a hard day's ceramic shopping.

La Scala (☎ 0933 5 77 81; Scalinata Santa Maria del Monte; meals €25; 🕮 closed Sun) Situated in Caltagirone's ceramic heart, on the long flight of steps leading to the Chiesa di Santa Maria del Monte, this is an atmospheric place to enjoy fresh pasta and local wines.

Il Palazzo dei Marchesi di Santa Barbara (☎ 0933 2 24 06; www.imarchesidisantabarbara.it; Via San Bonaventura 22; meals €25-30) Sitting inside a grand palazzo, this is Caltagirone's poshest restaurant. The lighting is a little unforgiving, but the food is good, and the service attentive and friendly. Try the *caponata* (a combination of tomatoes, aubergines, olives and anchovies) for starters, and follow it up with a creamy aubergine risotto. A fillet with seasonal mushrooms is a delicious main. The desserts are a feast of *cannoli* (pastry tubes stuffed with sweet ricotta) and *semifreddi* (literally 'semifrozen'; a cold, creamy dessert).

Shopping

There are about 120 ceramics shops located all over town. The highest concentration is found around the Scalinata di Santa Maria del Monte and Piazza Umberto I. See p162 for more information on Caltagirone's ceramics.

Le Maioliche (☎ 0933 5 31 39; www.varsallona.it; Discesa Collegio 1) This reliably creative and innovative local ceramicist produces some interesting designs as well as the more traditional *testa di Moro* (Moor's head; see above).

Getting There & Away

Caltagirone is served by SAIS Autolinee buses from Enna (€4.40, 1½ hours, three daily Monday to Saturday, one Sunday) and Palermo (€9.70, three hours, two daily Monday to Saturday, one Sunday). There's an AST bus from Syracuse (€4.90, three hours, one daily Monday to Friday) and buses from Piazza Armerina (€2.75, one hour, eight daily Monday to Saturday, one Sunday).

The town is also served by trains from Gela (€3.05, 40 minutes, nine daily) and Catania (€5.05, 1¾ hours, 10 daily).

THE WESTERN INTERIOR

You'll get no clearer sense of the effect of poverty in Sicily than when travelling through the western interior. Unlike other parts of the island, this area has never known prosperity and has been largely ignored by Sicily's conquerors and city builders. For centuries the bleached landscapes were divided into large *latifondi* (landed estates), and today it is still an area of rolling hills dotted with small towns. It receives fewer visitors than any other spot on the island and, although the tourist authorities have done their optimistic best to promote the area for its wild and natural beauty, it is difficult to imagine anything changing for a long time.

CALTANISSETTA

pop 60,900 / elev 568m

A big and busy town, Caltanissetta is the provincial capital of the western interior, but it has been a victim of the misfortune and Mafia meddling that has tainted this whole region of Sicily.

It was originally a Saracen settlement, and was captured and subsequently reorganised by the Normans in 1086. The city was badly damaged in the war and now contains little of historical or cultural interest. Today it is a market town grown prosperous on sulphur mining; when the industry collapsed in the 1970s, potassium and magnesium mining took its place. Either way there is nothing picturesque about Caltanissetta. Still, it is the transport hub of the region and you will undoubtedly pass through it.

Orientation

Caltanissetta's train station is west of town on Piazza Roma. The bus station is close by, around the corner on Via Colaianni.

Information

Provincial Tourist Office (☎ 0934 53 04 11; Corso Vittorio Emanuele II 109; ☒ 10am-noon Mon-Fri, 10am-noon & 4-6pm Wed) Located just off Piazza Garibaldi, this office is more involved with regional statistics.

Tourist Office (☎ 0934 2 10 89; Viale Conte Testasecca 20; ☒ 9am-1pm Mon-Fri, 9am-1pm & 4-6pm Wed) The better of the two offices. It is about 300m north of the train station.

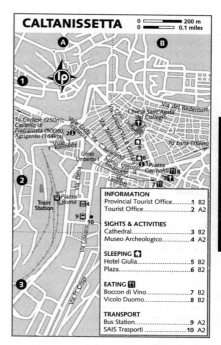

Sights

The centre of Caltanissetta is Piazza Garibaldi, a scruffy square singularly lacking any life. It's dominated by the huge **cathedral** on one side and the Town Hall on the other. The cathedral has a late-Renaissance appearance that breaks the baroque mould, but substantial alterations made in the 19th century have ruined the overall effect. Inside (if you find the church open) are frescoes by Guglielmo Borremans.

The most interesting sight in town is the **Museo Archeologico** (☎ 0934 2 59 36; Via Colaianni 3; adult/concession €2.50/1.50; ☒ 9am-1pm & 3.30-7pm, closed last Mon of month), about 100m east of the train station. The displays are mostly from prehistoric times and include finds from digs conducted in the 1950s, including vases, tools and rare terracotta figurines from the Bronze Age, and early Sicilian ceramics. Also of interest are finds from a number of necropolises spread about Caltanissetta's hinterland. One such necropolis was known by the Arabs as Gebel Habib, meaning 'Mountain of Death'. The museum was closed at the time of research.

To the west of town, but within easy walking distance of Piazza Garibaldi, are the ruins of the **Castello di Pietrarossa**, precariously balanced on a rocky outcrop. There isn't much left of the castle but the walk and the views from the rock are pleasant enough.

Sleeping & Eating

Hotel Giulia (☎ 0934 54 29 27; www.hotelgiulia.it in Italian; Corso Umberto I 85; s/d €42/60; P) This small hotel is the best option in town. Centrally located with friendly staff and plain but comfortable rooms, it represents good value. It also has a good restaurant, Ristorante Archetto, around the corner.

Plaza (☎ /fax 0934 58 38 77; Via B Gaetani 5; s/d €46/65; P ⚄) A modern hotel with large, bald rooms. Still, it's close to the centre of town and the train and bus stations, and the rooms are comfortable enough.

Boccon di Vino (☎ 0934 58 27 64; Corso Umberto I 146; meals €20; ⚇ closed Sun) This new little wine bar–cum–trattoria has a reasonably priced menu that changes daily. There's good antipasto and mixed grill, or you could just opt for a glass of wine and some nibbles.

Cortese (☎ 0934 59 16 86; Viale Sicilia 158; meals €25; ⚇ closed Mon) Cortese is another good restaurant serving local specialities such as *pasta con frutti di mare e funghi* (pasta with seafood and mushrooms).

Vicolo Duomo (☎ 0934 58 23 31; Piazza Garibaldi 3; meals €30; ⚇ closed Sun & lunch Mon) An extraordinarily good restaurant for Caltanissetta, way above the standard of anything else in town. Tucked in a corner of Piazza Garibaldi and decorated along stylish modern lines, it is full of contented diners lingering over their delicious food until well after 4pm. It has the Slow Food Movement badge of approval.

Getting There & Away

The town is well served by buses and trains from all corners of the island. **SAIS Trasporti** (☎ 0934 56 40 72; Via Colaianni) serves Agrigento (€7.80, 1¼ hours, 10 daily Monday to Saturday) and Catania (€7.80, 1½ hours, nine daily Monday to Saturday). It has its own

ticket office, opposite the bus station. Buses depart from the station. SAIS Autolinee serves Enna (€3.30, one hour, three daily Monday to Saturday); purchase your tickets in the café in the bus terminal. Astra has buses to Piazza Armerina (€2.70, one hour, five Monday to Saturday); buy tickets on the bus.

There are also trains to/from Agrigento (€4.25, 1½ hours, 10 daily), and also to/from Enna (€2.65, 40 minutes, seven daily). Note that you are better off getting the bus to Enna, because the length and steepness of the road connecting Enna's train station and town centre can be taxing.

If you plan on travelling into the western province from Caltanissetta, you're better off organising your own transport.

WEST OF CALTANISSETTA

The area west of Caltanissetta is wild and lawless, a Sicilian Timbuktu in terms of its remoteness. Two of Sicily's most powerful dons lived out their lives comfortably here: Don Calógero Vizzini, Sicily's first postwar Mafia mayor, lived in **Villalba**, 35km west, while Don Genco Russo, his successor in the 1950s and '60s, lived down the road in **Mussomeli** (20km south of Villalba). Both men ran their hideously depressed towns like personal fiefdoms, portraying themselves as Robin Hood figures. Vizzini's tombstone even cheekily laments the death of a gentleman.

The imposing 14th-century **Castello Manfredonico**, just to the east of Mussomeli, is a reminder of other feudal oppressors. Set on a rocky crag that rises from the flat fields, it has wonderful views of the valley.

To reach Villalba take the SS122b north from Caltanissetta, turn off onto the SS121 to Santa Caterina Villarmosa, then turn onto the SS121, which will take you directly to Villalba. If you continue along this road for 5km you will reach Vallelunga Pratameno, which borders on the vast and beautiful **Regaleali estate** (www.tascadalmerita.it). This winery is still largely run like a feudal estate by the Tasca family and you can spend a wonderful week here enrolled in Anna Tasca's cookery course (see p52).

Mediterranean Coast

The Mediterranean coast is one of Sicily's most contradictory areas, with stunning natural and archaeological beauty cheek-to-cheek with the ugly face of brutal modern development. The gorgeous Valley of the Temples and Agrigento's sandy beach have Gela's industrial wasteland and Agrigento's cement tower blocks as their backdrop, but travel a little further west and you'll discover the beauty of the Scala dei Turchi – an amazing, glowing-white limestone cliff which curves against the blue of the sky and the sea. The quiet beach at Eraclea Minoa has one of Sicily's better camp sites, while Sciacca celebrates the carnival like no-one else around. The Pelagic Islands of Lampedusa and Linosa offer quiet and isolation (outside of the high season) and some amazing diving. Lampedusa, often caught on film, is also caught in immigration controversy, thanks to its position between Africa and Europe. This area is also the birthplace of some of Sicily's most famous intellectuals, such as Greek philosopher and physiologist Empedocles, writer Luigi Pirandello and novelist Leonardo Sciascia.

The Mediterranean coast has also been in the grip of a mesmerising torpor: its landscape is scattered with skeletons of unfinished housing projects and roads. The mafiosi of the 1980s moved from Palermo forming a new organisation known as *La Stidda* (meaning 'star'), infiltrating southern towns like Agrigento and Gela. Consequently, the whole town council of Gela had to be suspended for 'criminal ties' back in 1992, though its progressive new mayor is improving the town's shady reputation.

MEDITERRANEAN COAST

HIGHLIGHTS

- Have your socks knocked off by the formidable ruins of Agrigento's **Valley of the Temples** (p261)
- Be awestruck by the beauty that is the **Scala dei Turchi** (p268)
- Swim, scuba dive and sunbathe in the dreamy blue waters off **Lampedusa** (p270)
- Soak up the sun and get a full-body mud mask on the beach at **Eraclea Minoa** (p269)
- Dance around at the cacophonous and varicoloured carnival at **Sciacca** (p277)

Sciacca ★ Eraclea Minoa ★ Scala dei Turchi ★ ★ Agrigento

Lampedusa ★

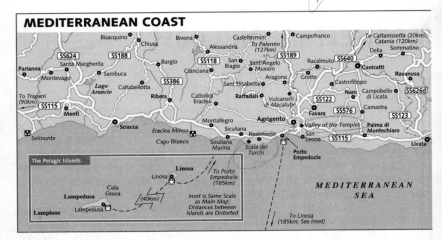

MEDITERRANEAN COAST

AGRIGENTO & AROUND

AGRIGENTO
pop 55,900 / elev 230m

Busy, brutish and beleaguered, Agrigento is Sicily's oldest tourist site (first put on the map by Goethe in the 18th century) thanks to the magnificent Greek ruins, the Valley of the Temples. Unfortunately overshadowed by towering modern apartment blocks, this splendid ancient site loses much of its immediate impact. It is only when you get down among the ruins that you can appreciate their monumentality.

Agrigento itself is obscured by the aesthetic myopia of the 1960s and 1970s, but despite this, this compact medieval town is deserving of more than just a cursory glance. In ancient times the Greek poet Pindar (5th century BC) declared the people of Akragas (Agrigento) 'built for eternity but feasted as if there were no tomorrow'. Nowadays the modern town, with its savvy inhabitants, has more in common with the character rather than the aesthetics of its ancient counterpart. It is one of the most lively and aggressive towns in Sicily and if you are up for Naples you will be able to handle the *furbi* (cunning) Agrigentans whose notorious crime families are reputedly key players in the multibillion-dollar narcotics trade.

History

Established by settlers from Gela and Rhodes in 581 BC, Akragas was conceived as a Greek lookout post to monitor potential Carthaginian invasions. This threat was temporarily eliminated following a resounding victory at the Battle of Himera in 480 BC, after which the building of the Temple of Zeus began with a fresh slew of slave labour. At the time, it was reckoned that Akragas was home to 200,000 citizens. Pindar described the city as 'the most beautiful of those inhabited by mortals'.

The good fortune of Akragas came to an abrupt end in 406 BC, when the old enemy Carthage finally overcame Greek resistance. However, it was reclaimed in 338 BC by the Corinthian general Timoleon, who instituted a liberal and democratic regime. The Romans took the city in 210 BC and renamed it Agrigentum, encouraging the farming (hence the name) and trading sectors. They thus laid the foundations for the city's future as an important centre of commerce under the Byzantines.

In the 7th century the bulk of Agrigentum's inhabitants moved up the hill to the site of the present-day city, virtually abandoning the old town. Although experts are still at a loss as to exactly why such a shift occurred, it has been suggested that it was to fend off the island's latest conquerors from North Africa, the Saracens. Despite its best efforts, Agrigento fell to the Saracens at the start of the 9th century.

Agrigento did not change much until the 19th century, when the western half of the city was built. In the 20th century the urban

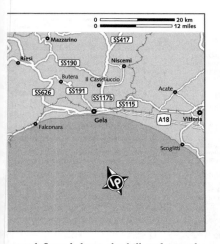

sprawl flowed down the hill and into the valley. The town was heavily bombarded by the Allies in WWII, and the postwar period saw the bulk of the unimaginative rebuilding still visible today. This effort was particularly ruinous for the Valley of the Temples as construction affected the valley's appearance, leading to accusations that Agrigento's cultural and environmental heritage was being destroyed.

Orientation

All public transport arrives at and departs from the centre of town. Intercity buses arrive in Piazza Rosselli, just off the northern side of Piazza Vittorio Emanuele. The train station is about 300m south, on Piazza Marconi. Lying between the two is the green oasis of Piazzale Aldo Moro, situated at the eastern end of Via Atenea, the main street of the medieval town. Frequent city buses run to the Valley of the Temples south of the town (see p268).

Information

There are banks on Piazza Vittorio Emanuele and along the main street, Via Atenea. Outside of banking hours, you can try the exchange office at the post office and another at the train station, although the rates are mediocre.

Ambulance (☎ 0922 40 13 44, 118)

Information booth Piazzale Aldo Moro (Map p262; ☺ 9am-1pm & 3-7pm); Valley of the Temples (Map p263; ☺ 8am-7.30pm summer only) The booth in Piazzale Aldo Moro has more maps and a little more information than the tourist office if pushed, while the booth in the Valley of

Temples has a map of the archaeological park and information on guides.

Internet Train (Map p262; ☎ 0922 40 27 83; www .internettrain.it; Cortile Contarini 7; per hr €6; ☺ 9.30am-9pm Mon-Sat) Excellent internet point with 10 fast, flat-screen computers and all the accessories, with scanners and digital-picture-download facilities.

Main tourist office (Map p262; ☎ 0922 2 04 54; www.agrigento-sicilia.it; Via Cesare Battisti 15; ☺ 8.30am-1.30pm Mon-Fri) Staff have maps and brochures, but are not overly helpful.

Ospedale Civile San Giovanni di Dio (Map p262; ☎ 0922 40 13 44; Via Giovanni XXII)

Police (questura; Map p262; ☎ 0922 59 63 22; Piazzale Aldo Moro 2)

Post office (Map p262; Piazza Vittorio Emanuele; ☺ 8.30am-6.30pm Mon-Fri, 8.30am-12.30pm Sat)

Sights
VALLEY OF THE TEMPLES (VALLE DEI TEMPLI)

One of Sicily's premier attractions, the Valley of the Temples (Map p263) is a Unesco World Heritage–listed complex of temples and old city walls that remain from the ancient city of Akragas. The site is a reason in itself to visit the Mediterranean coast of the island. The five Doric temples actually stand along a ridge, not a valley, designed to be visible from all around and a beacon for homecoming sailors. In varying states of ruin, the temples give a tantalising glimpse of what must truly have been one of the most luxurious cities in Magna Graecia. After visiting the area, Goethe waxed lyrical: 'We shall never in our lives be able to rejoice again, after seeing such a stupendous view in this splendid valley.' The most scenic time is in February and March when the valley is awash with almond blossoms.

Orientation & Information

The **archaeological park** (Map p263; ☎ 0922 49 72 26; adult/concession €6/3, incl archaeological museum €10/5; ☺ 9am-7pm) is divided into eastern and western zones by the main SS118 road (Via dei Panoramica Templi) leading to the temples from town. A very useful website with lots of information on the site and guides is www.lavalledeitempli.it.

By the entrances to the two zones is the car park and **main ticket office** (Piazzale dei Templi) where you can inquire about guided tours (see p265) or pick up an audio guide (€5, English and Italian only). There are also public toilets and a convenient

MEDITERRANEAN COAST

AGRIGENTO

0 — 300 m
0 — 0.2 miles

To Vulcanelli di
Macalúbe (8km);
Aragona (11km);
Sant'Angelo Muxaro

Via Imera

Piazza
Don
Minzoni

Piazza
Bibbirìa

Via Duomo

Via Santa Marta

Via S.
Domenica

Via Matteotti

Via Giuseppe Garibaldi

Piazza
Lena

Via Fodera

Piazza
Pirandello

Piazza
Rosselli

Via Porta di Mare

Via Dante

Piazza
Revanusella

Piazza
San
Francesco

Via San Francesco

Piazza
Vittorio
Emanuele

Via Atenea

Via Saette

Via Madonna
degli Angeli

Via Callicratide

Via Acrone

Via Empedocle

Piazzale
Aldo Moro
Pirandello

Via A Manzoni (Circonvallazione)

Piazza
Marconi

Piazzale
San Calogero

Viale della Vittoria

Train Station

Via Giovanni XXII

Via Petrarca

Via Essèneto

SS118

Viadotto Akragas

See Valley Of The Temples Map (p263)

To Casa Natale
di Pirandello (2km)

To Hotel Kaos (3km);
San Leone (5km)

INFORMATION
Information Booth................1 C3
Internet Train.....................2 C3
Main Tourist Office.............3 C3
Ospedale Civile San Giovanni di
Dio.............................4 D3
Police...............................5 C3
Post Office........................6 D3

SIGHTS & ACTIVITIES
Cathedral..........................7 A2
Chiesa di Santa Maria dei Greci..8 B2
Michele Gallo.....................9 A3
Monastero di Santo Spirito..(see 22)
Museo Civico..................(see 22)

SLEEPING
Antica Foresteria Catalana.....10 B2
Atenea 191........................11 B2
Camere a Sud......................12 C3

Hotel Amici.......................13 C3
Hotel Bella Napoli...............14 B3

EATING
Da Giovanni.......................15 D3
Kalòs..............................16 D3
L'Ambasciata di Sicilia..........17 B3
La Forchetta......................18 C3

DRINKING
Cafe Girasole.....................19 C3
Tempio di Vino....................20 C3

ENTERTAINMENT
Teatro Pirandello................21 B2

SHOPPING
Monastero di Santo Spirito......22 C3

TRANSPORT
Bus Ticket Booth.................23 D3
Intercity Bus Station............24 D2

MEDITERRANEAN COAST

bar/restaurant (Piazzale dei Templi) amid the usual souvenir stands. Fittingly, this rugby-scrum of a piazza used to be the ancient agora. A better entrance is on Via Panoramica near the Temple of Hera where there is also a ticket office.

To get around all the temples you will need a whole day plus another half day to enjoy the Museo Archeologico (see p264). The site is perpetually busy, although the earlier you get there the better. Late evening is also a good time as the temples are bathed in a light of amber hue, which is a magnificent sight from any angle. The site is boiling hot in July and August, so stock up on water and wear a hat and plenty of sunscreen.

The Eastern Zone
The temples that stand unfettered and unenclosed in the eastern zone are the most spectacular of all. The first of these is the **Temple of Hercules** (Tempio di Ercole), immediately inside the entrance and to the right. Its origin is uncertain but it is believed to be the oldest of the lot, dating from the end of 6 BC. Eight of its 38 columns have been raised and you can wander around the remains of the rest.

Moving east past the remains of the ancient walls, the next temple along the path is the **Temple of Concord** (Tempio della Concordia), which is the only one to survive the unforgiving hands of time and history relatively intact. It was built around 430 BC

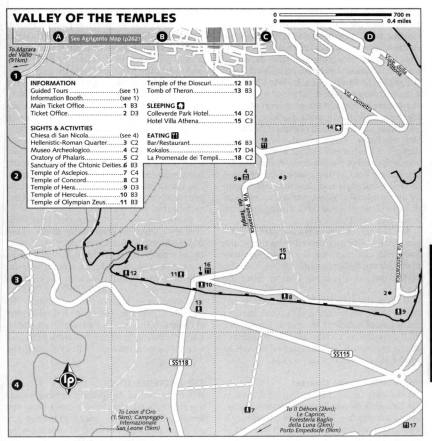

VALLEY OF THE TEMPLES

0 — 700 m
0 — 0.4 miles

See Agrigento Map (p262)

INFORMATION
Guided Tours ....(see 1)
Information Booth....................(see 1)
Main Ticket Office....................**1** B3
Ticket Office............................**2** D3

SIGHTS & ACTIVITIES
Chiesa di San Nicola................(see 4)
Hellenistic-Roman Quarter.......**3** C2
Museo Archeologico.................**4** C2
Oratory of Phalaris...................**5** C2
Sanctuary of the Chtonic Deities.**6** B3
Temple of Asclepios.................**7** C4
Temple of Concord...................**8** C3
Temple of Hera.......................**9** D3
Temple of Hercules...................**10** B3
Temple of Olympian Zeus.......**11** B3

Temple of the Dioscuri.............**12** B3
Tomb of Theron.......................**13** B3

SLEEPING
Colleverde Park Hotel..............**14** D2
Hotel Villa Athena..................**15** C3

EATING
Bar/Restaurant........................**16** B3
Kokalos...................................**17** D4
La Promenade dei Templi.........**18** C2

To Mazara del Vallo (91km)

Viale della Vittoria

Via Demetra

Via Panoramica dei Templi

Via Panoramica

SS118

SS115

To Leon d'Oro (1.5km); Campeggio Internazionale San Leone (5km)

To Il Déhors (2km); Le Caprice; Foresteria Baglio della Luna (2km); Porto Empedocle (9km)

MEDITERRANEAN COAST

and was converted into a Christian basilica in the 6th century; thankfully, the new tenants reinforced the main structure, giving it a better chance of surviving an earthquake. In 1748 the temple was restored to its original form. The architect in charge of the restoration, Tommaso Fazello, gave the temple its name – it is traditionally visited by brides and grooms on their wedding day.

At the eastern end of the ridge, a further 400m on, is the **Temple of Hera** (Tempio di Hera), partially destroyed by an earthquake in the Middle Ages. Just behind the eastern end is a long altar originally used for sacrifices. The traces of red are the result of fire damage, most likely during the Carthaginian invasion of 406 BC.

Across the path from the ruins is a little temple set on a high base. It is known as the **Tomb of Theron** (Tomba di Therone), the Greek tyrant of Agrigento, but in fact the structure dates from around 75 BC, during the Roman occupation, nearly 500 years after the tyrant's death.

The Western Zone

Across Via dei Panoramica Templi is the entrance to the western zone, the main feature of which is the crumbled remains of the **Temple of Olympian Zeus** (Tempio di Zeus Olimpico; 9am-5pm). Covering an area measuring 112m x 56m, with columns 20m high, it would have been the largest Doric temple ever built had its construction not been interrupted by the

Carthaginian sack of Akragas. Ironically, the foundations for the temple had been laid by Carthaginian prisoners captured after the Battle of Himera nearly 100 years previously. The incomplete temple was later destroyed by an earthquake. Lying flat on his back amid the rubble is a telamon, a sculpted figure of a man with arms raised, intended to support the temple's weight. One of several planned for the temple, the figure is 8m long.

Further on is the smaller **Temple of the Dioscuri** (Tempio dei Dioscuri; 🕑 9am-5pm), also known as the Temple of Castor and Pollux. It was built towards the end of the 5th century but was destroyed by the Carthaginians, later restored in Hellenistic style and then destroyed again by an earthquake. What you see today dates from 1832, when it was rebuilt using materials from other temples.

Just behind the temple is a complex of altars and small buildings believed to be part of the Santuario di Demetra e Kore. The **Sanctuary of the Chthonic Deities** (Santuario delle Divine Chtoniche; 🕑 9am-5pm), as it is known, dates from the early 6th century BC.

Back at the crossroads just inside the entrance to the temples, the path south leads to the **Temple of Asclepios** (Tempio di Esculapio), off the second fork to the left. The smallest of all the temples, it is distinguished by having solid walls instead of a colonnade.

Hellenistic-Roman Quarter

To the east of the Museo Archeologico is the **Hellenistic-Roman Quarter** (Quartiere Ellenistico-Romano; admission free; 🕑 8.30am-7pm), featuring a well-preserved street layout which was part of urban Akragas (and later, under the Romans, Agrigentum). The regular grid is made up of *plateiai* (main streets) intersected at right angles by *stenopoi* (secondary streets), all of which were laid out towards the end of the 4th century BC. The Romans didn't alter the layout but added their own embellishments, including mosaic floors and stuccowork. They were also responsible for adding water and heating pipes, and introduced drainage facilities for rainwater and sewage.

MUSEO ARCHEOLOGICO

About halfway up the road from the archaeological park and towards town is the **Museo Archeologico** (Map p263; ☎ 0922 40 15 65; adult/concession €6/3; 🕑 9am-7pm), housing a large collection of well-explained (in Italian and English)

artefacts from the excavated site. Room *(sala)* 1 contains an archaeological plan of ancient Akragas – which is helpful if you want a sense of the scale of the old city. Room 3 features a rich collection of ceramics in both black and red dating from the 6th to the 3rd centuries BC. Of particular note is the *krater*, a red ceramic chalice from 490 BC. Room 6 has a telamon standing 7.75m tall (a definite highlight) and the heads of three others, plus an excellent small-scale reconstruction of their temple, giving the visitor a sense of how extraordinary this place would have been. Room 9 features a fine *ephebus* (a statue of a young boy), sculpted in 470 BC from white marble. The last rooms hold artefacts from around the province – be sure to check out the wonderful ceramic bowls and bronze helmets.

In the grounds of the museum is the 13th-century Cistercian **Chiesa di San Nicola**, (Map p263) which has a fine Gothic doorway. Inside, in the second chapel on the right, you'll find a Roman sarcophagus, which bears a wonderful relief of the myth of Phaedra. On the church's esplanade stands an ancient Odeon called the Ekklesiasterion, built in the 3rd century BC for public meetings. Alongside it is the **Oratory of Phalaris** (Oratorio di Falaride; Map p263), a temple dating from the 1st century BC that was converted into an oratory during the Middle Ages.

THE MEDIEVAL TOWN

Roaming around Agrigento's narrow, winding streets is relaxing after a day among the temples. On Via Santo Spirito, at the top of a set of winding steps north off Via Atenea, is the Cistercian **Monastero di Santo Spirito** (Monastery of the Holy Spirit; Map p262), founded around 1290. A handsome Gothic portal leads inside, where you can see some fine stuccowork by Giacomo Serpotta plus a statue of the *Madonna incoronata* (Virgin Enthroned) by Domenico Gagini. Upstairs, the small **Museo Civico** (Map p262; ☎ 0922 40 14 50; admission free; 🕑 9am-1.30pm & 4.30-6.30pm Mon-Sat), contains a poorly labelled miscellany of objects. The church is usually open the same hours as the museum but if it isn't ring the bell next door (No 2), where you can also buy cakes and pastries baked on the premises by the resident nuns (see p267).

To the east of Via Duomo is the small **Chiesa di Santa Maria dei Greci** (Map p262; admission free; 🕑 8am-noon & 3pm-dusk Mon-Sat), accessed through a lovely garden with palm trees and

---

SHH! WE'RE IN A CHURCH!

By virtue of a remarkable acoustic phenomenon known as *il portavoce* (the carrying voice), even the faintest sound carries in Agrigento's cathedral, but the system only seems to work in the favour of the priest standing in the apse. Should any parishioner have been whispering in the back row near the cathedral door, the priest would have been able to hear their every word even though he stood some 85m away! Try it and see.

---

cypresses. It was built in the 11th century on the site of a 5th-century Doric temple dedicated to Athena. Inside are some badly damaged Byzantine frescoes and the remains of the original Norman ceiling. Opening hours are not strictly adhered to. If you find it closed, check with the custodian at Salita Santa Maria dei Greci 1 (to the right as you face the church). You might need to give a tip to the custodian for this.

About 300m northwest of the church is Agrigento's magnificent **cathedral** (Map p262; admission free; ☾ erratic), built in the year 1000. It is dedicated to the town's first archbishop, the Norman San Gerlando (St Gerland). It has been radically restructured over the centuries, and has an adjoining unfinished 15th-century bell tower. Inside is the saint's tomb, set in the right wing of the transept. Keep your eyes up for the wonderful Norman ceiling. The cathedral also contains a letter from the Devil, who is reputed to have used all his wiles to engineer the downfall of the Virgin of Agrigento. He wrote to her promising her all the treasure in the world, but steadfast in her purity the Virgin dobbed him in to the priest, who still holds this mysterious missive.

Tours

A guide can make a tour of the temples or the town of Agrigento much more interesting and easier to understand. All of the tourist offices in Agrigento can provide you with a list of multilingual guides. Alternatively, you can arrange guides at the main entrance to the archaeological park. The official rate is €84 for half a day.

An excellent English-speaking guide, 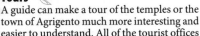**Michele Gallo** (Map p262; ☎ 0922 40 22 57, 0360 39 79 30; www.sicilytravel.net; Via Dante 49; half day €90, temples &

museum €120) can organise individual and group itineraries according to travellers' interests. Itineraries can also be arranged to areas of interest around Agrigento and include literary tours, such as tracing the life and work of Luigi Pirandello, Agrigento's most famous writer.

Festivals & Events

Check with the tourist office for more information on the two festivals below.

Sagra del Mandorlo in Fiore (Festival of the Almond Blossom) The city's big annual shindig is a folk festival, celebrated on the first Sunday of February, when the Valley of the Temples is cloaked in almond blossoms.

Festa di San Calogero (Feast of St Calogero) A week-long festival during which the statue of St Calogero, who saved Agrigento from the plague, is carried through the town while spectators throw loaves of spiced bread at the saint. Begins on the first Sunday in July.

Sleeping

AGRIGENTO

Accommodation in Agrigento tends to be overpriced and poor value for money, a result of the deluge of people who visit the Valley of the Temples. High season is between April and October and you will need to book in advance during this period. Here are some of the better and cheaper options.

Hotel Amici (Map p262; ☎ 0922 40 28 31; www .hotelamici.com; Via Acrone 5; s €35-45, d €60-80; ⊠) This is a good budget option in Agrigento, especially if you want to stay close to town. The rooms are plain but spotlessly clean, the beds are comfortable and breakfast is included in the price.

Hotel Bella Napoli (Map p262; ☎ /fax 0922 2 04 35; www.hotelbellanapoli.com in Italian; Piazza Lena 6; s/d €35/65; ⊠) This is an affordable, affable and atmospheric option run by the same people as the neighbouring Antica Foresteria Catalana. Breakfast is an extra €3.

our pick **Camere a Sud** (Map p262; ☎ 349 638 44 24; www.camereasud.it; Via Ficani 6; s €40-45, d €60-70; ⊠) A lovely, recently refurbished B&B in the centre of Agrigento, Camere a Sud has modern rooms that are simply and stylishly decorated – a play between traditional décor and contemporary textiles, with splashes of bright colour to liven things up. The communal kitchen is well-equipped and the sumptuous breakfast is served on the terrace in the warmer months.

Atenea 191 (Map p262; ☎ 0922 59 55 94; www .atenea191.com in Italian; Via Atenea 191; s €40-50, d €60-80; ⊠) Atenea 191 is a wonderful modern B&B

with tasteful rooms that feature flower-pot stencils across the walls, pretty floral linen, and in some, frescoed ceilings and traditional floor tiles. Many rooms have fantastic views of the valley, there's a great roof terrace, a huge communal kitchen and disabled access.

Antica Foresteria Catalana (Map p262; ☎ /fax 0922 2 04 35; www.albergoanticaforesteriacatalana.com in Italian; Piazza Lena 5; s €45, d €75-85; ✂) This decent and well-priced option tries for the 'authentic' antique look. It has exposed brickwork, wrought-iron beds, quaint bits of furniture and pastel-coloured walls, making the rooms a notch above average. Breakfast is an extra €3.

VALLEY OF THE TEMPLES

Most of Agrigento's plusher hotels are out of town, around the Valley of the Temples or near the sea. You'll need your own transport to get around if you're staying here.

Hotel Kaos (off Map p263; ☎ 0922 59 86 22; Contrada Luigi Pirandello; s/d from €100/150; P ✂ ✈) A large hotel in a restored villa set in beautiful, mature gardens, situated by the sea about 2km from the temples. The rooms are slightly dilapidated, but with reconstruction work underway perhaps there are brighter times ahead. There is, however, a huge swimming pool that compensates for some of the sad décor.

Hotel Villa Athena (Map p263; ☎ 0922 2 69 66; www .athenahotels.com; Via Ugo La Malfa 3; s €105-130, d €160-210; P ✂ ✈) Agrigento's most famous hotel and the only one situated inside the archaeological park. Once the home of Alexander Hardcastle (1920s), who devoted his life to the excavations, it has a peerless position overlooking the temples. The rooms are perhaps past their best, but the location makes this place extra special.

Colleverde Park Hotel (Map p263; ☎ 0922 2 95 55; www.colleverdehotel.it; Via Panoramica dei Templi 21; d from €120-170; P ✂) Set in lush gardens, this is a good family option, with wonderful views of the temples. The location is better for those who have a car, since the hotel is situated halfway between the town and the valley. The rooms are comfortably modern.

Foresteria Baglio della Luna (off Map p263; ☎ 0922 51 10 61; www.bagliodellaluna.com; Contrada Maddalusa; s/d from €150/200; P ✂) This handsome converted *baglio* (manor house) is Agrigento's best hotel. Full of character and comfort, the interior is tastefully decorated with antiques and chintz, and the restaurant, Il Déhors

(opposite), is rated as one of the best in Sicily. It is a little tricky to find, but check the website for exact directions.

SAN LEONE

The nearest camp sites are in the small coastal town of San Leone, 3km south of Agrigento.

Campeggio Internazionale San Leone (off Map p263; ☎ 0922 41 61 21; www.campingvalledeitempli.com; per person €5-7, tent €5-7; ✂ closed Nov-Feb; ☐ ✈) A well-equipped camp site, with a swimming pool, pizzeria, internet point, and bus shuttle to the Valley of the Temples and nearby beaches. It's situated on a magnificent stretch of golden sand, within cycling distance (5km) of the Valley of the Temples. To get there, take bus 2 (€0.85) from in front of Agrigento's train station; you'll then have to walk about 1km east along the beach at San Leone.

Eating
AGRIGENTO

Agrigentans are often referred to as *né carne né pesce* (neither fowl nor fish), and this pretty much reflects their eating habits. You are just as likely to get rabbit, pasta with fennel, broad beans and artichokes as you are to get stuffed swordfish or pilchards. Agrigento itself is famous for the unctuous Arab sweet *cuscusu* (looks like semolina couscous but is made of almonds and pistachio) and they sure do love their ice-cream brioches!

La Forchetta (Map p262; ☎ 0922 59 45 87; Via San Francesco 9; meals €15; ✂ closed Sun) A budget eatery, the Fork serves the cheapest grub in town, with simple pastas and meat fillets to follow. The cramped dining room is often packed with locals who come for the everchanging daily specials and the relaxed atmosphere.

L'Ambasciata di Sicilia (Map p262; ☎ 0922 2 05 26; Via Giambertoni 2; meals €20; ✂ closed Sun) The Ambasciata offers typical Sicilian fare, although the prepackaged desserts are a disappointment. If you can, get a table on the small outdoor terrace, which has splendid views of the town and the temples below.

Kalòs (Map p262; ☎ 0922 2 63 89; Piazzale San Calogero; meals €25; ✂ closed Sun) This is a top-end restaurant serving quality cuisine close to the centre of town. The whopping service charge of 20% is a bit steep, especially when the place can feel a little funereal early in the evening.

Da Giovanni (Map p262; ☎ 0922 2 11 10; Piazzetta Vadalà 2; meals €25; ✂ closed Sun) A reliable option with piazza seating, smooth service, classic

Sicilian dishes and mind-blowing *cassata* (sponge cake with ricotta and fruit). It gets quite busy on Saturday evenings, when bookings are a must.

VALLEY OF THE TEMPLES

There are some great upmarket spots near the temples, especially if you can nab a table with a view of the ruins illuminated at night.

Kokalos (Map p263; ☎ 0922 60 64 27; Viale Magazzeni 3; pizza €6-8) If you have a car, head for this trattoria/ pizzeria, on the road to San Leone, where the area's best pizza is dished up. It also serves the local *cavatelli* (a type of homemade pasta). The views of the Temple of Concord are impressive too.

La Promenade dei Templi (Map p263; ☎ 0922 2 37 15; Via dei Panoramica Templi; tourist menu €15-20) This is a good café/restaurant popular with locals for a morning coffee, and the best eatery near the temples away from the madding crowds. There is also a pleasant rooftop terrace.

Le Caprice (off Map p263; ☎ 0922 41 13 64; Via Cavaleri Magazzeni; meals €30; ☺ closed Fri) Le Caprice, long one of Agrigento's better restaurants, has a garden location complete with pool and swans. It is renowned for its seafood and the mixed seafood grill is certainly worth its reputation. A glass of the local white is perfect on a hot summer evening.

Il Déhors (off Map p263; ☎ 0922 51 13 35; Contrada Maddalusa; meals €35; ☺ closed Mon) The restaurant of the Foresteria Baglio della Luna takes its lead from the *monsù* cooking of the 1800s, when French influences began to reach the Sicilian dinner table. The menu includes sole, lobster and meats such as pheasant, lamb and kid. There are delicious pâtés and plenty of buttery sauces. Excellent.

Leon d'Oro (off Map p263; ☎ 0922 41 44 00; Viale Emporium 102; mains €35-40; ☺ closed Mon) A truly excellent restaurant that deserves its high prices, perfectly mixing the fish and fowl that typify Agrigento's cuisine. Try the *coniglio in agrodolce* (rabbit in a sweet-and-sour sauce) or the *triglia e macco di fave* (mullet with broad beans).

Drinking

Cafe Girasole (Map p262; Via Atenea 68-70; ☺ closed Sun) A popular café-cum-wine-bar in the heart of the medieval town serving late breakfasts, light lunches and, in the evenings, cocktails

and table snacks. Has a good atmosphere and outdoor seating.

Tempio di Vino (Map p262; ☎ 0922 59 67 86; Via San Francesco 11/13; ☺ closed Sun) A sweet *enoteca* in a pretty piazza. Enjoy a cool white Inzolia, and munch on olives and spicy salami as you listen to laid-back jazz.

Entertainment

Teatro Pirandello (Map p262; ☎ 0922 2 03 91; Piazza Pirandello) This theatre is mostly given over to the work of the town's great playwright, Pirandello. The main theatre season is during the winter months of October to March. Ask at any of the tourist offices for details.

Shopping

ourpick **Monastero del Santo Spirito** (Map p262; Via Santo Spirito) The monastery is home to nuns who bake heavenly pastries, including *dolci di mandorla* (almond pastries), pistachio *cuscusu* and *bucellati* (rolled sweet dough with figs). These treats are expensive but worth it for the taste and the experience. Press the doorbell, say '*Vorrei comprare qualche dolci*' (I'd like to buy a few cakes) and see how you go.

Getting There & Away

BUS

For most destinations, the bus is the easiest way to get to and from Agrigento. The intercity bus station (Map p262) is on Piazza Rosselli, just off Piazza Vittorio Emanuele, as is the ticket booth (Map p262). **Cuffaro** (☎ 0922 41 82 31) runs daily buses to Palermo (€7, two hours, seven daily Monday to Saturday, two Sunday). **Lumia** (☎ 0922 2 04 14) has departures to Trapani (€10, four hours, three daily Monday to Saturday, one Sunday).

SAIS Trasporti (☎ 0922 59 52 60) runs buses to Catania (€11, three hours, 14 Monday to Friday, seven Saturday and Sunday), Caltanissetta (€5, 1¼ hours, five Monday to Saturday, one Sunday). There are also buses to Palermo's Falcone-Borsellino airport (€9, two hours and 25 minutes, three Monday to Friday).

CAR & MOTORCYCLE

Agrigento is easily accessible by road from all of Sicily's main towns. The SS189 (the SS121 from Palermo) links the town with Palermo, while the SS115 runs along the coast and eventually to Syracuse. For Enna, take the SS640 via Caltanissetta.

MEDITERRANEAN COAST

Driving in the medieval town is nearly impossible. The main street is pedestrianised from 9am to 8pm and traffic is rerouted around Via Gioeni. There is metered parking at the train station (Piazza Marconi) and Piazza Rosselli.

TRAIN
There are plenty of trains daily to and from Palermo (€7, 2½ hours, 11 daily) and Catania (€12, 3½ to 4½ hours, five daily), although you are better off taking the bus which is faster. Train services to Gela (€6.50, three hours, 10 daily) are frequent and convenient. The train station has left-luggage lockers (€2.50 per 12 hours).

Getting Around
City buses run to the Valley of the Temples from in front of the train station. Take bus 1, 2, or 3 (€0.85, valid for 1½ hours, every 30 minutes) and get off at either the museum or further downhill at the Piazzale dei Templi. Bus 1 continues to Caos and then Porto Empedocle (€1.70). Bus 2 continues to San Leone. There are also regular buses running from the train station to the cathedral, for those who prefer not to walk up the hill.

CASA NATALE DI PIRANDELLO
Southwest of Agrigento in the suburb of Caos, about 2km along the busy road to Porto Empedocle, is the birthplace of one of the heavyweights of Sicilian (and world) literature, Luigi Pirandello (1867–1936). His early career was taken up with the writing of short stories and novels, but he concentrated on writing for the theatre after WWI. His works include such masterpieces as *Sei personaggi in ricerca di un autore* (Six Characters in Search of an Author) and *Enrico IV* (Henry IV), which are considered some of the most important plays written in the Italian language. In 1934 he was awarded the Nobel Prize for Literature.

Casa Natale di Pirandello (☎ 0922 51 11 02; admission €2; 🕙 9am-1pm & 2-7pm) is the villa in which Pirandello was born and spent most of his summers, now converted into a museum containing a lot of memorabilia. It also hosts occasional exhibitions of his manuscripts and letters, and every year there is a **Settimana Pirandellana** (Pirandellana Week) in early August when his plays are performed in a theatre near the villa (in Piazzale Caos). For information on theatrical events ask at any tourist office in Agrigento.

The ashes of Pirandello are kept in an urn buried at the foot of a pine tree, which lost its top half in a violent storm a few years ago.

ARAGONA & THE VULCANELLI DI MACALUBE
Head north from Agrigento along the SS189 towards the small farming town of Aragona, a typical Sicilian town of tiny alleys and secluded piazze with a lovely **Chiesa Madre** full of stuccowork. However, the real interest here lies 3km to the south of town – the bizarre **Vulcanelli di Macalube** are fascinating

THE MARVELOUS SCALA DEI TURCHI
It's incredible how many visit Agrigento and wander around the temples, but leave without seeing one of the most spectacular sights in the area: the Scala dei Turchi.

The curving, blindingly-white rock is made out of limestone and clay, and it contrasts against the blue sky and indigo sea quite spectacularly; you'll be awe-struck by its sheer scale and deliciousness. You'll see people running up the smooth stone; some lying and sunbathing on the whiteness; and others walking around exploring its coves and curves, running their hands along the smooth chalky surface. The sunsets are particularly incredible.

The story behind the name comes from a legend that this was the hiding place for Turkish and Arab pirates during strong winds and bad weather. They are also meant to have used the rock as their landing area during the island's battles with the Saracens.

There are two sandy beaches surrounding the Scala, and the one behind the rock is the better of the two. Take a picnic to make a full day out of it. There's a restaurant just by the steps that take you down to the beach from the road.

To get here from Agrigento, you'll need your own transport. Drive towards Porto Empedocle then follow the signs for Realmonte. You should see signs for the 'Lido Majarata' and 'Scala dei Turchi'.

DETOUR: ERACLEA MINOA

Despite the scant 6th-century-BC ruins a trip to Eraclea Minoa makes a wonderful detour, taking you through some gorgeous rural countryside, down to Sicily's most photogenic beach and one of the island's best camp sites.

Take the signposted exit on the SS115, which will bring you to a T-junction. Turn left and wend your way uphill through acres of vineyards until you reach another junction at the top of the promontory. The road ahead will take you down to the beach, while a right turn will take you to the **archaeological park** (admission €2; ☙ 9am-1hr before sunset) along the headland. There are great views of the beach from this road. The ruins are relatively scarce – the crumbling remains of the soft sandstone theatre are covered with protective plastic – but the views and singing scrub full of the intense chirrups of cicadas are gorgeous.

To reach the beach return to the junction and head downhill (2km). At the bottom of the hill you will have to turn right along a one-way road, then take a left turn at the big sign for **Lido Garibaldi**, which will bring you out on the golden sand, next to a beachfront café (with toilets) and the wonderful, eucalyptus-shaded camp site, **Eraclea Minoa Village** (☎ in summer 0922 84 60 23, in winter 0922 2 91 01; www.eracleaminoavillage.it; per person €8-14.50, d in a bungalow €55-95). Backed by a deep green band of cypress trees and the white marl cliffs of Capo Bianco to the west, it is a heavenly spot and very quiet outside July and August. There's a natural mud rock at the western end of the beach, where you can scrape the mud off the rock (with the aid of a bit of sea water) and rub it onto your skin – you'll see all the locals doing the same. Dry off in the sun then rinse in the sea, and have at least ten years removed in ten minutes. It's great refreshment for the skin and it'll save you the euros that spas charge for this very treatment. But do beware – you'll look like a green monster while the mud's drying.

---

minivolcanoes about half a metre high and chock-full of bubbling mud. To walk to the site, take the last left south out of Aragona (signposted) and follow the road for about 1km. At the first fork, take a left down a dirt road. When the road forks again, take a right and keep going until you reach a sign saying '*Proprietà Privata*' (Private Property). Walk 300m or so up the path and then you'll see a fenced-off field on your right. As you approach it, you will notice that the field is actually a greyish expanse of clay that looks eerily like the surface of the moon. This is caused by a rare geographical phenomenon known as sedimentary vulcanism. It is possible to walk around the *vulcanelli*, but watch your step.

Although this is private property, visitors are welcome if they stick to the path and the *vulcanelli*. If you see someone on the property, ask for permission: '*Lei dispiace se visito i vulcanelli?*' (Do you mind if I visit the *vulcanelli*?).

SANT'ANGELO MUXARO

This tiny town is famous for the prehistoric **rock tombs** *(tholos)* that litter the hillside on its southern side. They date from the 11th to the 5th century BC and resemble stone beehives. The largest one is known as the **Tomba del Principe** (Tomb of the Prince). Whatever

treasures they once contained have long since disappeared into the display cases of Europe's museums or into private hands. The tombs are always accessible.

From Agrigento, take the SS118 out of Agrigento and follow the signs for the turn-off near Raffadali. To get here from the north, take the SS188 west from Lercara Friddi and turn south (towards Agrigento): Sant'Angelo Muxaro is about 50km down the road.

THE PELAGIC ISLANDS

pop 5950

The Pelagic Islands (Isole Pelagie) earned their name from the Greek *pelagos*, meaning 'sea', and they are surrounded by a fabulous sea of luminous aqua depths (the cleanest in Italy) that shimmers in the endless sunshine. The islands lie on the very edge of the continental shelf separating Africa from Europe. While Linosa balances on the European shelf, the last peak in Etna's volcanic chain, Lampedusa lies on the African shelf and is known as 'a gift from Africa to Europe'. It isn't the only gift heading from Africa to Europe these days, and the island has of late been caught in a political maelstrom of illegal immigration as desperate refugees try to reach the European shores.

MEDITERRANEAN COAST

The archipelago's most popular island, Lampedusa, is overrun with visitors in July and August. To escape the crowds, you might consider skipping across the water to the small volcanic island of Linosa, where the black beaches are quieter and the swimming is great. Tiny Lampione is little more than an uninhabited pimple and isn't on the ferry route.

History

The islands have a somewhat chequered history, made famous by their one-time princes, the Tomasi family, who were given Lampedusa in 1661 (hence the name Giuseppe Tomasi di Lampedusa, of *Il gattopardo* fame). In 1839 they tried to sell it to the British but King Ferdinand II of Naples jumped in and forked out 12 million ducats to stop the British gaining yet another strategic foothold in the Mediterranean. The islands were bombed in 1943 by the Allies and the Americans later set up a military base here, which itself was the target of a bomb attack in 1986, when Libya's Colonel Gaddafi launched a couple of wobbly missiles that landed out to sea.

Getting There & Away

AIR

You can fly direct to Lampedusa from Palermo. **Meridiana** (☎ inside Italy 199 11 13 33, from outside Italy 0789 5 26 82; www.meridiana.it), **Air One** (☎ 091 702 01 11; www.flyairone.it) and **Alitalia** (☎ 848 86 56 41; www.alitalia.com) fly twice daily to Lampedusa from Palermo (from €40 one way, one hour). You can buy tickets at Falcone-Borsellino airport (31km west of Palermo) or contact a travel agency, who might scout around for a good deal.

BOAT

You can get to the islands by ferry from Porto Empedocle, 10km from the Valley of the Temples archaeological park. SAL Buses (€1.70) leave Agrigento's train station for Porto Empedocle every 30 minutes or so from 6.25am to 8.30pm, which is inconvenient given the later ferry departures. You can buy bus tickets on the bus. The 20-minute bus journey brings you to Piazza Italia on Via Roma. This is about 100m north of the ferry dock, which runs along Via Quattro Novembre. Alternatively you can get a taxi from Piazzale Aldo Moro in Agrigento for about €6. Call ☎ 0922 2 18 99 or ☎ 0922 2 66 70 for a taxi. Both Siremar and Ustica Lines

run ferries to Lampedusa and Linosa. Both ticket offices are on the quayside.

Siremar (☎ 0922 63 66 83; Lungomare Rizzo; ☺ 9am-1pm & 4.30pm-midnight Mon-Thu & Sat, 9am-1pm & 4.30-8pm Fri, 8pm-midnight Sun) has one-way fares to Lampedusa costing €42.30 and to Linosa €35.30. Although you can take your car (from €49 one way), it's best to leave it on the mainland at a parking station near the port (see below). The ferry leaves Porto Empedocle at 11.59pm, arriving in Linosa at 5.45am and Lampedusa at 8.15am. From June to September there are daily departures in both directions but the rest of the year there is no ferry out to the islands on Friday and no return ferry on Saturday. For the outward, night-time journey consider reserving a cabin with toilet for €20.50.

Ustica Lines (☎ 0922 63 61 10; www.usticalines.it; Lungomare Rizzo) runs a faster, four-hour hydrofoil service to the islands, which departs at more humane times. In high season (1 May to 31 October) hydrofoils depart daily for Lampedusa (€49) at 4pm and Linosa (€31). Services are reduced to twice weekly (Wednesday and Saturday) in April, November and December, and depart at 8am.

Parking at the Port

Alfonso Stagno (☎ 0922 63 60 29) has two garages near the port where parking costs €15 per day. Phone a couple of days beforehand to book a space. You can rent vehicles pretty cheaply on Lampedusa should you need to.

Getting Around

Ustica Lines runs a hydrofoil between Lampedusa and Linosa from 1 May to 31 October (€18, one hour, twice daily). The hydrofoil departs Lampedusa at 9.30am and 5.30pm and departs Linosa at 10.45am and 6.45pm. You can buy your ticket at the **Agenzia Marittima Strazera** (☎ 0922 97 00 03; Via F Riso 1) on Lampedusa. On Linosa, tickets are available from **Agenzia Cavallaro** (☎ 0922 97 20 62; Via Re Umberto 46).

LAMPEDUSA

Lampedusa is a rocky, sparsely covered and, in winter, wind-whipped place that was wonderfully captured in Emanuele Crialese's 2002 film, *Respiro*. Not so long ago, in the 19th century, the island was covered with farmland, but years of mismanagement have destroyed the local ecology, leaving only baking rock and

---

STORMY WATERS

It is not only moneyed tourists who have their sights set on the crystal-clear waters of Lampedusa, but also thousands of people escaping the poverty and political turmoil of Africa's failed states. In 2004 a record number of 10,000 asylum seekers landed on the island during the summer months, trebling the island's population and sending the Italian government into a tailspin. These numbers are more or less steady every year, as confirmed by the fact that 2007 saw about 7000 people rescued by Italian coastguards. Ten immigrants died in a crossing in August 2007 and more than 2500 people were rescued in July alone.

During his days in power, Silvio Berlusconi made a deal with one-time renegade Colonel Gaddafi to return illegal immigrants to holding camps in Libya, much to the dismay of the UN Refugee Agency – Libya has a long record of human-rights abuses. Images of handcuffed refugees being loaded on to cargo planes sent the UN envoy Juergen Humburg hotfoot to Lampedusa, but he was denied access to the island's high-security detention centre, which is ringed by spirals of razor wire. The situation got so bad, and the planeloads of returning immigrants so many, that even Libya had trouble coping with the numbers and flights had to be temporarily suspended.

Lampedusa is undoubtedly the frontline in the continuing European immigration crisis. Many of the refugees who are locked up in Lampedusa's dour detention centre are simply escaping some of the worst poverty in the world, but it doesn't look like there is a different solution on the horizon.

---

scrub bush. There is no sight of any particular interest in the town itself and most people come here for the wonderful sea and sand.

Orientation

Whether arriving by ferry or by plane, all visitors disembark on Lampedusa, in the town of the same name. If you arrive by ferry, it's a 10-minute walk up to the old town or a 15-minute walk west to the harbour at Porto Nuovo, where you'll find many of the hotels. The airport is not much further away on the southeastern edge of town. The bus station, handy if you want to visit beaches around the island, is on Piazza Brignone in the centre of town.

Information

Banco di Sicilia (Via Roma 129) Has an ATM.
Ente Turismo (☎ 0922 97 11 71; www.enteturismo lampedusa.it; Via Anfossi 3) Try this travel agency if the tourist office is closed. Ente can book hotels, arrange excursions, and help hire boats and scooters. Excellent website.
First Aid (☎ 0922 97 06 04)
Pharmacy (☎ 0922 97 01 95; Via Vittorio Emanuele 35; ☒ 9.30am-12.45pm, 5-7.30pm & 10-11pm)
Police (questura; ☎ 0922 97 00 01; Via Roma 37)
Post Office (Piazza Piave; ☒ 8.30am-1pm & 4-7pm Mon-Sat) Doubles as a Telecom office.
Tourist Office (☎ 0922 97 13 90; Via Vittorio Emanuele 89; ☒ Apr-Oct) Keeps erratic hours but otherwise supplies good information on the island. Linked to Ente Turismo.

Sights & Activities

The main area of activity on the island is the busy, picturesque port surrounded by a kasbahlike warren of streets. Beyond this you have your pick of beaches, such as **Cala Croce**, the first bay west of the town, or **Isola dei Conigli** (Rabbit Island), one of several beaches on the southern side of the 11km-long island. It's an easy swim away (you can even walk it if the tide is out), otherwise a scooter is a good idea. Isola dei Conigli is also part of a dedicated nature reserve, unique in Italy in that it is the only place where *Caretta caretta* (loggerhead sea turtles) lay their eggs (between July and August). You will be lucky to see one, though, as these timid creatures generally only come in when no-one's about.

The only other excursion is to the centre of the island and the **Santuario di Porto Salvo**, a small church nestled in a lush garden. It houses the Madonna of Porto Salvo, which is carried out in procession every year on 22 September to commemorate the first settlement on the island (1843).

The waters of Lampedusa are crystal clear and brimming with different kinds of fish. Consequently, diving is very popular. **Lo Verde Diving** (☎ 0922 97 19 86; Via Sbarcatoio) and **Mediterraneo Immersion Club** (☎ 0922 97 15 26; Via A Volta 8), both on the harbour front, organise gear rental and diving trips around the island. Expect to pay around €55 per day for a complete set of equipment.

MEDITERRANEAN COAST

Sleeping

Cheap accommodation can be hard to find and you will usually be expected to stay for a minimum of three nights in July and August. The small guesthouses are often full in summer and closed in winter. The tourist office has lists of all hotels and room rentals and many can be viewed on the website www .lampedusa.to (in Italian).

La Roccia (☎ 0922 97 09 64; www.laroccia.net; camp site per person €8, d in bungalow €37) An excellent camp site with very high standards and dozens of on-site facilities, including diving in the transparent waters. It is located at Cala Greca, which is 3km west of town past Guitgia beach. There are also cabins, chalets and caravans available here.

Hotel La Perla (☎ 0922 97 19 32; www.laperlahotel.net; Lungomare L Rizzo 1/3/5; per person incl half board €58-122; 🖫) A comfortable hotel with spacious rooms and balconies overlooking the sea, La Perla is central and open year-round. The décor is predominantly blue-and-white marine style, with wicker sofas and tasteful knick-knacks. There's also a decent restaurant that overlooks the sea.

Hotel Sirio (☎ 0922 97 04 01; Via Antonello da Messina; per person incl half board €86; 🖫) Friendly and family-run, the Sirio is situated between Guitgia Bay and the harbour. It has sunny rooms and a warm atmosphere, but it is the cooking that makes this place a real find, with delicacies prepared by Nonna Caterina. You can sample roasted sea urchins, stuffed calamari, pasta with mullet, and ricotta tart, and the hotel can even organise a culinary tour of the island. Good value for this expensive island.

'U Piddu (☎ 0922 97 09 01; fax 0922 97 10 50; Via Madonna 10; d per person per week incl half board €680-1060; 🕙 closed Oct-Apr; 🖫) Good value for longer stays (during the low season), this low-slung, Mexican-style adobe complex is dreamy, with elegant terraced rooms and a patio surrounded by dramatic cacti. The hotel also has its own scooters and private boat, and boat excursions are included in the price of the room.

Hotel Cupola Bianca (☎ /fax 0922 97 12 74; www .italiaabc.it/az/cupolabianca; Contrada Madonna; per person incl half board €120-150; 🖫) Lovely location in a fresh green garden dotted with palm trees. The garden sets the atmosphere for the *Arabian Nights* décor of the small cottages, complete with pointy Eastern-style arches and wrought-iron four-poster beds. Catamaran excursions and diving are also possible.

Eating

There are plenty of places to eat, but prices are higher here than anywhere else in Sicily. At night during summer, Via Roma's cafés and restaurants are chock-a-block with tourists tucking into all manner of fish dishes and the ubiquitous couscous. Most places are open during summer but are closed November to March.

Al Gallo d'Oro (Via Vittorio Emanuele 45; meals €20) A cheap and cheerful place, with a good tourist menu, the Golden Cockerel is popular for a simple dinner or lunch.

Da Nicola (☎ 0922 97 12 39; Via Ponente, on the road to the Isola dei Conigli; meals €25) The only thing you can eat here is the most delicious and freshest fish, served home-style in a simple and down-to-earth environment. No nonsense or frills.

Trattoria Pugliese (☎ 0922 97 05 31; Via Cala Pisana 3; meals €25-30) If you fancy a change from all that fish, this is a good alternative, serving up tasty pasta dishes with a north-Italian twist. The chef is from Puglia so you're guaranteed something different.

Le Mille e Una Notte (☎ 0922 97 15 55; Lungomare L Rizzo 133; meals €35) Specialising in Arabic and North African–style couscous, the 'A Thousand and One Nights' is a favourite for lovers of the semolina dish. It is served with meat and fish or even sweet – as a salad with kiwi or pomegranate.

Gemmelli (☎ 0922 97 06 99; Via Cala Pisana 2; meals €40; 🕙 closed Oct-Jun) A top-class restaurant offering a plethora of fish dishes including bouillabaisse, paella and couscous. Excellent food and good ambience.

Getting Around

Getting around Lampedusa is easy; the island is only 11km long. You can walk into town from the airport. Most hotels and camp sites, however, arrange courtesy buses that transport guests from the airport to their accommodation. You can also get a taxi, which costs €3 to €6.

From June to September, orange minibuses (€1.75) run regularly from Piazza Brignone to the different beaches around the island. Alternatively, you can rent a bicycle, scooter or even a car from one of the many rental outlets around town. **Licciardi Autonoleggi** (☎ 0922 97 07 68; Via Siracusa) is a few steps from the docks at Porto Vecchio. It rents scooters for €15 a day and cars from €30. You can also rent bicycles from there for €5 per day.

LINOSA

Linosa is essentially the summit of a dormant volcano that has been extinct for nearly 2000 years. Its black beaches and rocky coves don't attract nearly as many as visitors as Lampedusa, but they are worth checking out if you fancy getting away from the crowds that flock to the larger island. Linosa is slowly building up its own tourist trade and is a popular day trip from Lampedusa.

Linosa Club (☎ 0922 97 20 66; Contrada Calcarella; d per person incl half board from €80; ☙ closed Oct-May) is a good hotel, the only one on the island, and has lots of sporting facilities and a restaurant. Prices decrease outside August.

Trattoria da Anna (☎ 0922 97 20 48; Via Vittorio Veneto; meals €25-30) is a pleasant little trattoria run by the eponymous Anna herself, whose cooking is highly regarded. She can also help you find accommodation in studio apartments, which are available to rent year-round.

EAST OF AGRIGENTO

GELA

pop 72,500

Once the engine room of the great Greek colony that eventually pushed westwards to found Akragas, Eraclea Minoa and Selinunte, Gela was renowned during its colonial days for its artistic excellence and entrepreneurial spirit, which still makes it an unsentimental modern city today. Gela was settled by colonists from Rhodes and Crete in 689 BC, and Greek know-how mixed with the local Sicilian culture helped the city prosper, producing wines, olive oil and ceramics. However the city was sacked by Carthage (405 BC) and then completely destroyed by the tyrant Finzia of Agrigento (282 BC), who relocated the entire population of Gela to Agrigento. Far from that being the end of its woes, the city was destroyed again by WWII bombing, as it was chosen for the Allied landings of July 1943.

Since then, Gela has spearheaded Sicily's ill-fated oil industry. Gulf Oil strikes in the 1950s saw the rapid and ill-thought-out establishment of huge refineries at Syracuse, Augusta, Gela and Agrigento. Although Gela's plant provides employment for the majority of the city, it has not brought about the dreamt-of riches but has rather transformed the town into a mess of tangled steel and industrial mayhem. In recent years Gela has stood out as one of Sicily's more progressive cities, twice electing its mayor Rosario Crocetta, an openly gay, left-wing politician, who has vowed to improve Gela's reputation and carry on his work against the Mafia.

Orientation & Information

The ancient city or acropolis occupies the western slopes of the city near the Capo Soprano fortifications. Four kilometres east of this, down Corso Vittorio Emanuele, the main thoroughfare of the historic town, you will find the archaeological museum. A nicer walk is along the seafront.

Should you need it, there is a **tourist office** (☎ 0933 91 15 09; Via Palazzi).

Sights

There is really only one reason for coming to Gela and that's to visit the **Museo Regionale Archeologico** (☎ 0933 91 26 26; Corso Vittorio Emanuele; adult/concession €6/3; ☙ 9am-1pm & 3-7pm, closed last Mon of the month). The museum contains artefacts from the city's ancient acropolis but is rightly famed for its unique collection of red-and-black *kraters*, Gela's speciality between the 7th and 4th centuries BC. Gela's terracotta was famed throughout the Greek world for the delicacy of its designs and superb figurative work. This museum's collection, the largest in the world, is simply staggering. Other treasures of the museum include the Navarra collection of ancient vases from the 8th to the 6th century, the most important of its kind in Italy, and some 600 silver coins minted in Agrigento, Gela, Syracuse, Messina and Athens. At one time the collection numbered over 1000 coins, but it was stolen in 1976 and only about half of it was recovered. More recently, the city has acquired three unusual terracotta altars. These were found in 2003 in a 5th-century-BC warehouse, which had been buried under 6m of sand. The quality and state of preservation is amazing.

Right at the other end of Corso Vittorio Emanuele (turn left on Via Manzoni and follow the road to the sea for about 4km), you will find the remains of the ancient **Greek fortifications** (admission €3; ☙ 9am-1hr before sunset) at Capo Soprano. Built by the tyrant of Syracuse, Timoleon, in 333 BC, they are in a remarkable state of preservation, most likely

MEDITERRANEAN COAST

MEDITERRANEAN COAST

the result of being covered by sand dunes for thousands of years until they were discovered in 1948. The 8m-high walls were built in antiquity to prevent huge amounts of sand being blown into the city by the blustery sea wind. Today many of the walls are in ruins and the authorities have planted trees to act as a buffer against the encroaching sand. It makes for a pretty site planted with mimosa and eucalyptus trees, perfect for a picnic. Some 500m from the walls, next to the hospital, are Sicily's only surviving **Greek baths** (Via Europa; ☺ always open), which date from the 4th century BC.

Sleeping & Eating

If you wish to stay in Gela, try **Hotel Sole** (☎ 0933 92 52 92; Via Mare 32; s €20-35, d €30-50; ☒), one of the few accommodation options in town. The rooms are decent enough, though by no means charming.

There are pizzerie and restaurants along the main street, but the best place to eat and sleep is 20km from Gela on the SS117 to Caltagirone, at the **Vecchia Masseria** (☎ 0935 68 40 03; SS117, Cutuminello Rd; s €55-85, d €40-70; P ☒ ☒). It's a charming place, in the middle of the countryside. Rustic and tasteful, it's quite large-scale. The rooms are elegant, soothing and spacious, and the reputed restaurant specialises in traditional Sicilian cooking. Bizarrely, you can do archery here too, or if you don't fancy that, just chill out at the lovely pool.

Getting There & Away

Gela is easily reached by train and bus from every town on the Mediterranean coast. There are dozens of trains from Agrigento to Gela (€6.25, three hours, 10 daily). All buses in Gela run from Piazza Stazione, in front of the train station (ask at the Autolinee office across the street for a timetable). SAL services run to Agrigento (€3.25, 1½ hours, four daily) while SAIS Autolinee goes to Palermo via Enna and Piazza Armerina (€11.65, 2½ to three hours, four Monday to Saturday, three Sunday).

AROUND GELA

As the first Italian town to be liberated in WWII, the coast around Gela is dotted with pillbox defences. The best beaches are to the west of the town beyond the so-called Gela Riviera, and are wild and unspoilt.

The best of these are in **Falconara**, 20km west of Gela, along the SS115. It has two superb beaches, Manfria and Roccazzelle, overlooked by the impressive 14th-century Castello di Falconara, still owned by the aristocratic Falconara family and available to rent through **Think Sicily** (☎ in UK 020-7377 8518; www.thinksicily.co.uk). Another easy detour is 8km inland along the SS117b. The road takes you through the wonderfully fertile **Campo Geloi** (Gela Plains), which first attracted the Greeks to this side of the island. The plains are broken up by the dramatically tumbledown keep, **Il Castelluccio** (☺ 9am-1pm & 3-7pm, closed last Mon of month), which was built by Frederick II. It is said to be haunted. It's accessible with the same ticket as Museo Archeologico in Gela.

To the northwest (12km along the SS191) lies the lovely hill village of **Butera**, with its hilltop position crowned by a powerful Norman castle. Prosperous and content under the Spanish rule of the Branciforte family, Butera lacks the down-at-heel atmosphere of many rural towns in the south. It has a lovely town church, the Chiesa Madre, with some modest treasures, a Renaissance triptych and a painting of the Madonna by Filippino Paladino. Built on a steep hill it has good views over the Gela plains to the coast.

The Branciforte residence still stands in nearby **Mazzarino**, and the town has a clutch of churches sheltering more works of art by Paladino and the ostentatious funerary monuments of the Branciforte princes. In the 1960s, the town hit the headlines for its Mafia activity, all the more shocking for the involvement of local friars who were accused of extortion, intimidation and even murder. Imprisoned for acting as Mafia messengers, the friars admitted to delivering threats via the confessional.

WEST TO AGRIGENTO

Along the SS115 between Agrigento and Gela are the towns of **Licata** and **Palma di Montechiaro**, black spots in the Agrigentan hinterland. Palma is famous as the home of the princes of Lampedusa, made famous by writer Giuseppe Tomasi di Lampedusa in *Il gattopardo* (The Leopard). The family's 17th-century ancestral palace has not been occupied for some time, although the Chiesa Matrice still stands and can be visited.

WEST OF AGRIGENTO

SCIACCA
pop 40,600

Sciacca is one of the oldest spa towns in Italy. The spas were enjoyed by the Phoenicians, Greeks and Romans before the Arabs arrived and named it Xacca (meaning 'Water'). Like spa towns around the world, Sciacca has a gentle air and is popular with aging Italians who come to cure their rheumatism in the mineral-rich mud. A belvedere overlooks the harbour – home of Sciacca's working fishing port – and there's a pleasant day's strolling to be had through the weaving streets of the town.

Orientation

Sciacca still retains much of its medieval layout, which divided the town into quarters, each laid out on a strip of rock descending towards the sea. To the north of Via G Licata is Terravecchia, a maze of streets and alleyways. Between Via G Licata and the town's central artery, Corso Vittorio Emanuele, is a narrow strip containing most of the town's fine buildings and churches. Below the terrace of Piazza Scandaliato (halfway along Corso Vittorio Emanuele) is the traditional quarter of fishermen, ceramists and potters, which descends right down to the jetty.

Information

Banca Commerciale Italiana (Corso Vittorio Emanuele 106) Has an ATM.
Hospital (☎ 0922 9 43 76; Viale della Vittoria) Near to the public gardens.
Police (questura; ☎ 0925 96 50 11; Piazza Luigi Sturzi 2) Just outside the eastern gate to the old city.
Post Office (Corso Vittorio Emanuele 104)
Tourist Office (☎ 0925 2 27 44; Corso Vittorio Emanuele 84) This office supplies a map of the town and very limited tourist information.

Sights

The main street of Sciacca, Corso Vittorio Emanuele, is lined with impressive palazzi. The most imposing is the **Palazzo Steripinto**, recognisable by its diamond-point rustication and twin-mullioned windows. It was built in the Catalonian-Sicilian style at the beginning of the 16th century. Right in the heart of town, Vittorio Emanuele runs past the terraced **Piazza Scandaliato**, a central meeting place for locals, with splendid views of the sea below.

At the square's western end stands the **Chiesa di San Domenico**, an 18th-century reconstruction of a church built in the 16th century, while to the northeast of Piazza Scandaliato is the town's **cathedral** (admission free; ☉ 7.30am-noon & 4.30-7.30pm), first erected in 1108 and rebuilt in 1656. Only the three apses survive from the original Norman structure. The unfinished baroque façade features a set of marble statues by Gagini.

Other attractive churches here include the small, 14th-century **Chiesa di Santa Margherita**, of which the superb Gothic portal is the only surviving original feature, and the **Chiesa del Carmine**, an interesting building with an odd-looking rose window from the 13th century and a fine dome of green majolica tiles that was added in the early 19th century.

Below the town is the **artisan quarter**, rather down-at-heel, though much of the old town is slowly being renovated. Sciacca's ceramists are some of the best on the island and the risers on the steps leading down to the port are adorned with locally produced ceramic tiles. There is nothing specific to see here, but the dock is a lively place cluttered with fishing vessels and little bars. There are also numerous ceramics shops around the Piazza Scandaliato area, should you want to get down to some shopping.

About 3km east of the city (take bus 1 or 4 from the Villa Comunale) is the **Castello Incantato** (Enchanted Castle; ☎ 0925 9 93 04; admission free; ☉ 10am-noon & 4-8pm Tue-Sat), actually a large park with thousands of heads sculpted in wood and stone. The mind behind this bizarre collection was a local farmer and sculptor called Filippo Bentivegna, whose story is beset by woe. While living in America, he was ditched by his fiancée and later beaten up so badly that he was thought dead. He returned to his hometown of Sciacca in 1917 and devoted the rest of his life (he died in 1967) to exorcising the memories of his American experiences through sculpture, each head supposedly representing one of his enemies. He was certainly an eccentric, and liked to be treated as a king, going so far as to demand that people address him as '*Eccellenza*' (Your Excellency).

Activities

The main thing to do in Sciacca is take to the waters at the **Nuovo Stabilimento Termale** (☎ 0925 96 11 11; Via delle Nuove Terme; ☉ 9am-1pm Jun-Oct), where you can undergo a vast range of treatments – from hydrotherapy in a 32°C pool to

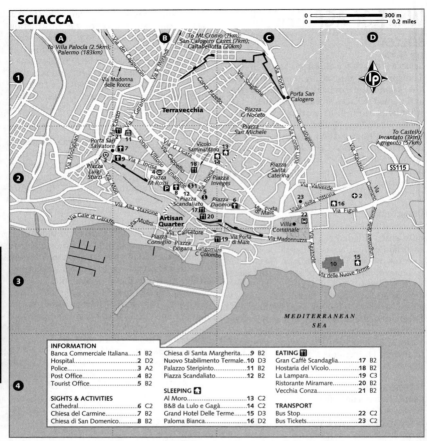

SCIACCA

mud packs and sweating it out in the natural hot caves of San Calogero on Monte Cronio.

Festivals & Events
Held the week before Lent, **Carnevale** is Sciacca's big festival. The highlight is a parade of huge papier-mâché figures mounted on floats, famous throughout Italy for their gaudy expressions. See opposite for more.

Sleeping
Sciacca does not have a great selection of hotels and most of them tend to be fairly dated.

Paloma Blanca (☎ 0925 2 51 30; fax 0925 2 56 67; Via Figuli 5; s/d €38/65; 🔄) A bizarre tower-block hotel on the eastern side of town, with a loud and cheerful landlady and a dilapidated 1970s

interior that gives you the feeling of being an extra on the set of *The Shining*. It's pretty much an emergency sleep-over place that'll do for one night. The rooms are aged and faded, with tiny bathrooms that offer the unique opportunity of sitting on the toilet and showering at the same time (as a space-saving device). The dining area – a large, chandeliered hall – must have been lavish once.

our pick B&B da Lulo e Gagà (☎ 0925 8 66 64; Vicolo Muscarnera 9; d €60; 🔄) This is a true find and a delight for any traveller. The wonderful Lulo and Gagà run this place that consists mainly of one apartment inside a little house that's completely decorated with Lulo's original and quirky works of art (think owls made of varicoloured pebbles, mosaic-framed mirrors

SCIACCA CARNIVAL

Sciacca's carnival is famed throughout Sicily for its flamboyance and fabulous party atmosphere. It's a carnival that requires a lot of preparation from the town's inhabitants – the grotesque papier-mâché figures are made by hand for months in advance, using traditional methods from generations ago.

There are several different theories about the carnival's origins and traditions. Some say that the celebration stems from Monte Cronio – named after the Greek god of time – where the ancient Romans used to celebrate the Saturnalia. The Romans are said to have burnt the king of the Saturnalia on the last day of the festival – a tradition that survives today, when the King of the Carnival, represented by the mask of Peppi Nappa, gets torched, after which everyone tucks into spicy local sausages. Others claim that the eating of sausages points to the carnival being an act of defiance against the ecclesiastical rule forbidding the consumption of meat on Shrove Tuesday.

The festival opens with carnival king Peppi Nappa receiving the city's keys. The technicolour floats are then released into the streets – they have new decorations added to them every year, though the main characters always represent current-day political and social personalities, making the carnival a sort of political satire. You'll have to be either pretty clued-up on Sicilian and Italian politics or have a good local interpreter with you to get the benefit of this. The floats go around the winding streets of the old town, while masked men and women run around them and dance to locally composed music. Satirical poetry is read aloud, and the fact that it's all in Sciacca's dialect means that you'll (again) need a strong local connection to understand the humour.

Don't miss out on this spectacle if you're in town during the carnival season – it's a unique opportunity to dance about, drink some wine, eat sausages and witness Sciacca's pride in its local history.

etc). There's a kitchen upstairs, where breakfast is prepared and served on the lovely terrace. Lulo is thinking of letting two of his wonderful self-contained cave apartments from summer 2008. These are 10 minutes' walk away from the B&B, and have more of the colourful Mediterranean-inspired works of art. Book well in advance and enjoy this unique place.

our pick **Al Moro** (☎ 0925 8 67 56; www.almoro.com; Via Liguori 44; s €55-65, d €80-95; ❀) An excellent new addition to Sciacca's fledgling accommodation scene, Al Moro is stylish and good-looking. It sits inside an old palazzo, and the owners have kept some of the original features, such as wooden-beam ceilings, which give it a lovely feeling. The 10 rooms are in baptism-white, with neat little bathrooms and a complimentary bottle of Sicilian red to greet you. The breakfast is quite sumptuous and there's a wine bar too, where you can taste an array of Sicilian offerings.

Grand Hotel delle Terme (☎ 0925 2 31 33; www.grandhoteldelleterme.com in Italian; Via delle Nuove Terme; s €59-79, d €100-143; ❀ ❐) Set on a cliff just east of the public gardens, the Grand Hotel is a decent choice that offers free admission to the thermal spa next door. The hotel itself is an uninspiring modern building left behind in the 1970s, but there are plenty of comforts to be had here.

Villa Palocla (☎ 0925 90 28 12; www.villapalocla.it in Italian; Contrada Raganella; s €70-80, d €115-135; P ❀ ❐ ❒) The nicest hotel in the environs of Sciacca, this 18th-century villa is surrounded by orange groves and retains its baronial feel with a cobbled courtyard and wrought-iron balconies. The interior is pure country house with lots of floral fabrics, ceramic floor tiles and dark wood.

Eating

The best places to eat are in and around the port, where relatively inexpensive trattorie serve up abundant menus of (mostly) seafood dishes.

Gran Caffè Scandaglia (☎ 0925 2 10 82; Piazza Scandaliato 5-6; breakfast €3.50) This is the perfect place for a breakfast in the shade, overlooking the harbour. Soft pastry, caffè latte in tall glasses and fresh orange juice are delicious, as are all the ice creams. You'll have the local seniors for company, who congregate here in the mornings to discuss politics and their physical ailments of the day.

Vecchia Conza (☎ 0925 2 53 85; Via Conzo 37; meals €15-20; ☒ closed Mon) Near the entrance to the old town, this is an attractive trattoria that is popular with lunching locals. It serves up the typical pasta dishes, though you should go for something with seafood and mains of fish – this is a fishing port after all. A relaxed place that's perfect for a satisfying lunch.

La Lampara (☎ 0925 8 50 85; Vicolo Caricatore 33; meals €20; ☒ closed Mon) If you're dying to try some of that fresh fish caught by the locals on a daily basis, go for La Lampara, one of a clutch of superfresh fish restaurants down at the port. It's a good place in a perfect location just opposite the docks and serves lovely pasta as well as seafood.

Ristorante Miramare (☎ 0925 2 60 50; Piazza Scandaliato 6; meals €20, pizza €5.15-6.20) Popular with local elderly folk, this restaurant and pizzeria sits on the corner of Sciacca's lovely belvedere. It's a place with simple traditional dishes, such as pasta with tomatoes and seafood, good fresh fish and decent pizza. The harbour views are lovely and it's best to get here for an early-evening supper to watch the sun go down.

Hostaria del Vicolo (☎ 0925 2 30 71; www.hostaria delvicolo.com in Italian; Vicolo Sammaritano 10; meals €35; ☒ closed Sun evening & Mon) Tucked away in a tiny alley in Sciacca's old town is this formal restaurant that offers a culinary *tour de force*: heavy tablecloths, noiseless service and an ample wine list. The menu is Sicilian traditional with modern twists, and the fresh pasta is great as *primo* – try the *taglioni* (long, flat pasta) with clams and *gamberoni* (king prawns). For mains, try the *merluzzo ai fichi secchi* (cod with dried figs), exquisitely moist and sweet. The desserts are less pleasing, such as pricey (€5) watermelon ice cream sprinkled with chocolate chips – a not particularly good combination.

Getting There & Away

Lumia (☎ 0922 2 04 14) buses run between Sciacca and Agrigento (€5.25, two hours, nine Monday to Saturday, two Sunday). There are also daily buses to Trapani (€7.50, two hours, two daily). All buses arrive at the Villa Comunale on Via Figuli and leave from Via Agatocle. You can buy your tickets at the small bar at Viale della Vittoria 22. Sciacca is not served by trains.

AROUND SCIACCA

Nineteen kilometres northeast of Sciacca is the beautiful village of **Caltabellotta** (850m). The highest point in the town is the ruin of the Norman castle where the peace treaty that ended the Sicilian Vespers was signed in 1302. Viewed from this lofty perch the terracotta roofs of the town cling to the cliffside like a perfect mosaic. It is quite spectacular. Below the bulk of the Norman castle is the restored Chiesa Madre with its original Gothic portal and pointed arches, and below that stands the Chiesa di San Salvatore. All around are lofty views over often mist-shrouded valleys, covered by flowers in springtime. On the edge of the village lies the derelict monastery of San Pellegrino, from where you can view the necropolises that stud the mountainside.

Lumia buses serve Caltabellotta from Sciacca (€2.45, 50 minutes, five Monday to Friday) and Agrigento (€5.75, 3½ hours, three Monday to Friday).

Directory

CONTENTS

ACCOMMODATION

Accommodation in Sicily ranges from the sublime to the ridiculous, with prices to match. You may find yourself in a national monument, the one-time home of a prince or an ugly Mafia-built '60s block. Hotels and *pensioni* make up the bulk of accommodation, although there is a huge gulf between the luxury of top-end hotels and numerous poky and pricey budget options. A number of good B&Bs, villa rentals, hostels and *agriturismi* (farm stays) have appeared in recent years, making it more possible to stay in good places for less money.

In this book we've used 'budget' to describe hotels with double rooms under €80, 'midrange' to describe doubles between €80 and €180, and 'top end' to cover hotels above €180. Unless otherwise stated, prices are for en suite rooms and include breakfast. We have quoted price ranges for the highest-priced standard rooms from low season (November to March) to high season (August).

During August or in rural accommodation you might have to pay for half or full board. Half board will include breakfast and lunch, while full board means that all meals are included in the price you pay for your room.

Prices fluctuate wildly depending on the season. The peak tourist times are Easter, summer and Christmas. It is advisable to

---

PRACTICALITIES

- Sicily uses the metric system for weights and measures.
- Buy or watch videos on the PAL system.
- Plugs have two round pins; the current is 220V, 50Hz.
- If your Italian's up to it, try *Il Giornale di Sicilia* for uncompromising coverage of corruption and political scandals, international news and a terrific listings page with details of all cinemas, theatres, festivals and other events. Other good newspapers include Milan's *Corriere della Sera*, Turin's *La Stampa* and Rome's *La Repubblica*.
- Tune into RAI-1 (1332AM or 89.7 FM), RAI-2 (846AM or 91.7 FM) and RAI-3 (93.7 FM), which combine classical and light music with news broadcasts and discussion programmes; the BBC World Service is on medium wave at 648kHz, short wave 6195kHz, 9410kHz, 12,095kHz and 15,575 kHz, and on long wave at 198kHz.
- Switch on to watch Italy's commercial stations Canale 5, Italia 1, Rete 4 and La7, as well as state-run RAI-1, RAI-2 and RAI-3.

book in advance during these periods. Prices rise around 5% to 10% annually and drop by about 20% in low season.

To make a reservation, hotels usually require confirmation by fax or letter, as well as a credit-card number.

Agriturismi & B&Bs

Agriturismo is a holiday on a working farm. Traditionally, families rented out rooms in their farmhouses and it is still possible to find this type of accommodation, although many *agriturismi* have now evolved into quite sophisticated accommodation. All *agriturismi* are operating farms and you will usually be able to sample the local produce. To search for reputable *agriturismi* log on to www.agriturismo-sicilia.it.

B&Bs have really sprouted all over Sicily in recent years. Options include everything from restored farmhouses, city palazzi and seaside bungalows to rooms in family houses. Tariffs cover a wide price range, typically €40 to €70 for a single, €65 to €150 for a double.

For more information log on to the website of **Bed & Breakfast Sicily** (www.bed-and -breakfast-sicily.it).

Camping

Camp sites in Sicily vary in terms of facilities: some are well organised and well laid out, while others are simply an empty space where you can pitch a tent, with facilities that consist of little more than a toilet-and-shower block.

Even basic camp sites can be dear once you add up the various charges, but they generally work out cheaper than a double room in a one-star hotel. Prices range from around €5 to €10 per adult, plus €5 to €20 for a site. You'll often have to pay to park

---

A WORD OF WARNING

Always try to book in advance in B&Bs since many of the owners don't live in the same building and no-one may be around if you arrive unannounced. There is usually a telephone number outside the front door, which you can call if you do pop in without booking. If you're sticking around for a couple of weeks and changing beds often, it's worth investing in a pay-as-you-go SIM card, which will make calls cheaper.

---

your car and there is sometimes a charge to use the showers and electricity. In the major cities, camp sites are often a long way from the historic (or city) centre.

Independent camping is generally not permitted. But, out of the main summer tourist season, independent campers who try to be inconspicuous and don't light fires shouldn't have too much trouble. Always get permission from the landowner if you want to camp on private property. Camper vans are popular throughout Sicily.

Full lists of camp sites are available from local tourist offices or **Touring Club Italiano** (TCI; www.touringclub.it). TCI publishes an annual book, *Campeggi in Italia*, listing all camp sites in Italy, and the Istituto Geografico de Agostini publishes the annual *Guida ai Campeggi in Europa*, sold together with *Guida ai Campeggi in Italia*. These books are available in major bookshops in Sicily. Otherwise, log on to www.camping.it.

Hostels

Youth hostels *(ostelli per la gioventù)*, of which there is only a handful in Sicily, are run by the **Associazione Italiana Alberghi per la Gioventù** (AIG; ☎ 064 87 11 52; www.ostellionline.org; Via Cavour 44, Rome), which is affiliated to **Hostelling International** (HI; www.iyhf.org). You need to be a member but you can join at one of the hostels. Nightly rates vary from €15 to €25 including breakfast. A meal will cost €8. Accommodation is in segregated dormitories, although some hostels offer family rooms (at a higher price per person).

Hostels are generally closed from 10am to 3.30pm. Check-in is from 6pm to 10.30pm, although some hostels will allow you a morning check-in before they close for the day (confirm beforehand). Curfew is 11.30pm or midnight. It is usually necessary to pay before 9am on the day of your departure, otherwise you could be charged for another night.

Hotels & Guesthouses

There is often no difference between a *pensione* (guesthouse) and an *albergo* (hotel). However, a *pensione* will generally be of one- to three-star standard, while an *albergo* can be awarded up to five stars. *Locande* (inns) and *affittacamere* (rooms for rent) are cheaper and are not included in the star classification system, although in some areas

(such as the Aeolian Islands) the standard
is very high.

While the quality of accommodation can
vary a great deal, one-star hotels/*pensioni*
tend to be very basic and usually do not have
a private bathroom. Standards at two-star
places are often only slightly better, but rooms
will generally have a private bathroom. Once
you arrive at three-star accommodation, you
can assume that standards will be reasonable. Four- and five-star hotels offer facilities such as room service, laundry, parking
and internet.

Overall, prices are highest in major tourist
destinations such as Taormina, the Aeolian
Islands and Cefalù. Prices can soar in the high
season at beach resorts and during Easter,
as Sicily is a very popular destination with
Italians on Easter holiday. The cost of a single
room (*camera singola*) starts at €40. A double
room with twin beds (*camera doppia*) and a
double room with a double bed (*camera mat-
rimoniale*) will cost from around €60. Make
a complaint to the local tourist office if you
believe you're being overcharged.

Tourist offices have booklets listing all local
accommodation, including prices.

Mountain Refuges

Around Etna and Piano Battaglia in the
Madonie Park there is a number of *rifugi*
(mountain chalets), most of which are open
year-round. In Sicily these operate as small
hotels with dormitory and double-room accommodation. The price per person for an
overnight stay and breakfast is €25 to €30,
and €50 for full board.

On Etna there is also a number of unstaffed,
ranger-maintained *bivacchi* (shelters), which
are always open and a good place to lay your
sleeping bag.

The **Club Alpino Italiano** (CAI; www.cai.it in Italian)
is a good source of information and is affiliated with some of these refuges. Members of

organisations such as the Australian Alpine
Club and British Mountaineering Council
can enjoy discounted rates for accommodation and meals by obtaining (for a fee) a
reciprocal-rights card.

Rental Accommodation

Renting an apartment in Sicily is quite easy.
In coastal resorts such as the Aeolian Islands
or tourist haunts like Syracuse, tourist offices will have lists of local apartments and
villas for rent. Renting short-term accommodation is not necessarily cheap, hovering around €1000 per month, although this
can drop to around €600 per month for a
long-term rental.

BUSINESS HOURS

Generally, shops open from around 9am
to 1pm and 3.30pm to 7.30pm (or 4pm to
8pm) Monday to Saturday. Some stay closed
on Monday mornings. Big department
stores, such as Rinascente, and most supermarkets have continuous opening hours
from 9am to 7.30pm Monday to Saturday.
Some even open 9am to 1pm on Sunday.
Smaller shops open on Saturday morning
until about 1pm.

Businesses such as travel agencies usually open 9am to 12.30pm or 1pm, and 4pm
to 7pm.

Banks tend to open 8.30am to 1.30pm
and 2.45pm to 3.45pm (or 3pm to 4.30pm)
Monday to Friday. They are closed on weekends, but it is always possible to find an exchange office open in the larger cities and in
major tourist areas.

Major post offices open 8.30am to 6pm
Monday to Friday and also 8.30am to
12.30pm on Saturday. Smaller post offices
generally open 8.30am to 1.30pm Monday
to Saturday.

Farmacie (pharmacies) are usually open
8.30am to 1pm and 4pm to 8pm. They are
always closed on Sunday and usually on
Saturday afternoon, but are required to display
a list of *farmacie* in the area that are open.

Bars (in the Italian sense; that is, coffee-
and-sandwich places) and cafés generally
open 7am to 8pm, although some stay open
after 8pm and turn into pub-style drinking
and meeting places. *Enoteche* (wine bars), on
the other hand, usually don't open until the
evening, around 7pm, and stay open until
about midnight (or later in summer).

LIVE LIKE A KING

You don't have to be a prince to be treated like royalty. In recent years Sicily's aristocracy and moneyed classes have flung open the doors of their fabulous palazzi and country villas, providing the well-heeled traveller with a unique holiday experience.

Prices for villas are not cheap (especially in summer), although the cost is more reasonable if you are in a large group. Prices for a four- to six-person villa start from €1200 per week in winter and can rise as high as €4000 per week in high season.

- **Bravo Holiday Residences** (☎ in US 866 265 5516; www.hipvillas.com) Get out your credit cards for these beauties. Bravo takes the biscuit for exclusive Sicilian villas such as Don Arcangelo all'Olmo and the stunning Villa Tasca, if you can afford the US$20,000 price tag!
- **Cuendet & Cie Spa** (☎ 057 757 63 30; www.cuendet.com) Cuendet is one of the major villa-rental companies in Italy offering villas in Sicily. In the UK you can order Cuendet's catalogues and make reservations by calling ☎ 0800 891 573. In the USA Cuendet bookings are handled by **Rentals in Italy** (☎ 805 987 5278; 1742 Calle Corva, Camarillo, CA 93010).
- **Cottages & Castles** (☎ in Australia 61 3 9853 1142; www.cottagesandcastles.com.au) This Australian agency has a portfolio of villa rentals throughout Italy, including a respectable clutch of Sicilian houses in Cefalù, Taormina and Syracuse. The company also has agents in New Zealand and across Europe.
- **Dolce Vita Villas** (☎ in UK 44 020-7436 0426; www.dolcevitavillas.com) Run by two smooth Italian operators, Dolce Vita Villas offers a range of top-end rentals, from the slick Villa Carruba in Taormina to a faux-19th-century manor house at Trecastagni, near Mt Etna.
- **Think Sicily** (☎ in UK 44 020-7377 8518; www.thinksicily.co.uk) Devoted exclusively to Sicily, this company holds the most comprehensive portfolio of Sicilian treasures, including a 14th-century palazzo in the heart of Palermo, a swanky condo in Mondello and domed *dammusi* (low-level dwellings made of thick volcanic rock) on Pantelleria.

Discos and clubs might open around 10pm but often there'll be no-one there until midnight. Restaurants open roughly from noon to 3pm and 7.30pm to 11pm. Restaurants and bars are required to close for one day each week (the day varies between establishments, although Monday is a popular choice).

Museum and gallery opening hours vary, although there is a trend towards continuous opening hours from around 9.30am to 7pm. Many close on Monday.

CHILDREN
Practicalities

Sicilians love children, but there are few special amenities for them. Ask staff at tourist offices if they know of any special family activities and about hotels that cater for children. Discounts are available for children (usually aged under 12 but sometimes based on the child's height) on public transport and for admission to sights.

Book accommodation in advance to avoid any inconvenience, and when travelling by train make sure to reserve seats to avoid finding yourselves standing up for the entire journey. You can hire car seats for infants and children from most car-rental firms, but you should always book them in advance.

You can buy baby formula in powder or liquid form (€18 for 1kg), as well as sterilising solutions such as Milton at *farmacie*. Disposable nappies (diapers) are widely available at supermarkets, *farmacie* and sometimes in larger *cartolerie* (stores selling paper goods). A pack of around 30 disposable nappies costs about €10. Fresh cow's milk is sold in cartons in bars that have a 'Latteria' sign and in supermarkets. If it is essential that you have milk, carry an emergency carton of UHT milk, since bars usually close at 8pm. In Sicily people generally use UHT milk.

See p287 for information on eating with children.

Sights & Activities

Successful travel with children can require special effort. Don't try to overdo things, and organise activities that include the children – older children could help you plan these. Try to think of things that will capture their imagination such as the archaeological sites at Selinunte (p126), the mosaics at Monreale (p99) and the Greek temples in Agrigento (p261); other good bets are the volcanoes of Etna (p208), Stromboli (p176) and Vulcano (p167), and snorkelling or boat trips around the numerous offshore islands are always popular. Even the hydrofoil is something of an event. In numerous cities (Palermo, Syracuse and Cefalù) there is the traditional Sicilian puppet theatre – a great way to keep kids amused, but always remember to allow some free time for playing. Most city parks have some sort of play area.

For more information see Lonely Planet's *Travel with Children* or look up the websites www.travelwithyourkids.com and www.family travelnetwork.com.

CLIMATE CHARTS

Sicily has a mild Mediterranean climate, defined by hot, dry summers followed by mild winters with light rainfall. However, climatic conditions vary across the island. The finest weather is usually found around the coast. The southern and western coasts are hotter due to their proximity to North Africa. They are also occasionally affected by the Saharan *scirocco* (sirocco or desert wind), usually in the springtime. The Tyrrhenian Coast is shielded to a large extent by the mountainous interior, while the Ionian Coast is considered to have the best weather of all.

Sicily's interior presents a different story. Summer days are dry and hot, although at altitude the air is surprisingly fresh and even cold in the evenings. On the highest mountains (Mt Etna and the Madonie) there is substantial snowfall in January.

See p17 for information on the best times to visit Sicily.

COURSES

Sicily is not well known for holiday courses, least of all language courses. It does, however, have a growing reputation as a food destination and there are a number of very good cooking courses on offer (see p52 for details).

If you are determined to learn Italian in Sicily there are a few institutions that run courses. The University of Catania has the well-regarded **Scuola di Lingua e Cultura Italiana per Stranieri** (☎ 095 710 27 08; www.unict.it/slci/it_home .htm; Piazza Dante 32). It offers 40 hours of Italian language and culture classes for €300. If you fancy learning the language in beautiful Taormina, **Babilonia** (☎ 094 22 34 41; www.babilonia .it; Via del Ginnasio 20) is a good school that offers classes in Italian language, literature, history and art history. A one-week standard language course (five hours per day) costs €350. Otherwise the most popular destination for language courses is Cefalù, where **Kulturforum** (☎ 092 192 39 98; www.kulturforum.it; Corso Ruggero 55) runs a standard two-week Italian course (20 hours) for €240. Private lessons and longer courses can also be arranged.

If you need to find accommodation, all the schools can help you.

CUSTOMS

Duty-free sales within the EU no longer exist. Under the rules of the single market, goods bought in and exported within the EU incur no additional taxes, provided duty has been paid somewhere within the EU and the goods are for personal use.

Travellers entering Italy from outside the EU are allowed to import the following duty free: 200 cigarettes, 1L of spirits, 2L of wine, 60mL of perfume, 250mL of *eau de toilette,* and other goods up to the value of €175. Anything over this limit must be declared on arrival and the appropriate duty paid (it is advisable to carry all your receipts with you).

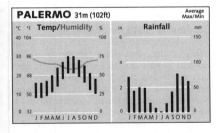

PALERMO 31m (102ft)

CATANIA 17m (56ft)

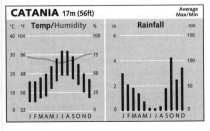

DANGERS & ANNOYANCES

Racism

As with nearly all European countries, Italy has seen a disturbing rise in racism. For decades Italy was one of the world's largest exporters of immigrants but now, as the first port of call for refugees from the Balkans, Eastern Europe and North Africa, it has become a net importer of people. For such a homogenous society with one of the lowest birth rates in Europe, the sudden influx has been traumatic and there are now an estimated half-million *clandestini* (illegal immigrants) in the country.

Historically, Sicilians have been fairly tolerant of their large North African community, but the vast numbers of immigrants landing on the beaches of Lampedusa are souring relations. Travellers should be aware of this at key entry points on the Sicilian coast, most notably at Agrigento and Trapani; if subjected to any racial discrimination you should report it to your embassy immediately.

Theft

This can be a problem for travellers in Sicily – groups of pickpockets and bag snatchers operate in Palermo especially, though you should keep an eye on your belongings in most towns and cities.

Wear a money belt under your clothing. Keep all important items, such as money, passport and tickets, in your money belt at all times. If you are carrying a bag or camera, wear the strap across your body and have the bag on the side away from the road to deter snatch thieves who operate from motorcycles and scooters.

Motorists are not immune to thieves either. Parked cars are the easiest prey, particularly those with foreign numberplates or rental-company stickers. Naturally, *never* leave valuables in your car. It is also preferable to park in a secure parking lot.

Always report theft or loss to the police within 24 hours, and ask for a statement otherwise your travel insurance company won't pay out. Emergency numbers are listed throughout this book.

Traffic

Sicilian traffic, particularly in Palermo, is second only to Naples as the most chaotic in Europe. The unprepared tourist is likely to be in for a shock when first confronted with the sheer lunacy of local motorists, who have seemingly never heard of road rules. The honking of car horns is incessant.

If you must drive in the city, you'll need to develop nerves of steel pretty quickly. For the virgin driver in Sicily, the best day to make your maiden voyage is Sunday when everyone stays resolutely at home. It is also a good idea to plan on leaving or arriving in big cities between 2pm and 4pm, when everyone is having lunch and the streets are relatively quiet.

Drivers are not keen to stop for pedestrians, even at pedestrian crossings. Sicilians simply step off the footpath and walk through the (swerving) traffic with determination – it is a practice that seems to work, so if you feel uncertain about crossing a busy road, wait for the next local. In the major cities, roads that appear to be for one-way traffic have special lanes for buses travelling in the opposite direction – always look both ways before stepping out.

DISCOUNT CARDS

Senior Cards

Senior citizens are often entitled to public-transport discounts, but usually only for monthly passes (not daily or weekly tickets). The minimum qualifying age is 65 years.

Admission to all of Sicily's major sites, museums and archaeological parks is free for the over-60s. The only place they may be asked for some ID is at the Cappella Palatina in Palermo.

Student & Youth Cards

Free admission to galleries and sites is available to under-18s. Discounts (usually half the normal fee) are available to EU citizens aged between 18 and 25 (you may need to produce proof of your age). An ISIC (International Student Identity Card) is no longer sufficient at many tourist sites as prices are based on age. A passport or driving licence is better, otherwise the **Euro<26** (www.euro26.org) card is universally acceptable. An ISIC card will still prove useful for cheap flights and theatre and cinema discounts. Similar cards are available to teachers (ITIC). For nonstudent travellers who are under 25, there is the **International Youth Travel Card** (IYTC; www.istc.org), which offers the same benefits.

Student cards are issued by student unions, hostelling organisations and some youth-travel agencies. **Centro Turistico Studentesco e Giovanile** (CTS; ☎ 06 44 11 11; www.cts.it in Italian), the youth and travel organisation, has branches in Sicily that can issue ISIC, ITIC and Euro<26 cards. You have to join the CTS first, which costs €28.

EMBASSIES & CONSULATES

It's important to realise what your embassy (of the country of which you are a citizen) can and can't do to help if you get into trouble. Generally speaking it won't be much help in emergencies if the trouble you're in is remotely your own fault. Remember that you are bound by the laws of the country you are in. Your embassy will not be sympathetic if you end up in jail after committing a crime locally, even if such actions are legal in your own country.

In genuine emergencies you might get some assistance but only if other channels have been exhausted. For example, if you need to get home urgently, a free ticket is highly unlikely – the embassy would expect you to have insurance. If you have all your money and documents stolen, it might assist with getting a new passport, but a loan for onward travel is out of the question.

Most countries have an embassy in Rome, and several also maintain consulates in Palermo. Passport inquiries should be addressed to the Rome-based offices. Most embassies and consulates are open from 8.30am or 9am to 5pm Monday to Friday. The immigration section is usually only open in the mornings from around 8.30am to 11.30am.

Australia (☎ 068 5 27 21; www.italy.embassy.gov.au; Via Antonio Bosio 5, 00161 Rome)

Canada (☎ 064 4 59 81; www.canada.it; Via Zara 30 Rome)

France (☎ 066 8 60 11; www.france-italia.it in French & Italian; Via Giulia, 251 Rome)

Germany Palermo (Map pp78-9; ☎ 091 625 46 60; Viale Scaduto 2d); Rome (☎ 064 9 21 31; www.deutsche botschaft-rom.it in German & Italian; Via San Martino della Battaglia 4)

Ireland (☎ 066 97 91 21; Piazza di Campitelli 3 Rome)

Japan (☎ 064 8 79 91; Via Quintino Sella 60 Rome)

Netherlands Palermo (Map p82; ☎ 091 58 15 21; Via Roma 489); Rome (☎ 063 22 11 41; www.olanda.it in Dutch & Italian; Via Michele Mercati 8)

New Zealand (☎ 064 41 71 71; www.nzembassy.com; Via Zara 28 Rome)

Spain (☎ 066 84 04 01; Palazzo Borghese, Largo Fontanella Borghese 19 Rome)

UK Palermo (Map p82; ☎ 091 32 64 12; S Tagiavia & Co, Via Cavour 121); Rome (☎ 064 220 00 01; www .britishembassy.gov.uk; Via XX Settembre 80a)

USA (☎ 064 67 41; www.usembassy.it; Via Vittorio Veneto 119a-121 Rome)

FESTIVALS & EVENTS

Sicily's calendar is full to bursting with events that range from colourful traditional celebrations with a religious and/or historical flavour, through to festivals celebrating the performing arts, including opera, music and theatre. The biggest events appear in the following list.

January
Befana (Epiphany) The town of Piana degli Albanesi, near Palermo, celebrates the festival of *La Befana* with a colourful parade that culminates in a firework display.

February
Carnevale (Carnival) During the week before Ash Wednesday, many towns stage carnivals and enjoy their last opportunity to indulge before Lent. The popular festivities in Sciacca are renowned throughout Sicily for imaginative floats. The party in Taormina is also pretty good.

Festa di Sant'Agata (Feast of St Agatha) There are hysterical celebrations in Catania, when one million Catanians and tourists follow a silver reliquary of the saint through the main street. Held 3 to 5 February. See p201.

Sagra del Mandorlo in Fiore (Festival of the Almond Blossom) A folk festival in Agrigento with open-air performances of drama and music. Held first Sunday in February. See p265.

April
Pasqua (Easter) Holy Week in Sicily is a very big deal and is marked by solemn, slow-moving processions and passion plays. Trapani's procession of *I Misteri* is the island's most famous, but there are similar ones worth checking out in Enna and in towns throughout the island.

Grand Prix (Motor Racing) The circuit is around Lago di Pergusa near Enna. Racing begins its season on the last weekend of April and runs till the end of October. See p244.

May & June
Festival of Greek Classical Drama Syracuse boasts the only school of classical Greek drama outside Athens and the shows attract some of Italy's finest performers. See p222.

Infiorata (Flower Festival) To celebrate the arrival of spring, Noto decorates its streets with colourful designs made with flower petals. Held third Sunday in May. See p230.

July & August
Festino di Santa Rosalia (Feast of St Rosalia) Palermo pulls out all the stops in the celebration of its patron saint. Amid the street celebrations – music, food, dancing and partying – the saint's relics are paraded from the city's cathedral. Held 10 to 15 July. See p91.

Taormina Arte (Taormina Art) This festival held in July and August hosts films, theatrical events and music concerts from an impressive list of international names. For information, log on to www.taormina-arte.com (in Italian). See p193.

Palio dei Normanni (Medieval Pageant) Piazza Armerina celebrates its Norman past on 13 and 14 August as it commemorates Count Roger's taking of the town from the Arabs in the 13th century. There are costumed parades, a procession into the town and even a joust. See p250.

September

Pelegrinaggi (Pilgrimages) This is the month for many of Sicily's pilgrimages. The most important are on 4 September (Palermo to Monte Pellegrino) and 8 September (Cefalù to the church at Gibilmanna in the Madonie mountains).

November

Ognissanti (All Souls Day; Festa dei Morti or Day of the Dead) Includes a children's toy fair and lots of pupe (sticky sugar figurines). Held 1 November.

December

Festa di Santa Lucia (Festival of St Lucy) This annual procession on 13 December commemorates Syracuse's patron saint. During the festival an enormous silver statue of the saint wends its way from the cathedral to Piazza Santa Lucia accompanied by fireworks. See p223.

Natale (Christmas) During the weeks preceding Christmas there are numerous religious events. Many churches set up elaborate cribs or nativity scenes known as presepi; these are particularly good in Caltagirone and Erice.

FOOD & DRINK

Throughout this book, prices are quoted for meals, which includes a *primo* (first course), *secondo* (second course) and dessert. We've used the term budget to describe places where you can get a main course for around €8 to €10 per person, which generally means that your whole meal will cost below €20 to €25 per person with drinks. Midrange places offer main courses between €9 and €15, resulting in a bill between €25 and €40 per person; while mains at top-end restaurants tend to exceed €15, going as high as €22 in places like Taormina (total meal cost over €40 per person). Some of the price ranges overlap as pasta dishes tend to be around €8 on all menus, the higher prices being confined to fish and meat main courses.

In very touristy places like Agrigento, Cefalù and Taormina numerous establishments offer a tourist menu that includes a

---

> **WATER**
>
> While tap water is reliable and safe throughout the country, most Sicilians prefer to drink *acqua minerale* (bottled mineral water). It will be either *frizzante* (sparkling) or *naturale* (still) and you will be asked in restaurants and bars which you prefer. If you want a glass of tap water, ask for *acqua dal rubinetto.*

---

starter, main course and dessert (and sometimes coffee or half a jug of house wine). These are always competitively priced (around €15 to €20 per person) but are hardly *haute cuisine,* and the selection is limited to one or two choices. Top-end restaurants also offer set menus, including all courses and coffee but no wine. These are generally expensive (between €25 and €50 per person), although they offer a good selection and the standard of the food is exceptionally high.

Within each section, restaurants are listed in order of budget.

Where to Eat & Drink

Restaurants in Sicily are divided starkly between casual bars or trattorie, the haunt of the working classes, and formal *ristoranti,* usually well decorated with excellent service and a wealthy clientele. Young professionals prefer to pose in *enoteche* (wine bars) or in a new breed of more casual restaurants.

In general eating establishments follow the same pattern as those on the mainland. Cheap trattorie serve simple, hearty menus; the more upmarket *ristoranti* generally have a wider selection of dishes and higher prices. It is best to check the menu, usually posted by the door, for prices. Don't judge the quality of a place by its appearance. You are just as likely to eat your most memorable meal at a place with plastic tablecloths in a tiny backstreet as in a smart restaurant.

Tavole calde (literally 'hot tables') serving street fare are popular hang-outs. In these places, what you see is what you get: brioche, *cornetti* (Italian croissants), *panini* (bread rolls with simple fillings) and *spuntini* (snacks). You can round off your meal with an ice cream – a crowd outside a *gelateria* is always a good sign.

Wine bars are popular and usually offer a limited menu (often charcuterie and cheese) to accompany a selection of wines. The general idea is to sample wines by the glass, which will, they hope, encourage you to buy a bottle or two.

Most eating establishments have a *coperto* (cover charge) of usually €1 to €3 per person; some include a *servizio* (service charge) of 10% to 15%.

For more on what to eat in Sicily, see p45.

Vegetarians & Vegans

While vegetables take pride of place on the Sicilian table, the notion of vegetarianism is quite foreign to Sicilians. You will have to pick and choose your way carefully through the menu or quiz your host on the most appropriate dishes. Most eateries serve a good selection of vegetable antipasti, pasta dishes and *contorni* (vegetable side orders). Vegans will be in for a tougher time, with many dishes featuring some sort of animal product (butter, eggs or animal stock).

Eating with Kids

You'll be hard pressed to find a children's menu in Sicilian restaurants. It's not that children aren't welcome because they are just about everywhere. Local children are treated very much as adults and are taken out to eat from a young age. You'll often see families order a *mezzo piatto* (half-plate) instead. Virtually all restaurants are perfectly comfortable tailoring a dish to meet your child's tastes.

High chairs are not easily available so bring one along if you can. While children are often taken out it's expected that they be well behaved and that they're disciplined if they are not.

GAY & LESBIAN TRAVELLERS

Although homosexuality is legal in Sicily it is not particularly well tolerated – though some say that attitudes are improving. There are a few gay and/or lesbian clubs and bars, mostly in Taormina and Catania (apparently the new gay capital). Palermo is lagging behind, though you'll find a couple of bars and clubs here too.

Overt displays of affection by homosexual couples can attract a negative response. Yet physical contact between men (and women), such as linking arms and kissing on the cheek, is commonplace and very much part of Sicilian life. It is best to bear this strange

dichotomy in mind when travelling throughout the island.

Gay-friendly bars and clubs can be tracked down through national gay organisations or the national monthly magazine *Pride*, published by Circolo Mario Mieli in Rome (available at gay and lesbian organisations and bookshops). The international gay guide, *Spartacus International Gay Guide*, has listings of gay venues all over Italy. The website http://it.gay.com (in Italian) lists gay bars and hotels, or get hold of a copy of *Guida Gay Italia* (www.metropolis.it/guidagay/guida200 .asp, in Italian). It is sometimes available at newsstands in Palermo and Catania.

If you want to track down the small (but growing) gay scene in Palermo, contact **ARCI-GAY & ARCI-Lesbica** (☎ 051 644 70 54; www.arcigay.it; Piazza di Porta Saragozza 2, 20123 Bologna), an Italian association based in Bologna.

HOLIDAYS

Most Sicilians take their annual holiday in August, deserting the cities for the cooler seaside or mountains. This means that many businesses and shops close for at least a part of the month, particularly during the week around Feast of the Assumption (Ferragosto) on 15 August. The Easter break (Settimana Santa) is another busy holiday period for Sicilians, especially as the rest of Italy seems to descend on the island, along with numerous school groups doing the tour of the churches.

Individual towns have public holidays to celebrate the feasts of their patron saints. National public holidays in Sicily include the following:

New Year's Day (Anno Nuovo) Celebrations take place on New Year's Eve (Capodanno)
Epiphany (Befana) 6 January
Good Friday (Venerdì Santo) March/April
Easter Monday (Pasquetta/Giorno dopo Pasqua) March/April
Liberation Day (Giorno della Liberazione) 25 April; marks the Allied victory in Italy
Labour Day (Giorno del Lavoro) 1 May
Republic Day (Giorno del Repubblica) 2 June
Feast of the Assumption (Ferragosto) 15 August
All Saints' Day (Ognissanti) 1 November
Feast of the Immaculate Conception (Concezione Immaculata) 8 December
Christmas Day (Natale) 25 December
St Stephen's Day (Boxing Day, Festa di Santo Stefano) 26 December

DIRECTORY

INSURANCE

A travel-insurance policy to cover theft, loss and medical problems is a good idea. It may also cover you for cancellation of and delays in your travel arrangements. Paying for your ticket with a credit card can often provide limited travel accident insurance and you may be able to reclaim the payment if the operator doesn't deliver. Ask your credit-card company what it will cover.

Some insurance policies offer lower and higher medical-expense options; the higher ones are chiefly for countries such as the USA, which have extremely high medical costs. See p305 for more details.

Some policies specifically exclude 'dangerous activities', which can include scuba diving, motorcycling and even trekking. A locally acquired motorcycle licence is not valid under some policies.

You may prefer a policy that pays doctors or hospitals directly, rather than you having to pay on the spot and claim later. If you have to claim later make sure you keep all documentation. Some policies ask you to call (reverse charges) a centre in your home country, where an immediate assessment of your problem can be made.

Check that the policy covers ambulances or an emergency flight home.

For details of car insurance, see p302.

INTERNET ACCESS

Wi-fi access is increasingly popular in Sicily and most of the top-end hotels will have wi-fi, as will some of the smaller hotels and B&Bs.

You'll find internet cafés throughout Sicily (some of them are listed in the town information listings in this book). Otherwise check out www.netcafeguide.com for an up-to-date list. Expect to pay about €6 per hour and to have to show ID – the staff will record your details in their book (as part of the new antiterrorism laws).

LEGAL AGE

- ▣ Driving: 18
- ▣ Voting: 18
- ▣ Drinking: 16
- ▣ Sex: 14 (heterosexual and homosexual)

For more useful internet addresses, see p21.

LEGAL MATTERS

For many Sicilians, finding ways to get around the law (any law) is a way of life. They are likely to react with surprise, if not annoyance, if you point out that they might be breaking the law.

The average tourist will probably have a brush with the law only if robbed by a bag snatcher or pickpocket.

Drink & Drugs

Sicily's drug laws are for the most part lenient on users and heavy on pushers. If you're caught with drugs that the police determine are for your own personal use, you'll be let off with a warning and, of course, the drugs will be confiscated from you. If the police determine that your intention was to sell the drugs, you could find yourself in prison. It's up to the police to decide whether you're a pusher, since the law is not specific about quantities. The sensible option is to avoid illicit drugs altogether. Sicilian attitudes to drug use are very conservative for the most part.

The legal blood-alcohol limit is 0.05% and random breath tests do occur. Penalties for driving under the influence of alcohol can be severe.

Police

If you run into trouble in Italy, you're likely to end up dealing with either the *polizia statale* (state police) or the *carabinieri* (military police).

The *polizia* belong to a civil force: officers take their orders from the Ministry of the Interior and generally deal with thefts, visa extensions and permissions. They wear powder blue trousers with a fuchsia stripe and a navy blue jacket. Tourists who want to report thefts and people wanting to get a residence permit will have to deal with them. They are based at police stations.

The *carabinieri* are more concerned with civil obedience. They deal with general crime, public order and drug enforcement, and are therefore more visible on the street. They wear a black uniform with a red stripe and drive dark blue cars with a red stripe. Their police station is called a *caserma* (barracks), a reflection of their military status.

Although innocent queries are always dealt with politely, in Sicily the role of *carabinieri* is an especially difficult one as – along with the regular army – they are the vanguard in the fight against the Mafia. Consequently, they have a reputation for being harsh and sometimes heavy-handed.

Other varieties of police in Italy include the *vigili urbani,* basically traffic police, and the *guardia di finanza,* who are responsible for fighting tax evasion and drug smuggling. Their role in Sicily is vastly inflated compared with their role in the rest of Italy and they are given wide berth by many Sicilians. The ordinary tourist will have no occasion to deal with them. The *guardia forestale* or *corpo forestale* are responsible for enforcing laws concerning forests and the environment in general.

Addresses and telephone numbers of local police stations are given in the Information sections in this guide.

Your Rights

Italy has some antiterrorism laws that could make life very difficult if you happen to be detained by the police for any alleged offence. You can be held for 48 hours without a magistrate being informed and you can be interrogated without the presence of a lawyer. It is difficult to obtain bail and you can be held legally for up to three years without being brought to trial.

MAPS

For specialist trekking maps see the Sicily Outdoors chapter (p70).

The city maps in this book, combined with tourist-office maps, are generally adequate. More detailed maps are available in Sicily in big-city bookshops (the best places being Palermo, Catania and Syracuse). The best large-scale city maps are produced by Litografia Artistica Cartografica (LAC) at a scale of 1:3500 and cost €5.50. Michelin, de Agostini and Touring Club Italiano (TCI) also produce decent city maps.

The AA's *Road Atlas Italy* (1:250,000), available in the UK, includes Sicily. In Italy, the Istituto Geografico de Agostini publishes a comprehensive *Atlante Turistico Stradale della Sicilia* (1:250,000), which includes 145 city maps. TCI publishes an *Atlante Stradale d'Italia* (1:200,000) divided into three parts: Nord, Centro and Sud.

The best map of Sicily is published by TCI at a scale of 1:200,000. You can buy it in bookshops, airports and motorway cafés in Sicily. Michelin also has a very good map of Sicily (series number 565) at a scale of 1:400,000.

MONEY

Sicily's unit of currency is the euro (€). The euro is divided into 100 cents. Coin denominations are one, two, five, 10, 20 and 50 cents, €1 and €2. The notes are €5, €10, €20, €50, €100, €200 and €500. In all EU countries, all euro notes of each denomination are identical on both sides. Euro coins are identical on the side showing their value, but there are different obverses, each representing one of the euro-zone countries. For more information on the euro check out the website www.europa.eu.int/euro.

See Quick Reference on the inside front cover for a handy table of exchange rates or log on to www.oanda.com. Refer to p17 for a guide to costs.

Money can be exchanged in banks, post offices and exchange offices. Banks generally offer the best rates, but shop around as rates fluctuate considerably.

ATMs

Credit cards can be used in ATMs *(bancomat)* displaying the appropriate sign or (if you have no PIN number) to obtain cash advances over the counter in many banks – Visa and MasterCard are among the most widely recognised. Check what charges you will incur with your bank.

You'll find ATMs throughout Sicily and this is undoubtedly the simplest (and safest) way to handle your money while travelling.

If an ATM rejects your card, don't despair. Try a few more ATMs displaying your credit card's logo before assuming the problem lies with your card.

Cash

Don't bring wads of cash from home (travellers cheques and plastic are much safer). Bag snatchers and pickpockets prey on cash-flashing tourists, so your best bet is never to carry more than you need for a day or two. It is, however, an idea to keep an emergency stash separate from other valuables in case you lose your travellers cheques and credit cards. You will need cash for many day-to-day transactions – many small guesthouses, eateries and shops do not take credit cards and cash is a necessity at markets.

Credit & Debit Cards

Carrying plastic is the simplest way to organise your holiday funds.

Major cards, such as Visa, MasterCard, Eurocard, Cirrus and Eurocheque, are accepted throughout Sicily. They can be used for many purchases (including in some supermarkets) and in hotels and restaurants. Check any charges with your bank but, as a rule, there is no charge for purchases on major cards.

You should check the procedure on what to do if you experience problems or if your card is stolen. Most card suppliers will give you an emergency number you can call free of charge for help and advice.

Travellers Cheques

These are a safe way to carry your money because they can be replaced if lost or stolen. They can be cashed at most banks and exchange offices. American Express, Thomas Cook and Visa are widely accepted brands.

It's vital to keep your initial receipt, a record of your cheque numbers and the ones you have used, separate from the cheques themselves. If your travellers cheques get stolen, you'll need these documents to get them replaced. You must take your passport with you when cashing cheques.

POST

Sicily's postal service is notoriously slow, unreliable and expensive.

Stamps (francobolli) are available at post offices and authorised tobacconists (look for the official tabacchi sign, a big 'T', often white on black).

Main post offices in the bigger cities are generally open from around 8.30am to 6pm and Saturday mornings too. Tobacconists keep regular shop hours (see p281).

It can take up to two weeks for mail to arrive in the UK or USA, while a letter to Australia will take between two and three weeks. Postcards take even longer. Put them in an envelope and send them as letters.

You can also send letters express, using posta prioritaria, which guarantees to deliver letters within Europe in three days and to the rest of the world within four to eight days. For more important items, use registered mail

(raccomandato), or insured mail (assicurato), the cost of which depends on the value of the object being sent.

Information about postal services and rates can be obtained at www.poste.it.

SHOPPING

The most interesting places to shop in Sicily are at the markets; every town worth its salt has at least one. Palermo's Mercato della Vucciria (p85) is probably the most famous of all and many Palermitans also shop in one of the city's two other markets. Catania has an excellent produce market and Syracuse's is fine too. At most markets you can pick up virtually everything you need, from fish to frocks and all things in between.

As in Spain and Portugal, the Arabs brought a rich tradition of ceramic production to Sicily. Major ceramics centres include Caltagirone, Santo Stefano di Camastra and Sciacca. A love of gold, coral and turquoise jewellery reflects another Arab tradition most strongly in evidence on the west coast and in particular in Trapani and Cefalù, although Syracuse, Taormina and Messina are also excellent centres of handmade jewellery, with Sciacca coral a precious local commodity. Old-fashioned European traditions of lace and embroidery can be found in Palermo and Taormina, or rural towns like Erice and Caltanissetta.

But perhaps the best shopping to be done in Sicily centres around its food and wine. The Aeolian Islands, along with Syracuse, Taormina and Cefalù, have a substantial number of gourmet delis. Sicilian wines are also beginning to make an impression on the international market. For more details see p51.

For the ultimate memento you could always purchase one of Sicily's paladin puppets or a miniature model of the traditional Sicilian cart, painstakingly decorated with all kinds of colourful features. The originals are now collectors' items.

SOLO TRAVELLERS

There is more of a backpacking culture in the east of the island around Catania, Mt Etna and Syracuse and these are the best destinations for the solo traveller. In the west there are fewer facilities for single travellers. You may feel a little lonesome in some very family-orientated communities, although Sicilians are very friendly and helpful.

The main problem facing solo travellers is the dearth of single rooms in popular tourist spots. In these places you will probably find yourself paying pretty much a double-room rate. If you are on a budget you may want to consider hostel accommodation. Other than that, normal common-sense rules apply. Avoid unlit streets and parks at night and ensure your valuables are safely stored.

TELEPHONE
Mobile Phones

Italy uses GSM 900/1800, which is compatible with the rest of Europe and Australia but not with North American GSM 1900 or the totally different system in Japan (although some North American GSM 1900/900 phones do work in Italy). If you have a GSM phone, check with your service provider about using it in Sicily and beware of calls being routed internationally (very expensive for a 'local' call). The alternative is to link up with a local service provider.

Payphones & Phonecards

The partly privatised Telecom Italia is the largest phone company in the country and its orange public payphones are scattered all over the place. The most common accept only telephone cards (carte/schede telefoniche), although you will still find some that accept both cards and coins. Some cardphones now also accept special Telecom credit cards and even commercial credit cards.

Payphones can be found in the streets, train stations and some big stores, as well as in Telecom offices. Where these offices are staffed, it is possible to make international calls and pay at the desk afterwards. There are also cut-price call centres run by various companies that offer lower rates than Telecom payphones for international calls. You simply place your call from a private booth inside the centre and pay for it when you've finished.

You can buy phonecards at post offices, tobacconists and newsstands. They come in denominations of €1, €2.50, €5 and €7.50. Remember to snap off the perforated corner before using them.

Phone Codes

The international access code is ☎ 00 and the country code is ☎ 39.

Telephone area codes all begin with '0' and consist of up to four digits. The area code is followed by a telephone number of anything from four to eight digits.

Area codes are an integral part of all telephone numbers in Italy, even if you are calling within a single zone. For example, any number you ring in Palermo will start with ☎ 091, even if it's next door. When making domestic and international calls you must always dial the full number including the initial zero.

Numeri verdi (toll-free phone numbers) usually begin with ☎ 800 (some start with ☎ 199 or ☎ 848). Mobile-telephone numbers begin with a three-digit prefix such as ☎ 330, ☎ 335, ☎ 347 etc.

TIME

Sicily is one hour ahead of GMT. Daylight-saving time starts on the last Sunday in March, when clocks are put forward one hour. Clocks go back an hour on the last Sunday in October.

TOILETS

Public toilets are not exactly common in Sicily except at major tourist sites and archaeological parks. Most people use the toilets in bars and cafés – although you might need to buy a coffee first. In many places public toilets tend to be grim, usually with a broken or nonexistent loo seat. This means you will have to do a lot of hovering about.

TOURIST INFORMATION

The quality of tourist offices in Sicily varies dramatically. One office might have enthusiastic staff but no useful printed information, while indifferent staff in another might have a gold mine of brochures.

Sicily's regional **tourist office** (☎ 091 605 81 11; www.regione.sicilia.it/turismo; Piazza Castelnuovo 35) has its headquarters in Palermo. You can also find information on the website of the **Italian State Tourist Office** (ENIT; www.enit.it).

Throughout the island, three tiers of tourist office exist: regional, provincial and local. They have different names but offer roughly the same services, with the exception of the regional offices, which are generally concerned with promotion, planning and budgeting. Throughout this book, offices are referred to as 'tourist office' rather than by their elaborate and confusing titles. Most offices will respond to written and telephone requests for information.

Azienda di Promozione Turistica (APT) The regional – read main – tourist office should have information on the town you are in and the surrounding province.

Azienda Autonoma di Soggiorno e Turismo (AAST)
Otherwise known as Informazioni e Assistenza ai Turisti,
AAST is the local tourist office. These local offices have
town-specific information and should also know about bus
routes and museum-opening times.

Pro Loco This is the local office in small towns and villages and is similar to the AAST office.

Tourist offices are generally open 8.30am to
12.30pm or 1pm and 3pm to 7pm Monday to
Friday. Hours are usually extended in summer, when some offices also open on Saturday
or Sunday.

Information booths at most major train
stations tend to keep similar hours, but in
some cases operate only in summer. Staff can
usually provide a city map, a list of hotels and
information on the major sights.

As you would expect, offices in popular destinations such as Palermo, Catania,
Taormina, Syracuse and the Aeolian Islands
are used to dealing with visitors from all
over the world. They are usually well stocked
and staffed by employees with a working
knowledge of at least one other European
language; usually English but also French
or German.

TRAVELLERS WITH DISABILITIES

Sicily is not an easy island for disabled travellers. Even a short journey in a city or town
can become a major expedition if negotiat-
ing cobblestoned streets in many of Sicily's
undulating towns. Although many buildings
have lifts, they are not always wide enough to
accommodate a wheelchair.

Alitalia operates a courtesy wheelchair
service for infirm passengers in the airport –
useful, as you will almost certainly have to
change planes in Rome and Milan to get to
Sicily. This service needs to be booked when
you book your ticket and should be recon-
firmed the day before you travel. The Italian
travel agency CIT can advise of hotels with
special facilities. It can also request that wheelchair ramps be provided to meet your train if
you book travel through CIT.

The Italian State Tourist Office in your
country may provide advice on Italian
associations for the disabled and information on what help is available. It may also
carry a small brochure, *Services for Disabled
Passengers*, which details facilities at stations
and on trains. There's an airline directory
that provides information on facilities offered

by various airlines on the disability-friendly
website www.everybody.co.uk.

The following are some useful organisations:

Accessible Italy (☎ inside Italy 378 054 994 11 00,
outside Italy 39-3486 91 30 64; www.accessibleitaly.com)
A Turin-based company that specialises in holiday services
for the disabled, ranging from tours to the hiring of adapted
transport. There is also a branch in Rome called **La Viag-
geria** (☎ 067 158 29 45; Via Lemonia 161, 00174 Rome).

Consorzio Cooperative Integrate (CO.IN; ☎ 067 12
90 11; www.coinsociale.it) A Rome-based organisation
that focuses largely on the capital, but it can provide
information on transport and accessible accommodation
throughout Italy and can help plan itineraries.

Holiday Care Service (☎ in UK 44 0845 124 9971;
www.holidaycare.org.uk) This company produces an
information pack on Italy for the physically disabled and
others with special needs. The website also has lots of
useful resources.

Royal Association for Disability & Rehabilitation
(RADAR; ☎ in UK 44 020-7250 3222; www.radar.org
.uk) A UK-based charity that publishes *Holidays & Travel
Abroad: A Guide for Disabled People*, which provides a useful
overview of the facilities that are available for disabled
travellers throughout Europe.

VISAS

The following information on visas was
correct at the time of writing, but restrictions and regulations can change. Use the
following information as a guide only and
contact your embassy for the latest details.
Travellers may also visit the Lonely Planet
website, lonelyplanet.com, for useful links and
up-to-date information.

Italy is one of 15 European countries to
have signed the Schengen Convention, an
agreement where member countries have
abolished checks at their common borders.
The other Schengen countries are Austria,
Belgium, Denmark, Finland, France,
Germany, Greece, Iceland, Luxembourg, the
Netherlands, Norway, Portugal, Spain and
Sweden. Legal residents of one Schengen
country do not require a visa for another
Schengen country. Citizens of the UK and
Ireland are exempt from visa requirements
for Schengen countries. Nationals of a number
of other countries, including Canada, Japan,
New Zealand and Switzerland, do not re-
quire visas for visits of up to 90 days to any
Schengen country.

Various other nationals not covered by the
Schengen exemption can also spend up to 90

days in Sicily without a visa. These include Australian, Israeli and US citizens. However, all non-EU nationals entering Italy for any reason other than tourism (such as study or work) should contact an Italian consulate as they may need a specific visa. They should also insist on having their passport stamped on entry as, without a stamp, they could encounter problems when trying to obtain a *permesso di soggiorno* (residence permit; see right). If you are a citizen of a country not mentioned in this section, you should check with an Italian consulate whether you need a visa.

The standard tourist visa issued by Italian consulates is the Schengen visa, valid for up to 90 days. However, individual Schengen countries may impose additional restrictions on certain nationalities. It is therefore worth checking visa regulations with the consulate of each Schengen country you plan to visit.

It is mandatory that you apply for a visa in your country of residence. You can apply for no more than two Schengen visas in any 12-month period and they are not renewable inside Italy. It's a good idea to apply early for your visa, especially in the busy summer months.

Student Visas

Non-EU citizens who want to study at a university or language school in Sicily must have a study visa. These visas can be obtained from your nearest Italian embassy or consulate. You will normally require confirmation of your enrolment, proof of payment of fees and adequate funds to support yourself before a visa is issued. The visa will cover only the period of the enrolment. This type of visa is renewable within Sicily but, again, only with confirmation of ongoing enrolment and proof that you are able to support yourself – bank statements are preferred.

Permits

EU citizens do not require permits to live, work or start a business in Sicily. They are, however, advised to register with a police station if they decide to take up residence, in accordance with an anti-Mafia law that aims to keep a watch on everyone's whereabouts in the country. Failure to do so carries no consequences, although some landlords may be unwilling to rent a flat to you if you cannot produce proof of registration. Those considering long-term residence will eventually want to consider getting a work permit, a necessary first step to acquiring an ID card *(carta d'identità)*. While you're at it, you'll need a tax-file number *(codice fiscale)* if you wish to be paid in Sicily.

WORK PERMITS

Non-EU citizens wishing to work in Sicily will need to obtain a work permit *(permesso di lavoro)*. If you intend to work for an Italian company, the company must organise the permit and forward it to the Italian embassy or consulate in your home country; only then will you be issued with an appropriate visa.

If non-EU citizens intend to work for a non-Italian company, wish to go freelance or be paid in foreign currency, they must organise the visa and permit in their country of residence through an Italian embassy or consulate. This process can take several months so look into it early.

It is in any case advisable to seek detailed information from an Italian embassy or consulate about the exact requirements before attempting to organise a legitimate job in Sicily. Many foreigners don't bother with such formalities, preferring to try to work illegally *(al nero*, literally 'in the black'). See p294 for details.

RESIDENCE PERMITS

If you stay at the same address for more than one week, you are technically obliged to report to a police station and obtain a *permesso di soggiorno* (residence permit). Tourists who are staying in hotels do not need to do this, as hotel owners must register all guests with the police.

A *permesso di soggiorno* is only necessary if you plan to study, work (legally) or live in Sicily. Obtaining one is never pleasant, although for EU citizens it is fairly straightforward and success is guaranteed. Other nationals may find it involves long queues, rude police officers and the frustration of arriving at the counter to find that you don't have all the necessary documents.

The exact requirements, such as documents and *marche da bollo* (official stamps), can vary from one place to another. In general, you will need a valid passport containing a visa stamp indicating your date of entry into

DIRECTORY

Italy, a special visa issued in your own country if you are planning to study, four passport-style photographs and proof of your ability to support yourself financially.

It is best to go to a police station to obtain precise information on what is required.

WOMEN TRAVELLERS

Women travelling alone might well receive some unwanted attention from local lotharios, but the Sicilians are generally pretty relaxed. If you feel nervous about being a solo woman, wearing a wedding ring nearly always deters any unwanted interest. If you do get chatted to by a persistent man, the best response is usually to just ignore him, but if that doesn't work, politely say that you're waiting for your husband *(marito)* or fiancé *(fidanzato)* and, if necessary, walk away.

Women on their own should use their common sense. Avoid walking alone on deserted and dark streets, and look for centrally located hotels within easy walking distance of places where you can eat at night. Women should not hitch alone.

The *Handbook for Women Travellers* (1995) by M and G Moss is recommended reading.

WORK

It is illegal for non-EU citizens to work in Sicily without a work permit but trying to obtain one can be time consuming. EU citizens are allowed to work in Sicily but they still need to obtain a residency permit from the main police station in the town where they have found work (see p293 for more information). The main challenge will not be bureaucracy but the economy – unemployment in Sicily is officially 20%; in reality it's more like 30% – the highest of any region in Italy. Frankly, other than being sent here by a company, teaching a little English or doing bar work at a summer resort, you won't have much luck securing employment.

Virtually the only source of work available to foreigners in Sicily is teaching English but, even with full qualifications, an American, Australian, Canadian or New Zealander might find it difficult to secure even a temporary position. There are language schools in Palermo, Catania and a few larger towns, but teaching positions don't often come up. Most of the more reputable schools will only hire people with a work permit *(permesso di lavoro)* and will require a Teaching English as a Foreign Language (TEFL) certificate. It is advisable to apply for work early in the year to be considered for positions that become available in October (language-school years correspond roughly to the Italian school year: late September to the end of June).

Some people pick up private students by placing advertisements in shop windows and on university noticeboards. Rates of pay vary according to experience. You can use other ads as a yardstick.

Further reading resources include *Work Your Way Around the World* (2003) by Susan Griffith and *Live and Work in Italy* (2003) by Victoria Pybus.

Transport

CONTENTS

GETTING THERE & AWAY

The best (and fastest) way to get to Sicily is by air. If you live in Europe, there are a number of budget airlines flying to Palermo. If you're coming from outside Europe, you should be able to pick up a reasonably priced fare to Rome or Milan from where you can pick up an onward connecting flight to Sicily. An adventurous alternative is to arrive by boat from Naples, Genoa or Livorno. Flights, tours and rail tickets can be booked online at www .lonelyplanet.com/travel_services.

ENTERING THE COUNTRY

Falcone-Borsellino airport at Palermo is small and efficient, so entering Sicily shouldn't be a problem or particularly stressful. If you're entering Sicily from outside Europe and catching a connecting flight in Rome or Milan, all airport formalities will take place there and the Sicilian leg of your journey will be considered an internal flight, meaning it should be a pretty painless procedure.

Boarding a ferry to Sicily from mainland Italy is almost as easy as getting on a bus, although you might want to consider pre-booking your passage if you are travelling in the high season, especially if you have a vehicle. You don't need to show your passport

THINGS CHANGE...

The information in this chapter is particularly vulnerable to change. Check directly with the airline or a travel agent to make sure you understand how a fare (and ticket you may buy) works and be aware of the security requirements for international travel. Shop carefully. The details given in this chapter should be regarded as pointers and are not a substitute for your own careful, up-to-date research.

on these internal routes but you should keep some photo ID handy.

AIR

You can get cheap flights with Ryanair and easyJet even in the highest of seasons (June to September), though if you're flying with the bigger airlines you'll be paying more (and getting more comfort). The months of April, May and October are the shoulder season, while low season is November to March. Holidays such as Christmas and Easter also see a huge jump in prices. If you are travelling to Sicily from outside Italy you may have to change carrier at either Rome or Milan.

Roughly speaking a return fare to Palermo will cost you from UK£50 on a budget airline from the UK (depending on when you book).

If you're flying to Rome and then Palermo or Catania, count on spending about US$400/800 (low/high season) from North America; C$900/1800 from the Canadian east and C$1200/2000 from the Canadian west coast; and A$1600/2200 from Australia.

The local airlines Meridiana, Volare and Air One also fly from around Europe to Palermo and Catania, via Rome.

Airports & Airlines

Sicily's two main airports are **Falcone-Borsellino** (☎ 091 702 04 09; www.gesap.it) outside Palermo, and **Fontanarossa** (☎ 095 34 05 05; www.aeroporto.catania.it) in Catania. There's also the small **Vincenzo Florio Airport** (☎ 0923 84 25 02) at Birgi, near Trapani, only used for domestic flights within Sicily.

TRANSPORT

CLIMATE CHANGE & TRAVEL

Climate change is a serious threat to the ecosystems that humans rely upon, and air travel is the fastest-growing contributor to the problem. Lonely Planet regards travel, overall, as a global benefit, but believes we all have a responsibility to limit our personal impact on global warming.

Flying & Climate Change

Pretty much every form of motor travel generates CO_2 (the main cause of human-induced climate change) but planes are far and away the worst offenders, not just because of the sheer distances they allow us to travel, but because they release greenhouse gases high into the atmosphere. The statistics are frightening: two people taking a return flight between Europe and the US will contribute as much to climate change as an average household's gas and electricity consumption over a whole year.

Carbon Offset Schemes

Climatecare.org and other websites use 'carbon calculators' that allow jetsetters to offset the greenhouse gases they are responsible for with contributions to energy-saving projects and other climate-friendly initiatives in the developing world – including projects in India, Honduras, Kazakhstan and Uganda.

Lonely Planet, together with Rough Guides and other concerned partners in the travel industry, supports the carbon offset scheme run by climatecare.org. Lonely Planet offsets all of its staff and author travel.

For more information check out our website: lonelyplanet.com.

The island is not served by intercontinental flights and only budget airlines fly directly into Sicily. Alitalia serves both Palermo and Catania. The biggest number of flights coming directly into Palermo are from airlines such as Ryanair and easyJet, both flying from London Stansted. British Airways and Air Malta have a direct flight from London Gatwick to Catania. You can also fly into both cities with Lufthansa's competitive local partner, Air One. Meridiana has numerous flights between mainland Italy and Sicily. From May to October, both airports are served by a number of charter flights (British Midlands and JMC Airlines), although airline schedules can be restrictive.

AIRLINES FLYING TO/FROM SICILY

Air Berlin (AB; ☎ 848 39 00 54; www.airberlin.com)
Air Malta (KM; ☎ 091 625 58 48; www.airmalta.com)
Air One (AP; ☎ 199 20 70 80; www.flyairone.it)
Alitalia (AZ; ☎ 022 31 41 81; www.alitalia.com)
British Airways (BA; ☎ 199 71 22 66; www.british airways.com)
British Midland (BD; ☎ 44-1332 85 4000; www .flybmi.com)
easyJet (EZY; ☎ 0905 821 09 05; www.easyjet.com)
Evolavia (7B; ☎ 899 00 09 29; www.evolavia.com)
Hapag-Lloyd Express (X; ☎ 01805 09 35 09; www .hlx.com)

JMC Airlines (JMC; ☎ 0870 750 57 11; www.jmc.com)
Lufthansa (LH; ☎ 066 568 40 04; www.lufthansa.com)
Meridiana (IG; ☎ 199 11 13 33; www.meridiana.it)
Ryanair (FR; ☎ 899 89 98 44; www.ryanair.com)
Tunis Air (TU; ☎ 091 611 18 45; www.tunisair.com.tn)
Volare (VE; ☎ 199 41 45 00; www.volareweb.com in Italian)

Tickets

If you book early or at the right time, the budget airlines have some excellent offers.

Full-time students and people aged under 26 (under 30 in some countries) can get discounted fares. You need a document proving your date of birth or an International Student Identity Card (ISIC) when buying your ticket. Other cheap deals are the discounted tickets released to some travel agents and specialist discount agencies.

Also check the online agents such as www.travelocity.co.uk, www.cheaptickets .com, www.travelcuts.com and www.expedia .com, which can offer some great deals.

Australia

There are no direct flights between Australia and Sicily so you will need to change planes at some point in Italy. Cheap flights from Australia to Europe generally go via Southeast Asian capitals. Qantas, along with Alitalia, offer the only direct flights from Melbourne and Sydney to Rome, but if you are looking for a bargain fare you will probably end up on either Thai Air or Malaysia Airlines. Flights from Perth are generally a few hundred dollars cheaper.

Quite a few travel offices specialise in discount air tickets. Some travel agencies, particularly smaller ones, advertise cheap air fares in the travel sections of weekend newspapers, such as the *Age* in Melbourne and the *Sydney Morning Herald*.

Canada
As with Australia and America, there are no direct flights to Sicily and you will have to connect through Rome or Milan. Alitalia has direct flights to Rome and Milan from Toronto and Montreal. Scan the budget travel agencies' advertisements in the *Toronto Globe & Mail*, the *Toronto Star* and the *Vancouver Province*.

Air Canada flies daily from Toronto to Rome, direct and via Montreal. European airlines British Airways, Air France, KLM and Lufthansa all fly from Canada to their respective home countries and then travel onward to Italy. Given Lufthansa's partnership with Air One, this may be the most cost-effective way to go.

Continental Europe
All national European carriers offer services to Italy. The largest of these, Air France, Lufthansa and KLM, have representatives in major European cities. Italy's national carrier, Alitalia, has a huge range of offers from all European destinations and can then connect you with one of their internal flights to Sicily.

The local Italian airlines Air One and Meridiana offer routes from either Palermo or Catania to a few European destinations, including Madrid, Barcelona, Valencia, London Gatwick, Trieste and Geneva, but even these flights will require a change in Rome or Milan.

New Zealand
Air New Zealand flies direct from Auckland to Italy, otherwise Qantas or Alitalia flights from Australia are the most direct way to get to Italy and then Sicily.

UK & Ireland
Discount air travel is big business in the UK. Advertisements for many travel agencies appear in weekend newspapers, such as the *Independent* and the *Guardian* on Saturday, and the *Sunday Times,* and in publications such as *Time Out* and the *Evening Standard.*

A couple of major airlines now operate direct routes to Palermo or Catania. Ryanair and easyJet fly twice daily from Stansted to Palermo and both British Airways (four weekly flights) and Air Malta (three weekly flights) offer flights from London Gatwick to Catania. British Midland flies out of London to Palermo and Catania, while JMC Airlines flies from Manchester or London to Catania only, usually on Friday or Saturday. There are also dozens of Alitalia flights between London and Milan or Rome, where you will have to transfer onto another plane to continue your journey to Sicily. Meridiana also offers flights to London Gatwick via various Italian cities.

Ryanair flies to Trapani from Dublin on a daily basis. There is now talk of the budget airline including flights to Comiso airport (in the Ragusa province), though this was still very much in the pipeline at the time of writing.

USA
Both the enormous **American Airlines** (www.aa.com) and **Delta Airlines** (www.delta.com) have regular flights travelling from New York to Milan and Rome, while **United Airlines** (www.united.com) has a service from Washington to Rome.

Discount travel agencies in the USA are known as consolidators, and San Francisco is the ticket consolidator capital of America although some good deals can be found in other big cities. The *New York Times, LA Times, Chicago Tribune* and *San Francisco Examiner* produce weekly travel sections containing numerous travel agencies' ads.

For discount and rock-bottom options to Europe from the USA it may be worth investigating stand-by and courier flights. Stand-by flights are often sold at 60% of the normal price for one-way tickets.

Online travel agencies www.expedia.com and www.travelocity.com are useful and reliable North American online-booking agencies, but there are plenty of others.

TRANSPORT

LAND
Sicily's location means getting there overland involves travelling the entire length of Italy, which can either be an enormous drain on your time or, if you have plenty to spare, a wonderful way of seeing Italy on your way to Sicily. At some point you are going to have to stop at a mainland port and travel over the water by boat (most people go from Villa San Giovanni or Reggio di Calabria in Calabria, to Messina). Buses are usually the cheapest option, but services are less frequent and considerably less comfortable than the train.

If you are travelling by bus, train or car to Italy it will be necessary to check whether you require visas to the countries you intend to pass through.

Border Crossings
The main points of entry to Italy are the Mt Blanc tunnel from France at Chamonix, connecting with the A5 for Turin and Milan; the Grand St Bernard tunnel from Switzerland (SS27), which also connects with the A5; and the Brenner Pass from Austria (A13), which connects with the A22 to Bologna. Mountain passes in the Alps can be closed in winter and sometimes in autumn and spring, so the tunnels are more reliable. Bring snow chains in winter.

Regular trains on two lines connect Italy with main cities in Austria and on into Germany, France or Eastern Europe. Those crossing the frontier at the Brenner Pass go to Innsbruck, Stuttgart and Munich. Those crossing at Tarvisio in the east proceed to Vienna, Salzburg and Prague. Trains from Milan head for Switzerland and on into France and the Netherlands. The main international train line to Slovenia crosses near Trieste.

Continental Europe
BUS
There is no direct service to Sicily from outside Italy. **Eurolines** (www.eurolines.com) is a consortium of European coach companies that operates across Europe but only goes as far as Rome, where you will have to change carrier. You can contact Eurolines in your own country or in Italy. Its multilingual website gives comprehensive details of prices, passes and travel agencies where you can book tickets.

Another option is the UK-based **Busabout** (☎ 020 7950 1661; www.busabout.com), which covers

at least 60 European cities and towns and offers passes of varying duration, allowing you to use its hop-on, hop-off bus network. Passes can be bought at travel agencies such as STA Travel. Travellers under the age of 26 and students get a discount of around 13%.

The frequency of departures and the number of stops available increase between April and October. You can book onward travel and accommodation on the bus or on their website.

From Rome, **Interbus** (☎ 06 481 96 76; www .interbus.it in Italian; Saistours, Piazza della Repubblica 42) runs one service weekly on Sunday from Piazzale Tiburtina to Messina (€33, 9½ hours, one per week), and then on to Palermo or Catania, all via Naples.

SAIS Autolinee (☎ in Bologna 051 24 21 50, in Pisa 050 4 62 88; www.saisautolinee.it in Italian) has buses from Bologna to Messina (€54, 14 hours, via Florence and Siena) and from Pisa to Messina (€54, 15 hours) all the way down the eastern coast (via Florence, Siena and Perugia). SAIS also has buses from Naples to Sicily.

In Rome, you can get tickets and information at the **Eurojet agency** (☎ 06 474 28 01; Piazza della Repubblica 54), or go to the bus station at Piazzale Tiburtina. Booking is a must.

CAR & MOTORCYCLE
Driving to Sicily is a pricey proposition, especially once you cross the border into Italy, which has the most expensive motorway tolls (from the French or Swiss borders to Naples it'll cost around €50) as well as the most expensive petrol in Europe (see p302 for prices). Furthermore, it's quite a drive to get to the ferry terminal at Villa San Giovanni, from where you'll cross the Straits of Messina into Sicily: you might make the trip from the French or Swiss borders in around 17 hours but only if you keep to the motorways, drive flat out (remember that the speed limit in Italy is 130km/h) and avoid the worst of the traffic – during the holiday seasons it'll be a minor miracle if you do.

Although Italy is a popular motorcycle destination, the mania has not quite reached Sicily – although there is a strong motorcycle contingent constantly racing around the hairpin bends of Mt Etna. Still, with a bike you rarely have to book ahead for ferries and can enter restricted traffic areas in cities. Crash helmets are compulsory. Unless you're touring, it is probably easier to rent a bike once you have reached Sicily. See p301 for details on driving in Italy and car and motorcycle rental.

An interesting website loaded with advice for people planning to drive in Europe is www.ideamerge.com. If you want help with route planning, try www.euroshell.com.

TRAIN

Not quite as tough-going as travelling by bus, one major advantage of getting to Sicily by train is the greater options you have en route, including more frequent departures and the possibility of breaking up your journey so it isn't one long slog.

The *Thomas Cook European Timetable* is a rail traveller's bible, giving a complete listing of train schedules. It is updated monthly and is available from Thomas Cook offices and agents worldwide. It is always advisable, but sometimes compulsory, to book seats on international trains to and from Sicily. Some of the main international services include transport for private cars – an option worth examining to save wear and tear on your vehicle before it arrives in Sicily. On overnight hauls you can book a *cuccetta* (couchette) for around €18 to €25.

If you're travelling to Sicily from anywhere outside Italy you'll have to change trains somewhere along the line in Italy; the handiest place is Rome, although there are also trains for Sicily that depart from Milan and Turin (which travel via Rome). From both Rome and Milan you should take an Intercity or Eurostar train to Sicily.

A one-way adult fare from Rome to Palermo on a EuroCity (EC) or Intercity (IC) train costs €78/55 for 1st/2nd class (11 hours, about nine daily). The equivalent from Milan costs €122/101 (19 hours, at least one daily). The *espresso* train from Rome to Messina costs €59/43 (about nine hours, five daily); from Milan to Messina with Eurostar (ES) costs €114/93 (14 hours, at least two daily). For train information in Rome, call ☎ 147 88 80 88 (open 7am to 9pm) or go to the information office at any train station.

UK

CAR & MOTORCYCLE

From the UK, you can take your car across to France either by ferry or the Channel Tunnel car train, **Eurotunnel** (☎ 08705 353 535;

www.eurotunnel.com). The latter runs 24 hours, with up to four crossings (35 minutes) each hour between Folkestone and Calais in the high season. You pay for the vehicle only and fares vary according to the time of day and season, but you could be looking at paying as much as UK£312 (valid for one year).

UK drivers holding the old-style green driving licence will need to obtain an International Driving Permit (IDP) before they can drive in Europe. For breakdown assistance both the **AA** (☎ 0870 600 0371; www.theaa .co.uk) and the **RAC** (☎ 08700 106 382; www.rac.co.uk) offer comprehensive cover in Europe.

TRAIN

The excellent passenger-train service **Eurostar** (☎ 08705 186 186; www.eurostar.com) travels from London to Paris and Brussels. Alternatively, you can get yourself a train ticket that includes crossing the Channel by ferry, Seacat or hovercraft. After that, you can travel via Paris and southern France or by swinging from Belgium down through Germany and Switzerland. The journey from London to Palermo takes 35 hours and costs around UK£300 (€420).

For the latest fare information on journeys to Italy, including the Eurostar, contact the **Rail Europe Travel Centre** (☎ Europe tickets & inquiries 08708 371 371; www.raileurope.co.uk) or **Rail Choice** (www.railchoice.com).

Alternatively, log on to the website www .seat61.com – this man has surely been on every train in the world!

SEA

Regular car/passenger ferries cross the strait between Villa San Giovanni and Messina and from Reggio di Calabria to Messina. Hydrofoils run by the railways and Ustica Lines connect Messina directly with Reggio di Calabria (see p188 for details). Sicily is also accessible by ferry from Valencia (Spain), Genoa, Livorno, Naples and Cagliari, and from Malta and Tunisia.

Ferry prices are determined by the season and are considerably more expensive from June to September. In high season, all routes are busy and you need to book several weeks in advance through each company or at travel agencies throughout Italy. Offices and telephone numbers for the ferry companies are listed in the Getting There & Away sections for the relevant cities. The incredibly helpful search

TRANSPORT

TRANSPORT

engine **Traghettionline** (☎ 010 58 20 80; www.traghetti online.net) covers all the ferry companies in the Mediterranean; you can also book online.

Grandi Navi Veloci (www1.gnv.it) Genoa (☎ 010 58 93 31); Livorno (☎ 058 640 98 94); Palermo (☎ 091 58 74 04) These are luxury ferries servicing Valencia (once weekly), Livorno (three weekly) and Genoa (daily) to Palermo.

Tirrenia Navigazione (☎ call centre 199 12 31 99; www.tirrenia.it in Italian) The main company servicing the Mediterranean and all Italian ports. Its ferries to and from Sicily include Palermo–Cagliari, Palermo–Naples, Trapani–Cagliari and Trapani–Tunisia.

Trenitalia (☎ 090 66 16 74; www.trenitalia.it; ferry terminal) Runs at least 20 fast boats a day from Villa San Giovanni and Reggio di Calabria to Messina. The boats bear the old Ferrovie dello Stato or a newer Bluvia insignia.

TTT Lines (☎ 095 746 21 87; www.tttlines.it in Italian) Based in Naples, TTT Lines has a daily car ferry from Naples to Catania leaving at midnight Monday to Saturday and 7.30pm on Sunday.

Ustica Lines (☎ 0923 2 22 00; www.usticalines.it) Ustica Lines' services include a daily hydrofoil from Naples to the Aeolian Islands and a June-to-September ferry from Naples to Trapani via Ustica.

Virtu Ferries (☎ 356 31 88 54; www.virtuferries.com; 8 Princess St, Ta'Xbiex, Malta) Virtu runs ferries between March and October from Malta to Catania and Pozzallo, just south of Syracuse.

The following table shows some mainland to Sicily ferry crossings (prices quoted for the high season; check individual websites for exact quotes at your travel time).

Route	Adult/Car	Duration
Genoa-Palermo	from €59/99	20hr
Livorno-Palermo	from €53/89	17hr
Malta-Catania	€81/130	3hr
Malta-Pozzallo	€99/110	1½hr
Naples-Catania	€40/92	10½hr
Naples-Palermo	€40/85	11hr
Naples-Trapani	€83	6½hr
Reggio di Calabria-Messina	€3/20	25min
Tunisia-Trapani	€60/100	11hr

GETTING AROUND

You can reach all of the major – and most of the minor – destinations in Sicily by train or bus. Services are generally efficient and cheap, although some of the slower trains tend to chug along in no real rush. In Sicily, your own wheels will give you the most freedom. A car allows you to stray off the main routes to discover out-of-the-way hill towns

or deserted beaches. The limited motorway (autostrada) system is toll free except for certain tracts between Messina and Catania, and Palermo and Messina (see boxed text, p190), but the extensive network of state roads can be clogged with traffic. You should also be aware that petrol is expensive and that the stress of driving and parking your car in the bigger Sicilian cities could easily ruin your trip.

To get to the offshore islands there is an extensive system of regular hydrofoils and ferries between June and the end of September. The frequency of services slows considerably in winter, when many of the islands close down. For Pantelleria and the Pelagic Islands, planes are probably a better bet – they are now cheaper than the ferries and a lot faster.

AIR

Boat trips to Sicily's offshore islands are frequent and reliable, but you may want to catch planes for Pantelleria and the Pelagic Islands if your time is limited. Local airlines Air One, Alitalia and Meridiana (for details see p296) operate flights out of Palermo and Trapani for Pantelleria and from Palermo for Lampedusa. All these flights cost from €40 one way.

Tickets can be bought at the airport or booked through any travel agency, including Sestante CIT and Centro Turistico Studentesco e Giovanile (CTS), details of which are given in the relevant regional chapters.

BICYCLE

Cycling can be a great way to see the countryside as well as get around busy town centres. There are no special road rules for cyclists. Helmets and lights are not compulsory but you would be wise to equip yourself with both. You cannot cycle on the autostrada. If you plan to bring your own bike, check with your airline for any additional costs. The bike will need to be disassembled and packed for the journey. Make sure you include a few tools, spare parts and a very solid bike lock.

Bikes can be taken very cheaply on trains for around €5, although only certain trains will take them. Fast trains (Intercity and Eurostar) will generally not accommodate them so they must be sent as registered luggage, which can take a few days. Bikes can be transported free on ferries to Sicily.

In the UK, **Cyclists' Touring Club** (☎ 08708 730 060; www.ctc.org.uk) can help you plan your own bike tour or organise guided tours. Membership costs UK£32.

Bikes are available for hire in most towns and many places have both city and mountain bikes. Rental costs for a city bike start at €5 per day or €25 per week; a good mountain bike will cost around double the price. See Getting Around under the relevant cities in this guide for more information.

BOAT

Sicily's offshore islands are served by *traghetti* (ferries) and *aliscafi* (hydrofoils). Services for the Aeolian Islands run from Milazzo; for the Egadi Islands from Trapani; for the Pelagic Islands from Porto Empedocle near Agrigento; and Ustica is served from Palermo and Trapani. See the Getting There & Away sections in the relevant regional chapters for details.

On overnight services (such as to the Pelagic Islands or Pantelleria), travellers can choose between cabin accommodation (men and women are usually segregated in 2nd class, although families will be kept together) or a *poltrona*, an airline-type armchair. Deck class is available only in summer and only on some ferries, so ask when making your booking. Restaurant, bar and recreation facilities are available on the larger ferries. All ferries carry vehicles.

The following companies serve Sicily's offshore islands:

Navigazione Generale Italiana (NGI; ☎ 090 928 34 15, www.ngi-spa.it in Italian) A ferry-only service operating out of Milazzo for the Aeolian Islands.

Siremar (☎ 091 749 31 11; www.siremar.it in Italian) Ferries and hydrofoils mainly to the Aeolian Islands from Milazzo. However, it also runs services to the Egadi Islands and Pantelleria from Trapani and to the Pelagic Islands from Porto Empedocle, as well as a useful service to Ustica from Palermo and a fast boat to Pantelleria from Mazara del Vallo (June to September only).

Ustica Lines (☎ 0923 2 22 00, for the Aeolian Islands only 090 924 91 99; www.usticalines.it in Italian) Ustica Lines specialises in a hydrofoil service. Its boats serve Ustica, Pantelleria and the Egadi Islands from its base in Trapani; the Aeolian Islands from Milazzo and Messina; and now the Pelagic Islands from Porto Empedocle.

BUS

Bus services within Sicily are provided by a variety of companies and vary from local routes linking small villages to intercity connections.

By utilising the local services, it is possible to get to just about any location on the island. Buses are usually a more reliable and faster way to get around if your destination is not on a main train line (trains tend to be cheaper on major routes).

It is usually possible to get bus timetables from local tourist offices. In larger cities, most of the main intercity bus companies have ticket offices or operate through agencies. In some smaller towns and villages, bus tickets are sold in bars – just ask for *biglietti per il pullman* – or on the bus. Note that in Sicily some minor bus routes are linked to when local markets are open: in rural areas this can often mean leaving incredibly early or finding yourself stranded after 2pm!

Major companies that run long-haul services include **Interbus** (☎ 091 616 90 39; www.interbus.it) and **SAIS Autolinee** (☎ 091 616 60 28; www.saisautolinee.it), both of which serve Naples and Rome. Interbus also owns Segesta. Although it is not usually necessary to make reservations on buses, do so in the high season for overnight or long-haul trips. Contact details and costs are listed throughout this book.

CAR & MOTORCYCLE

Roads are generally good throughout the island and there is a limited network of motorways (autostrade). The main west–east link is the A19, which extends from Palermo to Catania. The A18 runs along the Ionian Coast between Messina and Catania, while the A29d goes from Palermo to the western coast, linking the capital with Trapani and (through the western interior) Mazara del Vallo along the A29. The A20 runs from Palermo to Messina; at the time of writing it was still incomplete between Cefalù and Sant'Agata di Militello and it is doubtful it will be finished any time soon. Drivers usually travel at very high speeds in the fast (left-hand) lane on motorways, so use that lane only to pass other cars.

There's a cheap toll to use the A18 and A20 motorways. See p190 for costs.

To really explore the island, travellers will need to use the system of state and provincial roads. *Strade statali* (state roads) are single-lane highways and are toll free; they are represented on maps as 'S' or 'SS'. *Strade provinciali* (provincial roads) are sometimes little more than country lanes, but provide access to some of the more beautiful scenery

TRANSPORT

and the many small towns and villages. They are represented as 'P' or 'SP' on maps.

Automobile Associations

The **Automobile Club Italiano** (ACI; www.aci.it in Italian) no longer offers free road-side assistance to tourists. Residents of the UK and Germany should organise assistance through their own national organisations, which will entitle them to use ACI's emergency assistance number (☎ 803 116) for a small fee. Without this entitlement, you'll pay a fee of €80 if you call ☎ 803 116.

If you are hiring a car from a reputable company, it will usually give you an emergency number of its own to call in the case of any breakdown.

Bringing Your Own Vehicle

To drive your own vehicle in Sicily you need an International Insurance Certificate, also known as a Carta Verde (Green Card); your car insurance company will issue this. You should also always carry proof of ownership of a private vehicle.

Every vehicle travelling across an international border should display a nationality plate of its country of registration. A warning triangle (to be used in the event of a breakdown) is compulsory throughout Europe. A first-aid kit, a spare-bulb kit and a fire extinguisher are also recommended.

Driving Licence

EU member states' driving licences are recognised in Sicily. If you hold a licence from another country, you should obtain an International Driving Permit (IDP) too. Your national automobile association can issue this and it is valid for 12 months.

Fuel

The cost of fuel (petrol) in Sicily is very high – €1.35 for a litre at the time of writing. Petrol is called *benzina*, unleaded petrol is *benzina senza piombo* and diesel is *gasolio*. There are plenty of petrol stations in and around towns and on national road networks.

Hire

You have to be aged 21 or more (23 or more for some companies) to hire a car in Sicily. However, it is cheaper to arrange car rental before leaving your own country, for instance

through some sort of fly/drive deal. The most competitive multinational and national car-rental agencies are as follows:

Auto Europe (☎ 1888 223 55 55; www.autoeurope .com)

Autos Abroad (☎ 44 8700 66 77 88; www.autosabroad .com)

Avis (☎ 02 754 19 761; www.avis.com)

Budget (☎ 1800 472 33 25; www.budget.com)

Europcar (☎ 06 481 71 62; www.europcar.com)

Hertz (☎ 199 11 22 11; www.hertz.com)

Maggiore (☎ 06 229 15 30; www.maggiore.it in Italian)

No matter which company you hire your car from, make sure you understand what is included in the price (unlimited kilometres, tax, insurance, collision-damage waiver and so on) and what your liabilities are. It is also a very good idea to get fully comprehensive insurance to cover any untoward bumps or scrapes that are quite likely to happen.

You'll have no trouble hiring a small motorcycle such as a scooter (Vespa). There are numerous rental agencies in the cities (where you'll also usually be able to hire larger motorcycles for touring) and at tourist destinations such as seaside resorts. The average cost for a 50cc scooter (for one person) is around €25 per day or €130 per week.

Most agencies will not rent motorcycles to people aged under 18. Note that many places require a sizable deposit and that you could be responsible for reimbursing part of the cost of the bike if it is stolen.

Insurance

Third-party motor insurance is a minimum requirement in Italy. The Green Card, an internationally recognised proof of insurance obtainable from your insurer, is mandatory. Ask your insurer for a European Accident Statement form, which can simplify matters in the event of an accident. A European breakdown assistance policy is a good investment. In Italy, assistance can be obtained through the **Automobile Club Italiano** (ACI; ☎ 24hr info line 15 18, 06 49 11 15; www.aci.it in Italian).

Road Rules

In Sicily, as throughout continental Europe, you drive on the right-hand side of the road and overtake on the left. Unless otherwise indicated, you must always give way to cars entering an intersection from the right. It is compulsory to wear seat belts if fitted

ROAD DISTANCES (KM)

	Agrigento	Caltanissetta	Catania	Cefalù	Enna	Erice	Marsala	Mazara del Vallo	Messina	Palermo	Ragusa	Sciacca	Syracuse	Taormina	Trapani
Agrigento	---														
Caltanissetta	58	---													
Catania	165	112	---												
Cefalù	133	100	180	---											
Enna	91	33	83	109	---										
Erice	182	231	318	176	264	---									
Marsala	132	195	305	181	228	48	---								
Mazara del Vallo	91	190	324	211	223	67	19	---							
Messina	258	204	95	159	180	352	337	387	---						
Palermo	126	133	208	73	135	112	121	126	226	---					
Ragusa	131	126	101	218	130	308	256	215	201	250	---				
Sciacca	57	115	240	215	148	125	109	64	340	183	181	---			
Syracuse	218	159	60	231	131	378	350	309	160	260	78	275	---		
Taormina	214	162	47	206	135	365	355	321	53	255	157	287	115	---	
Trapani	157	225	312	168	234	6	31	69	324	104	284	127	355	359	---

to the car. If you are caught not wearing a seat belt, you will be required to pay an on-the-spot fine.

Random breath tests now take place in Sicily. If you're involved in an accident while under the influence of alcohol, the penalties can be severe. The blood-alcohol limit is 0.05%.

The autostrade speed limits are 130km/h and on all nonurban highways 110km/h. In built-up areas the limit is 50km/h. Speeding fines follow EU standards and are proportionate with the number of kilometres that you are caught driving over the speed limit. Fines can cost up to €260.

You don't need a licence to ride a scooter under 50cc but you must be aged 14 or more. You can't carry passengers or ride on motorways, and the speed limit is 40km/h. To ride a motorcycle or scooter up to 125cc, you must be aged 16 or more and have a licence (a car licence will do). Helmets are compulsory. For motorcycles over 125cc you need a motorcycle licence.

On a motorcycle you will be able to enter restricted-traffic areas in Sicilian cities without any problems and traffic police generally turn a blind eye to motorcycles parked on footpaths. There is no lights-on requirement for motorcycles during the day.

HITCHING

In Sicily it can be pretty tough to get a lift, as most motorists tend to be mistrustful of anyone standing on the side of the road and very few, if any, Sicilians (or Italians) would do it. It is illegal to hitch on Sicily's motorways but quite acceptable to stand near the entrance to the tollbooths. Never hitch where drivers can't stop in good time or where you might cause an obstruction. Look presentable, carry as little luggage as possible and hold a sign in Italian indicating your destination.

LOCAL TRANSPORT

All the major cities and towns have good local (bus) transport systems; Palermo and Catania also have a metro.

Bus & Metro

City bus services are usually frequent and reliable. You must always purchase bus tickets

TRANSPORT

TRANSPORT

before you board the bus and validate them once on board. It is common practice among Sicilians and many tourists to ride on the buses for free by not validating tickets. However, if you get caught with a nonvalidated ticket, you can be fined on the spot (up to €25 in Palermo and Catania). Having said that, officers are very lenient towards tourists.

The metro systems in Palermo and Catania are limited and don't service destinations of real interest to most visitors. You must buy tickets and validate them before getting on the train. You can get a map of the networks from tourist offices in Palermo and Catania.

You can buy tickets at most *tabaccherie* (tobacconists), at many newsstands and at ticket booths. Tickets generally cost €0.80 to €1 for two hours.

Taxi

Taxis are very expensive in Sicily. If you need a taxi, you can usually find one in taxi ranks at train and bus stations or you can telephone taxi companies direct (numbers are listed in the Getting Around sections of the major cities). However, if you book a taxi by phone, you will be charged for the trip the driver makes to reach you. Taxis will stop when hailed on the street.

Rates vary from city to city. A good indication of the average is Palermo, where the minimum charge is €3.50. After that it's €2.20 for the first kilometre, then €0.70 per kilometre thereafter. There is a surcharge of €1.70 from 10pm to 6am. All this usually means you will be paying about €12 for the shortest of taxi rides.

TRAIN

Travelling by train in Sicily may be slow, but it is simple, cheap and generally efficient. **Trenitalia** (☎ 848 88 80 88; www.trenitalia.it), previously the Ferrovie dello Stato (FS; the State Railway Service) is the partially privatised state train system that runs most of the services in Sicily.

There are several types of train. Intercity (IC) trains are the fastest, stopping only at major stations. The *diretto, interregionale* and *espresso* stop at all but the most minor stations, while the *regionale* (also called *locale*) is the slowest of all, halting at every stop on the line. Eurostar Italia (ES) does not run in Sicily. There is one private line in Sicily, the **Ferrovia Circumetnea** (☎ 095 54 12 50; www.circumetnea .it), which does a circuit of Mt Etna.

Travellers should note that all tickets must be validated *before* you board your train. Simply punch them in the yellow machines installed at the entrance to all train platforms. If you don't validate them you risk a fine. This rule does not apply to tickets purchased outside Italy.

There are left-luggage facilities or lockers at most of the bigger train stations. They are usually open 24 hours or close only for a few hours after midnight. Charges are from €3.10 per day per piece of luggage.

Costs & Classes

Apart from the standard division between 1st and 2nd class on the faster trains (generally you can get only 2nd-class seats on *locali* and *regionali*), you usually have to pay a supplement for travelling on the fast Intercity trains.

As with tickets, the price of the supplement is in part calculated according to the length of the journey and is usually between 20% and 25% of the ticket price. You can pay the supplement separately from the ticket. If you don't buy a supplement before you board you can get one from the conductor but it will cost you closer to 40% of the ticket price.

Sample prices for one-way train fares are as follows (return fares are generally double).

From	To	1st/2nd class
Catania	Agrigento	€12
Catania	Syracuse	€5
Messina	Catania	€10.50/8.20
Palermo	Agrigento	€7
Palermo	Catania	€14.50/12
Palermo	Messina	€18/14.50

Reservations

It is recommended that you book train tickets for long trips, particularly if you're travelling on weekends or during holiday periods (see p285), otherwise you could find yourself standing in the corridor for the entire journey.

In 1st class, booking is often mandatory (and free). Where it is optional (which is more often, but not always, the case in 2nd class), you may pay a €2.60 booking fee. Tickets can be booked at the ticket booths at the station or at most travel agencies.

Train Passes

It is not worth buying a rail pass if you are only travelling in Sicily, since train fares are reasonably cheap and the network isn't big enough to justify the expense.

Health

CONTENTS

BEFORE YOU GO

While Italy has excellent health care, prevention is the key to staying healthy while abroad. A little planning before departure, particularly for pre-existing conditions, will save trouble later. Bring medications in their original, clearly labelled containers. A signed and dated letter from your physician describing your medical conditions and medications, including generic names, is also a good idea. If carrying syringes or needles, be sure to have a physician's letter documenting their medical necessity. If you are embarking on a long trip, make sure your teeth are OK (dental treatment is particularly expensive in Italy) and take your optical prescription with you.

INSURANCE

If you're an EU citizen, an EHIC (European Health Insurance Card) is available online (UK citizens see www.ehic.org.uk) or from health centres in your country, and covers you for most medical care but not emergency repatriation home or nonemergencies. Citizens from countries outside the EU should find out if there is a reciprocal arrangement for free medical care between their country and Italy. If you do need health insurance, make sure you get a policy that covers you for the worst possible scenario, such as an accident requiring an emergency flight home. Find out in advance if your insurance plan will make payments directly to providers or reimburse you later for health expenditures abroad.

RECOMMENDED VACCINATIONS

No jabs are required to travel to Sicily. The WHO, however, recommends that all travellers be covered for diphtheria, tetanus, measles, mumps, rubella and polio, as well as hepatitis B.

INTERNET RESOURCES

Age Concern (www.ageconcern.org.uk) Advice on travel for the elderly.
Fit for Travel (www.fitfortravel.scot.nhs.uk) General travel advice for the layperson.
International Travel and Health (www.who.int/ith) This publication by the WHO is revised annually.
Marie Stopes International (www.mariestopes.org .uk) Information on women's health and contraception.
MDtravelhealth.com (www.mdtravelhealth.com) Travel health recommendations for every country; updated daily.

IN TRANSIT

DEEP VEIN THROMBOSIS (DVT)

Blood clots may form in the legs during plane flights, chiefly because of prolonged immobility (the longer the flight, the greater the risk). The chief symptom of DVT is swelling or pain of the foot, ankle or calf, usually, but not always, on just one side. When a blood clot travels to the lungs, it may cause chest pain and breathing difficulties. Travellers with any of these symptoms should immediately seek medical attention as the condition can be lethal. To prevent the development of DVT on long flights, you should walk about the cabin, exercise the leg muscles while sitting, drink plenty of fluids and avoid alcohol and tobacco.

JET LAG

To minimise jet lag, try drinking plenty of nonalcoholic fluids and eating light meals. Upon arrival, get exposure to natural sunlight and adjust your schedule (for meals, sleep etc) to local time as soon as possible.

HEALTH

IN SICILY

AVAILABILITY & COST OF HEALTH CARE

Excellent health care is readily available throughout Italy, but standards can vary. Pharmacists sell over-the-counter medication for minor illnesses and give valuable advice. They can also advise when more specialised help is required and point you in the right direction. In major cities you are likely to find English-speaking doctors or a translator service.

If you need an ambulance anywhere in Sicily call ☎ 118. For emergency treatment, go straight to the *pronto soccorso* (casualty) section of a public hospital, where you can also get emergency dental treatment.

TRAVELLER'S DIARRHOEA

If you develop diarrhoea, be sure to drink plenty of fluids, preferably in the form of an oral rehydration solution such as Dioralyte. If diarrhoea is bloody, persists for more than 72 hours, or is accompanied by fever, shaking, chills or severe abdominal pain, you should seek medical attention.

ENVIRONMENTAL HAZARDS
Bites, Stings & Insect-Borne Diseases

Italian beaches are occasionally inundated with jellyfish whose stings are painful but not dangerous. Dousing the affected area in vinegar will de-activate any stingers that have not fired. Calamine lotion, antihistamines and analgesics may reduce the reaction and relieve pain.

Italy's only dangerous snake, the viper, is found throughout the country except on Sardinia. To minimise the possibilities of being bitten, always wear boots, socks and long trousers when walking through undergrowth where snakes may be present. Don't put your hands into holes and crevices, and be careful when collecting firewood. Viper bites do not cause instantaneous death and an antivenin is widely available in pharmacies. Keep the victim calm and still, wrap the bitten limb tightly, as you would for a sprained ankle, and attach a splint to immobilise it. Seek medical help, if possible with the dead snake for identification. Don't attempt to catch the snake if there is a possibility of being bitten again. Tourniquets and sucking out the poison have now been comprehensively discredited.

Always check for ticks all over your body if you have been walking through a potentially tick-infested area, as they can cause skin infections and other more serious diseases such as Lyme disease and tick-borne encephalitis. If you find a tick attached to your body, press down around the tick's head with tweezers, grab the head and gently pull upwards. Avoid pulling the rear of the body as this may squeeze the tick's gut contents through the attached mouth parts into the skin, increasing the risk of infection and disease. Lyme disease begins with the spreading of a rash at the site of the bite, accompanied by fever, headache, extreme fatigue, aching joints and muscles, and severe neck stiffness. If untreated, symptoms usually disappear but disorders of the nervous system, heart and joints can develop later. Treatment works best early in the illness – medical help should be sought. Symptoms of tick-borne encephalitis include blotches around the bite, which is sometimes pale in the middle, and headaches, stiffness and other flulike symptoms, as well as extreme tiredness, appearing a week or two after the bite. Again, medical help must be sought.

Leishmaniasis is a group of parasitic diseases transmitted by sandflies and found in coastal parts of Italy. Cutaneous leishmaniasis affects the skin tissue and causes ulceration and disfigurement; visceral leishmaniasis affects the internal organs. Avoiding sandfly bites by covering up and using insect repellent is the best precaution against this disease.

Heatstroke

Heatstroke occurs following excessive fluid loss when there is inadequate replacement of fluids and salt. Symptoms of the illlness include headache, dizziness and tiredness. Dehydration is already happening by the time that you feel thirsty – aim to drink sufficient water to produce pale, diluted urine. To treat heatstroke, drink water and/or fruit juice, and cool the body with cold water and fans.

Hypothermia

When the body loses heat faster than it can produce it, hypothermia can set in. Proper preparation, however, will reduce the risks of getting it. Even on a hot day in the mountains, the weather can change, so carry waterproof garments, warm layers and a hat, and inform others of the route you will be taking. Hypothermia starts with shivering, loss of judgment and clumsiness. Unless rewarming occurs, the sufferer's condition deteriorates into apathy, confusion and coma. Stop further heat loss by seeking shelter, warm dry clothing, hot sweet drinks and shared bodily warmth.

TRAVELLING WITH CHILDREN

Make sure children are up to date with routine vaccinations and discuss possible travel vaccines well before departure as some vaccines are not suitable for children under one year of age. Lonely Planet's *Travel with Children* includes travel health advice for younger children.

WOMEN'S HEALTH

Emotional stress, exhaustion and travelling through different time zones can all contribute to an upset in the menstrual pattern.

If using oral contraceptives, remember that some antibiotics, diarrhoea and vomiting can stop the pill from working. Time zones, gastrointestinal upsets and antibiotics do not affect injectable contraception.

Travelling during pregnancy is usually possible but always consult your doctor before planning your trip. The most risky times for travel are during the first 12 weeks of pregnancy and after 30 weeks.

SEXUAL HEALTH

Condoms are readily available but emergency contraception is not, so take the necessary precautions.

HEALTH

Language

CONTENTS

SICILIANO OR ITALIANO?

Although standard Italian may be Sicily's official language and is spoken almost universally on the island, most locals (more than 70%) speak Sicilian among themselves. Sicilian is referred to as an Italian dialect, but is sufficiently different as to warrant being termed a language in its own right; even if you're fluent in Italian, you'll find it almost impossible to understand. Luckily, Sicilians will readily revert to Italian when speaking to anyone from the mainland or abroad, although the occasional Sicilian word will still creep in.

Some Sicilians have studied English at school, but English speakers are generally hard to find beyond the more popular tourist resorts, where staff at hotels, restaurants and tourist offices usually have a basic grasp of the language. Any attempt on your part to get to grips with Italian will greatly enhance your stay on the island, no matter how many mistakes you make.

For information on food and dining, which includes useful words and phrases in Italian, see p45. If you're interested in studying Italian while in Sicily, see p283. If you'd like a more comprehensive guide to the language, get hold of a copy of Lonely Planet's *Italian Phrasebook*.

ITALIAN

Italian is a Romance language related to French, Spanish, Portuguese and Romanian, all of which are directly descended from Latin. The Romance languages belong to the Indo-European group of languages, which includes English. Indeed, as English and Italian share common roots in Latin, you will recognise many Italian words.

Sicily has a strange relationship with the Italian language. Although it is commonly accepted that modern standard Italian developed from the Tuscan dialect, Sicilians rightly assert that the first literature in the 'common vernacular' (Italian, as opposed to Latin or Greek) was produced in Sicily (at the court of Frederick I in the 13th century). Exponents of the Sicilian school of poetry, mostly court officials-turned-poets, were a source of inspiration to many of the early Tuscan writers. After the Middle Ages, works by prestigious writers from the mainland's north, such as Dante, Petrarch and Boccaccio, contributed to the steady elevation of Tuscan as the dominant written vernacular. History shows that Tuscany's status as the political, cultural and financial power base of the nation ensured that the region's dialect would ultimately be installed as the national tongue.

The Italian of today is something of a composite. What you hear on the radio and TV, in educated discourse and indeed in the everyday language of many people is the result of centuries of cross-fertilisation between the dialects, greatly accelerated in the postwar decades by the modern media.

BE POLITE!

If you have more than the most fundamental grasp of the Italian language, you need to be aware that many Sicilians still expect to be addressed in the third person formal (*lei* instead of *tu*). Also, it is not considered polite to use the informal greeting *ciao* when

SPEAKING IN TONGUES

Along with all Italian dialects, Sicilian belongs to the Italo-Romance language group. However, centuries of foreign occupation have exposed it to linguistic influences from many and varied sources, including Albanian, Arabic, French, Greek, Norman, Spanish and northern Italian dialects.

The grammatical structure of Sicilian is somewhat different from standard Italian: there's no single verb conjugation for the future tense – instead, Sicilian uses a form akin to 'I have (to do something)'; and the simple past (a literary form only in standard Italian) is used for the past perfect tense in everyday speech. Pronunciation is difficult, and it is commonly claimed that only a Sicilian can pronounce the double 'd' that regularly substitutes the standard Italian double 'l' – the classic Sicilian protestation of sincerity, *La bella madre e veramente* (By the beautiful mother and truly), becomes *La bedda madre e beramante*.

Sicilian is also coloured with a rich range of metaphors and proverbs, some of which date back to the days of Arabic occupation. The English 'All things in moderation' in Sicilian reads *Nun essiri duci sinno ti mancianu, nun essiri amaru sinno ti futanu* (Don't be too sweet lest you be eaten, don't be too sour lest you be shunned). The Sicilian way to say 'Make the most of what you've got' is *Camina chi pantofuli fino a quannu nun hai i scarpi* (Walk in your slippers until you find your shoes).

Sicilians are also known for their epithets, which are used as insults of varying strength in a range of situations. If you want to call someone crazy, you refer to them as *stunato*; if there's an excess of drink involved, it's most likely that they're *scribbi di patata* – literally, taken over by the 'spirit of the potato', a reference to the distillation of some alcoholic drinks from that vegetable. If you want to curse someone, you refer to them as having *u mal'occhio* (the evil eye), and if you really want to slander a Sicilian man, refer to him as *cornuto* (with horns), meaning that he is a cuckold. While not an exclusively Sicilian insult, it suggests a loss of honour that is about as ignominious as it gets on the island – so be careful at whom you direct it!

addressing strangers unless they use it first; it's better to say *buongiorno* (or *buona sera*, as the case may be) and *arrivederci* (or the more polite form, *arrivederla*). This is true of most of Italy, but in Sicily inappropriate use of the informal can be considered gravely impolite, and in some cases downright insulting – especially when talking to an older person. You'll find that the younger generation are less likely to be troubled by this, but we have used the formal address for most of the phrases in this guide. Where the informal mode is included, it is indicated by 'inf' in brackets.

GENDER

Italian nouns have both masculine and feminine forms (usually ending in '-o' and '-a' respectively), and adjectives change according to the gender of the noun they modify. Where both gender forms are given in this guide, they are separated by a slash, the masculine form first.

PRONUNCIATION

Surprisingly – especially after you hear the near-incomprehensible dialect – a Sicilian speaker's pronunciation of standard Italian is refreshingly clear and easy to understand, even if you have only a limited command of the language. Vowels are pronounced more openly than in mainland Italy, and there's a tendency to emphasise consonants, so that a word like *buongiorno* (good day) sounds something like 'bawn-jaw-rrno'. The French influence also means that in certain parts of Sicily, particularly the west, the 'r' is not as rolled as it is in standard Italian: locals pronounce 'Trapani' the way an English-speaker would, without rolling the 'r'.

Setting aside the vagaries of Sicilian pronunciation and dialect, Italian is not difficult to pronounce once you learn a few easy rules. Although some of the more clipped vowels, and stress on double letters, require a bit of practice for English speakers, it's easy enough to make yourself understood.

Vowels

a	as in 'art', eg *caro* (dear); sometimes short, eg *amico/a* (friend)
e	short, as in 'let', eg *mettere* (to put); long, as in 'there', eg *mela* (apple)
i	short, as in 'it', eg *inizio* (start); long, as in 'marine', eg *vino* (wine)

o   short, as in 'dot', eg *donna* (woman);
        long, as in 'port', eg *ora* (hour)
u   as the 'oo' in 'book', eg *puro* (pure)

Consonants

The pronunciation of many Italian consonants is similar to that of their English counterparts. Pronunciation of some consonants
depends on certain rules:

c   as the 'k' in 'kit' before **a**, **o** and **u**; as
        the 'ch' in 'choose' before **e** and **i**
ch   as the 'k' in 'kit'
g   as the 'g' in 'get' before **a**, **o**, **u** and **h**;
        as the 'j' in 'jet' before **e** and **i**
gli   as the 'lli' in 'million'
gn   as the 'ny' in 'canyon'
h   always silent
r   a rolled 'rr' sound
sc   as the 'sh' in 'sheep' before **e** and **i**; as
        'sk' before **a**, **o**, **u** and **h**
z   as the 'ts' in 'lights', except at the
        beginning of a word, when it's as the
        'ds' in 'suds'

Note that when **ci**, **gi** and **sci** are followed by
a, **o** or **u**, the 'i' is not pronounced unless the
accent falls on the 'i'. Thus the name 'Giovanni' is pronounced jo-*va*-nee, not 'jee-o-
va-nee'.

A double consonant is pronounced as a
longer, more forceful sound than a single
consonant.

Word Stress

Stress is indicated in our pronunciation
guide by italics. Word stress generally falls
on the second-last syllable, as in spa-*ghet*-ti,
but when a word has an accent, the stress
falls on that syllable, as in cit-*tà* (city).

ACCOMMODATION

I'm looking for a ...	*Cerco ...*	*cher*·ko ...
guesthouse	*una pensione*	*oo*·na pen·*syo*·ne
hotel	*un albergo*	oon al·*ber*·go
youth hostel	*un ostello per la gioventù*	oon os·*te*·lo per la jo·ven·*too*

Where is a cheap hotel?
Dov'è un albergo a buon prezzo?
do-*ve* oon al·*ber*·go a bwon *pre*·tso

What is the address?
Qual'è l'indirizzo?
kwa·*le* leen·dee·*ree*·tso

Could you write the address, please?
Può scrivere l'indirizzo, per favore?
pwo skree·*ve*·re leen·dee·*ree*·tso per fa·*vo*·re

Do you have any rooms available?
Avete camere libere?
a·*ve*·te *ka*·me·re *lee*·be·re

May I see it?
Posso vederla?
po·so ve·*der*·la

Where is the bathroom?
Dov'è il bagno?
do·*ve* eel *ba*·nyo

I'm/We're leaving today.
Parto/Partiamo oggi.
par·to/par·*tya*·mo o·jee

I'd like (a) ...	*Vorrei ...*	vo·*ray* ...
bed	*un letto*	oon *le*·to
single room	*una camera singola*	oo·na *ka*·me·ra *seen*·go·la
double room	*una camera matrimoniale*	oo·na *ka*·me·ra ma·tree·mo·*nya*·le
room with two beds	*una camera doppia*	oo·na *ka*·me·ra *do*·pya
room with a bathroom	*una camera con bagno*	oo·na *ka*·me·ra kon *ba*·nyo
to share a dorm	*un letto in dormitorio*	oon *le*·to een dor·mee·*to*·ryo
How much is it ...?	*Quanto costa ...?*	*kwan*·to *ko*·sta ...
per night	*per la notte*	per la *no*·te
per person	*per persona*	per per·*so*·na

CONVERSATION & ESSENTIALS

Hello.	*Buon giorno.*	bwon *jor*·no
	Ciao. (inf)	chow
Goodbye.	*Arrivederci.*	a·ree·ve·*der*·chee
	Ciao. (inf)	chow
Yes.	*Sì.*	see
No.	*No.*	no
Please.	*Per favore/*	per fa·*vo*·re
	Per piacere.	per pya·*chay*·re
Thank you.	*Grazie.*	*gra*·tsye
That's fine/	*Prego.*	*pre*·go
You're welcome.		
Excuse me.	*Mi scusi.*	mee *skoo*·zee
I'm sorry.	*Mi scusi/*	mee *skoo*·zee/
	Mi perdoni.	mee per·*do*·nee

What's your name?
Come si chiama?   *ko*·me see *kya*·ma
Come ti chiami? (inf)   *ko*·me tee *kya*·mee

My name is ...
Mi chiamo ...   mee *kya*·mo ...

Where are you from?
Da dove viene?   da *do*·ve vye·ne
Di dove sei? (inf)   dee *do*·ve se·ee

I'm from ...
Vengo da ...   *ven*·go da ...

I (don't) like ...
(Non) Mi piace ...   (non) mee *pya*·che ...

Just a minute.
Un momento.   oon mo·*men*·to

DIRECTIONS

Where is ...?
Dov'è ...?   do·*ve* ...

Go straight ahead.
Si va sempre diritto.   see va *sem*·pre dee·*ree*·to
Vai sempre diritto. (inf)   *va*·ee *sem*·pre dee·*ree*·to

Turn left.
Giri a sinistra.   *jee*·ree a see·*nee*·stra

Turn right.
Giri a destra.   *jee*·ree a *de*·stra

at the next corner		
al prossimo angolo		al *pro*·see·mo *an*·go·lo
at the traffic lights		
al semaforo		al se·*ma*·fo·ro

behind	*dietro*	*dye*·tro
in front of	*davanti*	da·*van*·tee
far (from)	*lontano (da)*	lon·*ta*·no (da)
near (to)	*vicino (di)*	vee·*chee*·no (dee)
opposite	*di fronte a*	dee *fron*·te a
beach	*la spiaggia*	la *spya*·ja
bridge	*il ponte*	eel *pon*·te
castle	*il castello*	eel kas·*te*·lo

SIGNS	
Ingresso/Entrata	Entrance
Uscita	Exit
Informazione	Information
Aperto	Open
Chiuso	Closed
Proibito/Vietato	Prohibited
Camere Libere	Rooms Available
Completo	Full/No Vacancies
Polizia/Carabinieri	Police
Questura	Police Station
Gabinetti/Bagni	Toilets
Uomini	Men
Donne	Women

cathedral	*il duomo*	eel *dwo*·mo
island	*l'isola*	*lee*·so·la
(main) square	*la piazza*	la *pya*·tsa
	(principale)	(preen·chee·*pa*·le)
market	*il mercato*	eel mer·*ka*·to
old city	*il centro*	eel *chen*·tro
	storico	*sto*·ree·ko
palace	*il palazzo*	eel pa·*la*·tso
ruins	*le rovine*	le ro·*vee*·ne
sea	*il mare*	eel *ma*·re
tower	*la torre*	la *to*·re

HEALTH

I'm ill.	*Mi sento male.*	mee *sen*·to *ma*·le
It hurts here.	*Mi fa male qui.*	mee fa *ma*·le kwee
I'm ...	*Sono ...*	*so*·no ...
asthmatic	*asmatico/a*	az·*ma*·tee·ko/a
diabetic	*diabetico/a*	dee·a·*be*·tee·ko/a
epileptic	*epilettico/a*	e·pee·*le*·tee·ko/a
I'm allergic ...	*Sono*	*so*·no
	allergico/a ...	a·*ler*·jee·ko/a ...
to antibiotics	*agli antibiotici*	*a*·lyee an·tee·bee·*o*·tee·chee
to nuts	*ai noci*	a·ee *no*·chee
to peanuts	*alle arachidi*	*a*·le a·*ra*·kee·dee
to penicillin	*alla penicillina*	*a*·la pe·nee·see·*lee*·na

antiseptic	*antisettico*	an·tee·*se*·tee·ko
aspirin	*aspirina*	as·pee·*ree*·na
condoms	*preservativi*	pre·zer·va·*tee*·vee
contraceptive	*contraccetivo*	kon·tra·che·*tee*·vo
diarrhoea	*diarrea*	dee·a·*re*·a
medicine	*medicina*	me·dee·*chee*·na
sunblock cream	*crema solare*	*kre*·ma so·*la*·re
tampons	*tamponi*	tam·*po*·nee

LANGUAGE

EMERGENCIES

Help!
Aiuto! — a·yoo·to

There's been an accident!
C'è stato un incidente! — che sta·to oon een·chee·den·te

I'm lost.
Mi sono perso/a. — mee so·no per·so/a

Go away!
Lasciami in pace! — la·sha·mi een pa·che
Vai via! (inf) — va·ee vee·a

Call ...!	Chiami ...!	kee·ya·mee ...
a doctor	un dottore/	oon do·to·re/
	un medico	oon me·dee·ko
the police	la polizia	la po·lee·tsee·ya

LANGUAGE DIFFICULTIES

Do you speak English?
Parla inglese? — par·la een·gle·ze

Does anyone here speak English?
C'è qualcuno che parla inglese? — che kwal·koo·no ke par·la een·gle·ze

How do you say ... in Italian?
Come si dice ... in italiano? — ko·me see dee·che ... een ee·ta·lya·no

What does ... mean?
Che vuol dire ...? — ke vwol dee·re ...

I understand.
Capisco. — ka·pee·sko

I don't understand.
Non capisco. — non ka·pee·sko

Please write it down.
Può scriverlo, per favore? — pwo skree·ver·lo per fa·vo·re

Can you show me (on the map)?
Può mostrarmelo (sulla pianta)? — pwo mos·trar·me·lo (soo·la pyan·ta)

NUMBERS

0	zero	dze·ro
1	uno	oo·no
2	due	doo·e
3	tre	tre
4	quattro	kwa·tro
5	cinque	cheen·kwe
6	sei	say
7	sette	se·te
8	otto	o·to
9	nove	no·ve
10	dieci	dye·chee
11	undici	oon·dee·chee
12	dodici	do·dee·chee
13	tredici	tre·dee·chee
14	quattordici	kwa·tor·dee·chee
15	quindici	kween·dee·chee
16	sedici	se·dee·chee
17	diciassette	dee·cha·se·te
18	diciotto	dee·cho·to
19	diciannove	dee·cha·no·ve
20	venti	ven·tee
21	ventuno	ven·too·no
22	ventidue	ven·tee·doo·e
30	trenta	tren·ta
40	quaranta	kwa·ran·ta
50	cinquanta	cheen·kwan·ta
60	sessanta	se·san·ta
70	settanta	se·tan·ta
80	ottanta	o·tan·ta
90	novanta	no·van·ta
100	cento	chen·to
1000	mille	mee·le

PAPERWORK

name	nome	no·me
nationality	nazionalità	na·tsyo·na·lee·ta
date of birth	data di nascita	da·ta dee na·shee·ta
place of birth	luogo di nascita	lwo·go dee na·shee·ta
sex (gender)	sesso	se·so
passport	passaporto	pa·sa·por·to
visa	visto	vee·sto

QUESTION WORDS

Who?	Chi?	kee
What?	Che?	ke
When?	Quando?	kwan·do
Where?	Dove?	do·ve
How?	Come?	ko·me

SHOPPING & SERVICES

I'd like to buy ...
Vorrei comprare ... — vo·ray kom·pra·re ...

How much is it?
Quanto costa? — kwan·to ko·sta

I don't like it.
Non mi piace. — non mee pya·che

May I look at it?
Posso dare un'occhiata? — po·so da·re oo·no·kya·ta

I'm just looking.
Sto solo guardando. — sto so·lo gwar·dan·do

It's cheap.
Non è caro/cara. — non e ka·ro/ka·ra

It's too expensive.
È troppo caro/a. — e tro·po ka·ro/ka·ra

I'll take it.
Lo/La compro. — lo/la kom·pro

Do you accept credit cards?	*Accettate carte di credito?*	a·che·*ta*·te *kar*·te dee *kre*·dee·to

I want to change ...
Voglio cambiare ...
vo·lyo kam·*bya*·re ...

money	*del denaro*	del de·*na*·ro
travellers cheques	*assegni dee viaggio*	a·*se*·nyee dee vee·*a*·jo
more	*più*	pyoo
less	*meno*	*me*·no
smaller	*più piccolo/a*	pyoo *pee*·ko·lo/la
bigger	*più grande*	pyoo *gran*·de

I'm looking for ... *Cerco ...*   *cher*·ko ...

a bank	*un banco*	oon *ban*·ko
the church	*la chiesa*	la *kye*·za
the city centre	*il centro*	eel *chen*·tro
the ... embassy	*l'ambasciata di ...*	lam·ba·*sha*·ta dee ...
the market	*il mercato*	eel mer·*ka*·to
the museum	*il museo*	eel moo·*ze*·o
the post office	*l'ufficio postale*	loo *fee*·cho po·*sta*·le
a public toilet	*un gabinetto*	oon ga·bee·*ne*·to
the tourist office	*l'ufficio di turismo*	loo·*fee*·cho dee too·*reez*·mo

TIME & DATES

What time is it?	*Che ore sono?*	ke *o*·re *so*·no
It's (8 o'clock).	*Sono (le otto).*	*so*·no (le *o*·to)
When?	*Quando?*	*kwan*·do
in the morning	*di mattina*	dee ma·*tee*·na
in the afternoon	*di pomeriggio*	dee po·me·*ree*·jo
in the evening	*di sera*	dee *se*·ra
today	*oggi*	*o*·jee
tomorrow	*domani*	do·*ma*·nee
yesterday	*ieri*	*ye*·ree
Monday	*lunedì*	loo·ne·*dee*
Tuesday	*martedì*	mar·te·*dee*
Wednesday	*mercoledì*	mer·ko·le·*dee*
Thursday	*giovedì*	jo·ve·*dee*
Friday	*venerdì*	ve·ner·*dee*
Saturday	*sabato*	*sa*·ba·to
Sunday	*domenica*	do·*me*·nee·ka
January	*gennaio*	je·*na*·yo
February	*febbraio*	fe·*bra*·yo
March	*marzo*	*mar*·tso
April	*aprile*	a·*pree*·le
May	*maggio*	*ma*·jo
June	*giugno*	*joo*·nyo
July	*luglio*	*loo*·lyo
August	*agosto*	a·*gos*·to
September	*settembre*	se·*tem*·bre
October	*ottobre*	o·*to*·bre
November	*novembre*	no·*vem*·bre
December	*dicembre*	dee·*chem*·bre

TRANSPORT
Public Transport
What time does the ... leave/arrive?
A che ora parte/arriva ...?
a ke *o*·ra *par*·te/a·*ree*·va ...

boat	*la nave*	la *na*·ve
(city) bus	*l'autobus*	*low*·to·boos
(intercity) bus	*il pullman*	eel *pool*·man
plane	*l'aereo*	la·*e*·re·o
train	*il treno*	eel *tre*·no

I'd like a ... ticket.
Vorrei un biglietto ...
vo·*ray* oon bee·*lye*·to ...

one-way	*di solo andata*	dee *so*·lo an·*da*·ta
return	*di andata e ritorno*	dee an·*da*·ta e ree·*toor*·no
1st class	*di prima classe*	dee *pree*·ma *kla*·se
2nd class	*di seconda classe*	dee se·*kon*·da *kla*·se

I want to go to ...
   Voglio andare a ...   vo·lyo an·*da*·re a ...
The train has been cancelled/delayed.
   Il treno è soppresso/   eel *tre*·no e so·*pre*·so/
   in ritardo.   een ree·*tar*·do

the first	*il primo*	eel *pree*·mo
the last	*l'ultimo*	*lool*·tee·mo
platform (two)	*binario (due)*	bee·*na*·ryo (*doo*·e)
ticket office	*biglietteria*	bee·lye·te·*ree*·a
timetable	*orario*	o·*ra*·ryo
train station	*stazione*	sta·*tsyo*·ne

Private Transport
I'd like to hire a/an ...
Vorrei noleggiare ...
vo·*ray* no·le·*ja*·re ...

car	*una macchina*	oo·na *ma*·kee·na
4WD	*un fuoristrada*	oon fwo·ree·*stra*·da
motorbike	*una moto*	oo·na *mo*·to
bicycle	*una bici(cletta)*	oo·na *bee*·chee (*kle*·ta)
diesel	*gasolio/diesel*	ga·zo·lyo/*dee*·zel
petrol	*benzina*	ben·*dzee*·na

ROAD SIGNS

Dare la Precedenza	Give Way
Deviazione	Detour
Divieto di Accesso	No Entry
Divieto di Sorpasso	No Overtaking
Divieto di Sosta	No Parking
Entrata	Entrance
Passo Carrabile	Keep Clear
Pedaggio	Toll
Pericolo	Danger
Rallentare	Slow Down
Senso Unico	One Way
Uscita	Exit

Where's a service station?
Dov'è una stazione di servizio?
do·*ve* oo·na sta·*tsyo*·ne dee ser·*vee*·tsyo
Please fill it up.
Il pieno, per favore.
eel *pye*·no per fa·*vo*·re
I'd like (30) litres.
Vorrei (trenta) litri.
vo·ray (*tren*·ta) *lee*·tree
Is this the road to ...?
Questa strada porta a ...? *kwe*·sta *stra*·da *por*·ta a ...
(How long) Can I park here?
(Per quanto tempo) Posso parcheggiare qui?
(per *kwan*·to *tem*·po) po·so par·ke·*ja*·re kwee
Where do I pay?
Dove si paga?
do·ve see *pa*·ga
I need a mechanic.
Ho bisogno di un meccanico.
o bee·*zo*·nyo dee oon me·*ka*·nee·ko
The car/motorbike has broken down (at ...).
La macchina/moto si è guastata (a ...).
la *ma*·kee·na/*mo*·to see e gwas·*ta*·ta (a ...)
The car/motorbike won't start.
La macchina/moto non parte.
la *ma*·kee·na/*mo*·to non *par*·te

Also available from Lonely Planet:
Italian Phrasebook

I have a flat tyre.
Ho una gomma bucata.
o oo·na *go*·ma boo·*ka*·ta
I've run out of petrol.
Ho esaurito la benzina.
o e·zo·*ree*·to la ben·*dzee*·na
I've had an accident.
Ho avuto un incidente.
o a·*voo*·to oon een·chee·*den*·te

TRAVEL WITH CHILDREN

Is there a/an ...?
C'è ...?
che ...
I need a/an ...
Ho bisogno di ...
o bee·zo·nyo dee ...
 baby change room
 un bagno con fasciatoio
 oon *ba*·nyo kon fa·sha·*to*·yo
 car baby seat
 un seggiolino per bambini
 oon se·jo·*lee*·no per bam·*bee*·nee
 child-minding service
 un servizio di babysitter
 oon ser·*vee*·tsyo dee be·bee·*see*·ter
 children's menu
 un menù per bambini
 oon me·*noo* per bam·*bee*·nee
 (disposable) nappies/diapers
 pannolini (usa e getta)
 pa·no·*lee*·nee·(oo·sa e *je*·ta)
 formula (milk)
 latte in polvere
 la·te in *pol*·ve·re
 (English-speaking) babysitter
 un/una babysitter (che parli inglese)
 oon/oo·na be·bee·*see*·ter (ke *par*·lee een·*gle*·ze)
 highchair
 un seggiolone
 oon se·jo·*lo*·ne
 potty
 un vasino
 oon va·*zee*·no
 stroller
 un passeggino
 oon pa·se·*jee*·no

Do you mind if I breastfeed here?
Le dispiace se allatto il/la bimbo/a qui?
le dees·*pya*·che se a·*la*·to eel/la *beem*·bo/a kwee
Are children allowed?
I bambini sono ammessi?
ee bam·*bee*·nee so·no a·*me*·see

Glossary

abbazia – abbey
affittacamere – rooms for rent
agora – marketplace, meeting place
agriturismo – farm stay
albergo – hotel
alimentari – grocery shop, delicatessen
anfiteatro – amphitheatre
ara – altar
arco – arch
autostrada – motorway, freeway

badia – abbey
baglio – manor house
bancomat – ATM
belvedere – panoramic viewpoint
benzina – petrol
borgo – ancient town or village; sometimes used to
mean equivalent of *via*

cambio – money exchange
camera – room
campanile – bell tower
campeggio – camp site
campo – field
cappella – chapel
carabinieri – police with military and civil duties
Carnevale – carnival period between Epiphany and Lent
casa – house
case abusive – literally, 'abusive houses'; illegal
construction usually associated with the Mafia
cava – quarry
centro – centre
chiesa – church
CIT – Compagnia Italiana di Turismo; Italian national
travel agency
città – town, city
clientelismo – system of political patronage
comune – equivalent to municipality or county; town or
city council
contrada – district
corso – main street, avenue
cortile – courtyard
Cosa Nostra – Our Thing; alternative name for the Mafia
CTS – Centro Turistico Studentesco e Giovanile; Centre for
Student & Youth Tourists

dammuso – low-level dwelling made of thick volcanic
rock topped by a small whitewashed domed roof
diretto – direct; slow train
duomo – cathedral

enoteca – wine bar, wine shop

fangho – mud bath
faraglione – rock tower
ferrovia – train station
festa – festival
fiume – river
fontana – fountain
foro – forum
fossa – pit, hole
funivia – cable car

gola – gorge
golfo – gulf
grotta – cave
guardia medica – emergency doctor service

IC – Intercity; fast train
interregionale – long-distance train that stops
frequently
isola – island

lago – lake
largo – small square
latomia – small quarry
lido – beach
locale – slow local train; also called *regionale*
locanda – inn, small hotel
lungomare – seafront road, promenade

mare – sea
mattanza – ritual slaughter of tuna
mercato – market
molo – wharf
monte – mountain
municipio – town hall, municipal offices
museo – museum

Natale – Christmas

oratorio – oratory
ospedale – hospital
osteria – inn

palazzo – palace, mansion
parco – park
Pasqua – Easter
passeggiata – evening stroll
pensione – small hotel
piazza – square

piazzale – large open square
ponte – bridge
porta – gate, door
porto – port

questura – police station

reale – royal
regionale – slow local train; also called *locale*
rifugio – mountain hut
riserva naturale – nature reserve
rocca – fortress; rock

sagra – festival, generally dedicated to one food item or theme
sala – room

santuario – sanctuary
scalinata – staircase, steps
spiaggia – beach
stazione – station
strada – street, road

teatro – theatre
tempio – temple
tonnara – tuna-processing plant
torre – tower
traghetto – ferry, boat
treno – train

via – street, road
viale – avenue
vicolo – alley, alleyway

Behind the Scenes

THIS BOOK

The 1st edition of Lonely Planet's *Sicily* was written by Fionn Davenport. Sally O'Brien updated the 2nd edition and Paula Hardy the 3rd edition. This 4th edition was updated by Vesna Maric. This guidebook was commissioned in Lonely Planet's London office, and produced by the following:

Commissioning Editor Paula Hardy
Coordinating Editors Sasha Baskett, Laura Stansfeld, Louisa Syme
Coordinating Cartographer Csanad Csutoros
Coordinating Layout Designer Clara Monitto
Managing Editors Imogen Bannister, Bruce Evans
Managing Cartographer Mark Griffiths
Managing Layout Designer Adam McCrow
Assisting Editors Laura Crawford, Robyn Loughnane, Kirsten Rawlings
Assisting Cartographers Anita Banh, Anna Clarkson, Joshua Geoghegan, Malisa Plesa, Peter Shields
Cover Designer Pepi Bluck
Project Manager Rachel Imeson
Language Content Coordinator Quentin Frayne

Thanks to Lisa Knights, Annelies Mertens, Trent Paton, Celia Wood

THANKS
VESNA MARIC

My gratitude is as always to Rafael, my perfect companion. Also thanks to my mother and Susana for coming along for the fun and the running around. *Grazie mille* to Sandro and Vitea for being my islands in a sea of strangers, and for always helping and being kind. Big thanks also to Gabriel for calling me when chatting was much needed. *Grazie* to Ale and Simo for the fun and hospitality, and to Graziano for lots of good tips.

OUR READERS

Many thanks to the travellers who used the last edition and wrote to us with helpful hints, useful advice and interesting anecdotes:

A Jose Daniel Anadon, Moshe & Nili Arad, Silvia Ascarelli **B** Peter Badame, Mirjam Bakker, Sophie Beaupere, Saleem Begg, Peter Bennett, Jeanett Borsdal, Floris Brandriet, Robert Braunrath, Johannes Burr **C** Victoria Cambridge, Jim Campbell, Keith Campbell, Alison Coulby, Neil Courtney, Julie Crowe **D** Natalie David, Leonard Dorin, K T Dunlop **E** Ron Whaley England **F** Carole Feldman, Marvin Feldman, Lorenzo Frusteri, Geer Furtjes **G** Paul Gardner, Christina Geissler, D E Gray, Christian Greve, Arend De Groote **H** Michael Hahn, Liv Hamilton, Clare Hampton, Charlene Hiss, Nam Holtz, Andrew Hood, Irmgard Huber **J** Mark Jackobson,

THE LONELY PLANET STORY

Fresh from an epic journey across Europe, Asia and Australia in 1972, Tony and Maureen Wheeler sat at their kitchen table stapling together notes. The first Lonely Planet guidebook, *Across Asia on the Cheap,* was born.

Travellers snapped up the guides. Inspired by their success, the Wheelers began publishing books to Southeast Asia, India and beyond. Demand was prodigious, and the Wheelers expanded the business rapidly to keep up. Over the years, Lonely Planet extended its coverage to every country and into the virtual world via lonelyplanet.com and the Thorn Tree message board.

As Lonely Planet became a globally loved brand, Tony and Maureen received several offers for the company. But it wasn't until 2007 that they found a partner whom they trusted to remain true to the company's principles of travelling widely, treading lightly and giving sustainably. In October of that year, BBC Worldwide acquired a 75% share in the company, pledging to uphold Lonely Planet's commitment to independent travel, trustworthy advice and editorial independence.

Today, Lonely Planet has offices in Melbourne, London and Oakland, with over 500 staff members and 300 authors. Tony and Maureen are still actively involved with Lonely Planet. They're travelling more often than ever, and they're devoting their spare time to charitable projects. And the company is still driven by the philosophy of *Across Asia on the Cheap*: 'All you've got to do is decide to go and the hardest part is over. So go!'

Aviva Jacobs, Colin Jones **K** Gael Kennedy, Thierry Kim, Jonathan Koomey, Sandra Koreman, Monika Kruzel, Maxene Kupperman-Guinals **L** Peter Lack, Ghislaine Leger-Lemieux, Ana Lombardo, D Lowe **M** Marco Marco, Penny Mavor, Manuela Mayer, John McCutcheon, Ryan McDonald, Nancy McMichael, Taco Melissen, Alexandre Millepied, Jan Minkenberg **N** Trilce Navarrete, George Nelis, Thomas Neuman **O** Christoph Ostermann-Pflueger **P** Elke Parsa, Annemarie Pemmer, Massimiliano Puglisi **R** Caitlin Rathburn, Christian Reuther, Jim Robinson, Patricia Ruthven, Adele Ryan **S** Patricia Salvo, Andrew Sanders, Marcello Sannucci, Bob Skocpol, John Spuches, Ernest Stricker, P Sylva **T** Brad Thompson, Renée Du Tilly **V** John van Druten, Haidé Costa I Villaró **W** Ruud De Waay, Jessica Weber, Chris Wells, Lorraine Welsh, Sue Williams, Judith Wilson, Geraldine Wooller **Z** Veronica Zito, Marco Zoli

ACKNOWLEDGMENTS

Many thanks to the following for the use of their content:

Globe on title page ©Mountain High Maps 1993 Digital Wisdom, Inc.

Internal photographs p11 by Panoramic Images/Getty Images. All other photographs by Lonely Planet Images, and by Rafael Estefania p6, p7, p8, p9, p10; John Elk III p5; Bethune Carmichael p6, p10; Holger Leue p12.

All images are the copyright of the photographers unless otherwise indicated. Many of the images in this guide are available for licensing from Lonely Planet Images: www.lonelyplanet images.com.

Index

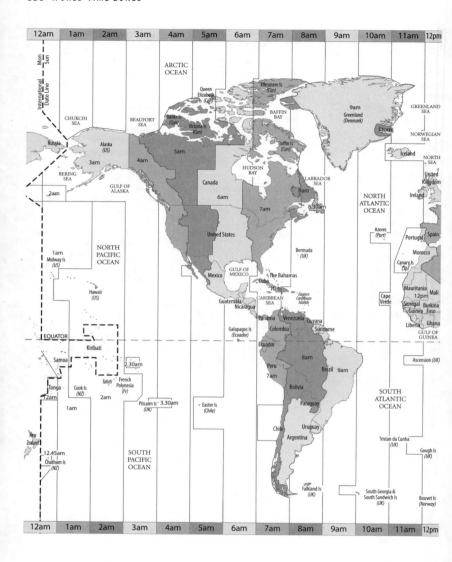

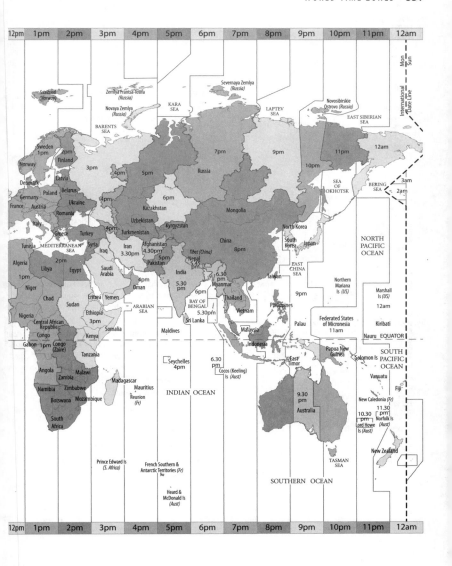

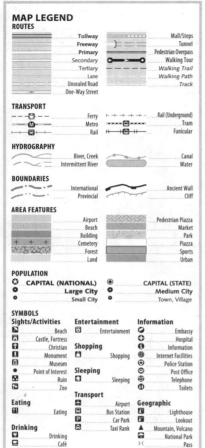

MAP LEGEND

ROUTES

Tollway	Mall/Steps
Freeway	Tunnel
Primary	Pedestrian Overpass
Secondary	Walking Tour
Tertiary	Walking Trail
Lane	Walking Path
Unsealed Road	Track
One-Way Street	

TRANSPORT

Ferry	Rail (Underground)
Metro	Tram
Rail	Funicular

HYDROGRAPHY

River, Creek	Canal
Intermittent River	Water

BOUNDARIES

International	Ancient Wall
Provincial	Cliff

AREA FEATURES

Airport	Pedestrian Piazza
Beach	Market
Building	Park
Cemetery	Piazza
Forest	Sports
Land	Urban

POPULATION

○ CAPITAL (NATIONAL)	◉ CAPITAL (STATE)
● Large City	● Medium City
● Small City	○ Town, Village

SYMBOLS

Sights/Activities	Entertainment	Information
Beach	Entertainment	Embassy
Castle, Fortress		Hospital
Christian	Shopping	Information
Monument	Shopping	Internet Facilities
Museum		Police Station
Point of Interest	Sleeping	Post Office
Ruin	Sleeping	Telephone
Zoo		Toilets
Eating	**Transport**	
Eating	Airport	**Geographic**
	Bus Station	Lighthouse
Drinking	Car Park	Lookout
Drinking	Taxi Rank	Mountain, Volcano
Café		National Park
		Pass
		River Flow
		Waterfall

LONELY PLANET OFFICES

Australia
Head Office
Locked Bag 1, Footscray, Victoria 3011
☎ 03 8379 8000, fax 03 8379 8111
talk2us@lonelyplanet.com.au

USA
150 Linden St, Oakland, CA 94607
☎ 510 893 8555, toll free 800 275 8555
fax 510 893 8572
info@lonelyplanet.com

UK
2nd Floor, 186 City Road,
London ECV1 2NT
☎ 020 7106 2100, fax 020 7106 2101
go@lonelyplanet.co.uk

Published by Lonely Planet Publications Pty Ltd
ABN 36 005 607 983

© Lonely Planet Publications Pty Ltd 2008

© photographers as indicated 2008

Cover photograph: Rugged landscape near Piazza Armerina, Sicily, Trevor Wood/Gettty Images. Many of the images in this guide are available for licensing from Lonely Planet Images: www.lonelyplanet images.com.